Phil Edmonston

LEMON-AID

2012|2013

USED CARS and TRUCKS

Phil Edmonston

LEMON-AID

2012|2013

USED CARS and TRUCKS

DUNDURN
TORONTO

Editing: Jade Colbert, Stacey Curtis, Cy Strom
Design: Jack Steiner
Printer: Webcom

1   2   3   4   5   16   15   14   13   12

Conseil des Arts   Canada Council
du Canada   for the Arts

Canada

ONTARIO ARTS COUNCIL
CONSEIL DES ARTS DE L'ONTARIO

We acknowledge the support of the **Canada Council for the Arts** and the **Ontario Arts Council** for our publishing program. We also acknowledge the financial support of the Government of Canada through the **Canada Book Fund and Livres Canada Books**, and the Government of Ontario through the **Ontario Book Publishers Tax Credit** program, and the **Ontario Media Development Corporation**.

Care has been taken to trace the ownership of copyright material used in this book. The author and the publisher welcome any information enabling them to rectify any references or credits in subsequent editions.

J. Kirk Howard, President

Printed and bound in Canada.
www.dundurn.com

Dundurn Press
3 Church Street, Suite 500
Toronto, Ontario, Canada
M5E 1M2

Gazelle Book Services Limited
White Cross Mills
High Town, Lancaster, England
LA1 4XS

Dundurn Press
2250 Military Road
Tonawanda, NY
U.S.A. 14150

CONTENTS

KEY DOCUMENTS

SECRETS, SURPRISES, AND SAFETY DEFECTS

Who Do You Trust?

Tokyo Electric Power Co., or Tepco, announced on national TV that all was well: The utility was on top of the accident. No radiation had been released into the atmosphere. Return to regular programming.

Mainstream media dutifully reported that story. But not Shiraishi's "Our Planet TV," which soon broadcast a live interview with five Japanese reporters in Futaba City, a community near the stricken plant. The reporters, who had covered the Chernobyl disaster, told a very different tale.

"They held up Geiger counters showing the level of radiation was almost beyond calculation," said Shiraishi, a former network TV journalist who co-founded the Internet venture in 2001, hosts the show and reports many of its stories. "They'd never seen anything like it."

LOS ANGELES TIMES
DECEMBER 18, 2011
http://articles.latimes.com/2011/dec/18/world/la-fg-japan-distrust-20111218

In researching this 42nd annual edition of *Lemon-Aid*, I see that the auto industry is still up to its old tricks: lying to customers about fuel economy and safety; giving less car but asking for more money; and making owners pay for repairs that are caused by factory screw-ups.

Radioactive cars?

You bet.

But don't expect Japanese automakers who routinely ignore claims of sudden acceleration and catastrophic brake failures to be any more truthful about their radioactive cars. They know some of their contaminated vehicles and parts were shipped to Chile and Russia, where they were turned back.

Since few ports scan for radiation, the Associated Press estimates that 1 percent of all shipped vehicles, parts, and accessories (powertrains, hybrid parts, radios, and tires) will be radioactive and will show up in other countries, including North America.

The March 11, 2011 nuclear plant meltdowns in Japan show that, just as in war, truth is the first casualty of natural disasters. You can expect governments and corporations to lie through their teeth in order to protect their own interests.

Prudent new and used car shoppers should be wary of Japanese vehicles built or exported from Japan after March 11. Instead, choose a model manufactured in Canada, the United States, or Mexico. You can confirm where a vehicle was built by looking at the date of manufacture plate (usually affixed to the driver's inside door jamb, near where the oil change stickers are found).

Japanese-made car parts are sold to automakers around the world. This means auto parts installed by dealers for any make of vehicle could be contaminated due to parts suppliers' close proximity to the Fukushima nuclear facilities.

So far, there is no agreement as to how much radiation poses a health threat since the effects vary and cancers can be slow-growing. *Lemon-Aid*'s position is that Canada must be proactive and install radiation screening for imported vehicles at all major ports of entry.

Even if Ottawa says there is "no threat" from radioactive Asian imports, other countries and independent medical research disagree. Radiation from the Fukushima blast represents a real danger to North Americans, but especially to children, says the most recent independent health study, released December 19, 2011 and found at *www.radiation.org/press/pressrelease111219FukushimaReactor-Fallout.html*):

> An estimated 14,000 excess deaths in the United States are linked to the radioactive fallout from the disaster at the Fukushima nuclear reactors in Japan, according to

a major new article in the December 2011 edition of the *International Journal of Health Services*. This is the first peer-reviewed study published in a medical journal documenting the health hazards of Fukushima.

Authors Joseph Mangano and Janette Sherman note that their estimate of 14,000 excess U.S. deaths in the 14 weeks after the Fukushima meltdowns is comparable to the 16,500 excess deaths in the 17 weeks after the Chernobyl meltdown in 1986. The rise in reported deaths after Fukushima was largest among U.S. infants under age one. The 2010–2011 increase for infant deaths in the spring was 1.8 percent, compared to a decrease of 8.37 percent in the preceding 14 weeks.

Just six days after the disastrous meltdowns struck four reactors at Fukushima on March 11, scientists detected the plume of toxic fallout had arrived over American shores. Subsequent measurements by the U.S. Environmental Protection Agency (EPA) found levels of radiation in air, water, and milk hundreds of times above normal across the U.S. The highest detected levels of Iodine-131 in precipitation in the U.S. were as follows (normal is about 2 picocuries I-131 per liter of water): Boise, ID (390); Kansas City (200); Salt Lake City (190); Jacksonville, FL (150); Olympia, WA (125); and Boston, MA (92).

Epidemiologist Joseph Mangano, MPH MBA, said: "This study of Fukushima health hazards is the first to be published in a scientific journal. It raises concerns, and strongly suggests that health studies continue, to understand the true impact of Fukushima in Japan and around the world. Findings are important to the current debate of whether to build new reactors, and how long to keep aging ones in operation."

Mangana is executive director, Radiation and Public Health Project, and the author of 27 peer-reviewed medical journal articles and letters.

Internist and toxicologist Janette Sherman, MD, said: "Based on our continuing research, the actual death count here may be as high as 18,000, with influenza and pneumonia, which were up five-fold in the period in question as a cause of death. Deaths are seen across all ages, but we continue to find that infants are hardest hit because their tissues are rapidly multiplying, they have undeveloped immune systems, and the doses of radioisotopes are proportionally greater than for adults.

There's more:

1. "China rejects ship from California with 'abnormal' radiation—Had only been in Tokyo for a few hours": *http://enenews.com/china-rejects-ship-from-california-with-abnormal-radiation-had-only-been-in-tokyo-for-a-few-hours*, March 29, 2011.
2. "Vancouver, Canada radiation tests show iodine-131 in rainwater at almost 100 times above US drinking water limit": *http://enenews.com/recent-radioactivy-testing-vancouver-canada-shows-iodine-131-rainwater-almost-100-times-above-drinking-water-limit*, April 8, 2011.

3. "Chile finds radiation in Korean cars—Tests show up to a level 5 on radioactive index, level 9 needed for alert": *http://enenews.com/ chile-finds-radiation-ship-south-korea-tests-show-level-5-radioactive-index-level-9-needed-alert*, May 2, 2011.

4. "Vancouver Paper: Health Canada detected massive amounts of radioactive material from Fukushima—Iodine-131 spiked above maximum allowed limit at 4 of 5 sites": *http://enenews.com/vancouver-paper-health-canada-detected-massive-amounts-of-radioactive-material-from-fukushima-iodine-131-spiked-above-maximum-allowed-limit-at-4-of-5-sites*, August 4, 2011.

5. "Member of Parliament: Health Canada 'negligent' on Fukushima radiation threats": *http://enenews.com/canadian-member-parliament-health-canada-negligent-fukushima-radiation-threats-important-media-raises-issue*, August 5, 2011.

6. "Egypt finds shipment from Japan with radioactive electric and mechanical instruments—Exceeded legal limit—Authorities trying to keep radiation from spreading": *http://enenews.com/egypt-finds-shipment-japan-radioactive-electric-mechanical-instruments-exceeded-legal-limit-authorities-trying-keep-radiation-spreading*, August 10, 2011.

7. "Tires found to be radioactive": *http://tirereview.com*, December 2, 2011.

Secret Warranties

"Secret warranties," often called "goodwill" policies by automakers, are still used to placate some customers when poor-quality components fail after the warranty expires. This practice has nothing to do with goodwill. It's simply a cynical way to make the factory's mistake a selling tool for the dealer. The reasoning is simple: customers will stay loyal to a dealer who pretends to bend the rules in giving out a free repair (even though the failure is caused by a factory-related defect that should be disclosed to all owners).

SPECIAL COVERAGE ADJUSTMENT–CATALYTIC CONVERTER WARRANTY EXTENSION

BULLETIN NO.: 10134   DATE: NOVEMBER 17, 2010

2006–07 Chevrolet Malibu equipped with 2.2L Engine (L61)
2006–07 Pontiac G6 equipped with 2.4L Engine (LE5)
CONDITION: Some customers of 2006–07 model year Chevrolet Malibu vehicles with a 2.2L engine (L61) and Pontiac G6 vehicles equipped with a 2.4L engine (LE5) may comment about the illumination of the indicator lamp. This may be due to erosion of the mat within the catalytic converter.
SPECIAL COVERAGE ADJUSTMENT: This special coverage covers the condition described for a period of 10 years or 120,000 miles (193,000 km), whichever occurs first, from the date the vehicle was originally placed in service, regardless of ownership. The repairs will be made at no charge to the customer.

Automakers have thousands of secret warranties applicable to used cars. These warranty extensions pay for repairs used to correct manufacturing or design defects. GM's catalytic converter "secret warranty," for example, represents an $800 savings, but few motorists know it exists.

In Part Two of this guide we have an extensive, revised list of secret warranties that are still in effect for thousands of 1995–2012 cars, trucks, SUVs, and vans.

Less Car, More Money

Carmakers are also cheapening or "decontenting" their products to make more profits. This has been especially true with Toyota starting in the late '90's, and has been carried over to the early entry-level Mercedes B- and C-Class models, as well as the redesigned 2012 Ford Explorer and Fiesta, Honda's Civic, the Hyundai Sonata, and its twin, the Kia Optima. In fact, these last five cars are better buys used (2011 and earlier), than new.

Five Cars Better Used Than New

2011 Ford Explorer

2011 Ford Fiesta

2011 Honda Civic

2011 Hyundai Sonata

2011 Kia Optima

A Bankrupt Saab Story

As predicted by *Lemon-Aid* a decade ago, Saab finally declared bankruptcy last December and stopped paying for warranty coverage for all its vehicles in the U.S. and Canada. The company is expected to be sold piecemeal for parts.

General Motors says it will cover any warranty remaining on vehicles sold under its ownership of Saab, which ended in February 2010. GM estimates its warranty will cover a majority of the about 48,000 Saabs still under warranty in the U.S. and the 9,000 Saabs in Canada. Saab owners can also hold their selling dealer responsible for damages arising from the bankruptcy or from manufacturing defects without any time limitation (see Part Two).

Saab was originally a division of Svenska Aeroplan Aktiebolaget (English: *Swedish Aeroplane Limited*), which had been created in 1937 to build fighter planes to protect Sweden's neutrality leading up to WWll. Shortly before the war ended, Saab created an automobile division and brought out its first cars in 1947. GM bought 50 percent of the company in 1989 and the rest in 2000, but Saab continued to lose huge sums of money until it was sold at a loss to Dutch luxury carmaker Spyker as part of GM's bankruptcy reorganization in 2010.

Auto Parts Price-Fixing

Have you looked at your latest repair bill and asked "Why in the heck are parts prices so high?" Well, according to justice officials on four continents, the answer may be that the high prices have been secretly "cooked" among parts suppliers. A number of class actions have recently been filed in the U. S. against Honda and Toyota and many of the suppliers listed below. Owners seeking information as to how they can get compensation will find a summary at the end of Part Two in *Pending Cases*.

Price-fixing probes among dozens of law enforcement agencies are also in full swing. The global investigation is looking into allegations that 19 suppliers secretly conspired to fix prices or allocate customers, market shares, or geographic areas. The parts involved were sold to automakers, dealers, and independent repair agencies.

Companies of interest to justice officials are mostly based in Europe, Japan, and the United States. Components targeted in the probe are ball bearings, electrical and electronic systems, heat exchangers, occupant safety devices, power management systems, refrigerants, small motors, and wiring harnesses and systems.

Auto Parts Price-Fixing (Companies of Interest to Probers)

Autoliv Leoni	DuPont Magna (Cosma)
Calsonic Kansei	*Furukawa Electric Mitsuba
Delphi	Hitachi Auto
Denso Mitsubishi Electric	Honeywell

Lear	Sumitomo Electric
Schaeffler	T.RAD
SKF	Valeo

*In a plea deal with U.S. Department of Justice officials last September, three Furukawa executives were sent to jail and the company was fined $200 million for price-fixing and bid-rigging over a 10-year period. Shuji Hayashida, who was CEO of U.S. subsidiary American Furukawa Inc. for most of the alleged collusion period, will not get any government protection under the plea and may face new charges.

Sources tell me that Furukawa operated in Canada during the past decade and may have committed similar antitrust violations in Canada that it pled guilty to in the States.

Canada's federal Competition Bureau should investigate whether violations of Canadian law (Section 45) occurred and take the appropriate action against Furukawa and other companies named as companies "of interest" in the U.S. Justice Department's investigation.

Section 45 is the cornerstone cartel provision of Canada's *Competition Act*. It makes it a criminal offence when two or more competitors or potential competitors conspire, agree or arrange to fix prices, allocate customers or markets, or restrict output of a product. This offence is known as a conspiracy, and is punishable by a fine of up to $25 million, imprisonment for a term of up to 14 years, or both.

2012–2013 *Lemon-Aid Guide* highlights

1. A listing of free online sources for showing current values for used cars, trucks, SUVs, and vans.
2. A comparison of fuel-economy claims in Canada and the States.
3. The disclosure of Mercedes' two new secret "goodwill" warranties that cover premature corrosion damage on 2006–07 B-Class compacts and the free replacement of the camshaft adjustment solenoid and wiring harness on 2001–05 C230 models.

REPLACE CAM ADJUSTMENT SOLENOID, ADAPTER HARNESSES

CAMPAIGN NO. 2009100001   DATE: APRIL 2011

INSTALL CAMSHAFT ADJUSTMENT SOLENOID(S) ADAPTER HARNESS(ES)
Models 170/203, Model Years 2001–04/2002–05
This Service Campaign has been initiated because Daimler AG (DAG), the manufacturer of Mercedes-Benz vehicles, has determined that due to the settling properties of the seal of the camshaft adjustment solenoid specification, oil may enter the engine wiring harness(es) through the electrical connection of the camshaft adjustment solenoid from capillary action. Dealers will install camshaft adjustment solenoid(s) adapter harness(es) at the next workshop visit.

Mercedes' service bulletin tries to restrict its responsibility to the replacement of the solenoid and adapter harness, but the company is also fully liable for all other damages caused by the above-recognized defect.

4. *Lemon-Aid's* "Endangered Species List" has been expanded to include Jaguar, Land Rover, Volvo, the Mercedes-Benz not-so-smart Smart Car, and now bankrupt Saab.

5. 2011–12 model automobiles that have "chin-to-chest" head restraints, blinding dash reflections, dash gauges that can't be seen in sunlight, and a painful wind-tunnel roar if the rear windows are opened while underway.

6. Why Audis are beautiful to behold, but hell to own (biodegradable transmissions, rodent-snack wiring, and mind-boggling depreciation).

7. New Canadian jurisprudence that holds General Motors liable for occupant injuries caused by inadvertent airbag deployment.

8. Other recent jurisprudence that gives arbitrators more leeway in considering poor automotive design as a "material defect."

9. Why the Supreme Court of Canada has called one company "the insurance company from hell" and slapped it with a million-dollar punitive damages judgment.

10. An exhaustive library of case law to support the use of electronic data recorders as proof in criminal and civil cases.

11. Why ethanol and hybrid fuel-saving claims have more in common with Mother Goose than the Society of Automotive Engineers.

12. How to get a refund if your Honda hybrid is a gas guzzler.

13. A new, extensive list of the best cars for senior drivers, along with lists of the optional features that are worth the extra cash—and the ones that are simply a "pain in the tailpipe."

14. Hundreds of new service bulletins and safety complaints.

15. More online resources not commonly known to buyers.

Lemon-Aid may taste a bit tart for some, but don't ignore its advice. The *Used Car and Truck Guide* tells you which cars are overpriced and by how much. Plus, the *Guide* can work wonders if you just place it on the sales agent's desk as you haggle.

Why have the bestselling *Lemon-Aid* guides been so trusted over the past 42 years?

It's all because the guides use tips from whistleblowers, owner complaints, court decisions, government findings, and hard-to-get internal carmaker service bulletins to expose safety- and performance-related defects, sales scams, and "secret" warranties, and because *Lemon-Aid* is updated each year.

Past guides warned of Toyota's "sudden unintended acceleration" years before the U. S. Department of Transportation fined Toyota $48 million for delaying its recall. In Canada, our class-action testimony four years ago forced General Motors to refund millions of dollars to Canadians stuck with overheating 1995–2004 V6 engines.

In the spring of 2011, we made Chrysler recall 300,000 2003–2011 Ram pickups to fix their "death wobble," an uncontrollable shimmy caused by uneven roadways and potholes. This recall ended Chrysler's nine years of stonewalling owner complaints and fruitless government investigations.

Keep this consumer victory in mind next time someone says, "you can't win" when battling a car company.

With *Lemon-Aid* by your side, *"Yes, you can."*

Phil Edmonston

April 2012

Part One
"BEATERS" AND BARGAINS

GM's Volt has been a resounding flop: less than half of the number of cars projected have been sold. GM says the average Volt owner makes $170,000 per year.

The Chevy Volt: An Electric Edsel?

Each Chevy Volt electric car sold thus far may have as much as $250,000 in state and federal dollars in incentives behind it—a total of $3 billion altogether, says James Hohman, assistant director of fiscal policy at the Mackinac Center for Public Policy.

GM has estimated they've sold 6,000 Volts so far. That would mean each of the 6,000 Volts sold would be subsidized between $50,000 and $250,000. If battery incentives are included in the analysis, the potential government subsidy per Volt increases to $256,824.

The $3 billion total subsidy figure includes $690.4 million offered by the state of Michigan and $2.3 billion in federal money. That's enough to purchase 75,222 Volts with a sticker price of $39,828.

"This might be the most government-supported car since the East-German Trabant," said Hohman.

MICHIGAN CAPITOL CONFIDENTIAL (CAPCON)
WWW.MICHIGANCAPITOLCONFIDENTIAL.COM/16192
DECEMBER 21, 2011

Cheap and Simple: Buy Used

Buying a used vehicle is easier than buying new and you can end up with reliable wheels for less than half what the car originally cost. Plus, there is less of a show-room shakedown—confusing figures, payment plans, and costly "extras"—awaiting you. You get a car that has already been scratched, dented, and corroded, but this saves you from that sickening feeling when new-car imperfections first appear.

Most cars sold in Canada are used: While new-car sales were up some 6.6% over last year to 1.557 million, that's still far short of 2003's peak of 1.703 million. Used-car sales, though, are going through the roof. In fact, the 2.89 million previously owned "bargains" and "beaters" sold in 2010 was an-all time high.

About 30 percent of the car fleet in Canada—about 6 million of the 21.4 million cars on the road—are 10 years old or older. The transformation from new to used occurs as soon as the sales title passes from dealer to a second owner, thus thro-retically making every car sold a used-vehicle. The beauty of this instant morphing from new to used is that it creates a huge pool of inexpensive used vehicles and competing sellers who expect you to haggle.

And price haggling is encouraged because depreciation gives buyers a large margin to bring prices down. In fact, most private owners discover they can get about 20 percent more by selling their trade-in privately than what most dealers would offer. Dealers also make more money selling used vehicles than they make selling new cars and trucks, and they aren't burdened by such things as the manufactur-er's suggested retail price, freight charges, options loading, high floor plan interest rates, reduced commissions, and warranty charge-backs. The savings generated by these simpler transactions often go straight into the dealer's and buyer's pockets.

Car dealers get their vehicles from fleets, lessees, wholesalers, trade-ins, and private sales. Some of the less reputable dealers will buy at auction vehicles that other dealers unloaded because they weren't good enough to sell to their own customers. Other dealers will set up "curb-sider" scams where they sell used vehicles from private homes, using their employees as shills.

The 2008 Ford Escape 4×4 SUV (*left*) and the 2008 Hyundai Tucson (*right*) are small SUVs recommended by *Lemon-Aid*. Both vehicles sold new for about $28,000. The Escape, though, took a bigger depreciation hit and is now worth only about $13,000, or $2,000 less than Hyundai's 4×4. Going more upscale, the $30,000 2008 Honda CR-V SUV now sells for an impressive $17,000—more than half its original price after four years. Why? Because buyers are willing to pay a premium for what they consider better-made Asian vehicles—no matter if some come from South Korea and once were considered bottom-of-the-heap, quality-wise.

Although a bit pricey, when it comes to reliability, it's hard to beat the CR-V's quality control, practicality, ideal ride height, fuel economy, and easy entry and exit. A redesigned 2012 will likely drive down the resale values of earlier renditions, although the numb steering and circa 1995 navigation system could be a turn-off for many.

Going into 2012, Chrysler, Ford, and GM dealers have an abundance of "young" three-year-old off-lease vehicles at unusually low prices because the buy-back prices at lease end were set low as the recession loomed. On the other hand, dealers now selling import brands are chronically short of product because owners keep these vehicles three to four years longer and use the buy-back option for themselves. The majority of private sales are comprised of vehicles six years or older, while independent used-car dealers get most of their profit from selling anything that can be driven away.

Asian Car "Bargains"?

The bad news is that most Asian small car prices are about 10 percent higher ($1,000–$1,500) this year due to a limited supply of both new and used vehicles and higher fuel costs, which drives car buyers toward reliable, fuel-frugal Asian makes. Some Asian companies have lost market share, while Detroit auto manufacturers are awash in profits.

Fewer new cars means higher used car prices will continue through early 2012, particularly for buyers of small and family-sized vehicles who will be at a disadvantage due to the weakened competition. Fortunately, prices are expected to level off as supply increases in the spring of 2012.

Japan's auto meltdown: buying strategies

Used Honda Civics are more in demand than ever now that the redesigned 2012 has been trashed by most independent consumer rating groups. Toyota is regaining its sales footing after being mauled by incessant safety recalls and product shortages. Meanwhile, South Korean automakers like Hyundai and Kia have been riding a surge of record sales over the past few years. This is now even more likely to continue as a result of *Consumer Reports'* April 2011 Annual Auto Issue which gives a Recommended green light to most of Hyundai's cars and SUVs and a few (Omigod!) Kias. Korean brands presently outsell European brands in North America. Naturally, used Hyundais and Kias will continue to be in short supply.

Think global, buy local

New cars sold in 2012 will be garnished with hefty rebates and other sales incentives, which will drive down the costs for used vehicles. Particularly good buys will be Asian automakers' discounted vehicles manufactured in North America, which will be unaffected by the supply, servicing, and parts problems impacting imported models. A three-year-old, Ontario-built Honda Civic, or Toyota Matrix or Corolla will be good choices.

Used Hondas are least likely to have servicing problems since last year 92 percent of Honda's Canadian sales came from domestically manufactured cars like the Civic, Acura, and Ridgeline pickup. Mazda Canada is also well situated to service its products: its two best-selling models in Canada, the Mazda3 and Mazda5, are both manufactured in Hiroshima, Japan, far away from the quake's epicentre, and unaffected by the Fukushima fallout. Subaru and Suzuki models are also solid choices, having emerged unscathed because their Japanese operations are far from the earthquake-ravaged area.

Buying a used Toyota or Nissan is a bit riskier. Nearly half the vehicles Toyota sells worldwide are built in Japan and many of its parts suppliers are gone. Moreover, Nissan's engine plant is situated near the stricken Fukushima Daiichi nuclear plant, and Nissan's assurance that it will test all cars and some parts for radiation contamination before releasing them for export isn't all that reassuring.

Some fuel-efficient cars, like the Toyota Yaris, Prius hybrid, and Honda Fit, may be particularly risky buys because they are made in Japan. The Fit is unique in the sense that it will be built in China and imported into Canada this year and then some manufacturting will shift to Mexico, starting with the 2014 model year.

Chinese-made Fits do not receive as high ratings for quality control as do the Mexican-made model. Again, check the date and place of manufacture sticker found on the driver's door jamb.

The Honda Civic is Canada's favourite small car. In the States, it's the Toyota Corolla that rules the small-car roost. Downsized SUVs—such as the Subaru Forester, the Honda CR-V, and the Toyota RAV4—make up almost half of our small-car market but account for only one-quarter of sales south of the border. As far as minivans go, we believe that less is more and, therefore, favour small imports over Detroit's unreliable front-drives and rear-drive gas hogs. The exceptions are trucks and sports cars (yes, the 2011 Mustang beats the pants off the Chevy Camaro).

VEHICLES THAT WILL LAST 15 YEARS OR MORE

Ford Crown Victoria, Escape, Grand Marquis, Mustang, and Ranger	Mazda 323 and 626, B-Series trucks, Miata, and Protegé
GM Chevy Van, Express, Savana, and Vandura	Nissan Frontier and Sentra
Honda Accord, Civic, CR-V, Odyssey, and Ridgeline	Toyota Camry, Corolla, Echo, Solara, and Tercel
Jeep Wrangler and YJ	

Despite higher fuel costs that vary from $1.30 to $1.45 a litre as of April 2012, Canadians are still in love with their cars. Back in the '70s, the average car racked up 160,000 km before it was dropped off at the junkyard. In the '90s, the average car reached 240,000 km before it was recycled. Nowadays, new models are expected to see 300,000 km before they're discarded. In the 2011 sales table below, most of the bestsellers are models recommended by *Lemon-Aid* and should last at least 15 years. Carmakers with sales trending downward will offer the most sales incentives.

SALES LEADERS IN CANADA 2010–2011

Rank	Best-Selling Vehicle	2011	2010	% Change
#1	Ford F-Series	96,325	97,913	−1.6%
#2	Dodge Ram	64,297	54,267	+ 18.5%
#3	Honda Civic	55,090	57,501	−4.2%
#4	Dodge Grand Caravan	53,406	55,306	−3.4%
#5	GMC Sierra	46,680	45,457	+ 2.7%
#6	Hyundai Elantra	44,970	34,556	+ 30.1%
#7	Ford Escape	44,248	43,038	+ 2.8%
#8	Chevrolet Silverado	40,523	41,737	−2.9%
#9	Mazda 3	37,224	47,740	−22.0%
#10	Toyota Corolla	36,663	38,680	−5.2%
#11	Chevrolet Cruze/Cobalt	33,900	3,184	+ 965%
#12	Dodge Journey	29,021	23,785	+ 22.0%
#13	Volkswagen Jetta	26,749	14,758	+ 81.3%
#14	Ford Focus	25,736	23,452	+ 9.7%
#15	Honda CR-V	25,076	24,930	+ 0.6%
#16	Hyundai Santa Fe	24,121	27,882	−13.5%
#17	Chevrolet Equinox	22,468	19,261	+ 16.7%
#18	Hyundai Accent	22,280	24,017	−7.2%
#19	Toyota RAV4	21,550	22,810	−5.5%
#20	Ford Fusion	18,404	19,364	−5.0%
#21	Ford Ranger	16,381	19,653	−16.6%
#22	Hyundai Sonata	16,343	13,856	+ 17.9%
#23	Jeep Wrangler	15,636	11,062	+ 41.3%
#24	Ford Edge	15,633	17,040	−8.3%
#25	Kia Sorento	15,105	10,214	+ 47.9%
#26	Toyota Matrix	14,895	19,093	−22.0%
#27	Nissan Versa	14,497	15,743	−7.9%
#28	Hyundai Tucson	14,309	12,923	+ 10.7%
#29	Nissan Rogue	14,191	13,199	+ 7.5%
#30	Kia Forte	13,984	13,578	+ 3.0%

Source: *Manufacturers*

Note: Cruze was a 2011 model; Cobalt was dropped.

The above chart doesn't show which vehicles flopped in 2011. However, some Ford, Dodge/Ram, Chevrolet, Buick, Lincoln, and Cadillac models all reported sale losses when compared with November 2010. Buick was one of the worst sellers with a 29 percent decline.

Buick may owe its present-day survival to China, where it has been the prefferred luxury car of Chinese digntaries for over five decades. Last year, the brand was among the biggest in the booming Chinese market, accounting for sales of more than 447,000, or more than four times Buick's volume in the U.S.

Some other ailing automakers are Saab, Suzuki, Volvo: all three *Lemon-Aid* rated as Not Recommended last year.

A Good Time to Buy

There are lots of reasons why 2012 is a good year to buy a used car or truck—as long as you stay away from some of the rotten products. Fortunately, there's not as much late-'70s and early-'80s junk out there as there once was, and models from 2006 and later are safer and come loaded with extra convenience and performance features, like standard electronic stability control, increased roof crashworthiness, and safer front and side full-torso airbags. Additionally, there are a lot of cheap vehicles to choose from as sellers compete with lower new-car prices, and a growing off-lease inventory.

But dealers aren't giving anything away. For example, they are selling fuel-efficient small cars for more than last year since gas prices are creeping higher and major Asian automakers are still rebuilding their supplier supply lines. This has forced smart shoppers to buy slightly older, downsized vehicles, or to shop the South Koreans, to keep costs manageable.

But lower fuel consumption and cheaper prices aren't the only factors to consider. Vehicle quality and dependability are equally important. Sure, you can prance around telling your friends how you "stole" that five-year-old Chrysler Caravan, GM Venture/Montana, or Ford Windstar/Freestar—until you have to spend $3,500 for engine or transmission work (or both, in GM's case). Granted, some of the junk is fairly well known, and vehicles are safer now; however, many Detroit models are loaded with nonessential convenience and performance features that fail around the fifth year of ownership. Chief among these are navigation systems,

HARD TO MANUALLY OPEN/CLOSE SIDE SLIDING DOORS	
BULLETIN NO.: 23-007-10	DATE: JUNE 9, 2010

OVERVIEW: This bulletin provides diagnostic steps to determine if the sliding door motor is adding resistance to the mechanical operation of the sliding door.
MODELS: 2001–07 Town & Country/Caravan/Voyager

Chrysler's sliding door fix will require an hour's labour, plus $200 for the door motor. No "goodwill," just a goodbye.

BULLETIN NO: T-SB-0280-10   **DATE: OCTOBER 4, 2010**

SLIDING DOOR OPERATING EFFORT

SIENNA 2004–10

INTRODUCTION: Some 2004–10 Sienna vehicles may exhibit a condition where one or both sliding doors do not open or close smoothly. Please follow the instructions in this bulletin to inspect the sliding door lock assemblies and replace the affected components as needed.

In Service Bulletin No: T-SB-0094-10, Toyota gives similar coverage to fix rattling side doors for the same model years.

adaptive cruise control, tire pressure sensors, ABS, automatic sliding side doors, and sunroofs. Among these defects, the sliding door and sunroof failures are the easiest to get repaired for free via a small claims court lawsuit.

Toyota has had frequent sliding door failures through the 2010 model year. Its sliding door fixes may take over four hours and are covered by secret "goodwill" warranty extensions given to those customers who rant and rave the most after their warranty has expired.

Luxury Lemons

But let's not pick on just Ford, GM, and Chrysler. European automakers make their share of lemons as well. For example, J.D. Power and Associates and *Lemon-Aid* readers have consistently ranked Mercedes' quality as worse than average.

Dear Phil: I am writing about our experience with a 2006 B-Class we purchased in 2009. We chose the B-Class because of Mercedes' reputation for quality and excellent service.

We were distressed to discover that—due to a manufacturing defect—all 5 doors were rusting internally.

We contacted our local dealership and asked for our vehicle to be assessed for repairs under the 'goodwill' warranty applicable to this situation. We were eventually told that Mercedes would pay only 80% of the repairs, leaving us with with a cost of approximately $1,800.

R. S.
Ontario

Premature rusting is a big problem affecting many different Mercedes models. To the company's credit, they will pay for most of the corrective repairs even if the base warranty has expired. Still, the remaining payout is unacceptable for the average owner.

If you have been a steady reader of *Lemon-Aid* since 1991, you've been wary of Mercedes' poor quality for almost two decades and probably saved money buying a Lincoln Town Car or Toyota Avalon instead. BMW owners have proven to be some of the most satisfied with their cars' overall dependability when compared with most other European makes, including Audi, Jaguar, Porsche, Saab, Volkswagen, and Volvo.

Lincoln's front-drive Continental (a failure-prone Taurus in disguise) and Mercedes' unreliable luxury cars and SUVs are proof positive that there's absolutely no correlation between safe, dependable transportation and the amount of money a vehicle costs, especially with most front-drive Lincoln and Cadillac luxury cars. Rear-drive Lincolns and Cadillacs, however, have always performed well after many years of use.

Chrysler "luxury" means beautiful styling and lousy quality control. Its luxury rear-drives, like the 300 and Magnum that once sold at a 10 percent premium, are now piling up on dealers' lots due to their reputation as gas-guzzlers with serious automatic transmission, fuel, and suspension system problems, as well as body deficiencies. It's hard to believe, but a 2009 Chrysler 300 Touring that originally sold for $32,095 is now worth barely $15,500. Depreciation also takes a pretty big bite out of Asian luxury car values: a 2008 Lexus IS 250 that once cost $32,000 now sells for $20,000.

Four Decades of Hits and Misses

Hits

Acura—CL Series and Integra; **BMW**—135i, 3 Series, and 5 Series; **Chrysler**—Colt, 2000 and later Neons, Stealth, and Tradesman vans (invest in an extended warranty for the automatic transmission); **Ford**—Crown Victoria, Econoline vans, Escape, 1991 and later Escorts, Freestyle/Taurus X, Grand Marquis, Mustang V6, and Ranger; **GM**—Cruze, Enclave, Equinox, Express, Firebird, Rainier, Savana, Terrain, Traverse, and Vandura; **Honda**—Accord, Civic, CR-V, Element, Fit, Odyssey, Pilot, and Ridgeline; **Hyundai**—Accent, Elantra, Genesis, Santa Fe, Tiburon, Tucson, and Veracruz; **Kia**—Forte, Rondo, and Soul;

For the best Mustang performance fuel economy, you must get the redesigned 2011 V6-equipped version. It dumps the lethargic, archaic (four-decades-old), 9.8 L/100 km 210 hp 4.0L V6 in favour of a sizzling 305 hp 3.7L V6 that increases fuel economy to 7.6 L/100 km.

Lexus—All models; **Lincoln**—Mark series and Town Car; **Mazda**—323, 626, Mazda3, Mazda5, Mazda6, Miata, Protegé, and Tribute; **Mitsubishi**—Outlander; **Nissan**—Altima, Frontier, GT-R, Leaf, Murano, Rogue, Sentra, Versa, Xterra, and X-Trail; **Subaru**—Impreza, Legacy, Outback, and Forester; **Suzuki**—

Aerio, Esteem, Kizashi, Swift, and SX4; **Toyota**—Avalon, Camry, Corolla, Cressida, Echo, Highlander, Matrix, Sienna, Sequoia, Tercel, and Venza; **VW**—Jetta TDI

Misses

Audi—A3, A4, A6, A8, and Q7; **BMW**—7 Series, Mini Cooper, and X5; **Chrysler**—200, 300, Avenger, Caravan, Charger, Dakota, Durango, Grand Caravan, Intrepid, LHS, Magnum, Neon, New Yorker, Pacifica, PT Cruiser, Sebring, Sprinter, and Town & Country; **Daewoo**—All models; **Fiat**—500; **Ford**—Aerostar, Contour, Explorer, F-150, 2003 and later Focus, Mystique, Sable, Taurus, Tempo, Topaz, and Windstar/Freestar; **GM**—Avalanche, Aveo, Canyon, Catera, Cimarron, Cobalt, Colorado, CTS, Envoy, Fiero, G6, Grand Prix, HHR, Impala, the Lumina/ Montana/Relay/Silhouette/Terraza/Trans Sport/Venture/Uplander group of minivans, Malibu, SRX, STS, TrailBlazer, and Volt; **Hyundai**—Excel, Pony, pre-2006 4-cylinder Sonatas, and Stellar; **Infiniti**—G20; **Jaguar**—All models; **Jeep**—Cherokee, Commander, Compass, Grand Cherokee, Journey, and Patriot; **Kia**—Rio, Sedona, Sephia, Sorento, Spectra, and 2006 and earlier Sportages; **Lada**—All models; **Land Rover**—All models; **Lincoln**—Continental front-drive; **Mercedes-Benz**—190, B-Class C-Class, CLK, GL-Class (V8), M series, R-Class, S-Class, and SLK; **Merkur**—All models; **Nissan**—240Z, 250Z, 260Z, pre-2005 Altimas, Armada, Cube, Juke, Quest, Titan; **Porsche**—All models; **Saab**—All models; **Saturn**—L-Series, ION, Relay, S-Series, and VUE; **Suzuki**—Forenza, Samurai, Verona, and X-90; **Toyota**—Previa and RAV4; **VW**—EuroVan, Passat, Golf, Rabbit, and Touareg

The GM Lumina, Montana, Relay, Silhouette, Terraza, Trans Sport, Venture, and Uplander are likely the worst minivans ever built. *The Truth About Cars* (*www.thetruthaboutcars.com*) said this in August 2006, almost three years before GM's bankruptcy: "In short, the Uplander's performance doesn't even deserve the noun.... If bankruptcy is the only way to stop GM from inflicting crap vehicles like the Uplander on unsuspecting rental car drivers and (God forbid) buyers, then I can't help but wish the world's largest automaker a speedy Chapter 11."

Note in the list above how many so-called premium luxury brands have fallen out of favour and have been orphaned by shoppers and then abandoned by the automakers themselves. Their hapless owners are left with practically worthless, unreliable cars that can't be serviced properly.

Also, keep in mind that some Japanese makes from Honda, Lexus, Mazda, Nissan, and Toyota have had a resurgence of engine and transmission problems, in addition to an apparent overall decline in reliability and safety.

For example, Nissan engineers have worked overtime during the past six years to correct Quest glitches, and Toyota's Tacoma and Tundra pickups have had such serious corrosion, sudden acceleration, drivetrain, and suspension problems that the automaker has continually recalled the vehicles and even bought back at 150 percent of their resale value those trucks too rust-cankered to repair.

Evidently, as they capture more of the market share, most Japanese automakers are coasting on their earlier reputations and cutting back on quality, thereby committing the same mistake Detroit did 40 years ago when it switched to front-drives and let quality be damned. That said, the Asian automakers are still ahead of American manufacturers in terms of quality control.

Top 10 Safety and Reliability Problems

In spite of the hand-wringing over the Chrysler and GM bankruptcies in 2009, the purchase of Ford's Volvo division by Chinese interests, and the closing of Pontiac, Saab, and Saturn by GM, I have no sympathy for these automakers. They were warned repeatedly over the past four decades, by *Lemon-Aid* and by independent journalists, that the dangerous junk they were selling and their cheapskate warranty handouts would lead to their downfall.

Over the past decade, many factory-related safety defects have afflicted major auto manufacturers, but these are the top 10:

1. Airbags that deploy when they shouldn't and don't deploy when they should (all automakers)
2. Sudden, unintended acceleration (all automakers)
3. Sudden loss of braking (all automakers)
4. Sudden steering loss (Chrysler)
5. Sudden electrical shutdown (all automakers)
6. Minivan sliding door failures (all automakers)
7. Fire of unknown origin (all automakers); cruise-control/master cylinder fires (Ford)
8. Automatic transmissions that won't hold a vehicle parked on a hill, or jump out of gear (Ford, Audi, and Volkswagen)
9. Fuel leaks (all automakers)
10. Leaking tire valve stems (all automakers)

I've spent 42 years battling automakers and dealers who lie through their teeth as they try to convince customers, financial analysts, and journalists that their vehicles are well made and that the "few" defects reported (like those shown above) are caused mainly by the proverbial nut behind the wheel, poor maintenance, or abusive driving. That's why the auto industry gets little support from consumers— a lie is one thing Canadian consumers won't buy.

Chrysler Automatic Transmissions

Since the early '90s, practically all models in Chrysler's front-drive lineup have had disposable automatic transmissions. What adds insult to injury, though, is that Chrysler regularly stiffs its customers with transmission repair bills that average about $3,000—about half the average vehicle's worth after five years—when the warranty expires. Since this is far less than what a new car or minivan would cost, most owners pay the bill and then hop onto the transmission merry-go-round, replacing the same transmission at regular intervals. Go ahead, ask any transmission shop.

Leaking Tire Stems from China

Here's one example, among many, of why *Lemon-Aid* is so distrustful of auto parts imported from China.

Just when you thought Ford had learned its lesson from the hundreds of millions of dollars it paid out for faulty Firestone tires that caused Ford Explorer rollovers over a decade ago, the automaker repeats its error. This time, it's cracked, leaking tire valve stems imported from China. Made by Topseal, a subsidiary of the Shanghai Baolong Automotive Corporation, these stems were used on many of Ford's 2007 model vehicles—including the Ford Explorer. NHTSA has logged hundreds of complaints from car owners.

Although Ford says leaking tire stems is not a safety issue, Explorer rollover hearings almost a decade ago proved that any variation in tire pressure could easily cause an SUV rollover.

Faced with this danger, owners of Fords and other vehicles manufactured from late 2005 through 2008 should get their tire stems inspected and replaced if they were made by Topseal. Also, if you have bought a replacement tire or valve stem, you should check up on its country of origin.

The cost of the replacement should be borne jointly by the selling dealer and Ford of Canada after they are notified by registered letter that a refusal of the claim will mean a quick trip to small claims court. Lawsuits have been filed against several tire retailers and Dill Air Controls Products LLC, the North Carolina–based distributor of Topseal valves to retail tire stores and other distributors. These lawsuits should be airtight winners (pun intended), inasmuch as Dill admitted liability on its website at *www.dillaircontrols.com/tovalvesteminstallers.html*:

> We are diligently investigating concerns raised regarding how certain snap-in valve stems produced overseas in the second half of 2006 withstand exposure to high ozone levels. If you replace one valve stem for being cracked, we recommend replacing all four valve stems on the vehicle.

Airbag Failures

Airbags often fail to deploy when they should, deploy too late, or deploy when they shouldn't, leaving accident victims seriously—and sometimes fatally—injured. And, consumer advocates say, studies show automakers and the federal government could care less.

An investigation conducted by the *Kansas City Star* found that NHTSA is doing very little to protect consumers from the threat of airbag failure, and that even when it does take action, the process for issuing airbag recalls is painfully slow.

The *Star*'s analysis of NHTSA's accident database between 2001 and 2006 showed at least 1,400 people died in front-impact car accidents after airbags failed to deploy. And this number is on the conservative side, as the newspaper did not count accidents that involved side-impact crashes where the airbag did not work, nor did it count fatal crashes that involved principal impacts to the left or right fender, accidents where victims died after being ejected, or when a crash involved a vehicle rollover. The *Kansas City Star* investigators also did not count airbag failure if a vehicle caught fire or was submerged in water. Had the *Star* included such accidents in its investigation, the death toll would have risen by more than 4,000 fatalities.

The newspaper's investigation also found that the number of accident fatalities that occurred when an airbag did not inflate has risen dramatically over the past several years. Since 2001, the number of deaths in accidents where airbags failed has gone up by about 50 percent. And in 2006, there was a 14 percent increase in such fatalities. Still, NHTSA does not see the failure of so many airbags as a problem. According to the *Star*, when told about the 1,400 fatalities, a NHTSA spokesperson told the newspaper, "It's not a surprise to us."

Toyota "Lurch-Mobiles"

Toyota Motor Corp. says the gas pedal design in more than 4 million Toyota and Lexus vehicles makes them vulnerable to being trapped open by floor mats, thus explaining why the vehicles hesitate and then surge when accelerating from a stop. But anecdotal reports from Toyota owners, interviews with auto safety experts, and a *Los Angeles Times* review of thousands of federal traffic safety incident reports, point to another, more plausible culprit: the electronic throttles that replaced mechanical systems nine years ago. A survey of safety incidents recorded by NHTSA confirms this theory:

> Traffic slowed as it approached an entrance ramp. I applied pressure to the brakes to disengage the cruise control and slow vehicle, nothing happened. Did this several times and also tried to turn cruise off from steering column lever. Cruise did not disengage, car did not slow, my 2009 Lexus RX350 ran into the rear end of the rock hauler truck in front of me.

The *Times* found that reports of sudden acceleration in many Toyota and Lexus vehicles shot up almost immediately after the automaker adopted the so-called drive-by-wire system. Total complaints of sudden acceleration for the Lexus and Camry in the 2002–04 model years averaged 132 a year. That's up from an average of 26 annually for the 1999–2001 models, the *Times* review found.

The average number of sudden acceleration complaints involving the Tacoma jumped more than 20 times, on average, in the three years after Toyota introduced drive-by-wire in these trucks in 2005. Increases were also found on the hybrid Prius, among other models.

"These incidents are coming in left and right where you can't blame the floor mats," says Sean Kane, president of the consulting company Safety Research and Strategies. "So they are chipping away at a problem that is widespread and complicated without having to unravel a root cause that could be very expensive."

Diesel Defects

All three Detroit manufacturers have had serious injector problems with their newest diesel engines. Ford is covering repair costs through a variety of "goodwill" programs, while GM and Chrysler argue that their recent bankruptcy absolves them from any liability.

Nevertheless, J.D. Power's 2004 Vehicle Dependability Study found that Ford and Chevrolet diesel pickups were worse performers than similar gas models, while Dodge and GMC trucks were better overall. Owners of Volkswagen diesels reported up to twice as many engine problems as did owners of VWs that burn gas.

Chrysler

Although Chrysler's Cummins engine has been the most reliable diesel sold by American automakers, it also has had some serious manufacturing flaws, involving lift-pump failures that compromise injector-pump performance. Here's how independent mechanic Chuck Arnold (*chuck@thepowershop.com*) describes the problem:

> Low fuel pressure is very dangerous because it is possible for the engine to run very well right up to the moment of failure. There may be no symptom of a problem at all before you are walking. If you notice extended cranking before startup of your Cummins 24-Valve engine you should get your lift pump checked out fast. Addition of fuel lubricant enhancing additives to every tank of fuel may minimize pump damage and extend pump life. Finally, Cummins and Bosch should re-engineer their injector pump to make it less sensitive to low-fuel-pressure-induced failure. Existing safety systems designed to limit performance or signal engine trouble need to be redesigned to work when fuel pressure is inadequate so that very expensive injector pumps are not destroyed without warning.

Incidentally, Chrysler's "Customer Satisfaction Notification No. 878" authorized the free replacement of lift pumps in some 2000 and 2001 Dodge pickups.

Tell the judge: They did it then, they should do it again.

Ford

F-Series 2003 and 2004 model year trucks equipped with the 6.0L Power Stroke diesel engine were so badly flawed that they couldn't be fixed, forcing Ford to buy back over 500 units. Wary customers are snapping up Ford's earlier 7.3L diesels, which are apparently more reliable, though less powerful (275 hp versus 325 hp). Power Strokes have a history of fuel injectors that leak into the crankcase, and, on the 7.3L diesel, water can leak into the fuel tank, causing the engine to seize. Other glitches affect the turbocharger, the fuel injection control pressure sensor, and the engine control software.

> The 6-liter Power Stroke diesel V8, built by a unit of Navistar for Ford, commands nearly half the U.S. market for diesel pickups. But a raft of problems and repeat trips to dealerships for repairs has left some owners upset, threatening Ford's efforts to rebuild a reputation for quality vehicles.
>
> Soon after the new engines went on sale in November in heavy-duty Ford pickups and the Ford Excursion sport-utility vehicle, owners started reporting problems. Among the costliest is fuel seeping into the engine's oil supply in amounts large enough to ruin the engine. Other complaints included engines that ran roughly or stalled, lack of power at low speeds and harsh shifts.
>
> JUSTIN HYDE
> *REUTERS*, AUGUST 20, 2003

One Ford dealer mechanic has seen it all:

> You name it, we've seen it. Oil "blowing" into the cooling system (fortunately, not the other way around), numerous running problems, tubes blowing off the turbos, and oil leaks. We had one truck with 8 miles [13 km] on it that we had to pull the engine on. It was a truck going to Hertz, so it wasn't a big deal to the customer, Ford owned [it] anyway, but still, it was a new truck coming off the autohauler sounding like it had a 5 hp air compressor running under the hood and a dead skip.
>
> We're pulling heads off of a 6.0 now with 4,000 miles [6,400 km] on it. All these problems I've mentioned are on trucks with less than 20,000 miles [32,000 km]. My diesel tech constantly wishes that since they had worked all the kinks out of the 7.3, Ford would have kept it. So far, we've had six buybacks. The one we're pulling the heads off of now will be the next. Before this, I only had one buyback, in four years.

After years of stonewalling and rejecting *Lemon-Aid*'s criticism and owners' refund claims for faulty 6.0L diesel truck engines, Ford now agrees that its engines were crap and has demanded that the supplier of these engines, International Engine

Group, pay the automaker compensation for the defective diesels. Ironic, isn't it? Ford is now doing to International what many angry owners of Power Stroke 6.0L-diesel-equipped trucks threatened to do to Ford. And, as in the Ford Explorer/Firestone tire debacle, neither company will admit guilt, or even apologize to owners for their shoddy product.

Ford's 2008–09 6.4L diesels are continuing to use faulty fuel injectors that may leak fuel into the engine crankcase, causing the oil level to rise and possibly damage the engine. Ford set up a "goodwill" warranty extension (Campaign 09B08) to replace these leaking injectors for free, but that program expired in September 2010. Nevertheless, Ford is now paying for replacements under a "goodwill" warranty on a case-by-case basis. What does all this mean? Don't take no for an answer.

ENGINE–LACK OF POWER

BULLETIN NO.: 10-2-2   **DATE: FEBRUARY 15, 2010**

FORD: 2008–10 F-Super Duty
ISSUE: Some 2008–10 6.4L F-Super Duty vehicles may experience a lack of power during acceleration and perhaps the illumination of the check air filter message in instrument cluster message center. The lack of power condition may occur when the air filter element becomes packed with snow, thereby restricting required air flow to the engine. This service bulletin allows for the free installation of a protective grill under the base warranty.
NOTE: THE WINTER GRILL COVER MUST BE REMOVED WHEN TEMPERATURES ARE GREATER THAN 50°F (10°C) (32°F (0°C) WHEN TOWING) OR ENGINE DAMAGE CAN RESULT. THE SNOW DEFLECTOR GASKET CAN REMAIN INSTALLED IN THE VEHICLE YEAR-ROUND.

ENGINE–REDUCED POWER

BULLETIN NO.: 08-06-04-054A   **DATE: JANUARY 7, 2010**

2007–10 Silverado and Sierra 2500/3500 Series Equipped with Duramax Diesel Engine (RPO LMM)
SUBJECT: Snow or Ice Ingestion into Air Cleaner Element, Malfunction Indicator Lamp (MIL) Illuminated, Engine Power is Reduced Message Displayed, DTC P0101 Set (Perform Repair as Outlined).

Also, both Ford and General Motors have had problems with snow accumulation in the air filter element, restricting air passage to the engine and possibly causing severe engine damage. Both companies are liable for the free repair of any damage called by this poor design. Or did they imagine Canada was a snow-free zone?

General Motors

GM's diesel engine failures primarily affect the 6.5L and 6.6L Duramax engine. The 6.5L powerplants are noted for cracked blocks, broken cranks, cracks in the main webbing, cracked cylinder heads, coolant in the oil, loss of power, hard starting, low oil pressure, and oil contamination. Duramax 6.6L engines have been plagued by persistent oil leaks and excessive oil burning, and by defective turbochargers, fuel-injection pumps, and injectors, causing seized engines, chronic stalling, loss of power, hard starts, and excessive gas consumption. To its credit, GM has a Special Policy program that extends the warranty to 11 years on injection pumps installed in 1994–2002 models. GM also extended the fuel injector's warranty coverage for owners of 2001 and 2002 Duramax 6600–equipped pickup trucks. Another program, Special Policy #04039, was set up in June 2004 to give additional warranty protection for seven years from the date the vehicle was placed into service, or for 330,000 km (200,000 miles)—whichever comes first. Finally, anecdotal reports from diesel owners tell *Lemon-Aid* that engine head gasket repairs or replacements are covered by a "goodwill" policy for up to 7 years/160,000 km.

Why Smart Canadians Buy Used

It simply costs too much to own a new car or SUV. In fact, many of my readers tell me that the cost of their new car exceeded the downpayment on their first mortgage. No wonder that of the 4.4 million automobiles that were sold in Canada in 2010, most were second-hand (2. 9 million).

The Cherolet Silverado (above) and its GMC Sierra twin are noted for their overall durability. Too bad their diesel engines were so screwed up.

More vehicles are being traded because more are available. R.L. Polk Data says an incredible 17.9 percent of the light trucks manufactured in the last 25 years are still in service (almost three times the rate for cars). GM trucks have the most longevity: 21.7 percent of all the Chevrolet pickups sold 25 years ago are still on the road.

Read on for more reasons why Canadians increasingly prefer to buy used vehicles rather than new ones.

Less Initial Cash Outlay, Slower Vehicle Depreciation, "Secret" Warranty Repair Refunds, and Better and Cheaper Parts Availability

New-vehicle prices average around $30,000 and insurance can cost almost $2,000 a year for young drivers. CAA calculates that once you add financing costs, maintenance, taxes, and a host of other expenses, the yearly outlay in 2010 for a small-sized car like a Chevrolet Cobalt driven 18,000 km a year is $6,257, or $7.14 a day; a Dodge Grand Caravan may cost about $8,568 a year, or $23.47 per day; and, surprisingly, a Toyota Prius hybrid, touted for its fuel frugality, hovers in the middle with a yearly outlay of $7,333, or $20.09 a day.

For a comprehensive though depressing comparative analysis of all the costs involved in owning a vehicle over one- to 10-year periods, access Alberta's consumer information website at *www.agric.gov.ab.ca/app24/costcalculators/vehicle/getvechimpls.jsp*.

Don't forget the savings. Used vehicles aren't sold with $1,600–$2,000 transport fees or $495 "administration" charges, and you can legally avoid paying some sales tax when you buy privately. That's right: You'll pay at least 10 percent less than the dealer's price, and you may avoid the federal Goods and Services Tax that in some provinces applies to dealer sales only.

Depreciation works for you

If someone were to ask you to invest in stocks or bonds guaranteed to be worth less than half their initial purchase value after three to four years, you'd probably head for the door. But this is exactly the trap you're falling into when you buy a new vehicle that will likely lose up to 60 percent of its value after three years of use.

When you buy used, the situation is altogether different. That same vehicle can be purchased three years later, in good condition and with much of the manufacturer's warranty remaining, for less than half its original cost.

Secret warranty refunds

Almost all automakers use secret "goodwill" warranties to cover factory-related defects long after a vehicle's original warranty has expired. This creates a huge fleet of used vehicles that are eligible for free repairs.

We're not talking about merely a few months' extension on small items. In fact, some free repairs—like those related to Mercedes engine sludge and GM diesel engines—are authorized up to 11 years or more as part of "goodwill" programs. Still, most secret warranty extensions hover around the five- to seven-year mark and seldom cover vehicles exceeding 160,000 km. Yet there are exceptions, like the secret catalytic converter warranty that will pay for the converter's replacement up to 10 years, or 120,000 miles (193,000 km), on all Chevrolet Malibu and Pontiac G6 models.

Incidentally, automakers and dealers claim that there are no "secret" warranties, since they are all published in service bulletins. Although this is technically correct, have you ever tried to get a copy of a service bulletin? Or, if you did manage to get a copy, did the dealer or automaker say the benefits are applicable only in the States? Pure weasel speak!

Parts

Used parts can have a surprisingly long lifespan. Generally, a new gasoline-powered car or minivan can be expected to run with few problems for at least 200,000–300,000 km (125,000–200,000 miles) in its lifetime and a diesel-powered vehicle can easily double those figures. Some repairs will crop up at regular intervals along with preventive maintenance, and your yearly running costs should average about $1,000. Buttressing the argument that vehicles get cheaper to operate the longer you keep them, the U.S. Department of Transportation points out that the average vehicle requires one or more major repairs after every five years of use. Once these repairs are done, however, the vehicle can then be run relatively trouble-free for another five years or more, as long as the environment isn't too hostile. In fact, the farther west you go in Canada, the longer owners keep their vehicles—an average of 10 years or more in some provinces.

Time is on your side in other ways, too. Three years after a model's launch, the replacement parts market usually catches up to consumer demand. Dealers stock larger inventories, and parts wholesalers and independent parts manufacturers expand their output.

Used replacement parts are unquestionably easier to come by after this three-year point through bargaining with local garages, carefully searching auto wreckers' yards, or looking on the Internet. And a reconditioned or used part usually costs one-third to half the price of a new part. There's generally no difference in the quality of reconditioned mechanical components, and they're often guaranteed for as long as, or longer than, new ones. In fact, some savvy shoppers use the ratings in Part Three of this guide to see which parts have a short life and then buy those parts from retailers who give lifetime warranties on their brakes, exhaust systems, tires, batteries, and so on.

Buying from discount outlets or independent garages, or ordering through mail-order houses, can save you big bucks (30–35 percent) on the cost of new parts and another 15 percent on labour when compared with dealer charges. Mass merchandisers like Costco are another good source of savings; they cut prices and add free services and lifetime warranties (on brakes, mufflers, and transmissions).

Body parts are a different story. Although car company repair parts cost 60 percent more than certified generic aftermarket parts, buyers would be wise to buy only original equipment manufacturer (OEM) parts supplied by automakers in order to get body panels that fit well, protect better in collisions, and have maximum rust resistance, says *Consumer Reports* magazine. Insurance appraisers often substitute cheaper, lower-quality aftermarket body parts in collision repairs, but *Consumer Reports* found that 71 percent of those policyholders who requested OEM parts got them with little or no hassle. The magazine suggests that consumers complain to their provincial Superintendent of Insurance if OEM parts aren't provided.

With some European models, you can count on a lot of aggravation and expense caused by the unacceptably slow distribution of parts and by the high markup. Because these companies have a quasi-monopoly on replacement parts, there are few independent suppliers you can turn to for help. And junkyards, the last-chance repository for inexpensive car parts, are unlikely to carry foreign parts for vehicles that are more than three years old or are manufactured in small numbers.

Finding parts for Asian and domestic cars and trucks is no problem because of the large number of vehicles produced, the presence of hundreds of independent suppliers, the ease with which relatively simple parts can be interchanged from one model to another, and the large reservoir of used parts stocked by junkyards.

Insurance Costs Less

The price you pay for insurance can vary significantly, not only between insurance companies but also within the same company over time. But one thing does remain constant: The insurance for used vehicles is a lot cheaper than new-car coverage, and through careful comparison shopping, insurance premium payouts can be substantially reduced.

Beware of "captive" brokers

Although the cost of insurance premiums for used cars is often one-third to half the cost of the premiums you would pay for a new vehicle, using the Internet to find the lowest auto insurance quote and accepting a large deductible are critical to keeping premiums low.

Use InsuranceHotline.com

InsuranceHotline.com is the largest online quoting service for car insurance in Canada. *InsuranceHotline.com* represents 80 percent of the Canadian auto insurance, home insurance, and life insurance market for consumers searching for the lowest rate. At no charge, the agency will run applicants' profiles through its database of 30 insurance companies to find the insurer with the lowest rate.

Surprisingly, some of the vehicles with the poorest reliability, durability, and fuel economy ratings, such as GM's Hummer, have good insurance rates and don't see the same multiplication of premiums in the case of a ticket or accident (in which case, your premiums can almost quadruple). When rates for a 2006 Hummer and a 2006 Honda Civic were calculated, the Civic driver saved only $49 compared to the Hummer premium. But add a police ticket and accident to the equation, and the Civic owner could pay over $2,500 more.

Here are some other *InsuranceHotline.com* findings:

- A family car under $35,000 can cost more to insure than one over $35,000.
- SUVs under $35,000 don't always cost more to insure than a family car or a small luxury model.
- Luxury cars mean luxury premiums, costing on average about $500 more annually to insure than family cars, SUVs, muscle cars, or hybrids.
- Hybrids' fuel savings can be wiped out by higher-cost insurance premiums that rival what you would pay to insure a muscle car.

Auto theft in Canada: The list you don't want to be on

According to the Insurance Bureau of Canada, automobile theft costs Canadians close to $1 billion every year, including $542 million for insurers to fix or replace stolen cars, $250 million in police, health care, and court system costs, and millions more for correctional services.

Thieves generally steal cars for one of four reasons:

1. For sale abroad: Stolen cars are often immediately packed—with their vehicle identification numbers (VINs) still intact—and shipped abroad, where they are sold for many times their original market value.
2. For sale to unsuspecting consumers: Stolen cars may be given a new identity with false vehicle identification plates, and then sold to unsuspecting consumers. They can also be dismantled and sold for parts.
3. To get somewhere: This is commonly, but inappropriately, referred to as "joyriding." Auto theft of any kind is still a crime, and innocent people do get hurt or killed as a result.
4. To commit another crime: Stolen cars used to commit other crimes are often recovered—abandoned and badly damaged—within 48 hours of their theft.

CANADA'S MOST STOLEN VEHICLES OF 2011

The top 10 most frequently stolen vehicles in Canada are:

1. 2009 Toyota Venza 4-door
2. 1999 Honda Civic SiR 2-door
3. 2000 Honda Civic SiR 2-door
4. 2006 Ford F-350 Pickup Truck 4WD
5. 2002 Cadillac Escalade EXT 4-door AWD
6. 2006 Chevrolet TrailBlazer SS 4-door 4WD
7. 2007 Ford F-350 Pickup Truck 4WD
8. 2001 Pontiac Aztek 4-door AWD
9. 1998 Acura Integra 2-door
10. 1999 Acura Integra 2-door

Source: Insurance Bureau of Canada

"Although many high-end, four-wheel-drive vehicles like the BMW X6, Toyota RAV4, and Lexus RX350 don't appear in the top ten," says Rick Dubin, Vice-President, Investigations at the Insurance Bureau of Canada, "thieves are stealing them in greater numbers than ever before. There is a demand for vehicles like these in Ghana, Nigeria, Dubai, Lebanon, the Middle East, and Eastern Europe. Organized criminals are shipping the vehicles overseas, and as a result, the recovery rate for stolen vehicles in Canada continues to decline, even though there are fewer thefts in total."

Incidentally, *Insurance hotline.com* got insurance quotes for the above most stolen vehicles and discovered their premiums didn't reflect their higher risk. Says *Insurance hotline.com* spokesperson Tammy Ezer:

Car insurance quotes have been prepared on all 10 cars, based on one identical driving profile—40 year old male, living in Toronto, Ontario with a clean driving record. The cost to insure the below cars, in order from lowest to highest insurance rates, are (order of most stolen vehicle list in brackets):

1. 2001 Pontiac Aztek 4-door AWD (8)
2. 2006 Ford F350 Pickup Truck 4WD (4)
3. 2007 Ford F350 Pickup Truck 4WD (7)
4. 2009 Toyota Venza 4-door (1)
5. 2002 Cadillac Escalade EXT 4-door AWD (5)
6. 1998 Acura Integra 2-door (9)
7. 1999 Acura Integra 2-door (10)
8. 2006 Chevrolet TrailBlazer SS 4-door 4WD (6)
9. 1999 Honda Civic SiR 2-door (2)
10. 2000 Honda Civic SiR 2-door (3)

The most-stolen vehicle, a 2009 Toyota Venza 4-door, is in fact the fourth cheapest vehicle to insure of all the stolen vehicles. Although there might now be a stigma that the Venza will cost more to insure because it has a high rate of theft, this does not seem to be the case based on the rates currently available within our network. Honda Civics appear to have the highest insurance rates compared to the other vehicles on the list, which may be caused by the amount of claims processed against these vehicles or perhaps the safety features on these vehicles since they are older cars, in addition to the fact that they appear on the top 10 stolen cars list. Comparing car insurance quotes is the best way for consumers to save money on auto insurance. Even if they find out that they cannot save money, they will have peace of mind knowing that they are currently paying a favourable rate.

CANADA'S LEAST STOLEN VEHICLES OF 2010

2003 Buick Le Sabre 4-door
2006 Buick Rendezvous 4-door AWD
2007 Buick Terraza EXT
2009 Chevrolet Impala 4-door
1999 Ford Escort Wagon
2007 Ford Freestyle Wagon
2002 Ford Thunderbird Convertible 2-door
2006 Ford/Mercury Crown Victoria/Grand Marquis 4-door
2004 Hyundai XG 350 4-door
2009 Kia Sportage 4-door 2WD

The Insurance Bureau of Canada claims that individuals steal less expensive cars because they are easier to steal and tend not to have alarm systems. More data on which vehicles are stolen the most and the least and accident claims stats on a model and year basis are just a click away at *www.ibc.ca*.

Insured collision repairs

The Automobile Repair Regulatory Council says the owner of a motor vehicle damaged in an accident has the right to choose the shop that will do the repairs. Do not waste your time or that of several shops getting several estimates. Select a repair facility you feel comfortable with, then notify your agent or insurance company, or ask the shop to call on your behalf. Your insurance adjuster may require that the damage to the vehicle be inspected. This can be done at an insurance drive-in claim centre or at the shop you have chosen.

Here are some things to inspect yourself, before driving away:

- Check the appearance of the repaired area close up and at a distance.
- Examine the paint for colour match, texture, and overspray.
- Take a test drive to check mechanical repairs.
- Check that the vehicle is clean.

If you are not satisfied, mention your concerns immediately and follow up with a written claim and a time period for the work to be completed.

Notify your insurance company

Before you sign any work orders, notify your insurance company or agent, and tell them where the damaged vehicle can be inspected. Most collision and repair centres guarantee their work to some degree, which may not include the paint job. Ask to see a copy of the shop's guarantee and have any information you do not understand clarified. As for the paint warranty: Try to get at least a one-year guarantee.

Choosing a qualified repair shop

Look for signs that indicate repair technician certification and training. Membership in professional trade associations indicates that the shop is keeping up with the latest repair procedures. Also, affiliation with automobile associations like the AMA, BCAA, or CAA is a plus, because you can use the association to exert pressure when the repair takes too long, or the work isn't done properly. In Part Two you will find jurisprudence where one auto club was found liable for the negligence of one of its member garages (see page 110).

Defects Can't Hide

You can easily avoid any nasty surprises by having your chosen used vehicle checked out by an independent mechanic (for $85–$100) before you purchase. This examination protects you against any of the vehicle's potential hidden defects. It's also a tremendous negotiating tool, since you can use the cost of any needed repairs to bargain down the purchase price.

It's easier to get permission to have the vehicle inspected if you promise to give the seller a copy of the inspection report should you decide not to buy it. If you still can't get permission to have the vehicle inspected elsewhere, walk away from the deal, no matter how tempting the selling price. The seller is obviously trying to put one over on you. Ignore the standard excuses that the vehicle isn't insured, that the registration plates have expired, or that the vehicle has a dead battery.

You Know the Past, Present, and Future

Smart customers can easily run an Internet history check on a vehicle and its previous owners through CarProof ($49.95, or $64,95 if you want ICBC vehicle claims history info, as well) and then read through *Lemon-Aid* to get answers to the following questions before signing a contract: What did the vehicle first sell for, and what is its present insured value? Who serviced it? Has it had accident repairs? Are parts easily available? How much of the original warranty or repair warranties are left? Does the vehicle have a history of costly performance-related defects? What free repairs are available through "goodwill" warranty extensions? (See "Secret Warranties/Internal Bulletins/Service Tips" in Part Three.)

Quick and Cheap Justice

Lawyers win, regardless of whether you win or lose. And you're likely to lose more than you'll ever get back using the traditional court system in a used-car dispute.

But if you're just a bit creative, you'll discover there are many federal and provincial consumer-protection laws that go far beyond whatever protection may be offered by the standard new-vehicle warranty. In fact, Nova Scotia just passed its own Lemon Law. Furthermore, buyers of used vehicles don't usually have to conform to any arbitrary rules or service guidelines to get this protection.

Let's say you do get stuck with a vehicle that's unreliable, has undisclosed accident damage, or doesn't perform as promised. Fortunately, small claims courts have a jurisdiction limit of $10,000–$25,000—more than enough to cover the cost of repairs, or compensate you if the vehicle is taken back. That way, any dispute between buyer and seller can be settled within a few months, without lawyers or excessive court costs. Furthermore, you're not likely to face a battery of lawyers standing in for the automaker and dealer in front of a stern-faced judge. You may not even have to face a judge at all, since many cases are settled through court-imposed mediators at a pretrial meeting that's usually scheduled a month or two after filing.

Choosing Safe "Wheels"

Looking through Part Three can help you make a list of safe and reliable buys to consider before you even leave the house.

The best indicator of a car's overall safety is the NHTSA's front, side, and rollover, crashworthiness ratings, applicable to most vehicles made and sold over the past several decades in North America. You will then want to compare NHTSA scores with similar crash tests carried out by the Insurance Institute for Highway Safety.

IIHS crashes vehicles differently and rates head restraint effectiveness and roof crush resistance as well. Results from these two agencies are posted for each model rated in Part Three. Readers who wish to go directly to the respective website of either group should click on *safercar.gov* or *www.iihs.org/ ratings*.

However, there are many other national and international testing agencies that you may consult, and they can be found at *www. crashtest.com/netindex.htm*. This site shows the results of early crash tests of cars that were sold in Australia, Europe, and Japan

2008 Smart Fortwo: Front- and side-impact results and rollover findings are worrisome.

and that are just now coming to the North American market. Take the Mercedes Smart Car as an example: Nowhere in Mercedes' or Chrysler's sales brochures did I see a reference to the Smart's unimpressive "Acceptable" frontal crash test rating for early models, or any mention that during the 2008 Smart Fortwo's side-impact test the driver-side door unlatched and opened. A door opening during a side-impact crash increases the likelihood of occupant ejection and massive injuries or death.

Of course, no one expects to be in a collision, but NHTSA estimates that every vehicle will be in two accidents of varying severity during its lifetime. So why not put the averages on your side?

Reliable, Cheap, and "Green" Buys

Consider these important points when making your choice:

- The 21.3 million cars and light-duty trucks on Canada's roads today are responsible for 12 percent of the nation's greenhouse gas emissions.
- Nationwide, 5,000 deaths per year are attributed to smog pollutants, which alone cost the Ontario economy $10 billion in health care costs and business losses, according to the Ontario Medical Association.
- By purchasing a used vehicle, you are already doing a lot for the environment by not adding to the vehicle population. Nevertheless, in choosing a fuel-efficient, safe small car, you are also protecting your life and your wallet.

Unfortunately, our federal and provincial governments have wasted millions of dollars in giving cash incentives in several misguided attempts to encourage motorists to buy small cars, to promote the use of ethanol, and to scrap cars and trucks that are 10 years or older.

The Canadian House of Commons' Standing Committee on Industry, Science and Technology confirmed "Cash for Clunkers" rebates would not help the environment and would waste money. In its *Study of the Crisis in the Automotive Sector in Canada*, which it released in March 2009, the Committee concluded that the only "green" that would result would be the dollars going from car buyers' wallets into car dealers' pockets:

The Automotive Industries Association of Canada (AIA) claimed that a scrappage program either as an environmental or safety measure was flawed. Although its members supported the federal government in offering incentives for Canadians to purchase new vehicles, it opposed taking older cars off the road for a number of economic reasons:

- Replacement parts purchased for repair of older cars are often recycled or remanufactured components which keep replacement parts prices competitive and are good for the environment by reducing waste and saving energy costs;
- A strong inventory of recycled and remanufactured parts keeps repair prices down for consumers and provides options for keeping their cars on the road. Motorists in this economic downturn do not want to take on more debt and added insurance costs with the purchase of a new vehicle;
- Scrappage incentives would hurt thousands of independent repair shops, auto restorers, customizers and their customers across the country who depend on the used car market. The automotive aftermarket provides thousands of Canadian jobs and generates millions of dollars in local, provincial and federal tax revenues;
- The program will reduce the number of used vehicles available for low-income individuals and drive up the cost of the remaining vehicles; and
- The premise that existing trucks and SUVs must be scrapped in order to save energy is short-sighted. The reduced "carbon footprint" argument does not factor-in the energy and natural resources expended in manufacturing the existing car, spent scrapping it and manufacturing a replacement car.

Here are *Lemon-Aid*'s picks of the top cheap, reliable, and environmentally friendly used cars, SUVs, trucks, and vans. Regrettably, no vehicles made by Chrysler or General Motors made this list, due to their poor quality.

Ford Escape/Mazda Tribute—A gas-saver; Escape Hybrid is outstanding but pricey. **Ford Focus**—Model years 2005–11 are more reliable and fuel-efficient; earlier buys are toxic. **Ford Fusion**—Similar to the Lincoln MKZ and Mercury Milan, this family-sized car offers good fuel economy, better-than-average reliability, and a reasonable retail price. The gas/electric hybrid is particularly fuel-efficient. **Honda Civic**—Up to 2011, a reliable fuel miser; pricey, but dealers will haggle this year. **Honda Fit**—A good-performing minicar; 2009 model year vehicles get power and interior upgrades. **Honda Odyssey**—Better engineered and better performing than Toyota's Sienna; some price haggling. **Hyundai Accent**—Cheap, with good fuel economy, but not-so-great acceleration. **Hyundai Elantra/Tiburon**—Reliable, cheap, roomy; gives fair gas mileage. **Hyundai Sonata**—In exchange for good fuel economy, you put up with a busy ride and numb steering. **Hyundai Tucson**—A reliable and versatile downsized SUV; horsepower may be overstated. **Mazda5**—A mini-minivan that carries six passengers and burns fuel like a compact car. **Nissan Sentra**—Reasonably priced, reliable, and provides average fuel economy. **Nissan Versa**—A reliable "jumbo shrimp"; roomy for a small car, and hoards fuel; a bit pricey. **Suzuki Aerio and Swift**—Cheap, cheap, and cheap; for urban dwellers only. **Toyota Corolla**—Reliable, spacious, and comfortable; 1997–2009 models were not as well built. **Toyota Echo**—Economical and bland, but more reliable and cheaper than a Yaris. **Toyota Tercel**—A cheap fuel-sipper that's not as refined as a Honda Fit or Nissan Versa. **VW TDI**—Cheap to run, and simple to service through the 2007 models.

Note: We don't recommend gas-electric engine hybrids (except for the Ford Escape Hybrid SUV), such as the Toyota Prius, Honda Insight, or Civic Hybrid. Their fuel economy can be 20–40 percent worse than the automakers report, their long-term reliability is unimpressive, battery replacement costs may be $3,000, and their retail prices are almost double what a Toyota Corolla would cost. A 2009 Prius that originally sold for $27,400 is now worth a paltry $20,000, while a 2009 Corolla CE that sold for $14,565 will command $10,500. Hmm…And, with the Corolla, you won't ever need to buy a battery pack. Oh, what a feeling!

Cars for Seniors

Drivers over 80 are the fastest-growing segment of the driving population. According to Candrive, the Canadian Driving Research Initiative for Vehicular Safety in the Elderly, there are currently about 3 million senior drivers in Canada, and their numbers are expected to double by 2040.

A quarter of Canadians 85 and older have a driver's license and it is estimated that by 2030 there will be roughly 15,000 centenarians driving in Canada.

Husbands do the bulk of family driving, which usually involves short trips (11–17 km per day, on average) for medical appointments and visits to family, friends, and shopping malls. This puts older women, who tend to outlive their husbands, in a serious bind because of their lack of driving experience—particularly in rural areas, where driving is a necessity rather than a choice.

Seniors, like most drivers, want cars that are reliable, relatively inexpensive, and fuel efficient. Additionally, older drivers need vehicles that compensate for some of the physical challenges associated with aging and provide crash protection in accidents that are more common with mature drivers (side impacts, for example). Furthermore, as drivers get older, they find that the very act of getting into a car (sitting down while moving sideways, without bumping their heads or twisting their necks) demands considerable acrobatic skill. And don't even ask about shoulder pain when reaching up and over for the shoulder belt.

Driving Through the Ages

Accident death rates are much higher for older occupants than for younger age groups. This is because our fragility increases as we age, and our ability to withstand the forces involved in crashes become much lower. Of course, our driving skills also deteriorate as we age:

At age 40: Thought processing starts slowing down, multitasking becomes more difficult, night and peripheral vision worsens, and glare blinds you for a longer period of time.

At age 50: Nine in 10 people use bifocals, reaction time slows, and distractions increase.

At age 60: Muscle strength and range of motion decrease by as much as 25 percent. Hearing acuity is reduced.

At age 70: Arthritic joints may make movement painful and restrict mobility, and conditions such as stroke, Parkinson's disease, hypertension, and diabetes may impair cognitive ability or affect behaviour.

Access and Comfort

Drivers with arthritic hands often have to insert a pencil into their key ring to twist the key in the ignition.

Since hand and grip strength can be a problem for seniors, make sure your ignition lock doesn't require that much effort. A thicker steering wheel also requires less hand and wrist strength to grip and handle to make turns. Power locks, trunk and tailgate closers, mirrors and windows are a must, especially if the vehicle will be operated with hand controls. A remote keyless fob will allow entry without fumbling with the door lock. Cruise control can be helpful for those with lower-body mobility challenges. Also, consider vehicles with adjustable pedals, a tilt steering column, and a height-adjustable, power-assisted driver's seat with memory.

Ideally, you want to balance lumbar support with the ability to reach the pedals and see over the dashboard, without putting stress on muscles that are losing some flexibility.

Some vehicle types are more senior-friendly:

Four-door vehicles—Doors are lighter and easier to open than two-door coupes.

Performance sports cars—Usually have seats with more heavily padded side and thigh bolsters, which force occupants to "climb out" of their seats.

SUVs, trucks, and vans—Easier to get in and out of than a sedan, since the higher seats require less bending. Minivans offer a higher seat, plus a more easily reached lower door.

Look for vehicles that are easy to enter and exit, with door openings that are wide enough for easy access. Ensure that the door catches when opened on a slight incline so that it doesn't close as you are exiting. Vans, SUVs, and trucks should also have a low step-up and an easily reached inside-grip handle, as well as other handles located throughout the interior. Other vehicles need low thresholds beneath the doors because many older drivers have a great deal of difficulty lifting their legs to get out. The trunk or rear cargo area should also have a low liftover and room to stow a wheelchair or scooter.

Drivers with limited mobility need a seated position that is close to standard chair height: not too low so that you fall into it, and not too tall that you have to climb up and then back down. Concave bucket seats may complicate exiting the vehicle, though heated seats with lumbar support are great for drivers with back pain.

Bench seats are preferable because they're roomier and easier to access. Incidentally, some General Motors' vans may be fitted with a removable Sit-N-Lift feature that provides a motorized, rotating lift-and-lower passenger seat accessed through the middle door.

Safety Features for Older Drivers

- A low beltline (the lower edge of the glass area) improves the driver's downward sightlines, making parking easier. As drivers age, reduced flexibility in the shoulders and neck can restrict head movement, so having more glass area is a huge help.
- Large, wide-angle side mirrors and rear-view mirrors help compensate for reduce vision caused by minor strokes and glaucoma, limited range of motion, or difficulties twisting to check for blind spots while merging or backing up. A rear-mounted camera helps when backing up; however, the rear image may be distorted, making it impossible to judge distance accurately.
- The driver's seat should be mounted high enough to give a commanding view of the road (with slower reaction times, seniors need earlier warnings). The driver's seat must offer enough rearward travel to attenuate the force of an exploding airbag, which can be particularly hazardous to older or small-statured occupants, and anyone recovering from surgery. Adjustable gas and brake pedals are a must for short-legged drivers.
- Head restraints shouldn't force your chin into your chest.
- Cars that are brighter and lighter in colour are easier for other drivers to see at night and when it rains.
- Look for bright dashboard gauges that can be seen in sunlight, and instruments with large-sized controls. Drivers with diminished vision and sensitivity to glare will find extendable sun visors helpful.
- Remote-controlled mirrors are a must, along with adjustable, unobtrusive head restraints and a non-reflective front windshield (many drivers put a cloth on the dash-top to cut the distraction). Make sure that the brake and accelerator pedals aren't mounted too close together.
- A superior crashworthiness rating is essential, as well as dual-stage torso- and

head-protecting side airbags, since many intersection collisions involving mature drivers occur when drivers are making a turn into oncoming traffic. The extra head protection can make a critical difference in side impacts. Dual-stage and dual-threshold airbags are recommended to attenuate the force of the airbags' deployment.

- The deployment force depends on crash severity, distance from the driver and passenger, and weight of the driver.
- Look for headlights that give you a comfortable view at night, as well as dash-mounted turn signal indicators that are easily seen and heard. Ensure that the vehicle's knobs and switches are large and easy to identify and that the gauges are sufficiently backlit that they don't wash out in daylight or produce too much glare at night.
- Features that are especially important to drivers wearing bifocals: A blue-green light colour that measures 505 nanometres is the ideal gauge colour in terms of being easiest to see. The belief that instruments illuminated or marked in red are easiest to see is a myth. Also, be sure to check that the dash doesn't cause windshield glare (a common problem with light-coloured dash panels).
- An antilock braking system, or ABS, prevents wheels from locking during emergency braking. Drivers using ABS can stop the car and retain control without "pumping" the brakes, which can be challenging for older drivers.
- Electronic traction and stability control (ESC) is a feature that helps prevent loss of control in turns, or during a sudden stop, especially on slippery roads. ESC allows drivers to compensate for slower reaction times and make quick corrections. Vehicles that come with ESC are listed on the National Highway Safety Administration website: *www.safercar.gov.*
- Having an easily accessed, full-sized spare tire and a user-friendly lug wrench and jack stand is also important.

Features of Limited Utility

Car buyers are warned that some safety, performance, and convenience features may not work as well as advertised and may issue false, distracting alerts, or be costly to service. A chief offender is Ford's new MyTouch and SYNC options found on many cars in its 2011–12 lineup. Owners find these features very buggy, slow, and not-at-all intuitive to use. Some compare these options to the miserable performance of BMW's iDrive system used a decade ago and then quickly changed to quell an owner rebellion.

Says one Ford owner:

> Ford's MyTouch infotainment system integrates multiple controls and info readouts via what used to be the entertainment system in what is a way busier approach than reaching over towards the center stack to make adjustments via rotary knobs or push buttons. I don't need to be cursoring up and down through menu options—while I am driving in heavy traffic, period. It isn't as bad as texting while driving, but it is close.

Other devices of dubious utility are some navigation systems, voice-recognition, rear obstacle cameras, blind-spot monitors, lane changing alerts, tire-pressure monitoring systems, and poorly-positioned head-restraints.

Good "Senior" Car Choices

Audi A8—This luxurious car's Multi-Media Interface controls all features of the car. The keyless startup, seat heaters, ventilated and massaging front seats will help you a lot.

BMW 7 Series—This luxurious sedan is ideal for arthritis sufferers. It features 20-way adjustable front seats, heated power rear seats, rear and front parking sensors, and a buttonless shifter.

Ford Five Hundred—This car features a tall seating position, which is ideal for people with stooping and bending problem. There is also a power-adjustable driver seat, rear parking sensors, and adjustable pedals. The trunk is spacious and can hold walkers and scooters with ease.

Honda Civic Hybrid—This eco-friendly car has a host of features that will give you an enjoyable ride. It features satellite navigation, three-point seat belts, and front head restraints.

Honda CR-V—Senior-friendly features include backup camera, tilt-and-telescoping steering wheel, height-adjustable driver seat, and heated passenger and driver and seats.

Infiniti M35—The car features heated driver and passenger seats, tilt-and-telescoping steering wheel, height-adjustable driver seat, keyless ignition, and a 10-way power-adjustable driver seat.

Lexus LS 460—This car features a voice-activated navigation system, 12-way power-adjustable driver seat, advanced parking guidance system, keyless ignition, and heated passenger and driver seats.

Mercedes-Benz S550—Features include 14-way power-adjustable driver seat, backup camera, keyless ignition, night vision, and tilt-and-telescoping steering wheel.

Toyota Avalon—This roomy sedan is a favourite among seniors. It has a number of senior-friendly features like tilt-and-telescoping steering wheel, heated power passenger and driver seats, and keyless ignition.

Toyota Camry and Hybrid—Features tilt-and-telescoping steering wheel, keyless ignition, eight-way power-adjustable driver seat, and manual-adjustable lumbar support.

Toyota Prius—If you are suffering from arthritis, this car's keyless ignition system is a big help. It also features touch-screen controls and backup camera display for parking.

Toyota Sienna—This car, seating seven or eight passengers, is roomy and senior-friendly. It offers a Mobility Upgrade Package with wheelchair or scooter lift.

Where to Go for More Information

Simple assistive devices are available to make driving safer and easier. Items such as seatbelt adjusters, handibars, or expanded mirrors are available either in home catalogs or at medical supply or auto parts stores. Other items that do not require a specialist to install are easy-locking seatbelts, visor extenders, steering wheel covers to improve grip, seat and back support cushions to relieve back pain or improve the ability to see over the steering wheel, keyless ignitions, and doors that automatically lock and open. (See: *www.colonial medical.com.*)

- The National Mobility Equipment Dealers Association (NMEDA) supports the use of safe, reliable vehicles and modifications to enhance accessibility for people with special needs. (See: *www.nmeda.org.*)
- The National Highway Traffic Safety Administration (NHTSA) addresses automotive safety issues for persons with disabilities. (See: *www.nhtsa.dot.gov/cars/rules/adaptive.*)
- See AAA's "Safe Features for Mature Drivers" (*www.aaaexchange.com/Main/Default.asp?CategoryID=18&SubCategoryID=86&ContentID=388*).
- AAA's list of vehicles and their options suitable for seniors can be accessed at *www.aaapublicaffairs.com/Assets/Files/20083211031180.SFMD-VehicleListv6.2.pdf.*

Fuel Economy Fantasies

The mileage promised on car stickers is grossly inflated, sometimes by as much as 30 percent. *Consumer Reports* now admits that hybrids alone account for fuel consumption discrepancies that average 12 L/100 km (19 mpg) worse than the city-driving rating given by the U.S. Environmental Protection Agency.

But Chrysler, Ford, GM, Honda, Lexus, and Toyota don't tell the average buyer that their so-called fuel-frugal hybrids and ethanol-friendly or diesel-powered vehicles are simply high-tech, feel-good PR machines that often don't hold their values as well as conventionally powered comparable models. Not only does it cost much more than advertised to run vehicles equipped with special engines and alternate fuels, but poor reliability and higher servicing costs also give these "green" vehicles a decidedly lemony flavour.

Yet most public environmental protection groups and government agencies, seconded by the major automobile clubs, genuflect whenever the hybrid, ethanol, or diesel alternative is proposed.

Once again, we have to be wary of the lies. Toyota, for example, seldom mentions the fact that its hybrid battery packs can cost about $3,000 (U.S.) to replace, or that *Automotive News*, *Car and Driver*, and Edmunds have also found that diesel and hybrid fuel consumption figures can be 30–40 percent more than advertised.

Why am I so hard on ethanol? After all, in its 2007 budget the federal Conservative government committed $2 billion in incentives for ethanol, made from wheat and corn, and for biodiesel. The Canadian Renewable Fuels Association says ethanol is "good for the environment," a position echoed by the Manitoba and Saskatchewan governments, which emphasize that ethanol "burns cleaner" than gasoline.

Hogwash! Environment Canada's own unpublished research says ethanol "burns no cleaner than gasoline."

Scientists at Environment Canada studied four vehicles of recent makes, testing their emissions in a range of driving conditions and temperatures. "Looking at tailpipe emissions, from a greenhouse gas perspective, there really isn't much difference between ethanol and gasoline," said Greg Rideout, head of Environment Canada's toxic emissions research. The study was broadcast by CBC on March 30, 2007, and can be found at *www.cbc.ca*.

Scientists found no statistical difference between the greenhouse gas emissions of regular unleaded fuel and 10 percent ethanol blended fuel. Although they did note a reduction in carbon monoxide, a pollutant that forms smog, emissions of some other gases, such as hydrocarbons, actually increased under certain conditions.

Other drawbacks of ethanol: It's hard to find (there are only two outlets in all of Canada), it eats fuel line and gas tank components, it performs poorly in cold climates, it gives you 25–30 percent less fuel economy than gasoline, and it adds to world hunger (the crop used to produce one SUV fill-up of ethanol could feed a person for a year).

Smart drivers should continue to ignore automaker gas-saving hype, hunker down, and keep their paid-for, reliable, gas-guzzling used vehicles, because the depreciation savings will more than offset the increased cost of fuel.

When and Where to Buy

When to Buy

In the fall, dealer stocks of quality trade-ins and off-lease returns are at their highest level, and private sellers are moderately active. Prices are higher, but you'll have a greater choice of vehicles. In winter, prices decline substantially, and dealers and private sellers are generally easier to bargain with because buyers are scarce and weather conditions don't allow sellers to present their wares in the best light. In spring and summer, prices go up a bit as private sellers become more active and increased new-car rebates bring more trade-ins.

Private Sellers

Private sellers are your best source for a cheap and reliable used vehicle because you're on an equal bargaining level with a vendor who isn't trying to profit from your inexperience. A good private sale price would be about 5 percent *more* than the rock-bottom wholesale price, or approximately 20 percent *less* than the retail price advertised by local dealers. You can find estimated wholesale and retail prices in Part Three.

Remember, no seller, be it a dealer or a private party, expects to get his or her asking price. As with price reductions on home listings, a 10–20 percent reduction on the advertised price is common with private sellers. Dealers usually won't cut more than 10 percent off their advertised price.

It is also a good idea to draw up a bill of sale that gives all the pertinent details of your used-car transaction. See the following page for one that you may use as your guide.

Buying with Confidence

No matter whom you're buying a used vehicle from, there are a few rules you should follow to get the best deal.

First, have a good idea of what you want and the price you're willing to pay. If you have a preapproved line of credit, that will keep the number crunching and extra fees to a minimum. Finally, be resolute and polite, but make it clear that you are a serious buyer and won't participate in any "showroom shakedowns."

Here's a successful real-world technique used by Kurt Binnie, a frequent *Lemon-Aid* tipster:

PLEASE PRINT CLEARLY

Bill of Sale

- **Sections 1 and 2 must be completed** in order to make this Bill of Sale acceptable for vehicle registration. Completion of section 3, on the back of this form, is optional.
- Two copies of this Bill of Sale should be completed. The buyer keeps the original and the seller keeps the copy.
- Alterations or corrections made while completing the vehicle information section should be initialled by the buyer and seller.

SECTION 1

SELLER(S) INFORMATION

Name(s) *(Last, First, Second)*			Telephone Number ( )

Address	Street	City / Town	Province / State	Postal Code / Zip Code

Personal Identification:

VEHICLE INFORMATION

Year	Make	Model or Series	Style

Vehicle Identification Number (VIN) / Serial Number	Body Color	Roof Color	Odometer Reading

BUYER(S) INFORMATION

Name(s) *(Last, First, Second)*			Telephone Number ( )

Address	Street	City / Town	Province / State	Postal Code / Zip Code

Personal Identification:

This vehicle was sold for the sum of:

_____ Dollars $ _____

(Sum written in full)

(Subject to the terms and special conditions which appear in Section 3 on the back of this form)

SECTION 2

Dated at: _____
City / Town   Province / State   Country

on _____ .

I certify that all information shown above is true to the best of my knowledge.

_____	_____
Signature of Buyer	Signature of Seller

_____	_____
Signature of Buyer	Signature of Seller

_____	_____
Signature of Witness	Signature of Witness

REG3126 (2008/09)

Imagine the surprise of the used-car salesman when I pulled out my BlackBerry and did a VIN search right in front of him using Carfax [*Lemon-Aid* recommends the Canadian firm CarProof]. Threw him right off balance. Carfax results for Ontario vehicles give a good indication, but not the complete MTO [Ministry of Transportation,

Ontario] history. I bought the UVIP [Used Vehicle Information Package]...before closing the deal. For the car I ended up buying, I didn't even tell the sales staff that I was running the VIN while I was there. I was able to see it wasn't an auction vehicle or a write-off. This technique should work with pretty much any WAP [Wireless Application Protocol] enabled phone.

Kurt's letter goes on to describe how he avoids negotiations with sales staff and managers. He figures out the price he's willing to pay beforehand, using a combination of book values and the prices listed at *www.autotrader.ca*. He then test drives the vehicle, runs the VIN through his BlackBerry, and then makes a point-blank, one-time offer to the dealer. He has also found that used-car staff often have no knowledge about the vehicles on their lots beyond their asking price, and they make no distinction between cars manufactured early or late in the model year. An alert buyer could get a car built in August 2002 for the same price as one from September 2001, since they're both used 2002 cars.

 ## Primary Precautions

Get a printed sales agreement, even if it's just handwritten, that includes a clause stating that there are no outstanding traffic violations or liens against the vehicle. It doesn't make a great deal of difference whether the car will be purchased "as is" or certified under provincial regulation. A vehicle sold as safety certified can still turn into a lemon or be dangerous to drive. The certification process can be sabotaged if a minimal number of components are checked, the mechanic is incompetent, or the instruments are poorly calibrated. "Certified" is not the same as having a warranty to protect you from engine seizure or transmission failure. It means only that the vehicle met the minimum safety standards on the day it was tested.

Make sure the vehicle is lien-free and has not been damaged in a flood or written off after an accident. Flood damage can be hard to see, but it impairs ABS, power steering, and airbag functioning (making deployment 10 times slower).

Canada has become a haven for rebuilt U.S. wrecks. Write-offs are also shipped from provinces where there are stringent disclosure regulations to provinces where there are lax rules or no rules at all.

If you suspect your vehicle is flood-damaged, is a rebuilt wreck from the States, or was once a taxi, there's a useful Canadian search agency called CarProof that can give you a complete history of any vehicle within a day.

CarProof (www.carproof.com)

Operating out of London, Ontario, CarProof's services cost between $34.95 and $64.95, plus taxes per report. Information requests can be completed overnight—or sometimes within minutes—online. Contact the company through its website, or if you prefer to talk, call 519-675-1415.

In most provinces, you can do a lien and registration search yourself, but it's hardly worth the effort considering the low cost and comprehensive nature of CarProof's services.

If a lien does exist, you should contact the creditor(s) listed to find out whether any debts have been paid. If a debt is outstanding, you should arrange with the vendor to pay the creditor the outstanding balance, or agree that you can put the purchase price in a trust account to pay the lender. If the debt is larger than the purchase price of the car, it's up to you to decide whether you wish to complete the deal. If the seller agrees to clear the title personally, make sure that you receive a written relinquishment of title from the creditor before transferring any money to the seller. Make sure the title doesn't show an "R" for "restored," since this indicates that the vehicle was written off as a total loss and may not have been properly repaired.

Even if all documents are in order, ask the seller to show you the vehicle's original sales contract and a few repair bills in order to ascertain how well it was maintained. The bills will show you if the odometer was turned back and will also indicate which repairs are still guaranteed. If none of these can be found, leave. If the contract shows that the car was financed, verify that the loan was paid. If you're still not sure that the vehicle is free of liens, ask your bank or credit union manager to check for you. If no clear answer is forthcoming, look for something else.

Don't Pay Too Much

Prices for used large and mid-sized cars, trucks, and SUVs are falling as gas prices go higher. But this price drop hasn't been as severe with small cars and trucks, mini-minivans, downsized SUVs, or wagon crossovers. Their prices on the used-car market are relatively stable and are expected to stay that way through the summer.

If you'd like to save even more when buying used, consider these tips:

- Choose a vehicle that's five years old or more and has a good reliability and durability record. Don't buy an extended warranty that may become worthless. The money you save from the extra years' depreciation and lower insurance premiums will make up for some additional maintenance costs.
- Look for discounted off-lease vehicles with low mileage and a good reputation.
- Buy a vehicle that's depreciated more than average simply because of its bland styling, unpopular colour (dark blue, white, and champagne are out; silver is in), lack of high-performance features, or discontinuation.
- Buy a cheaper twin or rebadged model like a fully loaded Camry instead of a

Lexus ES, a Toyota Matrix in lieu of a Pontiac Vibe, or a Chevrolet Silverado instead of a GMC Sierra.

- Buy a fully equipped gas hog. Your $30,000 savings on a large SUV or pickup will pay the gas bill many times over, and the vehicle can be easily resold a few years down the road, with only moderate depreciation.

Price Guides

The best way to determine the price range for a particular model is to read the *Lemon-Aid* values found in Part Three. From there, you may wish to get a free second opinion by accessing Vehicle Market Research International's Canadian used-car prices at *www.vmrcanada.com*. It is one of the few free sources that list wholesale and retail values for used cars in Canada. The site even includes a handy calculator that adjusts a vehicle's value according to model, mileage, and a variety of options.

Black Book and *Red Book* price guides, found in most libraries, banks, and credit unions, are essential to anyone buying or selling a used vehicle. Both guides are easily accessible on the Internet. To read the *Canadian Black Book* values, simply copy the following URL into your web browser: *www.canadianblackbook.com/used-cars.html*. This site lists the vehicle's trade-in and future value, as well as the asking price based upon your Canadian postal code. No other identification is required.

Now, if you want to use the *Canadian Red Book Vehicle Valuation Guide*, which seems more attuned to Quebec and Ontario sales, you can order single copies of their used car and light truck wholesale and retail price guide for $19.95 at *www.canadianredbook.com* (an annual subscription costs $105). There are no restrictions as to who may subscribe.

You may also go to *Auto Trader* magazine's website at *www.autotrader.ca* to see at what prices other Canadians are trying to sell your chosen vehicle.

Don't be surprised to find that many national price guides have an Eastern Ontario and Quebec price bias, especially the *Red Book*. They often list unrealistically low prices compared with what you'll see in the eastern and western provinces and in rural areas, where good used cars are often sold for outrageously high prices or are simply passed down through the family for an average of eight to 10 years. Other price guides may list prices that are much higher than those found in your region. Consequently, use whichever price guide lists the highest value when selling your trade-in or negotiating a write-off value with an insurer. When buying, use the guide with the lowest values as your bargaining tool.

Cross-Border Sales

Shopping in the States for a used car or truck won't save you much money with cheaper, entry-level small cars. However, sports cars, luxury vehicles, SUVs, large trucks, and vans bought in the States can save you tens of thousands of dollars, now that the Canadian dollar is flirting with parity to the American greenback.

Here's what to do:

1. Check with Ottawa to see if the used vehicle you covet can be imported into Canada (call the Registrar of Imported Vehicles at 1-888-848-8240, or visit their website at *www.riv.ca*).
2. Take a trip across the border to scout out what is available from all dealers. Compare your findings with what's offered by Canadian cross-border brokers.
3. Verify if the price is fair once taxes and transport charges are considered.

Hire a broker or deal directly with the dealer. Be wary of private sellers, because your legal rights may be more limited in cross-border transactions.

Rental and Leased Vehicles

Next to buying privately, the second-best choice for getting a good used vehicle is a rental company or leasing agency. Due to our slumping economy, Budget, Hertz, Avis, and National are selling, at cut-rate prices, vehicles that have one to two years of service and approximately 80,000–100,000 km on the odometer. These rental companies will gladly provide a vehicle's complete history and allow an independent inspection by a qualified mechanic of the buyer's choice, as well as arrange for competitive financing.

Rental vehicles are generally well maintained, sell for a few thousand dollars more than privately sold vehicles, and come with strong guarantees, like Budget's 30-day money-back guarantee at some of its retail outlets (including three in B.C.). Rental-car companies also usually settle customer complaints without much hassle so as to not tarnish their images with rental customers.

Rental agencies tend to keep their stock of cars on the outskirts of town near the airport (particularly in Alberta and B.C.) and advertise in the local papers. Sales are held year-round as inventory is replenished. Late summer and early fall are usually the best times to see a wide selection because the new rentals arrive during this time period.

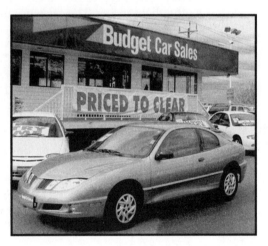

Even rental agencies are in the used-car business.

Vehicles that have just come off a three- or five-year lease are much more competitively priced than rentals, generally have less mileage, and are usually as well maintained. You're also likely to get a better price if you buy directly from the lessee, rather than going through the dealership or an independent agency. But remember that you won't have the dealer's leverage to extract post-warranty "goodwill" repairs from the automaker.

Repossessed Vehicles

Repossessed vehicles frequently come from bankrupt small businesses or sub-prime borrowers who failed to make their finance payments. They are usually found at auctions, but finance companies and banks sometimes sell them as well. Canadian courts have held that financial institutions are legally responsible for defects found in what they sell, so don't be at all surprised by the disclosure paperwork that will be shoved under your nose. Also, as with rental car company transactions, the combination of these companies' deep pockets and their abhorrence of bad publicity means you'll likely get your money back if you make a bad buy. The biggest problem with repossessed sport-utilities and pickups is that they may have been damaged by off-roading or neglected by their financially troubled owners. Although you rarely get to test drive or closely examine these vehicles, a local dealer may be able to produce a vehicle maintenance history by running the VIN through their manufacturer's database.

New-Car Dealers

New-car dealerships aren't bad places to pick up good used cars or trucks. Sure, prices are about 20 percent higher than those for vehicles sold privately, but rebates and zero percent financing plans can trim used-car prices dramatically. Plus, dealers are insured against selling stolen vehicles or vehicles with finance or other liens owing. They also usually allow prospective buyers to have the vehicle inspected by an independent garage, offer a much wider choice of models, and have their own repair facilities to do warranty work. Also, if there's a possibility of getting post-warranty "goodwill" compensation from the manufacturer, your dealer can provide additional leverage, particularly if the dealership is a franchisee for the model you have purchased. Finally, if things do go terribly wrong, dealers have deeper pockets than private sellers, so there's a better chance of winning a court judgment.

Provinces are also cracking down on dealers who sell defective used cars. In addition to Nova Scotia's recently enacted "Lemon Law," Alberta now requires a thorough mechanical inspection of every used car sold by dealers. Under the revised regulations, a mechanical assessment will be completed by licensed journeyman technician with a trade certificate as an Automotive Service Technician or Heavy Equipment Technician under the *Apprenticeship and Industry Training Act*.

A mechanical fitness assessment will be valid for 120 days from the time of completion. This is a change from 14 days for the previous certificate. The extended time period recognizes the broader nature of the assessment. More information about the amendments to the vehicle inspection regulation is available on the Alberta Transportation website at *www.transportation.alberta.ca* (under the "Drivers and Vehicles" tab).

MECHANICAL FITNESS ASSESSMENT

ALBERTA MOTOR VEHICLE INDUSTRY COUNCIL

As required by Vehicle Inspection Regulation (A/R 211/2006)

Dealer: _____ AMVIC License Number: _____

Address: _____

VEHICLE INFORMATION

Year: _____ Make: _____ Model: _____ Previous Province of Registration: _____

Vehicle Identification Number: _____ Odometer Reading: _____ ☐ (km / mi ☐

☐ Truck ☐ Motorcycle ☐ Bus ☐ Van ☐ Light Truck ☐ Auto ☐ Motorized RV ☐ Other

Please check mark (✓) each item as C = Complies N = Non-Compliant N/A=Not Applicable

Powertrain	C	N
Accelerator		
Fuel System		
Exhaust		
Transmission		
Front/Rear/Spindles Axles		
Clutch		
Fluid Levels (power steering, brake)		
CV Joints		

Lamps	C	N
Head Lamp Hi Beam		
Head Lamp Lo Beam		
Head Lamp Location		
Daytime Running Lamps		
Tail Lamps		
Brake Lamps		
Turn Signal Lamps		
Hazard Warning Lamps		
Licence Plate Lamp		

Instruments	C	N
Speedometer/Odometer		
Indicator Lamps		
Horn		
Hi Beam Indicator		

Brakes	C	N
Parking/Emergency Brake		
Hydraulic System		
Vacuum System		
Drum Brakes		
Disc Brakes		
Shoes/Pads		
Anti-Lock (if OEM equipped)		

Steering	C	N
Steering Lash		
Steering Linkage		
Rack & Pinion		
Power Steering System		
King Pin		
Ball Joints		

Suspension	C	N
Leaf springs		
Struts and Shocks		
Coil spring		
Torsion Bar		
Independent/Multilink Rear		
Computer Controlled		
Diagnostic Trouble Codes		

Frame & Body	C	N
Hood Latch		
Door Latches & Hinges		
Bumpers		
Windshield Wipers & Washer		
Rear Wiper & Washer		
Windshield		
Windows		
Defrost/Heaters		
Mirrors		
Seats		
Seat Belts/Airbags		
Mudguards		
Window Glazing		
Structural Integrity		

Tires & Wheels	C	N
Tread Depth		
Tread Section		
Sidewalls		
Wheels		

Electrical	C	N
Wiring		
Battery		
Switches		
Alternator		

Technician Comments

Alberta's Mechanical Fitness Assessment is a good template of the kind of inspection buyers everywhere should demand from independent garages before they purchase a used vehicle.

"Certified" vehicles

The word "certified" doesn't mean much. Ideally, it tells us the vehicle has undergone some reconditioning that was monitored by the manufacturer. Of course, some dealers don't do anything but slap a "certified" sticker on the car and then inflate the selling price. Sometimes, an auto association will certify a vehicle that has been inspected and has had the designated defects corrected.

Used-car leasing

It isn't a good idea to lease either new or used vehicles. Leasing has been touted as a method of making the high cost of vehicle ownership more affordable, but don't you believe it. Leasing is generally costlier than an outright purchase, and, for most people, the pitfalls far outweigh any advantages. If you must lease, do so for the shortest time possible and make sure the lease is close-ended (meaning that you walk away from the vehicle when the lease period ends). Also, make sure there's a maximum mileage allowance of at least 25,000 km per year and that the charge per excess kilometre is no higher than 8–10 cents.

Used-Car Dealers

Used-car dealers usually sell their vehicles for a bit less than what new-car dealers charge. However, their vehicles may be worth a lot less because they don't get the first pick of top-quality trade-ins. Many independent urban dealerships are marginal operations that can't invest much money in reconditioning their vehicles, which are often collected from auctions and new-car dealers reluctant to sell the vehicles to their own customers. And used-car dealers don't always have repair facilities to honour the warranties they do provide. Often, their credit terms are easier (but more expensive) than those offered by franchised new-car dealers.

That said, used-car dealers operating in small towns are an entirely different breed. These small, often family-run businesses recondition and resell cars and trucks that usually come from within their communities. Routine servicing is usually done in-house, and more complicated repairs are subcontracted out to specialized garages nearby. On one hand, these small outlets survive by word-of-mouth advertising and wouldn't last long if they didn't deal fairly with local townsfolk. On the other hand, their prices will likely be higher than elsewhere due to the better quality of their used vehicles and the cost of reconditioning and repairing what they sell under warranty.

Auctions

First of all, make sure it's a legitimate auction. Many are fronts for used-car lots where sleazy dealers put fake ads in complicit newspapers, pretending to hold auctions that are no more than weekend selling sprees.

Furthermore, you'll need lots of patience, smarts, and luck to pick up anything worthwhile. Government auctions—places where the mythical $50 Jeeps are sold—are fun to attend but highly overrated as places to find bargains. Look at the odds against you: It's impossible to determine the condition of the vehicles put up for bid, prices can go way out of control, and auction employees, professional sellers, their relatives, and their friends usually pick over the good stuff long before you ever see it.

To attend commercial auctions is to swim with the piranhas. They are frequented by "ringers" who bid up the prices, and by professional dealers who pick up cheap, worn-out vehicles unloaded by new-car dealers and independents. There are no guarantees, cash is required, and quality is likely to be as low as the price. Remember, too, that auction purchases are subject to provincial and federal sales taxes, the auction's sales commission (3–5 percent), and, in some cases, an administrative fee of $75–$100.

If you are interested in shopping at an auto auction, remember that certain days are reserved for dealers only, so call ahead. You'll find the vehicles locked in a compound, but you should have ample opportunity to inspect them and, in some cases, take a short drive around the property before the auction begins.

The Internet

The Internet is a risky place to buy a used car. You don't know the seller, and you know even less about the car. It's easy for an individual to sell a car they don't own, and it's even easier to create a virtual dealership, with photos of a huge inventory and a modern showroom, when the operation is likely made up of one guy working out of his basement.

Rating systems are unreliable too. Ratings from "happy customers" may be nothing but ploys—fictitious postings created by the seller to give out five-star ratings and the appearance that the company is honest and reliable.

If you must use the Internet, get the seller's full name and a copy of their driver's licence, plus lots of references. Then go see the vehicle, take a road test, and have a mechanic verify if the car is roadworthy and able to pass a safety inspection.

Although you take an even bigger risk buying out-of-province or in the States, there are a few precautions you can take to protect yourself. First off, compare shipping fees with a Canadian automobile transporter like Hansen's (*www.lhf.com*), and put your money into an escrow account until the vehicle is delivered in satisfactory condition.

If the car is located in the United States, print out the tips found on eBay's website at *http://pages.ebay.ca/ebaymotors/explained/checklist/howtobuyUS.html*. The website takes you through each step in detail and will tell you if the vehicle is admissible in Canada and the likely modification requirements. If the vehicle needs modification, you should check with a mechanic for an estimate. You will also need to get a recall clearance letter from the dealer or automaker in order to pass federal inspection. Additional information can be obtained from the Registrar of Imported Vehicles (1-888-848-8240 or *www.riv.ca*).

Beware of phony eBay solicitations that are sent via doctored emails selling out-of-province vehicles. In the email the "owner" will even promise to deliver the car to you at no extra cost. Rather than paying through the relatively secure PayPal used in most legitimate transactions, you will be instructed to send payment through a Western Union or MoneyGram money transfer.

How prevalent is this scam? About a third of the ads in *Canadian Auto Trader* checked out several years ago by the non-profit Automobile Protection Association turned out to be phony. The most obvious indications these ads were placed by scam artists is that the same email address kept reappearing, or the listed phone number was a dummy.

Most of the fraudulent advertisements were placed outside Canada, apparently without the knowledge of the online sites that published them. Nevertheless, it's hard not to suspect some complicity because the ads are quite easy to verify by the hosting site. For example, *Wheels.ca* staffers refuse advertisers with an IP address outside of Canada and ad claims and contact information are constantly checked.

Another fraud is committed by phony overseas used-car buyers who take the delivery of the car and pay for it with a worthless cashier's cheque. Again, using PayPal will protect you from this scam.

There is some government help available to catch Internet used-car swindlers. PhoneBusters, the federal-provincial agency set up to deal with telephone and Internet scams (1-888-495-8501) has ties to the RCMP and OPP, and will investigate and arrest these high-tech crooks.

Here are some more tips for selling or purchasing vehicles online:

- Check out the listed phone number and ask for an address and independent reference.
- Insist that the car be inspected by a third party before closing the deal.
- Search the VIN or ad description using Google or *www.carproof.com*. Often the same wording or VIN will appear on different sites.
- Never use a money transfer service.
- Call the online escrow agency and speak with a representative before divulging any personal financial information.
- Be skeptical of eBay "second chance" offers.
- Always use the eBay "contact seller" process.
- Report all shady deals to the local RCMP detachment. Then, file a complaint with your local police service and at the same time voice your concerns with the Internet service provider (ISP) hosting the offensive material. The Canadian Association of Internet Providers (*www.caip.ca*) would also welcome your comments or concerns in regards to Canadian ISPs.

Canadian car sales websites

- *AMVOQ.ca*—Quebec used-car classifieds (in French)
- *AutoHunter.ca*—Alberta used-car classifieds
- *Autonet.ca*—New and used cars and trucks, new-car dealers, new-car prices, and reviews
- *AutoTrader.ca*—Used-car classifieds from all across Canada
- *BuySell.com*—Classifieds from all across Canada
- eBay Motors Canada (*http://cars.eBay.ca*)—The premiere site for used cars located in Canada or anywhere in the world
- North American Automobile Trade Association (*www.naata.org*)—This trade association lists dealers and brokers who will help you find a new or used cross-border bargain

- *RedFlagDeals.com*—A compendium of shopping tips, as well as advice on dealing with the federal and provincial governments
- Used Cars Ontario (*www.usedcarsontario.com*)—Used-car classifieds for major cities in Ontario, with links and articles

U.S. car sales websites
- *AutoTrader.com*—New- and used-car classifieds
- *Cars.com*—Ditto, except there's an "Advanced Search" option
- *CarsDirect.com*—One of the largest car-buying sites
- eBay Motors U.S. (*www.motors.ebay.com*)—Similar to the Canadian site
- *Edmunds.com*—Lots of price quotes and articles
- The Big Lot! (*www.thebiglot.com*)—Another large car-buying site

Financing Choices

You shouldn't spend more than 30 percent of your annual gross income on the purchase of a new or used vehicle. By keeping the initial cost low, there is less risk to you, and you may be able to pay mostly in cash. This can be an effective bargaining tool to use with private sellers, but dealers are less impressed by cash sales because they lose their kickbacks from the finance companies.

INTEREST RATES FOR A $15,000 USED CAR LOAN

Lender	36 Months	48 Months	60 Months
Bank of Nova Scotia	6.94	6.61	6.69
CIBC	7.25	7.50	7.75
Caisses Desjardins	7.89	7.89	7.89
Comtech Credit Union	5.99	5.99	5.99
Ont. Civil Service C.U.	4.99	4.99	4.99
Pace Savings & C.U.	6.00	6.00	6.00
TD Canada Trust	7.50	7.50	7.50

Credit Unions

A credit union is the best place to borrow money for a used car at competitive interest rates and with easy repayment terms. In fact, credit unions are jumping into car financing as the major automakers pull back. You'll have to join the credit union or have an account with it before the loan is approved. You'll also probably have to come up with a larger down payment.

Banks

Financing a car through a bank can mean either applying for a car loan or a line of credit. A loan will require a lien on your car and fixed monthly payments until the end of the term. Interest rates on car loans often vary considerably. According to *www.bankrate.com/funnel/auto*, the cost of a car loan taken out for three years in

Miami, Florida, goes from a low of 3.2 percent to a high of almost 12.99 percent with a $50–$200 spurious "document fee" added. The average new-car loan interest rate in the States is 5.913 percent (*www.bankrate.com/funnel/auto*).

In Canada, as of April 2012, the cheapest used car loans vary between 4.99 and 7.89 percent (*http://money.canoe.ca/rates/en/carloans.html*).

You can get a good idea on the different car-loan interest rates through an online comparison of bank rates. For purchases in the States, go to *www.bankrate.com*; Canadian loan interest rates are updated at *http://money.canoe.ca/rates/carloans.html*.

Since you are already online, email the lowest-interest lenders and get a loan commitment first, before you start shopping and the dealer's sales agent starts throwing different figures at you. Simply Google the bank's name and add "car loan interest rates."

Lines of credit, on the other hand, require no lien and offer the ability to pay a minimum each month, or as much as you can afford. The rates are often lower than traditional bank loans and there are no penalties for paying it off early, making it the preferred route for many car buyers.

Banks are always leery of financing used cars, but they generally charge rates that are competitive with what dealers offer.

In your quest for a bank loan, keep in mind that the loan officer will be impressed by a prepared budget and sound references, particularly if you seek out a loan before choosing a vehicle. If you don't have a preapproved loan, it wouldn't hurt to buy from a local dealer, since banks like to encourage businesses in their area.

The Internet offers help for people who need an auto loan and want quick approval but don't want to face a banker. For example, the Royal Bank website has a selected list of dealers who are empowered to process Royal Bank loans at their dealerships (see *www.rbcroyalbank.com/products/personalloans/installment_loan.html*).

Dealers

Cash may be king with some Canadian retailers, but not at your local car dealership. It's a myth that dealers will treat you better if you pay cash. Dealers want you to buy a fully loaded vehicle and finance the whole deal. And, now that auto loans are easier to get than they were in 2008 and 2009, dealers are financing everything in sight—especially used cars.

Still, not that many buyers have that kind of extra green lying around anyway. Fewer than eight percent of all car sales are cash deals, so that leaves financing through the dealer or a bank as the only options for most of us.

Dealer financing isn't the rip-off it once was, but still be watchful for all the expensive little extras the dealer may try to pencil into the contract, because, believe it or not, dealers make far more of a profit on used-car sales than on new-car deals. Don't write them off for financing, though—if they want to, dealers can finance your purchase at rates that compete with those of banks and finance companies, because they agree to take back the vehicle if the creditor defaults on the loan. Some dealers mislead their customers into thinking they can get financing at rates far below the prime rate. Actually, the dealer jacks up the base price of the vehicle to compensate for the lower interest charges. As bank and other financing choices dry up in some areas, a credit union or cash may be your only alternatives.

Dealer Scams

Most dealer sales scams are so obvious, they're laughable. But like the "Nigerian lost fortune" email rip-off, enough stupid people get sucked in to make these flim-flam practices profitable.

One of the more common tricks is to not identify the previous owner because the vehicle was used commercially, was problem-prone, or had been written off as a total loss after an accident. It's also not uncommon to discover that the mileage has been turned back, particularly if the vehicle was part of a company's fleet. Your best defence? Demand the name of the vehicle's previous owner and then run a VIN check through CarProof as a prerequisite for purchasing.

It would be impossible to list all the dishonest tricks employed in used-vehicle sales. As soon as the public is alerted to one scheme, crooked sellers use other, more elaborate frauds. Nevertheless, under industry-financed provincial compensation funds, buyers can get substantial refunds if defrauded by a dealer.

Here are some of the more common fraudulent practices you're likely to encounter.

Evading Sales Tax by Trimming the Price

Here's where your own greed will do you in. In a tactic used almost exclusively by small, independent dealers and some private sellers, the buyer is told that he or she can pay less sales tax by listing a lower selling price on the contract. But what if the vehicle turns out to be a lemon, or the sales agent has falsified the model year or mileage? The hapless buyer is offered a refund on the fictitious purchase price indicated on the contract. If the buyer wanted to take the dealer to court, it's quite unlikely that he or she would get any more than the contract price. Moreover, both the buyer and dealer could be prosecuted for making a false declaration to avoid paying sales tax.

Phony Private Sales ("Curbsiders")

Individual transactions account for about three times as many used-vehicle sales as dealer sales, and crooked dealers get in on the action by posing as private sellers. Called "curbsiders," these scammers lure unsuspecting buyers through lower prices, cheat the federal government out of tax money, and routinely violate provincial registration and consumer protection regulations. Bob Beattie, executive director of the Used Car Dealers Association of Ontario (*www.ucda.org*), once estimated that about 20 percent of so-called private sellers in Ontario are actually curbsiders. Dealers in large cities like Toronto, Calgary, and Vancouver believe curbsiders sell half of the cars advertised in the local papers. This scam is easy to detect if the seller can't produce the original sales contract or show repair bills made out over a long period of time in his or her own name. You can usually identify a car dealer in the want ads section of the newspaper—just check to see if the same telephone number is repeated in many different ads. Sometimes you can trip up a curbsider by requesting information on the phone, without identifying the specific vehicle. If the seller asks you which car you are considering, you know you're dealing with a curbsider.

Legitimate car dealers claim to deplore the dishonesty of curbsider crooks, yet they are their chief suppliers. Dealership sales managers, auto auction employees, and newspaper classified ad sellers all know the names, addresses, and phone numbers of these thieves but don't act on the information. Newspapers want the ad dollars, auctions want the action, and dealers want someplace they can unload their wrecked, rust-cankered, and odometer-tricked junkers with impunity. Talk about hypocrisy, eh?

Curbsiders are particularly active in Western Canada, importing vehicles from other provinces where they were sold by dealers, wreckers, insurance companies, and junkyards (after having been written off as total losses). They then place private classified ads in B.C. and Alberta papers, sell their stock, and then import more.

Buyers taken in by these scam artists should sue in small claims court both the seller and the newspaper that carried the original classified ad. When just a few cases are won in court and the paper's competitors play up the story, the practice will cease.

"Free-Exchange" Privilege

Dealers get a lot of sales mileage out of this deceptive offer. The dealer offers to exchange any defective vehicle for any other vehicle in stock. What really happens, though, is that the dealer won't have anything else selling for the same price and so will demand a cash bonus for the exchange—or you may get the dubious privilege of exchanging one lemon for another.

"Money-Back" Guarantee

Once again, the purchaser feels safe in buying a used car with this kind of guarantee. After all, what could be more honest than a money-back guarantee? Dealers using this technique often charge exorbitant handling charges, rental fees, or mechanical repair costs to the customer who bought one of these vehicles and then returned it.

"50/50" Guarantee

This can be a trap. Essentially, the dealer will pay half of the repair costs over a limited period of time. It's a fair offer if an independent garage does the repairs. If not, the dealer can always inflate the repair costs to double their actual worth and then write up a bill for that amount (a scam sometimes used in "goodwill" settlements). The buyer winds up paying the full price of repairs that would probably have been much cheaper at an independent garage. The best kind of used-vehicle warranty is 100 percent with full coverage for a fixed term, even if that term is relatively short.

 ## "As Is" and "No Warranty"

You will see from the jurisprudence in Part Two that these phrases are pure bluff, whether used in a dealer or private sale. Sellers insert these clauses much like parking lot owners or coat checkers at restaurants do when they put up signs warning that they have no responsibility to indemnify your losses. In fact, when you pay for a custodial service or a used vehicle, the commission the seller of that service or product receives requires that you be protected.

Remember, every vehicle carries a provincial legal warranty protecting you from misrepresentation and the premature failure of key mechanical or body components. Nevertheless, sellers often write "as is" or "no warranty" in the contract in the hope of dissuading buyers from pressing legitimate claims.

Generally, when "as is" has been written into the contract or bill of sale, it usually means that you're aware of mechanical defects, you're prepared to accept the responsibility for any damage or injuries caused by the vehicle, and you're agreeing to pay all repair costs. However, the courts have held that the "as is" clause is not a blank cheque to cheat buyers, and must be interpreted in light of the seller's true intent. Was there an attempt to deceive the buyer by including this clause? Did the buyer really know what the "as is" clause could do to his or her future legal rights? It's also been held that the courts may consider oral representations ("parole evidence") as an expressed warranty, even though they were never written into the formal contract. So, if a seller makes claims as to the fine quality of the used vehicle, these claims can be used as evidence. Courts generally ignore "as is" clauses when the vehicle has been intentionally misrepresented, when the dealer is the seller, or when the defects are so serious that the seller is presumed to have known of their existence. Private sellers are usually given more latitude than dealers or their agents.

Odometer Fraud

Who says crime doesn't pay? It most certainly does if you turn back odometers for a living in Canada.

Does anyone really believe this 1975 Pontiac Trans Am only has only 11,000 miles on the "clock"?

Estimates are that each year close to 90,000 vehicles with tampered odometers reach the Canadian marketplace—at a cost to Canadians of more than $3.56 million. This is about double the incidents one would expect based on a 2002 U.S. NHTSA study that pegs odometer fraud at 450,000 vehicles annually. NHTSA estimates that half of the cars with reset odometers are relatively new high-mileage rental cars or fleet vehicles.

Odometer fraud is a pernicious crime that robs thousands of dollars from each victim it touches. See, for example, *United States v. Whitlow*, 979 F.2d 1008, 1012 (5th Cir. 1992) (under sentencing guidelines, the court affirmed the estimate that consumers lost $4,000 per vehicle). The television news magazine *60 Minutes* once characterized it as the largest consumer fraud in America. Victims of this fraud are commonly the least able to afford it, since buyers of used cars include large numbers of low-income people. In addition, consumers generally are unaware of being victimized.

Odometer tampering involves several interrelated activities. Late-model, high-mileage vehicles are purchased at a low price. The vehicles are "reconditioned" or "detailed" to remove many outward appearances of long use. Finally, odometers are reset, typically removing more than 40,000 miles (64,000 km).

In addition to the cosmetic "reconditioning" of the car, the odometer tamperer "reconditions" the car's paperwork. Automobile titles include a declaration of mileage statement to be completed when ownership is transferred. To hide the actual mileage that is declared on the title when the car is sold to an odometer tamperer, the tamperer must take steps to conceal this information. These steps vary from simple alteration of mileage figures to creating transfers to fictitious "straw" dealerships to make it unclear who was responsible for the odometer rollback and title alteration. Alternatively, the odometer tamperers frequently destroy original title documents indicating high mileage and obtain duplicate certificates of title from state motor vehicle departments, upon which the false, lower mileage figures are entered.

Odometer fraud is practiced by a variety of people, including:

- Organizations that roll back (or "clock") the odometers on thousands of cars, wholesaling them to dealers who resell them to the public.
- Groups of individuals (commonly called "curbstoners") who buy cars, clock them, and sell them through the classifieds, passing them off as cars of a friend or relative ("I'm selling Aunt Sally's Buick for her").
- Individuals who only clock their own car to defeat a lease provision or cheat on a warranty.

Gangs of odometer scammers ply their trade in Canada because it seems as if no one cares what they do, and they stand to gain thousands of dollars, or 10 cents profit for each mile erased from the odometer on the resale value of a doctored car. Moreover, electronic digital odometers make tampering child's play for anyone with a laptop computer, or anyone who has sufficient skill to simply replace the dashboard's instrument panel.

Think: When was the last time you heard of a Canadian dealership being charged with odometer fraud? Probably a long time ago, if at all. And what is the punishment for those dealers convicted of defrauding buyers? Not jail time or loss of their franchise. More than likely, it'll be just a small fine.

Not so in the States. There, many victims can get compensation from dealers who sold cars with altered odometers, regardless of who was responsible for the alteration. For business and legal reasons, dealers frequently compensate consumers who purchased vehicles with altered odometers. U.S. federal law permits consumers to obtain treble damages or $1,500, whichever is greater, when they are victims of odometer fraud (49 U.S.C. section 32710). The courts have been liberal in protecting consumers in these kinds of lawsuits against dealers.

How to spot a car that's been to a "spin doctor":

- When calling a supposedly private seller, ask to see the car in the ad, without specifying which one.
- Ask the seller for a copy of the contract showing the name of the selling dealer and previous owner.
- Check the history of the car through CarProof.
- Look for uneven paint or body panels that don't line up. Do the doors, hood and trunk open and close easily? Do the bumpers and fenders sit squarely?
- Examine brake and gas pedal wear as well as the driver's door sill. Does their wear match the kilometres? An average tire lasts 80,000 kilometres; any premature wear signals an odometer turnback or chassis misalignment.
- On older vehicles that don't use a digital odometer, check to see if the numbers on the odometer are lined up and snug. If they jiggle when you bang your hand on the dash, have an expert check for fraud.
- Have the car inspected by a franchised dealer for that make of vehicle, and ask for a copy of the service records, noting the mileage each time the vehicle was serviced.

Misrepresentation

Used vehicles can be misrepresented in a variety of ways. A used airport commuter minivan may be represented as having been used by a Sunday school class. A mechanically defective sports car that's been rebuilt after several major accidents may have plastic filler in the body panels to muffle the rattles or hide the rust damage, heavy oil in the motor to stifle the clanks, and cheap retread tires to eliminate the thumps. Your best protection against these dirty tricks is to have the vehicle's quality completely verified by an independent mechanic before completing the sale. Of course, you can still cancel the sale if you learn of the misrepresentation only after taking the vehicle home, but your chances of successfully doing so dwindle as time passes.

Private Scams

A lot of space in this guide is dedicated to describing how used-car dealers and scam artists cheat uninformed buyers. Of course, private individuals can be dishonest, too. In either case, protect yourself at the outset by keeping your deposit small and by getting as much information as possible about the vehicle you're considering. Then, after a test drive, you may sign a written agreement to purchase the vehicle and give a deposit of sufficient value to cover the seller's advertising costs, subject to cancellation if the automobile fails its inspection. After you've taken these precautions, watch out for the following private sellers' tricks.

Vehicles That Are Stolen or Have Finance Owing

Many used vehicles are sold privately without free title because the original auto loan was never repaid. You can avoid being cheated by asking for proof of purchase and payment from a private seller. Be especially wary of any individual who offers to sell a used vehicle for an incredibly low price. Check the sales contract to determine who granted the original loan, and call the lender to see if it's been repaid. Place a call to the provincial Ministry of Transportation to ascertain whether the car is registered in the seller's name. Find out if a finance company is named as beneficiary on the auto insurance policy. Finally, contact the original dealer to determine whether there are any outstanding claims.

In Ontario, all private sellers must purchase a Used Vehicle Information Package at one of 300 provincial Driver and Vehicle Licence Issuing Offices, or online at *www.mto.gov.on.ca/english/dandv/vehicle/used.htm*. This package, which costs $20, contains the vehicle's registration history in Ontario; the vehicle's lien information (i.e., if there are any liens registered on the vehicle); the fair market value on which the minimum tax payable will apply; and other information such as consumer tips, vehicle safety standards inspection guidelines, retail sales tax information, and forms for bills of sale.

In other provinces, buyers don't have easy access to this information. Generally, you have to contact the provincial office that registers property and then pay a small fee for a computer printout that may or may not be accurate. You'll be asked for the current owner's name and the car's VIN, which is usually found on the driver's side of the dashboard.

There are two high-tech ways to get the goods on a dishonest seller. First, have a dealer of that particular model run a vehicle history check through the automaker's online network. This will tell you who the previous owners and dealers were, what warranty and recall repairs were carried out, and what other free repair programs may still apply. Second, you can use CarProof (*www.carproof.com*) to carry out a background check.

Wrong Registration

Make sure the seller's vehicle has been properly registered with provincial transport authorities; if it isn't, it may be stolen, or you could be dealing with a curbsider.

Summary: Be a Tough Customer

You can get a reliable used car, truck, or minivan at a reasonable price—it just takes some patience and homework. Prevent potential headaches by becoming thoroughly familiar with your legal rights, as outlined in Part Two, and by buying a vehicle recommended in Part Three. The following is a summary of the steps to take to keep your level of risk to a minimum:

1. Keep your present vehicle for at least 10 years. Don't get panicked over high fuel costs—depreciation is a greater threat to your pocketbook.
2. Sell to a dealer if the reduction in applicable taxes on your next purchase is greater than the potential profit of selling privately.
3. Sell privately if you can get at least 15 percent more than what the dealer offered.
4. Buy from a private party, rental car outlet, or dealer (in that order).
5. Use an auto broker to save time and money, but pay a set fee, not a commission.
6. Buy only a *Lemon-Aid*-recommended three- to five-year-old vehicle with some original warranty left that can be transferred.
7. Carefully inspect front-drive vehicles that have reached their fifth year. Pay particular attention to the engine intake manifold and head gasket, CV joints, steering box, and brakes. Make sure the spare tire and tire jack haven't been removed.
8. Buy a full-sized, rear-drive delivery van and then add the convenience features that you would like (seats, sound system, etc.) instead of opting for a more-expensive, smaller, less-powerful minivan.
9. Buy a vehicle recommended by *Lemon-Aid*, thereby foregoing the need to purchase a $1,500–$2,000 extended warranty; many of these warranty providers may be headed for bankruptcy.
10. Have maintenance repairs done by independent garages that offer lifetime warranties on brakes, exhaust systems, and automatic transmissions.
11. Install used or reconditioned mechanical parts, demand that original parts be used for body repairs, and insist upon choosing your own repairer.
12. Keep all the previous owner's repair bills to facilitate warranty claims and to let mechanics know what's already been replaced or repaired.
13. Upon delivery, adjust mirrors to reduce blind spots and adjust head restraints to prevent your head from snapping back in the event of a collision. On airbag-equipped vehicles, move the seat backward more than half its travel distance and sit at least 30 cm away from the airbag housing.

14. Ensure that the side airbags include head protection.
15. Make sure that both the dealer and automaker have your name in their computers as the new owner of record. Ask for a copy of your vehicle's history, which is stored in the same computer.
16. Go to *www.safercar.gov* and look up all the free confidential service bulletins applicable to your vehicle and compare that to the free Alldata index of bulletins at *www.alldatadiy.com/recalls/index.html*. Get true copies of all the recalls and service bulletins that are particularly significant to your needs from Alldata's site (*www.alldatadiy.com/buy*), The cost is $26.95 (U.S.) for a one-year subscription, or $44.95 for five years. A one-year subscription for additional vehicles costs $16.95 per vehicle. Overnight, you will be sent an Internet download or data disc of all your vehicle's service bulletins going back to 1982. This will keep you current as to the latest secret warranties, recalls, and troubleshooting tips for correcting factory screw-ups.

Part Two
LEGAL RIGHTS AND WRONGS

Saab is Not on the Verge of Collapse

"Saab is still producing [cars] and it is not on the verge of collapse," proclaimed Saab Chairman Victor Muller to auto journalists at a recent new model unveiling.

DAVID BOOTH

WWW.THEPASSINGLANE.CA/2011/04/SHOULD-SAAB-STILL-BE-MAKING-CARS.HTML

APRIL 4, 2011

Saab is Officially Bankrupt: BBC *Top Gear*

Saab's owners signed it into bankruptcy this morning. The company has been mortally wounded since April, when it ran out of cash, couldn't pay its suppliers and had to stop building cars. After eight months of extraordinary and desperate negotiations over potential rescues, last month it looked like Saab was safe. A sale was agreed with Chinese manufacturer Youngman and distributor Pang Da. But that deal has now been called off, triggering the bankruptcy. The stumbling block is General Motors. It has forbidden its designs to be used by the Chinese, so they have pulled out of the deal.

PAUL HORRELL

WWW.TOPGEAR.COM/UK/CAR-NEWS/SAAB-BANKRUPT-2011-12-19

DECEMBER 19, 2011

Think of this part of *Lemon-Aid* as your legal aid tool kit to help you fight against the lies and consumer abuses inherent in the auto industry.

Here's 42 years' worth of strategy, tactics, negotiation tools, and jurisprudence you may cite to hang tough and get an out-of-court settlement, or to win your case without spending a fortune on lawyers. If you do end up using a lawyer, the following roundup of successful lawsuits from French and English courts in Canada, as well as some important American decisions, will save you lots of research time and money.

Broken Promises

Used cars can turn out to be bad buys for various reasons: They were misrepresented by the seller, who sold for the wrong model year ("redated"), covered up damage, turned back the odometer, inflated fuel economy, lied about its previous use (not really driven only on Sundays by a little old lady, etc.); or they are afflicted with factory-induced defects like sudden acceleration or brake failures. In some cases, abusive driving or poor maintenance by the previous owner can make a vehicle unreliable or dangerous to drive. Misrepresentation is relatively easy to prove: you simply have to show the vehicle doesn't conform to the oral or written sales representations made before or during the time of purchase. These representations include sales brochures and newspaper, radio, television, and Internet ads. Omission of key information can also fall under misrepresentation.

Private sales can easily be cancelled if the vehicle's mileage has been turned back, if accident damage hasn't been disclosed, or if the seller is really a dealer pretending to be a private seller ("curbsiding"). Even descriptive phrases like "well-maintained," "driven by a woman" (whatever *that's* supposed to imply), or "excellent condition" can get the seller into trouble if misrepresentation was intended.

To get compensation or to have the car taken back, defects need to be confirmed by an independent garage examination that shows either that the deficiencies are premature, factory-related, or not maintenance-related or that they were hidden at the time of purchase. You can also make your proof by showing repetitive repairs for the same problem over a short period of time. It doesn't matter if the vehicle was sold new or used. In fact, many of the small claims court victories against automakers relating to defective paint, engines, and transmissions were won by owners who bought their vehicles used and then sued both the seller and the automaker.

Sure, automakers will sometimes plead they are not part of the chain of responsibility because they didn't sell the product to the plaintiff. Fortunately, as you will learn reading this section, Canadian judges do not buy that argument. Particularly if the defect was obviously factory-related and caused an injury or death.

Cases involving these kinds of failures are not that difficult to win in Canada under the doctrine of *res ipsa loquitur*, meaning "the thing speaks for itself," or in negligence cases, the liability is shown by the failure itself. Planes shouldn't fall and cars shouldn't suddenly accelerate or fail to stop. Under *res ipsa loquitur*, you don't have to pinpoint the exact cause of the failure, and judges are free to award damages by weighing the "balance of probabilities" as to fault.

This advantage found in Canadian law was laid out succinctly in the July 1, 1998 issue of the *Journal of Small Business Management* in its comparison of product liability laws on both sides of the border (see "Effects of Product Liability Laws on Small Business" at *www.allbusiness.com*):

> Although in theory the Canadian consumer must prove all of the elements of negligence (*Farro v. Nutone Electrical Ltd. 1990*; Ontario Law Reform Commission 1979; Thomas 1989), most Canadian courts allow injured consumers to use a procedural aid known as *res ipsa loquitur* to prove their cases (*Nicholson v. John Deere Ltd. 1986*; *McMorran v. Dom. Stores Ltd. 1977*). Under *res ipsa loquitur*, plaintiffs must only prove that they were injured in a way that would not ordinarily occur without the defendant's negligence. It is then the responsibility of the defendant to prove that he was not negligent. As proving the negative is extremely difficult, this Canadian reversal of the burden of proof usually results in an outcome functionally equivalent to strict product liability (*Phillips v. Ford Motor Co. of Canada Ltd. 1971*; Murray 1988). This concept is reinforced by the principal that a Canadian manufacturer does not have the right to manufacture an inherently dangerous product when a method exists to manufacture that product without risk of harm. To do so subjects the manufacturer to liability even if the safer method is more expensive (*Nicholson v. John Deere Ltd. 1986*).

In *Jarvis v. Ford* (United States Second Circuit Court of Appeal, February 7, 2002), a judgment was rendered in favour of a driver who was injured when her six-day-old Ford Aerostar minivan suddenly accelerated as it was started and put into gear. What makes this decision unique is that the jury had no specific proof of a defect. The Court of Appeal agreed with the jury award, and Justice Sotomayor (now a Supreme Court Justice) gave these reasons for the court's verdict:

> A product may be found to be defective without proof of the specific malfunction: It may be inferred that the harm sustained by the plaintiff was caused by a product defect existing at the time of sale or distribution, without proof of a specific defect, when the incident that harmed the plaintiff: (a) was of a kind that ordinarily occurs as a result of product defect; and (b) was not, in the particular case, solely the result of causes other than product defect existing at the time of sale or distribution.

> Restatement (Third) of Torts: Product Liability § 3 (1998). In comment c to this section, the Restatement notes:

> [There is] *no requirement that plaintiff prove what aspect of the product was defective.* The inference of defect may be drawn under this Section without proof of the specific defect. Furthermore, quite apart from the question of what type of defect was involved, the plaintiff need not explain specifically what constituent part of the product failed. For example, if an inference of defect can be appropriately drawn in connection with the catastrophic failure of an airplane, the plaintiff need not establish whether the failure is attributable to fuel-tank explosion or engine malfunction.

The jury awarded Ms. Jarvis $24,568 in past medical insurance premiums, $340,338 in lost earnings, and $200,000 in pain and suffering. For future damages, the jury awarded $22,955 in medical insurance premiums, $648,944 in lost earnings, and $300,000 for pain and suffering.

Two Warranties

Used-vehicle defects are covered by two warranties: the *expressed* or *written* warranty, which has a fixed time limit, and the *implied* or *legal* warranty, the application of which is entirely up to a judge's discretion based upon the vehicle's cost, how it was maintained, manufacturer and dealer assertions, the severity of the failure, and the extent of that failure's consequences.

Expressed

The expressed warranty given by the seller is often full of empty promises, and it allows the dealer and manufacturer to act as judge and jury when deciding whether a vehicle was misrepresented or is afflicted by defects they'll pay to correct. Rarely does it provide a money-back guarantee.

Some of the more familiar lame excuses used in denying expressed warranty claims are "You abused the car," "It was poorly maintained," "It's normal wear and tear," "It's rusting from the outside, not the inside," and "It passed the safety inspection." Ironically, the expressed warranty sometimes says there is no warranty at all, or that the vehicle is sold "as is." Fortunately, courts usually throw out these exclusions by upholding two legal concepts:

1. The vehicle must be fit for the purpose for which it was purchased.
2. The vehicle must be of merchantable quality when sold.

Not surprisingly, sellers use the expressed warranty to reject claims, while smart plaintiffs ignore the expressed warranty and argue for a refund under the implied warranty instead.

Implied

The implied warranty ("of fitness") is your ace in the hole. As clearly stated in the under-reported Saskatchewan decision *Maureen Frank v. General Motors of Canada Limited*, in which the judge declared that paint discoloration and peeling shouldn't occur within 11 years of the purchase of the vehicle, the implied warranty is an important legal principle. It is solidly supported by a large body of federal and provincial laws, regulations, and jurisprudence, and it protects you primarily from hidden defects that may be either dealer- or factory-related. But the concept also includes misrepresentation and a host of other scams.

This warranty also holds dealers to a higher standard of conduct than private sellers because, unlike private sellers, dealers and auto manufacturers are presumed to be aware of the defects present in the vehicles they sell. That way, they can't just pass the ball to the previous owner and then walk away from the dispute.

Dealers are also expected to disclose defects that have been repaired. For instance, in British Columbia, provincial law (the *Motor Dealer Act*) says that a dealer must disclose damages that cost more than $2,000 to fix. This is a good law to cite in other jurisdictions.

In spite of all your precautions, there's still a 10 percent chance you'll buy a lemon, says mobility services company Runzheimer International (a figure also cited by former GM VP Bob Lutz, who confirms that one out of every 10 vehicles produced by the Detroit automakers is likely to be a lemon).

Why the implied warranty is so effective

- It establishes the concept of reasonable durability (see "How Long Should a Part or Repair Last?" below), meaning that parts are expected to last for a reasonable period of time, as stated in jurisprudence, judged by independent mechanics, or expressed in extended "goodwill" warranties given by automakers in the past (examples: 10 years/193,000 km for catalytic converters; 7 years/200,000 miles for diesel injectors as expressed in one U. S service bulletin; and 7 years/160,000 km for engines and transmissions).
- It covers the entire vehicle and can be applied for whatever period of time the judge decides.
- It can order that the vehicle be taken back, or a major repair cost be refunded. One *Lemon-Aid* reader writes:

> I wanted to let you and your readers know that the information you publish about Ford's paint failure problem is invaluable. Having read through your "how-to guide" on addressing this issue, I filed suit against Ford for the "latent" paint defect. The day prior to our court date, I received a settlement offer by phone for 75 percent of what I was initially asking for.

- It can order that plaintiffs be given compensation for supplementary transportation, inconvenience, mental distress, missed work, screwed-up vacations, insurance paid while the vehicle was in the repair shop, repairs done by other repairers, and exemplary, or punitive, damages in cases where the seller was a real weasel.
- It is often used by small claims court judges to give refunds to plaintiffs "in equity" (out of fairness), rather than through a strict interpretation of contract law.

How do you know when a part or service hasn't lasted as long as it should and whether you should seek a full or partial refund? Sure, you have a gut feeling based on the use of the vehicle, the way you maintained it, and the extent of work that was carried out. But you'll need more than emotion to win compensation from garages and automakers.

You can definitely get a refund if a repair or part lasts beyond its guarantee but not as long as is generally expected. You'll have to show what the auto industry considers to be "reasonable durability," however.

This isn't all that difficult if you use the conservative benchmarks that automakers, mechanics, and the courts have recognized over the years—see the "Reasonable Part Durability" chart below.

Much of the chart's guidelines are extrapolated from the terms of automaker payouts to dissatisfied customers within the past three decades, and from Chrysler's original seven-year powertrain warranty, applicable from 1991 to 1995 and then reapplied since then. Other sources for this table include the following:

- Ford and GM transmission warranties, which are outlined in their secret warranties
- Ford, GM, and Toyota engine "goodwill" programs, which are laid out in their internal service bulletins
- Court judgments where judges have given their own guidelines as to what constitutes reasonable durability

REASONABLE PART DURABILITY

ACCESSORIES		Brake calipers/pads	30,000 km
Air conditioner	7 years	Master cylinder	100,000 km
Cruise control	5 years/100,000 km	Wheel cylinder	80,000 km
Door handles	10 years/160,000 km	**ENGINE AND DRIVETRAIN**	
Power doors, windows	5 years	CV joint	6 years/160,000 km
Radio	5 years	Differential	7 years/160,000 km
BODY		Engine (diesel)	15 years/350,000 km
Paint (peeling)	7–11 years	Engine (gas)	7 years/160,000 km
Rust (perforations)	7–11 years	Engine block	7 years/no mileage
Rust (surface)	5 years	Engine control module	15 years/240,000 km
Water/wind/air leaks	5 years	Engine sludge	8 years/180,000 km
BRAKE SYSTEM		Engine turbocharger	7 years/160,000 km
Brake drum	120,000 km	Fuel pump module	10 years/191,000 km
Brake drum linings	35,000 km	Oxygen sensor	10 years/191,000 miles
Brake rotor	60,000 km	Power steering	10 years/191,000 km

Radiator	4 years/80,000 km	ABS brakes	7 years/160,000 km
Transfer case	7 years/160,000 km	ABS computer	10 years/160,000 km
Transmission (auto.)	8 years/160,000 km	Seat belts	life of vehicle
Transmission (man.)	10 years/250,000 km	**STEERING AND SUSPENSION**	
Transmission oil cooler	5 years/100,000 km	Alignment	1 year/20,000 km
EXHAUST SYSTEM		Ball joints	10 years/160,000 km
Catalytic converter	10 years/193,000 km	Coil springs	10 years/160,000 km
Exhaust manifold	10 years/193,000 km	Power steering	5 years/80,000 km
Muffler	2 years/40,000 km	Shock absorber	2 years/40,000 km
Tailpipe	3 years/60,000 km	Struts	5 years/80,000 km
IGNITION SYSTEM		Tires (radial)	5 years/80,000 km
Cable set	60,000 km	Truck tie-rod ends	3 years/60,000 km
Electronic module	5 years/80,000 km	Wheel bearings	3 years/60,000 km
Retiming	20,000 km	**VISIBILITY**	
Spark plugs	20,000 km	Halogen/fog lights	3 years
Tune-up	20,000 km	Sealed beam	2 years
SAFETY COMPONENTS		Windshield wiper	5 years
Airbags	life of vehicle		

Airbags

Airbags usually carry a four-year warranty in Canada; however, automakers routinely offer "goodwill" warranty extensions for up to 10 years/100,000 miles. Mercedes-Benz Canada, for example, sent off a dealer notification on December 2010 advising dealers that it would cover airbag replacement or correct a faulty wiring harness connection for free on 2005 through 2008 models up to 10 years or 100,000 miles (160,000 km). The affected vehicles are model years 2005–06 ML (164), SLK (171), C (203), CLK (209), E (211), CLS (219), R (251), and 2005–08 G (463).

Owners who paid for the repair will be refunded their money upon presentation of an acceptable receipt from a Mercedes-Benz dealer. Independent garage receipts will likely be accepted if you push hard enough.

Here is part of a letter that was sent out to U.S. owners:

Dear Mercedes-Benz Owner,

In our continuing efforts to assure the proper performance of Mercedes-Benz products and to ensure the satisfaction of our customers, Mercedes-Benz USA, LLC (MBUSA) has decided to extend the warranty for the driver's air bag wiring...from the original 4 years/50,000 miles (whichever occurs first) to 10 years/100,000 miles (whichever occurs first). This warranty extension applies to these vehicles regardless of ownership. If, during this period, your vehicle should experience an illumination of the "Air Bag" light as described above, this warranty extension would cover the necessary repairs to correct those conditions.

RALPH S. FISHER
MERCEDES-BENZ USA, LLC
GENERAL MANAGER, CUSTOMER ASSISTANCE CENTER
DECEMBER 2010

Mercedes-Benz's admission that airbag systems should be trouble-free for 10 years/100,000 miles serves as an important benchmark for owners experiencing airbag-related failures. Owners of any make or model of vehicle can use this durability standard (what the automaker considers "reasonable durability") to haggle for a "goodwill" settlement or to win a small claims court petition.

Airbags cost thousands of dollars to fix or replace. They are one of the most failure-prone components found on late model vehicles. Insurance companies won't cover their replacement or repair cost unless a collision is involved. But even if they did refund the repair cost, why should you pay a higher insurance fee for a failure caused by the automaker's poor design or use of inferior quality electronics?

Inadvertent deployment may occur after passing over a bump in the road or slamming the car door, or, in some Chrysler minivans, simply by putting the key in the ignition. This happens more often than you might imagine, judging by the hundreds of recalls and thousands of complaints recorded on the National Highway Traffic Safety Administration (NHTSA) website.

Almost all vehicles have a data recorder.

Forget the assurances of auto manufacturers and the safety establishment. Airbag deployment can cause massive face and chest trauma, ruin your hearing and eyesight, and break bones. Granted, any personal injuries or cabin-area damages caused by airbag deployment are covered by your accident insurance policy. However, if the airbag fails to deploy, or there is a sudden deployment for no apparent reason, the automaker and the dealer should be held jointly responsible for all injuries and damages caused by the failure.

How do you prove that the airbag deployed improperly? Download the data from your "black box" Electronic Data Recorder (EDR) *immediately* after the incident. Further driving of the vehicle may cause the EDR crash data record to be over-written by the addition of new data.

You can use the car's data recorder (see pages 88–89) to prove that the airbag, brakes, throttle control failed prior to an accident. Simply hook a computer up and then download the data from your vehicle's EDR. This will likely lead to a more generous settlement from the two parties and will prevent your insurance premiums from being jacked up.

Once you get all of your proof assembled, including photos of interior damage or injuries caused by the airbag's inadvertent deployment or non-deployment, file suit in provincial court if it's obvious no settlement is in the offing. If your insurance company decides to pay all of your damages and doesn't want to subrogate your case before the courts, make sure you state that they cannot raise your rates following their decision not to sue.

If you do decide to sue, copy the following template Edmonton lawyers have used in their Statement of Claim against Toyota for inadvertent airbag deployment and read the recent Calgary court judgment in *Hutton v. General Motors* (see next page).

IN THE PROVINCIAL COURT OF ALBERTA
JUDICIAL DISTRICT OF EDMONTON

BETWEEN:

████████   Plaintiff

- and -

**TOYOTA CANADA INC., COMPANY #1,
COMPANY #2 and COMPANY #3**
Schedule "A"   Defendants

CIVIL CLAIM

1. The Plaintiff, ████████ ("the Plaintiff"), was at all material times to this action a resident of the City of Edmonton, in the Province of Alberta.
2. The Defendant, TOYOTA CANADA INC. ("Toyota"), is a body corporate incorporated under the laws of the Dominion of Canada and is in the business of designing, manufacturing, selling and repairing motor vehicles. At all material times to this action, Toyota was carrying on business in Canada and in the Province of Alberta.
3. The Defendant, COMPANY #1, is a body corporate and is in the business of manufacturing and supplying air bags and air bag assemblies to Toyota including the Supplementary Restraint System ("SRS").
4. The Defendant, COMPANY #2, is a body corporate and is in the business of manufacturing and supplying electrical systems to Toyota including the Electronic Control Unit ("ECU").
5. The Defendant, COMPANY #3, is a body corporate and is in the business of manufacturing and supplying sensing and diagnostic modules to Toyota including the Event Date Recorder ("EDR").
6. On or about the 11th day of July, 2009, the Plaintiff was operating his motor vehicle, a 2005 Toyota 4Runner ("the vehicle"), registration number JTEBT17R058022580, and while entering his driveway the driver and passenger side curtain airbags of the vehicle deployed and the driver's seat belt pretensioner deployed. The odometer reading at the time of deployment was 99,100 kilometres.
7. The said vehicle was purchased on April 4, 2005, and was subject to Toyota's New Vehicle Warranty (the "Warranty"). The Warranty covers repairs needed on any seatbelt or air bag system supplied by Toyota that is defective in material or workmanship and includes coverage for a period of 60 months or up to 100,000 kilometres, whichever comes first. On July 11, 2009, the said vehicle was within the Warranty period of 60 months and had an odometer reading of 99,100 kilometres.
8. Following the deployment of the air bags, the vehicle was examined by a Field Technical Consultant ("FTC") from Toyota. The inspection by the FTC included diagnostic testing on the ECU and SRS. Toyota concluded from the inspection that the incident was the result of the rollover sensor detecting the onset of a rollover event and not the result of a vehicle defect. No malfunction of the SRS was identified. Based on the inspection and conclusion of the FTC, Toyota has denied and continues to deny warranty coverage for the vehicle.
9. The said vehicle was equipped with an EDR. The EDR contains data useful for troubleshooting and records data in a crash or near car crash event. Data from the EDR, if obtained, could support or dispute the conclusion reached by Toyota through the inspection of the ECU and SRS. Toyota did not have a proper readout tool and was unable to download the vehicle's EDR and the EDR was not inspected.

continued on p. 72

10. As a result of Toyota's decision not to cover the vehicle under the Warranty, the Plaintiff has suffered damages including the cost of repairing the vehicle and reinstalling new air bags.

11. The damages to the Plaintiff were caused jointly and/or severally by the negligence of the Defendants, some particulars of which include the following:
    a. Failing to properly install the said air bags in the vehicle;
    b. Failing to properly test the said air bags of the vehicle;
    c. Using faulty products to manufacture the air bag, the SRS, the ECU and the EDR;
    d. Failing to properly test the SRS, ECU and EDR;
    e. Failing to properly inspect the SRS and the ECU;
    f. Failing to inspect the EDR and failing to make available and/or update information allowing for a reading of the EDR;

Toyota claimed in its standard, boilerplate denial of responsibility that it operated within a reasonable standard of care and that the deployment of the airbags was caused by the negligence of the plaintiff. Shortly after denying practically everything, Toyota settled out of court. This lawsuit was filed by Lawyer Sarah M. Lanceley from the Tarrabain & Company law firm (lawyers@tarrabain.com or www.tarrabain.com).

HUTTON V. GENERAL MOTORS OF CANADA LTD.

[2010] A.J. No. 1077
2010 ABQB 606
76 B.L.R. (4th) 225
33 Alta. L.R. (5th) 340
[2011] 4 W.W.R. 284
2 M.V.R. (6th) 120
501 A.R. 90
2010 CarswellAlta 1879
Docket: 0501 03764
Registry: Calgary
Alberta Court of Queen's Bench
Judicial District of Calgary
P.R. Jeffrey J.
Heard: March 22-29, and May 5, 2010.
Judgment: September 22, 2010.

HELD: The plaintiffs' 1997 Chevrolet Cavalier's air bag did not deploy as designed. Its deployment resulted from the same defects that a previous recall campaign purported to address. The recall campaign did not rectify the defect, but merely recalibrated the deployment mechanism in order to ensure that appropriate deployments would not be prevented. The campaign was not negligent, but was ineffective, as it left vehicles vulnerable to inadvertent deployments in certain circumstances. Negligence arose from the omission of important information about the residual risks, as the defendant presented information in a manner that left a false impression as to cause and effect. The defendant failed to warn users that the risk of inadvertent deployment had not been eliminated, failed to inform users of the scope of the residual risks, and the circumstances that would increase exposure to such risks. Had the plaintiffs been properly warned, the incident and resulting damages could have been avoided. In addition, had the defendant continued to research and address the other conditions associated with inadvertent air bag deployments, a solution would have been implemented prior to the plaintiffs' accident. The accident caused a lasting impact on Hutton, whose broken wrist still caused intermittent pain and clicking. She was awarded general damages of $35,000 and lost wages of $1,820. Wobst was entitled to damages of $3,511 for repairs to the vehicle and $225 for lost wages while assisting Hutton post-accident. Counsel:Louise Novinger Grant (Owner: Burnet, Duckworth & Palmer LLP, Calgary, Alberta, *www.bdplaw.com/*), Patricia E. Olyslager, for the Plaintiffs; Taryn Burnett, Kristian Duff, for the Defendant.

This is a noteworthy decision because it pertains to a used Cavalier; accident data from the electronic data recorder wasn't challenged by either party and was admitted as evidence; GM Canada could not shed responsibility onto GM USA; and compensation for lost wages and pain and suffering were awarded. Interestingly, the estimated costs to repair the car, replace the airbags, etc. were awarded, even though the vehicle was sold unrepaired.

This lengthy judgment cites much case law favourable to plaintiffs. It can be accessed for free online at *www.canlii.org*.

Emissions Components

Car companies have repeatedly gotten themselves into hot water for refusing to replace emissions parts free of charge. These parts are covered by the emissions warranty, a relatively generous warranty set up several decades ago by automakers with the approval of the U.S. Environmental Protection Agency, which also monitors how fairly the warranty is applied. Canada has approved the same warranty, but leaves enforcement to the States and the courts. The EPA has fined both Ford and Chrysler for rejecting legitimate claims for failed emissions parts covered by the EPA and thereby violating the warranty's provisions. The EPA has aggressively gone after other automakers and have entered into consent agreements with them to respect owner warranty rights.

Use the manufacturer's emissions warranty as your primary guideline for the expected durability of high-tech electronic and mechanical pollution-control components, such as powertrain control modules and catalytic converters. These guidelines are usually found in bulletins dealing with sudden acceleration, stalling, hard starts, foul exhaust odours, and excessive tailpipe emissions. First look at your owner's manual for an indication of which parts on your vehicle are covered. Buttress that information with what the U.S. government's online copy of the service bulletin says is covered (the service bulletins are available under the "Vehicle Owners" tab at *www.safercar.gov*). If you don't come up with much detailed parts information, ask the dealer service manager or automaker for a list of specific components covered by the emissions warranty. If you're stonewalled, invest $26.95 (U.S.) in an ALLDATA service bulletin subscription (available for 1982–2011 models).

Many of the confidential technical service bulletins (TSBs) listed in Part Three show parts failures that are covered under the eight-year emissions warranty, even though motorists are routinely charged for their replacement.

Make sure to get your emissions system checked out thoroughly by a dealer or an independent garage before the emissions warranty expires and before having the vehicle inspected by provincial emissions inspectors. In addition to ensuring you pass provincial tests, this precaution could save you up to $1,000 if both your catalytic converter and other emissions components are faulty.

Contact the Right People

Before we go any further, let's get one thing straight: A telephone call to a service manager or automaker usually won't get you much help. Auto manufacturers and their dealers want to make money, not give it back. Customer service advisors are paid to *apply* the warranty policy; don't expect them to *make* policy due to your claim's extenuating circumstances.

To get action, if you suspect a secret warranty applies or that your vehicle has a factory-related defect, you have to kick your claim upstairs, where the company representatives have more power. This can usually be accomplished by sending your claim to the legal affairs department (typically found in Ontario). It should be a registered letter, fax, or email—something that creates a paper trail and gets attention. What's more, that letter must contain the threat that you will use the implied warranty against the dealer and manufacturer and cite convincing jurisprudence to win your small claims court action in the same region where that business operates.

On the following pages are two sample complaint letters that show the type of ammunition you'll need in order to invoke the implied warranty and get a refund for a bad car or ineffective repairs.

Legal "Secrets" Only Lawyers Know

Send a claim letter to both the seller (if it's a dealer) and the automaker to let them work out together how much they will refund to you. Make sure you keep plenty of copies of the complaint and indicate how you can most easily be reached.

Unfair Contract Clauses

Don't let anyone tell you that contracts and warranties are iron-clad and cannot be broken. In fact, a judge can cancel an unfair sales contract or extend your warranty at any time, even though corporate lawyers spend countless hours protecting their clients with one-sided standard-form contracts. Judges look upon these agreements, called "contracts of adhesion," with a great deal of skepticism. They know these loan documents, insurance contracts, automobile leases, and guarantees grant consumers little or no bargaining power. So when a dispute arises over terms or language, provincial consumer protection statutes require that judges interpret these contracts in the way most favourable to the consumer. Simply put, ignorance can sometimes be a good defence.

Hearsay and Courtroom Tactics

Judges have considerable latitude in allowing hearsay evidence if it's introduced properly. But it is essential that printed evidence and/or witnesses (relatives are not excluded) be available to confirm that a false representation actually occurred, that a part is failure-prone, or that its replacement is covered by a secret warranty or internal service bulletin alert. If you can't find an independent expert, introduce this evidence through the automaker reps and dealership service personnel who have to be at the trial anyhow. They know all about the service bulletins and extended warranty programs cited in *Lemon-Aid* and will probably contradict each other, particularly if they are excluded from the courtroom prior to testifying. Incidentally, you may wish to have the court clerk send a subpoena requiring the deposition of the documents you intend to cite, all warranty extensions relevant to your problem, and other lawsuits filed against the company for similar failures. This will make the fur fly in Oshawa, Oakville, and Windsor, and will likely lead to an out-of-court settlement. Sometimes, the service manager or company

---

USED-VEHICLE COMPLAINT LETTER/FAX/EMAIL

WITHOUT PREJUDICE

Date: _____
Name: _____

Please be advised that I am dissatisfied with my used vehicle, a (state model), for the following reasons:

1.
2.
3.
4.
5.

In compliance with the provincial consumer protection laws and the "implied warranty" set down by the Supreme Court of Canada in *Donoghue v. Stevenson, Wharton v. GM*, and *Sharman v. Ford Canada*, I hereby request that these defects be repaired without charge. This vehicle has not been reasonably durable and is, therefore, not as represented to me.

Should you fail to repair these defects in a satisfactory manner and within a reasonable period of time, I shall get an estimate of the repairs from an independent source and claim them in court, without further delay. I also reserve my right to claim up to $1 million for punitive damages, pursuant to the Supreme Court of Canada's February 22, 2002, ruling in *Whiten v. Pilot*.

I have dealt with your company because of its honesty, competence, and sincere regard for its clients. I am sure that my case is the exception and not the rule.

A positive response within the next five (5) days would be appreciated.

(signed with telephone number, fax number, or email address) representative will make key admissions if questioned closely by you, a court mediator, or the trial judge. Here are three important questions to ask: Is this a common problem? Do you recognize this service bulletin? Is there a case-by-case "goodwill" plan covering this repair?

SECRET WARRANTY CLAIM LETTER/FAX/EMAIL

WITHOUT PREJUDICE

Date: _____

Name: _____

Please be advised that I am dissatisfied with my vehicle, a _____, bought from you on _____.

It has had the following recurring problems that I believe are factory-related defects, as confirmed by internal service bulletins sent to dealers, and are covered by your "goodwill" policies:

1.
2.
3.

If your "goodwill" program has ended, I ask that my claim be accepted nevertheless, inasmuch as I was never informed of your policy while it was in effect and should not be penalized for not knowing it existed.

I hereby formally put you on notice under federal and provincial consumer protection statutes that your refusal to apply this extended warranty coverage in my case would be an unfair warranty practice within the purview of the above-cited laws.

Your actions also violate the "implied warranty" set down by the Supreme Court of Canada (*Donoghue v. Stevenson* and *Longpre v. St. Jacques Automobile*) and repeatedly reaffirmed by provincial consumer protection laws (*Lowe v. Chrysler, Dufour v. Ford du Canada*, and *Frank v. GM*).

I have enclosed several estimates (my bill) showing that this problem is factory related and will (has) cost $_____ to correct. I would appreciate your refunding me the estimated (paid) amount, failing which, I reserve the right to have the repair done elsewhere and claim reimbursement in court without further delay. I also reserve the right to claim up to $1 million for punitive damages, pursuant to the Supreme Court of Canada's February 22, 2002, ruling in *Whiten v. Pilot*.

A positive response within the next five (5) days would be appreciated.

(signed with telephone number, fax number, or email address)

Automakers often blame owners for having pushed their vehicle beyond its limits. Therefore, when you seek to cancel the contract or get repair work reimbursed, it's essential that you get an independent mechanic or your co-workers to prove the vehicle was well maintained and driven prudently.

Reasonable Diligence

When asking for a refund, keep in mind the "reasonable diligence" rule that requires that a suit be filed within a reasonable amount of time after the purchase, which usually means less than a year. Because many factory-related deficiencies take years to appear, the courts have ruled that the reasonable diligence clock starts clicking only after the defect is confirmed to be manufacturer- or dealer-related (powertrain, paint, etc.). For powertrain components like engines and transmissions, this allows you to make a claim seven to 10 years after the vehicle was originally put into service, regardless of whether it was bought new or used. Body failures like paint delamination (see *Frank v. GM*) are reimbursable for up to 11 years. If there have been negotiations with the dealer or the automaker, or if either the dealer or the automaker has been promising to correct the defects for some time or has carried out repeated unsuccessful repairs, the deadline for filing the lawsuit can be extended.

Extra, Punitive Damages

Yes, you can claim for hotel and travel costs or compensation for general inconvenience. Fortunately, when legal action is threatened—usually through small claims court—automakers quickly up their out-of-court offer to include most of the owner's expenses because they know the courts will be far more generous. For example, a British Columbia court's decision gave $2,257 for hotel and travel costs, and then capped it off with a $5,000 award for "inconvenience and loss of enjoyment of their luxury vehicle" to a motorist who was fed up with his lemon Cadillac (see *Wharton v. Tom Harris Chevrolet Oldsmobile Cadillac Ltd. and General Motors of Canada Limited*; B.C. Supreme Court, Vancouver; 1999/12/02; Docket C982104). In the *Sharman v. Ford* case (see page 116), the judge gave the plaintiff $7,500 for "mental distress" caused by the fear that his children would fall out of his 2000 Windstar equipped with a faulty sliding door.

As of March 19, 2005, the Supreme Court of Canada confirmed that car owners can ask for punitive, or exemplary, damages when they feel the seller's or the automaker's conduct has been so outrageously bad that the court should protect society by awarding a sum of money large enough to dissuade others from engaging in similar immoral, unethical conduct. In *Prebushewski v. Dodge City Auto (1984) Ltd. and Chrysler Canada Ltd.* (2001 SKQB 537; QB1215/99JCS), the plaintiff got $25,000 in a judgment handed down December 6, 2001, in Saskatoon. The award followed testimony from Chrysler's expert witness that the company was aware of many cases where daytime running lights shorted and caused 1996 Ram pickups to catch fire. The plaintiff's truck had burned to the ground, and Chrysler refused the owner's claim, saying it had fulfilled its expressed warranty obligations, in spite of its knowledge that fires were commonplace. The plaintiff sued on the grounds that there was an implied warranty that the vehicle would be safe. Justice Rothery gave this stinging rebuke in his judgment against Chrysler and its dealer:

> Not only did Chrysler know about the problems of the defective daytime running light modules, it did not advise the plaintiff of this. It simply chose to ignore the plaintiff's requests for compensation and told her to seek recovery from her insurance company. Chrysler had replaced thousands of these modules since 1988. But it had also made a business decision to neither advise its customers of the problem nor to recall the vehicles to replace the modules. While the cost would have been about $250 to replace each module, there were at least one million customers. Chrysler was not prepared to spend $250 million, even though it knew what the defective module might do.

> Counsel for the defendants argues that this matter had to be resolved by litigation because the plaintiff and the defendants simply had a difference of opinion on whether the plaintiff should be compensated by the defendants. Had the defendants some dispute as to the cause of the fire, that may have been sufficient to prove that they had not willfully violated this part of the *Act*. They did not. They knew about the defective daytime running light module. They did nothing to replace the burned truck for the plaintiff. They offered the plaintiff no compensation for her loss. Counsel's position that the definition of the return of the purchase price is an arguable point is not sufficient to negate the defendants' violation of this part of the *Act*. I find the violation of the defendants to be willful. Thus, I find that exemplary damages are appropriate on the facts of this case.

> In this case, the quantum ought to be sufficiently high as to correct the defendants' behaviour. In particular, Chrysler's corporate policy to place profits ahead of the potential danger to its customers' safety and personal property must be punished. And when such corporate policy includes a refusal to comply with the provisions of the *Act* and a refusal to provide any relief to the plaintiff, I find an award of $25,000 for exemplary damages to be appropriate. I therefore order Chrysler and Dodge City to pay: Damages in the sum of $41,969.83; Exemplary damages in the sum of $25,000; Party and party costs.

Warranty Rights

The manufacturer's or dealer's warranty is a written legal promise that a vehicle will be reasonably reliable, subject to certain conditions. Regardless of the number of subsequent owners, this promise remains in force as long as the warranty's original time/kilometre limits haven't expired. Tires aren't usually covered by car manufacturers' warranties; they're warranted instead by the tiremaker on a prorated basis. This isn't such a good deal, because the manufacturer is making a profit by charging you the full list price. If you were to buy the same replacement tire from a discount store, you'd likely pay less, without the prorated rebate.

But consumers have gained additional rights following Bridgestone/Firestone's massive recall in 2001 of its defective ATX II and Wilderness tires. Because of the confusion and chaos surrounding Firestone's handling of the recall, Ford's 575 Canadian dealers stepped into the breach and replaced the tires with any equivalent tires they had in stock, no questions asked. This is an important precedent that tears down the traditional wall separating tire manufacturers from automakers in product liability claims. In essence, whoever sells the product can now be held liable for damages. In the future, Canadian consumers will have an easier time holding the dealer, the automaker, and the tire manufacturer liable, not just for recalled products but also for any defect that affects the safety or reasonable durability of that product.

This is particularly true now that the Supreme Court of Canada (*Winnipeg Condominium v. Bird Construction* [1995] 1 S.C.R. 85) has ruled that defendants are liable in negligence for any designs that result in a risk to the public's safety or health. Sometimes automakers plead that their compliance with federal automobile safety laws immunizes them from product liability claims, but this argument has been shot down countless times by the courts. (Type "auto safety standards liability" into an Internet search engine.)

Other Warranties

In the U.S., safety restraints such as airbags and safety belts have warranty coverage extended for the lifetime of the vehicle, following an informal agreement made between automakers and NHTSA. In Canada, however, some automakers have tried to dodge this responsibility, alleging that they are separate entities, their vehicles are different, and no U.S. agreement or service bulletin can bind them. That distinction is both disingenuous and dishonest and wouldn't likely hold up in small claims court—probably the reason why most automakers relent when threatened with legal action.

 Aftermarket products and services—such as gas-saving gadgets, rustproofing, and paint protectors—can render the manufacturer's warranty invalid, so make sure you're in the clear before purchasing any optional equipment or services from an independent supplier.

How fairly a warranty is applied is more important than how long it remains in effect. Once you know the normal wear rate for a mechanical component or body part, you can demand proportional compensation when you get less than normal durability—no matter what the original warranty says. Some dealers tell customers that they need to have original equipment parts installed in order to maintain their warranty. A variation on this theme requires that the selling dealer does routine servicing—including tune-ups and oil changes (with a certain brand of oil)—or the warranty is invalidated. Nothing could be further from the truth. Canadian law stipulates that whoever issues a warranty cannot make that warranty conditional on the use of any specific brand of motor oil, oil filter, or any other component, unless it's provided to the customer free of charge.

Sometimes dealers will do all sorts of minor repairs that don't correct the problem, and then after the warranty runs out, they'll tell you that major repairs are needed. You can avoid this nasty surprise by repeatedly bringing your vehicle to the dealership before the warranty ends. During each visit, insist that a written work order include the specific nature of the problem, as you see it, and a statement that this is the second, third, or fourth time the same problem has been brought to the dealer's attention. Write this down yourself, if need be. This allows you to show a pattern of non-performance by the dealer during the warranty period and establishes that the problem is both serious and chronic. When the warranty expires, you have the legal right to demand that it be extended on those items consistently reappearing on your handful of work orders. *Lowe v. Fairview Chrysler* (see page 111) is an excellent judgment that reinforces this important principle. In another lawsuit, *François Chong v. Marine Drive Imported Cars Ltd. and Honda Canada Inc.* (see page 110), a Honda owner forced Honda to fix his engine six times—until they got it right.

A retired GM service manager suggests another effective tactic when you're not sure that a dealer's warranty "repairs" will actually correct the problem for a reasonable period of time after the warranty expires. Here's what he says you should do:

> When you pick up the vehicle after the warranty repair has been done, hand the service manager a note to be put in your file that says you appreciate the warranty repair, however, you intend to return and ask for further warranty coverage if the problem reappears before a reasonable amount of time has elapsed—even if the original warranty has expired. A copy of the same note should be sent to the automaker....Keep your copy of the note in the glove compartment as cheap insurance against paying for a repair that wasn't fixed correctly the first time.

Extra-Cost Warranties

When a company goes bankrupt, its extended warranties become worthless unless successfully litigated. At best, payouts will be parsimonious. Supplementary warranties providing extended coverage may be sold by the manufacturer, the dealer, or an independent third party and are automatically transferred when the vehicle is sold. They cost between $1,500 and $2,000 and are usually a waste of money. You can protect yourself better by steering clear of vehicles that have a reputation for being unreliable or expensive to service (see Part Three), and using the threat of small claims courts when factory-related trouble arises. Don't let the dealer pressure you into deciding right away.

Generally, you can purchase an extended warranty any time during the period in which the manufacturer's warranty is in effect or, in some cases, shortly after buying the vehicle from a used-car dealer. An automaker's supplementary warranty will likely cost about a third more than warranties sold by independents. And in some parts of the country, notably B.C., dealers have a quasi monopoly on selling warranties, with little competition from the independents.

Dealers love to sell extended warranties, whether you need them or not, because dealer markup represents up to 60 percent of the warranty's cost. Out of the remaining 40 percent comes the sponsor's administration costs and profit margin, calculated at another 15 percent. What's left to pay for repairs is a paltry 25 percent of the original amount. The only reason that automakers and independent warranty companies haven't been busted for this Ponzi scheme is that only half of the car buyers who purchase extended service contracts actually use them.

It's often difficult to collect on supplementary warranties because independent companies frequently go out of business or limit the warranty's coverage through subsequent mailings. Provincial laws cover both situations. If the bankrupt warranty company's insurance policy won't cover your claim, take the dealer to small claims court and ask for repair costs and the refund of the original warranty payment. Your argument for holding the dealer responsible is a simple one: By accepting a commission to act as an agent of the defunct company, the dealer took on the obligations of the company as well. As for limiting the coverage after you have bought the warranty policy, this is illegal, and it allows you to sue both the dealer and the warranty company for a refund of both the warranty and the repair costs.

Psst..."Secret" Warranties Are Everywhere

Toyotas needing new pistons and rings, Ford Focuses with steering issues, and VWs that leak when it rains are among the vehicles covered in the latest TSBs unearthed by *Lemon-Aid*.

Automakers are reluctant to make free repair programs public because they feel that doing so would weaken confidence in their product and increase their legal liability. The closest they come to an admission is sending a "goodwill policy," "product improvement program," or "special policy" TSB to dealers or first owners of record. Consequently, the only motorists who find out about these policies are the original owners who haven't changed their addresses or leased their vehicles. The other motorists who get compensated for repairs are the ones who read *Lemon-Aid* each year, staple TSBs to their work orders, and yell the loudest.

Remember, vehicles on their second owners and repairs done by independent garages are included in these secret warranty programs. Large, costly repairs, such as blown engines, burned transmissions, and peeling paint, are often covered. Even mundane little repairs, which can still cost you $100 or more, are frequently included in these programs. If you have a TSB but you're still refused compensation, keep in mind that secret warranties are an admission of manufacturing negligence. Owners who have been refused compensation should send an email claim to the automaker and selling dealer (sample claim letter found in *Lemon-Aid*) and then file a small-claims court claim if no settlement is reached within a week

Here are a few examples of secret warranties that may save you thousands of dollars. More extensive listings are found in Part Three's model ratings.

BMW
2007–10 models equipped with a high-pressure fuel pump

Problem: Premature failure. **Warranty coverage:** BMW has extended the emissions warranty to 10 years/120,000 mi. (193,000 km), according to bulletin #SI B13 03 09, announced in BMW's November 2010 dealer letter.

Chrysler, Ford, General Motors, and the Asian Automakers
All years, all models

Problem: Faulty automatic transmissions that self-destruct, shift erratically, gear down to "limp mode," are slow to shift in or out of Reverse, or are noisy. **Warranty coverage:** If you have the assistance of your dealer's service manager, or some internal service bulletin that confirms the automatic transmission may be defective, expect an offer of 50–75 percent (about $2,500) if you threaten to sue in small claims court. Acura, Honda, Hyundai, Lexus, and Toyota coverage varies between seven and eight years.

All years, all models

Problem: Premature wearout of brake pads, calipers, and rotors. Produces excessive vibration, noise, and pulling to one side when braking. **Warranty coverage:** *Calipers and pads:* "Goodwill" settlements confirm that brake calipers and pads that fail to last 2 years/40,000 km will be replaced for half the repair cost; components not lasting 1 year/20,000 km will be replaced for free. *Rotors:* If they last less than 3 years/60,000 km, they will be replaced at half price; replacement is free up to 2 years/40,000 km.

General Motors
2006–07 Cobalt, G4/G5, and Ion

Problem: A faulty fuel pump module may produce a fuel odour or spotting on the ground. **Warranty coverage:** GM has extended the fuel pump warranty to 10 years/120,000 mi. (193,000 km), says TSB #09275A, issued March 3, 2010.

2002–06 Buick Rendezvous; 2000–05 Cadillac DeVille; 2003–06 Cadillac CTS; 2004–06 Cadillac SRX; 2005–06 Cadillac STS; 2006 Cadillac DTS

Problem: Roof rust perforation. **Warranty coverage:** GM will replace, repair, or repaint the roof for free up to 6 years/100,000 km.

2006–07 Malibu and G6

Problem: Catalytic Converter failure. **Warranty coverage:** Under Special Coverage Adjustment #10134, dated November 17, 2010, GM will replace the converter free of charge up to 10 years/120,000 mi. (193,000 km).

2005–06 G6, Malibu, and Malibu Maxx; 2008 G6, Malibu, Malibu Maxx, and Aura

Problem: Loss of power-steering assist. **Warranty coverage:** Under Special Coverage Adjustment #10183, dated July 20, 2010, GM will replace the failed components free of charge up to 10 years/100,000 mi. (160,000 km).

2001–02 Grand Prix, Impala, Monte Carlo, and Regal

Problem: Defective catalytic converters may cause vehicle to lose power or the dash warning light to come on. **Warranty coverage:** The converter warranty is extended to 10 years. Owners will also be reimbursed for previous converter/OBD system repairs or replacements.

Honda

2006–09 Civic

Problem: Engine overheats or leaks coolant because the engine block is cracking at the coolant passages. **Warranty coverage:** Honda will install a new engine block assembly free of charge under a "goodwill policy," as stated in its TSB #10-048, issued August 17, 2010.

1999–2003 Odyssey and Pilot

Problem: EGR valve contamination or EGR port clogging may cause engine surging or stalling. **Warranty coverage:** Honda will install a new EGR valve and a valve kit under a "goodwill" program applicable up to 8 years/160,000 km (TSB #05-026; Date: July 20, 2005).

2003–05 Odyssey

Problem: Premature paint peeling on vehicles painted dark blue. **Warranty coverage:** Honda will repaint the affected areas free of charge up to seven years, with no mileage limit. This warranty extension is covered in Honda Service Bulletin #08-031, issued May 21, 2008.

Mazda

2007–2011 CX7 and CX-9

Problem: These Mazdas may leak oil from the rear differential seal. In TSB 0300411 Mazda says the differential breather was placed too low and could easily become clogged by snow or water. **Warranty coverage:** A new differential with a raised breather covered by the breather boot will be installed for free on a case-by case basis.

Nissan
2007–2012 Altimas and Sentras and 2008-12 Rogues with 4-cylinder engines
Problem: A leak from the oil cooler may be a problem on some Nissans. In TSB NTB11015A Nissan says the leak is from the upper end of the oil cooler. **Warranty coverage:** Removing the cooler and replacing the gaskets under an extended warranty should fix the problem.

Toyota
2004–07 Prius
Problem: Faulty electric water pump. **Warranty coverage:** According to Limited Service Campaign #A0N, Toyota will replace the water pump free of charge until November 30, 2013. There is no mileage limitation.

1995–2000 Tacoma and Tundra
Problem: Rust-damaged structural frames. The excessive rusting is caused by inadequate anti-corrosion undercoating applied at the factory. **Warranty coverage:** According to the April 14, 2008 edition of *Automotive News*, Toyota will repair or buy back the affected pickups. Dealers will inspect all affected Tacomas and Tundras free of charge and apply an extended 15-year frame-rust warranty. Trucks with minor frame pitting will be repaired for free; trucks with more serious damage will be bought back at 150 percent of the "excellent" value listed in the U.S.-published *Kelley Blue Book* guide, regardless of the truck's condition.

2006–08 RAV4, 2007–08 Solara, 2007–09 Camry, 2007–2011 Camry Hybrid, 2009 Corolla, and 2009 Matrix
Problem: The 2.4L 4-cylinder engine may be an "oil-burner." In TSBs SB002411 and SB009411, the company said the problem was traced to the piston assembly. **Warranty coverage:** Toyota will replace the pistons and rings on a "goodwill," case-by-case basis.

Volkswagen
2009–11 Jettas and 2010–11 Golfs, all with the 2.0L TDI engine
Problem: The company says it may have a remedy for diesels that won't start in cold weather. In TSB 2111-06 Volkswagen confirms that some vehicles might not start if left in temperatures below freezing. Moisture from the air intake may condense in the intercooler. **Warranty coverage:** VW recommends adding a cold weather intercooler kit, that will be provided free of charge on a case-by-case basis.

Volvo

2007–10 S8; 2008–10 V70 and XC70, and 2010 XC60

Problem: Leaking coolant from the cylinder-head bleeder hose. Leakage may cause the engine to run hot and cause severe engine damage. **Warranty coverage:** According to Volvo Service Campaign #232, as announced in the company's November 30, 2010 internal dealer service bulletin, Volvo will replace the engine cylinder-head bleeder hose free of charge until November 30, 2012.

Free Recall Repairs

Vehicles are recalled for one of two reasons: Either they are potentially unsafe or they don't conform to federal pollution control regulations. Whatever the reason, recalls are a great way to get free repairs—if you know which ones apply to you and you have the patience of Job.

In North America, over 300 million unsafe vehicles have been recalled by automakers for the free correction of safety-related defects since American recall legislation was passed in 1966 (a weaker Canadian law was enacted in 1971). During that time, about one-third of the recalled vehicles never made it back to the dealership for repairs, because owners were never informed, didn't consider the defect to be that hazardous, or gave up waiting for corrective parts.

Subsequent American legislation targets automakers that drag their feet in making recall repairs. Owners on both sides of the border may wish to cite the NHTSA guidelines (left) for support.

> ### DEALER RECALL RESPONSIBILITY—FOR U.S. AND IPC (U.S. STATES, TERRITORIES, AND POSSESSIONS)
>
> The U.S. *National Traffic and Motor Vehicle Safety Act* provides that each vehicle that is subject to a recall must be adequately repaired within a reasonable time after the customer has tendered it for repair. A failure to repair within 60 days after tender of a vehicle is *prima facie* evidence of failure to repair within a reasonable time. If the condition is not adequately repaired within a reasonable time, the customer may be entitled to an identical or reasonably equivalent vehicle at no charge or to a refund of the purchase price less a reasonable allowance for depreciation. To avoid having to provide these burdensome remedies, every effort must be made to promptly schedule an appointment with each customer and to repair their vehicle as soon as possible.
>
> GM Bulletin No. 00064C, issued September 2002

If you've moved or bought a used vehicle, it's smart to pay a visit to your local dealership, give them your address, and get a report card on which recalls, warranties, and free service campaigns apply to your vehicle. Simply give the service advisor the vehicle identification number—found on your insurance card, or on your dash just below the windshield on the driver's side—and have the number run through the automaker's computer system. Ask for a computer printout of the vehicle's history (have it emailed to you or a friend), and make sure you're listed in the automaker's computer as the new owner. This ensures that you'll receive notices of warranty extensions and emissions and safety recalls.

Regional Recalls

Don't let any dealer refuse you recall repairs because of where you live.

In order to cut recall costs, many automakers try to limit a recall to vehicles in a certain designated region. This practice doesn't make sense, since cars are mobile and an unsafe, rust-cankered steering unit can be found anywhere—not just in certain rust-belt provinces or American states.

For instance, in 2001, Ford attempted to limit to five American states its recall of faulty Firestone tires. Public ridicule of the company's proposal led to an extension of the recall throughout North America.

Common safety defects

Wherever you live or drive, don't expect to be welcomed with open arms when your vehicle develops a safety- or emissions-related problem that's not yet part of a recall campaign.

For example, both Ford and Toyota have been cited for stonewalling customer safety complaints. In 2010, NHTSA hit Toyotoa with three fines, each for the maximum $16.4 million (U.S.), for dragging its feet on three different recalls. More fines are expected as Washington looks more closely into when Toyota first became aware of its sudden acceleration problems.

Ford is in deeper trouble with axle breakage on its 1998–2003 Windstar minivans, and NHTSA will have to share the blame. Although some 200 owners of 1999–2003 Ford Windstar minivans had filed complaints about broken rear axles years ago, NHTSA never opened a safety investigation after Ford assured safety investigators in Washington and Ottawa that even if the axle broke, drivers wouldn't lose steering control. Yet NHTSA's own driving tests not only showed a loss of steering but also concluded the Windstar would likely roll over. Still NHTSA did not open a formal inquiry. Only after the *New York Times* did a story on the axle defect in May did the safety agency begin a formal investigation, saying it had received 234 complaints and reports of two accidents. The axle failures were linked to corrosion damage primarily in snowbelt states where roads are salted in winter.

Industry insiders say Ford will likely join Toyota and be forced to pay the maximum $16.4 million for delaying its axle recall.

In late August, Ford finally recalled 612,000 Windstars from the 1998–2003 model years in the United States and Canada, and in November the safety agency issued an unusual warning to Windstar owners: Get rusty rear axles fixed quickly before they break.

Only one problem with that advice: Ford stopped production of Windstars in 2003 and replacement axles are often back-ordered for months.

Ford and Toyota aren't all that different from other automakers in putting profits before safety, except for the egregious nature of the scam perpetrated by these two automakers. Ford sold the fire-prone Pinto long after the fire danger was evident, and Toyota hushed up its Prius brake failures and sudden acceleration on almost their entire lineup of vehicles in order to generate windfall profits. In fact, Toyota internal documents boasted at one sales meeting that its lobbying of NHTSA saved the automaker $100 million (U.S.).

Let's do the math: Toyota has been fined a total of almost $50 million. On the other hand, Toyota saves $100 million by pressuring the government to drop or delay inquiries into the safety of its vehicles. Result: a $50 million U.S. profit from lobbying NHTSA alone.

No wonder automobile manufacturers and dealers take a restrictive view of what constitutes a safety or emissions defect and frequently charge for repairs that should be free under federal safety or emissions legislation. To counter this tendency, look at the following list of typical defects that are clearly safety-related. If you experience similar problems, insist that the automaker fix the problem at no expense to yourself, including paying for a car rental while corrective repairs are done.

- Airbag malfunctions
- Corrosion affecting safe operation
- Disconnected or stuck accelerators
- Electrical shorts
- Faulty windshield wipers
- Fuel leaks
- Problems with original axles, driveshafts, seats, seat recliners, or defrosters
- Seat belt problems
- Stalling or sudden acceleration
- Sudden steering or brake loss
- Suspension failures
- Trailer coupling failures

Recall campaigns in the U.S. force automakers to pay the entire cost of fixing a vehicle's safety-related defect for any vehicle purchased up to eight years before the recall's announcement. A reasonable period beyond that time is usually a slam dunk in small claims court.

Voluntary recall campaigns, frequently called "Special Service" or "Safety Improvement Campaigns," are a real problem, though. The government doesn't monitor the notification of owners; dealers and automakers routinely deny there's a recall, thereby dissuading most claimants; and the company's so-called fix, not authorized by any governing body, may not correct the hazard at all. Also, the voluntary recall may leave out many of the affected models, or unreasonably exclude certain owners.

Safety Defect Information

If you wish to report a safety defect or want recall info, you may access Transport Canada's website at *www.tc.gc.ca/roadsafety/recalls/search_e.asp*. Recall information is available in French and English, as is general information relating to road safety and importing a vehicle into Canada. Web surfers can now access the recall database for 1970–2008 model year vehicles, but, unlike NHTSA's website, the Transport Canada website doesn't list owner complaints, doesn't disclose defect investigations, doesn't show "voluntary warranty extensions" (read "secret warranties"), and doesn't provide service bulletin summaries. You can also call Transport Canada at 1-800-333-0510 (toll-free within Canada) or 613-993-9851 (within the Ottawa region or outside Canada) to get additional information.

If you aren't happy with Ottawa's treatment of your recall inquiry, try NHTSA's website. It's more complete than Transport Canada's (NHTSA's database is updated daily and covers vehicles built since 1952). You can search the database for your vehicle or tires at *www.nhtsa.dot.gov/cars/problems*. You'll get immediate access to four essential database categories applicable to your vehicle and model year: the latest recalls, current and past defect investigations, complaints reported by other owners, and a brief summary of TSBs.

"Black Box" Data Recorders

If your car has an airbag, it's probably spying on you. And if you get into an accident caused by a mechanical malfunction, you will be glad that it is.

Event data recorders (EDRs) the size of a VCR tape have been hidden near the engine, under the seat, or in the centre consoles of about 30 million airbag-equipped Ford and GM vehicles since the early '90s. Almost all domestic and imported cars now carry them. To find out if your car or truck carries an EDR, read your owner's manual, contact the regional office of your car's manufacturer, or go to *www.harristechnical.com/downloads/cdrlist.pdf*.

The data recorders operate in a similar fashion to flight data recorders used in airplanes: They record data from the last five seconds before impact, including the force of the collision, the airbag's performance, when the brakes were applied, engine and vehicle speed, gas pedal position, and whether the driver was wearing a seat belt.

Getting EDR Data

In the past, automakers have systematically hidden their collected data from government and insurance researchers, citing concerns for drivers' privacy. This argument, however, has been roundly rejected by law enforcement agencies, the courts, and car owners who need the independent information to prove negligence or simply to keep track of how and where their vehicles are driven. Car owners, rental agencies, and fleet administrators are also using EDR data to pin legal liability on automakers for accidents caused by the failure of safety components, such as airbags that don't deploy when they should (or do deploy when they shouldn't) and anti-lock brakes that don't brake.

One handy portable tool for downloading EDR data to any PC is made by the Vetronix Corporation and sells for $2,500 (U.S.). It's presently marketed to accident reconstructionists, safety researchers, law enforcement agencies, and insurance companies as a tool to assess culpability in criminal and civil trials. Car owners who wish to dispute criminal charges, oppose their insurer's decision as to fault, or hold an automaker responsible for a safety device's failure (airbags, seat belts, or brakes) will find this data invaluable—if the data hasn't been wiped clean by the dealer!

A Tool for Parents

One of the scariest days for parents is when their teenager passes the driver's licence exam. Today there are cell phones, satellite radios, flip-down DVD players, and other entertainment options to distract even the most seasoned drivers. Teenagers just learning the rules of the road are especially susceptible to these distractions, and even more so when other teens are in the car.

Electronic monitors are a constant reminder to teens that driving is a privilege that can be taken away if they don't drive safely.

It's now possible to electronically monitor your teenager's driving habits and the places he or she visits with a device called the Road Safety RS-1000 On-Board Computer (see *www.techedu. com/RoadSafety_RS-1000.asp*). It is a relatively inexpensive device that plugs into the data recorder and sets off an audible alarm when the driver exceeds a preset speed limit. The device also uses an accelerometer, similar to those used in automotive testing, to measure vehicle G-forces that are created by aggressive driving. As G-forces become excessive, an audible warning immediately tells the driver to back off. The only way to prevent the audible warning (and the embarrassment when friends are in the vehicle) is to drive safely.

The RS-1000 can be bought through Road Safety International's website. Devices cost $295 (U.S.). For vehicles manufactured in 1996 or later, anyone can install the system by simply plugging the on-board computer into the vehicle's OBD-II connector. The device will also work in 1995 and older vehicles, but it will require hard-wire installation by a qualified automotive technician. For more information, contact the company at *rsi@roadsafety.com* or 805-498-9444.

Safety Benefits

EDRs are not simply good tools for collecting safety data; they have also had a positive effect on accident prevention. A 1992 study by the European Union, cited by the Canada Safety Council, found that EDRs reduced the collision rate by 28 percent and costs by 40 percent in police fleets where drivers knew that they were being monitored.

The Art of Complaining

Step 1: Can We Talk?

Not likely. You can try phoning the seller or automaker, but don't expect to get much out of the call. Private sellers won't want to talk with you, and dealer customer service agents will tell you the vehicle was sold "as is." They simply apply the dealership's policy, knowing that 90 percent of complainers will drop their claims after venting their anger.

Still, try to work things out by contacting someone higher up who can change the policy to satisfy your request. In your attempt to reach a settlement, ask only for what is fair and don't try to make anyone look bad.

Speak in a calm, polite manner, and try to avoid polarizing the issue. Talk about cooperating to solve the problem. Let a compromise emerge—don't come in with a rigid set of demands. Don't insist on getting the settlement offer in writing, but make sure that you're accompanied by a friend or relative who can confirm the offer in court if it isn't honoured. Be prepared to act upon the offer without delay so that your hesitancy won't be blamed if the seller or automaker withdraws it.

Service manager help

Service managers have more power than you may realize. They make the first determination of what work is covered under warranty or through post-warranty "goodwill" programs, and they are directly responsible to the dealer and manufacturer for that decision (dealers hate manufacturer audits that force them to pay back questionable warranty decisions). Service managers are paid both to save the dealer and automaker money and to mollify irate clients—almost an impossible balancing act. Nevertheless, when a service manager agrees to extend warranty coverage, it's because you've raised solid issues that neither the dealer nor the automaker can ignore. All the more reason to present your argument in a confident, forthright manner with your vehicle's service history and *Lemon-Aid*'s "Reasonable Part Durability" table on hand (refer to page 66). Also, bring as many TSBs and owner complaint printouts as you can find from NHTSA's website and similar sources. It's not important that they apply directly to your problem; they establish parameters for giving out after-warranty assistance, or "goodwill."

Don't use your salesperson as a runner, since the sales staff are generally quite distant from the service staff and usually have less pull than you do. If the service manager can't or won't set things right, your next step is to convene a mini-summit with the service manager, the dealership principal, and the automaker's service rep, if he or she represents that make. Regional service representatives are technicians who are regularly sent out by the manufacturer to help dealers with technical problems. By getting the automaker involved, you can often get an agreement where the seller and the automaker pay two-thirds of the repair cost, even though the vehicle was bought used.

Get an independent estimate

Dealers who sell a brand of vehicle used that they don't sell new will give you less latitude. You have to make the case that the vehicle's defects were present at the time of purchase or should have been apparent to the seller, or that the vehicle doesn't conform to the representations made when it was purchased. Emphasize that you intend to use the courts if necessary to obtain a refund—most sellers would rather settle than risk a lawsuit with all the attendant publicity. An independent estimate of the vehicle's defects and repair costs is essential if you want to convince the seller that you're serious in your claim and that you stand a good chance of winning your case in court. Come prepared with an estimated cost of repairs to challenge the dealer who agrees to pay half the repair costs and then jacks up the price 100 percent so that you wind up paying the whole shot.

Step 2: Create a Paper Trail

If you haven't sent a written claim letter, fax, or email, you really haven't complained—or at least, that's the auto industry's mindset. If your vehicle was misrepresented, has major defects, or wasn't properly repaired under warranty, the first thing you should do is give the seller a written summary of the outstanding problems and stipulate a time period within which the seller can fix the vehicle or refund your money. Follow the format of the sample complaint letters on pages 75–76.

Remember, you can ask for compensation for repairs that have been done or need to be done, insurance costs while the vehicle is being repaired, towing charges, supplementary transportation costs such as taxis and rented cars, and damages for inconvenience. If no satisfactory offer is made, ask for mediation, arbitration, or a formal hearing in your provincial small claims court. Make the manufacturer a party to the lawsuit, especially if the emissions warranty, a secret warranty extension, a safety recall campaign, or extensive chassis rusting is involved.

Step 3: Mediation and Arbitration

If the formality of a courtroom puts you off, or you're not sure that your claim is all that solid and don't want to pay legal costs to find out, consider using mediation or arbitration. These services are sponsored by the Better Business Bureau, the Automobile Protection Association, the Canadian Automobile Association, and by many small claims courts where compulsory mediation is a prerequisite to going to trial.

Arbitration clauses

An increasing number of automobile sales contracts contain mandatory, binding arbitration provisions that force the buyer to use independent arbiters to settle disputes. Dealers and automakers favour this process because it's relatively inexpensive, decisions are rendered more quickly than through regular litigation, there is a less formalistic approach to the rules of evidence, jurisprudence isn't created, and the process is less public than an open courtroom trial.

The disadvantages to binding arbitration are many and include: loss of recourse to the courts, no appeals, no jurisprudence to guide plaintiffs as to the rules of law used in prior decisions (which often leads to quicker settlements or encourages litigants to stand by their principles), and the chumminess that often develops between arbiters and dealer/automaker defendants who may meet often over similar issues throughout the year—a familiarity that breeds contempt.

The most serious drawback with arbitration is that the other side can refuse to take back the car or pay the cost of repairs simply by arguing that the arbitration process was flawed because the arbitrator exceeded his or her mandate. This is what Ford of Canada claimed recently in refusing to take back a 2010 Focus that had abraded paint. Ford's appeal was tossed out of court.

Don't get the impression that binding arbitration is a useless tool to get redress. The Canadian Motor Vehicle Arbitration Plan has worked fairly well with some new car disputes. On the other hand it proved woefully ineffective in resolving the "death wobble" on Dennis Warren's 2007 Dodge Ram 2500 (see *http://www.cbc.ca/m/touch/news/story/2011/05/16/bc-dodgeproblem.html*).

Binding arbitration agreements can be useful in covering up design or production defects that are carried over year-after year, since plaintiff's must file their cases individually and cannot pool their resources.

Getting Outside Help

Don't lose your case because of poor preparation. Ask government or independent consumer protection agencies to evaluate how well you've prepared before going to your first hearing. Also, use the Internet to ferret out additional facts and gather support (*www.lemonaidcars.com* and its links are good places to start).

 Pressure Tactics

You can put additional pressure on a seller or garage, and have fun at the same time, by putting a lemon sign on your car and parking it in front of the dealer or garage, by creating a "lemon" website, or by forming a self-help group. Angry Chrysler and Ford owners, for example, have received sizeable settlements in Canada by forming the Chrysler Lemon Owners Group and Ford Lemon Owners Group.

Use your website or place a newspaper ad to gather data from others who may have experienced a problem similar to your own. This can help you set the foundation for a meeting with the automaker, or even for a class action lawsuit, and it pressures the dealer or manufacturer to settle. Websites are often the subject of news stories, so the media may pick up on yours.

Here's some more advice from this consumer advocate with hundreds of pickets and mass demonstrations under his belt: Keep a sense of humour, and never break off the negotiations.

Finally, don't be scared off by threats that it's illegal to criticize a product or company. Unions, environmentalists, and consumer groups do it regularly (it's called informational picketing), and the Supreme Court of Canada in *R. v. Guinard* reaffirmed this right in February 2002. In that judgment, an insured posted a sign on his barn claiming the Commerce Insurance Company was unfairly refusing his claim. The municipality of Saint-Hyacinthe, Quebec, told him to take the sign down. He refused, maintaining that he had the right to state his opinion. The Supreme Court agreed.

This judgment means that consumer protests, signs, and websites that criticize the actions of corporations or government cannot be shut up or taken down simply because they say unpleasant things. However, what you say must be true, and your intent must be to inform, without malice.

Even if you do respectfully protest your treatment following a used car purchase from a dealer, on rare occasions that dealer may file suit against you for defamation or libel. Generally, Canadian courts take a dim view of consumers and non-government organizations, like unions and environmental groups, being sued for protesting, or even picketing. Nevertheless, some dealers will sue, as you can see in the typical filing shown on the following page.

Fortunately, two other Supreme Court decisions buttress a citizen's right to engage in information protests or picketing. This assumes the protest is done without infringing upon the rights of others through actions such as assault, restricting access, defacing property, or harassing others.

The first decision overturned a lower court award of $1.5 million to a forestry executive who sued *The Toronto Star*. The *Star* alleged he had used political connections to get approval for a golf course expansion (*Grant v. Torstar Corp.*).

The Supreme Court struck down the judgment against the newspaper because that judgment had failed to give adequate weight to the value of freedom of expression. The court announced a new defense of "responsible communication on matters of public interest." In the court's opinion, anyone (journalists, bloggers, unions, picketers, etc.) can avoid liability if they can show that the information they communicated—whether true or false—was of public interest and they tried their best to verify it.

In another case, again involving a major Canadian newspaper, a former Ontario police officer sued *The Ottawa Citizen* after it reported he had misrepresented his search-and-rescue work at Ground Zero in New York City after the attacks of September 11, 2001. The Supreme Court reversed the $100,000 jury award because the judges felt the article was in the public interest (*Quan v. Cusson*).

CLAIM

1. The Plaintiff claims from the Defendants:

   a) General damages in the sum of $250,000.00;
   b) Punitive or exemplary damages in the sum of $250,000.00;
   c) Pre-Judgment and post judgment interest in accordance with the Courts of Justice Act;
   d) Costs on a substantial indemnity basis.

2. The Defendants, C████████ and J████████ purchased a 2003 model Hyundai motor vehicle from the Plaintiff, a registered and licensed motor vehicle dealer whose principal place of business is the Town of Arnprior in the County of Renfrew. The motor vehicle was purchased on July 15, 2008 and was the subject of a 3000 month or 3000 km third party warranty pertaining to some power train items only and to no other parts or components of the vehicle.

3. The purchasers declined to apply for or request additional warranty coverage which was offered to them by the Plaintiff and which warranty coverage is much more extensive and for a longer duration than the warranty coverage above-mentioned.

4. Following the purchase by the purchasers, some defects not covered by the warranty were brought to the attention of the Plaintiff which effected repairs at no charge, same being of modest value and cost. In addition, in approximately mid 2009, the car was repaired by the Plaintiff to replace a transmission and differential which showed obvious indicators of serious abuse. The cost for those repairs was $1,737.79 including all charges and taxes.

5. The Plaintiff has learned that the car has been used in at least two racing events on a speed test facility in the Province of Quebec. Such use constitutes abuse and not uncommonly results in failure of parts necessitating repair.

6. The Defendant ████████, has, ostensibly on behalf of purchasers or one of them, made various requests and demands of the Plaintiff to effect additional further repairs not covered by any warranty or guarantee. This Defendant has been of the view that such repairs should be carried out entirely at the expense of the Plaintiff and not at the expense of the purchasers or one of them. The Plaintiff has declined to effect those repairs without charge but has been prepared to repair at the normal charges for labour and parts.

7. Commencing in or about the month of November 2009, the Defendants, or one or more of them have entered various postings on the internet which are defamatory toward the Plaintiff and which postings were and are intended to cause loss and harm to the Plaintiff and which postings were made maliciously.

8. Since approximately the month of November 2009, and with regularity and frequency since a time in and until the present the Hyundai automobile has been driven and put on display in various locations in the Arnprior and surrounding areas bearing signage and lettering labeling the car as "OVER PRICED LEMON" purchased from "ARNPRIOR TRUCK CENTRE". The vehicle, further, bears a large picture of a lemon on the hood of the vehicle. All of the Defendants have operated and parked the vehicle bearing the signage and picture at various times and including parking the vehicle in the immediate proximity of the Plaintiff's place of business. These actions by the Defendants are intended to defame the Plaintiff and have defamed the Plaintiff. The Defendants carried out these activities with malice and with a view and intention that the Plaintiff would suffer financial harm and injury to its reputation.

9. Despite the Plaintiff having warned and cautioned the Defendant ████████, from carrying on the acts of defamation and which constitute liable, that Defendant has disregarded such warning and has continued to drive the motor vehicle bearing the signage and picture as described above as well as leave same parked in prominent and obvious locations on the same street as is located the Plaintiff's place of business.

10. The actions of the Defendants or one or more of them, as described, have caused harm and injury to the Plaintiffs reputation and its business and the Plaintiff has thereby suffered loss.

11. The Defendants or one or more of them deliberately or intentionally set out to cause damage to the Plaintiffs reputation and bring about financial loss and therefore such actions are malicious and justify an award of punitive or exemplary damages.

Safety Failures

Incidents of airbags that deploy for no reason, or don't deploy when they should, sudden unintended acceleration, and brake failure are among the top most frequent complaints logged by Transport Canada and NHTSA. However, the cause of these failures can be very difficult to diagnose, and individual cases are treated very differently by federal safety agencies. Sudden acceleration is considered to be a safety-related problem—stalling isn't always given the same priority. Nevermind that a vehicle's sudden loss of power on a busy highway (as happens with 2001–05 Toyota and Lexus models) puts everyone's lives at risk. The same problem exists with engine and transmission powertrain failures, which are only occasionally considered to be safety-related. ABS and airbag failures are universally considered to be life-threatening defects.

If your vehicle manifests any of these conditions, here's what you need to do:

1. Get independent witnesses to confirm the problem exists. Confirmation includes verification by an independent mechanic, passenger testimony, downloaded data from your vehicle's data recorder, and lots of Internet browsing using *www.lemonaidcars.com* and a search engine like Google. Notify the dealer or manufacturer by fax, email, or registered letter that you consider the problem to be a factory-induced, safety-related defect. Make sure you address your correspondence to the manufacturer's product liability or legal affairs department. At the dealership's service bay, make sure that every work order clearly states the problem as well as the number of previous attempts to fix it. (You should end up with a few complaint letters and a handful of work orders confirming that this is an ongoing deficiency.) If the dealer won't give you a copy of the work order because the work is a warranty claim, ask for a copy of the order number "in case your estate wishes to file a claim, pursuant to an accident." (This will get the service manager's attention.) Leaving a paper trail is crucial for any later claim, because it shows your concern and persistence and clearly indicates that the dealer and manufacturer had ample time to correct the defect.

2. Note on the work order that you expect the problem to be diagnosed and corrected under the emissions warranty or a "goodwill" program. It also wouldn't hurt to add the phrase on the work order or in your claim letters that "any deaths, injuries, or damage caused by the defect will be the dealer's and manufacturer's responsibility" since this work order (or letter, fax, or email) constitutes you putting them on formal notice.

3. If the dealer does the necessary repairs at little or no cost to you, send a follow-up confirmation saying that you appreciate the assistance. Also, emphasize that you'll be back if the problem reappears, even if the warranty has expired, because the repair renews your warranty rights applicable to that defect. In other words, the warranty clock is set back to its original position. You won't likely get a copy of the repair bill, because dealers don't like to admit that there was a serious defect present. Keep in mind, however, that you can get your complete vehicle file from the dealer and manufacturer by

issuing a subpoena, which costs about $75 (refundable), if the case goes to small claims or a higher court. This request has produced many out-of-court settlements when the internal documents show extensive work was carried out to correct the problem.

4. If the problem persists, send a letter, fax, or email to the dealer and manufacturer saying so, look for ALLDATA service bulletins to confirm that your vehicle's defects are factory-related, and call Transport Canada or NHTSA, or log onto NHTSA's website, to report the failure. Also, contact the Center for Auto Safety in Washington, D.C. at 202-328-7700 or visit *www.autosafety.org* for a lawyer referral and an information sheet covering the problem. To find an expert Canadian lawyer familiar with auto defects and sales scams, contact the non-profit Automobile Protection Association (contact info available at *www.APA.ca*).

5. Now come two crucial questions: Should you repair the defect now or later, and should you use the dealer or an independent? Generally, it's smart to use an independent garage if you know the dealer isn't pushing for free corrective repairs from the manufacturer, if weeks or months have passed without any resolution of your claim, if the dealer keeps claiming that it's a maintenance item, or if you know an independent mechanic who will give you a detailed work order showing the defect is factory-related and not a result of poor maintenance. Don't mention that a court case may ensue, since this will scare the dickens out of your only independent witness. A bonus of using an independent garage is that the repair charges will be about half what a dealer would demand. Incidentally, if the automaker later denies warranty "goodwill" because you used an independent repairer, use the argument that the defect's safety implications required emergency repairs to be carried out by whoever could see you first.

6. Take note of the manufacturer's own safety warnings. Dashboard-mounted warning lights usually come on prior to airbags suddenly deploying, ABS brakes failing, or engine glitches causing the vehicle to stall out. (Sudden acceleration, however, usually occurs without warning.) Automakers consider these lights to be critical safety warnings and generally advise drivers to immediately have the vehicle serviced to correct the problem (advice that can be found in the owner's manual) when any of the above lights come on. This bolsters the argument that your life was threatened, emergency repairs were required, and your request for another vehicle or a complete refund isn't out of line.

7. Use the balance of probabilities. Sudden acceleration can have multiple causes, is difficult to prove because it isn't easy to duplicate, and is often blamed on the driver mistaking the accelerator for the brakes or failing to perform proper maintenance. Yet NHTSA data shows that factory-related defects are often the culprit. For example, 1997–2004 Lexus ES 300/330s and Toyota Camrys may have a faulty transmission that may cause engine surging. So how do you satisfy the burden of proof showing that the problem exists and is the automaker's responsibility? Use the legal doctrine called "the balance of probabilities" (refer to page 65) by eliminating all of the possible dodges the dealer or manufacturer may employ. Show that proper maintenance has been

carried out, that you're a safe driver, and that the incident occurs frequently and without warning.

8. If any of the above defects causes an accident, the airbag fails to deploy, or you're injured by its deployment, ask your insurance company to have the vehicle towed to a neutral location and clearly state that neither the dealer nor the automaker should touch the vehicle until your insurance company and Transport Canada have completed their investigation. Also, get as many witnesses as possible and immediately go to the hospital for a check-up, even if you're feeling okay. You may be injured and not know it because the adrenalin coursing through your veins is masking your injuries. A hospital exam will easily confirm that your injuries are related to the accident, which is essential in court or for future settlement negotiations.

9. Peruse NHTSA's online accident database to find reports of other accidents caused by the same failure.

10. Don't let your insurance company settle the case if you're sure the accident was caused by a mechanical failure. Even if an engineering analysis fails to directly implicate the manufacturer or dealer, you can always plead the aforementioned balance of probabilities. If the insurance company settles, your insurance premiums will probably increase.

Paint and Body Defects

The following tips on making a successful claim apply mainly to paint defects, water and air leaks, and subpar fit and finish, but you can use the same strategy for any other vehicle defect that you believe is the automaker's or dealer's responsibility. If you're not sure whether the problem is a factory-related deficiency or a maintenance item, have it checked out by an independent garage or get a TSB summary for your vehicle. The summary may include specific bulletins relating to the diagnosis, correction, and ordering of upgraded parts needed to fix your problem.

1. If you know that your vehicle's paint problem is factory-related, take your vehicle to the dealer and ask for a written, signed estimate. When you're handed the estimate, ask if the paint job can be covered by some "goodwill" assistance. (Ford's euphemism for this secret warranty is "Owner Notification Program" or "Owner Dialogue Program"; GM's term is "Special Policy"; and Chrysler simply calls it an "Owner Satisfaction Notice." Don't use the term "secret warranty" yet. You'll just make everyone angry and evasive.)

2. Your request will probably be met with a refusal, an offer to repaint the vehicle for half the cost, or (if you're lucky) an agreement to repaint the vehicle free of charge. If you accept the half-cost offer, make sure that it's based on the original estimate you have in hand, since some dealers jack up their estimates so that your 50 percent is really 100 percent of the true cost.

3. If the dealer or automaker has already refused your claim and the repair hasn't been done yet, get an additional estimate from an independent garage that shows the problem is factory-related.

4. If the repair has yet to be done, mail or fax a registered claim to the automaker

(and send a copy to the dealer) claiming the average of both estimates. If the repair has been done at your expense, mail or fax a registered claim with a copy of your bill.

5. If you don't receive a satisfactory response within a week, deposit a copy of the estimate or paid bill and claim letter/fax before the small claims court and await a trial date. This means that the automaker/dealer will have to appear, no lawyer is required, and costs should be minimal (under $100). Usually, an informal pretrial mediation hearing with the two parties and a court clerk will be scheduled within a few months, followed by a trial a few weeks later (the time varies depending on region). Most cases are settled at the mediation stage. You can help your case by collecting photographs, maintenance work orders, previous work orders dealing with your problem, and TSBs and by speaking to an independent expert (the garage or body shop that did the estimate or repair is best, but you can also use a local teacher who teaches automotive repair). Remember, service bulletins can be helpful, but they aren't critical to a successful claim.

Other situations

- If the vehicle has just been repainted or repaired but the dealer says that "goodwill" coverage was denied by the automaker, pay for the repair with a certified cheque and write "under protest" on the cheque. Remember, though, if the dealer does the repair, you won't have an independent expert who can affirm that the problem was factory-related or that it was a result of premature wearout. Plus, the dealer can say that you or the environment caused the paint problem. In these cases, TSBs can make or break your case.
- If the dealer or automaker offers a partial repair or refund, take it. Then sue for the rest. Remember, if a partial repair has been done under warranty, it counts as an admission of responsibility, no matter what "goodwill" euphemism is used. Also, the repaired component or body panel should be just as durable as if it were new. Hence the clock starts ticking from the time of the repair until you reach the original warranty parameter—no matter what the dealer's repair warranty limit says.

Very seldom do automakers contest these paint claims before small claims court, instead opting to settle once the court claim is bounced from their customer relations people to their legal affairs department. At that time, you'll probably be offered an out-of-court settlement for 50–75 percent of your claim.

Stand fast, and make reference to the service bulletins you intend to subpoena in order to publicly contest in court the unfair nature of this "secret warranty" program (automakers' lawyers cringe at the idea of trying to explain why consumers aren't made aware of these bulletins)—100 percent restitution will probably follow.

Four favourable paint judgments

Dunlop v. Ford of Canada (No. 58475/04; Ontario Superior Court of Justice, Richmond Hill Small Claims Court; January 5, 2005; Deputy Judge M.J. Winer). The owner of a 1996 Lincoln Town Car purchased used in 1999 for $27,000 was awarded $4,091.64. Judge Winer cited the *Shields* decision (following) and gave these reasons for finding Ford of Canada liable:

> Evidence was given by the Plaintiff's witness, Terry Bonar, an experienced paint auto technician. He gave evidence that the [paint] delamination may be both a manufacturing defect and can be caused or speeded up by atmospheric conditions. He also says that [the paint on] a car like this should last ten to 15 years, [or even for] the life of the vehicle....

> It is my view that the presence of ultraviolet light is an environmental condition to which the vehicle is subject. If it cannot withstand this environmental condition, it is defective in my view.

Shields v. General Motors of Canada (No. 1398/96; Ontario Court, General Division; Oshawa Small Claims Court; July 24, 1997; Deputy Judge Robert Zochodne). The owner of a 1991 Pontiac Grand Prix purchased the vehicle used with over 100,000 km on its odometer. Beginning in 1995, the paint began to bubble and flake and eventually peeled off. Deputy Judge Robert Zochodne awarded the plaintiff $1,205.72 and struck down every one of GM's environmental/acid rain/UV rays arguments. Here are the other important aspects of this 12-page judgment that GM did not appeal:

1. The judge admitted many of the TSBs referred to in *Lemon-Aid* as proof of GM's negligence.
2. Although the vehicle already had 156,000 km on it when the case went to court, GM still offered to pay for 50 percent of the paint repairs if the plaintiff dropped his suit.
3. The judge ruled that the failure to protect the paint from the damaging effects of UV rays is akin to engineering a car that won't start in cold weather. In essence, vehicles must be built to withstand the rigours of the environment.
4. Here's an interesting twist: The original warranty covered defects that were present at the time it was in effect. The judge, taking statements found in the GM technical service bulletins, ruled that the UV problem was factory-related, existed during the warranty period, and represented a latent defect that appeared once the warranty expired.
5. The subsequent purchaser was not prevented from making the warranty claim, even though the warranty had long since expired from a time and mileage standpoint and he was the second owner.

Bentley v. Dave Wheaton Pontiac Buick GMC Ltd. and General Motors of Canada (Victoria Registry No. 24779; British Columbia Small Claims Court; December 1, 1998; Judge Higinbotham). This small claims judgment builds on the Ontario

Shields v. General Motors of Canada decision and cites other jurisprudence as to how long paint should last on a car. If you're wondering why Ford and Chrysler haven't been hit by similar judgments, remember that they usually settle out of court.

Maureen Frank v. General Motors of Canada Limited (No. SC#12 (2001); Saskatchewan Provincial Court; October 17, 2001; Provincial Court Judge H.G. Dirauf). I discuss this case on page 66.

Other paint and rust cases

Whittaker v. Ford Motor Company (1979) (24 O.R. (2d), 344). A new Ford developed serious corrosion problems in spite of having been rustproofed by the dealer. The court ruled that the dealer, not Ford, was liable for the damage for having sold the rustproofing product at the time of purchase. This is an important judgment to use when a rustproofer or paint protector goes out of business or refuses to pay a claim, since the decision holds the dealer jointly responsible.

Martin v. Honda Canada Inc. (March 17, 1986; Ontario Small Claims Court, Scarborough; Judge Sigurdson). The original owner of a 1981 Honda Civic sought compensation for the premature "bubbling, pitting, [and] cracking of the paint and rusting of the Civic after five years of ownership." Judge Sigurdson agreed with the owner and ordered Honda to pay $1,163.95.

Thauberger v. Simon Fraser Sales and Mazda Motors (3 B.C.L.R., 193). This Mazda owner sued for damages caused by the premature rusting of his 1977 Mazda GLC. The court awarded him $1,000. Thauberger had previously sued General Motors for a prematurely rusted Blazer truck and was also awarded $1,000 in the same court. Both judges ruled that the defects could not be excluded from the auto-maker's expressed warranty or from the implied warranty granted by British Columbia's *Sale of Goods Act*.

See also:

- *Danson v. Chateau Ford (1976)* C.P. (Quebec Small Claims Court; No. 32-00001898-757; Judge Lande)
- *Doyle v. Vital Automotive Systems* (May 16, 1977; Ontario Small Claims Court, Toronto; Judge Turner)
- *Lacroix v. Ford* (April 1980; Ontario Small Claims Court, Toronto; Judge Tierney)
- *Marinovich v. Riverside Chrysler* (April 1, 1987; District Court of Ontario; No. 1030/85; Judge Stortini)

Using the Courts

Nova Scotia's Used-Car "Lemon Law"

In 2011, Nova Scotia became the first Canadian province to require that used-car dealers identify rebuilt or previously damaged vehicles by placing labels on their windshields. Acting on consumer complaints, the provincial government introduced changes to the *Motor Vehicle Act* to ensure consumers know a used vehicle's history before they buy it.

Under the new law, dealers must clearly label vehicles that have been deemed unrepairable, are manufacturers' buybacks, or have been involved in a serious collision in Canada or the United States. Sellers who do not comply with the new legislation will be fined up to $1,000 per vehicle.

Unfortunately, the fines are ridiculously low and the new rules will not apply to private auto sales or trade-ins.

Sue as a Last Resort

If the seller you've been negotiating with agrees to make things right, give him or her a deadline and then have an independent garage check the repairs. If no offer is made within 10 working days, file suit in court. Make the manufacturer a party to the lawsuit only if the original, unexpired warranty was transferred to you; if your claim falls under the emissions warranty, a TSB, a secret warranty extension, or a safety recall campaign; or if there is extensive chassis rusting due to poor engineering.

Choosing the Right Court

You must decide what remedy to pursue: a partial refund or a cancellation of the sale. To determine the refund amount, add the estimated cost of repairing existing mechanical defects to the cost of prior repairs. Don't exaggerate your losses or claim for repairs that are considered routine maintenance. A suit for cancellation of sale involves practical problems. The court requires that the vehicle be "tendered," or taken back to the seller, at the time the lawsuit is filed. This means that you are without transportation for as long as the case continues, unless you purchase another vehicle in the interim. If you lose the case, you must then take back the old vehicle and pay storage fees. You could go from having no vehicle to having two, one of which is a clunker.

Generally, if the cost of repairs or the sales contract amount falls within the small claims court limit, file the case there to keep costs to a minimum and to get a speedy hearing. Small claims court judgments aren't easily appealed, lawyers aren't necessary, filing fees are minimal (about $125), and cases are usually heard within a few months.

Watch what you ask for. If you claim more than the small claims court limit, you'll have to go to a higher court—where costs quickly add up and delays of a few years or more are commonplace.

Small Claims Courts

Crooked automakers scurry away from small claims courts like cockroaches from bug spray, not because the courts can issue million-dollar judgments or force litigants to spend millions in legal fees (they can't), but because they can award sizeable sums to plaintiffs and make jurisprudence that other judges on the same bench are likely to follow.

For example, in *Dawe v. Courtesy Chrysler* (Dartmouth Nova Scotia Small Claims Court; SCCH #206825; July 30, 2004), Judge Patrick L Casey, Q.C., rendered an impressive 21-page decision citing key automobile product liability cases over the past 80 years. He awarded $5,037 to the owner of a new 2001 Cummins-equipped Ram pickup that suffered from myriad ailments. The truck shifted erratically, lost braking ability, wandered all over the road, lost power or jerked and bucked, bottomed out when passing over bumps, allowed water to leak into the cab, produced a burnt-wire and oil smell as the lights would dim, and produced a rear-end whine and wind noise around the doors and under the dash. Dawe had sold the vehicle and reduced his claim to meet the small claims threshold.

There are small claims courts in most counties of every province, and you can make a claim either in the county where the problem happened or in the county where the defendant lives and conducts business. Simply go to the small claims court office and ask for a claim form. Instructions on how to fill it out accompany the form. Remember, you must identify the defendant correctly, and this may require some help from the court clerk or a law student because some automakers name local attorneys to handle suits (look for other recent lawsuits naming the same party). Crooks often change their company's name to escape liability; for example, it would be impossible to sue Joe's Garage (2008) if your contract is with Joe's Garage Inc. (2004).

At this point, it wouldn't hurt to hire a lawyer or a paralegal for a brief walk-through of small claims procedures to ensure that you've prepared your case properly and that you know what objections the other side will likely raise. If you'd like a lawyer to do all the work for you, there are a number of law firms around the country that specialize in small claims litigation. "Small claims" doesn't mean small legal fees, however. In Toronto, some law offices charge a flat fee of $1,000 for a basic small claims lawsuit and trial.

Remember that you're entitled to bring to court any evidence relevant to your case, including written documents such as a bill of sale, receipt, contract, or letter. If your car has developed severe rust problems, bring a photograph (signed and dated by the photographer) to court. You may also have witnesses testify, but it's important to discuss witness testimony prior to the court date. If a witness can't attend the court date, he or she can write a report and sign it for representation in court. This situation usually applies to an expert witness, such as an independent mechanic who has evaluated your car's problems.

If you lose your case in spite of all your preparation and research, some small claims court statutes allow cases to be retried, at a nominal cost, in exceptional circumstances. If a new witness has come forward, additional evidence has been discovered, or key documents that were previously not available have become accessible, apply for a retrial. In Ontario, this little-known provision is Rule 18.4 (1).B.

Alan MacDonald, a *Lemon-Aid* reader who won his case in small claims court, gives the following tips on beating Ford (*MacDonald v. Highbury Ford Sales Limited*, Ontario Superior Court of Justice in the Small Claims Court London, June 6, 2000, Court File #0001/00, Judge J. D. Searle):

> In 1999 after only 105,000 km the automatic transmission went. I took [my 1994 Ford Taurus wagon] to Highbury Ford to have it repaired. We paid $2,070 to have the transmission fixed, but protested and felt the transmission failed prematurely. We contacted Ford, but to no avail: their reply was we were out of warranty period. The transmission was so poorly repaired (and we went back to Highbury Ford several times) that we had to go to Mr. Transmission to have the transmission fixed again nine months later at a further $1,906.02....

> My observations with going through small claims court involved the following: I filed in January of 2000, the trial took place on June 1 and the judgment was issued June 6.

> At pretrial, a representative of Ford (Ann Sroda) and a representative from Highbury Ford were present. I came with one binder for each of the defendants, the court, and one for myself (each binder was about 3 inches thick—containing your reports on Ford Taurus automatic transmissions, ALLDATA Service Bulletins, [and extracts from the following websites:] Taurus Transmissions Victims (Bradley website), Center for Auto Safety...Read This Before Buying a Taurus...and the Ford Vent Page....

> The representative from Ford asked a lot of questions (I think she was trying to find out if I had read the contents of the information I was relying on). The Ford representative then offered a 50 percent settlement based on the initial transmission work done at Highbury Ford. The release allowed me to still sue Highbury Ford with regards to the necessity of going to Mr. Transmission because of the faulty repair done by the dealer. Highbury Ford displayed no interest in settling the case, and so I had to go to court.

> For court, I prepared by issuing a summons to the manager at Mr. Transmission, who did the second transmission repair, as an expert witness....Next, I went to the law school library in London and received a great deal of assistance in researching cases pertinent to car repairs. I was told that judgments in your home province (in my case, Ontario) were binding on the court; that cases outside of the home province could be considered, but not binding, on the judge.

The cases I used for trial involved *Pelleray v. Heritage Ford Sales Ltd.*, Ontario Small Claims Court (Scarborough) SC7688/91 March 22, 1993; *Phillips et al. v. Ford Motor Co. of Canada Ltd. et al*, Ontario Reports 1970, 15th January 1970; *Gregorio v. Intrans-Corp.*, Ontario Court of Appeal, May 19, 1994; *Collier v. MacMaster's Auto Sales*, New Brunswick Court of Queen's Bench, April 26, 1991; *Sigurdson v. Hillcrest Service & Acklands (1977)*, Saskatchewan Queen's Bench; *White v. Sweetland*, Newfoundland District Court, Judicial Centre of Gander, November 8, 1978; *Raiches Steel Works v. J. Clark & Son*, New Brunswick Supreme Court, March 7, 1977; *Mudge v. Corner Brook Garage Ltd.*, Newfoundland Supreme Court, July 17, 1975; *Sylvain v. Carroseries d'Automobiles Guy Inc. (1981)*, C.P. 333, Judge Page; and *Gagnon v. Ford Motor Company of Canada, Limited et Marineau Automobile Co. Ltée. (1974)*, C.S. 422–423.

In court, I had prepared the case, as indicated above, and had my expert witness and two other witnesses who had driven the vehicle (my wife and my 18-year-old son). As you can see by the judgment, we won our case and I was awarded $1,756.52, including prejudgment interest and costs.

Key Court Decisions

The following Canadian and U.S. lawsuits and judgments cover typical problems that are likely to arise. Use them as leverage when negotiating a settlement or as a reference should your claim go to trial. Legal principles applying to Canadian and American law are similar; Quebec court decisions, however, may be based on legal principles that don't apply outside of that province. Nevertheless, you can find a comprehensive listing of Canadian decisions from small claims courts all the way to the Supreme Court of Canada at *www.legalresearch.org* or *www.canlii.org*.

You can find additional court judgments in the legal reference section of your city's main public library or at a nearby university law library. Ask the librarian for help in choosing the legal phrases that best describe your claim. LexisNexis (*www.lexisnexis.com*) and FindLaw (*www.findlaw.com*) are two useful Internet sites for legal research. Their main drawback, though, is that you may need to subscribe or use a lawyer's subscription to access jurisprudence and other areas of the sites.

Some of the small claims court cases cited in *Lemon-Aid* may not be reported. If that happens, contact the office of the presiding judge named in the decision and ask his or her assistant to send you a copy of the judgment. If the judge or assistant isn't available, ask for the court clerk of that jurisdiction to search for the case file and date referenced in *Lemon-Aid*.

 An excellent reference book that will give you plenty of tips on filing, pleading, and collecting your judgment is Judge Marvin Zuker's *Ontario Small Claims Court Practice 2011, 30th Anniversary Edition* (Carswell, 2010). Judge Zuker's book is easily understood by non-lawyers and uses court decisions from across Canada to help you plead your case successfully in almost any Canadian court. It costs $91 (CDN) and can be ordered from *www.fedpubs.com/subject/law/sm_claims.htm*.

Product Liability

Almost three decades ago, in *Kravitz v. GM* (the first case where I was called as a pro bono expert witness), the Supreme Court of Canada clearly affirmed that automakers and their dealers are jointly liable for the replacement or repair of a vehicle if independent testimony shows that it is afflicted with factory-related defects that compromise its safety or performance. The existence of a secret warranty extension or TSB also helps prove that the vehicle's problems are the automaker's responsibility. For example, in *Lowe v. Fairview Chrysler* (see page 111), TSBs were instrumental in showing an Ontario small claims court judge that Chrysler's history of automatic transmission failures went back to 1989.

In addition to replacing or repairing the vehicle, an automaker can also be held responsible for any damages arising from the defect. This means that loss of wages, supplementary transportation costs, and damages for personal inconvenience can be awarded. In the States, product liability damage awards often exceed millions of dollars. Canadian courts, however, are far less generous.

Implied Warranty Rulings

Reasonable durability

As outlined near the beginning of the chapter, this is that powerful "other" warranty that they never tell you about. It applies during and after the expiration of the manufacturer's or dealer's expressed or written warranty and requires that a part or repair will last a reasonable period of time. What is reasonable depends in a large part on benchmarks used in the industry, the price of the vehicle, and how it was driven and maintained. Look at the "Reasonable Part Durability" table on pages 68–69 for some guidelines as to what you should expect. Judges usually apply the implied or legal warranty when the manufacturer's expressed warranty has expired and the vehicle's manufacturing defects remain uncorrected.

Chevrier v. General Motors du Canada (October 18, 2006; Quebec Small Claims Court, Joliette District (Repentigny) No. 730-32-004876-046; Justice Georges Massol). You can find the full judgment (French) at *www.canlii.org*.

The plaintiff leased and then bought a 2000 Montana minivan. At 71,000 km the automatic transmission failed and two GM dealers estimated the repairs to be between $2,200 and $2,500. They refused warranty coverage because the warranty had expired after the third year of ownership or 60,000 km of use. The owner repaired the transmission at an independent garage for $1,869 and kept the old parts, which GM refused to examine.

A small claims court lawsuit was filed, and Judge Massol gave the following reasons for ruling against GM's two arguments that (1) there was no warning that a claim would be filed, and (2) all warranties had expired:

- GM filed a voluminous record of jurisprudence in its favour, relative to other lawsuits that were rejected because they were filed without prior notice. But the judge reasoned that GM could not plead a "failure to notify," because the owner went to several dealers who were essentially agents of the manufacturer.

• The judge also reasoned that the expiration of GM's written warranty does not nullify the legal warranty set out in articles 38 and 39 of the *Consumer Protection Act*. The legal warranty requires that all products be "reasonably durable," which did not appear to be the case with the plaintiff's vehicle, given its low mileage and number of years of use.

GM was ordered to pay the entire repair costs, plus interest, and the $90 filing fee.

Dufour v. Ford Canada Ltd. (April 10, 2001; Quebec Small Claims Court, Hull; No. 550-32-008335-009; Justice P. Chevalier). Ford was forced to reimburse the cost of engine head gasket repairs carried out on a 1996 Windstar 3.8L engine—a vehicle not covered by the automaker's Owner Notification Program, which cut off assistance after the '95 model year.

Schaffler v. Ford Motor Company Limited and Embrun Ford Sales Ltd. (Ontario Superior Court of Justice; L'Orignal Small Claims Court; Court File No. 59-2003; July 22, 2003; Justice Gerald Langlois). The plaintiff bought a used 1995 Windstar in 1998. Its engine head gasket was repaired for free three years later, under Ford's seven-year extended warranty. In 2002, at 109,600 km, the head gasket failed again, seriously damaging the engine. Ford refused a second repair. Justice Langlois ruled that Ford's warranty extension bulletin listed signs and symptoms of the covered defect that were identical to the problems written on the second work order ("persistent and/or chronic engine overheating; heavy white smoke evident from the exhaust tailpipe; flashing 'low coolant' instrument panel light even after coolant refill; and constant loss of engine coolant"). Judge Langlois concluded that "the problem was brought to the attention of the dealer well within the warranty period; the dealer was negligent." The plaintiff was awarded $4,941 plus 5 percent interest. This judgment included $1,070 for two months' car rental.

John R. Reid and Laurie M. McCall v. Ford Motor Company of Canada (Superior Court of Justice; Ottawa Small Claims Court; Claim No: #02-SC-077344; July 11, 2003; Justice Tiernay). A 1996 Windstar, bought used in 1997, experienced engine head gasket failure in October 2001 at 159,000 km. Judge Tiernay awarded the plaintiffs $4,145 for the following reason:

> A Technical Service Bulletin dated June 28, 1999, was circulated to Ford dealers. It dealt specifically with "undetermined loss of coolant" and "engine oil contaminated with coolant" in the 1996–98 Windstar and five other models of Ford vehicles. I conclude that Ford owed a duty of care to the Plaintiff to equip this vehicle with a cylinder head gasket of sufficient sturdiness and durability that would function trouble-free for at least seven years, given normal driving and proper maintenance conditions. I find that Ford is answerable in damages for the consequences of its negligence.

Dawe v. Courtesy Chrysler (Dartmouth Nova Scotia Small Claims Court; SCCH #206825; July 30, 2004; Judge Patrick L Casey, Q.C.). "Small claims" doesn't necessarily mean small judgments. This 21-page, unreported Nova Scotia small claims court decision is impressive in its clarity and thoroughness. It applies *Donoghue, Kravitz, Davis, et al.* in awarding a 2001 Dodge Ram owner over $5,000 in damages. Anyone with engine, transmission, and suspension problems or water leaking into the interior will find this judgment particularly useful.

Fissel v. Ideal Auto Sales Ltd. (1991) (91 Sask. R. 266). Shortly after the vehicle was purchased, its motor seized and the dealer refused to replace it, even though the car was returned on several occasions. The court ruled that the dealer had breached the statutory warranties in sections 11 (4) and (7) of the *Consumer Products Warranties Act*. The purchasers were entitled to cancel the sale and recover the full purchase price.

Friskin v. Chevrolet Oldsmobile (72 D.L.R. (3d), 289). A Manitoba used-car buyer asked that his contract be cancelled because of his car's chronic stalling problem. The garage owner did his best to correct it. Despite the seller's good intentions, the *Manitoba Consumer Protection Act* allowed for cancellation.

Graves v. C&R Motors Ltd. (April 8, 1980; British Columbia County Court; Judge Skipp). The plaintiff bought a used car on the condition that certain deficiencies be remedied. They never were, and he was promised a refund, but it never arrived. The plaintiff brought suit, claiming that the dealer's deceptive activities violated the provincial *Trade Practices Act*. The court agreed, concluding that a deceptive act that occurs before, during, or after the transaction can lead to the cancellation of the contract.

Hachey v. Galbraith Equipment Company (1991) (33 M.V.R. (2d) 242). The plaintiff bought a used truck from the dealer to haul gravel. Shortly thereafter, the steering failed. The plaintiff's suit was successful because expert testimony showed that the truck wasn't roadworthy. The dealer was found liable for damages for being in breach of the implied condition of fitness for the purpose for which the truck was purchased, as set out in section 15(a) of the New Brunswick *Sale of Goods Act*.

Henzel v. Brussels Motors (1973) (1 O.R., 339 (C.C.)). The dealer sold a used car, brandishing a copy of the mechanical fitness certificate as proof that the car was in good shape. The plaintiff was awarded his money back because the court held the certificate to be a warranty that was breached by the car's subsequent defects.

Johnston v. Bodasing Corporation Limited (February 23, 1983; Ontario County Court, Bruce; No. 15/11/83; Judge McKay). The plaintiff bought a used 1979 Buick Riviera that was represented as being "reliable" for $8,500. Two weeks after purchase, the motor self-destructed. Judge McKay awarded the plaintiff $2,318 as compensation to fix the Riviera's defects. One feature of this particular decision is that the trial judge found that the *Sale of Goods Act* applied, notwithstanding the fact that the vendor used a standard contract that said there were no warranties or representations. The judge also accepted the decision in *Kendall v. Lillico* (1969) (2 Appeal Cases 31), which indicates that the *Sale of Goods Act* covers not only defects that the seller ought to have detected but also latent defects that even his or her utmost skill and judgment could not have detected. This places a very heavy onus on the vendor, and it should prove useful in actions of this type in other common-law provinces with laws similar to Ontario's *Sale of Goods Act*.

General Motors Products of Canada Ltd. v. Kravitz, (1979) (1 S.C.R. 790). The court said the seller's warranty of quality was an accessory to the property and was transferred with it on successive sales. Accordingly, subsequent buyers could invoke the contractual warranty of quality against the manufacturer, even though they did not contract directly with it. This precedent was then codified in articles 1434, 1442, and 1730 of Quebec's *Civil Code*.

Morrison v. Hillside Motors (1973) *Ltd.* (1981; 35 Nfld. & P.E.I.R. 361). A used car advertised to be in "A1" condition and carrying a 50/50 warranty developed a number of problems. The court decided that the purchaser should be partially compensated because of the ad's claim. In deciding how much compensation to award, the presiding judge considered the warranty's wording, the amount paid for the vehicle, the model year of the vehicle, the vehicle's average life, the type of defect that occurred, and the length of time the purchaser had use of the vehicle before its defects became evident. Although this judgment was rendered in Newfoundland, judges throughout Canada have used a similar approach for more than a decade.

Neilson v. Maclin Motors (71 D.L.R. (3d), 744). The plaintiff bought a used truck on the strength of the seller's allegations that the motor had been rebuilt and that it had 210 hp. The engine failed. The judge awarded damages and cancelled the contract because the transmission was defective and the motor had not been rebuilt and did not have 210 hp.

Parent v. Le Grand Trianon and Ford Credit (1982) (C.P., 194; Judge Bertrand Gagnon). Nineteen months after paying $3,300 for a used 1974 LTD, the plaintiff sued the Ford dealer for his money back because the car was prematurely rusted out. The dealer replied that rust was normal, there was no warranty, and the claim was too late. The court held that the garage was still responsible. The plaintiff was awarded $1,500 for the cost of rust repairs.

Narbonne v. Glendale Recreational Véhicules (Quebec Small Claims Court; June 2, 2008; Reference: 2008 QCCQ 5325; Judge Richard Landry). Three years after the plaintiff purchased a travel trailer, the manufacturer sent a recall notice to the wrong address. Seven years after that, the vehicle broke down when the recalled part failed. The manufacturer said it had done its part in sending out the recall notice. The judge disagreed, and found the company responsible for the full cost of the repairs, lodging, and $500 for general inconvenience, for a total of $5,792.

"As is" clauses

Since 1907, Canadian courts have ruled that a seller can't exclude the implied warranty as to fitness by including such phrases as "there are no other warranties or guarantees, promises, or agreements than those contained herein." See *Sawyer-Massey Co. v. Thibault* (1907; 5 W.L.R. 241).

Adams v. J&D's Used Cars Ltd. (1983) (26 Sask. R. 40 Q.B.). Shortly after the plaintiff purchased a car, its engine and transmission failed. The court ruled that the inclusion of "as is" in the sales contract had no legal effect. The dealer breached the implied warranty set out in Saskatchewan's *Consumer Products Warranties Act.* The sale was cancelled, and all monies were refunded.

Leasing

Ford Motor Credit v. Bothwell (December 3, 1979; Ontario County Court, Middlesex; No. 9226-T; Judge Macnab). The defendant leased a 1977 Ford truck that had frequent engine problems, characterized by stalling and hard starting. After complaining for one year and driving 35,000 km, the defendant cancelled the lease. Ford Credit sued for the money owing on the lease. Judge Macnab cancelled the lease and ordered Ford Credit to repay 70 percent of the amount paid during the leasing period. Ford Credit was also ordered to refund repair costs, even though the corporation claimed that it should not be held responsible for Ford's failure to honour its warranty.

Salvador v. Setay Motors/Queenstown Chev-Olds (Hamilton Small Claims Court; Case No.1621/95). The plaintiff was awarded $2,000, plus costs, from Queenstown Leasing. The court found that the company should have tried harder to sell the leased vehicle, and at a higher price, when the "open lease" expired.

Schryvers v. Richport Ford Sales (May 18, 1993; B.C.S.C.; No. C917060; Justice Tysoe). The court awarded $17,578.47, plus costs, to a couple who paid thousands of dollars more in unfair and hidden leasing charges than if they had simply purchased their Ford Explorer and Escort. The court found that this price difference constituted a deceptive, unconscionable act or practice, in contravention of the *Trade Practices Act*, R.S.B.C. 1979, c. 406.

Judge Tysoe concluded that the total general damages awarded to the Schryvers for both vehicles would be $11,578.47. He then proceeded to give the following reasons for awarding an additional $6,000 in punitive damages:

> Little wonder Richport Ford had a contest for the salesperson who could persuade the most customers to acquire their vehicles by way of a lease transaction. I consider the actions of Richport Ford to be sufficiently flagrant and high handed to warrant an award of punitive damages.

> There must be a disincentive to suppliers in respect of intentionally deceptive trade practices. If no punitive damages are awarded for intentional violations of the

legislation, suppliers will continue to conduct their businesses in a manner that involves deceptive trade practices because they will have nothing to lose. In this case I believe that the appropriate amount of punitive damages is the extra profit Richport Ford endeavoured to make as a result of its deceptive acts. I therefore award punitive damages against Richport Ford in the amount of $6,000.

See also:

- *Barber v. Inland Truck Sales* (11 D.L.R. (3rd), No. 469)
- *Canadian-Dominion Leasing v. Suburban Super Drug Ltd. (1966)* (56 D.L.R. (2nd), No. 43)
- *Neilson v. Atlantic Rentals Ltd. (1974)* (8 N.B.R. (2d), No. 594)
- *Volvo Canada v. Fox* (December 13, 1979; New Brunswick Court of Queen's Bench; No. 1698/77/C; Judge Stevenson)
- *Western Tractor v. Dyck* (7 D.L.R. (3rd), No. 535)

Repairs: Faulty Diagnosis

Davies v. Alberta Motor Association (August 13, 1991; Alberta Provincial Court; Civil Division; No. P9090106097; Judge Moore). The plaintiff had the AMA's Vehicle Inspection Service check out a used 1985 Nissan Pulsar NX prior to buying it. The car passed with flying colours. A month later, the clutch was replaced and numerous electrical problems ensued. At that time, another garage discovered that the car had been involved in a major accident, had a bent frame and a leaking radiator, and was unsafe to drive. The court awarded the plaintiff $1,578.40 plus three years' interest. The judge held that the AMA set itself out as an expert and should have spotted the car's defects. The AMA's defence—that it was not responsible for errors—was thrown out. The court held that a disclaimer clause could not protect the association from a fundamental breach of contract.

Secret Warranty Rulings

It's common practice for manufacturers to secretly extend their warranties to cover components with a high failure rate. Customers who complain vigorously get extended warranty compensation in the form of "goodwill" adjustments.

François Chong v. Marine Drive Imported Cars Ltd. and Honda Canada Inc. (May 17, 1994; British Columbia Provincial Small Claims Court; No. 92-06760; Judge C.L. Bagnall). The plaintiff was the first owner of a 1983 Honda Accord with 134,000 km on the odometer. He had six engine camshafts replaced—four under Honda "goodwill" programs, one where he paid part of the repairs, and one via this small claims court judgment.

In his ruling, Judge Bagnall agreed with Chong and ordered Honda and the dealer to each pay half of the $835.81 repair bill for the following reasons:

> The defendants assert that the warranty, which was part of the contract for purchase of the car, encompassed the entirety of their obligation to the claimant, and that it

expired in February 1985. The replacements of the camshaft after that date were paid for wholly or in part by Honda as a "goodwill gesture." The time has come for these gestures to cease, according to the witness for Honda. As well, he pointed out to me that the most recent replacement of the camshaft was paid for by Honda and that, therefore, the work would not be covered by Honda's usual warranty of 12 months from date of repair. Mr. Wall, who testified for Honda, told me there was no question that this situation with Mr. Chong's engine was an unusual state of affairs. He said that a camshaft properly maintained can last anywhere from 24,000 to 500,000 km. He could not offer any suggestion as to why the car keeps having this problem.

The claimant has convinced me that the problems he is having with rapid breakdown of camshafts in his car is due to a defect, which was present in the engine at the time that he purchased the car. The problem first arose during the warranty period and in my view has never been properly identified nor repaired.

Automatic Transmission Failures (Chrysler)

Lowe v. Fairview Chrysler-Dodge Limited and Chrysler Canada Limited (May 14, 1996; Ontario Court, General Division; Burlington Small Claims Court; No. 1224/95). This judgment, in the plaintiff's favour, raises important legal principles relative to Chrysler:

- TSBs are admissible in court to prove that a problem exists and that certain parts should be checked out.
- If a problem is reported prior to a warranty's expiration, warranty coverage for the problematic component(s) is automatically carried over after the warranty ends.
- It's not up to the car owner to tell the dealer/automaker what the specific problem is.
- Repairs carried out by an independent garage can be refunded if the dealer/automaker unfairly refuses to apply the warranty.
- The dealer/automaker cannot dispute the cost of the independent repair if they fail to cross-examine the independent repairer.
- Auto owners can ask for and win compensation for their inconvenience, which in this judgment amounted to $150.

Court awards quickly add up. The plaintiff was given $1,985.94, with the addition of court costs and prejudgment interest, plus costs of inconvenience fixed at $150. The final award amounted to $2,266.04.

Tire Failures: Premature Wear

Blackwood v. Ford Motor Company of Canada Ltd., 2006 (Provincial Court of Alberta, Civil Division; Docket: PO690101722; Registry: Canmore; 2006/12/08; Honourable J. Shriar). This four-page judgment gives important guidelines as to how a plaintiff can successfully claim a refund for a defective tire.

The plaintiff bought a new 2005 Ford Focus. After 10 months and 22,000 km, his dealer said all four tires needed replacing at a cost of $560.68. Both the dealer and Ford refused to cover the expense under the 3-year/60,000 km manufacturer's tire warranty, alleging that the wear was "normal wear and tear." Judge Shriar disagreed and awarded the plaintiff the full cost of the replacement tires, plus the filing fee and costs related to the registered mail and corporate records address check. An additional $100 was awarded for court costs, plus interest on the total amount from the date of the filing.

False Advertising

Misrepresentation

Goldie v. Golden Ears Motors (1980) Ltd (Port Coquitlam; June 27, 2000; British Columbia Small Claims Court; Case No. CO8287; Justice Warren). In a well-written, eight-page judgment, the court awarded plaintiff Goldie $5,000 for engine repairs on a 1990 Ford F-150 pickup in addition to $236 court costs. The dealer was found to have misrepresented the mileage and sold a used vehicle that didn't meet Section 8.01 of the provincial *Motor Vehicle Act Regulations* due to its unsafe tires and defective exhaust and headlights.

In rejecting the seller's defence that he disclosed all information "to the best of his knowledge and belief" as stipulated in the sales contract, Justice Warren stated,

> The words "to the best of your knowledge and belief" do not allow someone to be willfully blind to defects or to provide incorrect information. I find as a fact that the business made no effort to fulfill its duty to comply with the requirements of this form.... The defendant has been reckless in its actions. More likely, it has actively deceived the claimant into entering into this contract. I find the conduct of the defendant has been reprehensible throughout the dealings with the claimant.

This judgment closes a loophole that sellers have used to justify their misrepresentation, and it allows for cancellation of the sale and damages if the vehicle doesn't meet highway safety regulations.

MacDonald v. Equilease Co. Ltd. (January 18, 1979; Ontario Supreme Court; Judge O'Driscoll). The plaintiff leased a truck that was misrepresented as having an axle stronger than it really was. The court awarded the plaintiff damages for repairs and set aside the lease.

Seich v. Festival Ford Sales Ltd. (1978) (6 Alta. L.R. (2nd), No. 262). The plaintiff bought a used truck from the defendant after being assured that it had a new motor and transmission. It didn't, and the court awarded the plaintiff $6,400.

Used car sold as new (demonstrator)

Bilodeau v. Sud Auto (Quebec Court of Appeal; No. 09-000751-73; Judge Tremblay). This appeals court cancelled the contract and held that a car can't be sold as new or as a demonstrator if it has ever been rented, leased, sold, or titled to anyone other than the dealer.

Rourke v. Gilmore (January 16, 1928; as found in *Ontario Weekly Notes,* vol. XXXIII, p. 292). Before discovering that his new car was really used, the plaintiff drove it for over a year. For this reason, the contract couldn't be cancelled. However, the appeals court instead awarded damages for $500, which was quite a sum in 1928!

Vehicle not as ordered

Whether you're buying new or used, the seller can't misrepresent the vehicle. Anything that varies from what one would commonly expect, or from the seller's representation, must be disclosed prior to signing the contract. Typical misrepresentation scenarios include odometer turnbacks, undisclosed accident damage, used or leased cars being sold as new, new vehicles that are the wrong colour or the wrong model year, and vehicles that lack promised options or standard features.

Chenel v. Bel Automobile (1981) Inc. (August 27, 1976; Quebec Superior Court, Quebec City; Judge Desmeules). The plaintiff didn't receive his new Ford truck with the Jacob brakes essential for transporting sand in hilly regions. The court awarded the plaintiff $27,000, representing the purchase price of the vehicle less the money he earned while using the truck.

Lasky v. Royal City Chrysler Plymouth (February 18, 1987; Ontario High Court of Justice; 59 O.R. (2nd), No. 323). The plaintiff bought a 4-cylinder 1983 Dodge 600 that was represented by the salesman as being a 6-cylinder model. After putting 40,000 km on the vehicle over a 22-month period, the buyer was given her money back, without interest, under the provincial *Business Practices Act.*

Used car fuel-economy misrepresentation

In Sidney v. 1011067 Ontario Inc. (c.o.b. Southside Motors), the court ruled that fuel economy misrepresentation can lead to a contract's cancellation if the dealer gives a higher-than-actual figure, even if it's claimed it was an innocent misrepresentation. In *Sidney*, the buyer was awarded $11,424.51 plus prejudgment interest because of a false representation made by the dealer regarding fuel efficiency. The plaintiff claimed that the defendant advised him that the vehicle could run 800–900 km per tank of fuel, when in fact the maximum distance was only 500 km per tank.

Car owners, panicked over soaring fuel prices, have been scammed by carmakers and dealers alike with bogus fuel economy claims.

Fortunately, the courts are cracking down on sellers who use false gas consumption figures to sell both new and used cars. For example, Ontario's revised *Consumer Protection Act,* 2002 (available through the province's searchable law database, *www.e-laws.gov.on.ca*), lets consumers cancel a contract within one year of entering into the agreement if a dealer makes a false, misleading, deceptive, or unconscionable representation. This includes false fuel economy claims.

Dealers cannot make the excuse that they were fooled or that they were simply providing data supplied by the manufacturer. The law clearly states that both parties are jointly liable, and therefore the dealer is presumed to know the history, quality, and true performance of what is sold.

Honda new car fuel-economy misrepresentation

Peters v. American Honda Motor Co. (http://s3.documentcloud.org/documents/289067/honda-civic-small-claims-court-ruling.pdf). In another judgment recently rendered in Los Angeles, the plaintiff was awarded $9,867 in damages because her 2006 Honda Civic Hybrid didn't deliver the 50 MPG promised in Honda's representations. But rather than go the class-action lawsuit route (there are five state class-actions, so far), she took her case to small claims court. She correctly believed there was a better chance of winning her case in a court with more relaxed standards, no attorneys' fees, and quick decisions. Plus, she could get a small-claims payout of up to $10,000—much more than the paltry few hundred dollars and a free video on frugal driving Honda offered to the class-action plaintiffs.

Peters argued successfully in her small-claims lawsuit that she had been defrauded by Honda (see *www.dontsettlewithhonda.org* for the full text of the 25-page judgment).

Additionally, in 2005, a year before Ms. Peters was sold her Civic Hybrid, Honda had already been sued for the exact same false advertising in *Paduano v. American Honda Motor Co., Inc.*, a case that Honda later settled for $50,000, plus another $50,000 in attorneys' fees!

Incidentally, new internal service bulletins show the Honda Accord Hybrid underwent a similar modification and now, like the Civic Hybrid, owners complain of getting extremely poor gas mileage.

Punitive Damages

Punitive damages (also known as "exemplary damages") awards the plaintiff compensation that exceeds his or her losses in order to deter those who carry out dishonest or negligent practices. These kinds of judgments have been quite common in the U.S. for almost 50 years, and they sometimes reach hundreds of millions of dollars.

Punitive damages are rarely awarded in Canadian courts and are almost never used against automakers. When they are given out, it's usually for sums less than $100,000. During the past decade, though, our courts have cracked down on business abuses and awarded plaintiffs amounts varying from $5,000 to $1 million.

In February 2002, the Supreme Court of Canada let stand an unprecedented million-dollar award against what one of the justices called "the insurer from hell." In *Whiten v. Pilot Insurance Co.*, the couple's home burned down and the insurer refused to pay the claim. The jury was so outraged that it ordered the company to pay $345,000 for the loss, plus $320,000 for legal costs and $1 million in punitive damages, making it the largest punitive damage award in Canadian history. The Supreme Court refused to overturn the jury's decision. This judgment scares the dickens out of insurers, who fear that they face huge punitive damage awards if they don't pay promptly.

In May 2005, the Supreme Court of Canada once again reaffirmed the use of punitive damages in *Prebushewski v. Dodge City Auto (1984) Ltd. and Chrysler Canada Ltd.* (2001 SKQB 537; Q.B. No. 1215). The Court backed the Saskatchewan court's $25,000 punitive damage award against Chrysler, rendered in Saskatoon on December 6, 2001, which cited egregious violations of provincial consumer protection statutes (see part of the judgment on page 78). The Supreme Court of Canada's confirmation of the judgment can be found at *http://scc.lexum.umontreal.ca.*

Canadian courts have become more generous in awarding plaintiffs money for mental distress experienced when defects aren't repaired properly under warranty. In *Sharman v. Formula Ford Sales Limited, Ford Credit Limited, and Ford Motor Company of Canada Limited,* Justice Sheppard of the Ontario Superior Court in Oakville awarded the owner of a 2000 Windstar $7,500 for mental distress resulting from the breach of the implied warranty of fitness, plus $7,207 for breach of contract and breach of warranty. The Windstar's sliding door wasn't secure and leaked air and water after many attempts to repair it. Interestingly, the judge cited the *Wharton* decision as support for his award for mental distress:

> The plaintiff and his family have had three years of aggravation, inconvenience, worry, and concern about their safety and that of their children. Generally speaking, our contract law did not allow for compensation for what may be mental distress, but that may be changing. I am indebted to counsel for providing me with the decision of the British Columbia Court of Appeal in *Wharton v. Tom Harris Chevrolet Oldsmobile Cadillac Ltd.*, [2002] B.C.J. No. 233, 2002 BCCA 78. This decision was recently followed in *T'avra v. Victoria Ford Alliance Ltd.*, [2003] B, CJ No. 1957.

> In *Wharton*, the purchaser of a Cadillac Eldorado claimed damages against the dealer because the car's sound system emitted an annoying buzzing noise and the purchaser had to return the car to the dealer for repair numerous times over two and a half years. The trial court awarded damages of $2,257.17 for breach of warranty with respect to the sound system, and $5,000 in non-pecuniary damages for loss of enjoyment of their luxury vehicle and for inconvenience, for a total award of $7,257.17. The Court of Appeal upheld the decision of the trial judge and Levine J.A. spent considerable time reviewing the law, but in particular the law relating to damages for breach of implied warranty of fitness: "The principles applicable to an award of damages for mental distress resulting from a breach of contract were thoroughly and helpfully analyzed in the recent judgment of the House of Lords in *Farley v. Skinner*, [2001]

3 W.L.R. 899, [2001] H.L.J. No. 49, affirming and clarifying the decision of the English Court of Appeal in *Watts v. Morrow,* [1991] I W.L.R. 142 1. Both of those cases concerned a claim by a buyer of a house against a surveyor who failed to report matters concerning the house as required by the contract. In *Watts,* the surveyor was negligent in failing to report defects in the house, and non-pecuniary damages of $6,750 were awarded to each of the owners for the inconvenience and discomfort experienced by them during repairs. In *Farley,* the surveyor was negligent in failing to discover, as he specifically undertook to do, that the property was adversely affected by aircraft noise. The House of Lords upheld the trial judge's award of non-pecuniary damages of $610,000, reversing the Court of Appeal, principally on the grounds that the object of the contract was to provide 'pleasure, relaxation, peace of mind, or freedom from molestation' and also because the plaintiff had suffered physical discomfort and inconvenience from the aircraft noise."

•

The reasons for judgment in *Farley* provide a summary and survey of the law as it has developed, in England, to date. They are helpful in analyzing and summarizing the principles derived from *Watts,* which are, in my view, applicable to the case at bar. In summary they are (borrowing the language from both *Watts* and *Farley):*

(a) A contract-breaker is not in general liable for any distress, frustration, anxiety, displeasure, vexation, tension, or aggravation which the breach of contract may cause to the innocent party.
(b) The rule is not absolute. Where a major or important part of the contract is to give pleasure, relaxation or peace of mind, damages will be awarded if the fruit of the contract is not provided or if the contrary result is instead procured.
(c) In cases not falling within the "peace of mind" category, damages are recoverable for inconvenience and discomfort caused by the breach and the mental suffering directly related to the inconvenience and discomfort. However, the cause of the inconvenience or discomfort must be a sensory experience as opposed to mere disappointment that the contract has been broken. If those effects are foreseeably suffered during a period when defects are repaired, they create damages even though the cost of repairs are not recoverable as such.

Application of Law to the Facts of This Case

In the *Wharton* case, the respondent contracted for a "luxury" vehicle for pleasure use. It included a sound system that the appellant's service manager described as "high end." The respondent's husband described the purchase of the car in this way:

"[W]e bought a luxury car that was supposed to give us a luxury ride and be a quiet vehicle, and we had nothing but difficulty with it from the very day it was delivered with this problem that nobody seemed to be able to fix.... So basically we had a luxury product that gave us no luxury for the whole time that we had it."

It is clear that an important object of the contract was to obtain a vehicle that was luxurious and a pleasure to operate. Furthermore, the buzzing noise was the cause of physical, in the sense of sensory, discomfort to the respondent and her husband.

The trial judge found it inhibited listening to the sound system and was irritating in normal conversation. The respondent and her husband also bore the physical inconvenience of taking the vehicle to the appellant on numerous occasions for repairs. The inconvenience and discomfort was, in my view, reasonably foreseeable, if the defect in the sound system had been known at the date of the contract. The fact that it was not then known is, of course, irrelevant.

The award of damages for breach of the implied warranty of fitness satisfies both exceptions from the general rule that damages are not awarded for mental distress for breach of contract, set out in *Watts* as amplified in *Farley*.

The justice continued and said at para. 63 "...awards for mental distress arising from a breach of contract should be restrained and modest."

The court upheld the trial judge's award of $5,000 in *Wharton* where the issue was a buzzing in the sound system.

In my view, a defect in manufacture which goes to the safety of the vehicle deserves a modest increase. I would assess the plaintiff's damage for mental distress resulting from the breach of the implied warranty of fitness at $7,500.

Judgment to issue in favour of the plaintiff against the defendants, except Ford Credit, on a joint and several basis for $14,707, plus interest and costs....

Provincial business practices acts and consumer protection statutes prohibit false, misleading, or deceptive representations and allow for punitive damages should the unfair practice toward the consumer amount to an unconscionable representation (see *Canadian Encyclopedic Digest* (3d) s. 76, pp. 140–45). "Unconscionable" is defined as "where the consumer is not reasonably able to protect his or her interest because of physical infirmity, ignorance, illiteracy, or inability to understand the language of an agreement or similar factors." This concept has been successfully used in consumer, environmental, and labour law.

- Exemplary damages are justified where compensatory damages are insufficient to deter and punish. See *Walker et al. v. CFTO Ltd. et al. (1978)* (59 O.R. (2nd), No. 104; Ontario Court of Appeal).
- Exemplary damages can be awarded in cases where the defendant's conduct was "cavalier." See *Ronald Elwyn Lister Ltd. et al. v. Dayton Tire Canada Ltd. (1985)* (52 O.R. (2nd), No. 89; Ontario Court of Appeal).
- The primary purpose of exemplary damages is to prevent the defendant and all others from doing similar wrongs. See *Fleming v. Spracklin (1921)*.
- Disregard of the public's interest, lack of preventive measures, and a callous attitude all merit exemplary damages. See *Coughlin v. Kuntz (1989)* (2 C.C.L.T. (2nd); B.C.C.A.).
- Punitive damages can be awarded for mental distress. See *Ribeiro v. Canadian Imperial Bank of Commerce (1992)* (Ontario Reports 13 3rd) and *Brown v. Waterloo Regional Board of Commissioners of Police (1992)* (37 O.R. 2nd).

In the States, punitive damage awards have been particularly generous. Whenever big business complains of an "unrestrained judiciary," it trots out a 20-year-old case where an Alabama BMW 500 series owner was awarded $4 million because his new car had been repainted before he bought it and the seller didn't tell him so. Under appeal, the owner was offered $50,000.

The case was *BMW of North America, Inc. v. Gore* (517 U.S. 559; 116 S. Ct. 1589; 1996). In this case, the Supreme Court cut the damages award and established standards for jury awards of punitive damages. Nevertheless, million-dollar awards continue to be quite common. In the following example, an Oregon dealer learned that a $1 million punitive damages award was not excessive under *Gore* and under Oregon law.

The Oregon Supreme Court determined that the standard it set in *Oberg v. Honda Motor Company* (888 P.2d 8; 1996), on remand from the Supreme Court, survived the Supreme Court's subsequent ruling in *Gore*. The court held that the jury's $1 million punitive damages award, 87 times larger than the plaintiff's compensatory damages in *Parrott v. Carr Chevrolet, Inc.* (2001 Ore. LEXIS; 1 January 11, 2001), wasn't excessive. In that case, Mark Parrott sued Carr Chevrolet, Inc. over a used 1983 Chevrolet Suburban under Oregon's *Unlawful Trade Practices Act*. The jury awarded Parrott $11,496 in compensatory damages and $1 million in punitive damages because the dealer failed to disclose collision damage to a new-car buyer.

See also:

- *Vlchek v. Koshel (1988)* (44 C.C.L.T. 314; B.C.S.C., No. B842974)
- *Granek v. Reiter* (Ontario Court, General Division; No. 35/741)
- *Morrison v. Sharp* (Ontario Court, General Division; No. 43/548)
- *Schryvers v. Richport Ford Sales* (May 18, 1993; B.C.S.C., No. C917060; Judge Tysoe)
- *Varleg v. Angeloni* (B.C.S.C., No. 41/301)
- *Grabinski v. Blue Springs Ford Sales, Inc.* (U.S. App. LEXIS 2073; 8th Cir. W.D. MO; February 16, 2000)

Pending Cases

- Honda and Toyota auto parts price-fixing class action (*www.lawyersandsettlements.com/case/honda-toyota-owners-file-auto-parts-price-fixing.html*)

An antitrust class action lawsuit was filed in Seattle, Washington last October on behalf of a group of Honda and Toyota automobile owners against eight auto-part suppliers after the federal government released information detailing an international price-fixing scheme that may have cost American purchasers and lessees of a wide range of cars millions of dollars in the form of inflated car prices over a 10-year period. The vehicles purchased by plaintiffs during the class period include a 2009 Honda CRV, a 2005 Toyota Prius, and a 2008 Toyota Camry.

The defendants supply automotive wire harnesses and related products in a wide range of Japanese- and American-built cars. According to the complaint, the defendants collectively dominate the global automotive wire harness systems market. Wire harnesses are used to direct and control electronic components, wiring and circuit boards in cars.

Among the defendants is Furukawa Electric who was cited in an agreement announced last week in which three Furukawa Electric's executives agreed to plead guilty and pay a $200 million fine for the company's participation in the scheme, and three of its executives also agreed to serve prison terms ranging from a year to 18 months in U.S. prison for their role. Other defendants include Delphi Automotive, Lear Corporation, Leoni Ag, and Sumitomo Electric Industries, S-Y Systems Technologies GMBH. Yazaki Corporation and Yazaki North America and Denso recently settled out of court for $470 and $78 million, respectively.

Canadian consumers who believe they were affected by the above-named suppliers or by Honda and Toyota engaging in antitrust practices are urged to file an online complaint with the federal Competition Bureau. The complaint form is available under Tools, Online Forms at *www.competitionbureau.gc.ca*. Affected auto owners may also file a small claims or class action lawsuit. Some Canadian law firms who have been successful in similar automobile class actions:

- Stevensons LLP
  144 Front Street, Suite 400
  Toronto, ON M5J 2L7
  Phone: 416-599-7900
  Email: *bkirkland@stevensonlaw.net*

- Koskie Minsky LLP
  20 Queen Street West, Suite 900, Box 52
  Toronto, ON M5H 3R3
  Phone: 1-877-398-0497
  Email: *gmclassaction@kmlaw.ca*

- The Merchant Law Group LLP
  Calgary, Edmonton, Fort McMurray, Montréal, Moose Jaw, Regina, Saskatoon, St.Catharines, Toronto, Vancouver/Surrey, Victoria, and Winnipeg.
  Phone: 1-8888-398-0497
  www.merchantlaw.com

Part Three

1981–2010
THE GOOD, THE BAD, AND
THE DANGEROUS

Rodents Snack on Honda Fit, Civic, and Pilot Wiring

I did a Google search ["automobile wiring and rodents" / "Honda wiring and rodents"]. The search turned up many references to this problem in Honda automobiles and other manufacturers' automobiles. The search also uncovered many references to the recent use of soy in automobile wiring covering. If this is true it could explain why my 2005 Element has not been attacked while my 2009 Fit has been. It would also indicate a glaring defect in some auto electrical wiring. I am now dealing with the problem by leaving my Fit in with my dogs and letting them urinate on the tires. As of now this seems to be working. Obviously this is a lousy solution to the problem.

A HONDA CIVIC AND FIT OWNER

Big Savings, Fewer Problems

No matter if you buy American, Asian, or European, new or used, you are taking on someone else's problems: the dealer's and automaker's, or the previous owner's. Fortunately, you likely already saved $10,000 (on the average three-year-old American family sedan) or more buying used, so you'll have plenty of cash reserve to repair run-of-the-mill glitches at cheaper, independent shops.

Plus, there's not much that can surprise you on a well-inspected vehicle that has been widely sold and can be easily serviced. There's a safety advantage as well, since the vehicle's crashworthiness has likely been tested and retested by a handful of different agencies and about 75 percent of the recalls have been carried out.

Best of all, there's the peace of mind knowing you won't get left in the lurch if the dealer or automaker goes bust—again.

A Car for Half the Price

Primarily, you buy used to save money and to have reliable transportation for a decade or more. A good used car or truck should cost you no more than one-third to one-half of its original selling price ($7,500–$15,000) and should be between three and five years old. A "new" used car must meet your everyday driving needs and have high crashworthiness and reliability scores. Annual maintenance should cost no more than the CAA-and-DesRosiers-estimated average of $800–$1,100, and the depreciation rate should have levelled off, so that subsequent years won't cut the car's price by more than a couple thousand dollars over the next few years, leaving you with some resale equity. Parts and servicing costs shouldn't be excessive either, which means checking out maintenance costs before you buy.

The best values come from Asian automakers (Japan and South Korea), followed by European vehicles (mostly BMW and Volkswagen). American models bring up the rear, led by Ford, followed closely by General Motors. Chrysler/Fiat comes a distant third.

Small cars and family sedans give the most performance and reliability for the price. Some of the better choices are the Ford Focus; Honda's Accord, Civic, and Fit; the Chevrolet Cruze; Hyundai's Accent and Elantra; Nissan's Altima; the Subaru Legacy; the Toyota Corolla; and Volkswagen's diesel-equipped TDI (with manual transmission).

Luxury models, large cars and minivans, and mid-sized and large SUVs represent the worst values among used vehicles. If interior room is your paramount concern, consider a Mazda5 microvan, a Subaru Outback or Forester, or a downsized Hyundai Tucson or Toyota RAV4.

The best values for your purchasing dollar among luxury cars are the BMW X3, Acura RDX and MDX, and Infiniti EX. Luxury vehicles that don't provide much value are models built by Cadillac and Lincoln.

Fuel economy isn't all that important when you are buying used, since all of your other savings should easily compensate for the extra fuel costs. We don't recommend most gas-electric engine hybrids: their retail prices are incredibly high; long-term reliability is problematic; fuel economy can be 40 percent worse than the automakers' reports; their expensive motors are predicted to have a high failure rate due to corrosion; battery replacement costs are estimated to run as high as $3,000 (U.S.) for the Toyota Prius and $10,000 for other makes; and their eight-year resale values are no better than similar vehicles equipped with conventional engines. Look again at a 2006 Toyota Prius that originally sold for $31,280. It is now valued at a disappointing $10,000, less than a third of its original price (and we're coming up to the expiration of that battery-pack warranty).

Fuel Economy: Unbelievable!

Take our Part Three fuel economy estimates with a large grain of salt and blame it on the feds, since Ottawa is in cahoots with automakers through bailouts, tax exemptions, "green car" rebates, and feel-good environmental stories.

Why shouldn't Natural Resources Canada and Transport Canada crow about how much more fuel-efficient cars in Canada have become?

Because it's not true. The Canadian mileage figures have been cooked by as much as 22 percent.

In November of 2011, CBC News and the Automobile Protection Association (APA) compared the Canadian and American fuel consumption ratings of various 2012 models. The survey showed that Canadian fuel-economy estimates were inflated by 16 to 22 percent compared to the U.S. estimates, for the same vehicles. Since this is L/100km, a lower number is better.

More accurate U.S. fuel economy figures can be found at: *www.fueleconomy.gov*, while the puffed-up Canadian figures reside at *http://oee.nrcan.gc.ca/transportation/tools/fuelratings/ratings-search.cfm*.

VEHICLE	U.S. CITY	U.S. HWY	CDN. CITY	CDN. HWY	% DIFF./HWY
Toyota Yaris hatchback	7.8	6.7	6.8	5.5	22%
Ford Fiesta hatchback	8.1	6.0	6.9	5.1	18%
Chevrolet Cruze 1.4T	9.0	6.2	7.8	5.2	19%
Honda Civic 1.8L	8.4	6.0	7.2	5.0	20%
Hyundai Sonata 2.4L	9.8	6.7	8.7	5.6	20%
Ford F150 3.5T AWD	15.7	11.2	14.0	9.6	20%
Dodge Grand Caravan	13.8	9.4	14.0	9.6	20%

APA President George Iny says Canadian numbers are generated by the industry from standardized lab tests, not real-life road conditions. Back in 2008 the U.S. government got rid of the test Canada's carmakers are still using to generate their estimates.

Since then, American cars have been more rigorously tested for real life conditions and the Environmental Protection Agency said some cars use 30 percent more gas than the previous tests showed.

Depreciation Is Your Friend

Not all cars and trucks are born with equal attributes, and they age (depreciate) at different rates. When buying new, you want a reliable model that depreciates slowly; when buying used, consider a vehicle that has prematurely lost much of its value but is still dependable and inexpensive to maintain. Fortunately, there are plenty of the latter on the market due to poor vehicle sales during the 2008 and 2009 model years.

On the other hand, used vehicles that hold their value well after four years aren't bargains now, but they'll have considerable equity in them should you have to sell due to a cash emergency. And yes, models that depreciate slowly are usually the more dependable vehicles that hold up better in the long run.

During the past year, rebates, cut-rate financing, subsidized leasing, and fluctuating fuel costs, along with poor reputations for quality, have depressed the residual values of most American cars and trucks. According to the *Automotive Lease Guide* (*www.alg.com*), Detroit-made vehicles that come off lease barely keep 37 percent of their sticker values after three years.

How *Lemon-Aid* Picks the "Best" and "Worst"

Lemon-Aid has been giving honest, independent, and dependable auto ratings for four decades by following these simple rules:

- Ratings should be used primarily as a comparative database when the low-ranked or recommended models reappear in different driving tests and owner surveys. The best rating approach is to combine a driving test with an owners' survey of past models (only *Consumer Reports* does this).
- We use the database of owner complaints collected by the National Highway Traffic Safety Administration (NHTSA) *safercar.gov* site. It's a treasure trove of auto-failure anecdotes that show which cars have repeated failures or outstanding recalls, or are part of an ongoing safety probe, and which particular component is faulty. It even suggests ways to get a free warranty extension to cover the repair, or to get a free replacement part.

ERRATIC FUEL GAUGE

BULLETIN NO.: TSB 08-2-9   DATE: APRIL 2, 2008

FUEL GAUGE OPERATION—MIL ON—DTCS P0460/P0463 OR INSTRUMENT CLUSTER MODULE DTC B1201

FORD: 2004–08 F-150; LINCOLN: 2006–08 Mark LT

ISSUE: Some 2004–08 F-150 and 2006–08 Mark LT vehicles, built before 12/3/2007, may exhibit erratic fuel gauge operation or illuminated malfunction indicator lamp (MIL) with diagnostic trouble codes (DTCs) P0460 or P0463, and/or Instrument Cluster Module DTC B1201. This may be caused by sulphur contamination in the fuel causing an open or high resistance in the fuel level sender.

SERVICE PROCEDURE: Install a new fuel level sender following the service procedure instruction sheet provided in the fuel sender kit.

WARRANTY STATUS: Eligible Under Provisions Of New Vehicle Limited Warranty Coverage And Emissions Warranty Coverage.

- The responses must come from a large owner pool (1.2 million responses from *Consumer Reports* subscribers, for example). Anecdotal responses should then be cross-referenced, updated, and given depth and specificity through NHTSA's safety complaint prism. Responses must be cross-referenced again through automaker internal service bulletins to determine the extent of the defect over a specific model and model-year range and to alert owners to problems likely to occur. This is how we discovered that millions of GM 1995–2004 cars and minivans had defective engine intake manifold gaskets and millions of Ford trucks and Lincolns had faulty fuel gauges.
- Rankings should be predicated on important characteristics measured over a significant period of time, unlike Car of the Year contests, owner-perceived values, or J.D. Power–surveyed problems assessed after only three months of ownership.
- Ratings must come from unimpeachable sources. There should be no conflicts of interest due to ties with advertisers or consultants, and no results gathered from self-serving tests done under ideal conditions, like previous years' Transport Canada and U.S. Environmental Protection Agency (EPA) fuel economy tests.
- Tested cars must be bought, not borrowed, and serviced, not pampered as part of a journalists' fleet lent out for ranking purposes. Also, all automakers need to be judged equally. (Toyota at one time did not accept weekend car journalist "roundup" tests as valid and refused to lend its vehicles to the events; thus, they were penalized.) Automakers must not be members of the ranking body.
- Again, we are wary of self-administered fuel economy ratings used by automakers in complicity with the federal government. *Automotive News* recently added its name to the list of skeptics when it found that Honda and Toyota hybrids get 20–40 percent less real-world gas mileage than advertised. The car industry publication discovered that hybrids need to be driven in a particular way in order to be fuel efficient, use more fuel than ordinary cars on short trips or when using air conditioning, and are affected by colder climates, resulting in increased fuel consumption way beyond what the ratings figures indicate. The EPA has admitted its fuel economy calculations were overestimated and has set up a website at *www.fueleconomy.gov* that contains recalculated figures for 1985–2007 model year vehicles that will leave you scratching your head.

Definition of Terms

We rate vehicles on a scale of one to five stars, with five stars being our top ranking. Models are designated as "Recommended," "Above Average," "Average," "Below Average," or "Not Recommended," with the most recent year's rating indicated by the number of stars beside the vehicle's name.

Recommended

We don't give this rating out very often, and we are quick to drop it if safety, servicing, or overall quality control decline. We don't believe for one moment that the more you spend, the better performing, more reliable, or safer the vehicle. For example, most Hondas are as good as Acuras, which cost thousands of dollars more for their luxury cachet. The same is true when you compare Toyota and Lexus. Even more surprising, some luxury makes, such as Jaguar, are "pseudo-luxe," because they may be merely dressed-up ordinary Fords sold at a luxury-car price. The extra money only buys you more features of dubious value and newer, unproven technology, such as rear-mounted video cameras, backing up "beepers," and other failure-prone electronic gadgetry.

In fact, the simplest choice is often the best buy. Chrysler's minivans and small Jeeps, Ford's Mustang, and Hyundai's Elantra and Tiburon get positive ratings because they are easy to find, fairly reliable, and reasonably priced—not the case with many overpriced Hondas and Toyotas.

Above Average/Average

Vehicles that are given an Above Average or Average rating are good second choices if a Recommended vehicle isn't your first choice, isn't available, or isn't within budget.

Below Average/Not Recommended

Many vehicles are given a Below Average rating by *Lemon-Aid* because we know they will likely be troublesome; however, we also believe their low price and reasonably priced servicing may make them acceptable buys to some do-it-yourselfers who have put aside sufficient money saved from the transaction to cover expected failures.

Vehicles with a history of unforeseeable, recurring, and expensive defects are most likely to be given a Not Recommended rating. They are best avoided altogether, no matter how low the price, because they're so likely to suffer from many durability and performance problems that you may never stop paying for repairs. Sometimes, however, a Not Recommended model will improve over several model years and garner a better rating (as the Ford Focus and Hyundai's Sonata—2012 excepted— and SUVs have done).

Incidentally, for those owners who wonder how I can stop recommending model years I once recommended, let me be clear: As vehicles age, their ratings change to reflect new information from owners and from service bulletins relating to durability and the automaker's warranty performance. For example, Nissan's Quest, Toyota's Sienna, and BMW's Mini have been downgraded for some years because new service bulletins and additional owner complaints show some disturbing trends in dependability and servicing performance. Unlike car columnists who can't change their ratings due to automaker pressure, I quickly warn shoppers of rating downgrades as soon as they're made through subsequent editions of *Lemon-Aid* and updates to my website, *www.lemonaidcars.com*, and alerts on Twitter (@lemonaidcars).

For 42 years, I have been an *active* consumer advocate, not a *passive* auto journalist. When I uncover fraud, unsafe designs, or failure-prone components, I first denounce the problem. Then I take a second step, one rarely taken by journalists: I become part of the story by mobilizing owners, lawyers, and independent mechanics to force an automaker to recall or reimburse.

My proudest achievement? Getting GM Canada to pay back millions of dollars to Canadian car owners stuck with "cooked" V6 engines afflicted by warped intake manifold gaskets in GM's 1995–2005 models. GM paid Canadians an estimated $40 million in repairs because the automaker used faulty engine gaskets made out of plastic to save a few pennies per car.

Throughout the year, I get refunds for buyers cheated by dealers and automakers. I lobby automakers to compensate owners of out-of-warranty vehicles either through formal warranty extension programs or on a case-by-case basis. I also publish little-known lawsuits, judgments, and settlements in *Lemon-Aid* to help car owners win their cases or get a fair settlement without my personal assistance.

Reliability data is compiled from a number of sources, including confidential technical service bulletins, owner complaints sent to me each year by *Lemon-Aid* readers, owners' comments posted on the Internet, and survey reports and tests done by auto associations, consumer groups, and government organizations. Some auto columnists feel this isn't a scientific sampling, and they're quite right. Nevertheless, the results have been mostly on the mark over the past four decades.

Not all cars and trucks are profiled; those that are new to the market or relatively rare may receive only an abbreviated mention until sufficient owner or service bulletin information becomes available. Best and worst buys for each model category (e.g., "Small Cars," "Medium Cars," and so on) are listed in a summary at the beginning of each rating section.

 ## Strengths and Weaknesses

ALERT! This year we have added an **ALERT!** section to clearly point out those vehicles that may be exceptional buys, or are seriously flawed, or require special maintenance.

With the Detroit automakers, engine head gasket, automatic transmission, brake, steering, and electrical failures are omnipresent. South Korean vehicles have weak transmissions, electrical systems, and electronic control modules. Japanese makes are noted mostly for their brake, door, AC, window, sound system, electrical, and fuel delivery glitches, though engine and transmission failures have been appearing more frequently, especially with Toyota and Lexus models built during the past decade. Finally, the European automakers are in a high-tech bind: Electronic demons constantly bedevil Audi, BMW, Jaguar, Land Rover, Mercedes, Saab, Volvo, and VW products, making them unreliable and costly to service after only a few years of ownership; plus, these vehicles are so complicated to diagnose and service that many mechanics simply throw up their hands in dismay. And with Volvo sold to the Chinese and Jaguar/Land Rover now an Indian subsidiary, servicing can only get worse.

Unlike other auto guides, *Lemon-Aid* knows where automotive skeletons are buried and pinpoints potential parts failures, explains why those parts fail, and advises you as to your chances of getting a repair refund under a "goodwill warranty" program. We also give parts numbers for upgraded parts (why replace poor-quality brake pads with the same failure-prone part?) and offer troubleshooting tips direct from the automakers' bulletins so that your mechanic won't replace parts unrelated to your troubles before coming upon the defective component that is actually responsible.

Parts supply can be a real problem. It's a myth that automakers have to keep a supply of parts sufficient to service what they sell, as any buyer of a Chevrolet/Daewoo Aveo, a front-drive Lincoln Continental, or a Ford Windstar/Freestar will quickly tell you. Additionally, apart from *Lemon-Aid*, there's no consumer database that warns prospective purchasers as to which models are "parts-challenged."

The "Secret Warranties/Internal Bulletins/Service Tips" sections and vehicle profile tables show a vehicle's overall reliability and safety, providing details as to which specific model years pose the most risk and why. This helps you direct an independent mechanic to check out the likely trouble spots before you make your purchase.

Vehicle History

This section outlines a vehicle's differences between model years, including major redesigns and other modifications. If a model is unchanged from one model year to the next, why pay a premium for it simply because it is one year newer? Or, if a vehicle was redesigned a few years ago, don't you want that vehicle a year after the redesign, when most of the factory kinks have been ironed out?

 ## Safety Summary

Here we list safety failures reported by owners and ongoing safety investigations. NHTSA complaints are summarized by model year, even though they aren't all safety-related. This summary can help you prove that a part failure is widespread and factory-related and then use that information for free "goodwill" repairs or in litigation involving accident damage, injuries, or death.

NHTSA records indicate other common safety-related failures that include vehicles with collapsing axles (Ford Windstar/Freestar, et al.), vehicles rolling away with the transmission in Park, sliding minivan doors that don't open when they should or open when they shouldn't, or electronic computer modules that cause a vehicle to "lag and lurch." The vehicle won't accelerate from a stop for a few seconds, and then it will lurch out into traffic after the accelerator has been floored to get the vehicle out of harm's way (2002–03 Toyota Camry).

Be wary. You are dealing with an industry that ignores cars suddenly accelerating out of control with no brakes, pickups that corrode so badly their suspension is unsafe, steering wheels that fly off, and, with GM Corvettes, steering assemblies that suddenly lock up and roofs that take flight once the car is underway.

In a nutshell, the auto industry continues to put profits before safety, unions value jobs over integrity, and all that governments care about is getting back their auto bailout investment.

If *Lemon-Aid* doesn't list a problem you have experienced, go to the NHTSA website's database at *www.safercar.gov/Vehicle+Owners* or *www.safercar.gov/ Vehicle+Shoppers* for an update. Your vehicle may be currently under investigation, or may have been recalled since this year's guide was published.

Automotive News says an estimated 72 percent of the 25 million vehicles recalled in 2005 were fixed. *Lemon-Aid* doesn't list most recalls because there are so many, and the info. can be easily obtained either from NHTSA at the above-listed sites or from Transport Canada (*www.tc.gc.ca/roadsafety/recalls/search_e.asp*). Dealers willingly give out recall info when they run a vehicle history search through their computers, since they hope to snag the extra repair dollars. Just make sure you ask the dealer to also check for a "customer satisfaction program," a "service policy," a "goodwill" warranty extension, or a free emissions warranty service.

Secret Warranties/Internal Bulletins/Service Tips

It's not enough to know which parts on your vehicle are likely to fail. You should also know which repairs will be done for free by the dealer and automaker, even though you aren't the original owner and the manufacturer's warranty has long since expired.

Welcome to the hidden world of secret warranties, found in confidential technical service bulletins (TSBs) or gleaned from owners' feedback.

Over the years, I've grown tired of service managers denying that service bulletins exist to correct factory-related defects free of charge. That's why I pore over thousands of bulletins each year and summarize or reproduce in *Lemon-Aid* the important ones for each model year, along with improved parts numbers. These bulletins target defects related to safety, emissions, and performance that service managers would have you believe either don't exist or are your responsibility to fix. If you photocopy the applicable service bulletin included in *Lemon-Aid*, you'll have a better chance of getting the dealer or automaker to cover all or part of the repair costs. Bulletins taken from *Lemon-Aid* have also been instrumental in helping claimants win in small claims court mediation and trials (remember, judges like to have the bulletins validated by an independent mechanic or by the dealer or automaker you are suing).

Service bulletins listed in *Lemon-Aid* cover repairs that may be eligible for express or implied warranty coverage in one or more of the following five categories (although the description of the repairs is not always specific):

1. Emissions express warranty (5–8 years/80,000–130,000 km)
2. Safety component express warranty (this covers seat belts, ABS, and airbags, and usually lasts from eight years to the lifetime of the vehicle)
3. Body express warranty (paint: six years; rust perforations: seven years)
4. Secret implied warranty (coverage varies from five to 10 years)
5. Factory defect/implied legal warranty (depends on mileage, use, and repair cost; may be as high as 11 years, according to GM paint delamination jurisprudence)

Use these bulletins to get free repairs—even if the vehicle has changed hands several times—and to alert an independent mechanic about defects to look for. They're also great tools for getting compensation from automakers and dealer service managers after the warranty has expired, since they prove that a failure is factory-related and, therefore, not part of routine maintenance or caused by a caustic environmental substance such as bird droppings or acid rain. In small claims court, the argument that bird droppings caused a paint problem usually loses credibility when only certain models or certain years are shown to be affected, pointing the finger at the paint process and quality.

Automakers' "bird poop" defence doesn't explain why birds apparently defecate only on certain model vehicles (Chrysler Caravans, Ford's Taurus and Sable, GM minivans, etc.). Nevertheless, the implied warranty requires that all automakers use the same durability standard or disclose at the time of sale that their vehicles aren't "bird-proofed."

In *Maureen Frank v. General Motors of Canada Limited,* the Saskatchewan small claims court judge ruled that paint finishes should last for 11 years. Three other Canadian small claims judgments have likewise extended the benchmark for second owners and to pickups. In those cases, the courts judged that seven years was an appropriate extension. Automakers will offer a free paint job or partial compensation for up to six years (no mileage limitation). Thereafter, most manufacturers will offer 50–75 percent refunds on the small claims courthouse's front steps.

The diagnostic shortcuts and lists of upgraded parts found in many service bulletins make them invaluable in helping mechanics and do-it-yourselfers to troubleshoot problems inexpensively and to replace the correct part the first time. Auto owners can also use the TSBs listed here to verify that a repair was diagnosed correctly, that the correct upgraded replacement part was used, and that the labour costs were fair.

Each annual edition of *Lemon-Aid* lists safety-related failures, crashworthiness scores, service bulletins, and prices of a range of model years. If your vehicle, perhaps a 1997 model, isn't included in this year's guide (which provides detailed information on 2002–11 models), consult an earlier edition.

Summaries of service bulletins relating to 1982–2012 vehicles can be obtained for free from the ALLDATA or NHTSA websites, but they are worded so cryptically that you really need the bulletins themselves. If you have a vehicle that's off warranty, you should get copies of the hundreds of pages of bulletins applicable to your model year, listing factory-related defects and diagnostic shortcuts. These bulletins can be ordered and downloaded from the Internet for $26.95 (U.S.) through ALLDATA at *www.alldatadiy.com/buy/index.html*. Or you can get the bulletin title for free from ALLDATA and then search for it on the Internet.

Vehicle Profile Tables

These tables cover the various aspects of vehicle ownership at a glance. Included for each model year are the vehicle's original selling price (the manufacturer's suggested retail price, or MSRP), the wholesale and retail prices you can expect to pay, reliability ratings (specific defective parts are listed in the "Strengths and Weaknesses" section), and details on crashworthiness.

Prices

Dealer profit margins on used cars vary considerably—giving lots of room to negotiate a fair price if you take the time to find out what the vehicle is really worth. Three prices are given for each model year: the vehicle's selling price when new, as suggested by the manufacturer; its maximum used price (▲), which is often the starting price with dealers; and its lowest used price (▼), more commonly found with private sellers.

The original selling price is given as a reality check for greedy sellers who inflate prices on some vehicles (mostly Japanese imports, minivans, and sport-utilities) in order to get back some of the money they overpaid in the first place. This happens particularly often in the Prairie provinces and British Columbia.

Used prices are based on sales recorded as of February 2011. Prices are for the lowest-priced standard model that is in good condition with a maximum of 20,000 km for each calendar year. Watch for price differences reflecting each model's equipment upgrades, designated by a numerical or alphabetical abbreviation. For example, L, LX, and LXT usually mean more standard features are included, progressively, in each model. Numerical progression usually relates to engine size.

Prices reflect the auto markets in Quebec and Ontario, where the majority of used-vehicle transactions take place. Residents of Eastern Canada should add 10 percent, and Western Canadians should add at least 15–20 percent to the listed price. Why the higher costs? Less competition, combined with inflated new-vehicle prices in these regions. Don't be too disheartened, though; you'll recoup some of what you overpaid down the road when you sell the vehicle.

Why are *Lemon-Aid*'s prices sometimes lower than the prices found in dealer guides such as *Red Book*? The answer is simple: Much like a homeowner selling a house, dealers inflate their prices so that you can bargain the price down and wind up convinced that you made a great deal.

I use newspaper classified ads from Quebec, Ontario, and B.C., as well as auction reports, to calculate my used-vehicle values. I then check these figures against *Red Book* and *Black Book*. I don't start with *Red Book*'s retail or wholesale figures because their prices are inflated about 10 percent for wholesale/private sales and almost
20 percent for retail/dealer sales (compare the two, and you'll see what I mean). I then project what the value will be by mid-model year, and that lowers my prices further. I'll almost always fall way under *Red Book*'s value, but not far under *Black Book*'s prices.

I include a top and bottom price to give you some margin for negotiation as well as to account for the regional differences in prices, the sudden popularity of certain models or vehicle classes, and the generally depreciated value of used vehicles.

Most new cars depreciate 50–60 percent during the first three years of ownership, despite the fact that good-quality used cars are in high demand. On the other hand, some minivans and most vans, pickups, and SUVs lose barely 40 percent of their value, even after four years of ownership.

Since no evaluation method is foolproof, check dealer prices against newspaper- and Internet-sourced private classified ads and then add the option values listed on the next page to come up with a fairly representative offer. Don't forget to bargain the price down further if the odometer shows a cumulative reading of more than 20,000 km per calendar year. Interestingly, the value of anti-lock brakes in trade-ins plummeted during the last few years as they became a standard feature on many entry-level vehicles.

It will be easier to match the lower used prices if you buy privately. Dealers rarely sell much below the maximum prices; they claim that they need the full price to cover the costs of reconditioning and paying future warranty claims. If you can come within 5–10 percent of this guide's price, you'll have done well.

In the table on p. 132, take note that some options—such as paint protector, rust-proofing, and tinted windows—have little worth on the resale market, though they may make your vehicle easier to sell.

Reliability

The older a vehicle gets (at five to seven years old), the greater the chance that major components, such as the engine and transmission, will fail as the result of high mileage and environmental wear and tear. Surprisingly, a host of other expensive-to-repair failures are just as likely to occur in new vehicles as in older ones. The air conditioning, electronic computer modules, electrical systems, and brakes are the most troublesome components, manifesting problems early in a vehicle's life. Other deficiencies that will appear early, due to sloppy manufacturing and harsh environments, include failure-prone body hardware (trim, finish, locks, doors, and windows), susceptibility to water leakage or wind noise, and peeling and/or discoloured paint. The following legend shows a vehicle's relative degree of overall reliability; the numbers lighten as the rating becomes more positive:

1	**2**	**3**	**4**	**5**
Unacceptable	Below Average	Average	Above Average	Excellent

VALUE OF OPTIONS BY MODEL YEAR

OPTION	2001	2002	2003	2004	2005	2006	2007	2008	2009
Air conditioning	$200	$200	$250	$300	$350	$400	$500	$600	$750
AM/FM radio & CD player	100	100	100	150	175	200	300	500	600
Anti-lock brakes	50	50	100	125	150	175	300	300	400
Automatic transmission	250	250	300	325	375	400	500	600	750
Cruise control	75	50	50	75	100	125	225	300	350
Electric six-way seat	50	50	100	125	150	175	200	400	450
Leather upholstery	50	100	200	225	325	400	500	800	900
Level control (suspension)	50	50	75	100	125	150	250	350	450
Paint protector	50	50	50	50	50	50	50	50	50
Power antenna	0	0	0	0	0	75	75	75	75
Power door locks	50	50	100	125	150	175	200	250	250
Power windows	50	50	100	125	150	175	225	250	250
Rustproofing	50	0	0	0	25	25	50	50	50
Stability control	100	125	150	150	150	175	225	275	300
Sunroof	50	50	50	75	125	150	300	500	500
T-top roof	150	200	300	400	500	700	800	1,000	1,000
Tilt steering	0	50	50	75	75	100	175	250	200
Tinted windows	0	0	0	0	25	50	50	50	50
Tires (Firestone)	–100	–100	–100	–100	–100	–150	–150	–150	–150
Traction control	50	100	125	150	175	275	400	500	500
Wire wheels/locks	50	75	100	125	150	175	275	300	350

Crashworthiness

Some of the main factors weighed in the safety ratings are a model's crashworthiness, its front and rear visibility, and the availability of safety features such as seat belt pretensioners, depowered airbags, airbag disablers, adjustable brake and accelerator pedals, integrated child safety seats, effective head restraints, and assisted stability and traction control.

NHTSA CRASH TESTS: Front, side, and roof crash protection figures are taken from NHTSA's New Car Assessment Program. For the front crash test, vehicles are crashed head-on at 57 km/h (35 mph) into a fixed barrier. NHTSA uses star rankings to show the likelihood, expressed as a percentage, of belted occupants surviving a crash without serious injury—the higher the number, the greater the protection.

SIDE CRASHWORTHINESS: NHTSA's side crash test represents an intersection-type collision with a 1,368 kg (3,015 lb.) barrier moving at 62 km/h (38.5 mph) into a standing vehicle. The moving barrier is covered with material that has give in order to replicate the front of a car.

ROOF STRENGTH: Roofs of light passenger vehicles weighing up to 2,722 kg (6,000 lb.) are required to withstand up to three times the weight of the vehicle (a strength-to-weight ratio of 3) on both the driver's and passenger's side of the vehicle. Heavier light-duty vehicles weighing 2,722–4,536 kg (6,000–10,000 lb.) need only withstand 1.5 times their own weight on the roof.

IIHS CRASH TESTS: The Insurance Institute for Highway Safety (IIHS) rates vehicles' frontal offset, side, and head-restraint/rear crash protection as "Good," "Acceptable," "Marginal," or "Poor." Head restraints may be rated for both front- and rear-seat occupants.

In the Institute's 64 km/h (40 mph) frontal offset test, 40 percent of the total width of each vehicle strikes a barrier on the driver's side. The barrier's deformable face is made of aluminum honeycomb, which makes the forces in the test similar to those involved in a frontal offset crash between two vehicles of the same weight, each going just less than 64 km/h.

IIHS's 50 km/h (31 mph) side-impact test is carried out at a slower speed than NHTSA's test; however, the barrier uses a front end that is shaped to simulate the typical front end of a pickup or SUV, which is deemed to give truer results. The Institute also includes the degree of frontal-impact head injury in its ratings.

While many automakers are making improvements, a few are going in the wrong direction. Seat/head restraints in recent Chrysler 300, Kia Amanti, and Nissan Altima tests have earned Marginal ratings, compared with Acceptable ratings for their earlier designs, which were tested in 2004. Furthermore, a disappointingly large number of other models have been rated Poor. They include the Acura TSX, BMW 5 Series, Buick LaCrosse (Allure in Canada) and Lucerne, Cadillac CTS and DTS, Chevrolet/Daewoo Aveo, Honda Accord and Fit, Hyundai Accent, Infiniti M35, Jaguar X-Type, Kia Rio, Mitsubishi Galant, Pontiac Grand Prix, Toyota Avalon and Corolla, and Suzuki Forenza and Reno.

ROLLOVERS: A vehicle's rollover resistance rating is an estimate of its risk of rolling over in a single-vehicle crash, not a prediction of the likelihood of a crash. The lowest-rated vehicles (one star) are at least four times more likely to roll over than the highest-rated vehicles (five stars) when involved in a single-vehicle crash.

SMALL CARS

"It's a car!" Toyota proclaims. And here we thought that was obvious. Then we had the opportunity to drive a preproduction Yaris around the artsy west Los Angeles suburb of Culver City and realized Toyota was indeed right: It's a car. And that's about it.

WWW.CARANDDRIVER.COM/REVIEWS/2012-TOYOTA-YARIS-FIRST-DRIVE-REVIEW

When Cheap Is Too Cheap

Your biggest risk in buying a small car is that, mesmerized by the low prices, you'll buy a bare-bones model that's too cheap. Sure, the extra dollars will feel great in

Yaris has less power than the Ford Fiesta, Honda Fit, and Kia Rio5, with a 0–100 km/h time that is beaten by most of the competition. Updated for 2012, the Yaris remains gutless.

your pocket and the fuel economy will be worth bragging about—until the engine blows, the tranny packs it in, the throwaway battery leaves you stranded, insufficient sound insulation drives you to distraction, or the skimpy seat padding becomes literally a pain in the butt. Yet, for just a few dollars more you could have gotten a newer version of the same model that would be much more durable and incorporate additional safety, performance, and convenience upgrades.

On the other hand, be wary of formerly Recommended cars that are past their prime. Take the Toyota Yaris, for example. It has been one of the top compact car picks in Canada for years. But Toyota hasn't added much to the car over that time, while Honda, Hyundai, and Mazda, among others, now sell small feature-packed, entry-level cars that cost less and outperform Toyota's stand-pat Yaris.

Small cars are mostly entry-level vehicles that attract budget-conscious shoppers and young, first-time buyers who eschew cachet for more cash savings. These customers want an affordable vehicle for daily commuting and don't need a lot of cargo or passenger space. Plus, a small car's tidy size makes it a sensible choice for buyers who drive and park in congested urban areas.

Therefore, it's a no-brainer that your first line of defence against high fuel prices isn't buying a Toyota Prius, a Honda Insight hybrid, or GM's $41,545 2012 Volt electric car. What you want instead is a cheap, small, crashworthy, reliable, and easy-to-repair used car. In the bargain, you'll be following the "reduce, reuse, and recycle" environmentalist creed.

Indeed, fuel-frugal 4-cylinder compact cars are primarily for city dwellers who want good fuel economy in the city/highway range of 9.3/5.9 L/100 km (30/48 mpg), easy manoeuvrability in urban areas, a relatively low retail price, and modest depreciation. A decade ago, owners wanting good gas mileage had to accept a cramped interior that would carry only two passengers in comfort, a car that would take eons to merge with traffic or pass other vehicles, and insufficient luggage capacity. As well, engine and road noise were fairly excessive on base models. In response to these shortcomings, many cars in this class, such as the Honda Civic and Toyota Echo, have been replaced during the past decade by much larger, more stylish iterations that rival the size of Honda's early Accord and Toyota's Camry. This upsizing made room for the introduction of better-performing, cheap and reliable "micro" small cars like the Honda Fit, Hyundai Accent, and Nissan Versa, which vary in size between Mercedes-Benz's Smart Car and BMW's Mini Cooper.

Safety is a mixed bag, however.

One of the more alarming characteristics of a small car's highway performance is its extreme vulnerability to strong lateral winds, which may make the car difficult to keep on course and require constant steering corrections that are both distracting and tiresome. On the other hand, crashworthiness is not necessarily compromised by a small size. In fact, evidence suggests that lighter-weight vehicles can be as safe as heavier ones.

In the October 17, 2005, edition of *Automotive News*, Robert Hall, professor emeritus of operations management at Indiana University, said the following:

> In the last 40 years, auto-racing speeds have increased, yet deaths have decreased significantly while the weights of the vehicles have gone down progressively. Why? Crushable fronts that absorb impact, "tubs" that shelter drivers after the entire car has disintegrated, a relocation of the front axle and, yes, crash bags. In this case, lighter is markedly safer.

Although most small cars are similar in appearance, the Japanese and South Koreans have brought out subcompacts with flashy new designs that have added much-needed flair to functionality.

The Nissan Cube (*left*) is an Average buy; the cheaper Kia Soul (*right*) is rated Above Average.

Traditional "ho-hum" small car styling was thrown out the window when the Nissan Cube debuted as a late-2009 model, and the Kia Soul joined the class as an early 2010. Both are tall four-door wagons that boast outstanding cargo and passenger space, thanks to their upright body architecture. A 2009 Cube that originally sold for $16,998 now goes for $10,000; a 2010 Soul that sold for $15,495 is now worth $9,500.

SMALL CAR RATINGS

Recommended

Honda Fit (2009–10)
Hyundai Elantra (2007–10)
Mazda3 (2006–10)

Suzuki SX4 (2007–09)
Toyota Echo (2000–05)

Above Average

Ford Focus (2005–10)
Honda Civic (2010)
Honda Fit (2007–08)
Hyundai Accent (2006–10)
Hyundai Elantra (1999–2006)
Mazda3 (2004–05)
Mazda5 (2006–10)
Mazda Protegé (1999–2003)

Nissan Sentra (2007–10)
Subaru Forester (2003–10)
Subaru Legacy, Outback (1999–2010)
Suzuki Aerio (2003–07)
Suzuki Swift, Swift+ (1999–2009)
Toyota/General Motors Matrix/Vibe
 (2005–10)

Average

BMW Mini Cooper (2008–10)
Honda Civic (1999–2009)
Hyundai Accent (2004–05)
Kia Rio, Rio5, Spectra, Spectra5
 (2009–10)
Nissan Sentra (2001–06)
Nissan Versa (2007–10)

Subaru Forester (1999–2002)
Subaru Impreza (1999–2010)
Suzuki Esteem (1999–2002)
Suzuki Verona (2004–06)
Toyota Yaris (2006–10)
Toyota/General Motors Matrix/Vibe (2002–04)
Volkswagen diesel models (2007–10)

Below Average

BMW Mini Cooper (2002–07)
Daewoo/General Motors Aveo, Aveo5,
 Lanos, Wave (2004–10)
Hyundai Accent (2001–03)
Kia Rio, Rio5, Spectra, Spectra5
 (2006–08)

Toyota Corolla (1997–2010)
Volkswagen Golf, Rabbit, Jetta, Cabrio (1999–2007)
Volkswagen diesel models (1999–2010)

Not Recommended

Chrysler Caliber (2007–10)

Daewoo Lanos, Nubira, Leganza
   (2000–02)

Ford Focus (2000–04)

Honda Civic Hybrid (2003–09)

Honda Insight (2001–06; 2010)

Kia Rio, Rio5, Spectra/Sephia, Spectra5
   (2000–05)

Subaru WRX/STi (2002–09)

BMW

MINI COOPER ★★★

BMW's Mini: A "cute" low-quality performer that can burn you in a number of ways.

RATING: Average (2008–10); Below Average (2002–07). "High performance" means low quality. With the Mini, you choose performance and cuteness over reasonable reliability and cheap, convenient servicing. **Ideal model year:** The 2008 Cooper convertible. Originally sold for $31,600; now priced at $13,000 less. **"Real" city/highway fuel economy:** *Manual 5-speed:* 9.0/6.2 L/100 km. *Manual 6-speed:* 7.3/5.4 L/100 km. *Automatic 6-speed:* 7.8/5.9 L/100 km. **Maintenance/repair costs:** Outrageously higher than average. **Parts:** Expensive and sometimes rare; God help you if the supercharger goes. BMW's Pony Express parts distribution system gives preference to 2008 and later model years, and dealers find it more profitable to stock 2008 or later model year parts. This is characteristic of every model that is redesigned every three years or so.

Older parts are back ordered until they run out. **Extended warranty:** A good idea, but no solution to the slow parts delivery. **Best alternatives:** *For performance:* Ford Mustang, Honda Civic Si, and Mazda3. *For fuel economy/ reliability:* Honda Civic; Hyundai Accent or Elantra; Mazda Protegé; Nissan Sentra; Suzuki Aerio, Esteem, or Swift; and Toyota Corolla. **Helpful websites:** *www.northamericanmotoring.com* and *www.mini2.com.*

 ## Strengths and Weaknesses

ALERT! Engine oxygen sensors have a 10-year/160,000 km secret warranty extension (2004–06 models). • Last January, 89,000 2006–11 model Minis in North America were recalled to replace the water pump, which could short-circuit and cause a fire. Make sure the recall "fix" has been done before buying a used Mini. • In another story from the NHTSA database, the Mini's tailpipe sticks out too far and may burn the legs of persons who unload cargo from the rear (a recent recall doesn't cover all the affected 2006–10 models):

> After a 30 minute drive, I parked and then pulled something out of the trunk. While reaching in, I burned my left shin on the tailpipe. I showed it a couple of days later to our burn unit director and he told me that it was a functional full thickness burn in an extremely dangerous location (because of the poor blood perfusion to the shin, healing is impaired and infection risk is high). It is a very common problem (a simple Google search will show this).

Base hatchbacks come with a 118 hp 4-cylinder engine, while S versions are equipped with a turbocharged 172 hp variant. Convertibles feature a standard 115 hp 4-banger, while the S sports a 168 hp version of the same powerplant. A 6-speed manual is standard on most models, but the 2007 added a 6-speed automatic that replaced the previous year's continuously variable transmission (CVT) and manifested many of the factory and supplier defects that often follow such upgrades. The 2007 hatchbacks come with front side airbags and side curtain airbags; convertibles are equipped with front side airbags with head and torso protection.

This is a typical fun-to-drive, small European car that doesn't sacrifice power and handling for fuel economy. Handling is a breeze: The car performs responsibly in all speed ranges with precise steering, minimal body lean, and hardly any front-end noseplow. The 2007 redesign smoothed out the car's choppy ride a bit but made the audio and climate controls more confusing than ever. The ride is still harsh, road and engine noise are omnipresent, body glitches are common, and rear interior room and comfort are sadly lacking.

According to *Automotive.com*, the 2007 S model with the turbocharger has 4 more horsepower than the 2006 S model with a supercharger; it also gets 16 percent better city gas mileage. Gone is the scream of the supercharger, and you'll have to live with the annoying engine hesitation caused by turbo lag.

About 90 percent of the 2008's components are new or upgraded, and the 2008 Mini is 19.5 cm (7.5 in.) longer and 4.4 cm (1.7 in.) wider for increased driver and passenger space. Another plus: 10 percent quicker steering makes the car a bit more nimble, while the slightly longer wheelbase improves performance.

The 2009 convertible was redesigned and given a power fabric top and heated-glass rear window. JCW models come with a 208 hp turbocharged 4-banger along with stronger brakes, a performance suspension, specific exhaust tuning, and 17-inch wheels.

What are the big problems afflicting this little car?

Owner complaints and internal service bulletins point to major highway performance and safety deficiencies on the 2002–07 models that are obviously factory-related. Owners report under-hood fires igniting when the car is underway or parked, chronic stalling, CVT breakdowns, power-steering failures, automatic window electrical shorts, prematurely worn side struts and brake calipers and rotors, constantly cracking windshields, and poor fit and finish and body design (for example, the hood scoop deforms due to heat from the turbo)—as well as expensive servicing and long waits for parts.

The picture isn't totally bleak: 2008–10 models are a bit better built, but there are still too many reports of fires, tailpipe burn injuries, and windshield cracks. Other common complaints concern the engine, the fuel system, premature clutch wear, poor-quality body hardware, and spontaneous sunroof shattering,

 Safety Summary

All models: Under-hood fires. • Airbag fails to deploy. • Frequent power-steering failures. • Automatic window failures and windshield stress cracks • Excessive engine noise, knock. • Many early manual and automatic transmission, clutch, and cable replacements:

> The manual transmission of my 2010 MINI Cooper E convertible failed with only 3,700 miles [5,954 km] on the odometer. Dealer claims problem is due to excessive wear and tear.

2003—CVT and steering failures continue. • In one incident, power-steering pump caught fire; in other reported incidents, it simply stopped working. • Electrical shorts cause inside lights and gauges to operate erratically. • Power windows open on their own. **2004**—Vent fan in motor catches fire. • More transmission trouble. • Power steering fails:

> *www.mini2.com* has reports of around 1 in 4 vehicles having this pump fail prematurely. I believe an investigation is important due to member reports of fires starting under the hood.

Manual transmission failure. • Power window doesn't roll down. • Windshield is easily cracked:

> While driving normally a very very small pebble size stone hits underneath the windshield wiper on the passenger's side. The windshield [immediately] spiders all over the window. I've been told all the problems with the BMW windshields were corrected, but I've heard from over 20 fellow MINI owners of random cracking and failures within the first 2,000 miles [3,200 km]!

Brake failure. • Hard to find horn button's "sweet spot." **2005**—Power-steering pump, transmission, clutch, and strut failures continue unabated:

> Complete catastrophic failure of the front passenger strut, strut tower, mount and lower control arm bushing caused by an imperfection on a public, well traveled road. Reports on enthusiast forums of over 216 others suffering the same failure on the same model car and a report in the Sept–Oct 2007 edition of *MC²* magazine citing the need to look for these common flaws on this model car when considering purchasing a used one.

Car continually loses power when cruising; owner is told the problem is a loose gas cap, but it isn't. • Windshield spontaneously cracks. • Sudden stalling ("limp home" mode) on the highway; Digital Motor Electronics component needs to be reprogrammed. • Front wheel rubbing noises when turning hard left or hard right. **2006**—Vehicle suddenly stalls on the highway. • Both strut mounts fail. • ABS and DSC systems don't work properly. • Passenger-side seatback won't lock in the upright position. • "Mushrooming" struts:

> "Mushrooming" is when the car gets a hard hit and the strut tower pushes up the metal where it is attached to [create] a bubble and damage the alignment.

Stalling and then sudden acceleration. • Engine seizes after driving through a rain puddle. • Windshield cracked (stress fracture) while one car was parked overnight; many other complaints of cracks, while BMW denies all liability. • One car suddenly veered out of control on the highway when brakes were applied. • Plastic fuel tank is easily punctured by road debris. **2006–07**—Passenger-side airbag is disabled when average-sized adult is seated. **2006–10**—Loud knocking diesel sound on a cold start. • Hood scoop deforms due to extreme heat. • Windshield stress fractures. • Transmission and fuel-pump failures. • Excessive heat in driver's footwell near the centre pillar. • Dunlop run-flat radial tubeless tires have side wall bubbling. **2008**—Passenger airbag is disabled even though a full-sized adult is seated. • Multiple transmission failures. • Premature tire failure. **2008–09**—Sunroof suddenly shatters:

> The back sunroof just exploded, sending fragment shards of glass blowing into my car. Drove to nearest gas station and covered the gaping hole in the sunroof. When I got home, I noticed that all edges of the broken glass point outward. I did not hit anything for this to have happened. The explosion was instantaneous and frightening.

2010—Vehicle caught fire while parked. • Airbag failed to deploy. • Sudden brake failure. *Cooper S:* **2009**—Electrical fire started in the dashboard area. • Airbag failed to deploy. • Several incidents where the engine timing belt tensioner failed. • Engine tends to lag and lurch when accelerating from a stop. **2010**—A fire ignited under the hood while the vehicle was being towed; a second engine compartment fire was reported while the car was parked in the garage. • Passenger-side airbag is deactivated even though a normal-sized adult is seated. • Parking brake won't hold on a slight incline. • Excessive engine noise, knock. *JCW:* **2009**—Cold start rattle or knock. • Deflectors under front bumpers are too rigid and fail at the seam where the rubber is fused to the hard plastic. • When it rains, front windows open on their own. • Passenger-side Disable Airbag warning light comes on when an average-sized adult is seated. *Clubman:* **2009**—Excessive engine rattling. **2010**—Water pump wiring harness may catch fire (see *www. northamericanmotoring.com*). • Under-hood fire reported while the car was underway.

Secret Warranties/Internal Bulletins/Service Tips

All models: 2002–06—Engine flaring on acceleration. • Hydraulic fluid leakage from the engine mount. **2005–06**—Troubleshooting instrument panel creaking. **2007**—Free crankcase breather retrofit and engine-cooling-fan fuse replacement. • Cruise control cuts out at 110 km/h. • Automatic transmission fluid leak. • Various driveability complaints. • An inoperative navigation system may require the replacement of the HIP module. • Diagnosing and repairing various electrical malfunctions. • Inoperative electric steering lock. • Steering rattles. • Front-end clunking when passing over bumps. • Rear axle knocking. • Water leaks onto the front carpet. • Tailgate hard to open or close. • Sunroof sunshade opens on its own. • Sunroof wind noise. • Instrument panel rattle. • Windshield whistling noise. **2007–08**—Fuel gauge brightness fluctuations. **2007–10**—Countermeasures to silence a speedometer buzz. **2008**—A front-end knocking noise may be caused by a defective engine mounting bracket. • Headlights flickering or moving up or down on their own is likely caused by a chaffed headlight wiring harness. **2009**—Surging in traffic traced to a fuel pressure pump/shaft defect. • A rear suspension knock or rattle may indicate that the inner diameter of the stabilizer bar mounts is too large. **2010**—A lit airbag warning light may be caused by a pinched wire located between the seat spring and the seat frame. • Manual transmission may have stiff diagonal gear shifts, making it hard to select gears. • Headlights may flicker while driving. • The steering wheel leather covering may peel off. • Excessive AC compressor noise (runs rough). Sunroof won't open in high temperatures. • Troubleshooting tips to silence squeaks from the rear seat backrest, roof rattles, and rear end knocking when going over bumps.

MINI COOPER PROFILE

	2003	2004	2005	2006	2007	2008	2009	2010
Cost Price ($)								
Cooper	25,200	22,700	23,500	23,500	23,950	22,800	22,800	22,700
Clubman	—	—	—	—	—	26,400	26,400	26,400
S	29,950	29,950	30,500	30,600	30,600	29,900	29,900	29,800
Convertible	29,950	29,950	30,500	30,600	30,600	31,600	31,600	29,850
Used Values ($)								
Cooper ▲	5,000	6,000	7,500	9,000	11,500	13,500	15,000	17,000
Cooper ▼	4,000	5,000	6,500	8,000	11,000	13,000	14,500	16,000
Clubman ▲	—	—	—	—	—	15,000	17,500	20,000
Clubman ▼	—	—	—	—	—	14,500	17,000	19,000
S ▲	6,500	8,000	10,500	12,000	14,500	17,000	21,000	23,500
S ▼	6,000	7,000	9,500	11,000	13,500	16,500	20,000	22,500
Convertible ▲	—	—	—	13,500	16,000	19,000	22,000	25,000
Convertible ▼	—	—	—	12,500	15,500	17,500	21,000	24,000
Reliability	2	2	2	2	2	3	3	3
Crash Safety (F)	4	4	4	4	—	5	4	4
Side	4	4	4	4	—	4	5	5
IIHS Side	—	—	—	3	3	3	3	3
Offset	5	5	5	5	5	5	5	5
Roof Strength	—	—	—	—	3	3	3	3
Head Restraints (F)	2	2	2	2	3	3	5	5
Rollover Resistance	4	4	4	4	—	5	5	5

Chrysler

CALIBER ★

bad buy

RATING: Not Recommended (2007–10). The Caliber is an unsafe, quality-challenged, underpowered fuel hog that will be replaced by the Dodge Dart, a new compact model based on the Fiat Alfa Romeo Giulietta. **"Real" city/highway fuel economy:** Very poor; in the 15.0/14.0 L/100 km range. **Maintenance/repair costs:** Likely to be higher than average once the warranty expires and Fiat takes over the dealer network. **Parts:** Easily found and relatively inexpensive now, but expected to be in short supply in the near future. **Extended warranty:** A good idea. **Best alternatives:** The Honda Civic; Hyundai Accent; Mazda3; Nissan Versa; Suzuki SX4; and Toyota Corolla, Echo, or Tercel. The 2008 SE 2.0L costs $6,500, much less than its $17,245 original selling price. The $1,000-cheaper 1.8L engine–equipped model is entirely out of its league, although the 5-speed manual transmission is a better performer than the CVT. **Helpful websites:** www.caliberforumz.com.

Strengths and Weaknesses

ALERT! Don't get suckered into buying a Caliber because it's cheap. Its overall poor performance and failure-prone components will quickly eat into your wallet or purse, and repeat visits to the service bay will eat up your time. Stay away from the discontinued AWD and SRT4 models. Poor parts availability and incompetent servicing are the Caliber's main faults.

This small four-door hatchback/wagon provides a good view of the road, thanks to its SUV-like raised seats. The ride is acceptable; however, handling is poor, and the noisy 1.8L, 2.0L, and 2.4L engines (148, 158, and 172 hp, respectively) lack low-end power for merging with traffic—which would be acceptable if there was a trade-off for good fuel economy, but there isn't. A more powerful 280 hp SRT4 debuted in 2008, but 2009 was its last year.

Reliability has never been Chrysler's strong suit, and the Caliber duplicates many of the quality and performance failures of Chrysler's earlier models. Interestingly, the AWD version is much less reliable than the front-drive versions. Nevertheless, expect numerous powertrain defects, like chronic stalling followed by sudden lurching and oxygen sensor and throttle bushing failures that cause the engine to run roughly or the throttle to stick.

Brake and electrical problems abound. The air conditioning system is failure-prone and costly to repair. Paint easily peels off at the car wash, and windshield cracks at the windshield wiper mounting are common. The tie rod end, 4-cylinder engine gaskets, and automatic transmission module fail. The suspension struts are of poor quality (four replacements in one year, reports one owner); owners also report excessive vibration caused by a defective idler pulley. Interior noise is omnipresent, and includes tire thumping; engine rattles; window-crank, door-hinge, and driver-seat squeaks; and radio-speaker and fender rattles (the fender may be missing a bolt). Poor body fit allows for wind and water to enter the car practically everywhere, but especially through the sunroof area when the drain gets "kinked."

Safety-related factory defects are legion, though crashworthiness is fairly good. NHTSA awarded the 2007–10 Caliber five stars for front- and side-impact occupant protection and four stars for rollover resistance. IIHS concluded that the Caliber gives Good frontal offset crash protection, but side and head-restraint protection is Marginal. Roof crashworthiness is rated Acceptable,

Caliber prices have fallen dramatically since the car was launched as a 2007 model. Buyers are afraid of the car's reputation for poor quality and are waiting to see the Dodge/Fiat replacement arriving this summer. Higher fuel prices may cause a small spike in the Caliber's selling price, but this will erode as the 2012 models approach and resale prices nosedive again. A 2010 base version that sold for $13,995 now sells for $8,200, while a 2009 SE now costs $6,000–$7,500. The same year SRT4 is valued at $10,500–$11,500. A 2008 R/T AWD will cost $7,500–

$8,500. The entry-level 2008 models are worth $1,500–$2,000 less. SRT4 models have lost the most value since they were dropped after 2009: selling originally for $25,000, a 2009 version can now be bought for $11,000; a 2008 will run $11,000 less than its original price, or $9,500.

Safety Summary

All models: 2007—Constant stalling. • There's an off-idle hesitation when pulling away from a traffic stop. • Tailpipe is cut too short; allows fumes to enter the cabin. • Premature wheel bearing replacement. • AC/heater produces a nauseating smell when activated. • Excessive highway vibration. • Gas-pedal bushing falls out, causing engine to surge; in one case, the assembly fell under the brake pedal, preventing braking. • ABS failure can cause an accident. • Cold, rainy weather prevents the power windows from rolling down. • Automatic door locks can lock you out if you exit the vehicle to close the garage door, for example. • Cold water, then hot water, drips onto passengers from the heater core:

> Hot water leaking from under the steering wheel. Husband sustained second and third degree burns.... It was determined that the AC condensation drain hose was clogged with debris which caused hot water to get inside the vehicle.

If a passenger's head is resting near the lock button when the door is unlocked, the force of the spring can injure the passenger. • One cannot drive with the rear windows down without hearing a painful, helicopter-like roar. **2007–08**—Airbags fail to deploy. **2008**—Seat belts often become unlatched because occupants mistakenly put the tongue into the latch housing. • Vehicle pulls sharply to the right when accelerating. • Stalling problem traced to a malfunctioning wireless control module. • Intermittent failure of the turn signals and fog lights. • Inaccurate fuel gauge. • Water collects in the tail lights. • As with the BMW Mini, the Caliber's tailpipe can burn the unwary:

> The exhaust pipe protrudes too far from the rear of the vehicle making it possible for small children to receive injury when the vehicle is hot. A small child in our home received a second degree burn when walking around the vehicle.

2009—In a collision, seat belt unlatched and airbag failed to deploy. • Accelerator pedal fell off while car was changing lanes. • The Caliber is a "tire-eater":

> The 2009 Dodge Caliber has no adjustments for rear camber and requires an after-market bolt installation for front. My 2009 Dodge Caliber 1B3HB28C69D116544, has eaten the inside edges off all 4 tires (scooped). This was written off as tire wear—ok on each Chrysler service. I noticed that the insides of the tires were scooped out when the wheels were turned out when I parked recently. Essentially, you as the owner get to replace four tires every 24,000 miles [38,600 km] and there seems to be no solid repair.

Many engine head gasket and automatic transmission failures. • Transmission line suddenly burst; Chrysler billed owner $450 U.S. for repairs. • Transmission slippage. *SRT4:* Poor braking performance. **2010**—Airbags failed to deploy. • Car suddenly accelerated while driver was making a low-speed turn. Brakes also failed and the vehicle crashed and burned. • Vehicle constantly stalls out and can take up to 10 minutes to restart. • Cracks gradually appear in the centre of the front windshield. • Difficult starting with key that was issued with the car.

Secret Warranties/Internal Bulletins/Service Tips

All models: 2007—A sticking accelerator pedal involves inspecting the accelerator pedal assembly bushings and replacing the pedal assembly, if necessary. • AC compressor noise or housing damage. • Water leaking from headliner. • Windshield crack diagnosis for warranty approval. **2007–08**—Engine won't start with wireless key feature. • Excessive engine vibration at idle may also be fixed by reprogramming the control module. • Squeak or groan sound when raising or lowering door glass. • Seat creak or squawk. • Whistling sound from the left side mirror. • Horizontal panel paint etching. **2008**—Manual transmission gear clashing. • Clutch pedal squeak troubleshooting. **2009**—*Manual SRT4:* **All years:** A "limp-in condition" or lack of turbo boost may require that the injector be replaced and the powertrain control module reprogrammed. **2007–09**—Poor handling, a rough ride, or leaky struts require that the jounce bumper and dust shield be replaced with a new design. Obviously, this should be done under warranty "goodwill." **2007–10**—Lower door hinges popping or groaning correction. • Fuel gauge fluctuation. **2010**—Fix for engine overheating; no AC.

Daewoo

Lemon-Aid does not recommend any cars by South Korean automaker Daewoo. The manufacturer marketed three cars in Canada from 2000 to 2002: the Lanos subcompact, the Nubira compact sedan and wagon, and the Leganza luxury sedan. All of these cars are rated Not Recommended because they are unreliable and expensive to maintain. Daewoo entered the North American car market in 1988, declared bankruptcy a year later, and was bought by General Motors in 2002. General Motors brought up production quality, but it was too little, too late. Today, Daewoo/GM continues to run in the rear of the pack. By the way, Daewoo depreciation is mind-boggling: An entry-level, $13,395 2002 Lanos is now worth about $700, and the top-of-the-line 2002 Leganza CDX that originally sold for $25,495 now sells for about $1,200.

Daewoo/General Motors

Daewoo skipped the 2003 model year in Canada and brought out three models under the GM banner as 2004 models. Chevrolet dealers sold the entry-level Aveo (a Lanos spin-off); the Optra, a compact based on the Daewoo Lacetti; and the Epica, a mid-sized vehicle based on Daewoo's Magnos. Suzuki sold the subcompact Swift+, based on the Kalos, and the Verona for GM.

AVEO, AVEO5, LANOS, WAVE

RATING: Below Average (2004–10). A failure-prone small car that has improved only marginally since General Motors bought Daewoo. Best used as a bare-bones urban runabout. Aveo5 is a similarly priced four-door hatchback base model. **Ideal model year:** The best of a bad lot, the 2008 Wave5 costs less than $6,000. **"Real" city/highway fuel economy:** 8.8/6.1 L/100 km. Owners report fuel savings may undershoot this estimate by about 10 percent. **Maintenance/repair costs:** Higher than average. **Parts:** Easily found and relatively inexpensive. **Extended warranty:** A good idea. **Best alternatives:** The Ford Focus (post-2007); Honda Civic or Fit; Hyundai Accent; Mazda3 or Protegé; Suzuki Aerio, Esteem, Swift+, or SX4; and Toyota Corolla or Echo. **Helpful websites:** *www.automotiveforums.com/f1439-aveo.html.*

Strengths and Weaknesses

ALERT! Be wary of chronic stalling and loss of power on all model years.

First launched by Daewoo as the Lanos, this nondescript, cheaply made, small South Korean car had few redeeming qualities. Both cars carry an underpowered 103 hp 1.6L 4-cylinder engine mated with a 5-speed manual or a 4-speed automatic. The powertrain and overall performance lack the refinement found with many other bantamweights anchoring the compact-car division. The engine is particularly noisy and strains going uphill with its maximum four-passenger load. Four *small* passengers. Around town, though, the car is peppy and nimble.

The 2004 Aveo's $1,700 price tag is very reasonable for a four-door that originally sold for $13,480. It saves buyers $800 over a $2,500 Toyota Echo that's comparatively priced new but depreciates slower. Don't worry if you pay a bit extra for a better-performing and more reliable Honda, Hyundai, Mazda, or Toyota—the difference means nothing when spread out over a number of years, and it will likely be refunded through a higher resale price.

Lanos owners complain of an unending series of powertrain failures, serious fit and finish deficiencies, and electrical short circuits. These problems have continued with the 2004 and later versions built under GM's supervision. Even up through the past few years, Daewoo DNA still causes transmissions to burn out, electrical systems to short-circuit, engines to stall, and brakes to fail. Fit and finish is about average for a stagecoach; owners report persistent water leaks and an unending symphony of squeaks, grunts, and rattles.

VEHICLE HISTORY: 2002—Daewoo goes bankrupt. GM buys Daewoo's assets and dumps the dealers. **2004**—A slightly longer sedan, the same puny engine, optional ABS, and no side airbags. **2006**—Standard front side airbags and larger optional wheels. **2007**—Longer and slightly restyled.

Safety Summary

All years: Airbags fail to deploy. • Sudden acceleration. • Stalling. • Brake failures. • Premature brake pad/rotor wearout. **2004–05**—Transmission failures. • Accelerator and brake pedal are mounted too close to each other. • Snapped side shock bolt. • Plastic thermostat splits, allowing engine to overheat. • Windshield cracking. • Door lock falls into the door's interior. **2006–08**—Passenger-side airbag is disabled by an average-sized seated adult. **2007**—Spark plug cables rub on engine bolt and cause the engine to misfire. • Cruise control works erratically. • Premature alternator failure. • Difficulty in shifting the vehicle out of Park (there's a bulletin covering this). • Premature brake rotor wearout. • More windshield cracks after chipping at the base. • A voltage spike burns out the headlights. • Automatic door locks won't open from the inside. • Faulty gas gauge. **2008**—Passenger-side Airbag light remains lit even though a fully grown adult is seated. • Hood pops open while car is underway. • Bent wheel rims cause excessive front-end vibration. • Sharp door handles on the driver's side can cut one's hand. • Door lock failures:

> After locking the doors, they sometimes do not open from within the passenger compartment. The contact carries a hammer in the vehicle in case she has to break the windows to exit the vehicle.

Brakes warp prematurely, causing excessive shuddering when braking; rear drums don't last long, either.• Instrument panel lights shut down. • Faulty tire pressure sensors. **2009**—Chronic stalling, loss of power:

> Out of the blue the engine will lose power again, there are never any warnings or Check Engine lights.... The problem has occurred at all speeds, including when on the freeway. We have already spent over $600 on various (so-called) fixes; including a complete fuel system cleaning (including the throttle body cleaning) none have ever helped.

2010—Airbag failed to deploy. • Vehicle suddenly accelerated when cruise control was activated while going uphill. Car sputters, then surges when accelerating. • When underway, vehicle will suddenly lose power. • Plastic back of in-dash radio melted. Windshield washer is useless at high speeds.

🔍 Secret Warranties/Internal Bulletins/Service Tips

2000–11—If the tire slowly goes flat, check first for aluminum wheel bead seat corrosion as the cause. • Troubleshooting shifting clunk noise. **2004–06**—Can't shift out of Park or remove ignition key. **2004–07**—Engine front end leaks oil. • Suspension squawk, rubbing noise on bumps. **2004–09**—Hoot, whistle, moan noise from the windshield/door area. **2004–10**—Front-end rattling when passing over bumpy roads. • Remedy for an erratic AC blower motor. **2004–11**—Transmission fluid contaminated by engine coolant and speedometer malfunction. **2005–08**—Radiator coolant leak correction. **2005–11**—If the Reduced Power dash light remains lit for no reason, chances are water has seeped into the system. **2006–08**—Troubleshooting a sticking throttle. **2007–08**—What to do when the vehicle won't shift out of Park. **2008–11**—Engine lack of power or rattling.

AVEO, AVEO5, LANOS, WAVE, WAVE5 PROFILE

	2002	2004	2005	2006	2007	2008	2009	2010
Cost Price ($)								
Aveo/Wave	—	13,480	13,595	11,995	12,995	12,995	13,970	14,150
Aveo5/Wave5	—	13,820	14,785	12,195	12,995	13,000	13,770	13,950
Lanos	13,395	—	—	—	—	—	—	—
Used Values ($)								
Aveo/Wave ▲	—	2,000	2,500	3,000	5,000	6,500	7,000	8,500
Aveo/Wave ▼	—	1,500	2,000	2,500	4,000	5,500	6,000	7,700
Aveo5/Wave5 ▲	—	2,500	3,000	3,500	5,000	6,000	7,000	8,000
Aveo5/Wave5 ▼	—	2,000	2,500	3,000	4,500	5,000	6,000	7,500
Lanos ▲	700	—	—	—	—	—	—	—
Lanos ▼	500	—	—	—	—	—	—	—
Reliability	1	2	2	2	2	2	2	2
Crash Safety (F)	—	5	5	5	5	5	5	5
Side	—	3	3	4	4	4	4	4
IIHS Side	—	—	—	—	2	2	2	2
Offset	—	—	—	—	3	3	3	3
Head Restraints	—	—	—	—	1	1	1	2
Roof Strength	—	—	—	—	—	—	2	2
Rollover Resistance	—	—	3	4	3	3	3	4

All ratings on a numbered scale where 5 is good and 1 is bad. See page 132 for a more detailed description.

Ford

FOCUS ★★★★

A Forrest Gump car: "Like a box of chocolates, you never know what you are going to get."

RATING: Above Average (2005–10); Not Recommended (2000–04). This is a Dr. Jekyll and Mr. Hyde car: Its first five years of production turned out unreliable, problem-prone vehicles that cost thousands of dollars to fix, when a correction could be found. Some models couldn't be driven through puddles because the low-mounted air-intake hose ingested water into the engine ($5,000 repair). Chronic stalling and powertrain breakdowns have also been a major problem. Owners say their Focus seems "possessed": It eats ignition keys and locks and unlocks doors on its own. Yet 2005 and later model vehicles have shown incremental improvement each year to the point that the latest versions are fuel-thrifty, handle well, and offer generous cargo space (hatchback). They are acceptable buys selling for exceptionally low prices. **Ideal model year:** A 2007 SES Wagon for about $6,000. It originally cost $17,099 and comes loaded with safety, performance, and convenience features. **"Real" city/highway fuel economy:** *Manual:* 8.6/6.1 L/100 km. *Automatic:* 9.0/6.7 L/100 km. *SVT:* 11.3/7.8 L/100 km, but owners say the automatic transmission cuts fuel economy by over 20 percent. **Maintenance/ repair costs:** Average for the 2005 and later versions; quite high for earlier models. **Parts:** Again, expensive and sometimes hard to find on early models. **Extended warranty:** Having a bumper-to-bumper warranty, or a rich uncle, is a prerequisite to owning a 2000–04 Focus. **Best alternatives:** Asian small cars are your best bet. Try the Honda Civic (it's softer-riding, quieter, and has a smoother-running engine) or Fit; Hyundai Accent or Elantra; Mazda3 or Protegé; Suzuki Aerio, Esteem, or Swift; and Toyota Corolla, Echo, or Tercel. **Helpful websites:** *www.focusfanatics.com.*

Strengths and Weaknesses

ALERT! Proven poor design of the front wheelwells causes debris to be thrown up against the doors, resulting in severe paint abrasion on 2008–11 models. Alberta courts ordered Ford to buy the car back (see the service bulletin on page 153).

Hailed as Europe's 1999 Car of the Year (a big mistake), Ford's 2000 Focus came to North America shortly thereafter as a premium small car. Its base engine, a 110 hp 2.0L 4-cylinder, was carried over to the Focus LX and SE, while the 130 hp twin-cam 2.0L (also used on the Escort ZX2 coupe) became the standard powerplant on the ZTS and ZX3. Both engines were given more power with the 2005 models and the beefed-up 151 hp 2.3L 4-cylinder.

VEHICLE HISTORY: 2002—Debut of a high-performance 170 hp SVT Focus with sport suspension and 17-inch wheels, and the ZX5, a four-door hatchback. **2004**—No more anti-skid system, and a 145 hp 2.3L 4-cylinder is added. **2005–07**—Totally revamped with a horsepower boost, new exterior and interior styling, and durable, more reliable components. ZX4 ST models offer standard ABS and traction control. **2008**—Restyled, with a number of new features. Hatchback and wagon models are dropped. **2009**—Ford's Sync system now standard on the SES and SEL models. **2010**—Ford's new standard safety features.

While early models are agile and fun to drive, the 130 hp 2.0L powerplant is barely sufficient for highway cruising, where passing and merging require a bit more power. The 2005–08 2.0L and 2.3L engines are a bit stronger and more reliable performers, but acceleration and overall road performance with the standard powertrain remain unimpressive. You can also expect an omnipresent engine buzz and some hard shifting with the automatic gearbox at any decent speed. Brakes grind when applied, and the front suspension creaks constantly. Uneven terrain causes the car to bounce about as if it were a baby harnessed in a Jolly Jumper.

This small car does handle well in city traffic, thanks to its tight turning radius and nimble steering. The small back-corner windows are also handy for keeping the rear visibility unobstructed. The car's unusually tall roofline gives ample headroom and allows for a higher, more upright riding position than you'll see with traditional small cars. Front and rear legroom is impressive as well, as long as the front passengers don't push their seats too far back.

The disappointing build quality of this car is highlighted by its easily broken, plasticky components. The car has convenient grab-and-pull door handles, but the centre armrest may be too high for some.

Fuel, electrical, powertrain, and brake system failures are commonplace for all model years. Service bulletins are replete with special instructions telling dealers how to practically rebuild the car to make it tolerably driveable. Expect excessive vibration; poor engine and transmission performance; chronic stalling; and 2003 SVT flywheel, pressure plate, and clutch assembly failures. Other problems: trunk and AC leaks; power-window failures; door mouldings that fall off; a fuel-door lid that breaks in half; hood latches that break off when the hood is closed; a trunk latch that sticks or suddenly opens; premature rotor and brake pad wear and squeaking; a seatback bar that digs into the driver's back; a driver's door that won't open from the inside (help!); interior panels that don't fit or align properly; excessive wheel, brake, engine, suspension, and steering-column noise; and a failure-prone ignition switch that won't turn, locks up, and eats keys (unlocking costs $300).

 ## Safety Summary

2000–02—Many complaints of chronic stalling with loss of brakes and steering. • Defective speed control causes sudden acceleration in spite of corrective recall. • Other sudden acceleration incidents ascribed to faulty power control module and driver's shoe being caught under the plastic console. • Sudden acceleration in Reverse. • Collapse of tie rod and axle, leading to loss of control. • Defective axle wheel bearing. • Sudden pull to the left when turning left. • Clutch pedal spring pops out, injuring driver. • Pedal falls on floorboard. • Transmission slippage and failure. • Smoking electrical wiring in dash. • In one instance, under-hood fire ignited after AC engaged. • Driver-side seat belt won't deploy. • Emergency brake often fails to engage because button on handle stays depressed. • One vehicle was cruising at 110 km/h when gas pedal fell off its mounting. • Frayed accelerator throttle cable snaps; cable also kinks, causing hesitation, acceleration, and surging. • Stabilizer bar suddenly breaks. • One car left in Park rolled downhill. • Rear end is very unstable in snow, feels wobbly under normal conditions, and throws rear passengers about. • Sudden, unintended acceleration, and then engine cuts out. • Engine shuts down while cruising on the highway. • New engine needed after rainwater ingested into engine because of low air-intake valve. • Transmission hard to shift into Second or Reverse in cold weather. • Fuel-tank leak due to cracked filler pipe. • No brakes. • Steering wheel locks while driving. • Broken rack and pinion. • Tie rod suddenly breaks off. • Front and rear wheels buckle. • Collapsed front wheel. • Rear hatch opens on its own. • Dash lights flicker, then quit. **2003**—Chronic stalling. • Reports of severe back trauma from seatback failure in rear-enders. • Transmission and axle failures. • Excessive vibration. • Trunk latch suddenly releases. **2004**—Car fire believed to be caused by faulty fuel-line connection. • Cruise control self-activates, causing vehicle to surge suddenly. • One car's hood flew up, shattering windshield while car was cruising on the highway. • Automatic transmission, bearings, and throttle body replaced during first year. • Total brake failure and frequent rotor, pad, and caliper replacements:

> Brakes failed on our 2004 Ford Focus ZX5 4-door hatchback as my wife went to stop at a stop sign leaving our development and was broadsided by a truck. This resulted in a total loss of vehicle and injuries sustained to my wife.

Chronic stalling and surging continues to be a problem. • Bent steering tie rod makes vehicle wander all over the road. • Wheel bearing failure. • No-start because ignition cylinder seized:

> I drove and parked the 2004 Ford Focus about 40 mins from my home. About 2 hours later, I went to get in my car and the steering wheel was locked. I inserted the key and it would not turn. Several people tried jiggling the steering wheel, stepping on the brake all to no avail.

Water entry destroys the horn. • Snow kills the windshield wiper motor. **2004–05**—Sudden, unintended acceleration. **2005**—Airbags fail to deploy. • Key won't turn in the ignition. • Broken motor mounts. • Sudden transmission clutch failure. • Fuel pump fuse blows repeatedly. • Decorative wheel lug nuts fly off. • Door locks and unlocks on its own. • Early wearout of rear brakes and tires. **2005–06**—Airbag light stays on for no reason. **2006**—Stuck accelerator. • Driver's seatback suddenly falls backwards. • Brake calipers cut into the rotor. • Wheel lug nuts break off. • Rear passenger door opens suddenly while car is underway:

> The rear passenger door opened unexpectedly... In addition, the latches failed to secure the rear liftgate.

Tail light bulb melts the plastic cover assembly. • Dashboard lights short out. **2007**—Airbag deploys for no reason. • One vehicle's front right wheel flew off with its struts attached. • Transmission suddenly downshifts or shifts into Neutral when cruising on the highway. • "Chopped" rear tires due to a faulty suspension. • Engine cylinders overheat and burn out the spark plugs. • Tire rim stem fails, causing a blowout in one instance (this is a common Ford problem with tire stems imported from China and used on most of Ford's vehicles). **2008**—Airbags fail to deploy. • Failure of the tire pressure warning system. • Faulty throttle body. • Defective power door locks. **2009–10**—Airbags failed to deploy. • Painful chin-to-chest head restraints. • Faulty throttle body causes vehicle to constantly stall. • Key sticks in the ignition. • Premature brake wearout. • Windshield wiper blades don't clear the windshield and often break off from the wiper arm. • Sunroof suddenly shattered. • Frequent door lock failures that imprison occupants. • Original equipment Kumho Solus tires don't last. • Rear tires wear out early ("cupping") due to lack of a rear adjustment kit ($300). • Suspension bottoms out easily. • Paint abraded on door bottoms due to poorly designed wheelwells (see the service bulletin on the next page).

Secret Warranties/Internal Bulletins/Service Tips

2002–10—Key sticks in the ignition cylinder; what to do. **2000–04**—Remedy for front suspension creak, crunch, grinding, or rattle. **2000–07**—Vehicle drifts or pulls to one side due to a misalignment of the front subframe. **2003–05**—If doors lock or unlock when they shouldn't, try cleaning the door-latch connectors. **2003–06**—Premature manual clutch wearout. • AC fluid leaks. **2005–07**—Slow fuel fill or early shutoff. **2006–07**—Rear-end rattling. • Water leaks onto the front/rear floor area. **2006–08**—Power steering fluid leaks. **2006–10**—If the trunk lid won't latch, the solenoid is the likely culprit, requiring that the latch assembly be replaced. **2007–08**—Tire valve stem free inspection or pro-rata tire replacement (see bulletin on the following page). **2008**—No Third or Fourth gear (automatic). • Water leaks onto the rear floor. • Front-end pop/click. • Interior door handle pulls loose. **2008–10**—Remedy for front-end noise when passing over rough roads and an engine ticking noise at idle. • An engine fuel rail or injector malfunction may be the cause of an idle ticking noise. • A click/pop noise heard from the front end may be caused by faulty front stabilizer bar end links in the front upper strut bearing area, and/or by the lower control arm. • Although Ford is emphatic that paint abrasion on the side of the car is the owner's responsibility, TSB #10-15-6, issued 08/16/10, says the affected area (rocker panels, or door bottoms) will be repainted under warranty (see service bulletin below). **2008–11**—Remedy for brake squeak, creak when passing over bumps. **2012**—In TSB 11-9-8 issued on September 20, 2011, Ford said that some drivers had noticed a tendency for the steering to wander above 72 km/h (45 mph). Ford announced that it will replace the steering gear free of charge.

LOWER BODY PAINT ABRASION/DAMAGE

BULLETIN NUMBER: TSB 10-15-6   DATE: AUGUST 16, 2010

PAINT DEGRADATION/ROAD ABRASION

Ford Focus 2008-11

ISSUE: Some 2008–11 Focus vehicles may experience paint damage or road abrasion on the rocker panel and on the side of the vehicle located slightly ahead of the rear tires on both 2 door and 4 door models. Rocker Panel, 1/4 panel, dog leg and/or rear door, dependent on model. This has been reported in geographical areas that commonly experience snow and ice conditions and use various forms of traction enhancers.

ACTION: follow the service procedure steps to correct the condition.

SERVICE PROCEDURE: per the warranty and policy manual paint damage caused by conditions such as chips, scratches, dents, dings, road salt, stone chips or other acts of nature are not covered under the new vehicle limited warranty. However, paint abrasion at the dog leg area due to the above circumstances is a unique condition on the focus and, as a result, repairs are eligible for basic warranty coverage.

Sometimes in court, Ford's lawyers don't know their right hand from their left hand. This Ford internal bulletin clearly says Ford accepts responsibility for premature paint abrasion on the Focus. But Ford lawyers told an Alberta Court they deny all responsibility (see page 92). No wonder the court threw the case out.

FOCUS PROFILE

	2002	2003	2004	2005	2006	2007	2008	2009	2010
Cost Price ($)									
S/E	15,970	16,275	16,475	—	—	14,799	15,999	14,799	14,999
ZX3S	17,390	17,550	17,775	17,555	17,599	—	—	—	—
ZX4 ST	—	—	—	—	22,995	—	—	—	—
Wagon SE	17,271	18,995	19,165	19,365	19,565	17,099	—	—	—

Used Values

S/SE ▲	2,000	3,000	3,500	—	—	7,000	8,000	9,000	10,200
S/SE ▼	1,500	2,500	3,000	—	—	6,000	7,500	8,500	9,500
ZX3S ▲	2,500	3,500	4,000	4,500	5,500	—	—	—	—
ZX3S ▼	2,000	3,000	3,500	4,000	5,000	—	—	—	—
ZX4 ST ▲	—	—	—	—	5,500	—	—	—	—
ZX4 ST ▼	—	—	—	—	4,500	—	—	—	—
Wagon SE ▲	2,500	3,000	3,500	4,500	5,000	6,500	—	—	—
Wagon SE ▼	2,500	3,000	3,000	4,000	4,500	5,000	—	—	—

Reliability	1	1	1	3	3	4	4	4	4
Crash Safety (F)	4	4	4	4	4	4	5	5	5
4d	5	5	5	5	5	5	4	4	4
Side	3	4	4	3	3	3	3	3	3
4d	3	4	4	3	3	3	5	5	4
IIHS Side	1	1	1	1	1	1	5	5	5
4d	1	1	1	1	1	1	3	3	3
Offset	5	5	5	5	5	5	5	5	5
Head Restraints	2	2	2	2	3	3	5	5	5
Rollover Resistance	4	4	4	4	4	4	4	4	4
4d	4	4	4	4	4	4	4	4	4

Honda

CIVIC, INSIGHT, CIVIC HYBRID   ★★★/★

RATING: *Civic:* Above Average (2010); Average (1999–2009). Most Civics have been downgraded from Above Average to Average due to their higher incidence of failures, highlighted by cracked engine blocks, a tire-eating rear suspension, and "in your face" sun visors, among other quality deficiencies. Following *Lemon-Aid*'s disclosure of Honda Canada's secret warranties applicable to some of the preceding deficiencies, Honda now says it will extend its warranties on a case-by-case basis to treat all claimants equally. *Civic Hybrid:* Not Recommended (2003–09). *Insight:* Not Recommended (2001–06; 2010). **Ideal model year:** A base 2010 or 2011 Civic sedan that originally sold for $15,990 or $14,990 (yes, the 2011 was cheaper) and now sells for about $11,000 or $12,500. **"Real" city/ highway fuel economy:** *Civic manual:* 7.5/5.7 L/100 km. *Civic automatic:* 8.0/5.7 L/100 km, though owners report they burn about 10 percent more. *High-performance SiR versions:* 9.2/7.0 L/100 km. *Hybrids:* These models get nowhere near their estimated 4.7/4.3 L/100 km fuel consumption; expect to burn as much as 30 percent more. See **ALERT!** below). **Maintenance/repair costs:** Average. Independent garages can carry out repairs, but the 16-valve engine's complexity means that more-expensive dealer servicing may be unavoidable. Owners should check the engine timing belt every 3 years/60,000 km and replace it every

100,000 km ($300). **Parts:** A bit more expensive than with most other cars in this class; airbag control modules and body panels may be back ordered for weeks. **Extended warranty:** A waste of money. **Best alternatives:** Honda Fit; Hyundai Accent or Elantra; Mazda3 or Protegé; Nissan Sentra; Suzuki Aerio, Esteem, or Swift; and VW Golf or Jetta TDI. **Helpful websites:** *www.civicforums. com* and *www.honda-tech.com.*

Strengths and Weaknesses

ALERT! A Los Angeles woman found her 2006 Honda Civic Hybrid wouldn't live up to its high-mileage promises and sued Honda to pay for not delivering the 50 mpg [4.8 L/100 km] it promised. She got about only 30 mpg.

But rather than go the class action lawsuit route as thousands of owners have done, last February she took her case to small claims court and won $9,867. The important precedent set by *Peters v. American Honda Motor Co.* is outlined on page 114.

The plaintiff believed she had a better chance of winning her case in a court where standards of proof are more relaxed, there are no attorneys' fees, and cases are decided quickly. Considering there are 200,000 affected Civic and Accord Hybrid owners eligible for some compensation, Honda could be faced with a series of judgments costing the automaker over $2 billion U.S.

Honda USA admits it overstated the Hybrid's fuel economy and has offered 2003–09 Civic Hybrid owners in the U.S. a settlement for a couple of a hundred dollars each, $500–$1,000 toward the purchase of a new Honda, and a free "frugal driving" video. Honda owners are underwhelmed by the offer and 2005–07 Accord Hybrid owners are now threatening to sue.

Civic

Canada's top-selling small car, Civics have distinguished themselves by providing sports car acceleration and handling with excellent fuel economy and quality control that is far better than what American, European, and most other Asian automakers can deliver. Other advantages: a comfortable ride; a roomy, practical trunk; high-quality construction; good front and rear visibility; bulletproof reliability; simple, inexpensive maintenance; and a smooth-shifting automatic transmission. Also, these cars can be easily and inexpensively customized for better driving performance, or to gain a racier allure.

Si models are Honda's factory hot rods (the Acura 1.6 EL is a Si clone), providing lots of high-performance thrills without the bills. Despite four-wheel disc brakes, the Si's mediocre braking and its lack of low-end torque are the car's main performance flaws. Its suspension may be too firm for some, and its spoiler may block rear visibility.

The 2001–04 Civic models move from the subcompact to the compact class and increase interior volume while providing seats that are wider and higher. They are also better performers than earlier models from a power and handling standpoint. Although steering feedback is a bit vague and over-assisted, the softly sprung suspension still gives the base car a floating feel, and there's excessive body lean when cornering at high speeds (EX and Si models have a firmer stance). Drivers will find that parking is more of a chore because the car's increased size makes it difficult to see its rear corners.

Honda quality control, like Toyota, has gone steadily downhill for well over a decade. Having said this, Honda's lineup has always been better-made than the rest of the Asian competition and much better built than what Detroit offers. Heading the list of owner complaints are engine crankshaft failures, transmission malfunctions, weak front springs and shocks, and early strut failure resulting in degraded handling. Owners also complain of AC failures, chronic water leaks, delaminated, bubbling paint, suspension knocks and squeaks, erratic fuel gauge readings, a subpar stereo system, a constantly lit Check Engine light, fuel and electrical system failures frequent brake repairs (rotor warpage and pad replacement), trunk hinges that steal storage room and damage cargo, a faulty engine computer module and oxygen sensor, and early replacement of the crankshaft pulley and timing belt.

Other common problems include windshield air leaks and noise; warped windshield mouldings; hard-to-access horn buttons; windows that fall off their tracks; side mirrors that vibrate excessively; headlights that can't be focused properly and are prone to water leaks; gas-tank fumes that leak into the interior; and premature rusting, uneven paint application, chalky spots, and paint peeling off.

Insight and Civic Hybrid

Stay away from used Honda hybrids. Build quality is inconsistent, the electrical and braking systems can be quite hazardous, maintenance is highly dealer-dependent, depreciation is a bit faster than with comparable makes, and fuel economy is illusory. *Consumer Reports* says the Civic Hybrid's fuel economy may fall short by at least 25 percent.

The Insight is a two-passenger hatchback coupe that uses a small electric motor to assist the 3-cylinder gasoline engine during hard acceleration. The engine recharges the battery pack when coasting or braking and returns to battery power when the car is stopped. The car is slow to accelerate, is tossed about by moderate crosswinds, has a harsh ride and little soundproofing, and has very little interior room and poor rear visibility. Toyota's Prius seats four and uses a more-versatile hybrid system, wherein the electric motor is dominant and gasoline and electric power vary, depending upon driving conditions.

After a three-year hiatus, the Insight returned as a 2010 second-generation model and sold at discount—$23,900. It is a much better built hybrid with more features than the previous model. A used 2010 goes for about $17,000, while a 2006 version sells for half as much. The 2010 is the better buy, but it hasn't proven itself sufficiently to be Recommended by *Lemon-Aid*.

The Civic Hybrid does offer some fuel savings—plus it's smooth-shifting, gives a comfortable ride, and provides good front and rear visibility—but it comes in second to the Ford Escape and Toyota Prius, two more-refined hybrids. If your main goal is fuel economy, good alternatives are the 2005 or later Ford Focus, the Civic DX and EX (equipped with a manual transmission), Mazda3 Touring, and Volkswagen Golf TDI.

According to Wikipedia, in October 2010 Vincentric performed a Hybrid cost of ownership analysis for the American market. This analysis compared the Hybrid's five-year cost of ownership to Honda's all-gas counterparts. The analysis showed that a 2010 Honda Civic Hybrid costs an additional $1,830 U.S. over a 2010 Honda Civic EX two-door coupe with automatic transmission.

Hybrid cold weather performance isn't as fuel-efficient as advertised, hilly terrain eats into fuel savings, and the AC increases gas consumption and shuts off at stoplights, encouraging drivers to sneak up on lights. Furthermore, the car's unique dual powerplants can make for risky driving and erratic braking, as this Hybrid owner warns:

> [With a] 2003 Honda Civic Hybrid on a snowy road, coming over a small rise while going around a moderate curve under 40 mph [64 km/h], the battery charging function, activated by driver taking foot off the gas before cresting the hill, produced progressively stronger engine braking effect on the front wheels, equivalent to an unwanted downshift and causing fishtailing and poor response to corrective steering, so that the car slid across the road and into a snow bank and concrete abutment, causing $6,000 (U.S.) in damage. If there had been oncoming traffic, there could have been serious injuries or fatalities.

There's limited long-term reliability data, repairs and servicing are very complicated to perform, and rescuers are wary of cutting through the 500-volt electrical system to save occupants. Honda Hybrid performance and overall quality issues include chipped paint, rough shifting; a rotten-egg smell that intrudes into the cabin; premature brake and rear strut wear; a constantly lit Airbag light; poor-quality radio speakers; and a rear bumper cover that may fall off, be misaligned, or come loose.

VEHICLE HISTORY: 2002—The 160 hp SiR sporty hatchback arrives. Improved fit and finish, a firmer suspension, and a rear stabilizer bar (except on the base model). Front suspension uses MacPherson struts, which increases interior space while watering down the car's sporty performance. Insight is given a CVT. **2003**—New gauges, a CD player for the HX, and the Civic Hybrid arrives. **2006**—Redesigned with an emphasis on new styling, new safety equipment, and more power. The sedan is larger outside and somewhat smaller inside; the coupe is a bit smaller overall. Side curtain airbags and ABS are standard features. **2007**—A sedan version of the sporty Si coupe arrives. **2008**—A new EX-L and high-performance MUGEN Si sedan are added to the lineup. **2009**—A minor restyling inside and out. **2010**—The suspension is more refined, less jarring, and interior trim has been upgraded.

Safety Summary

All models/years: Spoiler and head restraints restrict rear visibility, and large rear-view mirror restricts forward visibility for tall drivers. • Sudden acceleration and stalling, and a sticking accelerator pedal:

> All of a sudden the car lurched at a high speed three times, and I was trying to brake it to make it quit and it wouldn't quit or brake. My car bashed in the window of the 7/11 and my foot was not on the gas…it was a horrible experience. However, Honda dealer is saying they cannot find anything wrong with it. I was just on the forum and there are lurching problems.

Engine and transmission failures. • Airbags that fail to deploy, deploy inadvertently, or deploy with such force they cause severe injuries. • Ball joints don't have a castellated nut to secure the ball in position; the nut can back off, and the ball pulls out of the steering arm. • Dangerous instability on wet roads. • Faulty cruise control. • ABS failures and constant rotor and pad replacement. • Defective automatic transmissions. • Transmission may suddenly jump into Reverse. • Surging when brakes are applied. • Vehicle may roll away when parked on an incline. • Hood and trunk lids that come crashing down. • Inoperative door locks. • Cracked windshields. • Headlights and interior lights that suddenly go out. • Vehicle wanders all over the road. **All models: 2005**—The smallest pebble can puncture the AC condenser. **2006**—Defective upper rear control arms. **2006–07**—Sun visor split at the seam:

> I went online and found several blogs: *www.usrecallnews.com* and *www.civicforums. com* and *www.honda-tech.com,* filled with complaints from other Honda owners having identical problems.

2006–08—Cracked engine block:

> There is a big engine block crack with a lot of 2006–08 Honda Civics, many of the owners have already posted their problems on many forums. Many owners took the car back to the Honda dealership and Honda did repair it for free. But! I still think the government should do an inspection on it and tell Honda to set up a recall on this problem. Honda will fix the problem only if it's under the warranty…. It is a manufacturer's fault for using bad heating material on engine blocks. Here's a link to a forum site: *http://8thcivic.com/forums/mechanical-problems-technical-chat/42339-my-r18-block-cracked-check-yours.html.*

2007—Faulty upper rear control arms suddenly fall off or simply chew up the rear tires:

> My rear control arm broke for absolutely no reason. It snapped in half.... the quality of material used to put together the rear control arm was completely unsafe.... I did not hit anything on the road, and the piece just snapped.... Fortunately, I did not crash. This has been an experience that has been completely traumatic to myself, and I am in complete fear of driving any Honda now. I haven't had the money to replace the parts on my vehicle, because my car is out of warranty. This particular piece of the car should have definitely been in a recall.

Early wheel bearing failures. • Brakes detach from their mounts. • Airbag warning light comes on for no reason. • Windshield water leaks. 2008—Airbags fail to deploy. • Vehicle lunges forward when the brakes are applied. • Sun visors continue to melt, crack, or fall down due to a faulty hinge. • Rodents snack on Honda wiring:

> Rodents eat wires, fuel, brake lines. It seems the car companies have started using a newer material to replace the common plastic used in wire insulation and tubing with a soy-based product.

2009—Sudden, unintended acceleration with the steering locked:

> We then hit the third and final curb, the car went airborne again slamming into the building at about six feet high on the wall. All airbags deployed, the passenger window shattered and windshield cracked. Immediately after the crash I proceeded to place the car into park when the shifter itself came out. The car was still trying to drive itself through the building when we crashed.

Airbags deploy for no reason. • Sudden failure of the driver-side axle. • Prematurely worn-out brake pads and glazed rotors continue to be a common problem along with rapid tire wear and tire "cupping." • Poor rain performance and excessive wear with Bridgestone Turanza tires. • Early wearout of the front strut assemblies. • Reports of brake failures after passing over rough or bumpy roads. • Snow and ice accumulate on the inner walls of the front wheels, causing them to be out of balance; this makes the Civic practically uncontrollable at 80 km/h. • Road debris can easily damage the AC condenser; other vehicles have a protective screen:

> I was told that a rock hit my AC condenser. I was told that I would have to pay 700 dollars to fix it. While doing some research, I found out that this has happened to plenty of other Honda owners. I went back to the dealership and told them about the plenty of other Honda owners who suffered the same problem. I was still told that I would have to pay for it. When plenty of people have suffered the same problem, there is obviously a design flaw and we should not be punished for it and have to pay 700 dollars to fix it.

Loose steering rack bolts cause a clunking noise when turning. • Intermittent no-starts. • Sun visors continue falling down or "exploding":

> While driving at 70 mph [113 km/h] in interstate. The sun visor literally "exploded". Pieces of plastic from the back seam fell and the visor [dropped] right in my view almost causing me to have an accident. Had to pull over to keep it together as out of nowhere this thing [cracked] and fell on my face.

Seat head restraints force short occupants' chins into their chests. • Windshield distorts visibility. **2010**—While parking, the vehicle suddenly accelerated. • Airbags failed to deploy. Car pulls to the right once underway. • More reports of painful, dangerous head restraints:

> My head is being forced downward by the headrests. This occurs in all headrest positions, but is worse when adjusted right behind my head. I have tilted the seat back as far as I safely can and still be able to drive. I am 53 year old female, 5'3" tall, and wear bifocals. I am having difficulty focusing from tachometer to speedometer to road because I cannot move my head. I cannot tilt my head back at all because of the headrest. I also experienced a headache that evening as well due to eye strain… the NHTSA changed their headrest regulations in 2008. Test dummies for large males were used.

Key on a key chain got lodged in a hole at the back of the steering wheel, thereby locking the steering wheel. • Rear windshield suddenly exploded. • Sun visors will not stay up and they crack at the seam. • Driver's head restraint doesn't lock into place. • All doors and trunk lock unexpectedly. • AC condenser punctured by road debris. • Car sputters and stalls. • Shifter sticks when going from Reverse to Drive, Drive into Reverse, and vice versa. • Bridgestone Turanza tire blowout. • Transmission failure. • Cracked motor block. When brakes were applied the car suddenly accelerated. • Parking brake doesn't hold on a hill. • Premature brake wearout. • This car can be easily stolen due to its poorly designed trunk lock. Says one expert:

> A plastic cover that is around the valet trunk key lock can be removed and a small latch can be moved to the left and the trunk opens.

Insight: **2001–06**—Random events of power loss cause significant reduction of engine power when it is most needed. • CVT failure. • Steering becomes abnormally unstable when vehicle is driven above 50 km/h over uneven or grooved roadways. • Vehicle is prone to hydroplaning on wet roads. *Civic Hybrid:* **2003**—One vehicle lost all forward power while cruising on the highway. • Chronic stalling. • Excessive brake vibration; vigorous brake pumping needed to get adequate braking. • Seat belt locks up. • In cold weather, power windows won't roll back up until vehicle warms up. • Prematurely worn shock absorbers. • Driver's seat design can cause serious back pain. • The vehicle's strong electromagnetic field may be a health hazard:

With the use of a gaussmeter, an instrument used to measure electro magnetic fields, the consumer found that vehicle had a high electromagnetic field. The highest level occurred when the engine draws power from the battery via the integrated motor assist or when the battery was charging.

2005—Transmission slippage and frequent failures. **2007**—Windows cannot be rolled down while underway without producing a roar. **2007–09**—Front door glass comes out of its channel. **2010**—Airbags fail to deploy. • When coasting to a stop, vehicle suddenly accelerates. • Vehicle lags and lurches when accelerating. • Insufficient power to go uphill:

Car has small engine that needs assistance from electric motor. Electric motor helps the car during acceleration and climbing. The car should not charge the battery on climbs. As a result of this, extra load is added on the engine during climbs. With a 1300CC engine going up a grade, this could be very dangerous as you don't have enough power to climb at a certain rate other cars are capable of. If you visit insight-central.net there are a lot of complaints about this. Honda needs to re-program the cars not to force charge during climbs. I understand that if the battery was very low or drained that force-charging on climbs are a necessary evil. But my battery was 75% full!!!

Sudden brake failure. • Tire inflation warning comes on for no reason. • Excessive wearout of both front tires (a common Insight problem). • Weather stripping peels away from all over the car. • Low-beam headlights provide inadequate illumination. • Interior electronics produce a high-volume electric static noise that is painful to the ears. • There is no means of securing the gas cap or fuel access door. • More complaints about the chin-to-chest head restraints • Excessive haze and windshield glare in the rain.

Secret Warranties/Internal Bulletins/Service Tips

All models/years: Most Honda TSBs allow for special warranty consideration on a "goodwill" basis, even after the warranty has expired or the car has changed hands. Referring to the "goodwill" euphemism will increase your chances of getting some kind of refund for repairs that are obviously related to a factory defect. • Seat belts that are slow to retract will be replaced for free under Honda's seat belt lifetime warranty, says TSB #03-062, issued September 16, 2003. • Paint defect claims require an accompanying digitized (2 MB) photo before they can be considered. Tips for submitting a successful paint claim can be found in TSB #10-002, published January 20, 2010. **All models: 1999–2005**—Warped/deformed windshield moulding. Harsh shifts. **2001–04**—If vehicle won't move in Drive, it's likely caused by excessive Second clutch wear. **2001–05**—Starter grinds while engine cranks. • Inoperative or erratically operating power windows. • Driver's seat rocks back and forth. • Water leaks into the trunk. • Automatic transmission warranty extension:

A/T, CVT START CLUTCH WARRANTY EXTENSION

BULLETIN NO.: 07-049   DATE: FEBRUARY 5, 2008

WARRANTY EXTENSION: CVT START CLUTCH JUDDER

2001–05 Civic; 2001–05 Insight; 2003–05 Civic Hybrid

NOTE: Because of a class action settlement, the warranty extension coverage for CVT start clutch judder on 2002–05 Civic GXs and HXs with CVT, 2003–05 Civic Hybrids with CVT, and 2002–05 Insights with CVT purchased or leased between April 13, 2002, and November 7, 2006, is 7 years or 105,000 miles [170,000 km], whichever occurs first. For more information, refer to Service Bulletin 06-085, Warranty **EXTENSION:** Vehicle Warranty Mileage.

On affected vehicles, a momentary judder may be felt after accelerating from a stop, but only up to about 15 mph [24 km/h]. The most likely cause of the judder is a worn start clutch in the CVT (continuously variable transmission). To increase customer confidence, American Honda is extending the warranty for this potential problem to 7 years or 100,000 miles [160,000 km], whichever comes first. This extended warranty covers only CVT start clutch judder below 15 mph and CVT drive belt slippage (see Service Bulletin 07-050).

2006—Honda will replace for free until 2012 the defective auto-tensioner pivot bolt and reroute the drivebelt to prevent loss of steering or excessive noise. **2006–07**—Honda admits that rapid, uneven rear tire wear is caused by a manufacturing defect. The company will install for free a rear upper control arm kit, replace the flange bolts, and pay (prorated) for the replaced worn tires (TSB # 08-001, published July 22, 2009). • Water pump pulley bolts come loose (dealer

ENGINE OVERHEATS/LOSES COOLANT

BULLETIN NO.: 08-044   DATE: JULY 30, 2009

ENGINE OVERHEATS OR LEAKS COOLANT

2006–08 Civic—ALL except GX, Hybrid, and Si

SYMPTOM: The engine is leaking coolant and may be overheating.

PROBABLE CAUSE: The engine block is cracking at the coolant passages.

CORRECTIVE ACTION: Install a new engine block assembly.

WARRANTY CLAIM INFORMATION

OP#	Description	FRT
111100	Install a new engine block assembly	12.0
Q	Add for alignment	0.4

IN WARRANTY: The normal warranty applies.

FAILED PART: P/N 10002-RNA-A00

H/C 8143323

DEFECT CODE: 07601

OUT OF WARRANTY: Any repair performed after warranty expiration may be eligible for goodwill consideration by the District Parts and Service Manager or your Zone Office. You must request consideration, and get a decision, before starting work.

will install a water pump pulley kit free of charge). • Front-end noise. • Front door glass comes out of the channel. **2006–08**—Engine overheats or loses coolant; Honda will replace the engine at no charge under a "goodwill" warranty (see service bulletin on the previous page). • Honda admits that its sun visors split or come apart in TSB #08-023, published August 8, 2008. **2007–09**—Engine oil leak at the timing cover. • Inoperative power windows. **2006–10**—An engine knock or rattle may be caused by a faulty engine mount. • Clutch pedal pops, squeaks, or clicks.• Front end pop or clunk when passing over bumps. **2008**—Engine oil leak from the oil/air separator. **2009–10**—Horn blows for no reason.

CIVIC, INSIGHT, CIVIC HYBRID PROFILE

	2002	2003	2004	2005	2006	2007	2008	2009	2010
Cost Price ($)									
Civic	15,900	16,000	16,150	16,200	17,180	17,180	16,990	16,990	15,990
Si	19,902	20,700	20,800	21,600	25,880	26,380	26,680	26,680	25,880
SiR	—	25,500	25,500	—	—	—	—	—	—
Insight	26,000	26,000	26,000	26,000	26,000	—	—	—	23,900
Hybrid	—	28,500	28,500	28,500	25,800	26,250	26,350	26,350	—
Used Values ($)									
Civic ▲	2,500	3,500	4,500	5,500	6,500	8,000	9,500	10,500	12,000
Civic ▼	2,000	3,000	4,000	5,000	6,000	7,000	8,500	9,500	11,000
Si ▲	6,000	6,500	7,500	8,500	10,000	12,000	14,500	16,500	19,500
Si ▼	5,500	6,000	6,500	8,000	9,000	11,000	13,000	15,000	18,000
SiR ▲	—	8,000	8,500	—	—	—	—	—	—
SiR ▼	—	7,000	8,000	—	—	—	—	—	—
Insight ▲	4,500	5,000	6,000	7,500	9,000	—	—	—	17,000
Insight ▼	3,500	4,500	5,500	6,000	7,500	—	—	—	15,500
Hybrid ▲	—	6,000	7,500	9,000	11,000	12,500	13,500	16,000	—
Hybrid ▼	—	5,000	6,500	7,500	10,000	11,500	12,000	15,000	—
Reliability	3	3	3	3	3	3	3	3	4
Insight	—	3	3	3	3	—	—	—	3
Hybrid	—	—	—	4	4	4	4	4	4
Crash Safety (F)	—	5	5	5	5	5	5	5	5
4d	—	5	5	5	5	5	5	5	5
Insight	4	4	4	4	4	—	—	—	5
Side	2	5	4	4	4	4	4	4	4
4d	—	—	—	—	4	4	4	4	4
Insight	4	4	4	4	4	—	—	—	5
IIHS Side	—	—	—	—	3	3	3	3	3
Offset	—	—	—	—	5	5	5	5	5
Head Restraints	—	2	3	1	5	5	5	5	5

4d	—	**1**	**1**	**1**	5	5	5	5	5
Hybrid	—	**1**	**1**	—	5	5	5	5	5
Rollover Resistance	—	4	4	4	4	4	4	4	4
Insight	—	4	4	4	4	—	—	—	4

Note: Insight (hybrid) resale values don't hold up as well as regular-fuel Civic prices, although the Civic Hybrid does keep a high resale value. Surprisingly, high-performance Civics like the Si maintain the highest resale value. From a safety and crashworthiness perspective, the 2010 Insight is a much safer vehicle than the 2006 model.

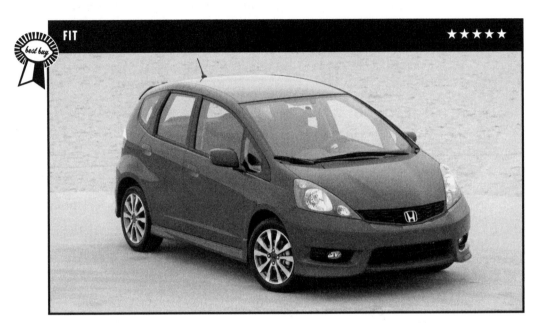

FIT ★★★★★

best buy

RATING: Recommended (2009–10); Above Average (2007–08). The Fit is a competent urban econocar that saves fuel without sacrificing reliability or driving performance. **Ideal model year:** The redesigned 2009 LX version. It sold originally for $17,380 and now goes for about $10,500. **"Real" city/highway fuel economy:** 7.1/5.7 L/100 km. Very few complaints that actual fuel consumption doesn't match fuel economy claims. **Maintenance/repair costs:** Lower-than-average maintenance costs. **Parts:** Reasonably available and relatively inexpensive. **Extended warranty:** A waste of money; the Fit is fairly dependable as is. **Best alternatives:** Honda Civic; Hyundai Accent, Elantra, or Tiburon; Mazda3 or Protegé; Nissan Sentra; Suzuki Esteem or Swift; and VW TDI. **Helpful websites:** *www.fitfreak.net.*

Strengths and Weaknesses

ALERT! Rodents snacking on Honda Civic and Fit wiring can cause over $1,000 worth of damage to your car's electronics. See: *www.wombatnation.com/2005/01/ mice-ate-my-car.* The Fit, launched as a 2007 model, is Honda's newest entry-level four-door hatchback. Powered by a 118 hp 1.5L 4-cylinder engine and coupled to a

All ratings on a numbered scale where 5 is good and **1** is bad. See page 132 for a more detailed description.

5-speed manual or automatic transmission, this small car provides better fuel economy than the Nissan Versa, is easily accessed, and has a surprisingly large interior for cargo, thanks to the clever seating arrangement (only a bit less room than in a Civic sedan). Highway performance is fairly good, with sufficient power and agile handling; city handling is better than with the larger Versa. Side curtain airbags and ABS are standard, and the Fit's reliability scores are a few points better than the Versa's.

The redesigned 2009 Honda Fit gained size and engine strength with an increase of 8 horsepower. A 5-speed manual transmission is standard, and a 5-speed automatic is optional; Sport models with an automatic transmission get steering wheel–mounted shift paddles, along with more aerodynamic styling, upgraded trim, and 16-inch alloy wheels. Safety features include ABS, traction control, an anti-skid system (new in 2009), front side airbags, and side curtain airbags.

A few complaints: Owners have endured painful chin-to-chest head restraints on all model years; gas-tank fuel sloshing underneath the driver's seat; automatic transmission gears that fail to engage smoothly; and the front side bumper falling off the vehicle. Many owners warn that the AC condenser is highly vulnerable to ($700) pebble damage and that the windshield spontaneously fractures.

 ## Safety Summary

2007—Engine raced and brakes failed after one vehicle passed over a speed bump. • Sudden steering loss:

> 2007 Honda Fit lost power steering without warning, becoming very hard to steer. Dealer reports code #61-04. There is a July 2009 service bulletin on this problem suggesting replacement of the EPS control unit, which has been done. An Internet search suggests this problem is common—there should be a recall, as serious accidents could occur as a result of sudden loss of power steering.

Power-steering control unit often fails when turning, causing a sudden loss of steering. • While one driver made a right-hand turn, the steering locked up because the ignition key was stuck in the steering-column orifice. • Turning the steering wheel right or left, or applying the brakes, may cause the engine to increase rpms. • After making a right turn, the automatic transmission fails to engage while the engine races for five seconds. • Automatic transmission hesitates when gearing down from 10 to 5 km/h in rolling stops for yield signs. • Sudden loss of engine power and sputtering said to be caused by defective coil packs. • Significant forward and rearward blind spots. • Angle at which foot must depress accelerator pedal can be painful; driver's seat position blamed. • Headlights are aimed too low, reducing visibility. • Failure of the right axle lift bearing. • Tires leak air. **2007–10**—Airbags fail to deploy:

> My son was involved in an auto accident in his 2007 Honda Fit Sport. He hit a truck stopped in the street while trying to avoid the truck. The impact occurred on the left

driver's side of the Honda Fit. The driver's side of the Fit was heavily damaged and the car was a total loss. My son had a serious head injury.

·

After a tear down by the body shop it was determined that the [airbag] sensors were installed at the sides at the front end of the frame rail. This is a very low position on this car since it's already low to the ground.... Had these sensors been placed at a higher elevation...the airbags would [likely] have gone off and the injuries would have been...minor. This design decision seems like it was developed to satisfy the frontal crash tests conducted by the Insurance Institute for Highway Safety.

2008—Sudden engine surging at low speeds when the brakes are applied. • Chronic stalling. • Dash lights stay on even if the headlights are off. • Defective headlight switch activates the high beams whenever the right turn signal is used. • The placement of the gas and brake pedals causes leg cramping. • Spongy brakes. • After a rain, rear carpeting and floor is soaked. • Tire jack bends sideways when used to lift the vehicle. 2009—Sudden, unintended acceleration. • Faulty Bridgestone Turanza EL470 tires (they develop side wall blisters). • Dunlop SP Sport tires show excessive treadwear and are prone to side wall bubbling. • Sun reflection from the dash impairs driver's view. • Headlight low beams do not engage. • Rodents eat up the Fit's wiring but leave alone a Honda Element parked nearby:

I did a Google search ["automobile wiring and rodents" / "Honda wiring and rodents"]. The search turned up many references to this problem in Honda automobiles and other manufacturers' automobiles. The search also uncovered many references to the recent use of soy in automobile wiring covering. If this is true it could explain why my 2005 Element has not been attacked while my 2009 Fit has been. It would also indicate a glaring defect in some auto electrical wiring. I am now dealing with the problem by leaving my Fit in with my dogs and letting them urinate on the tires. As of now this seems to be working. Obviously this is a lousy solution to the problem.

2010—Sudden acceleration with car in Reverse. • Sport model suddenly accelerated for no reason:

My online searches indicate that there have been reports of similar situations with prior-year models of the Honda Sport. I am certain there is an undiscovered problem with my car, and possibly others.

Sudden acceleration accompanied by loss of brakes. • Vehicle lurches and stalls. • In snowy weather, brakes lock up or fail to grab. • Brake and accelerator pedal are mounted too close together. • With headlights and heater blower running, the headlights dim significantly and the blower motor reduces its velocity. • Faulty door lock master switch not covered by recent recall. • Windshields develop cracks with minor or no impact. • Windshields also have long stress fractures, starting at the base on the passenger side and going to the centre of the windshield (replaced under warranty):

I was sitting in the parked car listening to the radio before work when I saw a foot long crack form half way up the right edge of the windshield horizontally toward the center of the windshield. There was practically no people or cars around and it was a clean straight line crack. I found an online forum on *Edmunds.com* where there were many people having stress crack issues with their fit windshields. I went to the dealer and they found a chip in the crack about the size of a pinhead, 2 inches in from the edge of the windshield. They claimed a stone hit the windshield to cause the chip and suggested contraction expansion of the glass caused the crack.

When closing the rear passenger door, the right front window shattered. • Carpeting falls apart and could get trapped under the brake or accelerator pedals. • Sport model seatbelt ratchets up and will not release. • Front seat head restraints cause a painful chin-to-chest seating position:

I ran Google search for Honda head rest complaints and found out that customers have been complaining about Honda's new head rests for the same very reason since 2007, for most of their models – from Accord and Odyssey to Fit. What makes the matter worse is that you cannot reverse the headrest as there are grooves only on one of the two support poles. By making head restraint extremely uncomfortable to use, Honda is forcing its customers to drive unsafely, specifically without head restraint. I spoke to service manager at my dealer and he told me that Honda does not have adjustable or reversible head restraint. He is also aware of the complaints from the customers. Solution should be easy to implement by making the head rest reversible for those like me with neck or back problems.

Be wary of loose front seat rail bolts allowing seat to move slightly when cornering or braking (see *www.fitfreak.net/forums/2nd-generation-ge-08-present/53493-2010-fit-seat-rocking-fix-2.html*).

Secret Warranties/Internal Bulletins/Service Tips

2007—Passenger seat won't slide. • Wind noise at top of windshield. **2007–08**—Steering may be more difficult due to a malfunctioning EPS control unit, says Honda Service Bulletin #09-043, published June 23, 2009. • Remedy for vehicles that pull or drift to one side of the road. • Tips on silencing under-dash gurgling noises. **2009**—Cracked front armrest repair. • Displayed fuel mileage is too high. • Troubleshooting a dash rattle. **2009–10**—Fuel filler door may not open. **2009–11**—AC blower motor operates only on "high speed." **2010**—Front seat rattle.

FIT PROFILE

	2007	2008	2009	2010
Cost Price ($)				
DX	14,980	14,980	14,980	14,480
LX	17,180	17,380	17,380	16,880
Sport	19,480	19,580	19,280	18,780

Used Values ($)

DX ▲	7,000	8,000	9,000	10,000
DX ▼	6,000	7,500	8,000	9,000
LX ▲	8,000	9,000	11,500	12,500
LX ▼	7,500	8,500	9,500	11,500
Sport ▲	9,000	10,500	12,500	15,000
Sport ▼	8,500	9,500	11,000	13,500

Reliability	5	5	5	5
Crash Safety (F)	5	5	5	5
Side	5	5	5	5
IIHS Side	5	5	5	5
Offset	5	5	5	9
Head Restraints	1	1	5	5
Roof Strength	—	—	3	3
Rollover Resistance	4	4	4	4

Hyundai

ACCENT ★★★★

RATING: Above Average (2006–10); Average (2004–05); Below Average (2001–03). Once the owner of a South Korean lemon grove populated by Ponys, Stellars, and Excels, Hyundai has used the past decade to leapfrog the competition and create high-quality, fuel-efficient, and reasonably priced vehicles. It got the product right, even if it did take almost a decade and involved pirating away Toyota's quality-control engineers. Hyundai now makes highly reliable cars with better warranties—at bargain prices. **Ideal model year:** Look for a loaded $5,500 2006 GL model. It originally sold for $13,495. **"Real" city/highway fuel economy:** 8.9/6.2 L/100 km. **Maintenance/repair costs:** Average. **Parts:** Reasonably priced and easily found. **Extended warranty:** Consider getting an optional powertrain warranty as protection from occasional engine head gasket and tranny failures. **Best alternatives:** Honda Civic; Hyundai Elantra; Mazda3 or Protegé; Nissan Sentra; Suzuki Esteem; and Toyota Echo or Corolla. **Helpful websites:** *www.hyundaiforum.com.*

 ## Strengths and Weaknesses

ALERT! Stay away from original-equipment Bridgestone Kumho tires. They have been blamed for poor traction and braking in wet or snowy conditions and premature wearout and sidewall splitting.

Launched as a '95 model, the early Accent was basically an Excel that had been substantially upgraded to provide decent performance and reliability at a phenomenally low price. Since that time, the car has increased in size and

Hyundai has added more equipment and performance features while increasing the car's overall quality and reliability. Of course, with its small 4-cylinder engine, the Accent is no tire-burner, but it will do nicely for urban commuting and grocery shopping. Consider investing in larger wheels and tires that equip the GT for safer highway handling. Overall, the Accent offers lots of performance for a very low price brought about by a faster than average rate of depreciation.

Other major drawbacks are so-so acceleration with the automatic transmission, little steering feedback, and limited rear seat access, especially with the hatchback versions.

VEHICLE HISTORY: 2003—A slightly larger engine; restyled front and rear ends. **2006**—Redesigned to be safer, larger, and more powerful (six more horses). Front side airbags, side curtain airbags, ABS, and four-wheel disc brakes are standard features.

Owner complaints are surprisingly rare; however, the following problem areas have been noted: faulty engine cooling system and cylinder head gaskets (engine overheating), engine sputtering, Check Engine light constantly comes on, and chronic automatic transmission failures (an extended transmission warranty is suggested for models no longer under warranty). One owner says the car cannot be aligned in the rear because there are no "adjustments" allowing for it. Owners also frequently complain of excessive front-end vibration; wheel bearing, fuel system, and electrical component failures; premature front brake wear; and excessive noise when braking, particularly an annoying clicking emanating from the rear brake drums. Paint, trim, and body hardware have also been subpar.

Recent models have been surprisingly trouble-free apart from a smattering of reports related to chronic stalling, loss of power when accelerating, excessive road vibrations (mostly a tire balance problem), prematurely worn Kumho original-equipment tires, and a transmission delay similar to Toyota's "lag and lurch" that causes the vehicle to lunge into gear.

Safety Summary

All years: Airbags fail to deploy, or deploy inadvertently. • Horn controls may be hard to find in an emergency. • Rear head restraints appear to be too low to protect occupants. **2004**—Sudden stalling and total loss of power while driving. • Airbag deploys when passing over railroad tracks. • Small original-equipment wheels and tires make the car unstable at high speeds or when cornering. • Automatic transmission downshifts abruptly or won't shift at all. **2005**—Fire ignites in the engine compartment. • Fuel sloshes out from the fuel-filler pipe. • Rear window shattered as one car was warming up. **2007**—Sudden acceleration. • One car sped forward when parking in a garage. **2007–08**—Passenger-side airbag is disabled even though seat occupant is an adult. **2008**—Vehicle "wobbles" when driven. • Motor surges when vehicle stops at a stoplight.• Front bumper spoiler flew off while one car was underway. • Turn signal switch malfunctions. • Groundhogs love to snack on Hyundai wiring:

My 2008 Accent I bought in February has groundhog problems. Two weeks ago, I saw a groundhog go under my car and several times after. About ten days ago, the transmission would stay in First gear and would not shift (when starting). When it finally did shift, at about 4K rpm, the transmission would remain in the higher gears. Trying to stop from a dead stop is quite slow. The Check Engine light also came on. I took the car into the dealer's. The repair man said that 3 of the cables were chewed. One for the trans., one for the brake level indicator, and one for the speedometer. The damage was not covered by Hyundai's warranty. They replaced the wires at $402.00. It's eight days later. I've lost the speedometer cable. For some reason these wires attract groundhogs.

2009—Airbags failed to deploy. Vehicle suddenly accelerated when driver braked for a red light. Transmission slipped out of Fourth gear into Neutral. Brake pedal sinks to the floor when braking. Over-responsive steering causes extensive wandering. **2010**—Excessive steering vibration and shudder believed to be caused by faulty motor mounts. • Brake failure following passing over a bump in the road. • Brakes don't work well on wet roads. • Brakes squeak, grind, and jerk car to the right when applied. • Inside walls of the Kumho Solus front tires wear out prematurely.

Secret Warranties/Internal Bulletins/Service Tips

1999–2004—A defective pulse generator may cause harsh, delayed, and erratic shifting, says TSB #03-40-022. • A TSB published in March 2004 says many automatic transmission breakdowns can be traced to faulty transaxle solenoids. **1999–2008**—Troubleshooting tips on correcting a steering pull or drift to one side and silencing a steering pump whine. **2000–06**—Automatic transaxle oil leak behind the torque converter. **2002**—Harsh or delayed automatic transmission shifting. **2006–09**—Silencing a creaking idle (manual transmissions) by replacing the clutch release lever fulcrum and applying grease to the clutch release bearing. **2007**—Remedy for a rough cold start/idle. • Free replacement of the clutch pedal ignition lock switch (service campaign T38). • Free Engine Control Module update. **2007–09**—Troubleshooting tips for a rough idle. **2008**—Sunroof clicking or ticking.

ACCENT PROFILE

	2002	2003	2004	2005	2006	2007	2008	2009	2010
Cost Price ($)									
L/GS	12,395	12,395	12,895	12,995	12,995	13,495	14,295	13,595	13,599
GL 4d	13,795	13,795	14,195	13,995	13,495	14,295	15,745	15,295	15,299
Used Values ($)									
L/GS ▲	2,500	2,500	3,000	3,500	4,500	5,500	7,000	8,500	9,500
L/GS ▼	2,000	2,000	2,500	3,000	3,500	4,500	6,000	7,000	8,500

	GL 4d ▲								
GL 4d ▲	3,500	4,000	4,500	5,000	5,500	6,000	7,500	9,000	10,000
GL 4d ▼	3,000	3,500	4,000	4,500	5,000	5,500	6,500	8,000	9,000
Reliability	1	1	4	4	5	5	5	5	5
Crash Safety (F)	4	—	5	5	—	—	—	—	—
4d	4	4	4	4	5	5	5	5	5
Offset	—	—	—	—	3	3	3	3	3
Side	—	3	4	4	4	—	—	—	—
4d	3	3	5	5	5	4	4	4	4
IIHS Side	—	—	—	—	1	1	1	1	1
Head Restraints	3	—	—	1	1	1	1	1	3
Roof Strength	—	—	—	—	3	3	3	3	3
Rollover Resistance	4	4	4	4	4	4	4	4	4

ELANTRA ★★★★★

RATING: Recommended (2007–10); Above Average (1999–2006). Named "Car of the Year" for 2012 (now, how'd that happen?). Asian quality on the cheap. Hyundai's Elantra has quietly gone about its business since 1991 providing reliable and cheap transportation for frugal car buyers. Now in its fifth generation, Elantra rivals the Japanese in quality and is generally much better than what Detroit offers. Another important advantage is that the Accent and Elantra fly under the radar for most buyers, meaning that more of them are available and they're much more reasonably priced than better-known Japanese brands. **Ideal model year:** For about $7,000, look for a 2007 GLS equipped with side curtain airbags, electronic stability control, and an unexpired warranty. If not available, go for a 2008 version. **"Real" city/highway fuel economy:** *Manual:* 8.9/6.4 L/100 km. *Automatic:* 9.6/6.7 L/100 km. **Maintenance/repair costs:** Average. Dealer servicing has improved considerably, and independent garages find the Elantra's simple mechanical layout quite easy to diagnose and service. **Parts:** Reasonably priced and easily found. **Extended warranty:** Yes, for the transmission, mainly. **Best alternatives:** Honda Civic or Accord; Hyundai Accent; Mazda3, Mazda5, or Protegé; Nissan Sentra; Suzuki Aerio, Esteem, or Swift; and Toyota Echo or Corolla. **Helpful websites:** *www.hyundaiforum.com.*

Strengths and Weaknesses

This conservatively styled, "high-end" front-drive sedan is a credible alternative to GM Saturns and the Mazda Protegé, Nissan Sentra, and Toyota Corolla. The redesigned 1996 and 2007 versions actually narrow the size, handling, and performance gap with the segment leader, Honda's Civic.

There is some excessive body lean when cornering, but overall handling is fairly good. Brakes are adequate, though sometimes difficult to modulate. Conservative styling makes the Elantra look a bit like an underfed Accord, but there's plenty of room for four average-sized occupants.

VEHICLE HISTORY: 2002—Debut of a GT hatchback. **2003**—The GT adds a four-door sedan. **2005**—A new base GLS hatchback comes online. **2006**—The sporty GT sedan is gone; front side airbags are standard, but no side curtain airbags. **2007**—Totally redesigned, restyled, and better-equipped, with more standard safety features. Elantra now comes only as a four-door sedan and gains width and height on a larger wheelbase. All models use a 4-cylinder engine with a manual transmission or an optional 4-speed automatic. ABS is standard, but traction control has been dropped. Side curtain airbags and front side airbags are now standard. **2008**—Given electronic stability control and brake assist; no more Limited version.

As with most Hyundai products, transmission failures are commonplace and have been the subject of numerous service bulletins (see the Accent "Secret Warranties/Internal Bulletins/Service Tips") and recalls. Airbag failures are another frequent complaint. Other problem areas include body deficiencies (fit, finish, and assembly), a leaking sunroof, paint cracking, engine misfire, oil leaks (some oil burning), hard starting, and warped brake rotors. The passing power in post-'95 automatics is perpetually unimpressive, and the trunk's narrow opening makes for a relatively small storage space.

That being said, the above-noted problems are in no way as severe or as frequent as what you would find with much of the Detroit competition.

The 2001–06 Elantras are noted for chronic stalling; early manual transmission clutch burnout; prematurely worn-out rear brake drums, cylinders, and shoes; and excessive brake noise and chassis vibration. Brake rotors are particularly vulnerable to rusting and premature wearout.

Owners also complain of tire thumping, paint/clearcoat cracking, delayed window defrosting, the dash front-panel console squeaking, rainwater seeping in under the door, the steering-wheel covering peeling away, a humming noise emanating from the corners of the windshield, and wind howling in the interior when encountering a crosswind.

Problems reported on the 2007–08 Elantras relate mostly to airbag malfunctions, early brake repairs, and a faulty fuel delivery system that causes frequent stalling. Body squeaks and rattles are still omnipresent. 2009–10 vehicles are mostly afflicted with airbag, brake, and powertrain problems.

 ## Safety Summary

All years: Airbags fail to deploy, or deploy for no reason. • Chronic stalling. • Erratic transmission shifting and excessive noise. • Sudden brake loss. • Warped front brake rotors, and master cylinder failure. • Gas and brake pedals are mounted too close together. • Passenger seat belt retracts and locks so that passengers are unable to move. **2002**—Seatback failure when one car was rear-ended. • While driving in a rainstorm, all interior and exterior lights shut off. **2003**—Engine surging while on the highway. • Headlights will read "dim" but will actually be on high. • Distracting windshield glare. • Seat belts fail to lock. **2004**—Under-hood fire. • Many complaints that the passenger-side front airbag is disabled when an average-sized adult is seated; recall doesn't correct the problem for all claimants. • Engine surging. • Stabilizer bar snaps, causing vehicle to fishtail. • In one incident, passenger seat collapsed in a frontal collision at moderate speed. • In another, the roof buckled while the car was underway. • Seat belt extenders not available. **2004–05**—Sudden, unintended acceleration. **2005**—Rear brake wheel-cylinder fluid leaks. **2005–06**—Faulty sensor continues to disable airbag when the seat is occupied; it is designed to disable the system only when an underweight occupant is seated. **2006**—Seat belt fails to lock in a collision. • Automatic transmission slippage. • Snow builds up in the wheels, causing severe vibration above 50 km/h. • Excessive vibration reported for other reasons. • Sunroof explodes for no reason. • Frequent headlight failures. • Faulty speedometer. **2007**—Car suddenly accelerates while parking. • Rear end sways, especially when carrying a full load. • Camber settings make the car oversteer. • Transmission shift lever locks in Drive or Park. • Seatback collapses in a collision. • Passenger seat belt may not unlatch. • Brake light suddenly goes out. **2008**—Sudden acceleration (sticking throttle sensor). • Gas pedal sticks under the floor mat. • Cruise control often resets itself at a much higher speed. • Car suddenly shuts off while underway, especially when turning; brakes don't work. • Airbag alert comes on for no discernable reason. • Chronic stalling continues even after fuel pump recall. • Horn cuts out. • Faulty brake light switch prevents shifting; earlier models were recalled for this problem. • Car doesn't downshift properly. • Emergency brakes don't hold the car on a hill. • Batteries frequently lose their charge. • Sudden steering loss. • Tire pressure sensor gives false alerts. **2009**—Airbags failed to deploy. • Gas pedal can get stuck under the floormat. • Stalling out due to a faulty fuel injector. • Brakes lock up when driving on loose, wet snow. • Vehicle oversteers when making steering corrections. • Inner sides of the front tires wear out prematurely. • Owners say original-equipment Solus all-weather tires constantly slide and lose contact with the road, causing the ABS to repeatedly engage. **2010**—Sudden unintended acceleration. • Airbags deployed for no reason. • Cruise control would not deactivate. • A sharp steering correction may make the car swerve out of control. • Suspension causes the car to bounce excessively, pull to the right side, and fishtail. • Windy conditions will cause the car to rock from side to side. • Blown head gasket at 29,000 km (18,000 miles). • Electric power steering failures. • Car continuously pulls to the right. • Water leaks from windshield area behind the dash and accumulates on the floor. • Premature tire failure. • Trunk lid opens by itself:

> My trunk opened suddenly many times over the past 10 months – either while driving and/or in the garage. Once where it was parked for four days and resulted in the battery discharging fully.

Secret Warranties/Internal Bulletins/Service Tips

2001–06—Automatic transmission delayed/harsh shifting into Park or Drive. **2002–04**—Poor engine performance when driving in high-altitude regions may require an upgraded fuel pump. **2003**—Corrosion in the front-door wiring connector. **2006–07**—Remedy for harsh/delayed transmission shifts. **2007**—Automatic transmission cannot be shifted into or out of Park. • Windshield water leaks are covered by a secret warranty:

CAMPAIGN T39—POTENTIAL WINDSHIELD WATER LEAK	
BULLETIN NO.: 07-01-004-2	DATE: FEBRUARY 2007

Elantra 2007
SUBJECT: Windshield glass water leak (Service Campaign T39).
IMPORTANT: Dealers must perform this campaign on all affected vehicles prior to customer retail delivery and whenever an affected vehicle is in the shop for any maintenance or repair.

2007–09—Silencing accelerator cable noise. • If the automatic transmission defaults into "limp home" Third gear, the transaxle solenoids could be faulty. • A front end noise heard when passing over bumps signals that front struts probably need to be changed.

ELANTRA PROFILE

	2002	2003	2004	2005	2006	2007	2008	2009	2010
Cost Price ($)									
GL	15,295	15,295	15,630	14,995	14,995	15,595	15,895	15,845	18,099
GLS/VE	16,995	16,995	17,525	17,365	17,365	23,095	20,595	20,595	20,999
GT	18,495	18,495	19,015	19,895	19,985	—	—	—	—
Touring	—	—	—	—	—	—	—	—	14,999
Used Values ($)									
GL ▲		2,500	3,000	3,500	4,000	5,000	6,500	7,500	10,500	11,500
GL ▼		2,500	2,500	3,000	3,500	4,000	5,000	6,500	9,000	10,500

GLS/VE ▲	3,500	4,500	5,000	5,500	6,000	7,500	10,000	11,500	14,000
GLS/VE ▼	3,000	4,000	4,500	5,000	5,500	6,000	9,000	10,500	13,000
GT ▲	4,000	5,000	5,500	6,000	7,000	—	—	—	—
GT ▼	3,500	4,500	5,000	5,500	6,000	—	—	—	—
Touring ▲	—	—	—	—	—	—	—	—	11,000
Touring ▼	—	—	—	—	—	—	—	—	9,500
Reliability	4	4	4	4	4	5	5	5	5
Crash Safety (F)	4	4	5	5	5	5	5	5	5
Side	3	5	5	6	5	4	4	4	4
IIHS Side	1	1	1	1	1	2	2	2	5
Offset	1	1	5	5	5	5	5	5	5
Head Restraints	1	1	1	1	1	3	3	3	5
Rollover Resistance	—	4	4	4	4	4	4	4	4

Kia

After going bankrupt in 1998, Kia was bought by Hyundai and now sells a full lineup that includes small cars, mid-sized sedans, a minivan, and several sport-utility vehicles. Hyundai's infusion of cash and better-quality components has ratcheted up the quality control on Kia's 2009–10 models and made them relatively dependable performers. Even venerable *Consumer Reports*, never seen as Kia-friendly, now recommends the car. On the other hand, the quality of the Amanti, Sedona, Sorento, and Spectra continues to be caught in a downward spiral.

RIO, RIO5, SPECTRA, SPECTRA5 ★★★

RATING: Average (2009–10); Below Average (2006–08); Not Recommended (2000–05). The 2006–10 and later models have more safety and performance features and are better built. The early Spectras and Rios don't offer even a modicum of the crashworthiness, safety features, performance, or reliability that other cars deliver for the same price or less. **Ideal model year:** The 2009 models are the best of the lot for standard performance and safety features at a reasonable price. **"Real" city/highway fuel economy:** *Manual:* 8.9/6.6 L/100 km. *Automatic:* 9.3/6.7 L/100. **Maintenance/repair costs:** Average. **Parts:** Average costs, and parts are easily found. **Extended warranty:** A bumper-to-bumper warranty is a must-buy on 2008 and earlier models, which wipes out your low sales-price savings. **Best alternatives:** *Rio, Spectra:* Honda Fit or Civic; Hyundai Accent or Elantra; Mazda3 or Protegé; Nissan Sentra; and Toyota Corolla, Echo, Tercel, or Yaris. *Spectra GS-X:* Hyundai Elantra GT; Mazdra3, Mazda5, or Protegé; and VW Golf. **Helpful websites:** *www.kia-forums.com.*

Strengths and Weaknesses

ALERT! A faulty passenger-side airbag sensor disables the front passenger airbag inadvertently on most Kia models built since 2002. If this occurs, demand warranty coverage up to 10 years/100,000 miles (193,000 km). The sensor is part of the supplementary restraint system, and Kia's negligence makes the company liable for the $500 cost both under the written and the implied warranty.

A bit smaller than the earlier Kia Sephia and Spectra, the Rio is one of the cheapest cars on the market and offers both sedan and wagon versions, a limited number of standard safety and performance features, and cheap interior and exterior materials. Versions from 2005 and earlier put a low base price before safety, reliability, and performance.

Rios are equipped with a weak 104 hp 1.6L 4-cylinder engine that gives adequate power only when teamed with a 5-speed manual transmission. Add an automatic transmission, and you'll need an hourglass to clock your speed. Options available include a 4-speed automatic transaxle; ABS; air conditioning; power steering, door locks, and windows; and fog lights. Side airbags are offered on only the most recent models.

Rios are highly manoeuvrable in city traffic and quite fuel efficient, but early models equipped with the 1.5L 4-cylinder engine are poorly suited for most driving tasks, and crashworthiness scores have been a mixed bag.

Rio owners report problems with the automatic transmission, seat belts, and electrical and fuel systems; frequent front-end alignments; unreliable tires; and weak, prematurely worn, noisy brakes.

Other areas of complaint include a busy, harsh ride; small door openings; small audio controls; a missing remote trunk release; weak and noisy engine performance; problematic entry and exit; slow and imprecise highway handling; low-budget interior materials; an optional tilt steering wheel that doesn't tilt much; limited passenger room, with little rear headroom or legroom; a small dealer network that complicates servicing and warranty performance; a small trunk opening that doesn't take bulky items and doesn't offer a pass-through for large objects; and poor body construction (stagnant water collects in the dash on the 2006 model).

Spectra

The Sephia became the Spectra in 2002, which was replaced by the Forte 2010. This five-passenger four-door came with new styling, an upgraded interior, and a new hatchback/four-door sedan body style based on the Mazda Protegé platform, housing Mazda's 4-cylinder powertrain.

In the spring of 2004, revamped Spectra models arrived with new styling, more power, and additional safety features, but they kept the 2004 designation. The

GSX hatchback is a well-equipped, sporty version of the Spectra, powered by a 125 hp 1.8L engine. It has more storage space and performs adequately on the highway. On the other hand, the engine is quite noisy, braking is subpar, and fit and finish is unbelievably bad.

Spectra owners' litany of complaints is similar to those of Rio owners: chronic stalling and surging, airbag failures, steering malfunctions, premature brake wear, brake failures, and fit and finish that is highlighted by poor-quality materials and slapdash workmanship.

Kia's products, unlike Daewoo's, do have a track record—and it's not good. In fact, *Consumer Reports* commented on the car's debut in its April 1999 New Car edition, "You'd have to search far and wide to find a car that's worse than this small Korean model." And the proportionally large number of safety-related complaints recorded by NHTSA through 2008 confirms *CR*'s early conclusion.

VEHICLE HISTORY: *Rio:* **2006**—A complete redesign gives the car more room, power, and safety features. A four-door hatchback called the Rio5 joins the lineup. The sole engine is a 110 hp 4-cylinder mated with a standard 5-speed manual transmission; a 4-speed automatic is optional. Front side airbags and side curtain airbags are standard, though anti-lock four-wheel disc brakes are optional. *Spectra:* **Mid-2004**—Considerably upgraded. **2005**—The Spectra5 hatchback arrives. **2006**—Standard cruise control on the SX and Spectra5. **2007**—A revised interior and a plug-in for digital audio players.

 Safety Summary

All models/years: Airbags fail to deploy. • Passenger-side airbag is frequently disabled when a normal-sized adult is seated. • Chronic stalling and engine surging. *Rio:* **2002–03**—Sudden steering loss. • No-starts, particularly in cold weather, due to faulty engine computer module. • Premature failure of the engine and transmission. • In damp weather, brakes grab abruptly and won't release, or they don't "catch" at all. • Steering-column bolt snaps. • Seat belt cuts across the driver's and passenger's throats. **2004**—Mass airflow sensor failures are the likely cause of chronic stalling. **2005**—Airbag deploys for no reason. • Child safety door lock failure (door could not be opened). **2007**—Sudden brake failure. **2008**—Sudden unintended acceleration. • Stalling caused by defective coil packs. Coil packs and the catalytic converter must be replaced under warranty. • Automatic transmission sticks in Third gear. Excessive brake fade when there are three occupants in the car. • Brakes lock up for no reason. • Steering suddenly locked up when going around a curve. • Premature failure of the lower ball joints and control arms. Heater blows cold air at idle. • Right rear passenger window shattered when the driver's door was closed. **2009**—Blown engine head gasket at 51,000 km (32,000 miles). • Automatic transmission won't shift out of Fourth gear. • Spongy brakes. Car unexpectedly veered off the road into a ditch. • Owners report tie-rod and ball joint failures while turning. • When it rains, water seeps through the inside trim on the passenger side where the airbag logo is found.

—ABS is activated whenever the brakes are applied, not just when needed. • Vehicle continuously drifts to the left when underway. Out-of-round Hankook Optimo original equipment tires. *Spectra:* **2005**—Steering locks up. • Defective tie-rods, struts, and sway bar linkage cause the vehicle to constantly pull to one side. • Key sticks in the ignition. • Cigarette lighter pops out of its housing and can start a fire in the cabin. • Front seat belt latches detach on their own. • Headlights frequently burn out. **2006**—One vehicle's side airbag deployed as door was closing. • Stalling caused by faulty alternators or malfunctioning engine computer. • Rear brakes suddenly lock up while cruising on the highway. *Rio:* **2007**—Engine fire ignites while vehicle is underway. • Sudden acceleration when brakes are applied. • Leaking gas tank; chronic stalling:

> Problems with the fuel tank and purge canister system. The normal operation of fueling the vehicle can cause the purge system to become filled with fuel. This created a dangerous situation by allowing fuel to be expelled or leak out of the tank or what the dealer called overflow onto the floor in my garage.

• Sudden brake loss. • Brake lights stay on after releasing the brake pedal, or don't come on at all. • Driver's side floor mats are not securely anchored. • Doors lock on their own:

> The contact exited the vehicle and shut the door with the keys still in the ignition. After a few seconds, all of the doors locked automatically with her 11-month-old child still in the vehicle.

• AC can leak Freon. • Faulty sway bar links. **2008**—Fire ignites in battery/fuse box area. • Airbag is disabled when the passenger seat is occupied. • Parking lights come on after vehicle is exited, causing battery to lose its charge.

Secret Warranties/Internal Bulletins/Service Tips

All models: 2003–04—TSB #013 addresses different remedies for curing hard starts in cold weather (reprogramming software is one field fix). *Rio:* **2006–07**—More remedies for poor cold starts or a rough idle. • Rear seatback may stick in the folded position. **2007**—Electronic control module upgrade to correct a rough idle. • Special campaign to silence rear-door glass-run channel wind noise. **2007–10**—Kia will replace defective weather stripping for free up to five years/160,00 km (100,000 miles) under Campaign SA045. **2008**—Troubleshooting a rough idle. **2009**—"Goodwill" campaign to replace the fuel cap. **2009–10**—How to silence a rear strut creaking noise. *Spectra:* **2006**—Key sticks in the ignition. **2006–07**—Troubleshooting tips for automatic transmission 2–3 gearshift shock, slip, or flare. **2006–08**—Correcting a rough idle. **2009**—"Goodwill" campaign to replace the fuel cap and fix the window crank handle.

	2002	2003	2004	2005	2006	2007	2008	2009	2010
Cost Price ($)									
S/EX	12,095	12,351	12,650	12,995	13,295	13,595	13,995	13,595	13,695
RS	13,095	13,251	13,550	13,995	—	—	—	—	—
Spectra	14,595	14,795	14,995	15,995	15,595	15,995	15,995	15,695	—
GSX	17,595	17,795	17,995	—	—	—	—	—	—
Used Values ($)									
S/EX ▲	1,500	2,000	3,000	3,500	4,500	5,000	6,000	7,500	8,500
S/EX ▼	1,500	1,500	2,500	3,000	4,000	4,500	5,000	6,500	7,500
RS ▲	2,500	3,000	3,500	4,000	—	—	—	—	—
RS ▼	2,000	2,500	3,000	3,500	—	—	—	—	—
Spectra ▲	2,500	3,500	4,000	6,000	7,000	8,500	9,500	10,500	—
Spectra ▼	2,000	3,000	3,500	5,500	6,000	7,500	8,500	9,500	—
GSX ▲	3,000	3,500	5,000	—	—	—	—	—	—
GSX ▼	2,500	3,000	4,000	—	—	—	—	—	—
Reliability	2	2	2	2	3	3	3	3	4
Crash Safety (F)	4	4	4	4	4	4	4	4	4
Spectra	4	4	4	4	4	5	5	5	—
Side	3	2	2	2	4	4	4	4	4
Spectra	3	3	4	4	4	4	4	4	—
IIHS Side	—	—	—	—	1	1	1	1	1
Spectra	—	—	1	1	1	1	2	2	—
Offset	—	—	—	—	3	3	3	3	3
Spectra	—	—	1	3	3	3	3	3	—
Head Restraints	—	—	—	—	1	1	1	1	3
Spectra	—	—	—	3	3	3	3	3	—
Roof Strength	—	—	—	—	3	3	3	3	3
Rollover Resistance	4	4	4	4	4	4	4	4	4

Mazda

MAZDA3, MAZDA5, PROTEGÉ ★★★★★/★★★★★

RATING: *Mazda3*: Recommended (2006–10); Above Average (2004–05). Owner complaints continue to be remarkably few in number. Nevertheless, make sure the AC cools the car sufficiently and the brake calipers and rotors are sound. *Mazda5*: Above Average (2006–10). Many of these small minivans are coming off-lease at bargain prices. *Protegé*: Above Average (1999–2003). These cars are plentiful at bargain prices. **Ideal model year:** A 2007 MazdaSpeed3. This sporty car delivers driving thrills without the garage bay bills. It's lightning-fast, user-friendly, European-stiff, and yet tame enough to handle that ultimate driver's

All ratings on a numbered scale where 5 is good and 1 is bad. See page 132 for a more detailed description.

The Mazda3.

challenge: stop-and-go city traffic. Cost? $30,995 in 2007. Today, you can drive it away for $11,500 to $12,500. Shoppers looking for the best Mazda5 choice should consider the 2008 Mazda5 GT for its sporty powertrain and refined performance. Originally sold for $24,815, it's now worth worth between $10,500 and $12,000. **"Real" city/highway fuel economy:** There isn't a lot of variation in fuel economy among the different model years, except for the turbocharged engine that wastes gas at a rate of 10.0/7.3 L/100 km. Owners say they burn about 10 percent more fuel than the following estimates indicate. *Mazda3 2.0L manual:* 8.5/6.2 L/100 km. *Mazda3 2.0L automatic:* 9.1/6.4 L/100 km. *Mazda3 2.3L manual:* 9.2/6.7 L/100 km. *Mazda3 2.3L automatic:* 9.8/7.5 L/100 km. *Mazda5 2.3L manual:* 10.6/8.0 L/100 km. *Mazda5 2.3L automatic:* 11.2/8.3 L/100 km. *Protegé manual 1.6L:* 8.5/6.7 L/100 km. *Protegé automatic 1.6L:* 9.3/6.9 L/100 km. *Protegé 2.0L manual:* 9.6/7.3 L/100 km. *Protegé 2.0L automatic:* 9.9/7.4 L/100 km. **Maintenance/repair costs:** Average. **Parts:** Reasonably priced and easily found. **Extended warranty:** Not necessary. **Best alternatives:** *Mazda3, Protegé:* Honda Civic; Hyundai Accent or Elantra; Nissan Sentra; Suzuki Aerio, Esteem, or Swift; and Toyota Echo or Corolla. *Mazda5:* Honda Odyssey, Hyundai Entourage, and Kia Sedona. **Helpful websites:** *www.mazdas247.com/forum/index.php.*

 ## Strengths and Weaknesses

ALERT! Although Mazda has made considerable progress in building reliable and well-performing vehicles, its warranty performance in Canada leaves much to be desired when compared with Mazda USA. Kurt Binnie, the owner of a 2007 Mazda6, tells his story:

Mazda Canada tell me that the transmission control module (TCM) is only covered by a 3 year warranty ... not the 5 year powertrain warranty offered in the States. In the US they spell out exactly which components are covered including the TCM. In Canada there's a pathetically small vague paragraph on what's covered. I was quoted a price of $1,500 plus labour.

After doing some research and balking at Mazda's "offer," they relented and covered the TCM under warranty and charged me $200 labour. I wonder how many owners would have simply paid up and shut up? (See *www. autos.ca/forum/index.php/topic,77195.0.html.*)

Protegé

Although 1996–2003 Protegés are far more reliable than most American-made small cars, automatic transmissions are their weakest link (a problem also seen with Ford's Escort and Hyundai's lineup), characterized by erratic shifting and locking up in Fifth gear. Owners also endure fuel-system glitches, electrical problems, front brake vibration, rotor warping, and premature pad wear. Other generic deficiencies are weak rear defrosting, chronic engine stalling (a secret warranty applies, up to seven years), AC failures, and body defects, including wind and water leaks into the interior.

Mazda3

An econobox with flair, the front-drive 2004 Mazda3 is the entry-level small car that replaced the Protegé. With considerable engineering help from Ford and Volvo, these cars use a platform and 4-cylinder engines that will also serve future iterations of the Ford Focus and Volvo S40. These pocket rockets are powered by three different 4-cylinder powerplants: a base 148 hp 2.0L, a 167 hp 2.5L, or a 263 hp 2.3L 4 turbo. Coupled with either a 5-speed manual or a 4-speed Sport-mode automatic transmission, the car offers spirited acceleration and smooth, sporty shifting. Handling is enhanced with a highly rigid body structure, front and rear stabilizer bars, a multi-link rear suspension, and four-wheel disc brakes. Interior room is also quite ample with the car's relatively long 263.9 cm (103.9 in.) wheelbase, extra width, and straight sides, which maximize headroom, legroom, and shoulder room.

The Mazda3 is a breeze to break into. Bizarre, but true—all it takes is a blow to the door on either side of any 2004–07 model, and the lock pops. The Internet is full of reports telling how easily the cars and their contents are stolen..

Mazda3 owner complaints are about average in number, which is still too high for a vehicle that is this simply made. There are some electrical shorts as well as numerous minor fit and finish deficiencies, and sporadic reports of prematurely worn-out transmission clutch assemblies. The rear seats provide limited footroom; the high deck reduces rear visibility; early brake pad and rotor replacements continue unabated; some drivers say the car's standard engine could use more passing power; and some Mazda dealers have been accused of overcharging for scheduled maintenance. Other reported problems: dashboards crack; window regulators break; the steering box makes a clicking/ticking sound; the dash and driver's door rattle; AC performance is wimpy; the driver's right knee rubs the console; there's excess brake dust on rear wheels; the Door Ajar light comes on for no reason; the gas and brake pedal are too close together; a front-end clunk is felt on hard acceleration; paint is unusually thin and aluminum rims peel; the passenger-side wiper may not clean the windshield sufficiently; fuel consumption is excessive, about 10 percent more than advertised; the 5-speed manual gearbox sometimes has trouble shifting from First to Second gear; a popping/creaking/rattling noise emanates from the rear end (hatch struts may be the culprit); and drivers easily catch the side of their shoe against the brake when accelerating (consider getting customized racing pedals). Original-equipment and Goodyear tires perform poorly in rain and slush (Michelin Pilot and Hakkapeliitta winter tires are better performers; check with *www.tirerack.com* for the best tire combination).

Mazda5

The Mazda5 is mainly a compact miniwagon that's based broadly on the Mazda3 and carries six passengers in three rows of seats. Used mostly for urban errands and light commuting, the "5" employs a peppy though fuel-frugal 153 hp 2.3L 4-cylinder engine hooked to a standard 5-speed manual transmission or a 4-speed automatic.

Since it debuted as a 2006 model, the Mazda5 has had few problems. It has all the advantages of a small minivan without the handling or fuel penalties. Furthermore, it's reasonably priced used and provides a comfortable ride and relatively quiet interior (except for omnipresent road noise—a common trait with small wagons). There are a few minuses, however. The small 4-cylinder engine doesn't have much torque for heavy loads or hill climbing, and towing isn't recommended. There isn't much room for two passengers in the third-row seat, either. There's also a history of automatic transmission and electrical malfunctions (but much fewer than with Honda or Toyota), prematurely worn-out brake rotors and pads, and fit and finish deficiencies.

NHTSA has received a steady stream of owner complaints concerning transmission malfunctions, the vehicle rolling downhill with the parking brake engaged, poor wet-road traction, and premature tire wear. However, one serious complaint that is repeated dozens of times in NHTSA's logs is the sudden loss of steering on both the Mazda3 and Mazda5. Apparently, both cars have been recalled to correct this defect, but owners say the problem persists.

VEHICLE HISTORY: 2004—Protegé is replaced by the 2004 Mazda3. *Mazda3:* **2004–07**—Mazda3 launches with two 4-cylinder engines: a base 148 hp 2.0L and a 160 hp 2.3L. **2007**—A new performance model equipped with the highly recommended traction/anti-skid control feature. **2010**—Standard head protection airbags. *Mazda5:* **2006**—Mazda5's first model year. **2007**—A more upscale wagon arrives. **2008**—A restyled interior and exterior and a 5-speed automatic transmission.

Safety Summary

All models/years: Airbags fail to deploy. • Chronic stalling. • Transmission failures and malfunctions. • If you stop or park on an incline, vehicle will likely roll away even with brakes applied. • Metal rods in driver's seat could cause severe back injuries in a rear-end collision. • Brake pedal pad is too narrow. **All models: 2003**—Brake pedal pushed almost to the floor before brakes work; they produce excessive noise. *Mazda3:* **2004**—Premature wearout of brake pads and rotors. • The transmission can be hard to shift, especially from Third to Fourth gear. • Transmission needs replacing during the first year. • Huge accumulation of brake dust on the rear wheels. • Brake rotors are prematurely grooved. • Chronic hard starts, stalling, and poor idling. **2004–05**—AC is inadequate; it doesn't cool the car and compromises acceleration. **2005**—When car stalls on the highway, both steering and brakes fail. • Brake failures. **2006**—Sudden acceleration when using the cruise control. • Engine failure due to defective lower engine rod. • Vehicle goes into Reverse when shifted into Fourth gear. • Brake and accelerator pedal mounted too close together. • Early rear brake pad and rotor replacement. • On one occasion, driver's seatback collapsed in a rear collision. • Tire rims are easily damaged when passing over potholes. **2007**—Gas tank puncture. • Warped front brake rotors. • Large rear blind spot. • Xenon headlights provide poor visibility. • Sudden failure of the MazdaSpeed3 engine:

> MazdaSpeed3 2007 has been having problems with engine mounting failures. It seems the engine mount is not bolted correctly or the bolt itself to the engine is defective. Mazda3 Forums [h]as some picture[s] provided by actual consumers who had this [happen] to their cars: *www.mazda3forums.com/index.php?topic=68463.0.*

2008—Parking brake won't hold the car on an incline. • Original-equipment Goodyear Eagle all-season tires don't give sufficient traction and wear out quickly. • Incorrect negative rear camber setting causes rear tires to wear out prematurely. • ABS goes on and off. • Power steering failure:

> In the power steering system the fuse that controls this valve blew for the first time on May 11, 2009. It has blown 2 additional times, including today in rush hour traffic. Unlike other manufacturers, when this fuse blows, the valve closes, cutting off all flow to the rack, disabling the power assist.

Fuel cap sticks. • Severe engine and steering wheel shake • Cabin air may be contaminated by toxic gases:

> I bought a 2008 Mazda3 4 months ago. The car began making me sick—bad headaches and loss of concentration.... I sent for a formaldehyde testing kit from a lab and tested the car after driving and getting really sick. The results came back positive with a .075 ppm (almost exact FEMA trailer litigation average).

Recalled steering repair parts are unavailable, for many. • Mazda aluminum tire valve stems are weak, vulnerable to corrosion, and will interfere with the low-pressure alert feature. • Gas cap seizing. **2010**—Serious water buildup in Mazda lights; bulbs are shorted out. • Premature clutch failure. • Driver's seat rocks fore and aft. • Early corrosion of tire valve stems. • Tire pressure warning light is constantly on. • Jack bent when used to lift the car. • Excessive rear suspension noise. • Excessive rear tire wear due to Mazda suspension design. *Mazda5:* **2006**—Driver's seat collapses in a rear-end collision. • Chronic engine overheating (faulty AC compressor?). • Hesitation when shifting. • Stalling in traffic believed to be caused by a defective PCM. • Leaking casing requires a transmission replacement. • Brake failures. • Sudden power-steering failure. • Leaking front struts. • Shocks, front stabilizer bushing, and damper wear out early. • AC compressor failure. • Doors freeze shut. **2007**—Car parked 3 metres from the house with the engine running suddenly accelerated, damaging the house. • Third-row safety belt anchor is placed too far forward to secure the passenger. • Fob-controlled door locks don't work. **2008**—Loose bolts in the rear right suspension. • Premature rear tire wear ("cupping"). • Power steering goes out sporadically. • Floor mat can catch the clutch pedal during gear changes. • Sunroof suddenly explodes while closed. **2009**—Engine compartment fire caused by improper length of wire in harness causing a loose connection to the controller unit. • Gas pedal stuck three times. • Frequent sudden power steering failures that return to normal if the car is restarted. • Parked vehicle rolled down a hill even though the emergency brake was applied. • Loose nut connecting the right rear anti-sway bar to the suspension. • Goodyear Eagle RS tires perform poorly in light snow conditions. • Broken fuel cap is a common problem.

Secret Warranties/Internal Bulletins/Service Tips

All models: 1999–2007—Troubleshooting tips for eliminating wind noise around windows. *Mazda3:* **2004**—Poor AC performance. • Mazda-upgraded shock absorbers will reduce suspension knocking when passing over bumps. • A splashing sound comes from the dash area. • Trunk lid difficult to open. • Power-window failures require a new window motor. • Fix for squeaking rear brakes. **2004–05**—Hard starts and poor idle are tackled in TSB #01-013/0. • Engine stalls at low rpms. • Possible causes for a noisy, smelly engine coming from any Mazda3 equipped with a manual transmission. • Installing countermeasure washers can stop drivetrain clicking. • Excessive engine vibration fix. • Rear brake squeal and grinding has been remedied with upgraded brake pads, says TSB #04-003/05. • Modified pads and a mounting support for the front brake calipers to correct front brake squeaking. • Front-door rattle correction guidelines. • One-touch window stops halfway down. **2004–06**—Hard starts in cold weather require a software recalibration. • Rough idle and engine hesitation. • Troubleshooting a snap or clunk noise when operating the windows. **2004–07**—Body vibration at cruising speed. • High power-steering effort. • Corroded wiper arm hinges. • Inability to adjust driver-seat manual lift. **2004–08**—No-start in Park. • Manual transmission grinding noise; pops out of gear. • Rough idle; engine stalls. • How to deal with brake noise, judder, and dragging. **2004–09**—Engine knocking noise on start or shutdown. • Front power window noise. • Cracked centre dash. • Vibration at cruising speed can be eliminated by installing countermeasure engine mount rubbers made by Mazda. This should be a free "goodwill" repair because the problem is of Mazda's own making. • Water in lights. **2004–10**—Front head restraint rattling. **2006–07**—Idle dip when AC cycles on. • Engine stalls or hesitates after a hot start (reprogram the PCM). **2006–08**—Coolant leaks. **2006–09**—AC no longer cools after a long drive. **2007–08**—Measures to correct difficult steering. • Clunking brakes. **2007–09**—High steering effort. **2007–11**—Remedy for front brake judder and excessive condensation in the headlamps. • Correction for a clunk or bang brake noise heard when vehicle is just starting out. **2008**—Silencing a ticking noise from the purge solenoid valve. **2009**—Engine oil leak between the engine and the automatic transmission bell housing. • Excessive noise generated by the manual transmission. *Mazda5:* **2004–08**—Moisture in lights. **2004–09**—Engine vibration at cruising speed. • **2006–07**—Stiff steering. • Intermittent engine stumble. • Engine stalls at low rpms. • Idle fluctuation and engine vibration. • Body vibration at cruising speeds. • Front suspension squeak, knock, or rattle. **2006–08**—Clunking brakes. • Rough idle, stalling. • Eliminating brake noise, judder, and dragging. **2006–09**—Engine knocking noise on start or shutdown. • AC no longer cools after a long drive. **2006–10**—Front/rear knock or rattle when driving over bumps • Front power window noise. • Front head restraint rattling. **2006–11**—Engine vibration at cruising speed. • Correction for a clunk or bang brake noise heard when vehicle is just starting out. **2006–12**—Troubleshooting excessive condensation in the headlamps. **2008**—Coolant leaks. **2008–12**—Remedy for front brake judder.

MAZDA3, MAZDA5, PROTEGÉ PROFILE

	2002	2003	2004	2005	2006	2007	2008	2009	2010
Cost Price ($)									
Protegé	15,795	15,795	—	—	—	—	—	—	—
Mazda3	—	—	16,195	16,295	16,495	16,795	16,895	14,895	15,995
MazdaSpeed3	—	—	—	—	—	30,995	31,095	29,360	32,995
Mazda5 GS	—	—	—	—	19,995	19,995	20,795	19,995	20,495
Mazda5 GT	—	—	—	—	22,795	22,895	24,815	23,295	24,295
Used Values ($)									
Protegé ▲	3,000	4,000	—	—	—	—	—	—	—
Protegé ▼	2,500	3,000	—	—	—	—	—	—	—
Mazda3 ▲	—	—	4,500	5,500	6,500	7,500	9,000	10,000	11,500
Mazda3 ▼	—	—	4,000	4,500	5.500	6,500	8,000	9,000	10,000
MazdaSpeed3 ▲	—	—	—	—	—	12,500	14,000	18,000	20,500
MazdaSpeed3 ▼	—	—	—	—	—	11,500	13,000	16,000	19,000
Mazda5 GS▲	—	—	—	—	7,000	8,500	10,000	12,500	15,000
Mazda5 GS▼	—	—	—	—	6,000	7,500	9,000	11,000	13,500
Mazda5 GT▲	—	—	—	—		9,500	11,500	13,500	17,000
Mazda5 GT ▼	—	—	—	—		8,000	10,000	12,000	15,500
MAZDA3									
Reliability	5	5	3	4	4	4	5	5	5
Crash Safety (F)	5	5	4	4	4	4	4	4	5

All ratings on a numbered scale where 5 is good and **1** is bad. See page 132 for a more detailed description.

Side	3	3	3	3	3	3	3	—	5
IIHS Side	—	—	—	1	1	1	1	—	5
Offset	3	5	5	5	5	5	5	—	5
Head Restraints (F)	3	3	2	2	2	2	2	2	5
Rollover Resistance	—	4	4	4	4	4	4	4	4

MAZDA5

Reliability	—	—	—	—	—	—	4	5	5
Crash Safety (F)	—	—	—	—	—	—	5	5	5
Side	—	—	—	—	—	—	5	5	5
Rollover Resistance	—	—	—	—	—	—	4	4	4

PROTÉGÉ

Reliability	3	4	—	—	—	—	—	—	—
Crash Safety (F)	5	5	—	—	—	—	—	—	—
Side	3	3	—	—	—	—	—	—	—
Offset	3	3	—	—	—	—	—	—	—
Rollover Resistance	—	4	—	—	—	—	—	—	—

Nissan

SENTRA ★★★★

RATING: Above Average (2007–10); Average (2001–06). The pre-2007 Sentras have been downgraded for their numerous safety and quality problems. Note the below-average side and head-restraint crashworthiness scores up to the 2006 models. **Ideal model year:** A 2010 base model for $10,000. **"Real" city/highway fuel economy:** *Manual 1.8L:* 8.5/6.1 L/100 km. *Automatic 1.8L:* 8.3/6.2 L/100 km. *Manual 2.5L:* 10.2/7.3 L/100 km. *Automatic 2.5L:* 10.2/7.7 L/100 km. **Maintenance/repair costs:** Average; anyone can repair these cars, although the high-performance versions require special skill and diagnostic software. **Parts:** Easily found and reasonably priced. Owners report slow delivery of recalled parts. **Extended warranty:** Not needed. **Best alternatives:** Honda Civic; Hyundai Elantra or Tiburon; Mazda3 or Protegé; Suzuki Esteem or Swift; and Toyota Echo or Corolla. High-performance enthusiasts should consider Sentra's 2007 and later SE-R and Spec V models, although the Honda Civic Si and MazdaSpeed are still the benchmark for the most performance for your dollar. **Helpful websites:** *http://forums.nicoclub.com/technical.html.*

Strengths and Weaknesses

ALERT! Standard electronic stability control is an important reason to buy a 2010 model, but keep in mind that not all models come with ESC.

The 2003–06 models are plagued by cylinder head gasket leaks; cracked #4 cylinder heads on the 1.8L engine; a misfiring #3 cylinder; early replacement of the engine serpentine belt; engine pinging and rattling; and automatic transmission, fuel-system, and electrical problems.

Front brake pads and rotors also wear out quickly; there's excessive noise, bouncing, and vibration caused by prematurely worn struts and control-arm bushings; the doors vibrate noisily; passenger-side windows leak; the hood allows water to leak onto the drivebelt; rear bumpers may fall off; there is excessive wind noise around the windshield moulding; and a poor AC design wastes fuel.

The 2007–09 Sentras are much improved from a quality control and crashworthiness standpoint, but some serious problems remain and new ones have appeared. The CVT is smooth and usually very responsive (though cold weather may adversely affect its performance), the ride is more comfortable, the interior trim has gone upscale, there are handy flip-forward rear-seat cushions and flat-folding rear seatbacks, and more attention has been paid to fit and finish. On the minus side, get used to limited passing power on the highway with base models, excessive engine noise in the higher revs, numb steering, mediocre manual shifting, instrument gauges that wash out in sunlight, and tight rear seating.

Quality is still problematic. Owners report that the engine may overheat without any warning lights coming on, or that the front brake calipers and warped brake rotors require frequent replacing. As well, fuel-delivery system glitches and poor acceleration with CVT may cause a loss of power, hard starting, and stalling. Other problems: power steering failures, defective rear beam axles, and premature rear tire wear due to faulty rear alignment.

VEHICLE HISTORY: 2002—The 145 hp SE model was replaced at the top of the line by the SE-R and SE-R Spec V; the latter offers a 180 hp engine, a limited-slip differential, and a sport-tuned suspension to compete against the Honda Civic SiR and Mazda's high-performance spin-offs. Four-wheel disc brakes also become a standard feature. **2003**—Arrival of the GXE, equipped with ABS, a 165 hp 2.5L engine, and front side airbags. **2007**—Redesigned with fresh styling, more power, a longer wheelbase, and added standard features, such as AC, side curtain airbags, four-wheel disc brakes (Spec V), ABS on higher-end models, a 6-speed manual transmission, an automatic CVT (2.0 SL), a 140 hp 2.0L that boosts horsepower by 14, and a sizzling 177 hp 2.5L 4-cylinder powerplant (SE-R) that's pumped up to 200 horses on the Spec V. **2009**—Standard anti-lock brakes. **2010**—Vehicle stability control and traction control available on 2.0 and 2.0 S models, standard on 2.0 SL and SE-R models.

 Safety Summary

All years: Airbags fail to deploy or deploy inadvertently. • Chronic stalling. • Sudden acceleration. • Complete brake failures. • Brake and accelerator pedals are set too close together. • Steering lock-up or failures. • Brakes don't last. • Horn blows on its own. **2004**—Erratic, rough idling. • Early automatic transmission replacement. • Keyless remote doesn't work, and back door doesn't open from the inside, apparently due to a short in the electrical system. **2005**—Rear wheel lock-up. • Warped rear brake drums. • Front seatback collapsed from a rear-end collision. • Frequent horn malfunctions. • Inoperative driver's door handle. **2006**—Automatic transmission stays in Neutral, or slips out of gear. • Door locks with the keys in the ignition. • Faulty front wheel bearings. • Defective window regulators. • Gas tank pressure forces fuel out of the tank. **2007**—One vehicle caught fire while driving on the highway. • Broken motor mounts and steering-column bolts (steering wheel turns without effect). • Cracked engine block. • Frequent power steering failures. • False illumination of the Low Tire Pressure light. • Poorly designed crossmember eats tires. **2008**—Vehicle bangs into gear after hesitating. • Rear-end toe out cannot be adjusted, making the rear end unstable on wet roads and gouging out the rear tires:

> I noticed the rear wheels tilt in at the top, especially the left rear wheel, at least 5 degrees negative camber (I am an insurance auto appraiser). It also appears to have slight [toe] in. This is a fixed non-adjustable beam axle that was set up wrong in the assembly jig and welded up wrong. After some research, [I discovered] this affects 07 and 08 models. The tires will wear out quickly on the inside of the tread (not too noticeable from the outside of the car), and may blow out. At best I will be replacing rear tires all the time.

Front struts wear out quickly. • Faulty original-equipment Bridgestone tires:

> Anyone with these tires should do a Google search of "Bridgestone Turanza problems" and "Bridgestone Turanza EL400 complaints." I have seen complaints from Toyota, BMW, Mercedes, Honda, and Nissan owners about these tires.

Tire Pressure warning sensor often comes on for no reason. • Seat belt buckle snaps back with excessive force, injuring occupants. • Bottom of the windshield is distorted. • Faulty rear-view mirror design:

> Blinded by the early morning sun and automatically reached for my sun visor. When I tried to pull it down it hit the rear view mirror and stopped in a position that blocked my entire forward view except for a few feet.

2009—Car accelerated forward even with driver's foot on the brake. • Front passenger airbag isn't disabled when a child is seated in the front seat. • Owners say vehicle swerves too much on the freeway. • Bridgestone Turanza tires keep setting off the low-tire-pressure sensor. **2010**—Car suddenly accelerated in Reverse. • Tie-rod snapped while parking. • Engine replaced at 59,200 km. • Engine surging. • Stalling/no-start recall parts not available. • Back end fishtails when cornering and bounces around over bumps:

> While exiting the highway and turning at approximately 35 mph [56 km/h], the contact drove over a road bump and the rear of the vehicle began excessively swerving from left to right. The rear wheels were lifted from the ground.

Loss of steering. • Car shuts down repeatedly due to electronic computer unit failures.

Secret Warranties/Internal Bulletins/Service Tips

2000–04—TSB #AT04-002, published March 10, 2004, says abnormal shifting of the automatic transmission is likely due to a defective control valve assembly. **2000–06**—Front-door windows may not work properly. **2002–05**—A 2–3 shift chirping noise can be silenced by pouring in two bottles of Nissan's special ATF transmission treatment fluid. Do this first, before spending big bucks on unneeded repairs, inspections, etc. **2004–08**—Leaking tire pressure sensors. **2005**—Fix for cold engine stumbling and stalling. **2007**—Doors are hard to open with the outside handle in cold weather. • Hard-to-close trunk lid. **2007–08**—AC compressor noise, poor cooling, and window fogging. **2007–09**—Coolant leaks from reservoir hoses. • Steering, suspension pop or clunk when turning. • Fixing an erratically operating sunroof. • Inoperative power-window "Auto Up" function. • Squeaking front seats. • Loose door weather stripping. **2007–10**—Diagnostic steps to troubleshoot drivebelt noise. • Radio stays on with ignition off. • Front seat creaking. **2007–11**—Erratic fuel gauge readings usually indicate a need to replace the fuel-level sensor unit. **2008–10**—Loose front seat head restraint. **2010**—Slower than normal acceleration. • Campaign PM053 covers the free replacement of the instrument cluster (the LED lamps don't last). **2010–11**—Trunk lid corrosion below chrome finisher.

SENTRA PROFILE

	2002	2003	2004	2005	2006	2007	2008	2009	2010
Cost Price ($)									
Sentra	15,598	15,598	15,798	15,598	16,698	16,798	16,798	14,798	14,798
SE-R	19,998	20,498	21,498	21,498	21,698	22,798	22,798	20,648	21,798
Spec V	21,498	21,998	21,998	21,998	22,198	24,298	22,798	22,048	23,198
Used Values ($)									
Sentra ▲	2,500	3,500	4,000	5,000	6,000	7,000	8,000	9,000	11,000
Sentra ▼	2,500	3,000	3,500	4,500	5,000	6,500	7,000	8,000	10,000
SE-R ▲	4,500	5,000	6,000	7,000	8,000	9,500	11,000	13,500	15,000
SE-R ▼	4,000	4,500	5,500	6,000	7,000	8,500	10,000	12,000	13,500
Spec V ▲	4,500	5,000	6,000	6,500	8,000	10,000	12,000	14,500	16,500
Spec V ▼	4,000	4,500	5,500	6,000	7,000	9,000	11,000	13,000	15,000
Reliability	3	3	3	3	3	3	4	4	5
Crash Safety (F)	4	4	4	4	4	5	5	5	5
Side	2	2	2	2	5	5	5	5	5
IIHS Side	1	1	1	1	1	5	5	5	3

Offset	3	3	3	3	3	5	5	5	5
Head Restraints	1	1	1	1	1	5	5	5	3
Roof strength	—	—	—	—	—	3	3	3	3
Rollover Resistance	4	4	4	4	4	4	4	4	4

VERSA ★★★

RATING: Average (2007–10). **Ideal model year:** A 2008 SL Hatchback for $5,500–$6,500 will steer you away from first-year production glitches, offer the best performance and fuel economy, likely have some of the original manufacturer's warranty left, and cost less than half what the car sold for new. **"Real" city/highway fuel economy:** 7.9/6.1 L/100 km. Owners have taken to task "puffed up" fuel economy claims. Drivers say that the Versa's fuel consumption is about 10 percent higher than what Canadian government figures show. **Maintenance/repair costs:** Lower-than-average maintenance cost. **Parts:** Easily found and not expensive. Recall campaign parts are slow to arrive. **Extended warranty:** Not needed. **Best alternatives:** Honda Civic or Fit; Hyundai Accent or Elantra; Mazda2, Mazda3, or Protegé; Suzuki Esteem or Swift; and Toyota Corolla or Echo. **Helpful websites:** *http://forums.nicoclub.com* and *www.nissanclub.com/forums/nissan-versa.*

Strengths and Weaknesses

ALERT! Be wary of the Continental Conti original-equipment tires; owners report they are not as durable as the competition:

> My 2010 Nissan Versa, with less than 10,000 miles [16,000 km] on it, has steel belts popping out the sidewalls of the Continental Contipro Contact P195/55 tires. Both front tires have belts popping out.

Also, think twice about buying a Versa with manual door locks:

> My 2010 Nissan Versa 4 door hatchback with manual door locks: only the driver side door can be unlocked from the outside. I had to wait 3 hours before being able to access my car because a van was parked too close on the driver side.

Versa is Nissan's entry-level small hatchback and sedan, first launched as a 2007 model. The 2008–09 models were carried over with few important changes. The 2010 1.8 SL Hatchback returned with standard stability control, an optional feature on the S version. Entry-level versions are powered by a 107 hp 1.6L 4-cylinder engine, while the SL models get a 122 hp 1.8L 4-banger. Coupled to a 6-speed manual transmission or a 4-speed automatic CVT, this small car gives decent fuel economy and a comfortable ride, is easily accessed, and is one of the roomiest econocars on the market. Side curtain airbags are standard, and first-year reliability has been acceptable. On the downside, the manual tranny isn't as smooth as the automatic CVT, handling is only so-so, wind and road noise are annoyingly loud, and brakes squeak continuously.

A 2007 base Versa S Hatchback sold new for $14,498 and is now worth $4,500–$6,000; a 2008 version sells for $6,000–$7,000; a 2009 S will fetch about $6,500–$8,000, and a 2010 now goes for $9,500. An all-dressed 2007 SL Hatchback sold for $17,098 and is now worth $6,000–$7,000; a 2008 will run you $6,500–$8,500; a 2009 is worth between $9,000 and $10,500; and a 2010 sells for approximately $11,000.

NHTSA awarded the 2007 four-door Versa hatchback four stars for occupant protection in a frontal impact, five stars in a side collision, and four stars for rollover prevention, which are better-than-average scores for a small car. 2008–10 hatchbacks and four-door models earned four stars for front, side, and rollover protection. IIHS gave the 2007–10 Versa its top rating for occupant protection in both frontal offset and side collisions and for head-restraint protection.

 ## Safety Summary

2007—A fire ignited in the rear wheelwell of one vehicle. • Airbag cover comes out of the dash. • No brakes. • In one incident, the vehicle shut down while cruising and the airbag deployed, knocking the driver unconscious. • The steering column of another vehicle had to be replaced twice. • Car veers left or right while cruising. • Car suddenly swerves out of control for no apparent reason. • Tie rod suddenly snaps, pulling the vehicle sharply to the right. • Gasoline spurts out of the filler neck when refuelling. **2007–08**—A fire in one vehicle originated in the front console area; other fires reported after the Check Engine light lit. • Vehicle seat belts fail to lock up in a sudden stop. • Airbags don't deploy when they should, or deploy when they shouldn't:

> Suddenly the airbag came out, she was scared, she applied the brakes and the car sped up, and she grabbed the emergency brake lever. The car stopped but she already hit other car, she had to go out through the passenger door.

Driver's side window "guillotine hazard": Express-up window doesn't easily retract and could strangle a child. • Doors lock/unlock on their own. • Many sudden front strut separations (suspension and steering loss). • CVT failures:

> Front axles "click" when making turns. CVT transmission cuts out or stalls when making turns and/or accelerating from a stop. Occurrence is 3–5 [times] weekly. I have taken this vehicle in for service 9–10 times. They have replaced the front axles and transmission with no improvement.

Faulty fuel pump and malfunctioning mass air flow sensor cause total loss of power while underway. • Windshield cracks first appear at the base on the passenger side and move upward. • Inadequate defrosting. • Instrument panel gauges wash out in daylight. • Horn doesn't blow unless it is tapped at exactly the right spot. • Original equipment Continental tire shredding. • Many complaints that the Tire Pressure warning light comes on even though the tires are properly inflated. **2009**—Airbags failed to deploy during a rear-end collision. • Loss of all braking capability. • Poor braking performance on ice. • Frequent replacement of prematurely worn brake rotors and pads. • Hard starts or no-starts even after the fuel pump and fuel pressure regulator were replaced. • Sudden stalling due to a faulty fuel pump. • Heater/defroster failure due to a faulty fan resistor. • Speedometer is difficult to read in daylight. • Vehicle tends to wander on the highway. • Early wearout of original equipment Continental Conti Pro Contact tires. • Tire air pressure sensor failures. • Noisy steering and delayed steering response when turning (see *http://x.nissanhelp.com/forums/versa/3861-versa-turning-right-problem-steering-column.html*). **2010**—Sudden unintended acceleration. Tire pressure alert comes on for no reason. Speedometer hard to see in daylight. Headlights and windshield wiper fail intermittently. Driver-side exterior door handle broke. Car is prone to fishtail. Severe vehicle shake around 80 km/h, and the vehicle wanders all over the road:

> Driving a Nissan Versa is like kayaking through the mirage of gorges...you have to be attentive all the time, it tends to slip to the left side of the road and won't stay in one lane. It is like trying to keep your boat/tube in one straight position while the boat keeps flying away...either left or right.

Secret Warranties/Internal Bulletins/Service Tips

2007—Front airbag cover not flush. • Inoperative driver-door mirror. **2007–08**—Tips on installing a child safety seat. • AC compressor noise and window fogging. • Hard starting; long cranking time. • Front-end pop. • Water leaks onto driver's side floor and front floor carpet. • Squeaking front seats and rear brakes. **2007–09**—A long crank time before starts is traced to a faulty fuel pressure regulator. • Coolant leaks from reservoir hoses. • Water leaks onto driver's side floor. • AC compressor noise in very cold weather. • Steering, suspension pop or clunk when turning. • Fixing an erratically operating sunroof. • Inoperative power-window "Auto Up" function. • Squeaking front seats. • Loose cowl end mouldings. **2007–10**—Can't remove key from ignition. • Tips on silencing rear brake squealing. • Front axle clicking when accelerating from a stop. • Erratic fuel gauge readings usually indicate a need to replace the fuel level sensor unit. • Front seatbacks won't recline. • Front seat has too much "play," or won't move forward or backward. • Front seat creak. **2007–11**—Steering, suspension pop or clunk when turning. **2008**—A sill cover plate will be installed at no charge to prevent water from entering the cabin. **2009–11**—Inoperative horn.

Subaru

FORESTER, IMPREZA, WRX/STI ★★★★/★★★/★

RATING: *Forester:* Above Average (2003–10); Average (1999–2002). *Impreza:* Average (1999–2010). *WRX/STi:* Not Recommended (2002–10). The WRX has tricky handling and serious, costly reliability issues (powertrain, brake, and steering). Except for the Forester, Subaru's model lineup is mostly the bland leading the bland. There's nothing remarkable about Subaru except for its early use of AWD for its entire lineup as a desperate move to stave off bankruptcy in the mid-'90s. This was a smart move because it gave buyers AWD versatility without the fuel penalty seen with larger engines. **Ideal model year:** Get a 2009 Forester ($16,000–$17,500) for its upgraded performance, safety features, and depreciated prices. The same advice applies to the 2009 Impreza WRX performance model ($18,500–$20,000), although diehard high-performance enthusiasts may well want to invest in a 2006 WRX STi sedan ($10,000–$11,500). In either case, a thorough WRX drivetrain and brake inspection is warranted, judging by past failures and a prevalence of "beaten up" WRXs. Buyers of the base Impreza would do well to stick to the upgraded 2006 and 2009 versions. **"Real" city/highway fuel economy:** *Forester turbocharged manual:* 13.0/9.3 L/100 km. *Forester turbocharged automatic:* 12.5/9.3 L/100 km. Generally, owners report the turbocharged Forester's actual gas consumption is often 20 percent higher than the above estimates. *Impreza 2.5L manual:* 11.2/7.7 L/100 km. *Impreza 2.5L automatic:* 10.6/7.6 L/100 km. *Forester:* 10.9/7.9 L/100 km. *WRX:* 11.8/8.0 L/100 km. **Maintenance/repair costs:** Average. Subaru sales have done extremely well during the last couple of years, keeping dealers in the fold and buying sufficient parts inventory. Expensive servicing is still sometimes hard to overcome because independent garages can't service key AWD components. **Parts:** Only powertrain parts are hard to find and costly. **Extended warranty:** Only for the powertrain. **Best alternatives:** If you don't need the AWD capability, you're wasting your money. Here are some front-drives worth considering: Honda Civic; Hyundai Elantra; Mazda3 or Protegé; Nissan Sentra; Suzuki Aerio, Esteem, or Swift; and Toyota Corolla or Echo. Some recommended small vehicles with 4×4 capability that are set on a car's frame, not a truck's (to provide more car-like handling and better fuel economy), include the GM Vibe, Honda CR-V, Hyundai Tucson, and Toyota Matrix. **Helpful websites:** *http://forums.nasioc.com.*

 ## Strengths and Weaknesses

ALERT! Subaru's unreliable WRX and STi are more "no-performance" than "high-performance"—be wary.

These well-equipped small cars have one of the most refined AWD drivetrains you'll find. With their four-wheel traction, they provide lots of storage space with the wagons, along with good fuel economy and responsive handling without any torque steer. On the other hand, Subaru makes you pay dearly for its seamless AWD capability: Expect clutch failures, poor body fit and finish, and unreliable braking that can get downright scary. Furthermore, small doors and entryways restrict rear access, the coupe's narrow rear window and large rear pillars hinder rear visibility, heat and air distribution is often inadequate, and legroom may be insufficient for tall drivers and passengers. Without their AWD capability, these cars would be back-of-the-pack used-car picks.

The full-time AWD Impreza is essentially a shorter Legacy with additional convenience features. It comes as a four-door sedan, a wagon, and an Outback Sport wagon, all powered by a 135 hp 2.2L or a 165 hp 2.5L 4-cylinder engine. The 2.5L performs much better with the Impreza and Forester than with the Legacy Outback. It is smooth and powerful, with lots of low-end torque for serious off-road use. The automatic transmission shifts smoothly. The manual transmission's "hill holder" clutch prevents the car from rolling backward when starting out. These Subarus hurtle through corners effortlessly, with a flat, solid stance and plenty of grip. Tight cornering at highway speeds is done with minimal body lean and no loss of control, and steering is precise and predictable.

Forester

Another Subaru spin-off, the Forester is a cross between a tall wagon and a sport-utility. Based on the shorter Impreza, the Forester added five horses to the Legacy Outback's 165 hp 2.5L engine and coupled it to a 5-speed manual transmission or an optional 4-speed automatic; the turbo-charged variant produces 224 horsepower. Its road manners are more subdued, and its engine provides more power and torque for off-roading than do most vehicles its size. One minus: cramped rear seating until the 2009 redesign added much-needed legroom.

The Subaru Forester.

The redesigned 2009 Canadian models also come with more standard features than what was offered to buyers in the U.S. For example, we get heated seats, air conditioning, power windows and mirrors, roof rails, electronic stability control and traction control, side curtain airbags, a tilt/telescoping steering wheel, height-adjustable driver's seat, privacy glass, and remote audio controls on the steering wheel. The Forester isn't perfect, but it beats most AWDs hands down.

WRX

An AWD car for the high-performance crowd, the WRX first showed up in 2001 as a 2002 model. It debuted as a goofy-looking, squat little wagon/SUV with a large rear end, a 227 hp 2.0L 4-cylinder engine mated to a high-boost turbocharger, lots of standard performance features, a sport suspension, an aluminum hood with a functional scoop, and higher-quality instruments, controls, trim, and seats. As time has passed, the engines have become more powerful and less reliable. Clutches have also become quite problematic. Subaru blames both of the above design deficiencies on driver abuse when the manufacturer turns down warranty repairs or grudgingly accepts to pay half the repair cost with a "goodwill" arrangement:

My 09 WRX, purchased in October, spun a bearing rod just over a month ago (had 6,001 miles [9,600 km] on it at the time). I live at altitude (8,200 ft.) and drive a roughly paved mountain road each day. This is not good on my tires, not one bit. Mike Shaw Subaru in Thorton, Colorado has finally gotten around to fixing the car. Took them one month, and I had a rental car for one week, but, they replaced the turbo and engine. One major repair is not covered by Subaru's limited warranty due to the "abusive or aggressive driving habits and/or vehicle modifications." Because of tire wear? Really?

VEHICLE HISTORY: All models: 2002—2.2L 4-cylinder is dropped, along with Subaru's pretensions for making affordable entry-level cars. Totally redesigned models include the 2.5 TS Sport Wagon, 2.5 RS sedan, Outback Sport Wagon, the WRX sporty sedan, and the Sport Wagon. There is no longer a two-door version available. *Forester:* **2003**—Improved interior materials, an upgraded suspension, and enhanced handling and ride quality. You'll also find larger tires and fenders, and revised head restraints and side-impact airbags. **2004**—A turbocharged 210 hp 2.5L 4-banger and a racier appearance. **2006**—More power and a slightly restyled interior and exterior. The 2006 turbocharged XT adds 20 hp, now up to 230 hp via a redesigned engine intake manifold; other models get eight more horses, for a total of 173 hp. A retuned suspension enhances ride smoothness and handling response, and there's improved braking feel on all models. Ground clearance is slightly increased, and an alarm system is now standard. **2008**—All models come with an engine immobilizer, and 2.5 XT models have a new front-end design and stability and traction control. **2009**—Completely redesigned with more of an SUV look, a larger interior and grille, wider-opening doors, wider rear glass, and a higher hood line. Other improvements include a more refined suspension, new seats, quicker steering, a lower-mounted powertrain for more stability, a larger fuel tank, and a short turning circle. *Impreza:* **2004**—New front end with larger headlights and a restyled interior and exterior. **2006**—A small horsepower increase, enhanced front end, additional airbags, and a freshened interior. **2008**—Fresh styling and additional safety features that include side curtain airbags. **2009**—Most models were substantially upgraded with added power, safety, and convenience features. The 2.5i added standard stability control and rear disc brakes. *WRX:* **2004**—A 300 hp engine comes on the scene. **2006**—2.5L gets 20 extra horses (up to 230 hp). **2009**—The automatic transmission is dropped and a new grille is added. **2010**—WRX got 41 more horses, a sportier performance suspension, and better tires. STi was given a similar suspension upgrade.

Subarus are noted for only average quality control, spotty, expensive servicing, and serious automatic transmission and brake deficiencies. There's also a history of premature clutch failures and shuddering, particularly after a cold start-up. Owners report paint peeling and chipping; poor engine idling; rear wheel bearing failures; doors that don't latch properly; a sunroof that won't close properly; frequent cold-weather stalling; catalytic converter failures; minor electrical short circuits; manual transmission malfunctions; excessive vibration caused by the alloy wheels; a windshield that cracks and scratches too easily; premature exhaust system rust-out and early brake caliper and rotor scoring and wear; and body panel and trim fit and finish deficiencies characterized by water leaks and condensation problems from the top of the windshield or sunroof.

Safety Summary

All models/years: Common complaints include sudden, unintended acceleration, stalling, transmission failures, steering loss, and airbag and brake malfunctions. • A mountain of complaints relative to loss of braking and premature wearout of key brake components. • Floor runner railings allow the front seats to unexpectedly move fore and aft. • Windshield is easily cracked, especially in freezing weather. **All models: 2003**—Very poor braking when passing over rough surfaces. • Seat belt ratchets tighter; refuses to unlock. **2004**—Vehicle won't go into gear. • Raw fuel smell in the cabin. • Car wanders all over the road because of defective suspension struts. **2005**—Chronic rear strut failure. • Side window shatters spontaneously. *Impreza:* **2008**—Fuel leak at the fuel pump/tank assembly flange. • Early steering rack failure ($1,400). • Broken clutch pedal assembly welds cause braking and clutch engagement problems. • Constant front wheel shimmy. • Rear end wobbles violently side to side when driving over packed snow or wet pavement. • Passenger-side seatbelt ratchets up to the point where it has to be taken off. • Rear doors may be hard to close. • Headlight high beams burn out. • Frost collects on the inside front windshield. • Visibility is impaired by a film that collects on the windshield in cool/cold weather. • Windshield wipers sometimes stop working and get caught up in each other. • Driver-side visor doesn't remain in position:

> Drivers sun visor rotates down unpredictably, blocking vision for average or tall drivers. A small bump can trigger this.

2009—Centre console electrical fire ignited while car was parked. • Total engine failure caused by rod knock/spun bearing. • Engine connecting-rod bearing failure. • Defective clutch pedal welds. • Firestone/Bridgestone tire sidewall bulges. • Gasoline spews out of the filler pipe when getting gas. • Frequent replacement of the clutch throwout bearing. • Inadequate rear window defrost. • The tire pressure warning system has to be reset twice a year at $50 a pop. **2010**—Engine #4 piston failure • Faulty air fuel sensor. *Forester:* **2002**—Dangerous delay, then surging, when accelerating forward or in Reverse. • Surging at highway speeds, and stalling at lower rpm. • Transmission failure; gears lock in Park intermittently. • Open wheel design allows snow and debris to pack in the area and throw wheel out of balance, creating dangerous vibration. • High hood allows water onto the engine. **2003**—Five doors but only one keyhole makes for difficult access when the keyless entry fails. **2004**—Hood latch released while one Forester was underway. **2005**—Car is too flimsy to protect occupants in a rollover:

> The symmetrical all wheel drive system of my 2005 Subaru Forrester XT failed, the vehicle fishtailed and drifted, resulting in a rollover, and severe bodily injury. The

vehicle was so flimsy, it was disgusting. Every door and window opening collapsed, glass flew everywhere. The ceiling collapsed on the passengers' heads.

Car hesitates and bucks in cold weather. • Cruise control fails to disengage. **2006**—One driver's seatback collapsed when vehicle was rear-ended. • Engine surges and sags, especially after a cold start. • Rear tailgate hydraulic struts fail, and the tailgate falls. • Gas station pumps don't shut off automatically when the car is fuelled. • Low-beam headlights fail to provide adequate illumination. **2006–07**—Passenger-side airbag disabled when an average-sized passenger is seated. **2007**—Cruise control fails to disengage. • Engine surges when vehicle goes downhill. • Vehicle surges forward as driver shifts the manual transmission from First to Second gear. • Transmission locks up. **2008**—Floor mat slides about and bunches up near the accelerator pedal. • Prematurely worn wheel bearings and hub assembly. • Steering over-corrects when turning. • No keyhole on the liftgate; in the event of an electrical failure, there is no way to open the trunk. *WRX:* **2002–03**—Chronic ABS failures. **2003**—Increased braking distance when brakes are applied on an uneven surface. **2004**—Turbocharger failure. • Loss of power on the highway. • Failure-prone, clunking struts will not rebound, causing the rear end to sag and degrading handling. **2004–05**—Difficulty shifting into Fifth gear:

I discovered that this is a common problem in 2004 and 2005 STIs. Apparently, Subaru of America put an inferior synchro in 5th gear. 1st, 2nd, 3rd, 4th, and 6th all have upgraded synchros. Starting in 2006, Subaru began putting the upgraded synchros in all 6 gears.

2005—Tricky handling. **2006**—Cracked oil pickup tube. • Premature manual transmission clutch failure. • Fuel-system lines and hoses continue to leak fuel. **2008**—ABS locks up the wheels when passing over snow. Frequent clutch failures. **2008–09**—Frequent early engine failures involving "blown" rods and pistons:

My STi had cracked ringlands on the # 2 and 4 pistons. Before I purchased this car Subaru issued a stop sale on all 2008 WRX's. [T]he car was repaired at a local dealership under a goodwill repair. In Mar 2010. Recently the engine has developed a knock. The dealership says that the rod bearing on CYL #4 had failed. This is the same issue that prompted Subaru to place a stop sale on the vehicles.

•

The Subaru STi series known at the GR is prone to breaking piston ringlands if detonation ever occurs, which happens easily on this engine, which is now tuned for more power yet fewer emissions. The ringland breakage results in power loss and extreme oil consumption due to blowby and if not noticed in time will lead to engine seizing. If driven aggressively enough, this seizing due to oil loss can happen in as few as 10 minutes. It is also possible for the ringland breakage to be so severe that that engine spray-coats a large section of roadway, making for the equivalent of a black ice condition for other traffic.

Secret Warranties/Internal Bulletins/Service Tips

All models/years: Automatic transmission pops out of gear. • At least three bulletins deal with manual transmission malfunctions. • Diagnostic and repair tips for transfer clutch binding and/or bucking on turns. • Troubleshooting a sticking anti-lock brake relay; this problem is characterized by a lit ABS light or the ABS motor continuing to run and buzz when the ignition is turned off. • Premature brake pad, caliper, and rotor wear. • A rotten-egg smell could be caused by a defective catalytic converter. It will be replaced, after a bit of arguing, free of charge for up to five years, as per the emissions warranty. **All models: 2003**—Defective 4EAT transmission parking pawl rod. **2006–10**—A service campaign disclosed in service bulletin number #WVU-31 will pay for the reprogramming of the engine control module on the Impreza, Legacy, Outback, and Forester. **2008–09**—Difficult fuel fill-up in cold weather. • Premature rusting around the liftgate area. • Front stabilizer bar rubbing noise. • Click noise heard coming from the bottom of the A-pillar. • Water leak onto the front floor. *Impreza:* **2008–10**—Rust stain on liftgate. **2008–11**—Rust stain on trunk lid below garnish. *Forester:* **2008**—Front stabilizer bar rubbing noise. **2008–10**—ECM update to improve catalyst efficiency. **2009–10**—Noise from B- and C-pillar trim. **2011**—Difficult starting. *WRX:* **2004–05**—Tips on silencing a noisy rear differential. **2007**—Remedy for hard acceleration surge. **2008**—High idle with clutch disengaged. • Rear quarter panel paint chipping.

FORESTER, IMPREZA, WRX PROFILE

	2002	2003	2004	2005	2006	2007	2008	2009	2010
Cost Price ($)									
Forester	28,395	28,395	27,995	27,995	27,995	26,995	26,995	25,795	25,995
Impreza	21,995	22,995	22,995	22,995	23,495	22,695	20,695	20,995	20,995
STI	—	—	—	47,995	48,995	48,995	48,995	39,995	39,995
WRX	34,995	34,995	35,495	35,495	35,495	35,495	32,995	30,995	30,995
Used Values ($)									
Forester ▲	4,500	5,500	7,000	8,000	10,000	12,500	15,000	17,500	20,500
Forester ▼	4,000	5,000	6,000	7,000	8,500	11,000	13,500	16,000	19,000
Impreza ▲	3,000	3,500	5,500	6,500	7,500	9,500	11,500	13,000	15,000
Impreza ▼	2,500	3,000	4,500	6,000	6,500	8,500	10,500	12,000	13,500
STI ▲	—	—	—	9,000	11,500	14,500	19,000	23,000	28,000
STI ▼	—	—	—	8,000	10,000	13,000	17,500	21,000	26,000
WRX ▲	5,000	6000	7,000	8,000	10,000	14,000	17,000	20,000	23,500
WRX ▼	4,500	5,000	6,000	7,000	8,500	12,500	15,500	18,500	22,000
Reliability	4	4	4	4	4	4	4	4	4
WRX, STi	2	2	2	2	1	1	1	1	1
Crash Safety (F)									
Forester	4	5	5	5	5	5	5	5	5
Impreza	4	4	—	—	4	4	5	5	5
Side (Forester)	5	5	5	5	5	5	5	5	5

All ratings on a numbered scale where 5 is good and **1** is bad. See page 132 for a more detailed description.

Impreza	4	4	—	—	4	4	5	5	5
IIHS Side									
Offset	—	5	5	5	5	5	5	5	5
Forester	5	5	5	5	5	5	5	5	5
Head Restraints	3	3	—	5	5	5	5	5	5
Forester	—	—	—	—	5	5	5	5	5
WRX	—	—	2	2	2	2	3	3	3
Roof (Forester)	—	—	—	—	—	—	—	5	5
Rollover Resistance									
Forester	3	3	4	4	4	4	4	4	4
Impreza	4	4	—	—	4	4	4	4	4

LEGACY, OUTBACK ★★★★

RATING: Above Average (1999–2010). An overpriced, competent full-time AWD performer for drivers who want to move up in size, comfort, and features. Available as a four-door sedan or five-door wagon, the Legacy is cleanly and conventionally styled; the AWD is what this car is all about. It handles difficult terrain without the fuel penalty or clumsiness of many truck-based SUVs, although it is a bit ponderous traversing normal highways. The Outback is a marketing coup that stretches the definition of "sport-utility" by simply customizing the all-wheel-drive Legacy to give it more of an outdoorsy flair. Interestingly, what was a $10,000 gap between the high-end and entry-level model narrows to a couple thousand dollars after a few years. **Ideal model year:** A 2010 Legacy offers the best combination of reliability, standard features, and an attractive price ($16,000–$17,500). **"Real" city/highway fuel economy:** *Manual:* 11.0/7.8 L/100 km. *Automatic:* 10.9/7.9 L/100 km. *3.0L 6-cylinder:* 12.4/8.4 L/100 km. Owners say their fuel consumption is about 15 percent more than these estimates. **Maintenance/repair costs:** Higher than average (imagine a $50 "reset" charge for each tire sensor recalibration and $35 for each tire stem). Repairs are dealer-dependent due to the unique AWD mechanism. **Parts:** Powertrain parts aren't easily found and can be costly. **Extended warranty:** Get an extended warranty to cover powertrain deficiencies after the base warranty has expired. **Best alternatives:** Honda CR-V and Hyundai Tucson or Santa Fe. **Helpful websites:** *www.subaruoutback.org.*

 ## Strengths and Weaknesses

Costing a bit more than the smaller Impreza, these Subaru models are well-appointed, provide a comfortable ride and acceptable handling with the right options, and have lots of cargo room. On the downside, owners report problematic automatic transmission performance when it's hooked to the base engine; sluggish performance from the 2.5L, undoubtedly because of the car's heft; sloppy handling on base models; excessive 4-cylinder engine noise; cramped back seats, with a tight fit for the middle rear-seat passenger; limited rear headroom for tall passengers; trunk hinges that can damage cargo and cut into storage space; seat belts that may be too short for large occupants; and very dealer-dependent servicing.

First launched in 1989 as front-drives, these compacts are a bit slow off the mark. The 5-speed is a bit "notchy," and the automatic gearbox is slow to downshift, has difficulty staying in Overdrive, and is failure-prone. Early Legacy models are noisy, fuel-thirsty cars with bland styling that masks their solid, dependable AWD performance. Actually, the availability of a proven 4×4 powertrain in a compact family sedan or wagon makes these cars appealing for special use.

VEHICLE HISTORY: 2002—The H6-3.0 VDC Outback sedan, equipped with a standard 3.0L engine, joins the lineup. **2003**—New front-end styling; GT gets an upgraded engine and a semi-manual Sport Shift; Outback suspension is upgraded to improve cornering and reduce front-end plow. **2005**—Larger, more power, and a few additional features. In fact, 2.5i models use a 168 hp 4-cylinder with a manual transmission or optional 4-speed automatic. However, a new 250 hp turbocharged version of that engine powers the Legacy 2.5 GT/GT Limited and Outback 2.5 XT models, and it's mated with a manual or an optional 5-speed automatic. The Outback 3.0 R sedan, L.L. Bean Edition wagon, and VDC Limited wagon come with only the 5-speed automatic and a 250 hp 3.0L 6-cylinder engine (up from 212 hp). The automatic transmissions include a manual-shift feature. On the safety front, all these Subarus have anti-lock brakes, front side airbags, and side curtain airbags. An anti-skid system is standard on the Outback 3.0 R VDC wagon but is otherwise unavailable. **2006**—A new sporty version of the GT, called the spec.B. **2007**—A 60/40 split-folding rear seatback. A slight restyling and revised dash; the automatic transmission is standard on the 3.0. A wagon body style is no longer offered. **2008**—A slightly restyled interior and exterior, plus steering wheel-mounted automatic transmission shift paddles. **2009**—The addition of the 3.0 R Limited, equipped with a 245 hp 6-cylinder engine and a power-adjustable driver's seat with lumbar support. **2010**—A completely redesigned car. It comes with a new platform that makes for a larger interior, new and revised engines, an optional CVT automatic transmission, and standard electronic stability control.

The 2010 revised engines include a 170 hp 2.5L 4-cylinder in the 2.5i, a 265 hp turbocharged 2.5L four in the 2.5GT, and a 256 hp 3.6L 6-cylinder in the 3.6R. The 2.5i comes as a Partial Zero Emission Vehicle and reduces emissions by as much as 90 percent compared with a conventional vehicle. The 2.5i uses a 6-speed manual transmission or Lineartronic CVT. The 2.5GT uses a 6-speed manual transmission exclusively, while the 3.6R models come with a 5-speed automatic transmission with manual shift mode.

Prior to the 2010 makeover, the 6-cylinder engine was only adequate with little reserve power. The automatic transmission shifted into too high a gear to adequately exploit the engine's power, and it was reluctant to downshift into the proper gear. The 2.5L engine is a better performer with the manual gearbox, although its shift linkage isn't suitable for rapid gear changes. The 4-cylinder has always had several drawbacks as well: It's noisy and rough-running, and it's tuned more for low-end torque than speedy acceleration. Fortunately, these drivetrain deficiencies were greatly ameliorated with the 2010 redesign.

Early base models don't handle well. They bounce around on uneven pavement, the rear end tends to swing out during high-speed cornering, and there's too much body lean in turns at lesser speeds. Higher-end models handle well, though there's some excessive lean when cornering. The GT's firmer suspension exhibits above-average handling.

The Legacy and Outback have had more than their share of reliability problems over the years. Powertrain defects can sideline the car for days. Engine and transmission problems keep showing up. Servicing can be awkward because of the crowded engine compartment, particularly on turbocharged versions.

Automatic transmission front seals and clutch breakdowns are most common through 2008; the transmission sometimes downshifts abruptly while descending a long grade or travelling on snow-packed highways, or suddenly shifts into Neutral when the car is underway; and the front brakes require frequent attention. Check Engine, Tire Pressure, and ABS warning lights come on constantly, for no reason. Shock absorbers, constant velocity joints, and catalytic converters also often wear out prematurely. Other problems that appear over most model years include chronic electrical and fuel-system malfunctions; hard starting, surging, and stalling in cold weather; starter and ignition relay failures; and snow packing inside the wheelwells, binding steering. Misadjusted door strikers make for hard closing/opening. Tire valve stems are expensive to replace (dealer charges $50 a pop), and there is no reset system for the Tire Pressure warning light so most owners simply let it stay lit. Owners also report that headlight illumination is inadequate, particularly with the 2008 Outback:

> When going downhill you can't see more than 20 feet [6 metres] ahead of the car. We immediately stopped for fear of hitting something in the road and not being able to see if the road stayed straight or turned....This car has the new projector lights and even on level road you can see a very definitive line of demarcation when driving at night.

Safety Summary

All models/years: Many reports of sudden acceleration in Drive and in Reverse, constant stalling followed by engine surging, severe pulling to one side, ABS brake failures, and the premature wearout of brake components. • Small horn buttons may be hard to find in an emergency. **All models/years:** Airbag malfunctions and excessive steering vibration. **2002**—While idling in Park, vehicle suddenly jumps into Drive. **2004**—Automatic transmission failure. • Seat belt comes undone during a collision. **2005**—Cruise-control failure. **2006**—Oil pickup tube shears off, causing major engine damage. • Fuel-pump fuse burns out repeatedly. • Early wearout of the rear brakes (front and rear rotors warped). • Windshield wipers come on and go off on their own, as if possessed. **2006–07**—Airbags fail to deploy. **2007**—Oil return line cracks and ignites a fire in the engine compartment:

The contact owns a 2007 Subaru Legacy. While driving 15 mph [24 km/h], oil leaked on the exhaust and caused a small engine fire.

2008—Shift shock when going from Second to Third or Third to Second. • High idle with clutch disengaged. • Gear slippage. • Premature wheel bearing failures. • When cruising downhill, headlights don't illuminate enough of the roadway to provide adequate lighting. • Vehicle rolled backward while in Park with the engine running. • Uncomfortable head restraints. • AC cycles erratically; the problem is so bad, the cabin won't cool:

> The manufacturer, Subaru of America has determined this is a "normal characteristic of the vehicle" although it took them over a month to come to this conclusion. Many other Subaru Legacy owners report this same problem online, however no fix seems to be coming.

2009—Airbag failed to deploy and seat belt failed to sufficiently restrain the driver. **2010**—Airbag failed to deploy. • Airbag is disabled on the front passenger side even though a normal-sized adult is seated. • Excessive steering vibration at 70+ km/h felt in the steering wheels of both Legacy and Outback. • Powertrain lags, lurches, and then stalls. Brake failure. • Severe knee trauma from a rear-ender that caused the driver's knee to be rammed into the sharp, hard plastic area under the steering wheel.

Secret Warranties/Internal Bulletins/Service Tips

All models/years: Troubleshooting tips on a sticking anti-lock brake relay; this problem is characterized by a lit ABS light or the ABS motor continuing to run/buzz when the ignition is turned off. • Diagnostic and repair tips for transfer clutch binding and/or bucking on turns. • Instructions on isolating the cause of excessive steering vibration when the vehicle reaches cruising speed. **All models: 2003**—Improved Sport Shift cold-weather operation. • Premature suspension corrosion:

> Certain rear suspension subframe components were produced with poor paint quality, which, after continued exposure to corrosive road salts for a period of several years, could result in rust-out of the component and possible breakage of the subframe. If such breakage occurs while the vehicle is being operated, control of the vehicle could be affected, increasing the risk of a crash. Remedy: Dealers will clean and rustproof the rear suspension subframe under a special service campaign.

2004—Possible causes of transfer clutch binding when cornering. **2005**—Seat belt warning chimes when seat is unoccupied. • Water leak from AC evaporator drain hose. **2005–06**—Radiator cooling fan relay #2 replacement. • Troubleshooting instrument panel squeaks. **2005–07**—How to fix front-door rattles and a right front wheel bearing squeak, squeal. **2005–08**—Sunroof sunshade rattles. **2005–09**—Water leaks onto the passenger-side floor. **2006**—Fixing rattles from the liftgate area. **2006–10**—Free reprogramming of the electronic computer module for better powertrain performance (Campaign #WVU-31). **2007**—Rear differential vent oil leak. • Transmission Temperature light flashing. • Rubbing noise when turning steering wheel. **2007–08**—Transmission shift-lever boot cracking. • Rear differential oil seepage. **2007–09**—Hesitation when accelerating. **2008**—Condensation buildup in the headlights is the likely cause of flickering headlights. **2010**—Shift lever hard to move out of Park. • Low power in Reverse on an incline. • Software for idle RPM drop. • Silencing seatbelt creaks and squeaks. • Driver seat rocking. • How to repair an inoperative seat lumbar support. • Sunroof stops halfway when opening. • Water leaks into headliner/map light area. **2010–11**—A fix for excessive steering-wheel shake when car is underway.

LEGACY, OUTBACK PROFILE

	2002	2003	2004	2005	2006	2007	2008	2009	2010
Cost Price ($)									
Legacy	27,395	27,295	27,295	27,995	28,495	26,996	26,996	26,995	23,995
Outback	31,995	37,995	26,995	32,995	32,995	30,995	30,995	30,995	28,995
Used Values ($)									
Legacy ▲	4,500	5,000	6,000	7,000	8,500	11,000	13,500	15,000	17,500
Legacy ▼	4,000	5,000	5,000	6,000	7,500	9,500	12,000	13,500	16,000
Outback ▲	6,500	7,000	8,000	10,000	11,500	13,500	15,500	18,000	21,500
Outback ▼	5,500	6,500	7,000	8,500	10,000	12,000	14,500	16,500	20,000
Reliability	3	3	3	3	4	4	4	4	4
Crash Safety (F)									
Legacy 4d	4	4	4	5	5	5	5	5	5
Side	4	3	3	—	—	5	5	5	5
Wagon	—	4	4			5	—	—	—
IIHS Side	—	—	—	2	5	5	5	5	5
Offset	5	5	5	5	5	5	5	5	5
Head Restraints	3	3	4	3	5	5	5	5	5
Roof strength	—	—	—	—	—	—	—	—	5
Rollover Resistance	4	4	4	—	—	4	4	4	5
Outback AWD	4	4	4	4	4	4	4	4	4

Suzuki

AERIO, ESTEEM, SWIFT, SWIFT+, SX4, VERONA ★★★★/★★★/★★★★

RATING: *Aerio:* Above Average (2003–07). *Esteem:* Average (1999–2002). *Swift, Swift+:* Above Average (1999–2009). *Verona:* Average (2004–06). *SX4:* Recommended (2007–10). Suzuki's earlier lineup has been downgraded one level because the company's poor sales and constant reorganization make for low resale

The Suzuki SX4. Pull the wheels and check the brake pads and rotors.

values and problematic servicing. Getting the most horsepower bang for your buck means shopping for a sport model or looking at the upgraded model from 2000 or later. Wagons are especially versatile and reasonably priced for the equipment provided. Both the base GL and upscale GLX come loaded with standard features that cost extra on other models. **Ideal model year:** Getting the most horsepower bang for your buck means shopping for a sport model or looking at more recent model years. Wagons are especially versatile and reasonably priced for the equipment provided. Both the SX4 JX and upscale JLX depreciate quickly and come loaded with standard features that cost extra on other models. A loaded 2008 JLX AWD, for example, costs $11,000 to $12,500, much less than its $22,695 original price. If you can spend a little extra, the revised 2010 SX4 ($12,000) comes with a more refined drivetrain and instrumentation. **"Real" city/highway fuel economy:** *Aerio manual:* 9.4/7.0 L/100 km. *Aerio automatic:* 9.3/7.0 L/100 km. *Aerio AWD automatic:* 9.9/7.6 L/100 km. *Swift manual:* 8.9/5.9 L/100 km. *Esteem manual:* 8.3/6.0 L/100 km. *Esteem automatic:* 9.0/6.3 L/100 km. *Swift automatic:* 9.1/6.3 L/100 km. *SX4 AWD manual:* 10.1/7.6 L/100 km. *SX4 AWD automatic:* 9.9/7.1 L/100 km. *Verona automatic:* 12.0/7.9 L/100 km. **Maintenance/repair costs:** Cheap to keep up and repair. **Parts:** Average costs, and most parts are easily found. **Extended warranty:** A toss-up. Some long-term powertrain protection would be helpful; buy your brakes from independents who give long warranties. **Best alternatives:** Honda Civic; Hyundai Accent or Elantra/Tiburon; Mazda3 or Protegé; Nissan Sentra; and Toyota Corolla or Echo. **Helpful websites:** *www.suzuki-forums.com* and *www.suzuki-forums.com/canada.*

Strengths and Weaknesses

ALERT! Suzuki has a small dealer network in Canada. Fortunately, if you are unhappy with the dealer's service most independent garages can take up the slack at a sizeable discount. • Before purchase, be sure to pull the wheels to check on the condition of the brake pads and rotors.

The Esteem is a four-door econocar that is ideal for cheapskates. Although it's a decade old and is a small step up from the Swift, it has a fairly spacious interior and stands out with its European-styled body and large array of such standard features as AC, a fold-down back seat, and remote trunk and fuel-door releases. Cargo space is also fairly good with the sedan and exceptional with the wagon's rear seats folded.

The small engine delivers respectable acceleration, and overall performance is acceptable, thanks to the Esteem's four-wheel independent suspension, which gives just the right balance between a comfortable ride and no-surprise handling.

Suzuki's more recent entry-level Aerio front-drive sedan and wagon replaced the Esteem for the 2003 model year. Equipped with optional all-wheel drive, it is one of the lowest-priced AWD vehicles available in Canada. Both models come with a 145 hp 4-cylinder engine that's among the most powerful standard engines in this class. Every Aerio comes with AC, power windows and mirrors, a tilt steering wheel, a CD player, and split-folding rear seats.

Suzuki's Ontario-built Swift was first launched in 1995 for the American and Canadian markets. It was dropped in the States in 2001 but remained in Canada as the Swift and the Swift+. The Swift+, essentially a GM/Daewoo Aveo knock-off, was first launched as a 2004 model. It has posted average reliability scores (surprising for a Daewoo), though crashworthiness info is quite sparse.

SX4

Launched as a 2007 model, the SX4 arrived with a 143 hp 4-cylinder engine and a 5-speed manual transmission, or optional 4-speed automatic. The SX4 is good for urban chores, although the engine could use more freeway power. The AWD system lacks low-range gearing, but it can be set for front-wheel drive only, for AWD, or for a locked-in front/rear power split. For extra safety, there's standard ABS with all-disc braking, Sport models have added traction/antiskid control, and all models have front and curtain side airbags.

Overall, the SX4 is well-equipped, fairly reliable, and relatively fuel-efficient. It handles well, gives a comfortable ride, provides generous cargo room, and has an adequate powerplant if not pushed. Things not to like: Rear seating is a bit tight, and engine and road noise intrude into the cabin area. Good alternative models are the Honda Fit or Hyundai Accent.

VEHICLE HISTORY: 2003—Aerio makes its debut. **2004**—The 145 hp 2.0L is replaced by a 155 hp 2.3L engine. Swift+ debuts. **2005**—Standard front side airbags and a host of new exterior styling touches. **2006**—ABS becomes a standard item. **2007**—Suzuki's smallest car, the Aerio, drops its hatchback, leaving a four-door sedan in base and premium trims. All Aerios still have a 155 hp 4-cylinder engine. Automatic-transmission models are available with all-wheel drive. ABS and front side airbags are standard, but side curtain airbags are not available. **2008**—Suzuki SX4 adds a sedan model to the existing four-door hatchback. The new sedan, called SX4 Sport, replaces Suzuki's Aerio sedan and comes with front-wheel drive only. **2009**—The SX4 hatchback adopts front-drive. **2010**—The revised 4-cylinder 2.0L engine gains seven horses and is coupled to a more economical 6-speed manual transmission. The clunky 4-speed automatic is replaced by the more efficient CVT transmission. An updated instrument cluster and climate control panel are also new this year.

Here are some of the drawbacks to owning one of these econoboxes: small tires compromise handling; power steering doesn't transmit much road feedback; the 4-speed automatic transmission may shift harshly and vibrate excessively between gear changes; and braking is mediocre for cars this light. Also, the SX4 has less storage space than Honda's Fit, and its raised floor can make loading more difficult.

Problems reported by Esteem and Aerio owners include paint delamination/peeling; fragile body panels and trim items; occasional electrical short circuits; premature clutch, tire, brake, and transmission wear; noisy front brakes and early wearout of brake pads and rotors; and wind and water intrusion into the engine and passenger compartment through the Aerio's air-intake breather.

 Safety Summary

All models/years: Many reports of airbag malfunctions and frequent brake servicing. *Aerio:* **2002**—Brake caliper may leak fluid. **2003**—Many complaints of broken, cracked, or bent aluminum wheel rims and wheel bearing failures. • Delayed shifts. • Vehicle refuses to go into Reverse gear. • CV axle joint separation. • Misaligned power-steering bracket. • Trunk pops up while driving. **2004**—Sudden unintended acceleration. **2005**—Front brake failure. • Excessive body shake caused by defective stabilizer bushing, bracket, and mount. **2006**—Emergency Brake light comes on for no reason. • Premature engine failures. • Serpentine belt failures (early symptom is excessive squealing). • Air intake sucks up water on flooded streets and causes serious engine damage, stalling:

> While driving 25 mph [40 km/h] on a rainy day, the vehicle shut off when it drove over a puddle. The vehicle was towed to the dealer and they stated that the failure was caused by water intrusion. They further stated that the rod failed and went through the aluminum motor. Both times the rod went through the motor, the water intrusion was caused by the air [breather] positioned under the motor.

2007—Premature wearout of the brake caliper may lead to brake failure. • Hard starting. • Brakes and tires continue to wear out prematurely. *SX4:* **2007**—Airbag light comes on for no reason (dealers charge over $80 to scan the system for what is a common Suzuki owner complaint). • When going uphill, the car downshifts a couple of times, then when passing over the crest, it resumes cruise control at an ever-increasing speed. • Sudden loss of brakes as engine surged. • Faulty tire pressure sensors. • Condensation drips/pours out of the AC unit. • **2007–09**—Faulty airbag sensor for the passenger front seat:

> Took to dealer, computer reset done. Lasted only 4 days, AIR BAG SYS FAULT lights on again. Taken back to dealer, service dept said the front passenger seat air bag sensor was faulty. Mileage 54,442 [87,600 km] not covered under warranty. Over $2,400 U.S. to fix issue. [A quick review of the Internet reveals this to be a common problem: *www.suzuki-forums.com*. Search SX4 airbag light.]

2008—When traction control kicks in, the car may fishtail. • Jack storage mount is easily broken in a collision, allowing the jack to fly about. **2009**—Several underhood fires reported. • Steering column locked while vehicle was underway. **2010**—The two roof frame supports on each side of the windshield block the driver's view of the road. • Tire pressure sensors corrode and split on the stem, leading to leaks. • Floor mats interfere with the brake and accelerator pedals. Sudden unintended acceleration when the brakes were applied.

Secret Warranties/Internal Bulletins/Service Tips

All models: Pops out of gear when driving (Fifth gear in manual trannies). • Battery discharge can be avoided by installing an upgraded alternator, says TSB #TS-03-06304. **2002–03**—Popping noise when turning. **2002–04**—Left driveshaft pops out of final drive. • Instruments don't display. **2004–06**—Suzuki admits that its own faulty suspension may cause abnormal tire wear (TSB #TS 05-11225). **2007–08**—Extended cranking to start. • Abnormal vibration can be felt with the shift lever when driving in Third gear. *SX4:* **2007**—Pops out of Fifth gear while driving. • Cold engine stall. • AC doesn't cool because the compressor clutch fails to engage. **2007–08**—Extended cranking time to start. **2007–09**—Water drips on the passenger floor when using the AC. **2009**—Countermeasures to apply when the Airbag warning light comes on for no reason.

AERIO, ESTEEM, SWIFT, SWIFT+, SX4, VERONA PROFILE

	2002	2003	2004	2005	2006	2007	2008	2009	2010
Cost Price ($)									
Aerio sedan	—	15,785	15,995	17,995	18,595	18,995	—	—	—
Aerio SX (AWD)	—	—	20,495	23,995	22,995	—	—	—	—
Esteem GL	16,195	—	—	—	—	—	—	—	—
Esteem GLX	19,795	—	—	—	—	—	—	—	—
Swift+	—	—	13,495	13,595	13,745	13,895	13,995	14,495	—
SX4 Sedan/Hatchback	—	—	—	—	—	15,996	17,195	17,395	17,695

SX4 JX	—	—	—	—	—	18,195	18,695	19,995	17,695
SX4 JLX AWD	—	—	—	—	—	21,495	22,695	23,195	24,695
Verona	—	—	22,995	22,995	22,995	—	—	—	—
Used Values ($)									
Aerio sedan ▲	—	3,500	5,000	5,500	6,500	8,000	—	—	—
Aerio sedan ▼	—	3,000	4,000	5,000	5,500	6,500	—	—	—
Aerio SX (AWD) ▲	—	—	6,000	6,500	8,000	—	—	—	—
Aerio SX (AWD) ▼	—	—	5,000	6,000	7,000	—	—	—	—
Esteem GL ▲	2,500	—	—	—	—	—	—	—	—
Esteem GL ▼	2,000	—	—	—	—	—	—	—	—
Esteem GLX ▲	3,000	—	—	—	—	—	—	—	—
Esteem GLX ▼	2,500	—	—	—	—	—	—	—	—
Swift+ ▲	—	—	3,500	4,500	5,000	5,500	6,500	8,000	—
Swift+ ▼	—	—	3,000	4,000	4,500	5,000	5,500	6,500	—
SX4 ▲	—	—	—	—	—	6,500	8,000	10,000	12,000
SX4 ▼	—	—	—	—	—	6,000	7,000	9,000	11,000
SX4 JX ▲	—	—	—	—	—	8,500	9,500	11,000	12,500
SX4 JX ▼	—	—	—	—	—	7,000	9,000	10,000	11,500
SX4 JLX AWD ▲	—	—	—	—	—	10,500	12,500	14,000	16,000
SX4 JLX AWD ▼	—	—	—	—	—	9,000	11,000	13,000	15,000
Verona ▲	—	—	3,500	4,500	5,500	—	—	—	—
Verona ▼	—	—	3,000	4,000	5,000	—	—	—	—
Reliability	3	4	4	4	4	4	4	4	5
Crash Safety (F)									
Aerio	—	—	4	—	—	—	—	—	—
SX4	—	—	—	—	—	—	4	4	4
Side (Aerio)	—	—	5	5	—	—	—	—	—
SX4	—	—	—	—	—	5	5	5	5
IIHS Side	—	—	—	1	1	1	—	—	—
SX4	—	—	—	—	—	5	5	5	5
Offset	5	5	5	5	5	5	—	—	—
SX4	—	—	—	—	—	5	5	5	5
Head Restraints	2	2	2	2	2	2	—	—	—
SX4	—	—	—	—	—	2	2	2	2
Roof strength (SX4)	—	—	—	—	—	2	2	2	2
Rollover Resistance	—	—	—	—	—	—	4	4	5

Toyota/General Motors

COROLLA, MATRIX/VIBE ★★/★★★

RATING: *Corolla:* Below Average (1997–2010). It's not just runaway cars with no brakes: Corolla quality has been on a downhill slide for more than a decade (see "Strengths and Weaknesses"). Since the 1997 model was "de-contented" through the use of lower-quality materials, there has been a noticeable reduction in quality control—though horsepower-enhanced engines make this a better performer than earlier versions. Interestingly, the Matrix/Vibe didn't go through a similar cheapening of the product, hence its higher *Lemon-Aid* rating. *Matrix/Vibe: Above Average (2005–10); Average (2002–04).* Aimed at the youth market, these versatile spin-offs don't provide enough horsepower to justify their sporty pretensions, and they aren't suitable for any place more rugged than Ontario's Highway 401. Nevertheless, both the Matrix and Vibe are decent performers. **Ideal model year:** There is no "ideal" Corolla, however, you won't get in much trouble with a $10,500 2010 base model with some unexpired warranty coverage. All of the Matrix/Vibes are good buys, particularly the 2009 entry-level Vibe. It sells for $8,500 to $10,000. A 2010 Matrix is the best buy from Toyota, but you will have to shell out about $12,500. **"Real" city/highway fuel economy:** *Corolla manual: 7.1/5.3 L/100 km. Corolla automatic: 8.1/5.8 L/100 km. Matrix manual: 7.7/6.0 L/100. Matrix automatic: 8.3/6.4 L/100 km. Matrix 6-speed manual: 9.5/6.8 L/100 km. Vibe manual: 7.7/6.0 L/100 km. Vibe automatic: 8.3/6.4 L/100 km. Matrix/Vibe AWD: 9.1/6.9 L/100 km.* Owners report that their fuel consumption is about 10 percent higher than these estimates. **Maintenance/ repair costs:** *Corolla:* Average, and repairs can be done anywhere. *Matrix/Vibe:* Powertrain and body part supply is a bit problematic now that GM has closed down the Pontiac division, plus owners complain that they cost more than similar parts used on other models. **Parts:** Electronic and powertrain parts can be expensive at the dealership; shop lower-priced independent suppliers. **Extended warranty:** Not needed. But you will be limited to Toyota dealers now that GM has shut down Pontiac. **Best alternatives:** Matrix/Vibe third-year depreciation is brutal—a bargain for buyers, but disappointing come trade-in time. Consider the Hyundai Accent or Elantra; Mazda3, Mazda5, or Protegé; Nissan Sentra; and Suzuki Aerio or SX4. For extra cabin storage space and all-wheel drive, check out the Suzuki Aerio AWD and Subaru Forester. **Helpful websites:** *www. toyotanation.com* and *www.toyotaownersclub.com.*

Strengths and Weaknesses

ALERT! Firestone Affinity and Goodyear Integrity tires have been troublesome. Check *www.tirerack.com* for some better-rated tires.

A step up from the Echo and Yaris, the Corolla has long been Toyota's standard-bearer in the compact-sedan class—many late '80s Corollas are still on our roads after 20+ years. Over the years, however, the car has grown in size, price, and refinement to the point where it can now be considered a small family sedan. All Corollas ride on a front-drive platform with independent suspension on all wheels.

For over a decade, Corollas have been afflicted by serious quality problems that include chronic stalling; brake and tire failures; an easily cracked windshield and windshield reflections; faulty strut assemblies; sudden acceleration; engine hesitation and surging; the suspension bottoming out; warped brake rotors and early brake pad wearout; poor steering (vehicle wanders all over the road); seat belt failures; hard starting; dash gauge "washout"; airbag malfunctions; poorly designed headlights that misdirect the light beam; and the transmission popping out of Drive into Neutral or refusing to shift at all.

VEHICLE HISTORY: 2003—Corolla is redesigned to be taller, wider, and longer; it gets a new 4-speed automatic transmission and five more horses. Matrix/Vibe launches. **2005**—A light restyling, and side curtain airbags are optional for all models. Toyota also launches its new high-performance Corolla XRS sedan. **2007**—Matrix/Vibe loses all-wheel drive. All sporty models are dropped. **2009**—The Matrix and Vibe are redesigned with new styling, more power, and the return of all-wheel drive. **2010**—Matrix returns with electronic stability control and traction control on the XR and AWD.

Matrix/Vibe

These practically identical small front-drive or all-wheel-drive sporty wagons are crosses between mini-SUVs and station wagons, but they're packaged like small minivans. Unlike the Matrix, which has soldiered on, GM dropped Vibe from its lineup when it shut down the Pontiac division.

The front-drive Matrix/Vibe is equipped with a 1.8L 132 hp engine, a 5-speed manual overdrive transmission, and lots of standard features; however, the weak, buzzy base engine can be felt throughout the car. The AWD models are about 10 percent heavier and are woefully power-challenged.

If you really need a bit more horsepower, get a model equipped with the 2.4L 158-hp 4-cylinder, but keep in mind that there are safer, better-quality high-performance choices out there, such as the Honda Civic Si, Mazda5, or a base Acura RSX. Other front-drives worth considering are the Ford Focus, Honda Civic, Hyundai Elantra or Tiburon, Mazda3, Nissan Sentra, and Suzuki SX4. The Subaru Impreza and Forester are two other good choices for the AWD variant.

 Safety Summary

All models/years: Chronic airbag malfunctions; they deploy when they shouldn't, or don't deploy when they should:

> [Our] [t]hirteen-year-old daughter sustained [a] severe traumatic brain injury after [a] head-on collision. Her airbag deployed, [but the] top of passenger-side airbag was completely blown apart from one side to the other, allowing her head to strike [the] dash. We both had seat belts on. I sustained bruising of [my] hips and right rib. She was in [a] coma and [is] just now beginning to move [her] left side. She still cannot sit up, stand, walk, talk coherently, eat, or do anything for herself.

Sudden, unintended acceleration:

> I have a 2007 Toyota Matrix and have 3 incidents of uncontrolled acceleration of over 70 mph [113 km/h] and uncontrolled deceleration when going 35 to 60 mph [56 to 97 km/h] in heavy traffic. I have been lucky enough to have avoided any accidents but last week came very close to hitting a tree. My car is not part of the recall. I have had trouble with my floor mats but this is not the problem with the accelerator. I took the car to the dealership and they said that there is nothing wrong with the accelerator.

Engine hesitation and surging. • Poor headlight illumination. • Engine compartment fires. • Gas fumes in the interior. • Brake and power-steering failures. • Excessive drifting and high-speed instability. • Premature control arm failure. • Seat belt releases in accident. • Rear wheel breaks at the axle. • Windshield cracks easily. • Premature tire side wall shredding. *Corolla:* **2002**—Fuel leakage.• While using cruise control, gas pedal suddenly goes to the floor. **2002–03**—Unable to shift out of Park. **2003**—Fire ignites because of loose fuel line. • One vehicle suddenly shut down while underway at 100 km/h; in another case, vehicle suddenly accelerated while cruise control was engaged. • Several owners report that a hole in the oil pan causes vehicle to stall. • Faulty seat belt wiring could cause a fire. • Floormat catches accelerator pedal. • Pedal goes soft when brakes are applied, and brakes lock up when coming to a gradual stop, resulting in extended stopping distances. • Rear welding breaks away from the frame, resulting in complete loss of control. • Shifter refuses to go into gear while driving; transmission sometimes goes from Drive to Neutral while driving. • In windy conditions, vehicle becomes hard to steer, veering left or right. • Glow-in-the-dark inside trunk release doesn't glow in the dark because it is rarely exposed to light (owner actually crawled inside trunk to test it out!). • Sunlight washes out dash readings. **2004**—Hand brake doesn't hold very well. • Front passenger-side windshield frame obstructs visibility. • Sun visor interferes with the rear-view mirror. • One vehicle's sunroof came unglued from the metal frame; glass from the sunroof flew off. **2004–05**—Brake and gas pedals mounted too close together. **2005**—Passenger-seat sensor is too sensitive and rings an alarm when there is the slightest pressure on the seat. • Water pools in the ventilation system causing mildew growth. • Car will not slow down when foot is taken off the accelerator pedal. • Low engine intake ingests water when going through puddles, causing severe engine damage. • Steering-wheel lock-up. • Excessive play in rear hub bearings. **2006**—AC condenser destroyed by small rocks:

> Toyota has issued a technical service bulletin indicating that the A/C condenser is not properly protected. The number for this problem is AC002-06. Additionally, the Toyota has redesigned the Corolla to correct this in 2007 by properly protecting the A/C condenser leaving the 2005–2006 customers in the dust. Toyota refuses to replace the condenser and wants to charge customers the full $600 replacement cost.

Gas pedal sticks under the floormat. **2006–07**—A defective throttle sensor/ECM unit is blamed for lurching acceleration, surging, stalling, and no starts:

> Many people complain about the same problem on the Internet and describe such cases where either the car's engine dies in the middle of the road, or the car leaves

people in the middle of nowhere and won't start at all (*www.toyotanation.com/ forum/showthread.php?t=201631*). Toyota has issued a technical service bulletin about this problem: TSB EG042-07 (*www.tundrasolutions.com/forums/attachments/ corolla-matrix/27763d1201041193-2006-obdii-code-p0607-06-corolla-tsb.pdf*). Information on the Internet suggests that faulty solenoids on the ECM board are causing the computer to go crazy.

•

At approximately 70–75 miles per hour [113–121 km/h] in the fast lane, probably while on cruise control, car began to accelerate, [I] hit the brake which had no effect, and if it had been on cruise control, it did not override the acceleration. I began to get closer to the car in front of me. I do not believe I initially tried to put the car into neutral. I turned off the car engine, the acceleration stopped, I hit the brake somewhat to get it down to a regular speed, put the car into neutral, started it while coasting, put it back into gear (manual transmission), and the crisis was over.

2008—Chronic stalling. • Poor steering. • Driver-side axle suddenly snapped:

The driver heard a loud bang as she slowly made a left turn. The vehicle was towed to the dealer. According to the work order, the end of the axle was broken off in the differential and the axle seal was leaking.

Tire and rim fly off vehicle while underway. • The rear heat shield mount between the exhaust and the fuel tank may rust out. • Driver's express window rollup feature doesn't have a safety mechanism to retract; it could possibly amputate a finger or strangle a child. • Normal braking causes the wheels to lock up. • Car window suddenly shattered while one vehicle was parked in mild weather. • Odometer/speedometer is hard to read in daylight. **2009**—Normally, NHTSA posts an average of 50 safety-related complaints per year for each model. The 2009 Corolla has racked up over 729 complaints, where about 75 would have been the norm over a year and a half. Most of the complaints are for sudden acceleration, no brakes, steering failures, and many of the other failures already listed for previous model years. Some new and unusual failures have also appeared, however. • Vehicle seems to float all over the road, hydroplanes, or swerves right to left. • Steering lock-up while vehicle is underway. • Water on the driver's side floor. • Premature wearout of Firestone Affinity Touring tires. *Matrix:* **2003**—Excessive steering wander; some torque steer (twisting) evident, especially on wet roads. • The manual shift lever's upward and forward position is counterintuitive and feels a bit ragged. • Instrument panel lights are dimmed by automatic sensor to the point where they are unreadable in twilight hours. • Automatic headlights turn on and go off for no apparent reason. **2004**—Hand brake doesn't hold very well. • Clutch failures with the manual transmission. • Car drifts out of control and crashes; steering is non-responsive:

Matrix drifted to the left while driving, resulting in the consumer losing control and the vehicle flipping over. As the consumer attempted once more to gain control of the steering, the vehicle veered off to the left, hit a ditch, went airborne, and flipped. Toyota determined that there were steering problems.

Dealers have blamed a defective steering yoke and poor-quality original-equipment tires for this instability and steering loss. • Warped front brake rotors. • Dashboard reflects onto the windshield. • Front bumper/spoiler drags on the ground over any uneven surface. • Ice collects in wheel rims, throwing tires out of balance. **2005**—Hard starting and chronic stalling. • Engine begins racing while vehicle is stopped. • Alloy wheel splits in half. **2006**—Frequent replacement of the engine control module, throttle body assembly, transmission, and clutch. **2006–07**—Original-equipment tires are notorious for premature wearout; faulty shocks, poor differential alignment, and a too-light rear end are blamed. **2007**—Gasoline fumes in the cabin caused by failure of the fuel-pressure regulator and fuel-injector seals. • Power-steering failure. • Goodyear Eagle original-equipment tires crack at the side wall. **2008**—Vehicle stalls out due to a defective computer module. • The left rear passenger window in one vehicle suddenly exploded. • On another occasion, entire rear quarter window spontaneously shattered. • Premature rear tire wear blamed on inaccurate rear alignment. **2009**—Stalling while underway. • Automatic transmission struggles going into First and Reverse. • Fuel gauge registers empty when the tank is actually full. **2010**—Matrix suddenly accelerated without brake or steering control. • Engine surging when the car was stopped at a red light. • Toyota refused owner's request to put in a brake over-ride feature. • Vehicle swerves side to side when underway. • Brakes have to be pumped repeatedly before they will work. *Vibe:* **2003**—Vehicle will roll while in Park. • Faulty ABS. • Dash gauges unreadable when driver wears sunglasses. • Automatic headlight sensor turns the headlights on and off about 20 times per day, depending on sun and shade variations. • When the lights go on, dash lights become unreadable. • Transmission indicator unlit at night. • After start-up, 15–20 seconds elapse before the automatic headlights and tail lights turn on. • Sunroof suddenly explodes. • Excessive condensation on interior glass. • Refuelling impossible without a large amount of fuel spitting out. • Rear outboard seat belts constantly tighten. **2004**—Too much steering play, making the Vibe, like its Toyota counterpart, highly unstable on the highway. • Rear-passenger seat belt may be hazardous to children:

> The rear-passenger seat belt twisted around the child's abdomen and would not release. Every time the child moved, it clicked tighter. The child had to be cut out of the seat belt.

Automatic door locks may not secure the door shut. • Instrument-cluster chrome finish reflects into windshield. • Power side window cracks as it is being raised. • Speedometer needle can't be seen on sunny days. • Wheel lug nuts may fail. • Many electrical shorts. • Loose firewall shield screws. **2005**—Poor rear visibility. • Hard starts. • Severe pulling to one side when accelerating or braking. • Mice can crawl into the dash, air vents. **2006**—Sudden loss of power due to a malfunctioning powertrain control module. • Driver-side window doesn't roll down completely; when it is lowered, it interferes with the door's operation. • Annoying dash reflection onto the windshield. **2007**—Stalling, hard starting caused by a defective throttle body/ECM. • Accelerator pedal too sensitive, leading to jerky acceleration. • Vehicle pulls to the left when underway, due to a misaligned rear end. • Windshield distortion. **2008–09**—About 100 complaints posted by NHTSA and most of these were carryovers from the sudden acceleration, brake failures, premature tire wear, and steering issues mentioned above. • Uneven wear of rear brake pads:

> Passenger side outer pad is positioned in an angle which causes premature wear of that pad while all other pads are wearing evenly. Such defect (caliper position) causes rotor damage and possible wheel lock. This is a second Vibe with the same problem that I've seen. The passenger side rear caliper needs to be adjusted and repositioned.

Secret Warranties/Internal Bulletins/Service Tips

All models/years: Steering-column noise may require the replacement of the steering-column assembly. • Toyota has developed special procedures for eliminating AC odours and excessive wind noise. These problems are covered in TSBs #AC00297 and #BO00397, respectively. **All models: 2009**—According to TSBs #SB002411 and #SB009411, excess oil consumption in the 2.4L 4-cylinder engine was traced to the piston assembly. Toyota will replace the pistons and rings on a "goodwill" case-by-case basis. *Corolla:* **2002–04**—Troubleshooting tips for fixing a poorly performing AC. **2002–07**—Repair tips for correcting a severe pull to one side when underway (TSB #ST005-01). **2003–05**—Ways to silence front- and rear-door wind noise and a rear hub axle bearing humming. **2003–07**—Remedy for engine compartment squeaks and rattles. • Rear hatch is slow to open. **2003–08**—Tips on silencing windshield, automatic transmission whistle or hoot, wind noise, and front brake rattling. **2003–11**—Remedy for a windshield ticking noise. **2004–06**—Front-seat movement correction. **2004–10**—Fixing front-seat squeaking. **2005–06**—Engine vibration/drone when accelerating. • Toyota's correction for hard starts (TSB #EGO53-06). • Grill mesh available to protect the AC condenser from road debris. **2005–07**—Troubleshooting tips to fix a harsh-shifting automatic transmission and hard starts. **2009–10**—Poor steering feel. • Steering clunk, pop noise. A-pillar rattles. • Premature front brake pad wear (see TSB on following page). *Matrix, Vibe:* **2003**—Loose or deformed front or rear glass door run. • AC doesn't sufficiently cool the vehicle. • Headlights come on when turned off. **2003–06**—Correction for rear-end whining, humming, or growling. **2005–06**—Troubleshooting no-starts. **2009**—Harsh downshift when stopping. • Instrument panel rattling. **2009–10**—No starts. • Condensation dripping from the dome lamp. *Vibe:* **2003**—Transmission shifts too early when accelerating at full throttle and the engine is cold. • Harsh shifting. • Water leak from the A-pillar or headliner area. **2003–04**—Harsh 1–2 upshifts. • Slipping transmission. **2003–08**—Silencing a hoot or whistle heard on light acceleration (replace the automatic transaxle cooler hoses).

BRAKES—PREMATURE FRONT BRAKE PAD WEAR

BULLETIN NO.: T-SB-0392-09

DATE: DECEMBER 3, 2009

YEAR(S)	MODEL(S)	ADDITIONAL INFORMATION
2009–2010	Corolla	

APPLICABILITY: Some 2009–2010 model year Corolla vehicles may exhibit premature pad wear. Use the following replacement pads to address this condition.

PREVIOUS PART NUMBER	CURRENT PART NUMBER	PART NAME	QTY
04465-02240 (NAP)	04465-12630	Pad, Kit Disc Brake, Front	1
04465-02220 (JPP)			
04945-12100 (NAP)	Same	Shim, Anti-Squeal, Front	1
04945-02150 (JPP)	Same		1
N/A	08887-80609	Disc Brake Caliper Grease (50 g Tube)	1

COROLLA, MATRIX/VIBE PROFILE

	2002	2003	2004	2005	2006	2007	2008	2009	2010
Cost Price ($)									
Base Corolla	15,765	15,290	15,410	15,490	15,715	15,785	14,565	14,565	15,460
Matrix	—	16,745	16,745	16,925	17,200	17,200	17,200	15,705	15,665
XR	—	24,115	24,210	24,550	24,825	21,465	21,465	19,180	20,575
XRS AWD	—	24,540	24,640	25,560	25,835	—	—	25,220	26,275
Vibe	—	20,995	21,150	19,900	19,900	19,950	19,210	22,995	—
GT AWD	—	27,000	27,140	25,670	25,670	—	—	24,995	26,155
Used Values ($)									
Base Corolla ▲	2,500	3,000	3,500	4,500	5,500	6,000	7,500	9,000	11,000
Base Corolla ▼	2,000	2,500	3,000	4,000	5,000	5,500	6,000	7,500	9,500
Matrix ▲	—	4,500	5,000	5,500	6,500	7,000	9,000	11,000	12,500
Matrix ▼	—	3,500	4,500	5,000	6,000	6,500	7,500	10,000	11,500
XR ▲	—	5,000	6,000	7,000	8,500	10,500	12,500	14,500	16,000
XR ▼	—	4,000	5,500	6,000	7,000	9,500	11,000	13,000	15,000
XRS AWD ▲	—	7,500	8,000	9,500	10,500	—	—	19,500	—
XRS AWD ▼	—	6,500	7,000	8,500	9,500	—	—	18,000	—
Vibe ▲	—	3,000	4,000	5,000	6,000	7,000	8,000	10,000	11,500
Vibe ▼	—	2,500	3,000	4,500	5,000	6,600	7,000	8,500	10,500
GT AWD ▲	—	3,500	4,500	5,000	5,500	—	—	13,000	14,500
GT AWD ▼	—	3,000	4,000	4,400	5,500	—	—	11,500	13,500
Reliability (Corolla)	2	2	2	2	2	2	2	2	2
Matrix/Vibe	4	4	4	5	5	5	5	5	5
Crash Safety (F)	4	5	5	5	5	5	5	4	4
Matrix	—	5	5	5	5	5	5	5	5

All ratings on a numbered scale where 5 is good and 1 is bad. See page 132 for a more detailed description.

Vibe	—	5	5	5	5	5	5	5	5
Side	4	4	4	4	4	4	4	5	5
Matrix	—	5	5	3	3	3	3	5	5
Vibe	—	5	5	3	3	3	3	5	5
IIHS Side	—	1	1	3	3	3	3	5	5
Offset	3	5	5	5	5	5	5	5	5
Head Restraints	2	3	3	1	1	1	1	5	5
Matrix/Vibe	—	—	—	—	—	—	—	3	3
Roof Strength	—	—	—	—	—	—	—	5	5
Matrix	3	4	4	4	4	4	4	4	4
Rollover Resistance	3	4	4	4	4	4	4	4	4

Toyota

ECHO, YARIS ★ ★ ★ ★ ★ / ★ ★ ★

best buy

The Toyota Echo.

RATING: *Echo:* Recommended (2000–05). *Yaris:* Average (2006–10). Both cars are practical and cheap, if you can get past the tall, function-over-form styling and rust-damaged ABS brakes of the newer Yaris. The Echo is an excellent alternative to the similarly styled, glitch-ridden early Ford Focus models and the discontinued Chrysler Neon and PT Cruiser. Now that the Echo has been replaced by the larger Yaris, Echo resale values have declined markedly, making it a cheap and reliable urban runabout. **Ideal model year:** For new safety and performance features, like traction control and an anti-skid system, look for a $9,500 high-mileage, upgraded 2010 Yaris LE with some factory warranty left. **"Real" city/highway fuel economy:** *Echo manual:* 6.7/5.2 L/100 km. *Echo automatic:* 7.1/5.5 L/100 km. *Yaris manual:* 7.0/5.5 L/100 km. *Yaris automatic:* 7.0/5.6 L/100 km. **Maintenance/**

All ratings on a numbered scale where 5 is good and 1 is bad. See page 132 for a more detailed description.

repair costs: Low, except for 2007–08 Yaris brake corrosion problems. **Parts:** Easily found and cheap. **Extended warranty:** A waste of money. **Best alternatives:** Honda Civic; Hyundai Accent; Mazda3, Mazda5, or Protegé; Nissan Sentra; and Suzuki Aerio. **Helpful websites:** *www.toyotanation.com* and *www.toyotaownersclub.com*.

 ## Strengths and Weaknesses

Echo

Toyota scrapped its highly recommended Tercel in favour of the 2000 Echo for a six-year run before it was replaced by the Yaris. Echo is an entry-level, five-passenger econocar that usually gives good fuel economy without sacrificing performance. Both two- and four-door models are available, and the car costs substantially less than the Corolla. The Echo also offers about the same passenger space as the Corolla, thanks to a high roof and low floor height.

The Echo is powered by a 108 hp 1.5L DOHC 4-cylinder engine, featuring variable valve timing (VVT) cylinder-head technology. Normally, an engine this small would provide wimpy acceleration, but thanks to the Echo's light weight, acceleration is more than adequate with the manual gearbox and acceptable with the automatic.

Standard safety features include five three-point seat belts (front seat belts have pretensioners and force limiters), two front airbags (sadly, side airbags are not available), four height-adjustable head restraints, rear child-seat tether anchors, and rear door locks.

Some of the negatives: The Echo's base tires provide poor wet traction, its narrow body limits rear bench seating to two adults, its tall profile and light weight make it vulnerable to side-wind buffeting, and its excessive torque steer makes for sudden pulling to one side when accelerating. There have also been a few complaints about rough idling, hard transmission shifts, broken door latches, leaking shock absorbers, engine ticking and rattling, some interior and brake squeaks, and a high-pitched whine and pulling to the right when underway.

Yaris

ALERT! Owners report serious brake corrosion with the 2007–08 Yaris. The following owner of a 2007 Yaris sums up the problem (*www.yarisworld.com/forums/showthread.php?t=11533*):

> Last winter, I was without ABS for about 2 months. They initially replaced the sensor for one of the rear wheels ($450+), but after a week, the problem came back. It took me about a month to take the car back in and their senior mechanic spent 2 hours on it and decided he couldn't fix it and they'd have to order in a new wiring harness since the connections were corroded. After a week, they got the new harness in, and that solved the problem. However, I was dinged another $250 for

the harness. Total was over $700+ to fix the problem. If I was in the market for another Yaris, I'd pass on the ABS.

Although it's not very refined mechanically or stylistically when compared with the Honda and Mazda competition, you can't beat a Yaris for giving good fuel economy and offering acceptable reliability. It does provide a comfortable ride, but rear entry/exit is a pain, handling is surprisingly sloppy, engine and road noise is omnipresent, adequate acceleration is not one of the options offered, and the car can be hard to control when buffeted about by side winds or when it gathers speed (hatchbacks, especially). Braking is another drawback. Stops seem to take forever without the optional anti-lock brakes. Acceleration with the 106 hp 1.5L 4-cylinder engine is acceptable, but you will have to contend with lots of engine and road noise entering into the cabin area as the car picks up speed. The positioning of the steering wheel and centre-mounted dash gauges may be hard for some drivers to accept, as well. Yaris models are selling at discount now that the Ford Fiesta, Honda Fit, and Mazda3 are eating into the small-car market, which Toyota once practically owned.

VEHICLE HISTORY: *Echo:* **2003**—A major restyling adds 4 cm to overall length, via new front and rear sheet metal, as well as revised bumpers, hood, front fenders, headlights, tail lights, trunk lid, and grille. *Yaris:* **2006**—Replaced Echo as a new 2006 model. **2008**—A "sporty" S hatchback arrives with the generic 106 hp 1.5L 4-cylinder engine hooked to a 5-speed manual or 4-speed automatic transmission. **2009**—A 4-door hatchback joins the lineup. **2010**—The two-door RS hatchback has been dropped. The four-door hatchback comes with standard vehicle stability control and brake assist; front-seat side and side curtain airbags are also standard. The four-door LE hatchback now has a 60/40 split-folding rear seat. Anti-lock brakes are a standard feature on the sedan.

 ## Safety Summary

All models/years: Airbag malfunctions. • Sudden, unintended acceleration:

> While driving, the Echo will accelerate to 60 mph [100 km/h] without [my] hitting the gas pedal. I have to put the vehicle in Neutral to stop it. I contacted [the] dealer, but he cannot locate the cause. The sudden acceleration incident occurred three times. The problem was not corrected by removing the cruise control.

Echo: **2002**—In one incident, sudden steering loss led to crash. • Vehicle often jumps out of Drive into Neutral. **2003**—Engine hesitates when shifting gears. • Chronic stalling when decelerating. • Dash lights not bright enough. **2005**—Brake failure caused by a warped brake rotor. • Vehicle won't remain in Overdrive. • Gasoline smell permeates the cabin. • Leaking shock absorbers. • Broken door latches. *Yaris:* **2006**—Dashboard fire. • Total brake failure. • Intermediate steering shaft fails. **2007**—Seat belt fails to retract. • In one incident, a child had to be cut free from a seat belt that continued to tighten around the child's body. • In cold weather, the manual transmission sticks in First gear. • On a hill, First gear will not prevent the vehicle from backing down the hill while parked. • Vehicle pulls to the left and the right when reaching 100 km/h. • Trunk lid may suddenly fall. • Driver's side door window explodes for no reason. **2007–08**—Premature brake sensor corrosion will shut down your ABS and break your budget. **2008**— Frequent stalling. • No brakes, or brakes lock up. • Car cannot be refuelled without gas overflowing. **2009**—Passenger-side airbag is disabled even when an average-sized passenger is seated. • Cruise control won't deactivate unless one stomps on the brake pedal. • Inaccurate fuel gauge reading shuts down the car. • Random stalling with manual transmission. • Brake failures. • AC produces disagreeable odours. • Ignition key sticks in the ignition and burns up the starter. **2010**— Traction control prevents car from going up hills in icy conditions and cannot be turned off unless fuse to traction control and ABS is removed. • While driving on the highway late at night, the driver-side window imploded. A Google search showed this to be quite common. • Stuck accelerator pedal. • Overly sensitive steering. • Interior and exterior lights malfunction intermittently. • A burning odour permeates the cabin. • Fuel pump and computer fuse failures. • Ignition key, key tumbler, and surrounding metal cylinder get very hot. • Car surged violently after hitting a patch of rough road; almost impossible to control steering.

Secret Warranties/Internal Bulletins/Service Tips

All models: 2003–11—Eliminating a windshield ticking noise. **2004–10**— Front seat squeak. *Echo:* **2002–05**—Fixes for a vehicle that pulls to one side. **2003–05**—AC evaporator leaks water into the cabin. *Yaris:* **2006–07**—Front windshield ticking noise. **2006–09**—Inability to shift out of Park. **2007**—Trunk lid full-open improvement. • Engine compartment rattle heard when car is put in Reverse. • Intermittent odour in the cabin. • Paint staining along horizontal surfaces. **2007–08**—Water on front and rear carpets. • Noise, vibration with the blower motor on. • Rattle from the upper instrument panel area. • ABS light stays on (corrosion alert). • Noise, vibration on acceleration, or when shifting gears. **2007–09**—Engine noise, vibration when vehicle accelerates. • Automatic transmission shift cable rattles in when car in Reverse. **2007–10**—AC blower motor noise and vibration. **2007–11**—Front end clunk.

ECHO, YARIS PROFILE

	2002	2003	2004	2005	2006	2007	2008	2009	2010
Cost Price ($)									
Echo hatch	14,084	13,690	12,995	12,995	—	—	—	—	—
Yaris	—	—	—	—	13,580	13,725	13,165	13,210	13,620
Used Values ($)									
Echo hatch ▲	1,500	2,000	2,500	3,000	—	—	—	—	—
Echo hatch ▼	1,500	2,000	2,000	2,500	—	—	—	—	—
Yaris ▲	—	—	—	—	4,000	5,000	7,000	8,500	10,000
Yaris ▼	—	—	—	—	3,500	4,500	6,000	7,500	9,000

Reliability	4	4	4	4	4	3	3	4	4
Crash Safety (F)	4	4	4	4	—	4	4	4	4
Yaris hatch	—	—	—	—	—	—	5	5	5
Side	3	3	3	3	—	3	3	4	4
Yaris hatch	—	—	—	—	—	—	5	5	5
IIHS Side (Yaris)	—	—	—	—	—	1	1	5	5
Offset (Yaris)	—	—	—	—	—	5	5	5	5
Head Restraints (Yaris)	—	—	—	—	—	2	2	2	2
Roof Strength	—	—	—	—	—	3	3	3	3
Rollover Resistance	4	4	4	4	—	4	4	4	4

Volkswagen

GOLF, RABBIT, JETTA, CABRIO, EOS/DIESEL MODELS ★ ★ / ★ ★ ★

RATING: Below Average (1999–2010). When the cars' transmission isn't trying to kill you (see **ALERT!** below), these econocars perform well during the first five years—then the electronics, emissions system, and brakes start to give you grief. Golfs are entry-level models that are the cheapest of the lot and depreciate fairly rapidly. A Jetta is a Golf with a trunk, the most popular configuration, which fetches fair resale prices. A Cabrio is a Golf without a roof; it depreciates steeply after its first five years. An Eos is an overpriced 2007 or later Cabrio, a car for impatient buyers with big wallets—expect a $10,000 depreciation after its first year on the market. *Diesel models:* Average (2007–2010). Below Average (1999–2006). Servicing for the new diesel system in these recent models takes considerable skill, and fixes don't last long. **Ideal model year:** Old-technology, pre-2007 diesels present fewer quality and servicing problems and are more reasonably priced, but they are only the best of a bad lot. The diesel system is less complicated than the newer units and if you want to junk the car after a few years, you can do so with minimal depreciation loss. Be careful of the newer TDIs: a 2009 Jetta TDI Wagon costing between $13,000 and $14,500 can easily hit you with a $10,000 engine repair bill and a forced diet of expensive new tires as you near that critical fifth year of ownership. **"Real" city/highway fuel economy:** *City Golf manual:* 9.8/7.1 L/100 km. *City Golf automatic:* 9.6/7.2 L/100 km. *Golf manual:* 9.8/7.2 L/100 km. *Golf automatic:* 9.6/7.2 L/100. *Golf TDI manual:* 6.2/4.6 L/100 km. *Golf TDI automatic:* 7.1/4.2 L/100 km. *GTI manual:* 9.8/6.9 L/100 km, or 11.1/7.3 L/100 km with the 6-speed. *Jetta 1.8 manual:* 9.9/6.9 L/100 km. *Jetta 1.8 automatic:* 10.8/7.4 L/100 km. *Jetta 2.0 manual:* 9.8/7.0 L/100 km. *Jetta 2.0 automatic:* 9.6/7.2 L/100 km. *Jetta 2.8 manual:* 11.1/7.3 L/100 km. *Jetta TDI manual:* 6.2/4.6 L/100 km. *Jetta TDI automatic:* 7.1/4.9 L/100 km. *Eos 2.0 manual:* 10.1/6.8 L/100 km. *Eos 2.0 automatic:* 10.3/6.9 L/100 km. *Eos 3.2 V6 automatic:* 10.8/7.5 L/100 km. *Diesel versions:* Although owners of gasoline-fuelled vehicles report that their consumption is about 15 percent higher than the estimates listed above, the

TDI engine still burns about 30 percent less fuel than an equivalent 4-cylinder gasoline engine and has an impressive range of 1,000 km (600 mi.) or more. You'll need that range, however, since only one fuel station out of three or four sells diesel fuel. Plus, diesel fuel is usually much more expensive than gasoline. This is where government subsidies and automaker rebates ought to be given, not with hybrids and electrics. **Maintenance/repair costs:** Maintenance costs are unreasonably high; for example, TDIClub (*www.tdiclub.com*) warns that power-steering fluid, brake fluid, and special automatic transmission fluid should be purchased only from the dealer for optimal performance, even though the VW power-steering fluid is many times more expensive than fluid sold by independents. Repairs have always been dealer-dependent, and even more so since VW changed its diesel technology in 2007. **Parts:** Expensive, and not generally available from independent suppliers. Recall campaign parts may be back ordered for months. **Extended warranty:** A smart idea. VW "Goodwill" warranty repairs are practically nonexistent in Canada. **Best alternatives:** Any small car that doesn't punish backseat passengers as much as this VW trio does. Try the Honda Civic; Hyundai Elantra or Tiburon; Mazda3, Mazda5, or Protegé; and Nissan Sentra. There is no viable diesel alternative. If a convertible tickles your fancy, consider a Mazda Miata or Toyota Solara. **Helpful websites:** *http://forums.vwvortex.com* and *http://volkswagenownersclub.com/vw*.

Strengths and Weaknesses

ALERT! Volkswagens equipped with a DSG manual/automatic transmission are failure-prone and lag and lurch in any gear. This owner reported the following life-threatening incidents to NHTSA:

> I own a 2009 Jetta TDI with a DSG transmission. I feel like I am going to get hit when I start from a stop. The transmission jumps and hesitates. I [have] been to the dealer without [it] being fixed. It is terrifying to drive a car that may or may not accelerate which also jumps in and out of gear!

Volkswagen are such weasels: Their confidential service bulletin below says this problem "seems to be a concern," causes only a "momentary" delay, and is a "normal" operating condition of the transmission.

Fuddle duddle. NO delay is acceptable. Delays are always life-threatening, and the concern to "some" means hundreds of scared people. Finally, this problem may be "normal" for VW, but it is certainly not acceptable to everyone else. And get this: "All 2004–11 models may be affected."

Stop the crap, VW.

In most cases, momentary delays (less than 1 second) while seeming to be a concern, are a normal operating condition of the transmission and repairs are not required.

DIRECT SHIFT GEARBOX (DSG), MOMENTARY DELAY WHEN ACCELERATING

BULLETIN NO.: 35 11 01　　　　　　　　　　　　　　　　　　　　　　　JUNE 6, 2011

MODEL(S)	YEAR	ENG. CODE	TRANS. CODE	VIN RANGE FROM	VIN RANGE TO
ALL	2004-2011	ALL	DSG	ALL	ALL

In most cases, momentary delays (less than 1 second) while seeming to be a concern, are a normal operating condition of the transmission and repairs are not required.

COMPLAINT		CAUSE		CORRECTIVE ACTION
Delay when accelerating from stop...	...when moving selector lever from position "N" or "P" to "D" and accelerating within less than 1 second. ...after heavy braking to a stop and accelerating immediately (within 1 second). i.e. when driving up to a Yield sign then accelerating.	1st, and reverse gears are on one shaft. 2nd gear is on the other shaft. The DSG cannot determine whether the vehicle will be driven forwards or backwards. Therefore, the gearbox has mechanically preselected reverse gear and 2nd gear. DSG only shifts down to 2nd gear.	DSG Starts out in 2nd gear and then changes into 1st gear during acceleration phase. Initial acceleration in 2nd gear could be perceived as inadequate.	No action required, operating as designed.
	...especially when on a slope	Oil level too low.		Check oil level according to Repair Manual.
Delay when accelerating from stop. Jerks when drive engages...	...in conjunction with reduced creeping capability	Inaccurate adaptation.		Perform basic settings using Guided Fault Finding (GFF).
Delay when accelerating from constant speed...	...when manually downshifting (especially gears 6 to 5 and 4 to 3) using Tiptronic function (steering wheel or shift lever) while simultaneously depressing accelerator pedal. No Kickdown. Cannot be reproduced in drive range "D".	The duration of downshifts for the DSG is comparable to other transmissions. Downshifts take place with multiple declutching. The reason for multiple declutching is to reach the synchronization speed of the engine for the selected gear as quickly as possible. To achieve this, multiple declutching is activated until the synchronization speed is reached. During this process, the vehicle does not accelerate. Depending on the driving situation, this process lasts for less than 1 second.		No action required, operating as designed.

COMPLAINT	CAUSE	CORRECTIVE ACTION
...when accelerating lightly (shortly after upshift).	The clutch is perceived to be slipping. Two gears are selected, the K1 and K2 clutches are in slip. There is a gearshift overlap, which is necessary to prevent a disruption of traction. This happens when changing gears from 5 to 6 to 5, if the vehicle is accelerated lightly right after 6th gear is selected, this makes gear selection more difficult for the gearbox control unit.	
(below 2500 RPM)... in the drive range "D", slowly pressing & holding accelerator at 2/3 pedal travel. No kickdown. No downshift occurs. Above 2500 RPM (complaint cannot be reproduced).	Possible engine misfire.	Check engine according to the Repair Manual using the VAS 5051 Diagnostic Tool.

Apart from having dangerous transmissions, these European small cars do give a comfortable ride and provide good fuel economy. On the other hand, rear passenger room is fairly restricted, and some models, like the GLI, don't provide enough power for most tastes. Both engines are easily started in cold weather, but here's the rub: Golfs and Jettas become less reliable as the end of the warranty approaches. What you save with less fuel consumption, you lose in the ever-mounting maintenance costs as the vehicle gains years and mileage. Finding a qualified independent repairer can offset the high maintenance charges, but qualified independents are rarer than hen's teeth. And 2007 and later models use new diesel technology that is best left to VW mechanics.

VEHICLE HISTORY: 2002—Debut of the more-powerful 1.8L 4-cylinder engine, a 5-speed automatic transmission, and an optional 6-speed manual transmission; 2.8L V6 horsepower boosted (200 hp). **2003**—Anti-skid system becomes standard with the V6 engine; GL gets power windows, heated power mirrors, and cruise control; GLS versions come with alloy wheels and a sunroof. **2004**—All-wheel-drive Golf arrives. **2005**—Jetta's GLI VR6 sedan and the limited-edition all-wheel-drive V6 Golf R32 are ditched. Mid-year, revamped Jettas with a larger platform, 150 hp 5-cylinder engine, four-wheel ABS disc brakes, and head-protecting side airbags arrive. **2006**—Turbocharged gasoline engine and rear side airbags. The Jetta 2.0T and GLI get the 200 hp turbocharged 4-cylinder and 6-speed manual transmission. Frequently stolen Xenon headlights are standard on the GLI and optional for the 2.0T. The Golf is renamed the Rabbit (the Rabbit name was last used in 1983). Arrival of a sporty two-door called the GTI. **2007**—Jetta GL's suspension is lowered by 2 cm (0.8 in.). Wolfsburg Edition joins the lineup with its sunroof, heated front seats, and 5-cylinder engine. **2008**—Jetta gets more power and a new model lineup that includes S, SE, and SEL versions, instead of the Base and 2.5. The GLI now carries a base 170 hp 2.5L 5-cylinder engine, an increase of 20 hp from 2007. GLI uses a turbocharged 200 hp 2.0L 4-cylinder. S and SE versions are available with a 5-speed manual transmission. GLIs use a 6-speed manual. A 6-speed automatic is standard on the SEL and optional on all other Jettas. The Rabbit gets 20 more horses. **2009**—Jetta adds a wagon and an available 140-hp 2.0L 4-cylinder turbodiesel engine. **2010**—Jettas and Golfs rust prematurely, usually around areas where panels join or chrome strips have been placed. Undercarriages suffer from deterioration and increasingly frequent mechanical/electrical failures after their fourth year in service. For example, starters often burn out because they are vulnerable to engine heat; fuel pumps self-destruct. As well, sunroofs leak, door locks jam, window cranks break, and windows bind. Owners also report engine head gasket leaks as well as water-pump and heater-core breakdowns. It's axiomatic that all diesels are slow to accelerate, but VW's Fourth gear often can't handle highway speeds above 90 km/h. Engine noise can be deafening when shifting down from Fourth gear.

VW reliability is below average and repair charges are onerous. Invariably, VW service managers blame owners, never the car. Still, it's hardly a secret that VW powertrains, brake components, and fuel and electrical systems have the half-life of a fruit fly, requiring expensive repairs that are often ineffective. Exhaust systems aren't very durable, body hardware and dashboard controls are fragile, the paint often discolours and is easily chipped, and window regulators constantly fail.

Similar quality shortcomings afflict Volkswagen's other divisions: Audis and Porsches are undoubtedly top-performing vehicles, but they're cursed by using similar failure-prone VW components (did someone mention the DSG transmission?) that can't be diagnosed or repaired at the corner garage. When the faulty part is found, it will likely be back ordered for weeks. Owners endure chronic electrical short circuits; heater/defroster resistor and motor failures; leaking transmission and stub-axle seals; and defective valve-pan gaskets, head gaskets, timing belts, steering assemblies, suspension components, and alternator pulleys. Body problems are legion, including air and water leaks, faulty catalytic converters, inoperative locks and latches, poor-quality body construction and paint, and cheap, easily broken accessories and trim items.

Owners also complain of noisy brakes and wheel bearings; malfunctioning gauges and accessories; fragile bumpers that become brittle and crack as the temperature falls; chronic automatic transmission/clutch and diesel-engine turbocharger problems; and leaky sunroofs and assorted water leaks from other areas (when it rains, both the front and rear floors are soaked).

Eos

A four-seater Jetta with a folding metal hardtop, the Eos is a pricey convertible that doesn't provide sporty handling and has limited rear passenger room. Powered by a peppy 200 hp 2.0L turbocharged 4-cylinder or a torquier 250 hp 3.2L V6 coupled to either a standard 6-speed manual or an automated manual DSG transmission ("Do you feel lucky, punk?"), the Eos provides the same superb handling and ride comfort as the Jetta—without the wind buffeting, wind and water leaks, and chassis flexing found with many convertibles. The 2008 models returned relatively unchanged and are the best buys within this group. The 2009 Eos dropped the VR6 version; all models now carry the 200 hp turbocharged 2.0L 4-cylinder.

 ## The Diesel Dilemma

People who buy a diesel-powered vehicle such as VW's TDI usually cite at least one of these three reasons for their decision: lower fuel costs, lower maintenance costs, and the popular notion that diesel engines are more durable. Unfortunately, none of these reasons stand up under close scrutiny:

> 2009 VW Jetta TDI fuel pump explodes sending metal shavings into the fuel system and engine. Causing the vehicle to stall in the middle of the interstate while driving. Dealership gave me repair quote of $10,000. I don't have the money to get my car fixed. I was told that this is an ongoing issue with these cars.

Higher operating costs

Diesel-fuelled vehicles do provide 20–30 percent better fuel economy than gasoline burners. But those savings are being progressively wiped out by higher diesel fuel prices and added maintenance costs (learn to say, "Top off the urea, please"). Diesel fuel costs are expected to go even higher as North American refiners are forced to produce cleaner, more expensive fuel.

Servicing price gouging

Diesel owners decry the high cost of regular maintenance and claim that parts and fluids can cost many times what a non-diesel engine requires. Furthermore, dealerships' service personnel are in a monopolist "take it or leave it" position because there are few independent mechanics available to service diesel cars—good diesel mechanics are rare in most dealerships, and diesel engine diagnostic tools and parts inventories are often wanting.

Reliability: The dark side of diesels

Automakers promote diesel engines for their fuel-efficient and dependable performance; however, independent studies and owner complaints indicate diesels burn more fuel than advertised, are more likely to break down than gasoline-powered engines, and produce emissions that exacerbate lung diseases like emphysema.

With the latest urea-dependent, cleaner-burning diesel system installed within the past few model years, no one knows what the final verdict on diesels will be. One thing is sure, though: Servicing will be more complicated and expensive, and you will be the dealership's captive customer because few independent mechanics will have the experience, tools, fluids, and service codes needed to service these new systems.

Safety Summary

All models/years: Golfs and Jettas, as well as many Audis, are easily stolen due to a flawed door lock mechanism design, reports *Lemon-Aid* reader and British Columbia resident Susan O.:

> Basically, it is a factory-installed flaw in the design that if you pop the silver cylinder off the only keyed door, you can remove the lock mechanism, which allows anyone to get into the vehicle. Further to that, you are also able to deactivate the alarm, so the VW/Audi owner would not hear anyone gaining entry.

NHTSA's database shows repeated reports of the following problems: fires; lights that go out; self-activating alarms; inadequate defrosting; AC mould and mildew smell; brake, tire, and AC failures; early replacement of brake pads; window regulator failure; inadvertent airbag deployment; transmission and wheel bearing failures; poor-quality body components; inoperable power windows; erratic cruise-control operation; Airbag light stays on for no apparent reason; electrical malfunctions leading to chronic stalling; airbags fail to deploy or cause severe injuries when they go off; and DSG manual transmission pops out of gear or tends to lag and lurch. Also, doors may open suddenly; hoods suddenly fly up; locks jam shut, fall out, or freeze; power-window motors and regulators self-destruct; cigarette lighters pop out of their holders while lit; the seat heater may burn a hole in the driver's seat; and battery acid can leak onto the power-steering reservoir and cause sudden steering loss. **All models: 2000–03**—Airbag cover pops off while driving. • Cracked oil pan. • Engine burns oil. • Hard starting. • Noisy, prematurely worn brakes. • Sudden headlight failure; poor headlight illumination. • Faulty power-window regulators cause windows to fall down into door panels. **2002**—Sudden, unintended acceleration. • Vehicle hesitates on acceleration. **2003**—One vehicle's driver's seat burst into flames. **2004**—Golf totally destroyed by a fire of unknown origin. • Jetta fire ignited in the seat-heater control, which was shut off at the time. • VW says engines need a special oil to prevent engine sludge. • Transmission clutch slipping. • There is such a long delay when shifting the automatic transmission in Reverse or Drive, the vehicle is free to roll as if it were in Neutral. • Harsh downshifts. • Transmission locks up between Third and Fourth gears. • Frequent electrical shorts (windows, lights, gauges, alarm system, etc.). • Dash gauges cannot be read in sunlight. • Distracting reflection from the chrome shifter panel. **2004–11**—DSG automatic transmission–equipped cars may buck or jerk when accelerating; there is often a one- or two-second delay after the gas pedal is pressed. **2005**—Engine surges when shifted into Reverse. • Faulty fuel gauges. • Driver's seat becomes unattached. **2006**—Fuel doesn't get to the engine. • Full throttle will only make the vehicle idle. • Engine is always ready to stall out. **2007**—Faulty water pump impeller causes the car to overheat. **2008**—"Lag and lurch": vehicle feels like it is going to stall out, and then it suddenly surges:

> There has been an intermittent fuel shutoff problem that results in a stall or a lurch that results in a near-stop. This occurs in low-speed, heavy traffic situations

with trailing throttle (typically no brake application)... I have since found identical complaints on several VW-interest forums on the web including Carspace Automatic forums and VWVortex forums, VW Rabbit Owners Club and Edmunds.com. This is a disgrace and an example of corporate irresponsibility.

Windshield wipers stop when the brakes are applied. • Faulty Continental tires. **2009**—Chronic stalling at all speeds. • Faulty steering box may cause excessive steering wheel shake (some, but not all, units were recalled). • Steering locks up while vehicle was underway; freed up when car was restarted. Dealer changed the steering unit. • Vehicle wanders ("floats") all over the road. • In one vehicle the Check Engine and Fuel Cap warning lights came on inexplicably; the fuel tank imploded while dealer was looking for the cause. • RPMs suddenly spike and then the vehicle stalls out. • Car shifts into Neutral while underway. • While the car is in Drive, driver can remove the ignition key and the car will roll freely on any sort of slope. • Driver-side rear door may not unlock. *TDI:* **2004**—Many reports of engine overheating, chronic stalling, and EGR/turbocharger failures:

> TDI engine will stall at times due to coolant leaking internally into [the] intake manifold through [a] faulty EGR cooler, causing vehicle to lose steering and brake assist. I have looked on VW web forums, and many owners have had a similar incident.

> •

> TDI engine and manual transmission: While driving, vehicle lost power intermittently. Pressed accelerator; no change in rpm—just idled. [The] "glow plug" flashed and [the] Engine Warning light...lit after [the] first two occasions, not on [the] third. Re-start solves problem for 30 seconds. Dealership was notified, but did not resolve the problem in two attempts. Vehicle is in for third attempt.

The EGR problem is so rampant and expensive to correct that VW owners are pleading for relief. Enterprising independent repair shops are seizing the opportunity to make a profit by offering cheaper fixes for the well-known turbocharger problems. • Stripped manifold bolts are another cause of the turbo's demise. **2005**—Clutch disengages from the flywheel. • TDI's fuel-filler pipe is too small for most truck stop gas stations. • Chronic surging and stalling. • Sunroof's drains clog, causing serious electrical problems and mould growth:

> Sunroof drains clog causing backup of water to settle on floors ruining carpet, causing mold. Water gets into door frames causing buckling of doors during winter months. Water damage also caused an electrical wiring short which caused an airbag failure as well as ruined two batteries. I have not used or opened the sunroof since for fear of more problems. I was informed that the cost to replace the carpeting again would be charged to me if the car had another water problem again due to the clogged drains.

2006—In a rear-ender, the driver's seatback collapsed and the airbag failed to deploy. • The vehicle stalls out when the accelerator pedal is depressed. Intercooler leaks oil:

Chaffing of the aluminum intercooler pipes by the perpendicular piece of plastic that extends to it from the front passenger side grill and touches the intercooler. Over time, the plastic rubs against the intercooler and eventually creates holes where oil leaks out. If left unchecked, this would lead to continued loss of oil, loss of boost and eventually failure of the turbo. Numerous Internet searches and looking on *www.TDIClub.com* show many occurrences of this problem. It is specific to the TDI version of the Golf since it has a turbo. At a minimum, the plastic needs to be trimmed and a piece of foam or something soft needs to be inserted so nothing hard can rub against the aluminum intercooler pipes.

Premature wear of rear pads and rotors. • Mould buildup due to a defective trunk gasket seal. **2009**—TDI chronic stalling and shutdown; diesel $10,000 failure due to shards of metal in the fuel lines:

Car had to be towed to VW. Upon receipt of the car, VW tried to accuse me of using "bad fuel" but then changed their story, once they did more research (and they found that many people across the US are having this problem). Volkswagen states that there is a complete fuel pump failure, with metal particulate in the fuel filters and system, and all components must be replaced (see *www.tdi-issues.com/hpfp-cases-tac68/2010-vw-jetta-tdi-gap186.htm#comment344*).

Faulty fuel pump blamed on owner:

After being in the shop now for six weeks the dealer has informed me that the problem is with the fuel system and that the fuel pump has failed. They say there is rust and other contamination in it and there must have been water in the system. VW has refused to cover it under the warranty. The cost of replacing the entire fuel system will be $8,000–$10,000. Having researched the issue online I have found that this is an often reported occurrence and a known problem with the 2009 Jetta TDIs. It appears that VW is covering the problem in many cases but not in others.... This problem is a point of discussion on numerous forums see *http://forums.tdiclub.com/showthread.php?t=286380*.... VW is trying to foist it off on the customers rather than taking responsibility for it. I may well need to file suit against the dealership to get this issue resolved.

Hard cold weather starts. • Premature, uneven rear brake wearout:

Brakes need to be replaced at 25,000 miles [40,200 km] and 50% of the miles were highway miles. Spongy brake pedal and heavy rear wheel brake dust reported to dealer 3 times when new and at the normal service intervals. VW dealer service manager said all 09 Jetta's rear brakes are wearing out between 20,000 and 30,000 miles [32,200–48,300 km]. Either rear brake design or materials are defective causing premature wear and failure.

2010—Airbag failed to deploy. • Chronic loss of power, stalling with TDI. • Repeated fuel pump failures. • Horn takes a second or so to sound. • Foot got stuck under the brake pedal. • Engine failure caused by poor engine design, says this NHTSA owner report:

> Inter-cooler design is defective in that it allows condensation and sludge to build within the charge air intake system which subsequently freezes and thaws with low ambient temperature and it moves further and further within the intake system until the condensate and sludge become drawn into the air intake manifold and becomes discharged into the cylinders causing the engine to hydro-lock and fail. Causing potential for permanent and catastrophic damage upon restart. Currently for this model, the repair is covered under the manufacturer's warranty along with replacement of the charge air inter-cooler system with a redesign. It remains to be seen whether this redesigned system indeed solves the root cause of this problem. However, if the car is beyond the years/miles of the original manufacturer's or extended warranty, VW will not subsidize the repairs to the engine, nor the replacement of the charge air system…even though the problem was directly caused by their design. The owner will be responsible for the large expense of getting the car running again.

Secret Warranties/Internal Bulletins/Service Tips

All models: 1997–2009—Class action settlement results in Service Actions implemented in 2007–08 to pay for and mitigate water damage to components and interiors of numerous models, and reimburse expenses; certain VW Passat and Audi A4 and A6 vehicles are included. Service Action for owners and lessees of certain Golf/GTI, Jetta, Jetta Wagon, and New Beetle vehicles to modify leaking sunroofs, provide refunds, and update maintenance recommendations for drainage systems. Lawyers are litigating the inclusion in the settlement of all 1997–2009 models. (See *www.WaterIngressSettlement.com* or *www.volkswagen-classaction.com*.) **1999–2006**—Possible reasons why the car won't start or is hard to start. **1999–2008**—Inoperative window regulator. • Noisy, binding sunroof. • Repair tips on fixing heated rear windshield lines that are inoperative. **1999–2012**—Troubleshooting brake pedal vibration, pulsation. **2003–10**—Causes for excessive vibration when braking (a warranty item, admits VW). • Headlights dim when vehicle is put into Idle. **2004–11**—DSG transmission lag and lurch troubleshooting (see **ALERT!** above). **2005–07**—Engine knocking noise. • Rattle from front passenger-side floor area. **2005–08**—Troubleshooting sound system malfunctions. • Fix for an inoperative seat heater. • Seized AC compressor. **2005–10**—Cooling fan runs on after ignition shut off. • Poor heater output. **2006–08**—Ice deforms leading edge of doors. **2007–10**—AC blower motor operates on high speed only. **2008**—Loose door mirrors; incorrect fold functions. • Engine cooling fan stays on. **2009–10**—No start, runs rough. *Rabbit, GTI, R32.* **2010**—Noise from the B-pillar area. • Front door gap causes some wind noise. • Can't open liftgate after locking. **2010–11**—Poor front seat heater performance.

GOLF, RABBIT, JETTA, CABRIO, EOS PROFILE

	2002	2003	2004	2005	2006	2007	2008	2009	2010
Cost Price ($)									
Cabrio/Eos	28,530	—	—	—	—	36,900	35,975	35,975	36,575
Golf/City	19,230	17,950	18,300	18,530	18,530	14,900	15,300	15,300	15,300
Jetta/City	21,490	24,260	24,520	24,750	24,975	16,700	16,900	16,900	22,175
Jetta TDI	23,220	23,450	25,860	26,080	26,310	—	—	24,275	24,475
Jetta TDI wagon	—	—	25,860	27,550	27,780	—	—	25,775	—
Rabbit	—	—	—	—	—	19,990	19,975	19,975	—
Used Values ($)									
Cabrio/Eos ▲	6,500	—	—	—	—	16,500	20,500	23,000	27,500
Cabrio/Eos ▼	5,500	—	—	—	—	15,000	19,000	21,500	26,000
Golf/City ▲	2,500	3,500	4,000	5,000	6,000	7,000	8,500	10,000	11,500
Golf/City ▼	2,500	3,000	3,500	4,500	5,000	6,000	7,000	9,000	10,500
Jetta/City ▲	5,500	6,000	6,500	7,500	8,000	9,500	10,500	12,500	16,500
Jetta/City ▼	5,000	5,500	6,000	7,000	7,500	8,500	9,500	11,500	15,000
Jetta TDI ▲	6,000	6,500	7,000	8,000	9,500	—	—	15,000	17,500
Jetta TDI ▼	5,500	6,000	6,500	7,500	8,500	—	—	13,500	16,000
Jetta TDI Wagon ▲	—	7,500	8,500	9,000	10,500	—	—	14,500	—
Jetta TDI Wagon ▼	—	6,000	7,500	8,500	9,000	—	—	13,000	—
Rabbit ▲	—	—	—	—	—	10,000	11,500	13,500	—
Rabbit ▼	—	—	—	—	—	8,500	10,000	12,000	—
Reliability	3	3	3	3	3	3	3	3	3
Crash Safety (F)									
Golf	5	5	5	5	5	—	—	—	4
Jetta	5	5	5	4	4	4	4	4	4
Rabbit	—	—	—	—	—	4	4	4	—
Side									
Golf	—	4	4	4	4	—	—	—	5
Jetta	4	—	—	5	5	5	5	5	5
Rabbit	—	—	—	—	—	5	5	5	—
IIHS Side (Golf)	—	—	—	—	—	—	—	—	5
Eos	—	—	—	—	—	5	5	5	5
Jetta	—	—	—	5	5	5	5	5	5
Rabbit	—	—	—	—	5	5	5	5	—
Offset									
Eos	—	—	—	—	—	5	5	5	5
Golf	5	5	5	5	5	—	—	—	5
Jetta	5	5	5	5	5	5	5	5	5
Rabbit	—	—	—	—	5	5	5	5	—
Head Restraints (F)									
Eos	—	—	—	—	—	2	2	5	5
Golf 2d	5	5	5	—	—	—	—	—	5
Golf 4d	3	3	3	—	—	—	—	—	5

All ratings on a numbered scale where 5 is good and **1** is bad. See page 132 for a more detailed description.

Jetta	3	3	3	3	3	2	2	5	5
Rabbit	—	—	—	—	3	2	2	5	—
Roof Strength									
Golf	—	—	—	—	—	—	—	—	5
Jetta	—	—	—	—	—	—	—	—	5
Rabbit	—	—	—	—	5	5	5	5	—
Rollover Resistance									
Golf/Jetta	4	4	4	5	4	4	4	4	4
Rabbit	—	—	—	—	—	4	4	4	—

MEDIUM CARS

The most popular size car sold in North America today, medium- or mid-size vehicles usually have wheelbases between 105 inches (267 cm) and 110 inches (279 cm). A mid-size car is a trade-off between size and fuel economy, offering more room and convenience features but a bit less fuel economy than a small car. Owners also get a full complement of important safety features like side curtain airbags and electronic stability control. As a result of their versatility, as well as both upsizing and downsizing through the years, these vehicles overlap with several car niches and encompass small trucks and downsized SUVs as well.

Hyundai's 1996–2010 Elantra is as good a mid-size car as you can find.

For example, in 1985 the U.S. Environmental Protection Agency classified the Honda Accord and Toyota Camry as compact, but since the 1990s, both have been classified as mid-size.

These cars are best for combined city and highway driving, with the top choices traditionally dominated by Japanese automakers: the Honda Accord; the Mazda5, Mazda6, and 626; and the Toyota Camry. South Korean automakers, however, are catching up fast, both in good times and bad, with Hyundai's Elantra and Sonata leading the pack.

But there are lots of bad cars in this group, too, and they belong mostly to the Detroit automakers. Take the Ford Taurus and Sable, for example. Bestsellers for many years and easily found for a few thousand dollars at most, these two models don't cost much because they are no longer built and have a well-deserved reputation for being lemons. Engine, transmission, brake, electrical, and body problems are legion, and repair costs for the automatic transmission alone can easily run about $3,500.

GM's mid-sized lineup is only marginally better. Cars like the Chevrolet front-drive Impala and Malibu are decent highway performers and relatively fuel-frugal, but their reliability is the pits. Chrysler is the Detroit automaker with the worst quality-control record of all. The Avenger, Dakota, Durango, Sebring, and most of their Jeeps and minivans have declined dramatically in quality during the past decade and are mediocre highway performers. Cheap, they are. But that's mainly because their upkeep costs so much. The only Chrysler model that may be a good buy if priced low enough is a Dodge truck (with an early diesel engine).

Bottom line? Stick with the Asian models for their dependability, solid highway performance, and high residual values.

MEDIUM CAR RATINGS

Recommended

Acura 1.6 EL, 1.7L EL (1999–2005)   Mazda6 (2009–10)
Hyundai Sonata (2009–10)

Above Average

Acura CSX (2006–10)   Mazda6 (2006–10)
Honda Accord (2007)   Nissan Altima (2008–10)
Hyundai Sonata (2006–08)   Toyota Solara (2006–08)

Average

Chrysler Avenger, Sebring (2007–10)   Mazda6 (2003–05)
General Motors Grand Prix,   Mazda 626 (1999–2002)
    Impala, Malibu, Malibu Hybrid   Nissan Altima (2002–07)
    (2008–10)   Nissan Altima Hybrid (2007–09)
Honda Accord (2006; 2010)   Toyota Camry (2010)
Honda Accord Hybrid (2005–07)   Toyota Solara (1999–2005)
Hyundai Sonata (1999–2005)

Below Average

Chrysler Avenger, Sebring (1999–2006)   Honda Accord (2008–09; 1999–2006)
General Motors Bonneville, Grand Prix,   Toyota Prius (2001–10)
    Impala, Intrigue, LeSabre, Lumina,   Volkswagen New Beetle (2008–10)
    Malibu, Monte Carlo,   Volkswagen Passat (1999–2010)
    Regal (1999–2007)

Not Recommended

Toyota Camry (1996–2009)   Volkswagen New Beetle (1999–2007)
Toyota Camry Hybrid (2007–10)

Acura

1.6 EL, 1.7 EL, CSX   ★★★★/★★★★★

RATING: *1.6 EL, 1.7 EL:* Recommended (1999–2005). The first Japanese automobile built exclusively in and for the Canadian market (manufactured in Alliston, Ontario), the EL is basically a gussied-up Honda Civic sold under the Acura

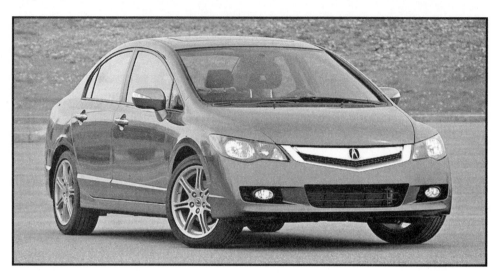

The Acura CSX.

moniker. The redesigned 2001 EL and later models offer the most reliability and performance for the least amount of money. They are the cheapest Acuras available and offer more features and a slightly more powerful, torquier engine than the Civic. As the Civic grew in size from a subcompact to a compact during the past decade, so did the EL. *CSX:* Above Average (2006–10), but watch out for transmission glitches. The CSX is a twin of the Civic Si, borrowing the engine and drivetrain from the Si but adding some luxury options, including leather seating. The CSX also features distinctive front and rear fascias. **Ideal model year:** If you want the performance thrills without the acquisition bills, seriously consider getting a $13,500–$15,000 2008 Type-S. You will be paying half the car's original cost. If you aren't bowled over by the Acura moniker, then choose a 2008 Honda Civic Si Coupe for $12,500–$14,000. **"Real" city/highway fuel economy:** *1.6L manual:* 7.8/6.1 L/100 km. *1.6L automatic:* 7.9/6.0 L/100 km. *1.7L manual:* 8.1/6.3 L/100 km. *1.7L automatic:* 7.9/6.0 L/100 km. *CSX 2.0L manual 5-speed:* 8.7/6.4 L/100 km. *2.0L manual 6-speed:* 10.2/6.8 L/100 km. *2.0L automatic:* 9.5/6.5 L/100 km. **Maintenance/repair costs:** Average. Repairs aren't dealer-dependent. **Parts:** Average costs, thanks to the use of generic Civic parts sold through more price-competitive independent suppliers. **Extended warranty:** Not needed. Best alternatives: Ford Fusion; Honda Civic EX or Si; Hyundai Elantra or Sonata; Mazda3, 5, or 6; and the Suzuki SX4. **Helpful websites:** *www.8thcivic.com/ forums/mechanical-problems-technical-chat.*

 ## Strengths and Weaknesses

ALERT! Buying the cheaper Civic version and keeping it "forever" will save the most money. However, once depreciation has taken its toll on both models, the higher-cost Acura's cachet means that the Acura will retain more of its value than the Civic.

VEHICLE HISTORY: 2002—Improvements to the redesigned 2001 model. **2003**—A retuned suspension and steering system for better handling and enhanced ride comfort through improved engine mounts and upgraded brakes. New features: adjustable head restraints and upgraded instrument clusters, armrests, and front seats. **2006**—CSX is launched. **2007**—Arrival of the high-performance Type-S, selling at a premium over the base CSX. The extra money buys 42 more horses, plenty of torque, a 3,000 rpm redline, and a 6-speed close-ratio manual gearbox. The car also gets stiffer springs, larger stabilizer bars front and rear, and a sport-tuned suspension system. **2008**—Electronic stability control is a big plus. **2009**—A restyled front end; standard 17-inch (43 cm) wheels and fog lights. **2010**—The CSX i-Tech becomes the base model.

EL

First generation ELs come with a peppy 127 hp VTEC 1.6L 4-banger that's both reliable and economical to run. Add the Civic's chassis and upgraded suspension components, and you have competent performance that's as good as or better than the Civic Si's. Weak points: a narrow interior, with seats and seatbacks that are not to everyone's liking; emergency braking that's only average; head restraints rated Poor by IIHS; an overly soft suspension; and excessive engine noise intruding in the passenger compartment.

The 1.6 and 1.7 EL have done quite well over the years they've been on the market. The cabin is quieter than the Civic's, the steering is quick and responsive, handling is quite nimble with 15-inch tires versus the Civic's 14-inchers, and the suspension is firmer. Braking and acceleration have also improved; however, the engine's maximum torque is reached at only about 5000 rpm, which means lots of downshifting with a full load of passengers and cargo. Interestingly, Honda recommends premium gasoline, yet the equivalent Civic gets by with regular fuel. One major safety complaint targets premature strut failures that degrade handling. Otherwise, the few owner complaints recorded have typically concerned premature suspension wear (mostly springs and bushings), merely adequate engine power, wind noise, easily dented body panels, malfunctioning accessories (AC, audio system, electrical components, etc.), and fragile trim items.

CSX

The 2006 CSX is a Civic twin and replaces the 1.7 EL. It is essentially a luxury compact for penny pinchers who can't afford the high prices and servicing costs of competitive German high-end performers. Acura differentiates the car from the Civic through exterior upgrades that include Acura rims, a double exhaust, chrome wheels and door handles, and a restyled front fascia. Other differences: The manumatic comes with cheap-feeling thin paddles mounted on the steering column, plus there are Lilliputian instrument controls, as well as heated leather seats.

A 155 hp 2.0L 4-cylinder engine, also used in the RSX, delivers power smoothly; however, acceleration times are merely middle of the pack. The BMW Mini

Cooper and 128i, Volvo C30, Audi A3 2.0T, and similarly priced Civic Si all give faster takeoffs.

Secret Warranties/Internal Bulletins/Service Tips

All models/years: Most Honda/Acura TSBs allow for special warranty consideration on a "goodwill" basis even after the warranty has expired or the car has changed hands. Referring to this euphemism will increase your chances of getting some kind of refund for repairs that are obviously related to a factory defect. Keep in mind that many Honda bulletins often apply to Acuras as well. So check out the Civic's and Accord's TSBs and safety complaints before assuming that the manufacturer doesn't recognize a particular Acura problem, or that it's your responsibility. **2006**—*Lemon-Aid* reader Larry says:

> The alloy wheels have a huge design flaw—the wheels have a groove in them on the inside. Stones, dirt, ice accumulate in here and throw off the balance which in turn wrecks the tires. I had to throw out a perfectly good set of tires last year (tires get cupped when you do traveling on unbalanced wheels) and it looks like I will probably have to throw this set out as well (maybe 15,000 km on them if I am lucky).

2006–07—Brake pedal feels hard in the morning or in cold weather. **2006–08**—Manual transmission Third gear failures. • Engine surges in first gear. • Oil leaks at the cylinder head cover. **2007–09**—Front door windows rattle.

1.6 EL, 1.7 EL, CSX PROFILE

	2002	2003	2004	2005	2006	2007	2008	2009	2010
Cost Price ($)									
1.6/1.7 EL	21,700	22,000	22,200	23,000	—	—	—	—	—
CSX	—	—	—	—	25,400	25,900	26,990	26,990	27,490
CSX Type-S	—	—	—	—	—	33,400	33,400	33,400	29,990
Used Values ($)									
1.6/1.7 EL ▲	4,500	6,000	7,000	7,500	—	—	—	—	—
1.6/1.7 EL ▼	4,000	5,000	6,000	7,000	—	—	—	—	—
CSX ▲	—	—	—	—	8,500	10,000	12,500	14,500	17,000
CSX ▼	—	—	—	—	8,000	9,000	11,500	13,000	15,500
CSX Type-S ▲	—	—	—	—	—	13,500	15,000	17,000	18,500
CSX Type-S ▼	—	—	—	—	—	12,000	13,500	15,500	17,500
Reliability	5	5	5	5	5	5	5	5	5

Note: These vehicles have not been crash tested, but should perform as well as the Civic Si.

Chrysler

AVENGER, SEBRING ★ ★ ★

RATING: Average (2007–10); Below Average (1999–2006). The Avenger and its better-appointed Sebring twin are not great performers, but they are so cheap and easily fixed, it's not hard to give them the nod as inexpensive basic transporters. Drive a hard bargain, though, because the money you save you'll need to keep in a cookie jar for upcoming transmission, brake and fuel system, and AC evaporator repair bills. The Sebring convertible is an attractively styled bargain ragtop that comes with water leaks and a symphony of squeaks and rattles due to the chassis flexing. **Ideal model year:** None. If you don't mind taking a "leap into the abyss" with your fingers crossed, shop around for a $14,000 Sebring 2009 Convertible. The number of complaints against this car registered with NHTSA is amazingly small). **"Real" city/highway fuel economy:** *Sebring convertible manual: 11.9/7.9 L/100 km. Sebring convertible automatic: 11.2/7.8 L/100 km. 2.4L sedan: 11.1/7.7 L/100 km. 2.7L sedan: 10.6/7.3 L/100 km.* Fuel savings may be lower by about 15 percent. **Maintenance/repair costs:** Average. **Parts:** Reasonably priced and good availability. **Extended warranty:** Yes. **Best alternatives:** Ford Fusion, Honda Accord, Hyundai Elantra or Sonata, and Mazda5 or Mazda6. **Helpful websites:** *www.chryslerforum.com/forum* and *www.topix.com/forum/autos/chrysler-sebring.*

Strengths and Weaknesses

ALERT! Stay away from the AWD model and carry extra warranty protection for automatic transmission breakdowns.

These coupes, sedans, and convertibles are mediocre buys mainly because they're so underpowered and basic. Defects affect body and mechanical components equally, and lead to serious long-term reliability and durability problems. Powertrains, platforms, safety features, and other mechanical components are shared among the entire lineup and can be bought easily from independent suppliers for much less than dealers charge.

VEHICLE HISTORY: 2002—Sebrings are joined by a 200 hp 2.7L V6 R/T sedan equipped with a manual 5-speed gearbox. **2003**—Four-wheel disc brakes. **2006**—Coupes are dropped. **2007**—The sedan is completely redesigned and the convertible is dropped for one model year. The sedan is a bit wider and 10 cm taller, offers more interior room (especially rear legroom) and a taller seating position, and has slightly less cargo volume. Buyers have a choice of three engines: a 2.4L 4-cylinder hooked to the ubiquitous gas-guzzling 4-speed automatic transmission; a 2.7L V6, also coupled to the 4-speed; and a more powerful, better performing 3.5L V6 mated to a 6-speed manumatic transmission. **2008**—A revamped Sebring convertible is resurrected with the 2007 Sebring upgrades. An optional AWD Limited sedan is offered. Sebring's sister car, the Dodge Avenger, returns as a four-door sports sedan after an eight-year absence; it had sold from 1995 to 2000 as a two-door coupe. **2009**—AWD model is axed. **2010**—Standard active head restraints, four-wheel disc brakes. The Limited sedan carries only the 3.5L V6.

And that's a good thing, because the 3.5L V6 is needed to overcome the power-hungry automatic transmission and to avoid a persistent 4-cylinder engine head gasket defect affecting all model years. In theory, the 6-speed transmission should be more economical; however, with the V6 it's overkill and it tends to shift too much, negating the fuel savings one would expect. Handling is so-so, and the ride is generally comfortable.

The 2.7L V6 would normally be a good alternative to the small 4-cylinder; however, it is subject to oil sludging and early failures of the engine primary timing-chain tensioner and tensioner O-ring. Opt for the 2.4L instead. Over the past decade, Avenger/Sebring owners report widespread automatic transmission failures, grinding when shifting, shuddering from a stop, and defaulting to Second gear. Other deficiencies in need of attention include loss of steering; engine oil leaks; sunroof malfunctions; premature brake wear, brake failures, and suspension replacement; ignition, electrical system, and PCM glitches; sloppy body construction (water leaks and lots of wind noise); and a clanking or rattling heard when turning over rough pavement. The driver-seat motor frequently burns out; replacement cost: $2,000. Scrapyard price: $200!

As with 2005–06 Corvettes, Sebring convertible tops can fly off on early models, plus they leak water and air and operate erratically. A faulty window regulator lets the window run off its track; poor design and sloppy construction allow water into the vehicle when the window is partly opened; and rear windshield sealant lets water leak into the vehicle. The side door mouldings melt; there's excessive brake dust; the chrome wheels and airbag coating peel; wheel rims are easily bent and leak air from normal driving; and a black goo oozes from body panels and the undercarriage.

2007–10 models have been beset by some brake, fuel system, and body defects; however, few safety-related complaints have been recorded for these model years. The upgraded 2007s improved brake performance and give a quieter ride. And while the 2.4L 4-cylinder coupled to the 4-speed automatic works hard, the acceleration is woefully unresponsive; the 6-speed transmission hooked to the 3.5L V6 works much more smoothly and delivers the power that's needed, but with excess noise. Post-2006 models also give a busy ride, respond slowly to steering corrections, and feel ponderous and ungainly on the road.

 Safety Summary

All years: Sudden, unintended acceleration. • Airbag malfunctions. • Chronic stalling. • Electrical short-circuits. • Horn blows on its own (costs $700 to fix). •

Steering and automatic transmission failures. • Brake failures. • Early replacement of brake pads and rotors. • Brake and gas pedals too close together. • Exploding windows. **2003**—Tapping brakes locks them up. • ABS failure. • Rodents can get into the heater blower area. • Headlights dim and shut off intermittently. **2004**—Electrical wiring in the rear defroster catches fire. • Firewall fuel line leakage. • Engine overheating. • Seat heater overheats. • Dash lights flicker, and headlights may suddenly go off. • Key sticks in the ignition. • Chrome door handles can cut fingers. • Bumper falls off. **2005**—Airbags deploy and start a fire. • Left front wheel breaks away from vehicle. • Filler pipe collapses while vehicle is refuelling. • Inaccurate fuel gauge readings. **2006**—Varmints chew on the soy-based electrical wiring (control sensor), which makes the engine lose power when the car accelerates. • Engine crankshaft seal failure at 74,000 km. • Fuel pump ($500) sends too much fuel to the engine, causing stalling and lagging when accelerating. • Water collects on the floor of the rear passenger area. • When one car reached 100 km/h, the convertible top blew away. **2007**—Four engine compartment fires reported; one fire attributed to a faulty cooling fan. • Excessive steering shimmy when braking. • ABS and traction control engage for no reason, almost pulling car off the road. • Cruise control failures. • Fuel odour in the cabin. • Instrument panel cluster won't illuminate, or dims unexpectedly. • While underway, the hood suddenly opens and flies backwards. **2008**—Convertible engine compartment fire. • Engine surges when the brake pedal is depressed. • Car accelerates and the cruise control fails to disengage when brakes are applied. • Defective PCM computer module. • Incorrect fuel gauge readings are one-quarter off when the fuel tank is almost empty. **2009**—Emergency brake didn't hold the car in Park. • All four TPS valve stems leaked and caused all four tires to go flat. • Vehicle loses power and then stalls; starter grinds. • Even at its highest setting, driver's seat is too low for driver to see over the hood. • Side window glare obstructs driver's vision. • Hard to secure child safety seats due to restricted accessibility and clearance.

Secret Warranties/Internal Bulletins/Service Tips

2002–04—Delayed gear engagement. **2003–04**—Harsh downshifts. **2004**—Driveability improvements to fix engine stumbling and rough running, idle fluctuations, and surging when at idle or coming to a stop. • Harsh 4–3 downshifts. • Low-speed transmission bumps. • Pop/clunk sound from front of vehicle; engine snapping noise. • Steering-column click. • Revised suspension lateral-control links. • Door clunk noise. • Power seat won't adjust; front seat movement. • Intermittent loss of accessories. **2004–05**—Inoperative AC. **2007–08**—Tips on silencing noisy seats and rear suspension rattles. • Sunroof water leaks. • Rear-door glass comes out of its track; won't roll up. • Front door glass flutter or rattle. • Engine surge or gear hunting upon deceleration. • Steering honk, moan, or grinding sound when making left turns (replace the power steering fluid reservoir). • Broken transmission gearshift-lever interlock spring retainer hook "freezes" lever in Park position. Customer Satisfaction Notification Program K16, dated August 2010, says steel reinforcement clip will be installed for free, if needed. **2007–09**—Difficult to fill fuel; nozzle shut off. • Horn honks or moans on hard left-hand turns. **2007–10**—AC leaks water onto passenger floor. • Lower door hinge popping, groaning noises. **2008**—Hard starts; no-starts. **2010**—Cold start is followed by rough idle. • Automatic transmission transfer gear beating noise. • Rear-door glass may make a "shuttering" noise when raised or lowered. • Trunk release operates even though vehicle is locked.

AVENGER, SEBRING PROFILE

	2002	2003	2004	2005	2006	2007	2008	2009	2010
Cost Price ($)									
Avenger SE	—	—	—	—	—	—	21,195	21,995	22,995
Avenger AWD	—	—	—	—	—	—	30,760	—	—
Sebring	23,320	23,610	24,115	24,560	24,880	22,995	22,995	22,995	23,995
Sebring V6	27,380	27,795	28,415	28,855	—	—	—	—	28,020
Convertible	33,580	34,305	35,195	35,795	36,115	—	29,995	29,995	30,665
Used Values ($)									
Avenger SE ▲	—	—	—	—	—	—	7,500	9,000	11,000
Avenger SE ▼	—	—	—	—	—	—	6,000	8,000	9,500
Avenger AWD ▲	—	—	—	—	—	—	9,500	—	—
Avenger AWD ▼	—	—	—	—	—	—	8,500	—	—
Sebring ▲	2,000	2,500	3,500	4,000	5,000	6,500	8,000	11,500	13,500
Sebring ▼	1,500	2,000	3,000	3,500	4,500	5,500	7,000	10,000	12,000
Sebring V6 ▲	3,500	4,500	5,000	6,000	—	—	—	—	15,500
Sebring V6 ▼	3,000	4,000	4,500	5,500	—	—	—	—	14,000
Convertible ▲	4,500	5,500	6,000	7,000	8,000	—	12,000	14,500	20,000
Convertible ▼	4,000	5,000	5,500	6,000	7,000	—	10,500	13,000	18,500
Reliability	2	2	2	2	2	3	3	3	3
Crash Safety (F)									
Avenger	—	—	—	—	—	—	5	5	5
Sebring 2d	4	4	4	4	—	—	—	—	—
Sebring 4d	5	5	5	5	5	5	5	5	5
Sebring cvt.	3	3	3	3	3	—	4	4	4
Side									
Avenger	—	—	—	—	—	—	5	5	5
Sebring	3	3	3	3	—	—	—	—	5
Sebring 4d	3	3	3	3	3	5	5	5	5
Sebring cvt.	3	3	3	3	5	—	5	5	5
IIHS Side									
Avenger	—	—	—	—	—	—	5	5	5
Sebring	3	3	3	3	3	5	5	5	5
Offset									
Avenger	—	—	—	—	—	—	5	5	5
Sebring	3	3	3	3	3	5	5	5	5

Head Restraints									
Avenger	—	—	—	—	—	—	3	3	5
Sebring	3	1	1	1	1	3	3	3	5
Sebring cvt.	—	—	—	—	—	—	2	2	—
Roof Strength	—	—	—	—	—	—	5	5	5
Rollover Resistance									
Avenger	—	—	—	—	—	—	4	4	4
Sebring 4d	—	4	4	4	—	—	4	4	4
Sebring cvt.	—	5	5	5	5	—	4	4	4

General Motors

BONNEVILLE, GRAND PRIX, IMPALA, INTRIGUE, LESABRE, LUMINA, MALIBU, MALIBU HYBRID, MONTE CARLO, REGAL ★ ★ ★

RATING: Average (2008–10); Below Average (1999–2007). These are the mid-size cars that pushed GM into bankruptcy a few years back: Their blandness, poor fuel economy, non-existent quality control, and mediocre highway performance made the cars so unwanted that even fleet buyers were turning them down. By the time GM began improving the 2008 Malibu and Impala, the company had lost the public's confidence. **Ideal model year:** An upgraded 2008 Chevrolet Impala 1LT or Malibu 2LT for $10,000. **"Real" city/highway fuel economy:** *Impala 3.5 V6L automatic: 8.0/6.7 L/100 km; Impala 3.9 V6L automatic: 12.0/7.4 L/100 km. Malibu 2.2L automatic: 9.9/6.6 L/100 km; Malibu 2.4L automatic: 9.4/5.9 L/100 km; Malibu 3.5L 6-cylinder automatic: 10.4/6.8 L/100 km; 3.6L 6-cylinder automatic: 12.4/7.8 L/100 km. LeSabre, Bonneville 3.8L 6-cylinder automatic: 11.9/7.3 L/100 km. Monte Carlo 3.4L 6-cylinder automatic: 11.8/7.1 L/100 km.* Owners report gas consumption isn't as good as the above figures. **Maintenance/repair costs:** Higher than average. **Parts:** Parts are more difficult to find and more costly because GM's bankruptcy has curtailed inventories for older models everywhere. Fortunately, repairs and parts procurement for the newer front-drive Impala and Malibu aren't as dealer-dependent. **Extended warranty:** Yes, mainly for the engine and automatic transmission. **Best alternatives:** Acura TSX; Ford Fusion; Honda Civic or Accord (choose the model year carefully and check out the tranny on both); Hyundai Elantra or Sonata; and a Mazda5 or 6. **Helpful websites:** *www.gminsidenews.com/forums* and *www.topix.com/forum/com/gm.*

 Strengths and Weaknesses

ALERT! Engine intake manifold gaskets continue to be troublesome on the Impala and Malibu; check out the engine compression before buying.

It's a shame these cars are so poorly made. Hopefully, the 2008–10 models will post better quality scores than previous iterations.

The rear-drive versions of these cars have been off the market for over a decade (but if you can get your hands on an early "classic" one (1984–87), they're highly recommended). The rear-drives were competent and comfortable cars, but they definitely came from a time when handling wasn't a priority and fuel economy was unimportant. Front-drive technology is not GM's proudest achievement.

Front-drive failures

Phased into the lineup in the '80s, GM front-drives are a different breed of car: less reliable and more expensive to repair than rear-drives, with a considerable number of mechanical (e.g., brake, steering, and suspension component) deficiencies directly related to their front-drive configuration. Nevertheless, acceleration is adequate, fuel economy is good, and handling is better than with their rear-drive cousins—except in emergencies, when their brakes frequently lock up or fail, notwithstanding ABS technology. The Detroit automakers' front-drive designs and manufacturing weaknesses make for unimpressive high-speed performance, a poor reliability record, and expensive maintenance costs. That's why most fleets and police agencies use rear-drives when they can get them, and GM is banking on supplying that clientele with new rear-drive police cars, similar to the old Caprice, in the near future.

GM's medium-sized front-drives aren't particularly driver-friendly. Many models have a dash that's replete with confusing push buttons and gauges that are washed out in sunlight or reflect annoyingly upon the windshield. At other times, there are retro touches, like the Intrigue's dash-mounted ignition, that simply seem out of place. The keyless entry system often fails, the radio's memory is frequently forgetful, and the fuel light comes on when the tank is just below the one-half fuel-level mark. The electronic climate control frequently malfunctions, and owners report that warm air doesn't reach the driver-side heating vents. Servicing, especially for the electronic engine controls, is complicated and expensive, forcing many owners to drive around with their Airbag, Service Engine, and ABS warning lights constantly lit.

Other major problem areas include weak shocks; warping rotors; leaking oil pans; rear brake/wheel lock-ups; excessive front brake pad wear; faulty electronic modules; rack-and-pinion steering failures; seizure of the rear brake calipers; early replacement of the suspension struts; automatic transmission failures and clunking; leaking and malfunctioning AC systems (due mainly to defective AC modules); and myriad electrical failures requiring replacement of the computer module.

The high-performance 3.4L V6, available since 1991, gives out plenty of power, but only at high engine speeds. Overall, the 3.8L V6 is a more suitable compromise. One major powertrain problem found in 1995–2008 models carrying 3.1L, 3.4L, 3.5L, 3.8L, and 3.9L V6 engines is head gasket leaks caused by cracking plastic intake manifolds.

Other deficiencies: Lots of road and wind noise comes through the side windows, thanks to the inadequately soundproofed chassis. Seating isn't very comfortable because of the lack of support caused by low-density foam and knees-in-your-face low seats combined with the ramrod-straight rear backrest. The ride is acceptable with a light load, but when fully loaded, the car's back end sags and the ride deteriorates.

On the one hand, 2002–05 models do have a comfortable ride; a nice array of standard features; an easily accessed, roomy interior; and a good choice of powertrains that includes a supercharged 3.8L engine. But on the minus side, they continue to have bland styling, noisy engines at high speeds, rear seating that's uncomfortable for three, and obstructed rear visibility because of a high-tail rear end.

Except for the automatic transmission upgrade, owners report that newer versions still have many of the same shortcomings seen on earlier front-drive models. Body construction is still below par, with loose door panel mouldings, poorly fitted door fabric, misaligned panels, and water accumulation in the backup lights. Other common problems are fuel-pump whistling, frequent stalling, vague steering, premature paint peeling on the hood and trunk, heavy accumulation of hard-to-remove brake dust inside the honeycomb-design wheels, scraped fenders from contact with the front tires when the wheel is turned, and hard starts due to delayed cranking.

The 3.1L engine is still problematic. Engine controls, faulty intake manifold gaskets (a chronic problem affecting the entire model lineup; see "Secret Warranties/Internal Bulletins/Service Tips"), and electronic fuel-injection systems have created many problems for GM owners. The 4-speed automatic transmission shifts erratically and sometimes slams into gear. The front brakes wear quickly, as do the MacPherson struts, shock absorbers, and tie-rod ends. Steering assemblies tend to fail prematurely, the electrical system is temperamental, the sunroof motor is failure-prone, and owners report water leaks from the front windshield. Front-end squeaks may require the replacement of the exhaust manifold pipe springs with dampers.

VEHICLE HISTORY: *Bonneville:* **2004**—A 275 hp V8 arrives; the 240 hp V6 is dropped. *Impala:* **2004**—An SS model arrives equipped with a 240 hp supercharged V6. **2007**—A 3.9L V6 with a tire-pressure monitor and GM's Active Fuel Management, which deactivates some cylinders to save fuel. Both features are surefire extra-maintenance items as the Impala ages. **2008**—Engine tweaked to run on E85 ethanol-blended fuel. **2009**—Standard thorax-protecting side-impact airbags and front seat belt pretensioners. **2010**—No more Impala EE. *Malibu:* **2004**—Completely redesigned. The sedan uses Saab's 9-3 platform and a base 145 hp 4-cylinder engine (a 200 hp V6 comes with the LS and LT) hooked to a 4-speed automatic transmission. A Maxx hatchback uses the same powertrain but adds a sliding rear seat with a reclining seatback, a cargo cover that transforms into a tailgate table, a glass skylight, four-wheel disc brakes, and head-protecting side curtain airbags. **2008**—Redesigned with new styling, more available power, and added safety features, including an anti-skid system. A gas/electric Hybrid makes its appearance. A standard 169 hp 2.4L 4-cylinder engine teams with a 4-speed automatic transmission on the entry-level models, though a 6-speed automatic comes with the LTZ Four. Optional on the LT and standard on the LTZ is a 252 hp 3.6L V6 that also teams with the 6-speed automatic. **2009**—Standard electronic stability control with brake assist and traction control and a 6-speed automatic tranny with the 2LT (optional on the 1LT). **2010**—No more Hybrid. Power-adjustable lumbar support replaces manual support. *Monte Carlo:* **2004**—A supercharged 3.8L SS. *Impala, Monte Carlo:* **2006**—Chevrolet updates its largest sedan and Monte Carlo coupe with new engines, upgraded suspensions, and revised exterior styling. The 3.5 models come with a 211 hp 3.5L V6 (an increase of 30 hp); LTZ sedans carry a 242 hp 3.9L V6; and Chevrolet SS models are equipped with a potent 303 hp V8 with Displacement on Demand, which cuts off four cylinders under light throttle conditions to save fuel. Supercharged models are dropped. All come with a 4-speed automatic transmission. Except for the SS, all models use bench seats for six-passenger capacity. The SS comes with front bucket seats only. Head-protecting side curtain airbags are standard in Impalas but unavailable in the Monte Carlo.

1995–2005 Impala, Lumina, and Monte Carlo

These models are popular two- and four-door versions of Chevy's "large" mid-sized cars, featuring standard dual airbags, ABS, and 160 hp V6 power. Powertrain enhancements have increased horsepower and fuel efficiency. A 3.1L V6 is the base engine, a standard 3.4L 210 hp V6 powers the coupe and is optional with the LS Lumina, and a 3.8L V6 equips the more upscale versions. The 2004 SS comes with a supercharged 3.8L engine that's hard to service and keep in parts.

1997–2003 Malibu

This front-drive medium-sized sedan is a boringly styled car that uses a rigid body structure to cut down on noise and improve handling. Standard mechanicals include a 2.4L twin-cam 4-cylinder engine and an optional 3.1L V6. The Malibu offers plenty of passenger and luggage space. Although headroom is tight, it can carry three rear passengers and gives much more legroom than either the Cavalier or Lumina.

Here are other points to consider: The base 4-cylinder is loud, handling isn't on par with the Japanese competition, there's lots of body lean in turns, outside mirrors are too small, there's no traction control, and the ignition switch is mounted on the dash (a throwback to your dad's Oldsmobile).

Malibu was redesigned for the 2004 model year, adding a companion hatchback body style and new features that include remote control engine starting and a rear seat that slides seven inches fore and aft. Its new platform houses a 145 hp 4-cylinder engine, while the LS and LT sedans carry a 200 hp V6. The hatchback

Maxx has a 6-inch-longer wheelbase and a bit shorter body. All of these design changes failed to improve the car's overall reliability.

1998–2002 Intrigue

Strikingly similar to the Alero, the Oldsmobile Intrigue was GM's replacement for the Cutlass Supreme and represents the most refined iteration of the front-drive platform once shared by the Century, Grand Prix, Lumina, and Regal. It's more luxurious than the Lumina and performs as well as the Accord, Camry, or Maxima. Its rigid chassis has fewer shakes and rattles than with GM's other models, and its 3.8L engine provides lots of low-end grunt but lacks the top-end power that makes the Japanese competition so much fun to toss around.

2004–10 Impala and Malibu

Impalas and Malibus perform quite similarly and share most of the same performance and quality problems. However, the Impala's poor suspension geometry and rear misalignment in the factory chews up tires and makes the vehicle difficult to control on slick highways:

> I made a left turn after being stopped at a stop light going approximately 5–10 mph [8–16 km/h] and back end continued the turn and car spun 180 degrees. Went to an Internet discussion board and noticed I'm not the only driver experiencing problem.

In addition to the generic front-drive problems listed previously, owners also report the following deficiencies with some of the latest Impalas and Malibus: side window whistling; failure-prone transmissions; unpredictable steering; annoyingly loud brake squeal; poor headlight illumination; excessive vibration at any speed; sensors failing throughout the vehicle; fuel-injector deposits that cause chronic stalling, poor idling, or hard starts; early wearout of the tires, brakes, alternator, steering assembly, and tire-pressure sensor; premature suspension strut failures (vehicle bottoms out with four or more passengers aboard); and early failures of the exhaust and intake manifold gaskets, now afflicting the 2006 through 2008 models equipped with 3.5L and 3.9L V6 engines.

Malibu Hybrid

The Malibu Hybrid arrived as a 2008 model and uses a 2.4L 4-cylinder gas engine with an electric motor/generator. The 4-banger is mated to a 4-speed automatic. It is classified as a "mild" hybrid because it can't run solely on its battery. Despite its complexity, there have been few owner complaints targeting the hybrid models. The biggest disappointment so far is that the car's gas consumption is far higher than the figures touted by Environment Canada and GM (8.5/6.2 L/100 km). *CanadianDriver.com* tested the Hybrid and found it burned an average of 11.0 L/100 km.

Other complaints posted relate to generic Malibu problems: premature brake wear, transmission breakdowns, and electrical shorts.

Safety Summary

All models/years: Airbag fails to deploy. • Sudden engine failure or overheating (faulty intake manifold). • Vehicle suddenly accelerates or stalls in traffic. • Frequent loss of braking, and premature rotor warpage and pad wearout. • Vehicle rolls downhill when parked on an incline. • Many incidents of total loss of steering or power steering. • Dash reflection in the windshield obstructs view. • Automatic trunk lid flies up and falls down on one's head. • Improper headlight illumination. • Horn is difficult to activate because of the hand pressure required. **All models: 2003**—Fire ignites when defogger activated. • Fire erupts in the rear deck speaker. • Shifter can be moved without key in the ignition or brakes applied. *Impala:* **2003**—Frequent complaints of dash area and engine compartment fires. • Front harness wires overheat; excessive current load from fuel pump may burn the ignition block wire terminal; inhalation injuries caused by the melting of the wiring harness plastic. • Electrically heated seat burns the driver's back. • The connection that goes to the brake pedal piston collapses, causing total brake failure. • When traction control is activated, wheel slip computer is also activated, and security system kills the engine and prevents it from restarting. • Driver-side wheels fall off. • Steering, ball joint, and lower, left, and right control arm failures. • AC refrigerant leaks into car interior. • In one incident, the driver-seat adjuster failed and the seat suddenly moved backward, causing loss of vehicle control. • Design of the rubber seal on the windows allows road salt to enter and short-circuit the window mechanism. **2004**—Crankshaft position sensor failures cause vehicle to stall and not restart. • Vehicle can be shifted out of Park without applying the brakes. • Vehicle hydroplanes easily, wanders all over the road, and jerks to one side when braking. • Steering wheel suddenly jerks to one side and resists driver's pull in the other direction. • Unreliable steering assembly. • Fuel-tank failures. **2005**—Inadvertent airbag deployment:

> A 2005 Chevy Impala police car was traveling on a gravel road in rural Ogle County, Illinois, when both front air bags deployed, the car never made contact with anything, there are at least 30 pictures of the car and the roadway. Since the 30th I personally have called General Motors about my concerns involving the rest of my 2005 squad cars, I've called every day since the 30th, with no response.

Fuel-pressure regulator may leak fuel. • Intermediate steering shaft is a sealed unit, yet requires frequent lubrication. • Steering-pump failure. • The transmission fails to hold the vehicle in Park or in Reverse on an incline. • Car can be shifted into any gear without depressing the brake pedal. • ABS failure. • Frequent traction-control system failures. • Automatic window could easily kill a child:

> The way that the window switch is designed it can easily shut on a child's body or body part.... When the consumer's son leaned his head out the window, his elbow hit the switch, and the window began to go up. The consumer suggested that a different type of switch be installed, the type that one would have to pull in order to close the window.

Inadequate headlight illumination. • AC blower seizes, causing an electrical fire. *Impala, Malibu:* **2006**—Seat belts fray and tear under normal use. • Early tie-rod replacements. • Doors unlock or lock on their own. • Car cannot be shut off. • Melted wiring harness. • Tire side walls blow out. **2007**—In one incident, airbags didn't deploy in a collision, despite OnStar being alerted that they had deployed. • One driver's seatback collapsed twice. • Automatic transmission slips, then bangs into gear. • In cold weather, shifter sticks in Park. • Brake rotors and pads wear out prematurely, and vehicle shakes excessively when braking. • Parking brake doesn't hold in Reverse or when parked on a slight incline. • Broken exterior door handle. • Faulty tire-pressure sensors ($600). • Original-equipment tire failures (Goodyear Eagle F1), and early wear on the inner sides of the rear tires:

> Talked to dealers. They said it was not a reported problem. Found out later that was BS. It's a suspension problem. So much so there is an aftermarket kit to correct the problem. I had to take car to tire dealer where they corrected problem. Reported problem to GM and got more BS.

•

> I am now buying the third set of rear tires in less than a year. The inside tread wears down to the wires every 13–16,000 miles [21,000–26,000 km]. The VIN on my car falls within the VINs listed on GM TSB 8032, however this car is not a police car. GM states that I must be hitting a pothole causing alignment problems. I must be hitting the same pothole at the same mileage all three times and it only affects the rear tires.

Intermediate steering shaft failures and steering lockups are quite common. • Tire pressure monitoring system gives incorrect readings. • Headlights and instruments lights intermittently dim or go out completely (see TSB #07-08-42-008). **2008**—Airbag alert light stays on for no reason. • Engine lags and lurches. • Automatic transmission line failure. • All seat belts fail to tension properly when vehicle stops abruptly. • When vehicle is shut off, it continues running. • Squirrely steering is still a problem due to the car's poor tracking. • Excessive tire wear (back tires first, then front tires) due to all four wheels being constantly out of alignment. • Steering shake. • Steering may freeze in cold weather. • Steering wheel jerks to the side. • Brake rotor warpage. • Remote starter won't work in cold weather. • Brake master cylinder leak. • Inadequate rear defroster. • Key jams in the ignition. • Water leak under the dashboard. • Sunroof explodes. • Hubcaps snap off the wheels. • Doors lock and unlock on their own; door lock motors burn out. **2009**—Transmission lag and lurch. • Excessive steering shake; sudden loss of steering capability. • Frequent replacement of the steering sway bar components. • Rear wheel bearing failures. • Doors lock and unlock on their own. • Power windows won't operate. • Poorly designed driver's seat causes severe back pain. • Bent wheel rims.

⌕ Secret Warranties/Internal Bulletins/Service Tips

All models/years: Reverse servo cover seal leak (transmission). • Keep in mind that some of the following service bulletins may apply to subsequent model years. **All models: 2001–07**—Correcting a shift shudder during light acceleration. **2005–06**—Engine knocking, ticking requires replacement of the flexplate and torque converter. **2006–07**—Troubleshooting tips to stop coolant loss and leaks from the 3.5L engine. **2006–08**—Correcting engine coolant loss and leaks, and a rear brake rattle. **2008–09**—Wet carpet on the passenger side. **2008–10**—Automatic transmission refuses to go into gear (see the following page). *Impala:* **2006–08**—GM bulletin #08-06-04-039, published August 7, 2008, says that if the car cranks but won't start, the likely culprit is a blown fuel pump fuse. • Coolant leaks that can cause engine overheating usually require that the engine head gasket be replaced. Again, this is a warranty item that is often covered up to 7 years/160,000 km under "goodwill" warranty extensions:

ENGINE—COOLANT LEAK/COOLANT LOSS

BULLETIN NO.: 08-06-01-012A   **DATE: NOVEMBER 19, 2008**

ENGINE COOLANT LEAK, LOSS OF COOLANT (REPLACE AFFECTED CYLINDER HEAD GASKET)

2006–07 Buick Terraza; 2006–07 Chevrolet Monte Carlo; 2006–08 Chevrolet Impala, Uplander; 2008 Chevrolet Malibu; 2006–08 Pontiac G6, Montana SV6; 2006–08 Saturn Relay; and the 2007–08 Saturn Aura All with a 3.5L or 3.9L engine

CONDITION: Some customers may comment on a coolant leak. The comments may range from spots on the driveway to having to add more coolant. Upon inspection, the technician may find that there is an external coolant leak coming from the top end of either cylinder head.

CORRECTION: If a leak is found to be coming from a cylinder head gasket, the gasket must be replaced. When replacing the gasket be advised that larger flange hex head bolts are now to be used at locations 5 and 8. The larger flange hex bolts are the same as the ones used at the other six locations. When installing the two large flange hex head bolts at locations 5 and 8 a new style lower intake manifold gasket that has provisions to allow for the larger flange bolts must be used. Caution: Failure to use the new lower intake manifold gaskets when installing the larger flange hex head bolts at locations 5 and 8 may result in the lower intake manifold not fitting properly, which may result in a leak condition.

2006–09—Rear suspension creak, clunk, pop noise. • Power-steering noise reduction measures. **2007**—Troubleshooting wind/road noise. **2007–08**—Engine squealing on start-up. • AC won't maintain desired temperature. • Ignition key cannot be removed. • No shift out of Park. • Undercar noises. • Rear speaker rattling. **2008**—Inaccurate fuel gauge readings. *Malibu:* **1999–2002**—Troubleshooting tips for plugging water leaks into the trunk and interior. **1999–2003**—Inoperative tail lights due to water intrusion. • Automatic transmission flaring. **2003**—Firm shifts, shudder, or no downshifts. **2004**—Noisy steering column, and lack of steering assist. • Ignition key hard to remove in cold weather. • Instrument panel rattle or buzz. **2004–05**—Steering pop or snap noise when turning. • Hood won't latch in the primary position. • A special lube must be applied to prevent door latches from freezing.

NO REVERSE, 3RD OR 5TH, CHECK ENGINE LIGHT ILLUMINATED, DTC P0776 (REPLACE 3-5 REVERSE CLUTCH PLATE (WAVED)

2008–09 Buick Enclave; 2008–09 Chevrolet Equinox, Malibu; 2009 Chevrolet Traverse; 2007–09 GMC Acadia; 2007–09 Pontiac G6; 2008–09 Pontiac Torrent; 2007–09 Saturn Aura, Outlook; 2008–09 Saturn VUE; All Equipped with 6T70/75 6-Speed Automatic Transmission (RPOs MH2, MH4, MH6 or MY9)

CONDITION: Some customers may comment about an SES light and/or no reverse and may also comment on a slip/flare or harsh shifts in drive range 3rd and/or 5th gear.

CAUSE: This condition may be caused by a broken 35R clutch wave plate allowing the apply piston to over-stroke, causing the piston to leak and causing loss of apply. This normally will not occur before approximately 32,000 km (20,000 mi). Debris generated by the condition can affect the operation of the speed sensors and other clutches.

2004–08—Front-end clunk or rattle when passing over small bumps at low speeds. 2006–07—TSB #10134A, published August 24, 2011, says that cars with the 2.2L 4-cylinder engine and those with the 2.4L 4-cylinder with 4-speed automatic transmission may have a deteriorating catalytic converter, causing the engine light to illuminate. The warranty will be extended to 10 years/192,000 km.

BONNEVILLE, GRAND PRIX, IMPALA, INTRIGUE, LESABRE, LUMINA, MALIBU, MALIBU HYBRID, MONTE CARLO, REGAL PROFILE

	2002	2003	2004	2005	2006	2007	2008	2009	2010
Cost Price ($)									
Bonneville	32,365	33,430	34,345	35,310	—	—	—	—	—
Grand Prix	28,050	28,277	28,125	27,865	25,885	25,595	26,230	—	—
Impala	24,875	26,020	26,810	26,405	24,685	25,230	25,695	26,625	27,320
Intrigue	28,365	—	—	—	—	—	—	—	—
LeSabre	32,960	33,720	33,935	34,550	—	—	—	—	—
Malibu	22,760	22,980	22,370	22,375	21,995	20,230	22,995	23,395	23,995
Malibu Hybrid	—	—	—	—	—	—	26,995	28,295	28,490
Malibu Maxx	—	—	26,320	26,495	25,595	25,930	—	—	—
Monte Carlo	26,525	27,620	28,200	27,840	24,685	25,231	—	—	—
Regal	29,080	29,980	29,975	—	—	—	—	—	—
Used Values ($)									
Bonneville ▲	3,000	3,500	4,000	4,500	—	—	—	—	—
Bonneville ▼	2,500	3,000	3,500	4,000	—	—	—	—	—
Grand Prix ▲	3,000	4,500	5,000	5,500	6,500	8,500	10,500	—	—
Grand Prix ▼	2,500	3,500	4,500	5,000	5,500	7,500	9,000	—	—
Impala ▲	3,500	4,500	5,500	6,500	7,500	9,000	10,500	13,000	15,500
Impala ▼	3,000	4,000	5,000	5,500	6,500	8,000	9,500	12,000	14,500
Intrigue ▲	2,500	—	—	—	—	—	—	—	—
Intrigue ▼	2,000	—	—	—	—	—	—	—	—

LeSabre ▲	3,500	4,000	5,000	6,500	—	—	—	—	—
LeSabre ▼	3,000	3,500	4,500	5,500	—	—	—	—	—
Malibu ▲	2,000	2,500	3,500	4,500	5,500	7,500	9,500	12,000	14,500
Malibu ▼	2,000	2,500	3,000	4,000	5,000	6,000	8,000	10,500	13,000
Malibu Hybrid ▲	—	—	—	—	—	—	12,500	14,500	17,000
Malibu Hybrid ▼	—	—	—	—	—	—	11,500	13,000	16,000
Malibu Maxx ▲	—	—	—	4,500	6,000	8,000	—	—	—
Malibu Maxx ▼	—	—	—	4,000	5,000	6,500	—	—	—
Monte Carlo ▲	3,000	3,500	4,000	4,500	6,000	7,500	—	—	—
Monte Carlo ▼	2,500	3,000	3,500	4,000	5,500	6,500	—	—	—
Regal ▲	3,500	4,000	4,500	—	—	—	—	—	—
Regal ▼	3,000	3,500	4,000	—	—	—	—	—	—

Reliability	1	1	1	2	2	2	2	2	3
Crash Safety (F)									
Bonneville 4d	4	4	4	—	—	—	—	—	—
Grand Prix 4d	4	4	3	3	5	5	5	—	—
Impala	5	5	5	5	5	5	5	5	5
LeSabre 4d	4	4	4	—	—	—	—	—	—
Malibu	4	4	4	5	5	5	5	5	5
Monte Carlo	—	5	5	5	5	—	—	—	—
Regal 4d	4	4	—	—	—	—	—	—	—
Side									
Bonneville 4d	4	4	4	—	—	—	—	—	—
Grand Prix	2	3	3	3	3	3	3	—	—
Impala	4	4	4	4	5	5	5	5	5
LeSabre 4d	4	5	4	—	—	—	—	—	—
Malibu	3	4	4	5	5	5	5	5	5
Monte Carlo	—	3	3	3	3	—	—	—	—
Regal 4d	3	3	—	—	—	—	—	—	—
IIHS Side									
Grand Prix	—	—	2	2	2	2	2	—	—
Impala	5	5	5	5	3	3	3	3	5
Malibu 4d	1	1	1	5	5	5	5	5	5
Offset									
Bonneville 4d	5	5	5	5	—	—	—	—	—
Grand Prix 4d	3	3	5	5	5	5	5	—	—
Impala	5	5	5	5	3	3	3	3	3
LeSabre	5	5	5	—	—	—	—	—	—
Malibu	—	1	5	5	5	5	5	5	5
Regal	3	3	—	—	—	—	—	—	—
Head Restraints									
Bonneville	1	1	1	—	—	—	—	—	—
Grand Prix	2	2	1	1	1	1	1	—	—
Impala	1	1	1	1	2	2	2	3	3
LeSabre 4d	1	1	1	—	—	—	—	—	—

All ratings on a numbered scale where 5 is good and 1 is bad. See page 132 for a more detailed description.

Malibu	2	1	3	3	3	3	2	2	5
Malibu Classic	1	1	1	—	—	—	—	—	—
Monte Carlo	2	2	—	—	—	—	—	—	—
Regal 4d	1	1	—	—	—	—	—	—	—
Rollover Resistance									
Bonneville	5	5	5	—	—	—	—	—	—
Grand Prix	4	4	4	4	4	4	—	—	—
Impala	4	4	4	4	4	4	—	4	4
LeSabre	—	—	5	—	—	—	—	—	—
Malibu	4	4	4	4	4	4	4	4	4
Monte Carlo	—	4	4	4	4	—	—	—	—

Honda

ACCORD/ACCORD HYBRID ★ ★ ★ / ★ ★ ★ / ★ ★ ★

RATING: *Accord:* Average (2010); Below Average (2008–09; 1999–2005); Above Average (2007); Average (2006). *Accord Hybrid:* A surprising gas-guzzler earns this hybrid an Average rating (2005–07). The Hybrid's first model year production also had a larger number of factory-related snafus than later models. It has been off the market for five years, which seriously compromises servicing and parts availability. Thoroughly check the automatic transmission, rear suspension, and brakes on all Accords. The number of safety-related defects on 2008 and 2009 models is many times that of the average for most cars. Most knee-jerk "anything Japanese is good" car guides give the Honda Accord and Toyota Camry equally positive ratings. Not *Lemon-Aid*. We know after looking through reams of confidential service bulletins and owner complaints that for the past decade Toyota has been asleep at the switch and allowed quality to decline in its lineup. Now we are seeing the same low quality in Honda models. Defects aside (and that's asking a lot), the Accord is one of the most driver-friendly, versatile compacts you can find. Think of it as a better-performing Toyota Camry that welcomes driver input and is an all-around good road performer. Nevertheless, *Lemon-Aid* has downgraded the ranking for 2008–09 models because of their many factory-related and redesign glitches. These deficiencies include expensive powertrain failures, sudden acceleration and stalling, loss of brakes, and airbag malfunctions. **Ideal model year:** A 2007 SE V6 sedan for about $10,500 is your best bet. It has worked out earlier revamping glitches from earlier redesigns and doesn't have the new set of problems inherent in the reworked 2008 model. **"Real" city/highway fuel economy:** *2.4L manual: 9.4/6.4 L/100 km. 2.4L automatic: 9.5/6.4 L/100 km. 3.0L 6-speed manual: 11.4/7.2 L/100 km. 3.0L automatic: 11.5/7.5 L/100 km. 3.5L V6 6-speed manual: 12.2/7.8 L/100 km. 3.5L V6 automatic: 11.0/6.9 L/100 km. Hybrid: 8.2/6.1 L/100 km.* Owners complain that, like with the Civic Hybrid, the Accord Hybrid's fuel economy figures are false. Anyone noting this problem with their Accord should use the *Peters v. Honda* judgment found on page 114 to claim compensation up to $10,000. **Maintenance/repair costs:** Average. Except for the Hybrid, repairs aren't dealer-dependent. Recall repairs have been delayed on some models because corrective parts are often unavailable. **Parts:** Higher-than-average costs, but non-Hybrid parts can be easily found for much less from independent suppliers. **Extended warranty:** Not needed, unless you are buying the Hybrid. **Best alternatives:** Acura CSX, EL, or Integra; Ford Fusion or Mercury Milan; post-2006 Honda Civic; Hyundai Elantra wagon, Sonata, or Tiburon; Kia Rondo; Mazda5 or Mazda6; Nissan Sentra; and 2005 or 2006 Toyota Camry. *Hybrids:* Ford Escape. **Helpful websites:** *www.honda-tech.com* and *www.hondaaccordforum.com/ forum.*

Strengths and Weaknesses

ALERT! The 2010 model year is the first time reports of factory-related defects declined to Average since 2007. Nevertheless, be wary of premature rear brake wear on 2008–09 models. Pull the wheels before buying the car.

Fast and nimble even without a V6, this is the mid-sized sedan of choice for drivers who want maximum fuel economy and comfort along with lots of space for grocery hauling and occasional highway cruising. With the optional V6, the Accord is one of the most versatile mid-sized cars you can find.

The gasoline-powered Accord doesn't really excel in any particular area; it's just very, very good at everything. It's smooth, quiet, mannerly, and competent, with acceptable fit and finish inside and out. Other strong points are comfort, ergonomics, and driveability. Like Toyota's lineup, there are powertrain and brake problems, and in recent years (2008–09 models especially) there have been an unusually large number of serious safety-related complaints reported to NHTSA. In this sense, Honda is mirroring Toyota's quality decline, although Honda's hasn't been as steep, and unlike Toyota's, consists almost entirely of automatic transmission and suspension/alignment failures.

Accord Hybrid

After successfully launching its 2003 Civic Hybrid, Honda introduced the 2005 Accord Hybrid. Equipped with a 255 hp V6 engine, the Hybrid is assisted as needed by an electric motor and a 5-speed automatic transmission. An innovative Variable Cylinder Management System automatically deactivates three cylinders when cruising or on deceleration. Like the Civic Hybrid, the Accord Hybrid can't be driven on electricity alone.

The primary complaint of Hybrid owners is that the vehicle gets nowhere near the advertised gas mileage; owners say it's about 30 percent worse than promised. Other Hybrid-specific complaints involve electrical short circuits and premature brake wear. Overall, though, there are proportionately fewer complaints from Accord Hybrid owners than from Toyota Prius and GM Malibu Hybrid owners, and the complaints are less serious in nature. Nevertheless, due to slow Hybrid sales, 2007 was the car's last model year.

VEHICLE HISTORY: 2003—This larger, totally restyled model offers a V6 and 6-speed manual tranny combo, and increased 4-cylinder and V6 horsepower (160 and 240 hp, respectively) with better fuel economy. **2004**—V6 models add traction control. Head-protecting side curtain airbags are standard on EX V6 models. **2005**—Honda introduces the Hybrid sedan and standard side curtain-type airbags, along with front torso airbags and better interior soundproofing. **2008**—More power and passenger space; no more Hybrid. Two engines are offered: A 2.4 L four with 177–190 horsepower, and a 3.5-L V6 that is rated at 268 horsepower. The V6 uses Honda's Variable Cylinder Management while cruising to conserve fuel. A standard four-cylinder engine hooked to a 5-speed manual or a 5-speed automatic transmission powers all models, though EX and EX-L sedans also provided a V6 coupled to either a 5-speed automatic or a 6-speed manual tranny. **2009**—The Accord's 2008 redesign sent safety complaints skyrocketing for both the 2008 and 2009 models. **2010**—The EX and EX V6 get an upgraded dual-zone climate control system.

The 2003 redesign manifested a continued decline in quality through the 2006 model year, resulting in the Accord losing its Recommended rating for all those years. Honda promised us better-performing, more durable transmissions in its redesigned 2003 models, but the company lied, and then later reluctantly extended the warranty up to eight years. Furthermore, some 2003–06 model year Accord owners say their cars have similar problems but haven't been included in the extended "goodwiil" warranty program; others complain that the corrective repairs haven't fixed the tranny problems and that they were forced to pay a high deductible, which should be Honda's responsibility.

Other problems related to the 2003 and later models' redesign: roof buckling; defective paint; frequent hard starts; warped brake rotors; erratic transmission shifts; a steering-column ticking; a defective CD changer; coolant in the engine oil pan; windshield creaks in cold, dry weather; brake shuddering, grinding, and squealing; a moonroof that doesn't close all the way; a popping noise heard when accelerating; wrinkled, bubbling door window moulding; doors closing on occupants as they leave the vehicle; an AC condenser that's easily punctured by road debris; stereo speaker hum or popping and frequent speaker blowouts; passenger-side seat heater coming on by itself and overheating; non-stop rattles, squeaks, and vibrations in door panels, tops of windows, and rear shelves, and in the B-pillars around the top seat belt anchor; engine-oil leaks onto the manual transmission clutch, causing shifting slippage (the problem is caused by a low vent valve on the 6-speed tranny); and the rear headliner becoming unglued and sagging, causing water to leak into the cabin and trunk (the carpeting and rear seat are saturated after moderate rainstorms).

The increase in engine, transmission, and brake failures is worrisome. To its credit, Honda puts a "goodwill" clause in almost all of its service bulletins, allowing service managers to submit any claim to the company long after the original warranty period has elapsed. Powertrain and brake repairs have often been covered by these secret warranties—after a little verbal jousting.

The Accord's 2008 redesign, carried over in 2009, has also sent safety complaints skyrocketing. Just one example: Owners report that the car's faulty suspension/steering geometry makes the vehicle dangerously unstable and chews up rear tires, accounting for a sixfold increase in NHTSA complaints for those model years.

Safety Summary

All models/years: Sudden acceleration, stalling. • Automatic transmission failures:

> Independent mechanic says Honda transmissions are poorly designed in that first the filter is hard to get to and that there is a very small hole for fluid to flow through and that once clogged with no fluid the transmission fails. Now he's rebuilding it and our supposed trusty Honda is going to cost us $2400.

Airbags fail to deploy, or deploy for no reason. • Check Engine light is always on. • Brake failures and premature front/rear brake wear. • Steering pulls to one side while driving. • AC compressor is easily damaged by pebbles on the highway, due to Honda's poor design. Honda says it's an insurance issue, but no—it's Honda's responsibility. • Defective door handles. **All models: 2002**—Seat belt won't retract, or continually tightens; in one incident, child had to be cut free. • Child safety seat can't be installed because buckle latch is located too far into the seat. • Vehicle pulls sharply when braking. • Trunk lid may suddenly fall. **2003**—Axle suddenly snaps. • Severe pulling to the right. • Console overheats and smells burnt. • Keys overheat in the ignition. • ABS and Traction Control lights stay lit, and corrective parts aren't easily found. • Rear vision is obstructed by head restraints, high rear deck, and roof pillar. **2004**—Higher than average number of safety-related incidents registered by NHTSA. • Several reports of fires igniting in the insulation material. • One report of fire igniting behind the right front tire while vehicle was underway. • Brake light bulb drops down into the trunk area and burns through luggage. • Axle collapses while vehicle is underway. • Vehicle accelerates when brakes are applied. • Engine surges when gears are shifted. • Steering suddenly locks up. • Seat belt failed to retract in a rear-end collision; several complaints allege the front seat belts failed to restrain occupants in frontal collisions. • Side window shatters after morning moisture is wiped off. • Driver's seat moves forward on its own. **2005**—Automatic transmission regularly slips out of gear and sometimes violently downshifts to Second. • Shifter slips by Drive mode into D3, or sticks in Second gear. • Right front wheel comes apart. • Cracks in the steering wheel just above the airbag. • Intermittent power-steering failure. • Honda's jack is a knuckle-buster that won't hold the car. Inoperative inside door handles trap occupants. **2006**—Less than average number of complaints posted (186). • Car will roll away in Park, unless emergency brake is set. Ignition key can be removed while vehicle is in gear. • Sharp door handles can cut occupants' hands. **2007**—Fewer than average safety-related defects reported (164). • Driver-side seat catches fire. • When accelerating, engine hesitates and then surges; sudden acceleration when vehicle is in Park. • Vehicle vibrates so badly that hands on the steering wheel go numb. • Rear brake pad pins become so rusted they won't let the brake pads release. • Dash lights and headlights flicker when the AC compressor cycles. Intermittent failure of the power door locks, especially when it rains. • Serious blind spots due to the design of the front windshield pillars. • Horn may not sound in cold weather. • LED tail lights are nausea-inducing for drivers behind you. **2008**—More than 815 safety-related incidents were reported to the U.S. government; 150 complaints would have been the norm over a three-year span. Most of these problems relate to sudden, unintended acceleration and brake failures. Other brake issues are brake squeaking, screeching, and grinding and the uneven and premature wearout of brake pads, calipers, and rotors:

> It is my understanding that for 2008 and 2009, Honda went to smaller rear pads and rotors and that's why they wear out so fast.... I looked at one web site, *carcomplaints.com*, and there are 517 complaints regarding premature brake wear for 2008 and 2009 Honda Accords, with a severity rating of 7.8 out of 10. Also car magazine *Motor Trend* had the same problem: *www.motortrend.com/roadtests/oneyear/112_0910_2008_honda_accord_test_verdict/index.html.*

Poorly designed head restraints result in painful "chin-to-chest" driving. • Lights dim or flicker. • Clearcoat used by Honda on its wheel rims causes the rims to corrode prematurely. **2009**—A higher than normal number of owner safety-related incidents posted. A large part of these complaints concern faulty airbags, front and rear brake failures (premature pad, caliper, and rotor wear), and uncomfortable head restraints:

> The feature to move the headrest forward in the event of a rear-end collision puts the upper-back region of the seat too far forward, creating a very uncomfortable region with little lower-back support. I find that my lower-back aches after an hour of driving, and needed to lean up against the steering wheel while driving to relieve the pain. I believe this is unsafe if the airbag deployed.

Engine surging; sudden acceleration. • In one incident, side airbag deployed five minutes after driver shut the door. • Broken axle. • Headlights dim or blink intermittently. • Seat wobbles back and forth. • Head restraint blocks rear view. • Sunroof glass was sucked out of the car during highway cruising. • Defective lock/unlock remote control. • Tire pressure sensor gives false alerts. **2010**—Faulty head restraint design forces driver to adopt a "chin-to-chest" driving position. • Painful lumbar support in the driver's seat. • Trunk lid won't stay up. • Front windshield fractured without any provocation. • Defective automatic transmission control module caused vehicle to go into Reverse and suddenly accelerate. *Hybrid:* **2005**—Transmission failure ($4,000 U.S.). • Defective motor mount. • Defective speedometer. • Instead of a spare tire, owners are given a can of sealant that won't work if the puncture is located outside the tread. **2006**—Car accelerates when brakes are applied. • Long hesitation when accelerating invites a rear-end accident. • Brake failure. • Engine MIL and other instrument panel warning lights come on for no reason. **2007**—Much like the Toyota Prius, Accord Hybrid brakes may fail after passing over a bump:

> Brakes have failed to stop car when I've gone over a bump—they vibrate and make noise, but do not stop the car. This has led to near accidents four times since I bought the car new over three years ago. A similar problem has occurred when brakes are wet and I'm trying to stop at low speed.

Secret Warranties/Internal Bulletins/Service Tips

All models/years: Accord service bulletins may also apply to the Hybrid. • Troubleshooting tips for vehicles that pull sharply to one side. **All models: 1999–2004**—V6 engine oil leaks (an extension of a problem first noticed on 1994–97 models). **1999–2006**—Vehicles may have broken rear stabilizer links; push for a "goodwill" adjustment. • Repair tips applicable to vehicles that pull/drift to one side. **2003**—Many automatic transmission failures. • Corrective action for coolant leakage into the engine oil pan; oil leaks at the cylinder head cover. • Troubleshooting ABS light illumination. • Inaccurate gauges. • Dash or pillar creaking or clicking. • Roof moulding channel leaks water; roof water leak fix. **2003–04**—If the brake pedal is stiff, a new booster vacuum hose may be required. • Loose steering or clunky steering response. **2003–05**—Low Fuel warning is activated even though fuel tank is a quarter full. **2003–06**—Guidelines for fixing dashboard/A-pillar creaks and clicks. **2003–07**—Drivetrain ping, rattle, squeal when accelerating. • Brake pedal is low and feels soft. **2003–08**—The 6-speed manual transmission grinds when shifted into Third gear, pops out of Third gear, or is hard to shift into Third gear. **2003–09**—Power-steering moan/whine. **2004**—Excessive engine vibration in idle. • Noisy steering. • No-starts and faulty power windows. • Door rattles. • Wheel bearing humming or growling. **2005–10**—Silencing a chirp coming from the engine timing belt area. **2007**—A fix for the manual transmission grinding or popping out of Third gear (TSB #08-020, dated 07/18/08). • Inadequate AC cooling. • Noisy rear window regulator. **2008**—The tire pressure warning system may give invalid warnings. Sudden unintended acceleration. • Excessive oil consumption. • Road debris continues to damage expensive AC compressors. • A flood of premature rear brake wearout reports has been received by NHTSA:

> I took my car for a regular service at the DCH Academy Honda and the service dealer told me that I need to replace rear brakes. It was very surprising that at 22K miles the rear brakes have gone. He told me about the complaints filed for the 2008-2009 and some 2010 models. I filed the complaint and found out that my VIN is not eligible for a reimbursement. I believe they should consider all the 2010 models. I don't know what is the criteria Honda has to identify faulty brakes. Clearly, Honda has a flaw in keeping track of their inventory or they are not willing to acknowledge customer complaints and act on the information.

Engine rattles on cold start-up. • Blower motor noisy or inoperative. • Carpet on the passenger's side pulls out from under the door sill trim. • If an owner reports a front brake squeal or judder, Honda will refinish the front brake discs and install new brake pads under a "goodwill" warranty, says Honda Service Bulletin #09-096, published December 24, 2009. **2008–09**—Troubleshooting an engine whining noise and a steering clicking. • Fix for an engine that ticks or knocks at idle. **2008–10**—Honda extends its brake repair up to the 2010 models and states the normal warranty applies. However, take a close look at the bulletin below where it says "Failed Part" and "Defect Code." This admission of a part failure or of a "defect" gives rise to Honda's liability beyond its normal warranty limitations under the legal *implied* warranty. That's the case to make in small claims court, should Honda reject your claim:

BRAKES—FRONT BRAKES SQUEAL/JUDDER

BULLETIN NO.: 09-096   DATE: MAY 28, 2010

2008–10 Accord
SYMPTOM: When the brakes are applied normally, the driver feels a juddering vibration through the steering wheel or brake pedal, and/or hears a squealing noise.
THE NORMAL WARRANTY APPLIES: Operation Number: 410820; Flat Rate Time: 0.9 hour; Failed Part: P/N 45022-SEA-J11; Defect Code: 00504; Symptom Code: 03503.

Hybrid: **2006–07**—Hybrids that lose power when accelerating need three different software updates. This will be done under a "goodwill" warranty at no charge to the customer, says Honda Service Bulletin #09-058, published July 30, 2009. Honda's 2006 Civic software update caused a dramatic drop in fuel economy and resulted in Honda USA paying almost $10,000 in compensation ordered by a California small claims court last January (see page 114). Accord Hybrid owners say they are also getting poor gas mileage, since the same revised engine/IMA battery software was installed in their Hybrids to extend IMA battery life (see following internal service bulletin):

IMA BATTERY SOFTWARE/HARDWARE UPDATES

BULLETIN NO.: 10-083   DATE: JULY 12, 2011

2005-07 Accord Hybrid; 2003-05 Civic Hybrid; 2006-08 Civic Hybrid
BACKGROUND: Due to improvements in battery manufacturing efficiency, once stocks of original IMA batteries are depleted, a new battery design will be available for IMA battery replacement. Both battery types require that its battery control software be matched to its IMA battery type. Failure to match the software with the battery will result in reduced IMA battery life
In addition, if the battery condition monitor (BCM) or the motor control module (MCM) is replaced or reprogrammed, matching IMA battery software must be installed in that control module to maximize the IMA battery's life.

Hmmmm...This battery software revision is what cut fuel economy almost in half. Accord Hybrid owners have the same legal rights to $10,000 damages in small claims court as do Civic Hybrid owners.

ACCORD, ACCORD HYBRID PROFILE

	2002	2003	2004	2005	2006	2007	2008	2009	2010
Cost Price ($)									
LX/SE sedan	23,000	25,000	25,100	25,500	26,301	26,501	25,090	25,090	24,790
EXi/EX V6	31,100	32,500	32,900	33,600	34,100	34,902	31,690	31,690	31,190
Hybrid	—	—	—	36,990	38,900	38,100	—	—	—
Used Values ($)									
LX/SE sedan ▲	4,000	5,500	6,500	8,000	9,500	11,000	14,000	16,000	18,500
LX/SE sedan ▼	3,500	5,000	6,000	7,000	8,500	10,000	13,000	14,500	17,000
EXi/EX V6 ▲	5,500	6,500	8,000	9,500	11,000	14,000	16,000	19,500	23,000
EXi/EX V6 ▼	5,000	6,000	7,000	8,500	10,000	13,000	14,500	18,000	21,500
Hybrid ▲	—	—	—	9,000	10,500	14,000	—	—	—
Hybrid ▼	—	—	—	7,500	9,500	12,500	—	—	—
Reliability	3	3	3	3	3	4	2	2	2
Crash Safety (F)	5	5	5	5	5	5	5	5	5
4d	5	5	5	5	5	5	5	5	5
Side (2d)	3	—	5	4	4	4	4	4	4
4d	5	5	4	4	4	4	5	5	5
IIHS Side	—	1	1	5	5	5	5	5	5
Offset	3	5	5	5	5	5	5	5	5
Head Restraints (2d)	—	1	1	1	1	1	5	5	5
Roof Strength	—	—	—	—	—	—	3	3	3
Rollover Resistance	5	4	4	4	4	4	5	5	5

Note: The Accord Hybrid's relatively rapid rate of depreciation is similar to that of the Civic Hybrid and Toyota Prius. Perhaps word is getting around that the promised fuel economy and quality is not to be believed.

Hyundai

SONATA ★★★★★

RATING: Recommended (2009–10); Above Average (2006–08); Average (1999–2005). Recent iterations of the Sonata haven't registered one-half the number of safety complaints of the highly rated Honda Accord or Toyota Camry. On the other hand, Sonata's crashworthiness ratings aren't impressive for some model years. **Ideal model year:** For maximum savings and the most safety features, I suggest you buy a 2010 4-cylinder Limited ($17,000–$18,500) with standard electronic stability control and traction assist. Or buy a dirt-cheap base 2007 Sonata for $8,000. By purchasing the 2007 version, you are avoiding many of the glitches found in 2006's redesign. **"Real" city/highway fuel economy:** *2.0 automatic: 8.7/5.7 L/100 km. 2.4 manual: 8.7/5.7 L/100 km. 2.4 automatic: 9.4/5.7 L/100 km. 2.7 6-cylinder automatic: 12.3/7.9 L/100 km. 3.3 6-cylinder automatic: 11.5/7.2 L/100 km.*

3.5 6-cylinder automatic: 13.9/8.4 L/100 km. Owners report fuel savings may undershoot these estimates by at least 10 percent, or up to 20 percent with the 3.5L engine. **Maintenance/repair costs:** Higher than average. Repairs aren't dealer-dependent. **Parts:** Average part costs; most parts are quickly found. **Extended warranty:** An extended transmission warranty is a smart buy. **Best alternatives:** Acura Integra, Honda Accord, Hyundai Elantra wagon, or the Mazda5, Mazda6, or 626. **Helpful websites:** *www.hyundai-forums.com* and *www.hyundai-forums.com/f70-4g-2006-sonata.htm.*

 ## Strengths and Weaknesses

ALERT! Don't buy this car without first checking the steering and low-beam headlights. Cost to replace the headlights: $910.

This mid-sized front-drive sedan went from bad to good in an incredibly short period. Could it be just a coincidence that major Hyundai quality improvements were initiated almost a decade ago, once Hyundai hired away a gang of Toyota's top quality-control engineers? Apparently, the pirated employees brought with them a bushel basket of internal quality reports that listed prominently Toyota's sudden acceleration, brake loss, lag and lurch powertrain, and truck corrosion issues. It's a moot point now. The papers were returned to Toyota's lawyers several years ago, following threats of legal action. Hyundai assured Toyota the documents went unread (wink, wink; nudge, nudge).

Corporate intrigue aside, the Sonata is a decent performer in most areas, with some notable exceptions, like the brakes, steering, fuel system, headlights, and fit and finish. Acceleration is impressive with the manual gearbox and passable with the automatic, if equipped with the 6-cylinder engine. Handling and performance are also fairly good, although emergency handling isn't confidence-inspiring, particularly because of the imprecise steering and excessive lean when cornering. As with early Hyundai models, reports for 2006–08 models continue to note the erratically shifting automatic transmission, the jamming manual tranny clutches, and endemic brake loss and premature wear.

VEHICLE HISTORY: 2002—GL is given four-wheel disc brakes. **2003**—Standard front side airbags. **2006**—A major redesign gives the Sonata new looks, more passenger room (especially rear-seat legroom), additional trunk space, and more power. The new 162 hp 2.4L 4-cylinder adds 24 more horses, while the 235 hp 2.7L V6 puts out 65 more horses. Traction and stability control, anti-lock four-wheel disc brakes, front side airbags, and head-protecting side curtain airbags are standard features. **2009**—Retuned suspension, redesigned interior, and a restyled exterior. The 4-cylinder gained 13 hp to 175, while the V6 added 15 hp to 249. Previous to 2009, 4-cylinder models also got the smoother-performing 5-speed automatic transmission used by the V6 models. **2010**—Electronic stability control and traction assist were important safety features added to the 4-cylinder Limited.

Throughout the Sonata's history, Hyundai's technical service bulletins have been replete with references to automatic transmissions that exhibit what Hyundai describes as "shift shock" as well as delayed shifting.

The 2006 through 2010 Sonatas have elicited very few quality-control and safety complaints, and represent the best buys. Nevertheless, airbags, steering, sun visors, suspension struts, power door locks, brakes (rotors and pads), automatic transmissions, and fuel- and electrical-system components still top the list of parts most vulnerable to premature failure or malfunctioning. Highway performance for some owners has also come under serious criticism:

> Bad pull to the left, replaced front strut. Assorted spring noises while driving. Tires feathering. No stability while driving; any kind of bumps mean you are wandering all over the road. Shimmy in steering wheel. With two passengers in the back seat the car lifts up in front and stability while driving is even worse. This has been occurring since it was new. Easy to lose control of vehicle, dealership acknowledges all tires feathering but say they cant fix it.

Fit and finish continue to be problematic. Interestingly, some of these problems, like disabled passenger-side airbags, short circuits, premature brake wear, and inadequate headlight illumination, have apparently been carried over to a lesser extent to the 2009 model year, according to NHTSA owner complaint records.

 Safety Summary

All years: Airbags don't deploy when they should, or deploy when they shouldn't. • Frequent automatic transmission failures. • Poor design of the car's anti-fogging feature:

> Sonata windows fog quickly, completely and frequently blinding the driver necessitating distracting changes to be made to balance multiple changes in outside to inside temps along roads. Defogging is achieved—only—with outside air intake vents open.

2002—Axle (U-bolt) fails while car is underway. • Seat belt latch releases when jostled by passenger's elbow. **2003**—Driver-side seat belt buckle suddenly releases. • Large rear-view mirror obstructs the view. **2004**—Gas fumes enter the cabin. • Stalling because of a faulty throttle sensor. • Early clutch failure. • Automatic transmission slippage and seizure. • Complete brake loss. • Rear wheel bearing seizure. • Seat belt comes loose during a collision. **2004–06**—Sudden, unintended acceleration. **2005**—Failure of the passenger-side front suspension. • No brakes. • Loose front passenger seat. • Vibration caused by loose engine mount bolts. • Excessive heat generated under the driver-side dash. **2006–07**—Sunroof glass explodes. **2006–08**—After recall repairs, front passenger-side airbag is still disabled even though an adult is seated. • Driver-side sun visor sags and continually drops down. **2007**—In one incident, cruise control would not disengage when the brakes were applied. • Vehicle rolls back on an incline while in Drive. • Headlights don't give enough light, and both the headlights and rear lights burn out quickly. **2007–08**—Premature brake pad and rotor wear:

> This condition is reported online by many other owners with as little as 20K [mi.] [32,000 km]. Dealer will not cover under warranty. Hyundai USA will only consider reimbursement after it is repaired first and preferably by a dealer. My dealer said it's a "design flaw with the pad retainer;" those online report corroded caliper mounting pins as the cause.

Rear brake pad comes apart. • Rear calipers freeze against the brake rotors. **2008**—Fire ignites from the wires in the trunk. • Driver's seat belt release latch doesn't operate properly. • Vehicle suddenly loses power when cruising at 100 km/h (throttle position sensor suspected). • When cruising in Third, transmission suddenly downshifts into First. **2009**—In two separate frontal collisions, front seat belts failed to tighten. • Sudden, unintended acceleration. • Clutch pedal will sometimes jam or not engage:

> The clutch on my 5 speed 2009 Hyundai Sonata is sporadically dropping to the floor and not allowing me to change gears. I was nearly hit from behind, as the car behind me assumed I'd be accelerating, but when the clutch drops (without much resistance) the linkage locks and I can't change gears.....

After cruise control is deactivated, it resumes at a higher speed. • Worn out and noisy rear brakes:

> They told me there is uneven wear on rear break pads and that the sliders are sticking causing the pads to stay compressed to rotor. They offered to "lube" them for me and replace pads for over $200.00.

Wiring harness caught fire. • Intermittent electrical short kills the dash lights. • Faulty throttle position sensor causes hard starts, loss of power, and stall-outs. • AC drains poorly, produces a musty smell. • Low-beam headlights have too narrow a beam. • Windshield suddenly shattered without cause. **2010**—Airbags fail to deploy. • Sudden, unintended acceleration causes airbag to deploy and seriously cut driver's wrists. • While in Reverse, vehicle suddenly accelerates. • Stallout while underway results in automatic transmission replacement. • Reports of the vehicle losing power on the road, requiring frequent replacement of throttle position sensors and electrical wiring harness. • Engaging the cruise control causes vehicle to accelerate to an unexpected higher speed. • Cruise control switch failures. • Defective fuel injector causes gasoline odour to permeate the cabin area. • Transmission upshifts when it's not necessary. • Car rolls backwards on an incline. • Rear middle brake light failure. • Car tends to both over- and under-steer. • Vehicle drifts to the left. • Loose, noisy steering wheel may suddenly stiffen up. • Hankook Optimo tires bulge and blow out at the sidewall. • Tire pressure warning system often comes on for no reason. • Low-beam headlights project a black line midway in the beam.

Secret Warranties/Internal Bulletins/Service Tips

All years: Troubleshooting tips for delayed engagement of the automatic transmission. • Harsh shifting when coming to a stop or upon initial acceleration likely caused by an improperly adjusted accelerator pedal switch transmission control unit. • A faulty air exhaust plug could cause harsh shifting into Second and Fourth gears on vehicles with automatic transmissions. • Brake pedal pulsation correction. • How to reduce brake noise. **1999–2006**—Attending to differential seal oil leaks. **2002**—Troubleshooting poor shifting and torque converter clutch malfunctions. • 2–3 shift flare. • Erratic operation of the automatic climate control. • Sticks in Second gear. **2003–04**—Low-speed driveline "bump." **2006**—Front drive axle snapping noise. **2006–07**—Front windshield creak or squeak. **2006–08**—Engine hesitation and misfire repair tips. • Remedy for seat creaking, squeaking. **2006–09**—Correction for a rough idle or display of the MIL warning light on vehicles equipped with the 3.3L engine. • The oil temperature sensor may leak. **2006–10**—Steering squeaks when turning. **2007–10**—Troubleshooting hard starts or a rough idle. **2008**—Correction for a steering wheel shimmy/vibration. **2009–10**—A water leak onto the passenger side front floor is likely due to a kinked AC drain hose.

SONATA PROFILE

	2002	2003	2004	2005	2006	2007	2008	2009	2010
Cost Price ($)									
Base	21,195	21,595	22,395	22,395	21,900	23,595	22,295	21,995	22,499
Used Values ($)									
Base ▲	3,000	4,500	5,000	6,000	7,000	8,500	10,500	12,500	14,500
Base ▼	3,000	3,500	4,500	5,000	6,000	7,500	9,500	11,500	13,500
Reliability	2	2	3	3	3	3	3	3	3
Crash Safety (F)	4	4	4	4	5	5	5	5	5
Side	4	4	4	4	5	5	5	5	5
IIHS Side	1	1	1	1	3	3	3	3	3
Offset	3	3	3	3	5	5	5	5	5
Head Restraints (F)	1	1	1	1	5	5	5	5	5
Roof Strength	—	—	—	—	2	2	2	2	2
Rollover Resistance	5	5	5	5	4	4	4	4	4

Mazda

MAZDA6, 626 ★★★★★/★★★★★/★★★

RATING: *Mazda6:* Recommended (2009–10); Above Average (2006–08); Average (2003–05). *626:* Average (1999–2002). **Ideal model year:** For enhanced highway performance, safety, and comfort, pick a 2008 Mazda6 GT for $14,000, or a 2006 Mazda6 V6 Sport Wagon GS for $9,500—another good choice. It will give you upgraded side airbags, anti-lock braking and traction control, and a 6-speed automatic transmission on some versions. **"Real" city/highway fuel economy:** *Mazda6 2.3 manual:* 9.6/6.7 L/100 km. *Mazda6 2.3 automatic:* 10.4/7.5 L/100 km. *Mazda6 3.0 manual:* 12.1/8.1 L/100 km. *Mazda6 3.0 automatic:* 12.3/8.1 L/100 km. *Mazda 626 2.0 manual:* 9.4/6.8 L/100 km. *Mazda 626 2.0 automatic:* 11.3/7.9 L/100 km. *Mazda 626 2.5 6-cyl. manual:* 11.8/8.5 L/100 km. *Mazda 626 2.5 6-cyl. automatic:* 12.2/8.5 L/100 km. There isn't a lot of difference in fuel consumption rates between these models. Although the newer versions are a bit more fuel-frugal, their higher price tag means any savings are illusory. Gas mileage may be 15 percent lower than advertised. **Maintenance/repair costs:** Average. Repairs aren't dealer-dependent, however, so save bagfuls of loonies by frequenting independent repair shops. **Parts:** Easily found, but sometimes costly; compare prices with independent suppliers. **Extended warranty:** An extended powertrain warranty is recommended as protection against mostly automatic transmission failures. **Best alternatives:** Acura CSX or RSX; Honda Accord; and the Hyundai Elantra, Sonata, or Tucson. **Helpful websites:** *www.mazdaforum. com/forum* and *www.mazdas247.com/forum/index.php.*

 Strengths and Weaknesses

ALERT! Tall drivers should be wary of the low headrests, which can be hazardous in a collision, and short drivers will want to ensure they can see adequately without getting dangerously close to the airbag housing.

626

Although far from being a high-performance vehicle, the 626 rides and handles fairly well, sips fuel, and still manages to accommodate four people in comfort. On the downside, complaints posted up to the 2002 model year for the 626 point out that there's too much body lean in turns; road noise intrudes into the cabin; the rear spoiler blocks rear visibility; the car is hard-riding over uneven pavement; the trunk opening isn't conducive to loading large objects; there's excessive torque steer (pulling) to the right when accelerating; and shifting isn't all that smooth, nor is the automatic gearbox very reliable.

Mazda6

The 2003 through 2010 Mazda6 offers the following powerplants: a 156 hp inline 4-cylinder, a 2.5L 170 hp inline 4-cylinder, a 212 hp V6, and a 272 hp turbocharged V6. All are adequate for most tasks but come up short for fuel economy. These Mazda engines can be hooked to a 5-speed or 6-speed manual or automatic transmission.

Don't get the idea that this is a warmed-over 626. It's set on an entirely new platform and carries safety and convenience features never seen by its predecessor, such as two-stage airbags and a chassis engineered to deflect crash forces away from occupants. The Mazda6's interior also allows for a comfortable ride and carries an unusually large trunk.

During its first year on the market, there was a wide range of owner complaints that have become fewer with more recent models. Owners mention various water leaks, omnipresent interior and exterior clunks (suspension), and a number of driveability concerns that include poor engine and transmission performance (clutch failures, predominantly).

Also, the 5-speed transmission is sometimes difficult to shift in its lower gears, hesitates when accelerating or decelerating, and gets stuck in gear. Many owners report dash rattles, paint bubbling, window motor failures, chronic stalling and hard starts, defective engine knock sensors, electrical shorts everywhere, noisy and prematurely worn brakes and steering, separation of the radiator's bottom seam, excessive condensation on the inside bottom of the front windshield, and waits of a month or more for replacement parts.

VEHICLE HISTORY: *626:* **2000**—Restyled and substantially improved with a small horsepower boost (5 hp) and enhanced handling, steering, and interior appointments. The 626 carried on until 2002, but there were no changes. *Mazda6:* **2004**—A four-door hatchback and wagon are added, along with passenger-side airbags. **2005**—Standard anti-lock braking and traction control; a 6-speed automatic transmission replaces the 5-speed unit for S models. **2007**—Standard side curtain airbags. **2008**—No more wagon or MazdaSpeed models. **2009**—Larger, with sportier handling.

 ## Safety Summary

All models/years: The 626's different iterations have registered far fewer complaints than their Asian, European, or American counterparts. Inadvertent airbag deployments, or airbags that fail to deploy in a collision. • Sudden, unintended acceleration. • Frequent automatic transmission malfunctions and failures with both the 626 and Mazda6. *626:* **2002**—One vehicle's driver-side seat belt unlatched during an accident. *Mazda6:* **2003**—Hard starts. • Steering failures. **2004**—Fuel line detaches from engine, even after fix:

> I have had two incidents where the fuel line has detached from inside the engine and the car has stalled and gasoline has poured out from underneath the car. The first time, the dealership told me that there was a recall and I should receive [notification] in the mail. I later found out there was no recall. They then fixed the car supposedly, and three months later it happened again.

Dangerous automatic transmission design cuts engine power when passing another vehicle. • Total brake failure. • Early severe brake rotor warpage. • Airbag light comes on due to cracked front sensors that short out from water ingress. • Rear windshield shatters because the defroster shorts out. • Electronic door lock often will not allow occupant to open car door from the inside (help!). **2005**—Harsh shifts, automatic transmission slippage, getting stuck in gear (has to be put into manual mode), and dropping into the next lower gear for no reason. • Manual transmission seizure. **2006**—Automatic transmission failure took a month to be repaired, in one incident. • Chronic stalling. • Car loses power when accelerating in cold weather (see *forum.mazda6club.com/index.php?showtopic=65171&st=0*). • Frequent replacement of brake pads and rotor. • Vehicle shifts from Sixth gear down to Third gear. **2007**—Hesitation when shifting gears. • Engine rear main seal oil leak; complete transmission failure due to a leaking seal at the torque converter. • One vehicle's engine threw a rod at 66,000 miles (106,000 km). • Lights and remote do not work in the rain; diagnosed as a junction box failure caused by rain. • Automatic windows will not reverse if they are closing on an object. **2008**—Rough idle, hesitation when accelerating. **2009**—Transmission replacement due to fluid leakage through weep hole. • Brake pedal goes to the floor without effect; premature wearout of brake pads, calipers, and rotors. • Corroded tire stems caused tire failure. • HID lights give inadequate field of illumination. **2010**—Underhood fire ignites while car is underway. • Tire pressure sensor failures. • Mushy brakes. • Brake rotors quickly go out of round. • Plastic bumper cracking creates a safety hazard. • The inner tail light lenses overheat, melt, and deform.

Secret Warranties/Internal Bulletins/Service Tips

626: **2002**—Rough idle, hesitation, and stumble. • Grinding, rubbing noise at front of vehicle. • Tips to silence wind noise around doors. *Mazda6:* **2003**—Doors hard to close in cold weather. • Sticking traction-control system switch. • Wind noise around doors. **2003–05**—Procedures to cure an engine camshaft ticking noise. • 1–2 gear shift shock with automatic transmission. **2003–06**—Rough idle and hesitation. • Excessive body vibration. **2003–07**—Pull or drift to the side when driving. **2003–08**—3.0L engine ticking. • Headlight lens condensation or water entry. • Steering shaft clunk. • Various wind noise concerns. • Unstable idle, engine stalling just after stopping. • Troubleshooting tips to correct brake noise, judder, and dragging. **2003–10**—Information relating to windshield flaws, scratches, cracks, etc. and the elimination of seatback creaking. • Front-seat head restraint rattling. • Noisy, wobbly seats. **2004**—Engine surging at 80 km/h. • Hesitation or rough idle at high altitudes. • Remedies for brake judder and moan. • Special Service Program #60 to replace the fan control module. • Special Service Program for evaporative emission-system leak monitoring failures. • Special Service Program for oxygen sensor failure. • Front suspension popping, clunking. **2005**—Surging at 60–90 km/h with the 2.3L 4-cylinder engine. **2005–08**—3.0L engine surging. • AC is inoperative when brakes are applied. **2006–07**—Front axle knocking noises in extreme cold. • Low-speed engine stalling. **2006–08**—No-start; inoperative AC or defroster. • Parking brake lever drops down after engagement in extremely cold climate. **2007–11**—Excessive water/condensation in headlamps. **2009**—Poor AC performance; engine runs hot. • Excessive manual transmission noise when shifting. • Transmission servo-cover fluid leaks. • Inaccurate fuel gauge. A Hyundai Campaign (MSP 22) will repair an electrical short that causes the wipers and headlights to work erratically. **2009–10**—Engine runs hot, poor AC performance. • Manual transmission hard to shift into Third or Fourth gear. • Diagnosing why the automatic transmission defaults to a "limp home" mode. • Silencing drivetrain squeak noises. • Premature front brake pad wear. • Rear door locks inoperative in freezing temperatures. • Front door speaker rattling. • An electrical short circuit may cause the horn to intermittently self-activate. • Rear taillight heat deformation. **2009–11**—Fix for front brakes that click or pop when applied. • Repair tips for an inoperative sunroof. **2010**—Free fix for A-pillar water leaks.

MAZDA6, 626 PROFILE

	2002	2003	2004	2005	2006	2007	2008	2009	2010
Cost Price ($)									
626	23,470	—	—	—	—	—	—	—	—
Mazda6	—	24,295	24,395	23,795	23,795	24,395	24,495	22,695	23,195
Mazda6 GT	—	—	—	29,795	29,895	30,295	29,895	27,695	33,495
Sport Hatchback	—	—	25,495	25,495	25,495	26,295	26,395	—	—
Sport Wagon	—	—	26,995	26,995	26,995	27,895	—	—	—
Used Values ($)									
626 ▲	3,500	—	—	—	—	—	—	—	—
626 ▼	3,000	—	—	—	—	—	—	—	—
Mazda6 ▲	—	4,500	5,000	6,500	9,500	11,000	13,000	15,000	17,500
Mazda6 ▼	—	4,000	4,500	5,500	8,000	10,000	11,500	13,500	16,000
Mazda6 GT ▲	—	—	—	8,500	10,000	11,500	14,500	18,500	23,000
Mazda6 GT ▼	—	—	—	8,000	9,000	10,500	13,000	17,000	21,500
Sport Hatchback ▲	—	—	5,500	7,000	9,000	10,500	13,000	—	—
Sport Hatchback ▼	—	—	4,500	6,000	8,000	9,500	12,000	—	—
Sport Wagon ▲	—	—	7,000	8,500	10,000	11,000	—	—	—
Sport Wagon ▼	—	—	5,500	8,000	9,000	10,500	—	—	—
Reliability	3	3	4	4	4	4	4	4	5
Crash Safety (F)	4	5	5	5	5	5	5	5	5
Side (626 4d)	3	—	—	—	—	—	—	—	—
Mazda6	—	3	3	3	4	4	4	5	5
IIHS Side	—	1	1	1	1	—	—	5	5
Offset	—	5	5	5	5	5	5	5	5
Head Restraints	2	2	2	2	2	2	2	2	2
Roof Strength	—	—	—	—	—	—	—	3	3
Rollover Resistance	—	5	5	5	5	5	5	5	5

Note: The 2003–05 Mazda6 models earn a higher score for head-restraint protection if the seats don't have a lumbar adjustment mechanism.

All ratings on a numbered scale where ☐5 is good and ■1 is bad. See page 132 for a more detailed description.

Nissan

ALTIMA, ALTIMA HYBRID ★★★★/★★★

RATING: Above Average (2008–10); Average (2002–07). *Altima Hybrid:* Average (2007–10). **Ideal model year:** Best choice would be a $10,000 to $11,000 2006 3.5 SE-R or a $9,000 SE version. **"Real" city/highway fuel economy:** *2.5 manual:* 10.3/7.3 L/100 km. *2.5 automatic:* 10.3/7.4 L/100 km. *3.5 manual:* 11.3/8.3 L/100 km. *3.5 6-speed manual:* 11.5/7.3 L/100 km. *3.5 automatic:* 12.3/8.3 L/100 km. *1.8 manual:* 8.8/6.2 L/100 km. *1.8 automatic:* 9.0/6.5 L/100 km. *2.0 manual:* 9.9/7.0 L/100 km. *2.0 automatic:* 9.8/7.2 L/100 km. *2.4 automatic:* 10.9/7.6 L/100 km. **Maintenance/repair costs:** Higher than average. Repairs are dealer-dependent. **Parts:** Owners complain of frequent parts shortages. Parts on earlier models are relatively inexpensive. **Extended warranty:** Get an extended warranty to protect you from automatic transmission failures and a host of other problems. **Best alternatives:** Acura Integra; later-model GM Cavalier or Sunfire; Honda Accord; Hyundai Elantra wagon, Sonata, or Tiburon; Mazda6; and 2005 or 2006 Toyota Camry. **Helpful websites:** *www.nissanforums.com.*

Strengths and Weaknesses

ALERT! Powertrain often gives a slow-poke performance.

Expect only average acceleration and fuel economy with the pre-2002 4-cylinder engine. It has insufficient top-end torque and gets buzzier the more it's pushed. In order to get the automatic to downshift for passing, for example, you have to practically stomp on the accelerator. Manoeuvrability is good around town but twitchy on the highway. There are few reliability problems reported with the 16-valve powerplant; however, the 5-speed manual transmission is sloppy and the automatic transmission's performance has been problematic. The uncluttered under-hood layout makes servicing easy. Body assembly is only so-so, with more than the average number of squeaks and rattles.

The 2002–10 models provide acceptable V6 acceleration (sometimes whether you want it or not), good braking, well laid-out instruments and controls, and better-than-average interior room and craftsmanship. Too bad their exceptional performance is hobbled by chronic stalling, unreliable transmission performance, premature brake failures, short circuits by the dozen, suspension glitches, and worse than average fit and finish.

Highway handling isn't impressive. The underpowered 4-cylinder engine isn't as refined as the competition and is noisy when pushed. The V6's acceleration overpowers this car and causes excessive rear-end instability and steering pull to one side. Brakes tend to lock up on wet roads; dash gauges wash out in sunlight; interior appointments lack panache; the dashboard reflects onto the windshield;

rear seating for three adults is snug, there's limited rear headroom, and obstructed rear visibility; and parts are often back-ordered. Quality problems multiply by the fifth year of use.

The car's 180 hp 2.5L 4-cylinder engine is almost as powerful as the competition's V6 powerplants, and the optional 245 hp 3.5L V6 has few equals among cars in this price and size class. And when you consider that the Altima is much lighter than most of its competitors, it's obvious why this car produces sizzling (and sometimes uncontrollable) acceleration.

VEHICLE HISTORY: 2002—Completely revised with two high-performance engines (a 180 hp 2.5L 4-cylinder or an optional 245 hp 3.5L V6), a larger interior, and a more-supple ride combined with sportier handling. Quality declines. **2005**—The sporty new SE-R model arrives with a 260 hp V6. Other V6 models now use a 5-speed automatic. Interior trim is upgraded throughout the lineup. **2007**—Restyled, more standard safety features, and the debut of Nissan's first gas/electric hybrid model. **2008**—ABS is a standard feature, and an all-new Coupe model comes on the scene. **2009**—A standard sunroof for the 3.5 SE and auto-locking power door locks across the board. **2010**—A redesigned model that now comes with a restyled front end; standard electronic stability control and traction assist; a CVT transmission for the V6 sedan; and a new name for the 3.5 SE, which becomes the 3.5 SR.

The engine, fit and finish, automatic transmission, fuel and electrical systems, and brakes (squealing and premature wearout of pads and rotors) continue to be troublesome on 2009–10 models. Owners report electrical glitches; excessive brake wear, noise, and pulsations; an annoying and hazardous dash reflection onto the windshield; and engine surging, stalling, and hard starting, possibly because of a defective engine crank sensor or throttle switch. Rear shocks are noisy and failure-prone; the ABS warning light stays lit; the clutch pressure plate throw-out bearing and flywheel may fail when downshifting into Fourth gear; and snow builds up in the small wheelwells, making steering difficult and causing excessive shimmy.

 Safety Summary

2001–03—Airbags fail to deploy. **2002–03**—Dealerships said to be aware of redesigned Altima's tendency to catch fire: fire erupted after collision; fire ignited because of a faulty fuel-injection system; fire ignited while vehicle was cruising on the highway. • One vehicle was idling and then suddenly went into Reverse and accelerated as groceries were being unloaded from the trunk (dash indicator showed car in Park). • Driver run over by his own car when it slipped into Reverse. • Sudden acceleration when brakes are applied. • Transmission slips and engine hesitates when accelerating. • Chronic stalling. • Windshield distortion. • Exhaust-pipe hanger pin catches debris that may ignite. • Crankshaft position sensor failure. • Tail lights constantly fail. • Seat belt fails to retract. • Instrument panel gauges wash out in sunlight. **2004**—Sudden stalling and hard starts. • Vehicle starts, but won't move forward. • Car is a hostage-taker:

The problem that I face now is that I cannot get out of my car!!!!!! I arrived home one day and found that the driver's side door would not open from the inside. I am 7 months pregnant and was very scared when I found this problem. What if there is ever a car fire or an accident and I cannot get out? You can open the door from the outside but not the inside. Hyannis Nissan claims it's a door latch problem and it had to be replaced. So since my warranty just ran out I have to pay $192.00 to get this repaired. Are you kidding me?

2005—Sudden, unintended acceleration while parking. • Seat belts failed to lock when one Altima was rear-ended. • Rear control bar breaks (see also TSB #NTB05-114b in "Secret Warranties/Internal Bulletins/Service Tips," following):

Rear passenger control bar (2 rods) broke at the weld while driving and caused my car to spin out of control, causing damage to the tire, and the rear housing. I was told it would not be covered under either warranty that I carry. I was told to turn it over to my insurance company. This same part has a recall in other states, just not Florida?

Transmission hesitates and then slams into gear. • Excessive steering vibration resolved:

I have a 2005 Nissan Altima 3.5 SL. Last summer I was having problems with the car's handling at highway speeds. I had the car aligned, replaced all 4 tires, one by one and was still having [problems] with the car—which was shaking at speeds over 60 mph [97 km/h]. I took it to the dealer again and they determined that the shaking was like a turbulence effect. The spoiler under the car was not allowing the wind to flow through properly.

2006—Many complaints that the 2.5L engine stops running without warning due to an overheated crankshaft position sensor (not included in an earlier recall). • Engine surges after vehicle comes to a complete stop. • Early strut and tie-rod failures. • Clutch pedal goes to the floor and stays there. • Dry-rotted tire valve stems. **2007**—Snapped stabilizer bar:

2007 Nissan Altima 3.5 SE rear sway bar snapped in two while driving. There was no damage to the surrounding area where the bar snapped. At close inspection, the bar is hollow inside. There are web blogs that I have found where other owners have experienced the same problem. See *wiki.answers.com/q/should_the_2007_Nissan_Altima_rear_sway_bar_be_recalled.*

Passenger-side airbag is disabled when an average-sized adult is seated. • Sudden steering lockup. • Defective tire-pressure sensor. • The Tire Pressure warning light comes on for no reason. **2007–08**—Unstable driver's seat moves side to side and fore and aft when the car turns, accelerates, or slows down. **2008**—Airbag shuts off when passenger seat is occupied. • Chronic stalling. • Defective automatic CVT (warranty extension for 10 years). • Sudden brake lock-up. • Leaking brake master cylinder. • Windshield wipers blur the windshield. • Continental ContiPro Contact tires perform poorly on snow-covered, wet highways. • Back doors don't close properly. **2009**—Sudden, unintended acceleration when brakes are applied. • Loss of power on the highway. • Airbags fail to deploy. • Passenger-side airbag is disabled when a normal-sized adult is seated. • Binding automatic transmission replaced under warranty. • Brake master cylinder leaks brake fluid into the brake booster:

> The low brake fluid light came on and I found out the brake master cylinder leaks brake fluid into the brake booster. There are no leaks at the calipers, hoses, or any other areas. This is a known issue with the 2007 and 2008 and there is an open investigation for those years but NHTSA does not include the 2009.

Corroded floorboards. • After a rain, water puddles inside the driver's door. **2010**—Many complaints that the CVT automatic transmission is slow to send power to the wheels and then surges. • Excessive steering vibration.

Secret Warranties/Internal Bulletins/Service Tips

All years: Diagnostic and correction tips for brake vibration and steering-wheel shimmy. • TSB #NTB99-028 outlines the procedures necessary to fix slow-to-retract seat belts. • TSB #NTB00-037a covers possible causes of the vehicle's pulling to the side. **2002–03**—Low power, poor running, and MIL stays lit. • Automatic transmission slips in Reverse and won't brake when in Drive 1 range. • Hard starting. • Excessive engine, fuel-sloshing, and suspension noise. • Inoperative AC; warm air flows from vents. • Poor heater performance. • AC drain hose may leak into interior. • Sunroof water leaks. • Wind noise from doors and sunroof. • Water leakage on front floor area. • Sunroof won't close at highway speeds. **2002–04**—The control valve assembly may be the culprit responsible for erratic shifting. **2002–05**—Secret 13-year extended warranty on the rear subframe:

CAMPAIGN—REAR SUSPENSION MEMBER, BUSHING REPLACEMENT

BULLETIN NO.: NTB05-114B   DATE: MARCH 24, 2006

VOLUNTARY SERVICE CAMPAIGN REAR SUSPENSION REPLACEMENT/BUSHING REPLACEMENT AND SEALING

On some model year 2002–05 Nissan Altima and 2004–05 Nissan Maxima vehicles, there is a possibility that corrosion of the rear sub-frame may occur. Corrosion is most likely in cold climates where heavy salting of roads is common practice in freezing conditions.... In severe cases, cracking of the rear sub-frame may occur, which may result in a knocking noise coming from the rear of the vehicle.... On most vehicles, Nissan will replace the rear sub-frame assembly. On some 2005 Model Year vehicles, where sub-frame replacement is not necessary, Nissan will replace and seal the front bushings and seal the rear bushings.

WARRANTY EXTENSION: To ensure the highest levels of customer satisfaction, Nissan is also extending the warranty for cracking of the rear sub-frame due to corrosion to a total of 13 years with unlimited mileage on all model year 2002–05 Nissan Altima and 2004–05 Nissan Maxima vehicles. Vehicles included in the Service Campaign (as described above) are also covered by the Warranty Extension.

2002–06—Hard starts or no-starts in cold weather. • Ticking noise from the engine area. • Oil cooler oil leaks do not require the replacement of the complete engine oil cooler assembly, says TSB #NTB06-029. • Pop, thump noise when operating front-door window. 2002–10—Exhaust shield rattles. 2003–05—Nissan's bulletin admits that a harsh-shifting condition is factory-related. 2004—Hard starts or no-starts may signal the need for a new fuel-pump assembly. 2004–08—Leak from the tire pressure monitor sensor. 2007–08—Erratic speedometer readings. • ABS and Brake lights lit. • Silencing front brake noise at slow speeds. • Sunroof seals poorly. • Front suspension rattling. • Inoperative "power up" window. 2007–09—Ignition may not turn to the On position (steering lock unit may need to be replaced under warranty or via "goodwill"). • Sunroof may operate erratically. • Inoperative power window "Auto Up" feature. • Front brake squealing or squeaking at low speeds; replace brake pads and install brake kit per TSB # NTB08-057B, published August 19, 2009. 2007–10— Driver's power seat moves side to side. • Troubleshooting tips for correcting fuel gauge malfunctions. • Door mirror wind noise. 2008–09—Driver seat may not move forward or backward. 2009—Nissan has set up a special Campaign (#PCO 44) to prevent the front windshield wipers from scraping the windshield. Parts and labour are Nissan's responsibility. Another Campaign (#PC005) provides free replacement of the rear suspension knuckle.

ALTIMA, ALTIMA HYBRID PROFILE

	2002	2003	2004	2005	2006	2007	2008	2009	2010
Cost Price ($)									
XE/S	23,498	23,798	23,798	23,798	24,698	24,398	24,499	25,998	27,348
GXE/SE	27,698	24,675	24,298	29,098	29,698	30,198	30,298	29,498	—
Coupe S	—	—	—	—	—	—	27,799	25,998	27,348
Coupe SE	—	—	—	—	—	—	31,398	29,798	—
Sedan 3.5 SE-R	—	—	—	21,498	29,698	—	—	—	—
Hybrid	—	—	—	—	—	32,998	33,998	32,298	33,398
Used Values ($)									
XE/S ▲	3,000	4,500	5,000	6,500	8,000	9,500	12,500	15,000	17,500
XE/S ▼	2,500	3,000	4,500	5,500	7,000	8,500	11,000	13,500	16,000
GXE/SE ▲	4,500	5,500	6,500	8,000	9,500	11,500	14,000	18,000	—
GXE/SE ▼	4,000	5,000	6,000	7,000	8,500	10,000	12,500	16,500	—
Coupe S ▲	—	—	—	—	—	—	13,500	16,500	19,500
Coupe S ▼	—	—	—	—	—	—	11,500	15,000	18,000
Coupe SE ▲	—	—	—	—	—	—	14,500	18,500	—
Coupe SE ▼	—	—	—	—	—	—	13,000	17,000	—
Sedan 3.5 SE-R ▲	—	—	—	7,500	9,500	—	—	—	—
Sedan 3.5 SE-R ▼	—	—	—	6,500	8,000	—	—	—	—
Hybrid ▲	—	—	—	—	—	11,500	14,000	19,500	21,500
Hybrid ▼	—	—	—	—	—	10,000	13,000	18,000	20,000

Reliability	3	3	3	3	4	4	4	4	4
Crash Safety (F)	4	4	4	5	5	5	4	4	4
4d	—	—	—	—	—	—	5	5	5
Hybrid	—	—	—	—	—	—	5	5	5
Side	3	3	3	3	3	5	5	5	5
4d	—	—	—	—	—	4	5	5	5
Hybrid	—	—	—	—	—	5	5	5	5
IIHS Side	1	1	1	1	1	5	5	5	5
Offset	5	5	5	5	5	5	5	5	5
Head Restraints (F)	3	3	3	3	3	2	2	3	3
Roof Strength	—	—	—	—	—	3	3	3	3
Rollover Resistance	4	4	4	4	4	4	5	5	5
4d	—	—	—	—	—	4	4	4	4
Hybrid	—	—	—	—	—	—	4	4	4

Toyota

CAMRY, HYBRID, SOLARA ★ / ★ ★

bad buy

RATING: *Camry:* Average (2010); Not Recommended (1996–2009). Toyota's sudden, unintended acceleration, loss of brakes, and airbags that fail to deploy are a triple whammy that may kill you. Sadder still, NHTSA logs show these three interconnected problems have carried over to the 2010 and 2011 model years.

Interestingly, when the 2007 model Camry was redesigned, quality control and safety took a serious hit with the exception of the Solara and Hybrid models. From falling sun visors to lurching powertrains, the company could have done much better, and knows it, as evidenced by a few contrite apologies issued by top Toyota executives. *Hybrid:* Not recommended (2007–10). Although not as failure-prone as the conventional Camry, the Hybrid's high cost and safety defects make it less affordable and more hazardous than the competition. *Solara:* Above Average (2006–08); Average (1999–2005). Almost identical to the Camry, the Solara has had almost no meaningful safety complaints and resale prices are relatively reasonable. **Ideal model year:** The Solara, a two-door Camry clone, was overpriced when bought new; however, the 2006–08 models are good buys because they are more reasonably priced as used cars and are likely to have some of the original factory warranty coverage left. Of all the model years, I'd go for a $9,000 2006 Solara V6 to get the maximum depreciation discount and a good array of standard features. **"Real" city/highway fuel economy:** *Camry, Solara 2.4 automatic:* 10.1/6.7 L/100 km. *Camry, Solara 3.3 6-cylinder:* 11.7/7.4 L/100 km. *Camry 2.2 manual:* 10.0/6.8 L/100 km. *Camry 2.2 automatic:* 9.0/6.5 L/100 km. *Camry 2.4 automatic:* 10.4/7.3 L/100 km. *Camry 3.0 automatic:* 11.9/7.3 L/100 km. *Camry Hybrid:* 5.7/5.7 L/100 km. These estimates may be off by as much as 20 percent. **Maintenance/repair costs:** Higher than average, but repairs aren't dealer-dependent. **Parts:** Can be more expensive than for most other cars in this class, making it worth your while to shop at independent suppliers. Parts availability is excellent. **Extended warranty:** Essential for 1997 and later model years. **Best alternatives:** Ford Escape Hybrid; Honda Accord; Hyundai Elantra wagon, Sonata, Tiburon, or Tucson; Mazda6; and Nissan Sentra. **Helpful websites:** *www.toyotanation.com/forum* and *www.toyotaowners.net.*

 ## Strengths and Weaknesses

ALERT! There is apparently still a "ghost in the machine." In a confidential 2006 memo published by CNN TV News in March, Toyota admitted its test vehicle suddenly accelerate due to an electronic glitch. Toyota says its document was mis-translated by CNN's translators. The engineering memo, filed in court, has led to several Toyota out-of-court settlements in the plaintiffs' favour (see *http://edition. cnn.com/2012/03/01/us/toyota-memo-acceleration-concerns/index.html*).

And, incidents are now reported with the 2011 and 2012 Toyotas:

> I braked the 2011 Toyota Camry really hard to the floor, but the car could not slow down and could not stop completely. The brake system in the 2011 Toyota Camry had obviously failed and the car was even accelerating during the last few seconds prior to the collision.

The Camry is basically a Japanese Oldsmobile (the old rear-drive kind); it drives and coddles you. Safety complaints aside, it's a good small family hauler because of its spacious, well-appointed interior, good fuel economy, and comfortable ride.

"De-contenting" hit Toyota's 1996–2004 lineup hard, resulting in many changes that cheapened the Camry and precipitated a huge increase in owner complaints over problems that had never appeared on Toyota vehicles before. Many of these defects continue to reappear to this day. Specifically, owners have endured leaky, noisy struts; self-destructing AC; excessive steering-wheel vibrations; warning lights that constantly come on; water leaking into the car after a hard rain; front power windows that often run off their channels; a suspension that bottoms out when carrying four adults; failure-prone engine head gaskets and automatic transmissions; moonroofs that are prone to water leaks and annoyingly loud wind noise; frequent hesitation or stalling out when accelerating or braking; charcoal canisters that need early replacement (covered by the emissions warranty, if you insist on it); and constantly irritating brake pulsations, plus brake components (pads, rotors, calipers, master cylinder, and the ABS valve) that wear out early. Side pillar rattling is also a chronic annoyance.

The 2007–09 models are particularly failure-prone, leading the pack in sheer number of complaints reported to NHTSA. Engine stalling and surging and transmission failures lead the list. Other problems relate to loose headliners/moulding; chronic water and air leaks; and poor-quality fit and finish, evidenced by poor paint application. Brake problems and electrical shorts continue unabated.

The 2010 models are a bit less troublesome, thanks to a flurry of goodwill warranty extensions used to placate owners. Nevertheless, these are still dangerous vehicles. Toyota's "lag and lurch" powertrain hazard is still in evidence on these more recent models, and safety defects affecting acceleration, brakes, and airbags haven't gone away.

VEHICLE HISTORY: 2002—Car gets larger and now carries a 157 hp 2.4L 4-cylinder engine. **2004**—SE version gets a 225 hp 3.3L V6 hooked to a revised 5-speed automatic, improved fuel injection, and additional soundproofing. The 3.0L V6 available in the LE and XLE also gets the new 5-speed automatic and gains 18 hp, giving it 210 hp. **2005**—Standard ABS, and an upgraded automatic transmission for models equipped with a 4-cylinder engine. Less effective rear drum brakes are kept on the entry-level models. **2007**—Totally redesigned, equipped with an all-new 268 hp 3.5L V6, or a more powerful (four more horses) 158 hp 2.4L 4-cylinder engine. This year's version has a longer wheelbase and is a bit wider and lower, with new exterior and interior styling. A hybrid model, equipped with the 2.4L 4-banger, makes its debut as well. **2010**—The 2.4L is replaced by a slightly more powerful 2.5L.

Camry Hybrid

The Hybrid combines a 2.4L 4-cylinder gas engine with a battery-powered electric motor (187 hp) and a CVT. Similar to Toyota's other hybrids, the Camry HV runs on one or both of its power sources, depending on driving conditions, and requires no plug-in charging.

Although the car is less fuel-thirsty than the base 4-cylinder Camry, it also costs about $6,000 more. And the kicker: Your first two years' depreciation will be $8,000. You will also become a captive customer of the hybrid-selling dealer.

Both the 2007 and 2008 Hybrid models have serious safety-related deficiencies caused by poor design. 2009 Hybrids are relatively trouble-free, with only six safety-related incidents reported. The two most worrisome failures are the aforementioned lag and lurch powertrain syndrome and the sudden downshifting/ surging associated with the cruise control as the vehicle passes over hilly terrain. Other complaints involve failure of the brakes and electrical system, subpar fit and finish, and poor-quality paint. Reports one angry Hybrid owner to NHTSA:

> Hybrid 2007 black paint is defective design technology. Toyota changed to a water-based paint two years ago, and the product is a manufacturer's defective design and process. Toyota is hiding this fact from its customer base.... Be honest, you paid a lot of money for a defective paint job and they know it.

Solara

Introduced in the summer of 1998 as a '99 model, the Solara is essentially a two-door coupe or convertible Camry that's longer, lower, and more bare-bones, with a more stylish exterior, sportier powertrain and suspension, and fewer quality problems. Most new Toyota model offerings, such as the Sienna, Avalon, and RAV4, are also Camry derivatives.

The Solara was redesigned for 2004 and adopted the latest Camry sedan platform and upgrades. Convertibles arrived with seating for four instead of five and resemble the two-seat Lexus SC 430 hardtop convertible. The 2007 Solaras underwent a mild front and rear restyling, got standard side curtain airbags and a coloured rear spoiler, and dropped the SE V6 model. For 2008, the Solara's last model year, only the SLE remained. The 4-cylinder engine was replaced by the 3.3L V6, coupled to a 5-speed automatic transmission.

Relatively rare on the used-car market, you have a choice of either four or six cylinders. Unfortunately, vehicles equipped with a V6 also came with a gimmicky rear spoiler and a headroom-robbing moonroof. The stiff body structure and suspension, as well as tight steering, make for easy, sports-car-like handling with lots of road feel and few surprises. Unfortunately, the 4-cylinder base engine in pre-2007 models is wimpy and constantly reminds you and everyone else that it's a Toyota. Get the V6 instead.

 Safety Summary

All models/years: Airbag fails to deploy, or is accidentally deployed. • Sudden acceleration when braking, shifting, or parking. • Stalling, then surging when accelerating or braking. • Car rolls away when parked on an incline. • Owners report that original-equipment Firestone tires fail prematurely. • Vehicle wanders all over the road or drifts into oncoming traffic. **All models: 2001**—Under-hood fire (left side) while vehicle is parked overnight. • Fire ignites from underneath vehicle while driving. **2001–02**—Brake pedal goes to floor with no braking effect. • ABS suddenly locks up when coming to a gradual stop. **2002**—An astounding 620 owner complaints up to May 2007. • One vehicle's starter caught on fire while vehicle was parked. • Faulty cruise control causes vehicle to suddenly accelerate. • Sudden acceleration without braking effect. • Defective rear brake drum. • Many owners complain of poor brake pedal design:

> Arm that holds up brake pedal is interfering with the driver's foot. Driver stated if consumer had a large size foot, it could easily get wedged and stuck on brake pedal. Foot gets caught between the floormat and the brake arm, needs to be redesigned.

Front right axle broke six months after a car was purchased. • High rear end cuts rear visibility. • Turn signal volume is too low. **2003**—Over 400 safety-related complaints were registered by NHTSA, mostly identical to the incidents detailed for the 2002 model. **2004**—Fire ignites in the side wheelwell. • Sudden, unintended acceleration when braking, using the cruise control, shifting from Park to Reverse, or pulling into a parking space:

Difficulty shifting from Park to Reverse, then upon shifting into Drive the car accelerated uncontrollably, would not stop, collided with a mobile home, airbags did not deploy, resulting in the death of one passenger and injury of driver.

•

While parking the car, the steering locked turning the car to the right. The car accelerated and surged despite depressing the brake (same as ODI PE04021), the car broke a metal flag pole, damaged a retaining wall, and fell seven feet [2 m] into a major street. The airbags did not deploy.

•

Caller's mother-in-law just got her car washed and when she pulled out of the car wash, the vehicle accelerated without warning. She pumped the brakes and tried to stop the car, and it would not stop. The car went into an 8-lane highway and was hit by an 18-wheeler and a pickup truck. Driver sustained injuries and so did the driver of the pickup truck.

Steering U-joint bearing falls out. • Steering knuckle defective:

Problem has been going on for two weeks. Now after taking it to an official Toyota dealer repair shop, problem still not fixed. Now at least two weeks to a month wait on part. Was told we were number 536 on waiting list, and was told it was not a safety issue in short term, but do not believe that. Steering is loose, and a catch occurs in steering. Passenger can even feel when this occurs. Dealer has reported three exact same problems with other Camrys in the same week.

Brake and gas pedal are mounted too close together. • Sudden brake failure. • Brake pedal goes all the way to the floor, and braking distance is increased. • When in Drive on a hill, the vehicle rolls backward. • When shifted into Reverse, vehicle goes forward. • When accelerating, engine and transmission will hesitate for up to four seconds, then will surge forward. This problem extends over several model years and also includes the Lexus ES 300/330. • Poorly designed, misadjusted headlights cause a blinding glare. • Backup lights are too dim. • Repeat failures of the cruise-control, odometer, and speedometer control modules. • Front passenger airbags are disabled even when a heavy adult sits in the seat. • Inside cabin hood release latch not attached to release mechanism. • The bumpers are easily dented. • Premature wearout of Firestone tires. • Original-equipment Goodyear Integrity "all-season" tires perform poorly in snow. • Unstable tire jack. • Are Camrys "rat-prone"? Read the following owner's complaint and decide for yourself:

O_2 sensors failed due to rodents or rabbits chewing the plastic wiring housing the internal electrical wires. O_2 sensors had to be replaced at a cost of about $600. The outside coatings, or sheaths, for the wiring is made of a soy-based plastic and possibly contains a "fish oil" in the sheath, which attracts rodents and rabbits, and they chew on the plastic wire coverings, thereby destroying the O_2 sensor's wiring mechanism. This problem is prevalent in the Denver and mountain state areas and should be corrected as the problem could lead to engine fires or engine failures. The wiring housing should be changed to a "retardant" type of wiring to prevent other incidents of this problem, and not just for Toyota but for all manufacturers.

2005—Vehicle hesitates and then surges. • Sometimes, the Camry will suddenly lurch forward when easing into a parking space:

> I was slowly turning right to park in front of a store with my foot on the brakes preparing to stop when my 2005 Camry accelerated, jumped the curb and crashed into a storefront window.

V6 has chronic hesitation problems at lower speeds. • Engine surges when slowing for a traffic light, or when applying moderate brake pressure. • Car constantly veers left. • Transmission shifts with a jolt when car slows down and then accelerates. • Brake pedal will sink to the floor intermittently. • Windshield has hash marks that obstruct vision when sun shines through. **2006**—225 safety-related complaints, which is about average for a five-year-old car, with most reports relating to sudden acceleration, brake failures, and airbag malfunctions. • Too much steering play, knocking noise. • Side windows fall down. **2007**—Over 1,166 safety-related complaints posted on NHTSA's website; 200 complaints would be normal for a 2007 model. • Top complaint categories are airbag failures, sudden, unintended acceleration, and loss of brakes or reduced braking. • Many reports that the car hesitates on takeoff; transmission slips. • Steering wheel binds. **2008**—231 safety-related complaints posted on NHTSA's website. • Passenger-side airbag is disabled when the passenger seat is occupied. • Sudden acceleration while parking the car and cruising on the highway. • Throttle response has intermittent delay. • Chronic stalling, hesitation, and surge. • 6-speed automatic transmission slippage. • Poor braking performance. • Excessive vibration once underway. • Rear window glare, and dash reflects onto the front windshield. **2009**—432 safety-related incidents reported; brakes, airbags, and unintended acceleration still appear as troublesome. *Hybrid:* **2007**—Only 79 safety incidents reported to NHTSA. This is less than half what one would normally see on the average three-year-old vehicle. • Sudden acceleration after floor mats were removed. • Chronic stalling. • Sudden loss of steering. • Cruise control malfunctions:

> The car's cruise control behavior on level ground is fine, but on rolling hills it's totally egregious, and indicates to me that this feedback control system may be close to instability and therefore potentially dangerous. I think that the control algorithm used is dreadfully sub-optimal, and has such long internal control-loop processing delays that its reactions to changing road conditions are alarming. What I find is the following behavior: The car substantially overshoots (by 10 mph [16 km/h] or more) the set speed on the downhill portion of each hill, but then waits so long before reacting to the beginning of the next uphill portion, that it then undershoots the set speed by such a large amount (5 mph [8 km/h] or more) that it has to "floor" the accelerator in order to catch up. Still on the uphill portion, it then proceeds to overshoot the set

speed again, before finally settling down to the desired speed. This cycle of events repeats over and over again as one negotiates rolling hills with the cruise control "on"... The cruise control's behavior could be fixed by a simple firmware update.

•

The speed [decreases] by as much as 5 mph [8 km/h] while descending...a hill, then as it begins to climb it quickly accelerates way over the target speed. This causes a whiplash effect to all passengers and may cause the driver to lose control and collide with vehicles.

While driving in the snow, the car's traction control feature cuts all power—a common complaint among owners. • Engine sludge requires an $8,000 rebuild; Toyota had this problem a decade earlier and refunded the repair costs under a secret goodwill warranty they later publicized. • Both sun visors fall at the pivot point. • Sun glares from the dash's stainless steel appliqué. • Oily residue coats interior windows. Dealer says it is the car's plastic trim and fabrics "outgassing":

The contact stated that the vehicle was emitting fumes that made her sick. However, she was unsure of the composition of the fumes. She went to the hospital three different times, and was admitted for a week each of the last two times. Her doctor said that she had chemical pneumonia or statis asthmaticus. Neither speed nor weather conditions were a factor.

A rock passed through a hole in the grille of one vehicle and destroyed the radiator. • Premature tire wear. • Long wait for replacement parts. **2008**—Only 25 incidents recorded by NHTSA. • Airbag deployment broke driver's finger and acid-like substance from the airbag ate into her leg tissue:

All surface skin & few layers deep gone! Eaten away like acid. I am sure 100% airbag powder soaked in at implosion and ate its way out! I never knew powder in "air" bags. At emergency room no one told me to cleanse legs. Went to wound care doctors & skin continued to disintegrate. On April 20 2010, had emergency surgery to remove necrotic area, not healing. Graft July 2010 not healing. Aug 31 took last bandage off, huge ugly scar, chunk of calf missing/deformity now. Airbag powder like caustic acid. Many people say they had blisters, too. Lawyers too said same. Most people cars are gone before anyone can investigate.

Fire ignited in the engine compartment. • Vehicle lunges forward when shifted into Reverse. • No brakes, or reduced braking capability. • Loss of power as car limped home; no data found in the car's black box. • Loss of steering control as car veered off into oncoming traffic. • When it rains the car leaks water, which soon fouls the cabin air. **2009**—Sudden acceleration and poor braking make encore appearances (along with one rodent report):

2009 Toyota Camry acceleration problem happened after recall fixes. Was pulling into parking space slowly when Acc. pedal dropped and engine able to stomp hard on brakes and not hit the building since hybrid gas part of engine disengages when the brake pedal is used.

•

Rodents chewing on biodegradable wire harness in 2009 Camry 4 door sedan hybrid. Complaint given to customer service mgr was inoperative gas gauge. No explanation given for entry points or solution other than replacement of wiring harness. Toyota customer experience center representative Emanual put customer on hold to review internal Toyota documents regarding issue, but refused to give document name, page number or file name.

Vehicle feels like it speeds up, instead of braking, just after passing over a speed bump. • Acceleration recall repair makes it hard to keep foot on the accelerator pedal. • Vehicle may shift over to gasoline power and runs with reduced power until battery is dead. **2010**—A whopping 319 safety-related incidents have been posted—almost double the norm. • Airbags fail to deploy. • Many unintended acceleration reports. • Stallout on the highway. • Automatic transmission lurches and lags during gear changes. • Premature failure of the suspension wheel struts. • Sudden brake failure. • Assembly-line whistle-blower tells of leaky brake lines cover-up. • Vehicle pulls to the left once underway. • Excessive steering-wheel vibration. • While vehicle was idling in Drive, vehicle rolled back and stalled. • Front end support bracket not welded to frame support. • Early blowout of Bridgestone Turanza tires. • Sun visor failures block driver's vision. • A foul sulfur smell comes from the heating system. • Windshield wiper started banging on left side of front pillar while operating.

Secret Warranties/Internal Bulletins/Service Tips

All models/years: Owner feedback over the last decade as well as dealer service managers who wish to remain anonymous tell me that Toyota has a secret warranty that will pay for replacing front disc brake components that wear out before 2 years/40,000 km. If you're denied this coverage, threaten small claims court action. **All models: 2002–06**—Plugging a front-door water leak. **2002–08**—Front power seat grinding and groaning. **2003–06**—Tips for silencing intermediate steering shaft noise. **2003–11**—Remedy for a rear windshield ticking noise. **2004–05**—Correction for drifting or pulling into oncoming traffic involves installing new springs and struts. **2004–08**—Front seat squeaking. **2006–09**—No shift from Park; multiple warning lights come on. **2007**—Engine oil leaks from the timing cover. • Rough idle, stalling. • Shift flare. **2007–08**—No crank; engine starts and dies. • Premature brake pad wear; squeaking rear brakes. • Excessive steering-wheel vibration, flutter, and noise. • Instrument panel rattle. Frame creaking noise. • Rear suspension squeaking, rubbing. • Engine oil leak from camshaft housing. • Engine ticking noises. • Torque converter shudder. • Moonroof knocking when underway. • Troubleshooting brake pulsation/vibration. • Rattle from trunk area. **2007–09**—Silencing engine ticking and floor pan creaking. • Inoperative moonroof. **2007–10**—Limited Service Campaign #90K will cover the full cost of replacement of the V6 engine VV-1 oil hose until March 31, 2013. • Braking vibration, pulsation can be reduced through the use of new brake pads and brake rotor R & R. Work should be paid for by Toyota, whether vehicle was bought new or used:

VIBRATION/PULSATION WHEN BRAKING

BULLETIN NO.: T-SB-0169-09   DATE: JUNE 4, 2009

Some 2007–10 Camry vehicles may exhibit a vibration or pulsation condition when braking. New front brake pads are available to address customer concerns. Follow the repair procedure below.

APPLICABLE WARRANTY: This repair is covered under the Toyota Comprehensive Warranty. This warranty is in effect for 36 months or 36,000 miles, whichever occurs first, from the vehicle's in-service date. Warranty application is limited to correction of a problem based upon a customer's specific complaint.

REPAIR PROCEDURE: Machine both front rotors with an on-car lathe to minimize rotor run-out. Make sure that the rotors are within minimum thickness. After machining the maximum allowed rotor run-out is 0.05 mm (0.002 inch). If the rotors are unserviceable or below minimum thickness replace the rotors.

A rattle or buzz coming from the driver's side dash may require an updated vacuum check valve. • Tips on correcting a roof knocking sound. • Intermittent noxious AC odours. • Loose sun visor mounts. **2007–11**—Uneven rear brake pad wear. • Water leaks from sunroof onto headliner and into footwell area. **2008–09**—TCM update for shift improvements. **2008–10**—Ignition coils may need replacing if the MIL alert is illuminated. **2010–11**—Wheel cover ticking, creaking. *Camry:* **2007–09**—The 2.4L 4-cylinder engine burns oil rapidly. *Hybrid:* **2007–09**—No shift from Park; multiple warning lights come on. • Water leaks onto headliner and footwell area. • Inoperative moonroof. **2007–10**—Ways to fix a knocking sound from the roof area. **2007–11**—The 2.4L 4-cylinder engine burns oil rapidly. *Solara:* **All years:** Water leaking into the trunk area. • Poor durability of rear-view mirrors. **2002–03**—Harsh automatic transmission shifts. • Excessive brake vibration. • Sliding-roof repair tips (TSB #BO002-03). • Power front seat feels loose (TSB #BO004-03). • Poor AC/heating. **2002–05**—Fuel door hard to open. • Remedy for rotten-egg exhaust smell. **2004–06**—Convertible top hard to close. **2004–08**—Water leaks at headliner and floor areas. **2007–08**—The 2.4L 4-cylinder engine may be an "oil-burner."

TSBs #SB002411 and #SB009411 say that excess oil consumption in the 2.4L 4-cylinder engine in several models was traced to the piston assembly. Toyota will replace the pistons and rings on a "goodwill" case-by-case basis.

CAMRY, HYBRID, SOLARA PROFILE

	2002	2003	2004	2005	2006	2007	2008	2009	2010
Cost Price ($)									
LE	23,755	24,800	24,800	24,990	24,990	25,800	25,900	23,400	24,900
LE V6	27,585	27,070	27,070	27,475	27,475	29,400	29,500	28,235	28,345

Camry Hybrid	—	—	—	—	—	31,900	32,000	30,660	30,900
Base Solara	28,175	28,175	28,800	26,850	27,545	29,200	—	—	—
V6	33,990	34,290	27,777	30,950	32,850	33,400	36,975	—	—
Convertible/SE	39,505	39,505	39,100	39,100	34,700	36,500	36,500	—	—
Used Values ($)									
LE ▲	4,000	5,500	6,500	8,000	9,500	11,500	13,500	16,000	18,500
LE ▼	3,500	5,000	6,000	7,000	8,500	10,000	12,000	14,500	17,000
LE V6 ▲	6,000	6,500	7,500	8,500	10,500	13,000	16,000	18,500	21,500
LE V6 ▼	5,500	6,000	7,000	7,500	9,000	11,500	14,500	17,000	20,000
Camry Hybrid ▲	—	—	—	—	—	13,500	17,000	20,000	23,000
Camry Hybrid ▼	—	—	—	—	—	12,000	15,500	18,500	22,500
Base Solara ▲	4,500	5,500	6,500	7,500	9,500	12,500	—	—	—
Base Solara ▼	4,000	5,000	6,000	7,000	8,000	11,000	—	—	—
V6 ▲	6,000	6,500	7,500	8,500	10,500	13,500	18,000	—	—
V6 ▼	5,000	6,000	7,000	8,000	9,000	12,000	16,500	—	—
Convertible/SE ▲	6,500	8,000	9,500	11,000	13,000	16,000	21,000	—	—
Convertible/SE ▼	5,500	7,000	8,500	10,000	11,500	14,500	19,500	—	—
Reliability	2	3	3	3	2	2	3	3	3
Crash Safety (F)	5	5	4	5	5	5	5	5	5
Solara	—	—	—	—	—	—	5	—	—
Side	2	3	4	4	4	5	5	5	5
Solara	3	3	5	5	5	—	5	—	—
IIHS Side	1	1	1	1	1	5	5	5	5
Solara Cvt.	—	—	3	3	3	3	3	—	—
Offset	5	5	5	5	5	5	5	5	5
Solara Cvt.	—	—	—	—	—	—	5	—	—
Head Restraints	—	—	2	2	2	2	2	2	2
Solara Cvt.	—	3	1	1	1	1	1	—	—
Roof Strength	—	—	—	—	—	5	5	5	5
Rollover Resistance	5	5	3	4	4	5	5	5	5

PRIUS ★★

RATING: Below Average (2001–10). A "runaway" success combining high-tech electronics with impressive fuel economy. Where the car disappoints is in its proclivity to run away (sudden, unintended acceleration), lose steering and braking capability, and burn out headlights at $300 apiece. Servicing is also highly dealer-dependent and expensive. **Ideal model year:** A side airbag-equipped 2007 that sells for less than half its original price. Put aside some of your savings from the purchase to buy an anchor you can throw out to brake the car. **"Real" city/highway fuel economy:** Transport Canada estimates fuel economy to be in the range of 4.5/4.6 L/100 km, though owners say they burn much more fuel than that, especially in cold weather or when running over hilly terrain. **Maintenance/repair costs:** Higher than average. **Parts:** Good luck. Parts are hard to find and mainly available only at exorbitant prices from some Toyota dealers. As Toyota accelerator, brakes, steering, and corrosion recalls mount, dealer inventory will be crowded out by recall parts, and mechanics will spend much of their time fixing the recalled vehicles. Get your 12-volt battery from any independent retailer; it'll cost way less. **Extended warranty:** A good idea. **Best alternatives:** Comparable high-mileage models include the Ford Focus, Ford Fusion Hybrid, Honda Civic, Toyota Echo, and Volkswagen Golf/Jetta diesel. **Helpful websites:** *http://priuschat.com/forums, www.toyotanation.com/forum* and *www.toyotaowners.net.*

 ## Strengths and Weaknesses

ALERT! Consider hiring a "car-sitter" when you go on vacation: The battery can drain its charge and be damaged if the vehicle isn't started and left in idle for a half-hour at least once every two weeks. Read more at *www.consumeraffairs.com/automotive/toyota_prius_battery.html.*

Seating five passengers, the Prius carries both a 4-cylinder gasoline engine and an electric motor, which work together or separately, depending on driving needs. The Prius accelerates from a stop using its electric motor alone. However, once underway, the gas engine becomes the sole power source. For merging or passing power, the electric motor may kick in to add additional power. Conversely, when coasting or braking, the gas engine may shut off, and the electric motor takes over as a generator to recharge the battery pack. While stopped, the gas engine stays off unless the air conditioner is in use. Prius's powertrain system uses a CVT, which has no gears but uses a system of belt and pulleys to deliver power to the wheels. When the wheels are moving, they charge the battery pack, which means the Prius never needs to be plugged into an AC outlet.

The 2001–03 models weren't particularly noteworthy and changed very little over the years. They did conserve fuel; however, these early models lacked power and interior room, and handled poorly. The 2004s were redesigned to provide more interior room and better handling. Power, though, was still anemic; rear passenger room remained fairly tight, handling still was not impressive, and worst of all there came a deluge of reports of sudden acceleration, brake and steering loss, and headlight failures that increased exponentially through the 2010 models. The 2006 models were little changed, but the 2007s got a major safety upgrade with new standard airbags. The 2008 models changed little, as steering and handling stayed sub-par, cargo room was Lilliputian, and acceleration remained wimpy and scary. The 2009 models got smaller wheels, and the 2010 Prius was redesigned to provide 22 percent more power along with a 7 percent improvement in fuel economy. The 1.5L 4-banger has been replaced by a 1.8L 4-cylinder engine. There's also more rear-seat legroom.

The Prius warranty includes 8-year/160,000 kilometre powertrain coverage, plus roadside assistance. The battery pack price has come down, but it is still quite expensive at $2,588 for the 2001 model and $2,299 or more for the second-generation hybrid (2002–09). See the letters about unreasonable battery pack costs in the Prius Chat website link above.

Buyers can expect rear seating that's cramped for three adults, minimal power for passing and merging, a rear windshield that cuts visibility, higher-than-average insurance premiums, 50 percent depreciation after three years, dealer-dependent servicing creating higher servicing costs, and sales and servicing that may not be available outside of large urban areas. The CVT has a mixed reliability record and cannot be easily repaired by independent agencies, and the engine is stall-prone and may suddenly accelerate when the brakes are applied. When the brakes do work as they should, they aren't very precise or responsive. Other safety concerns you may not discover until it's too late: The car is very unstable when hit by crosswinds; highway rescuers are wary of the car's 500-volt electrical system and are taking special courses to prevent electrocution; and rare, toxic battery components offset any positive environmental impact from cleaner and reduced emissions.

Other shortcomings

Toyota says the Prius is engineered to be as fuel-frugal, versatile, and hassle-free as possible. Unfortunately, Toyota has fallen far short of this goal. Some shortcomings: Acceleration is a mixture of yawning and screaming (also known as "lag and lurch"); handling is mediocre; braking is life-threatening; the steering is numb at best, nonexistent at worse; the steering-wheel position takes some getting used to; and seats could use better bolstering and lumbar support. Hatch struts weaken progressively, and there are frequent problems with the multifunction display, a screen in the dash that provides information about fuel consumption and manages some radio and climate-control functions.

Other failings include constant stalling, electrical system glitches, and tire failures. Plus the gas pump shuts off when refuelling, the fuel gauge is inaccurate, and the vehicle runs out of gas despite the gauge showing plenty of fuel in the tank.

A fuel-sipper?

Fuel economy is nowhere near what's advertised. In fact, it may be 30 to 40 percent less, say *Consumer Reports*, the Society of Automotive Engineers, and others, and they all agree gas consumption is higher in colder weather and over hilly terrain.

Consumer tests have shown that gas-electric hybrid cars in general are just a little more fuel-efficient (by fuel volume) than manual transmission–equipped diesels. Again, keep in mind that the ratings are all over the map and seldom come anywhere near the government-estimated fuel consumption figures. Diesel fuel has a significantly higher energy density than the gasoline used by the Prius, and in some countries diesel is less expensive than gasoline, so a diesel engine coupled to a manual transmission may be competitive with hybrid technology in some cases.

- A *Popular Mechanics* comparison (September 2008) shows that the 2009 Jetta TDI diesel has slightly better highway fuel economy than the 2008 Prius with 5.2 L/100 km (45.4 mpg) compared to 5.3 L/100 km (44.8 mpg). The Prius did better than the Jetta in city fuel economy, however: 5.3 L/100 km (44.7 mpg) compared to 7.4 L/100 km (32.0 mpg).
- UK's *Auto Express* magazine (August 2007) performed independent fuel efficiency tests on public roads on a number of hatchbacks and published its list of the 10 most efficient. The Prius landed 10th on the list. The Citroën C4 Coupe 1.6 HDi took first place.

 ## Safety Summary

All years: Most of the complaints logged by NHTSA from 2005–10 involve sudden acceleration accompanied by loss of braking. • Sudden acceleration when slowing down, and loss of braking:

> I have a 2005 and a 2009 Toyota Prius. On both of these vehicles, I have experienced the same [braking] problems which are being described in the news about the 2010 Prius model. I have never had an accident relating to this problem, but the potential is certainly there. The problem occurs when I am moving forward, have the brake slightly depressed, and I hit a pothole or speed bump.

Electric motor or Smart Key can cause pacemakers to fail. • Chronic stalling:

> I called Toyota corporate headquarters and was told they are unaware that this is a recurrent issue. This despite discussions in the press and on *hybridcars.com*. I am contacting you in case I am killed or injured before Toyota figures out that this is a serious and recurrent issue.

Extremely vulnerable to side winds. • Steering failure. • Floormat gets stuck between pedals. • Occupant accidentally bumped gearshift knob and put Prius into Dynamic Braking Mode, which almost caused a semi-truck to rear-end the car. • Poor emergency braking. Tail lights don't work. • Headlights fail prematurely. • Difficulty in fastening seat belts. **2002**—Early transmission replacement. • Car drifts from lane to lane. **2002–03**—Steering lockup and excessive steering shake (see *priuschat.com/forums/care-maintenancetroubleshooting/36358-03-power-steering. html*). **2003**—Floormat jams accelerator pedal. • Inaccurate fuel gauge. **2004**—Sudden acceleration and the simultaneous loss of brakes. • Malfunctioning computer causes many of the accessories and gauges to shut down or function erratically. **2004–07**—HID headlights go on and off intermittently, then go out for good:

> I took the car to the Toyota dealer, where they replaced the headlights for $990. A few weeks later the same thing happened, headlights cut out at night. I took the car back to the dealer, where they kept it for several days. They then returned the car, assuring me that the problem was solved. Since that time the driver's side headlight has gone out several times.

2005—Close to 500 complaints, or almost twice the average for a six-year-old car. • Loose screws in the steering column cause severe shake. **2005–06**—Airbag fails to deploy. **2006**—Yikes! Almost 900 complaints, when the average vehicle would generate no more than 200. • Cruise control won't disengage unless the driver slams on the brakes. **2007**—Almost 800 safety-related complaints posted to NHTSA's site when 150 incidents would be the average for a vehicle this age. **2008**—NHTSA has logged over 500 safety-related complaints, mostly concerning sudden, unintended acceleration and brake failures. **2009**—300 safety complaints registered by NHTSA. 150 complaints would have been the normal number. Most of the complaints relate to brake failures. • Airbag did not deploy in a fatal car accident. • Sudden loss of steering. • All electrics suddenly shut down. • Inaccurate fuel gauge readings. • Squirrels love the Prius:

> The contact owns a 2009 Toyota Prius. The contact stated that squirrels were able to chew through the wiring and the fuse box from under the vehicle. In addition, the squirrels had also chewed through the plastic radiator cover and support panel for the fan and the ABS warning light was illuminated as a result of the damages.

2010—Are you sitting down? Over 1,897 safety-related incidents have been posted by NHTSA; 100 complaints would have been normal. Most of these reports involve brake failures and sudden, unintended acceleration. • Airbags failed to deploy. • The rear-view mirror's auto dim feature is too sensitive and turns itself off for no reason. • Rear-view mirror hangs too low and obstructs forward visibility. • The dash lights go off when the headlights come on. • Thin plastic cover for oil pan is easily cracked. • The plastic front engine cover comes loose and drags on the ground. • Premature tire failure (Yokohama).

Secret Warranties/Internal Bulletins/Service Tips

All years: It is surprising that with so many serious defects, most Prius service bulletins are bereft of any reference to major deficiencies. **2000–08**—Multiple warning lights on; vehicle won't shift out of Park. • Steering pulls to the right. **2003–08**—Windshield back glass ticking. **2004–08**—Troubleshooting an engine knock and inaccurate fuel gauge readings. • Intermittent instrument display in cold weather. • Noxious AC odours. **2010**—Warped front engine under cover.

PRIUS PROFILE

	2002	2003	2004	2005	2006	2007	2008	2009	2010
Cost Price ($)									
Prius	29,990	29,990	29,990	30,330	31,280	31,280	29,500	27,400	27,800
Used Values ($)									
Prius ▲	4,500	5,000	6,000	8,000	10,000	12,500	15,500	18,500	21,000
Prius ▼	3,500	4,500	5,500	7,000	8,500	11,000	14,000	17,000	19,500

Reliability	2	2	2	2	2	2	2	2	1
Crash Safety (F)	3	3	5	5	4	4	4	4	4
Side	3	3	4	4	4	5	5	5	5
Offset	—	—	5	5	5	5	5	5	5
IIHS Side	—	—	1	1	1	5	5	5	5
Head Restraints	—	—	2	2	2	2	2	2	6
Rollover Resistance	4	4	4	4	4	4	4	4	4

Note: The Prius depreciates more quickly in its later years because buyers are wary of paying for the car plus a $2,500+ battery pack—an amount almost equal to the car's worth.

Volkswagen

NEW BEETLE   ★★/★

RATING: Below Average (2008–10); Not recommended (1999–2007), although a well-maintained 2006 or earlier diesel model will do if you have reliable, inexpensive servicing available. The New Beetle has always been a bad car that's both unreliable and expensive to troubleshoot. **Ideal model year:** A 2006 GLS TDI for about $9,000. **"Real" city/highway fuel economy:** *1.8 manual: 9.6/7.2 L/100 km. 1.8 automatic: 10.3/7.3 L/100 km. 2.0 manual: 9.8/7.0 L/100 km. 2.0 automatic: 9.6/7.2 L/100 km. 1.9 diesel manual: 6.2/4.6 L/100 km. 1.9 diesel automatic: 6.5/5.2 L/100 km.* Owners report gasoline fuel savings may undershoot these estimates by at least 10 percent, or 15 percent for diesel fuel. **Maintenance/ repair costs:** Average, but only a VW dealer can repair these cars. **Parts:** Usually easily found, since they're taken mostly from the Golf and Jetta parts bin, but body parts are harder to find. **Extended warranty:** A good idea. **Best alternatives:** Acura Integra, CSX, or RSX; Ford Fusion; Honda Accord; Hyundai Elantra wagon, Sonata, Tiburon, or Tucson; Mazda5 and Mazda6; and Nissan Sentra. **Helpful websites:** *http://newbeetle.org/forums/questions-issues-concerns-problems-new-beetle, http://forums.vwvortex.com,* and *http://volkswagenownersclub.com.*

Strengths and Weaknesses

ALERT! Stay away from any model carrying the Direct-Shift Gearbox (DSG) manumatic transmission. It is failure-prone and expensive to repair.

VW resurrected the Beetle as a 2000 model and produced a competent front-engine, front-drive compact car set on the chassis and running gear of the Golf hatchback. It's much safer than its predecessor, but, oddly enough, it's still afflicted with many of the same deficiencies that we learned to hate with the original. Without the turbocharger, the 115 hp 2.0L engine is underwhelming when you get it up to cruising speed (the 90 hp turbodiesel isn't much better), plus there's still not much room for rear passengers, engine noise is disconcerting, front visibility is hindered by the car's quirky design, and storage capacity is at a premium.

All ratings on a numbered scale where ☐ is good and **1** is bad. See page 132 for a more detailed description.

On the other hand, the powerful optional 1.8L turbocharged engine makes this Beetle an impressive performer; the heater works fine; steering, handling, and braking are quite good; and the interior is not as spartan or as tacky as it once was.

VEHICLE HISTORY: 2002—Introduction of the 180 hp Turbo S and a new Electronic Stabilization feature. **2003**—Convertible and turbodiesel arrive. **2004**—Upgraded head-protecting airbags and front head restraints, improved spoiler, and new wheels. The GLX model is axed. **2006**—The 115 hp 2.0L and 150 hp turbocharged 1.8L are replaced by a 150 hp 2.5L 5-cylinder engine. A hatchback TDI model with a 100 hp 1.9L turbodiesel is the only diesel model available. Standard anti-lock four-wheel disc brakes and front side airbags with head and torso protection, and an anti-skid system and traction control. **2007**—No more diesel-engine Beetles; all models come with a 150 hp 5-cylinder gasoline engine.

In a nutshell, here are the New Beetle's strong points: standard side airbags; easy handling; impressive braking; sure-footed and comfortable, though firm, ride; comfy and supportive front seats with plenty of front headroom and legroom; and a cargo area that can be expanded by folding down the rear seats.

On the minus side, owners have reported serious safety defects, powertrain performance is unimpressive, and body construction is second-rate. Some specific owner gripes: Frequent ECM failures; malfunctioning dash gauges; excessive engine and brake noise; faulty window regulators; early brake component replacement; limited rear legroom and headroom; axle oil pan and oil pump failures; difficult rear entry/exit; car is easily buffeted by crosswinds; skimpy interior storage and trunk space; diesel engines lack pep and produce lots of noise and vibration; faulty oxygen sensors cause the Check Engine light to come on; delayed shifts from Park to Drive, or failure to shift into Fourth gear; awkward-to-access radio buttons and door-panel-mounted power switches; coolant leaks onto the wiring harness also causing the Check Engine light to come on; the 2.0L engine runs out of steam around 100 km/h and may overheat; and optional high-mounted side mirrors, large head restraints, and large front roof pillars obstruct front and rear visibility. Also, interior vent louvres loosen and break, the hatchback rattles and sometimes fails to open, the AC disengages when decelerating, the AC fan motor howls and the engine makes a loud humming noise when the AC is turned on, front lights retain water and short out, and the low-slung chassis causes extensive undercarriage damage when going over a curb.

 Safety Summary

All models/years: Airbag malfunctions, electrical fires, chronic stalling, transmission failures, and steering lockups; the back glass suddenly shatters. **2002**—ABS failure. • Window goes up and down on its own. • Harsh downshifts; vehicle loses power (mass airflow sensor is the suspected cause). **2003**—Sudden acceleration, stalling. • Punctured fuel tank leaks fuel. • Excessive shake; constant pulling to the right (torque steer). • Rear windshield is hard to see through. • Head restraints sit too high to be comfortable, and obstruct rear visibility. • Open sunroof sucks exhaust into the cabin. • Left front strut slips down through the spindle, causing the spindle to hit the wheelwell. **2004**—Complete transmission failure. • Delayed shifting and long hesitation when accelerating. • Sudden stalling and loss of electrical power while underway. • Loss of steering. • Driver-side window lowers on its own. • On convertible models, the windows catch on the top when the doors are opened. **2004–05**—There are reports of the car suddenly accelerating when coming to a stop, or, conversely, losing power when accelerating. • Driver's window explodes. **2006**—Rear seat belt unlatches in a rear-end collision. • Rear engine mount failure. • Dual-mass flywheel blows apart in the manual transmission clutch assembly. • Brake pedal goes to the floor with no braking effect. • Right side of the windshield distorts the driver's view. **2007**—Vehicle lags and then surges when accelerating. • Frequent brake and brake master cylinder failures. Hard starting due to electrical failures. **2008**—Sudden acceleration when stopped at a traffic light. • Key won't turn in the starter; easy to break off the key in the ignition or damage the starter. **2009**—A fire ignited in the vehicle's front end while it was parked. • Sudden, unintended acceleration, vehicle crashed, and airbags failed to deploy. • Snapped motor mount bolts cause severe vibration throughout the vehicle and excessive engine noise. **2010**—Car slips out of gear. • No adapter for anti-theft lug nuts in spare tire kit. Nobody can repair a flat tire. • Back passenger side window sticks midway; cost: $880 U.S. to replace.

Secret Warranties/Internal Bulletins/Service Tips

1997–2009—Class action settlement results in Service Actions implemented 2007–08 to pay for and mitigate water damage to components and interiors of numerous models, and reimburse expenses. Service Action for owners and lessees of certain vehicles to modify leaking sunroofs, provide refunds, and update maintenance recommendations for drainage systems. Lawyers are litigating the inclusion in the settlement of all 1997–2009 models. (See *www. WaterIngressSettlement.com* or *www.volkswagen-classaction.com*.) **1999–2012**—Troubleshooting excessive brake vibration, pulsation. **2000–08**—Door windows may separate from regulators. **2000–11**—Removing nasty smells emanating from the air vents. **2001–08**—Inoperative or malfunctioning sunroof. **2003–05**—Corroded rotors may be the cause of excessive brake vibration. • Convertible top may not operate correctly. **2003–10**—Excessive brake vibration troubleshooting tips. **2004**—Hard starting, no-starts, or rough running when wet. **2004–07**—Transmission fluid leakage between case halves. **2004–11**—DSG delay on acceleration. **2005–10**—Poor heating. • Engine cooling fan stays on after the ignition has been shut off. **2006–07**—The 6-speed automatic transmission won't shift out of Park. **2006–08**—AC doesn't get cold enough. **2007**—Insufficient heater output at idle. **2007–08**—Cluster lights flicker with wipers on.

NEW BEETLE PROFILE

	2002	2003	2004	2005	2006	2007	2008	2009	2010
Cost Price ($)									
Base	21,950	23,210	23,690	23,910	24,490	22,780	21,977	21,976	24,175
Cabrio	28,530	29,250	29,610	30,160	29,880	27,790	26,975	26,975	29,175
Used Values ($)									
Base ▲	4,000	5,000	6,000	6,500	8,500	10,000	12,000	15,000	18,000
Base ▼	3,500	4,500	5,000	6,000	7,500	9,000	10,500	13,500	16,500
Cabrio ▲	5,500	6,500	7,500	9,000	10,500	12,000	14,000	18,000	22,000
Cabrio ▼	5,000	6,000	7,000	8,000	9,500	11,000	12,500	16,500	20,500
Reliability	1	1	1	1	1	1	3	3	3
Crash Safety (F)	4	4	4	4	4	4	4	4	4
Cabrio	—	5	4	—	—	4	4	4	4
Side	5	5	5	5	5	5	5	5	5
IIHS Side	—	—	1	1	1	1	1	1	1
Offset	5	5	5	5	5	5	5	5	5
Head Restraints (F)	5	5	3	3	3	3	3	3	3
Rollover Resistance	—	4	4	4	4	4	4	4	4
Cabrio	—	4	4	—	—	4	4	4	4

Note: Used diesel models will cost from $500 to $1,000 more than the gasoline-powered versions. They didn't start out that way, but higher fuel costs have pushed up their resale value. Also, seats with adjustable lumbar support scored 5 consistently.

PASSAT ★★

RATING: Below Average (1999–2010). About as unreliable and expensive to service as the New Beetle. Passats have lost their lustre to Japanese luxury cars, and they now depreciate more quickly than ever. But beware; their low price won't cover the extraordinarily high repair bills you'll get from Otto, Hans, and Ingrid who want to top up their Canada Pension Plans. **Ideal model year:** There is no "ideal" Passat. **"Real" city/highway fuel economy:** *1.8 manual: 9.8/6.9 L/100 km. 1.8 automatic: 11.7/7.3 L/100 km. 2.8 6-cylinder automatic: 12.7/8.3 L/100 km. 4.0 8-cylinder 6-speed manual: 14.0/8.9 L/100 km. 4.0 8-cylinder 6-speed automatic: 13.4/8.8 L/100 km.* **Maintenance/repair costs:** Higher-than-average costs; dealer-dependent. **Parts:** Parts and service are more expensive than average; long waits for parts are commonplace. **Extended warranty:** Yes, principally for the powertrain. **Best alternatives:** Acura Integra, CSX, or RSX; Ford Fusion; and Honda Accord. **Helpful websites:** *http://forums.vwvortex.com* and *http://volkswagenownersclub.com.*

All ratings on a numbered scale where 5 is good and 1 is bad. See page 132 for a more detailed description.

Strengths and Weaknesses

ALERT! Again, you want to stay away from the unreliable, complex, expensive-to-repair DSG engine. These cars invite "T-bone" and rear-end collisions. The DSG can leave you stranded anywhere, but worse, you may lose power just as you are merging with fast traffic, or pulling away from a traffic light, or turning at an intersection. **SCARY**.

These front-drive compact sedans and wagons use mechanical parts borrowed from the Golf, Jetta, and Corrado. A 2.8L V6 became the standard powerplant beginning with the '99 wagon. Its long wheelbase and squat appearance give the Passat a massive, solid feeling, while its styling makes it look sleek and clean. As with most European imports, it comes fairly well-appointed.

As far as overall performance goes, the Passat is no slouch when its powertrain isn't stalling, suddenly accelerating, or bucking and jerking you around like a bull ride at the Calgary Stampede. The multi-valve 4-cylinder engine is adequate, and its handling is superior to that of most of the competition. The 2.8L V6 provides lots of power when revved and is the engine that works best with an automatic transmission.

VEHICLE HISTORY: 2002—Given a 134 hp 2.0L turbocharged diesel coupled to either a front-drive or an all-wheel-drive powertrain. Also new is a 5-speed automatic transmission with manual capability. **2003**—W8 is given a 6-speed manual transmission. **2004**—A diesel powerplant joins the lineup, and AWD is offered on more models. **2005**—No more W8 series, GL models come with a turbodiesel only, and the GLX gets 17-inch wheels. **2006**—Redesigned with fresh styling, a larger interior, and more power. The turbocharged 2.0L picks up 30 more horses, while the 280 hp 3.6L V6 adds 90 more horses. V6 models come with an automatic transmission only. **2007**—Return of the popular Passat wagon. **2008**—Not much new, except for a 3.6L engine powering the 4Motion all-wheel drive and a standard 12-way power driver's seat. **2010**—New CC model arrives. It is a reasonably priced, coupe-styled, four-door sedan. The 3.5L V6 engine is no longer offered with the sedan. **2010**—Failure-prone DSG transmission arrives, and standard rear side airbags and rear seatbelt pretensioners equip the 2.0T models.

Passats have a history of automatic transmission failures, engine ignition coil/fuel-system stalling and no-starts, and engines gummed up by oil sludge—all costly to repair. Even when they're operating as they should, the Passat's manual and automatic gearboxes leave a lot to be desired; for example, the 5-speed manual transmission's gear ranges are too far apart (there's an enormous gap between Third and Fourth gear), and the 4-speed automatic shifts poorly with the 4-banger. Also, owners report that the transmission won't shift from lower gears, and as the car ages there are problems with MacPherson struts, clutch slave cylinder (leaks), the fuel and electrical systems, and the front brakes (rotor warpage, premature wear, excessive noise, brake booster failures, and master cylinder replacements). Additionally, engines often leak oil; early replacement of the power-steering assembly is often needed; fuel and computer module problems lead to hard starts and chronic stalling; and defective tie-rod and constant velocity joint seals allow debris to enter into the vehicle's system, effectively causing the premature wearout of internal components.

On the body side, the sunroof rattles; rear door mouldings warp easily; door speakers need frequent replacing; the front spoiler and rear trim fall off; the driver-seat memory feature fails; windshields may be optically distorted; trim and controls are fragile; heated seats are a pain in the...well, you know; water leaks persistently from the pollen filter; the fuel gauge malfunctions, indicating fuel in the tank when it's empty; the rear-view passenger-side mirrors are too small and cause several blind spots; and interior there's a helicopter-type wind noise when cruising with the windows or sunroof open.

Owners report that VW dealer servicing is the pits. Cars have to be brought in constantly to fix the same problems, recall campaign repairs are often slow because parts aren't available, and warranty coverage is spotty because VW headquarters doesn't empower or pay dealers sufficiently to take the initiative. Competent servicing and parts are particularly hard to find away from large cities, and many of the above-mentioned deficiencies can cost you an arm and a leg to repair.

 Safety Summary

All years: Sudden, unintended acceleration. • An incredible number of automatic transmission malfunctions, breakdowns, and early replacements. • Airbag light comes on for no reason. • Airbags fail to deploy, or deploy for no reason. One VW employee told U.S. federal investigators he was fired shortly after complaining about the airbag hazard:

> The driver-side head airbag (air curtain) of a 2003 Volkswagen Passat W8 sedan deployed spontaneously while I was driving the car...a few minutes later, when the car was stopped, the steering wheel airbag deployed spontaneously.... I suffered a permanent wrist injury and am suffering from post-traumatic stress syndrome.... The incident, which happened during a test drive, was reported to the management of the VW dealership for which I was working and to the VW of America by the management.

2000–03—Many reports of fires igniting in the engine compartment. • Excess raw fuel flows out of the exhaust system. • Hard starts and chronic stalling. • Check Engine light comes on intermittently, and then engine shuts down. • While cruising, vehicle speeds up; when brakes are applied, it slows down until foot is taken off the brake, then surges again. • Braking doesn't disengage cruise control. • Hesitation and long delays when accelerating. • Automatic transmission suddenly drops out of gear. • Many complaints of windshield distortion (there's an accordion effect, where objects expand and contract as they pass by). • Passenger window suddenly explodes just after being rolled up. • Windshield wipers cut out. • Plastic engine nose shield falls off. • Rear tire failure damages the fuel-filler neck, causing a fuel leak. **2002**—Premature CV joint failure. • Oil pan is easily punctured because of low ground clearance. • Some electrical and fuel-system glitches cause chronic stalling, loss of engine power. • Gas pedal remains stuck to the floor. • Brakes don't grab as well when vehicle is cold; premature brake wear. **2003**—Vehicle runs out of fuel despite the fuel gauge showing one-quarter tank of gas. • Super-heated seats. **2004**—Vehicle lurches forward when braking or accelerating. • Transmission control module and clutch failure. • Hard shifting. • Automatic transmission tends to hesitate and then jumps forward. • Prematurely worn rear brake pads. • Electrical short circuits shut off lights. • Seat heater burns through seat:

> The heated drivers seat in my 2004 VW Passat caught on fire and burned through my wife's jeans. This occurred after driving only 1/4 mile [0.4 km]. She felt something on her leg, and when she looked down there was smoke coming out of the seat. She stopped and got the fire out, but it had burned her (left a red mark on her leg), her jeans, and put a hole in the seat.

Insufficient space between the footrest and clutch pedal; foot gets trapped. • Windshield wiper collects snow and ice in wiper groove. • Water leaking into interior causes serious electrical shorts, primarily affecting the drivetrain:

> Water coming into front passenger seat resulting in damages to the TCM (transmission control module), wet carpeting, and rust under the passenger seat.

Low-mounted oil pan is easily damaged when passing over uneven terrain. **2005**—Chronic stalling may cause engine failure. • Seat belts fail to retract. **2006**—More safety incidents reported than is normal. • Several under-hood fires. • Sudden loss of power while cruising on the highway. • Engine over-revs when the AC is turned on; foot has to be kept on the brake pedal. • The bolt that holds the oil pump in place backs out and shears off, requiring an engine replacement. • Steering-column lock failure (lock control module: $2,400 (U.S.)). • Catalytic converter busted at a flange seam, damaging the brake vacuum tube with hot gases. • Tires wear out prematurely. • Trunk will not latch. • Airbag light is always lit. **2007**—Under-hood electrical harness fire. • Seat-warmer catches fire. • Vehicle recalled for sudden acceleration, but problem reappears after the fix. • Premature failure of the engine piston rings. • Oil pump socket broke, causing complete engine failure. • Engine over-revs when decelerating. • Chronic loss of power and misfiring. • Brakes slip and then grab when applied. • Subframe bolt failure. **2008**—Severe windshield distortion. • Sudden acceleration when slowing for traffic; problem identical to a recall campaign announced by VW for earlier Passats, but the involved car was excluded. • Chronic stalling cured only after the fuel pump is replaced. • Front axle and automatic transmission failure. • Car shifts into Neutral when stopping. • The 2.0L T engine is an oil-burner:

> I must frequently add oil to the engine and have brought it in to be serviced for this oil consumption issue several times. From research done online, this is not a problem unique to me.

2009—Underhood fire ignited while car was parked in a shopping mall. • Airbags failed to deploy. • Car suddenly shuts down on the highway; continues to do so after fuel pump was replaced several times. • While turning left, car suddenly accelerated. • Defective (threads stripped), missing motor mount bolts. **2010**—Lag-and-lurch DSG powertrain. • DSG transmission is very rough and jerky due to a faulty "Mechatronic Unit." • Vehicle often stalls out on the highway and cannot be restarted. • Frequent steering rack failures. • Wheel rim cracks cause the tires to lose air pressure. • Shiny chrome bezel around the shifter reflects a blinding light into the driver's eyes.

Secret Warranties/Internal Bulletins/Service Tips

All models/years: Failure-prone, malfunctioning automatic transmissions. **All models: 1997–2009**—Class action settlement results in Service Actions implemented 2007–08 to pay for and mitigate water damage to components and interiors of numerous models, and reimburse expenses. Service Action for owners and lessees of certain vehicles to modify leaking sunroofs, provide refunds, and update maintenance recommendations for drainage systems. Lawyers are litigating the inclusion in the settlement of all 1997–2009 models. (See *www.WaterIngressSettlement.com* or *www.volkswagen-classaction.com*.) **1999–2006**—Condensation inside exterior lights. **1999–2008**—Correcting excessive brake pulsation, vibration. **1999–2008**—Inoperative heated rear glass lines. **2000–11**—Removing smelly odours from vents. **2003–10**—Excessive vibration when braking. **2004–11**—DSG delay on acceleration. **2005–10**—Cooling fan continues to run after ignition has been turned off. • Poor heater output. **2006–07**—Airbag light constantly lit. • Front suspension creak. **2006–08**—Front-seat creaking, cracking. • Inoperative AC and seat heater. • Seatback creaking; inoperative lumbar support. • Front suspension knocking. • Rear cupholder hard to remove. • Back glass sunshade damaged or fails to work properly. **2006–09**—Wind noise from the top of the doors. **2006–10**—Inoperative front-seat back recliner. **2008**—Door mirrors loose or won't fold properly. • Inoperative keyless remote. • **2008–10**—AC blower motor only operates on high speed. **2008–11**—Silencing a front suspension knocking. **2008–12**—Rattling noise from engine, exhaust. *Diesels:* **2004–05**—Engine hesitation on acceleration.

PASSAT PROFILE

	2002	2003	2004	2005	2006	2007	2008	2009	2010
Cost Price ($)									
Sedan	29,550	29,550	29,550	30,190	29,950	29,970	27,476	27,476	27,775
Wagon	30,500	30,725	31,020	31,660	—	31,425	28,976	28,976	29,275
Used Values ($)									
Sedan ▲	4,000	5,000	7,000	8,500	10,000	12,000	14,000	17,000	20,000
Sedan ▼	3,000	4,500	5,500	7,500	9,000	10,500	12,500	15,500	18,500
Wagon ▲	5,500	6,500	7,500	9,000	—	12,500	14,500	18,000	21,000
Wagon ▼	5,000	6,000	7,000	7,500	—	11,000	13,000	16,500	19,500

Reliability	1	1	1	1	1	2	2	2	2
Crash Safety (F)	5	5	5	5	4	4	4	4	4
Side	4	4	4	4	5	5	5	4	5
IIHS Side	—	—	—	—	5	5	5	5	5
Offset	5	5	5	5	5	5	5	5	5
Head Restraints (F)	1	1	1	1	3	2	2	5	5
Roof Strength	—	—	—	—	5	5	5	5	5
Rollover Resistance	—	4	4	4	4	4	4	4	4

All ratings on a numbered scale where 5 is good and 1 is bad. See page 132 for a more detailed description.

LARGE CARS

This seems counterintuitive, but purchasing a used large car in the midst of a global recession may be the smartest buy of your life. Owners equate "large" with "gas-guzzler" and are dumping perfectly good cars for next to nothing due to high fuel prices and a weakening economy. Owners don't realize that the biggest operating expense is depreciation and smart used car buyers will save many times over the cost of fuel by purchasing a heavily depreciated large car.

Of course, these behemoths can't compete in a market of $1.50 a litre fuel costs and they get left at the post by more versatile crossover vehicles. These include the mini-van Mazda5, downsized sport-utilities like the Hyundai Tucson, and upscale, sporty coupes and sedans like the Hyundai Azera and Genesis. There are only two rear-drive Detroit choices left: Ford's once-popular, bland-leading-the-bland fleet anchor, the Grand Marquis, which was axed in 2008, and Chrysler's quality-challenged 300 series, Charger, and Magnum—three mediocre Chryslers that should have been axed a long time ago.

It's surprising Chrysler's large cars have stuck around this long. True, they are attractively styled, but their reputation as gas-guzzling, unreliable sedans places them several notches below the Ford and GM competition. Chrysler's desperate appeal to nostalgia and high-performance rear-drive enthusiasts has fallen flat. These fully featured cars equipped with Hemi V8 engines were done in by high fuel prices, poor quality control, and a shortened powertrain warranty. All three

Chrysler's "Jurassic Park" cars use raw, primitive power to carry an overweight platform that's out of sync with today's environment (shown above: the 2011 Chrysler 300).

Chryslers are now scheduled for radical redesigns by Chrysler/Fiat next year. You can bet, though, that if fuel prices continue to rise, instead of undergoing expensive redesigns, these large cars will be put back on the shelf next to the rear-drive Chevrolet Caprice and Ford's Grand Marquis and Crown Victoria.

Station Wagons (Full-Sized)

Once popular, full-sized rear-drive wagons—such as the GM Caprice and Roadmaster (both axed in 1996)—lost out to sport-utilities and minivans almost two decades ago and have now been reincarnated as crossover front-drives. If passenger and cargo space and carlike handling are what you want, a used minivan, light truck, downsized SUV, or compact wagon can meet your needs at little cost, and will probably still be around a decade from now.

Some disadvantages of large station wagons: atrocious gas consumption, sloppy handling, mediocre braking, and poor rear visibility. Also, rear hatches and rear brake supporting plates tend to be rust-prone, and the bodies become rattletraps.

LARGE CAR RATINGS

Below Average

Dodge Charger, SRT8 (2006–10)
General Motors Allure/LaCrosse, Lucerne (2006–10)

Not Recommended

Chrysler 300, 300C, 300M, Concorde, Intrepid, LHS, Magnum (1999–2010)

Chrysler

| 300, 300C, 300M, CHARGER, CONCORDE, INTREPID, LHS, MAGNUM, SRT8 | ★ / ★ ★ |

RATING: *300, 300C, 300M, Concorde, Intrepid, LHS, Magnum:* Not Recommended (1999–2010). Chrysler Group's lemon grove. If *Lemon-Aid* had a rating lower than one star, these models would earn it. *Charger, SRT8:* Below Average (2006–10). The Mercedes connection didn't mean that Daimler shared its top-quality front- and rear-drive components; the cars actually got worse. Chrysler has gone from subpar front-drive vehicles to sub-par rear-drive 300 and Magnum models that are just as unreliable. Sure, they look good, but that's about all these gas hogs offer. Although all these large cars are heavily discounted, factory glitches will steal away most of your savings—and endanger your life, too. Parts are rare, and mechanics cringe when these hard-to-service cars arrive in their service bays. **Ideal model year:** None. There is no "keeper" in this litter. **"Real" city/ highway fuel economy:** *Chrysler 300: 12.2/8.1 L/100 km. 300C: 12.6/8.6 L/100 km. 300C Hemi: 13.5/8.0 L/100 km. 300C Hemi AWD: 13.4/8.7 L/100 km. 300C Hemi SRT8: 16.0/10.6 L/100 km. Dodge Charger 2.7 6-cylinder: 11.3/7.7 L/100 km. Charger 3.5 6-cylinder: 12.2/8.1 L/100 km. Charger 3.5 6-cylinder AWD: 12.6/8.6 L/100 km. Charger 5.7 Hemi: 13.5/8.0 L/100 km. Charger 6.1 Hemi SRT8: 16.0/10.6 L/100 km. Concorde 2.7: 12.6/8.0 L/100 km. Concorde 3.5: 12.5/7.9 L/100 km. Intrepid 2.7: 11.0/7.4 L/100 km. Intrepid 3.5: 12.5/7.9 L/100 km.* **Maintenance/ repair costs:** Higher than average, but most repairs aren't dealer-dependent. **Parts:** Higher-than-average costs. Hemi engine parts are hard to find and cost an arm and a leg. Parts needed for the completion of safety recall repairs are often delayed. **Extended warranty:** Look for an extended warranty that offers bumper-to-bumper protection—usually a $2,000–$3,000 extra expense. **Best alternatives:** Ford Crown Victoria or Grand Marquis; GM Allure, LaCross, or Lucerne; and Hyundai Azera. The Lincoln Town Car is a good choice, as well. **Helpful websites:** *www.allpar.com* and *www.chargerforums.com/forums.*

Strengths and Weaknesses

ALERT! Before purchasing any one of these models, have an independent garage check the brake calipers and rotors (pull the wheels), the steering assembly, the condition of the transmission fluid, and the engine oil (look for sludge formation). Also, ensure that the tilted head restraints aren't a pain in the neck (especially on the 2009 and later SRT8).

All the cars in Chrysler's full-size lineup share the same chassis and offer most of the same standard and optional features. They provide loads of passenger space and many standard features, such as four-wheel disc brakes and an independent rear suspension. Unfortunately, since their 1998 redesign, base models are equipped with a hard-to-service, failure-prone, and wimpy 200 hp 2.7L V6 aluminum engine. Higher-line variants get a more powerful 225 hp 3.2L V6 powerplant or a 242 hp 3.5L V6. (Earlier models also carried a 153 hp 3.3L 6-banger, but 70 percent of buyers chose the 3.5L for its extra power.) Both variant engines provide plenty of low-end torque and acceleration, but this advantage is lost somewhat when traversing hilly terrain—the smaller V6 powerplant strains to keep up. The newer 5.7L and 6.1L Hemi engines have plenty of torque and spare power to handle steep inclines and merging; however, there is a tremendous fuel penalty to pay, in addition to serious engine and drivetrain malfunctions.

The early cars have better handling and steering response than the Ford Sable and Taurus or GM mid-sized front-drives, but the difference is marginal when you tote up the Chryslers' $3,000–$10,000 cost for powertrain, brake, and AC repairs.

Owner reports confirm that there are chronic problems with leaking 3.3L engine head gaskets, engine sludge gumming up the works of the 2.7L engine (change your oil more often than recommended), and noisy lifters wearing out prematurely around 60,000 km. Water pumps often self-destruct and take the engine timing chain along with them (a $1,200 repair). Complaints of engine surging and unintended acceleration are also frequent refrains for all model years. However, the one recurring safety problem affecting almost all model years concerns the steering system. As you can read at *www.daimlerchryslervehicleproblems.com* ("The Truth Behind Chrysler"):

> Chrysler has been under investigation by NHTSA for more than 55,000 warranty claims for steering problems with these vehicles and 1,450 reports of steering control problems, some including complete loss of steering control.

The 4-speed LE42 automatic transmission is a spin-off of Chrysler's failure-prone A604 version, and owner reports show it to be just as unreliable. Owners tell of chronic glitches in the computerized transmission's shift timing and other computer malfunctions, which result in early replacement and driveability problems (stalling, hard starts, and surging). AC failures are commonplace and costly to repair.

Rear visibility is quite poor and body problems abound. Expect exposed screw heads; lots of interior noise; power-window motor failures; distorted, poorly mounted windshields; steering-wheel noise when the car is turning; uneven fit and finish with misaligned doors and jagged trunk edges; poor-quality trim items that break or fall off easily; windows that come off their tracks or are misaligned and poorly sealed; and faulty door hinges that make the doors rattle-prone and hard to open.

VEHICLE HISTORY: 2002—The 300M Special performance model comes with a new grille, upgraded ABS, and more user-friendly child safety seat anchors. Concorde gets the LHS's styling and most of the other LHS amenities, including leather trim, ABS, high-tech gauges, traction control, 17-inch alloy wheels, and a 250 hp 3.5L V6. The LXi acquires the 3.2L V6 with a 234 hp variant of the 3.5L V6. **2003**—Intrepid gets a 244 hp 3.5L V6, Concorde horsepower goes to 250, and the 300M's power is boosted to 255 hp. **2005**—Debut of the rear-drive 300, 300C, and Magnum. **2007**—The wheelbase is lengthened and shared with the Dodge Charger sedan and Magnum wagon. **2008**—A slightly restyled exterior and interior. **2009**—The Hemi 5.7L V8 gets a few more horses (bringing the engine to 359 hp), as well as Variable Valve Timing, and a Multi-Displacement System to reduce fuel consumption. SRT8 adds a better climate-control system, heated seats, a remote start, and tilted head restraints. **2010**—300 Series loses front seat side airbags; the 300C adds standard Park Assist; and the SRT8 has an improved dash display.

300M

More show than go, this car is a near-luxury clone of the Chrysler Concorde. It uses the same front-drive platform as the Concorde, though the 300M is shorter and styled differently. It's powered by a 253 hp 3.5L V6 mated to Chrysler's AutoStick semi-automatic transmission. Mechanical and body deficiencies generally mirror those of the Concorde and Intrepid.

300, 300C, and Magnum

These rear-drive, full-sized, and feature-laden (standard ABS, traction control, and electronic stability control) sedans and wagons were first launched as 2005 models. Their first few years on the market were accompanied by a plethora of factory-related problems, as well as limited parts supply and problematic servicing due to the cars' new design and relatively small sales volume. The residual value for these cars is in freefall as more buyers flock to fuel-efficient front-drives.

The full-sized Chrysler 300 shares its platform with the sportier Dodge Magnum wagon and comes in three packages: the base model with a 190 hp V6; a Touring version with a 250 hp V6; and the high-performance 300C with a 340 hp V8 Hemi engine. The V8 employs Chrysler's Multi-Displacement System, which uses eight cylinders under load and then switches to 4-cylinder mode when cruising to save fuel. AWD is available on Touring and 300C models. V6-equipped models have a 4-speed automatic transmission. AWD and V8 versions use a 5-speed automatic with a manual shiftgate.

Charger and SRT8

Charger's rear-drive sedan shares its platform and engines with the Dodge Magnum and Chrysler 300. It seats five and comes in three trim levels: SE with a 3.5L V6, R/T with a 5.7L V8, and SRT8 with a 6.1L V8. The 5.7L V8 has Chrysler's Multi-Displacement System also. R/T and SRT8 models have firmer suspensions, and the SRT8 adds Brembo brakes and upgraded trim. An AWD joined the lineup for the 2007 model year, while the 2008 models returned relatively unchanged, except for some minor interior upgrades. For 2009, the horsepower for the SRT8's 5.7L engine was increased from 340 to 350 and the suspension was retuned.

 Safety Summary

All models/years: Airbag failures. • 2.7L engine suddenly self-destructs because of excess oil sludge and overheating. Owners describe the failure this way:

> The primary symptom is that the car heater, for no reason, does not blow hot air. If this has been happening it is likely that your car engine has been overheating and causing sludge to build up in the top half of the engine. Ultimately your engine will fail with very little warning. Some symptoms are: car starts to burn oil, very light traces of white smoke from exhaust, and the engine may seem to run a little rough at idle.

Cost for repairs averages $6,500 (U.S.). Two excellent websites that cover this problem from both a Canadian and an American perspective are *www.intrepidhorrorstories.blogspot.com/2003_11_01_archive.html* ("Dodge Intrepid Owner? Read This!") and *www.autosafety.org/article.php?did=961&scid=122.* • Engine rod bearing failure. • Chronic stalling, engine surging, and sudden, unintended acceleration. • Many reports of sudden transmission failures, often because of cracked transmission casings. • Transmission fluid leakage caused by defective transmission casing bolt. • Gas fumes enter the interior. • Windshields are often distorted and may fall out while vehicle is underway. • High rear windowsill obstructs rear visibility. • Headlights may be too dim for safe motoring, may cut out completely, or may come on by themselves. • Both ABS and non-ABS brakes perform poorly, resulting in excessively long stopping distances or the complete loss of braking ability. • Brake rotors rust prematurely and warp easily, and pads have to be changed every 15,000 km. • Overhead digital panel is distracting and forces you to take your eyes from the road. • Emergency brake pedal catches pant cuffs and shoelaces as you enter and exit the vehicle. **All models: 2002**—Steering drifts, sometimes takes undue effort, or squeaks and clunks. • Seat belt button is too sensitive; belt is easily unlatched inadvertently. **2005**—Seat heater can burn your butt. • Premature tire wear. • Chronic stalling and hard starting in vehicles with the Hemi engine. • Transmission hesitates, then slams into gear. • Steering freezes or breaks in low temperatures. • Stabilizer bar separation. • Persistent electrical shorts. • Lights suddenly shut off. • Horn doesn't work. • Pulling to the right while driving (the camber bolt service bulletin fix doesn't help). • Rear hatch seizes shut so that the owner has to crawl through the back of the vehicle to open it. • Sudden acceleration with the Hemi engine is particularly common among these more recently reported incidents:

> I have a new 2005 Dodge Magnum. The car has the 5.7L Hemi motor. My wife cranked the car and put it in reverse. She then depressed the accelerator and the engine did not respond with any rpm change until the accelerator pedal was depressed in excess of 50%. When the engine did respond, it was violent, causing the car to spin tires and accelerate backward at a high rate of speed, hitting another car in our driveway. This has happened about 6 times.

2006—Fire ignites in the wiring harness and in the trunk. • Seat warmer burns driver's back. • Faulty tie rod causes excessive front-end shake. • Vehicle rolls away when parked with emergency brake applied. **2007**—Check Engine light stays on, and emissions officials won't pass the car with light lit. Chrysler says the repair will cost $2,000. • Battery ignites a fire:

> Ground wire melted causing loss of electrical grounding leading to an electrical fire. Vehicle was a total loss. Fire began in front of vehicle even though battery actually located in trunk.

Transmission stuck in Park:

With only 44,000 miles [71,000 km] on the car, my gear would not shift out of Park. There is an override switch ("pink") that did not work as well. I got online to check to see if there were any recalls on this matter and there was not; however, when I checked online, I noticed several complaints and blogs about these cars with the same problem from 2005 to 2007.

Air intake is poorly designed and will suck water into the engine. • Excessive torque converter shudder. • Water leaks from the rear windshield area. • Tail light, fuse failures:

I am a master technician in the state of Calif. I have worked on Chryslers for 16 years. What burns me is this particular manufacturer uses a system called Star to hide defects from becoming full recalls to avoid cost. I am complaining about all Dodge, Chrysler 300, Magnum, Charger 3.5L models. The rear license plate harness retainer clip above the oversize 3.5L muffler comes loose and the two wire harness melts to the muffler and causes parklight/taillamp failure. The consumer will attempt in desperation to install fuses of a larger amp causing a major meltdown of the fusebox (wire domino of one wire in the fusebox melts to other sources). Well, I complained and was told to shut up by Chrysler!!! I've seen six [other] cases.

ESP/anti-lock brakes fail, causing the vehicle to slide on very little snow or rain. • Doors close without warning. • Limo conversions may be unsafe:

When is NHTSA going to look into the extra long limousine conversions being completed on the Chrysler 300 and Dodge Charger cars? Chrysler does not offer a limo conversion chassis like Lincoln and Cadillac. The axles, wheels, tires and brakes are seriously overloaded based on the federal door labels.... Operators are experiencing premature front end component failures and excessive tire wear. Does someone have to die before this industry practice is reviewed?

2008—One car exploded:

My 2008 300 Touring was parked in a parking lot. Then a fire started out of nowhere from under the hood. Then my car exploded from the front to the back through the exhaust pipe. I only had 6,100 or so miles [10,000 km] on my car.

Sunroof may also explode. • Another scary ESP/anti-lock brake story:

I rented a Chrysler 300 over this past weekend. I want you to know that it was the scariest ride I've had in a while. Have you ever tested the electronic stability program on ice? It not only does not work, it is extremely dangerous. I had to drive about 600 miles [1,000 km] on icy and windy Wyoming roads which proved to be quite scary in the 300 with ESP.

Excessive effort is needed to honk the horn. • Defective tire pressure sensors and valve stems. • Sudden loss of engine power. • No power for accessory features:

I have found that I have no accessory power while driving (no heat/AC, no radio, and no control of windows). I may actually have no accessory power from the time I start the car, as I often notice it within the first mile when I try to use an accessory. The only way to get the power back is to pull over, turn off the car and restart. Occassionally I have had to repeat this process several times to get the accessory power back.

Defective front seat belt buckle. • Hard to keep interior windows free from condensation. **2009**—Accelerator falls to the floor, and vehicle accelerates. • Defective steering pinion gear. • Horn doesn't sound if the vehicle isn't running. **2010**—Fire ignited in the engine compartment. • Side airbag failed to deploy when the car was T-boned. • Car stalls and cannot be restarted. • Driver memory seat doesn't return to its former position. • Steering-wheel-mounted horn and radio controls are often inoperative. *300M:* **2002**—Brake failure, then engine surges. • Sunroof explodes. • Right front wheel disconnects from vehicle. **2003**—Surging when stopped. • Rear visibility compromised by narrow rear windows. **2004**—Trunk collects water, interferes with spare-tire access. • Many complaints that the car always pulls to the right. • Seat belts do not restrain a child safety seat sufficiently. • Passenger-side airbag is disabled when average-sized passenger sits in the seat. • Driver's seatback suddenly reclined into the backseat while vehicle was underway. • Rear windows won't go down.

Secret Warranties/Internal Bulletins/Service Tips

All models: 1999–2004—Remedy for a 3.5L engine that stumbles or misfires (TSB #09-002-03). • Rear headliner sags or rattles. **2000–04**—Fuel tank slow to fill; this has been a chronic problem affecting five model years. **2002**—Transaxle limp-in; engine misfire; engine no-start. **2002–04**—Vehicles equipped with a 3.5L engine that has a rough idle when cold may need the PCM recalibrated or replaced, a free service under the emissions warranty (TSB #18-042-03). **2005–06**—Transmission shudder or buzz due to water contamination; torque converter may require replacement. • Headliner sags. **2005–07**—Dash squeak, rubbing sound. • Sunroof rattles. • Inoperative window "express up" feature. **2005–08**—Steering pulls to one side. **2006–07**—Water leaks from the A-pillar area. **2005–09**—Difficult fuel fill-up; nozzle shuts off. **2006–10**—Lower door hinge popping, groaning. **2007–10**—Harsh 4–3 shift; poor shift quality. • Lower door hinge popping, groaning. **2008–09**—How to reduce engine whistling. **2009**—Poor steering wheel returnability. **2010**—Inoperative side windows. **2009–10**—Inoperative remote start.

300, 300C, 300M, CHARGER, CONCORDE, INTREPID, MAGNUM, 300C SRT8 PROFILE

	2002	2003	2004	2005	2006	2007	2008	2009	2010
Cost Price ($)									
300	—	—	—	29,995	30,225	30,785	32,095	32,095	32,995
300C	—	—	—	43,095	43,595	44,190	45,595	45,595	46,745
300M	39,900	40,335	40,910	—	—	—	—	—	—
Charger	—	—	—	—	27,635	28,370	29,095	29,095	29,995

Concorde	29,690	30,240	30,775	—	—	—	—	—	—
Intrepid	25,765	25,095	25,615	—	—	—	—	—	—
Magnum	—	—	—	27,995	28,135	28,800	29,395	—	—
300C SRT8	—	—	—	—	44,790	45,690	46,395	46,595	54,845
Used Values ($)									
300 ▲	—	—	—	5,500	6,500	8,000	11,500	14,000	16,000
300 ▼	—	—	—	4,500	5,500	6,500	10,000	12,500	14,500
300C ▲	—	—	—	7,000	8,000	10,000	12,500	16,500	21,000
300C ▼	—	—	—	5,500	7,000	8,500	10,500	15,000	19,500
300M ▲	3,000	3,500	4,500	—	—	—	—	—	—
300M ▼	2,500	3,000	4,000	—	—	—	—	—	—
Charger ▲	—	—	—	—	6,500	8,500	10,000	13,500	15,500
Charger ▼	—	—	—	—	5,000	7,000	9,000	12,000	14,000
Concorde ▲	2,500	3,000	3,500	—	—	—	—	—	—
Concorde ▼	2,000	2,500	3,000	—	—	—	—	—	—
Intrepid ▲	1,500	2,000	2,500	—	—	—	—	—	—
Intrepid ▼	1,000	1,500	2,000	—	—	—	—	—	—
Magnum ▲	—	—	—	4,500	5,000	6,500	8,000	—	—
Magnum ▼	—	—	—	4,000	4,500	5,500	7,000	—	—
300C SRT8 ▲	—	—	—	—	9,500	12,000	15,000	21,000	25,000
300C SRT8 ▼	—	—	—	—	8,500	10,500	13,500	19,500	23,000
Reliability	1	1	1	1	1	1	1	1	2
Crash Safety (F)	4	4	4	5	5	5	5	5	5
300M	3	3	4	—	—	—	—	—	—
Side	4	4	4	4	4	4	4	4	5
IIHS Side	—	—	—	1	1	1	1	1	2
Offset	3	3	3	5	5	5	5	5	5
LHS/300M	3	3	3	—	—	—	—	—	—
Head Restraints									
300/Magnum	—	—	—	3	2	2	2	2	2
300M (F)	1	1	1	—	—	—	—	—	—
Intrepid (F)	4	4	4	—	—	—	—	—	—
Intrepid (R)	3	3	3	—	—	—	—	—	—
LHS	—								
Rollover Resistance									
300/Magnum	4	4	4	4	4	4	4	4	4
300M	4	4	4	—	—	—	—	—	—
Concorde	—	5	5	—	—	—	—	—	—
Intrepid	—	5	5	—	—	—	—	—	—

Note: All these vehicles are practically identical and should have similar crashworthiness scores, even though not every model was tested in each year.

All ratings on a numbered scale where ▢ is good and **1** is bad. See page 132 for a more detailed description.

General Motors

ALLURE/LACROSSE, LUCERNE ★★

RATING: Below Average (2006–10). The Allure/LaCrosse and Lucerne are similarly equipped large front-drive sedans that are hobbled by mediocre road performance and poor quality control. The Lucerne is the larger of the three cars and the model that has accumulated the most performance- and safety-related complaints. **Ideal model year:** *Allure/LaCrosse:* Smart used-car shoppers looking for the best combination of price and safety features should consider a 2008 Buick Allure CX for $9,000 to $10,500, or a 2008 Buick Lucerne CX for about $2,000 more. *Lucerne:* The 2006 first-year V6 model is no bargain when you look at its many first-year quality shortcomings. **"Real" city/highway fuel economy:** *LaCrosse 2.4 4-cylinder:* 10.8/6.5 L/100 km. *LaCrosse 3.6 V6:* 12.2/7.3 L/100 km. *LaCrosse AWD 3.6 V6:* 12.7/7.7 L/100 km. *Lucerne 3.9 V6:* 12.0/7.4 L/100 km. *Lucerne 4.6 V8:* 13.8/8.7 L/100 km. **Maintenance/repair costs:** Higher than average, but most repairs (Northstar engine and AWD components excepted) aren't dealer-dependent or prohibitively expensive. **Parts:** Higher-than-average costs for emissions, engine, and AWD repairs. **Extended warranty:** A good idea, especially on AWD-equipped cars. **Best alternatives:** Ford's Crown Victoria or Mercury Grand Marquis; Hyundai Azera or Genesis; a downsized SUV like the Ford Escape or Hyundai Tucson. Lincoln's Town Car is a good second choice. **Helpful websites:** *www.automotiveforums.com/vbulletin/f727.*

Strengths and Weaknesses

ALERT! In a startling announcement, GM says a clunk heard when the automatic transmission is shifted is a normal characteristic of all of its vehicles up to 2012. The company says any attempt to silence this noise is a waste of time and money (TSB # 99-04-20-002G, published May 6, 2011).

Allure/LaCrosse

GM's 2005–10 Allure/LaCrosse is a substantially upgraded and stiffened version of the Century and Regal, resulting in an improved ride and handling. The rack-and-pinion steering has proven to be troublesome, and the four-wheel disc braking system isn't very durable. NHTSA gives both 2010 cars five stars for front and side impacts; previous models received only three stars for side protection. 2010 models' rollover resistance scored four stars. IIHS says the 2005–2012 frontal offset crash protection is "Good" as is the 2010's side protection score and roof strength. 2005–09 models scored only a "Marginal" side rating. Head restraints for the 2003/2009 Allure/LaCrosse were also rated "Poor," though the revised restraints on the 2010s have a "Good" rating.

Lucerne

The Lucerne is a full-size car sold by GM's Buick division that replaced the Park Avenue and LeSabre in 2006. Buick's largest car shares its basic design with the Cadillac DTS. A 197 hp 3.8L V6 engine was standard in the CX, CXL, and CXL Special Edition V6 and then it was replaced by the 227 hp 3.9L V6. The Northstar 4.6L V8 ("hell to troubleshoot" and "parts are on back order") is standard in the CXL Special Edition V8 and CXS. The V8 added 17 horses in 2008 (to 275) and has remained relatively unchanged to this day. To say the Northstar has been a troublesome powerplant is an understatement. 2006–2010 Lucernes get five stars for frontal crash protection and rollover resistance. Side crashworthiness garners four stars from NHTSA. 2006–2011 Lucernes are "Good" in front crashes and "Acceptable" in side collisions. 2009–11 head restraints are "Marginal" and 2006–08 models are rated "Poor." All Lucernes use a 4-speed automatic transmission and seat six.

VEHICLE HISTORY: *Allure/LaCrosse:* **2006**—Adoption of new safety features, including ABS (CX and CXL models) and side curtain airbags. **2008**—Interior and exterior upgrades along with the LaCrosse Super V8 option and sport suspension. **2010**—A complete redesign and new name (LaCrosse—the name it always carried in the States). The engine lineup has changed, as well: The base CX LaCrosse uses a 2.4L 4-cylinder, but a new 3.0L direct-injection V6 is optional. It's a standard feature with the CXL, while the CXS uses a 3.6L direct-injection V6. The V8 engine has been dropped. All models use a 6-speed automatic transmission, though all-wheel drive is available on the CXL version along with a limited-slip differential for better control on slippery roads. *Lucerne:* **2008**—Adoption of a lane departure warning system. **2009**—A new 3.9L V6 engine, Bluetooth phone connectivity, and XM NavTraffic. **2010**—Not much new. Restyled door rocker panels and fog lights are shared with all Lucerne models, and instrument panel backlit gauges are upgraded.

Safety Summary

All models/years: No airbag deployment. • Faulty front passenger airbag sensor module. • Airbag light constantly lit. • Sudden, unintended acceleration with or without the cruise control engaged. • Chronic stalling (defective fuel pump or throttle position sensor). • No starts. • Chin-to-chest front head restraints. • Premature automatic transmission failure. • Loss of brakes. • Early replacement of the brake rotors and pads. • Light steering that allows the car to wander, pulling to the right when accelerating. • Defective steering-column intermediate shaft produces a screeching, clunking, crunching, or groaning noise. • Power-steering high-pressure fitting failures. • Excessive vibration on the highway. • Front strut bushing failures. • Early tie rod replacement. • Rear windshield exploded when the defroster was turned on. • Low-beam headlights suddenly go out. • Dash gauges can't be read in daylight. • Instrument panel lights and headlights are too dim. • Various reflections into the side mirror and rear windshield. • The fuel gauge gives incorrect readings. • Windshield wiper failures. • Heated windshield washer recall is inadequate; it disables the feature, instead of repairing the problem. • Snow and ice collects just below the front windshield wipers. • Weak, cheap plastic door handles. • Sun visor suddenly drops down. • Remote won't open the door locks; passenger had to climb out via the window. • Tires lose air. *Allure/LaCrosse:* **2006**—Engine camshaft failure. **2008**—Early replacement of steering and suspension components. **2009**—Passenger-side airbag malfunction. Sudden, unintended acceleration accompanied by loss of braking capability. **2010**—Underhood fire ignited. • Vehicle suddenly stalls out when under power. • Steering continually pulls the vehicle sharply to the left. • Electrical shorts cause the door locks, lights, and gauges to malfunction. • Defroster takes too long to be effective. • Steering locks up. • Head restraint on the front passenger seat obstructs the driver's view. • Heated seats suddenly came on, overheated, and burned the driver. • Opening a rear window at expressway speed produces a deafening roar.

Lucerne: **2006**—Defective motor mounts:

> These motor mounts are known to be defective and many bulletins have been posted, along with many known customers getting them replaced. I however have had ba[d] luck getting my local Buick dealership to replace them. The problem happens while taking off from a stop. The defective mounts cause the engine to vibrate and shake the car. This to me seems like a very dangerous issue to have to deal with.

Rear passenger door cannot be locked from the inside or out. • Chrome wheels corrode in valve stem openings causing air loss. • Excessive brake vibration and shimmy. **2007**—Front safety belts may not lock up. • Underside of the interior door handle can cut a hand. • Tire system sensor goes off for no reason. • Aluminum wheels lose air and chrome peels away. • Tire jack bent when lifting vehicle. **2008**—Acceleration is hard to modulate:

> I find it almost impossible to hold an even speed on the highway as it is constantly either speeding up or slowing down, and I have no perception of ever moving the pedal. At stop signs/lights it will sometimes leap out with a "jack rabbit" start which was totally unplanned for.

Steering wheel suddenly locks up. • Gas spews out of the filler pipe when filling up. • Instrument panel lights are dim or go dim while driving. • Ice builds up at the base of the windshield; the wipers become clogged with ice. **2009**—Sudden, unintended acceleration accompanied by loss of brakes and failure of the airbag to deploy:

> My wife was stopped waiting for a car to leave the parking lot. She had her foot on the brake ready to put it in Park. The car suddenly surged forward and she could not stop it with both feet on the brake. She hit a building and 3 vehicles before she was stopped by the 3rd vehicle. She was headed for another part of the building when she stopped. The air bags did not deploy. There was less than 600 miles on the car.

Premature failure of the front-end struts, lower control arm bushings, brake master cylinder, steering control module, and the StabiliTrak stability control. • Door stoppers don't hold doors open on an incline.

Secret Warranties/Internal Bulletins/Service Tips

Allure/LaCrosse: **2005–07**—Automatic transmission shudder when accelerating. **2005–08**—Countermeasures for harsh shifting and slipping. • Repair for a steering column clunk heard when turning. **2005–09**—Automatic transmission slips in gear; left-side axle seal leaks (see bulletin on following page). • Wind noise diagnostic tips. • Airbag warning light comes on intermittently. **2005–11**—Reduced power, as MIL alert lights up (see bulletin on following page). **2006–09**—Airbag warning light stays lit. **2007–09**—Steering gear mount to frame may make a pop, creak, or click noise. **2008**—Power steering leak may require the replacement of the steering gear cylinder line. • Tips on reducing tire vibration. **2008–09**—Poor AC performance. • Inaccurate fuel gauge readings. **2008–09**—V8 engine oil leak from the rear cover assembly area. **2009**—V8 engine valve tick noise remedy (replace the valve lifters). *Lucerne:* **2006–08**—Inoperative Park Assist feature. • Frayed headliner (front edge). **2006–09**—Airbag warning light stays lit (replace the right front seat belt buckle). • Vehicle pulls to the right when accelerating. • Bump, clunk on slow speed turns. • Front door won't open or unlock. • Inoperative inside and outside rear door handles. • Hard to view instrument panel cluster in sunlight. • Hard starts, no-starts (repair and re-route transmission wiring harnesses). **2006–11**—Reduced power as MIL alert lights up. **2007–10**—Low-speed automatic transmission moan or whine noise. **2009**—Parking Assist gives erratic visual and audio warnings. **2009–10**—Engine coolant leaks (replace coolant crossover pipe gaskets). • Campaign and service bulletin number: #10142, dated May 12, 2010, provides for the re-securing of the electronic brake control module at no charge to the vehicle owner. Courtesy transportation will also be provided. This is not a recall. • Oil leak at the front of the engine (replace the front cover seal). **2009–11**—Procedures outlined to reduce front brake rotor noise and pulsation.

SLIPS IN GEAR/AXLE SEAL LEAKS

BULLETIN NO.: 08-07-30-009B   **DATE: MAY 01, 2008**

SLIPS IN GEAR (REPLACE THIRD CLUTCH HOUSING WITH REVISED SERVICE PART)

2001–08 GM passenger cars with HYDRA-MATIC(R) front wheel drive 4T80-E automatic transmission.

CONDITION: Some customers may comment on a transmission oil leak and/or that the transmission slips in gear.

CAUSE: An oil leak may be caused by bushing wear in the third clutch housing, causing excessive fluid build-up at axe sea.

CORRECTION: DO NOT replace the transmission for above concerns. Instead, replace the third clutch housing with service P/N 8682114, which has revised bushing material to extend life and reduce left front axle seal leaks.

INTERMITTENT MALFUNCTION INDICATOR LAMP (MIL) ILLUMINATED, DTC P2138 WITH REDUCED ENGINE POWER (REPAIR INSTRUMENT PANEL (IP) TO BODY HARNESS CONNECTOR)

2005–11 GM Passenger Cars and Light Duty Trucks (Including Saturn); 2005–09 HUMMER H2; 2006–10 HUMMER H3; 2005–09 Saab 9-7X

CAUSE: This condition may be caused by water intrusion into the instrument panel (IP) to body harness connector, which carries the APP sensor signals to the ECM/PCM. This water intrusion results in a voltage difference between APP Sensor 1 and APP Sensor 2 that exceeds a predetermined value for more than a calibrated period of time, setting P2138.

NOTE: Aftermarket equipment can generate DTC P2138 and/or other DTCs, so verify that aftermarket equipment is not electrically connected to any of the APP sensor signal or low reference circuits or to any other ECM/PCM 5V reference or low reference circuits.

ALLURE, LACROSSE, LUCERNE PROFILE

	2005	2006	2007	2008	2009	2010
Cost Price ($)						
Allure/LaCrosse CX	25,200	26,295	26,395	26,495	26,995	32,795
Lucerne CX	—	30,995	31,210	31,790	31,995	33,095
Lucerne CXL	—	36,095	33,570	34,120	34,995	36,095
Used Values ($)						
Allure/LaCrosse CX ▲	—	7,500	9,000	10,500	14,000	19,500
Allure/LaCrosse CX ▼	—	6,000	8,000	9,000	12,500	18,000
Lucerne CX ▲	—	8,500	10,500	12,500	16,500	20,000
Lucerne CX ▼	—	7,500	9,000	11,000	15,000	18,500
Lucerne CXL ▲	—	9,500	11,000	13,500	17,500	22,000
Lucerne CXL ▼	—	8,500	9,500	12,000	16,000	20,500
Reliability	1	1	1	1	3	3

Note: The higher-end V8-equipped 2007 Lucerne CXS originally sold for $43,080, more than $12,000 more than the base Lucerne. Only $2,000 separates these 2007 models today.

All ratings on a numbered scale where 5 is good and 1 is bad. See page 132 for a more detailed description.

LUXURY CARS

Luxury in a Recession?

Sure, there's no better time to get luxury on the cheap.

Luxury vehicle sales are rebounding much more quickly than their non-luxury counterparts because they generally have more financially stable dealerships, better leasing and certified pre-owned programs, and a loyal customer base. Moreover, there is a shift in buyer interest from North America to emerging markets such as China, India, and Russia. For instance, General Motors now sells more vehicles in China than it does in the United States. Also, the entry-level luxury segment has been very competitive, mostly due to price-overlapping with well-equipped non-luxury cars.

Used Luxury

Used luxury cars can be great buys if you ignore most of the hype and remember that many high-end models don't give you much more than the lower-priced, entry-level versions, without all the options. For example, the Lexus ES 300 is a Toyota Camry with a higher sticker price; the Audi A4 isn't much different from the Volkswagen Passat; Lincoln's front-drive Continental uses mostly junky Ford Taurus and Sable powertrains; and the Acura 3.2 TL, Infiniti I35 (formerly called the I30), and Jaguar X-Type are fully loaded, high-tuned versions of the Honda Accord, the Nissan Maxima, and the European Ford Mondeo, respectively.

Both high- and low-end models project a flashy cachet, come loaded with high-tech safety, performance, and comfort features, and can be bought, after three years or so, for half of what they sold for as new. Furthermore, if you can get servicing and parts from independent garages, you'll save even more. On the downside, there are overpriced luxury lemons out there (such as the front-drive Lincoln Continental and the Cadillac Allanté and Catera) that aren't sold anymore and are unreliable, with hard-to-service engines and transmissions and servicing costs that rival the national debt.

Mercedes-Benz owners, for example, can't say they weren't warned. Almost two decades ago, a $5 million study conducted over five years by the Massachusetts Institute of Technology said that the German automaker had begun making lousy cars by committing the same assembly-line mistakes as American automakers: allowing workers to build poor-quality vehicles and then fixing the mistakes at the end. As one reviewer of *The Machine That Changed the World*, by James P. Womack, Daniel T. Jones, and Daniel Roos (HarperCollins, November 1991), wrote:

This study of the world automotive industry by a group of MIT academics reaches the radical conclusion that the much vaunted Mercedes technicians are actually a throwback to the pre-industrial age, while Toyota is far ahead in costs and quality by building the automobiles correctly the first time.

Readers of *Lemon-Aid* know from the internal service bulletins I quote extensively that Mercedes' C-Class compacts and M-Class sport-utilities have been plagued by serious factory defects, running the gamut from powertrain failures to fit and finish deficiencies.

Traditionally, the luxury-car niche has been dominated by American and German automakers. During the past decade, however, buyers have gravitated toward Japanese and South Korean models like the Lexus lineup, Hyundai's Genesis Coupe high-performance luxury model, and the Veracruz high-end SUV. This shift in buyer preference has forced Chrysler out of the market and has made Ford consider closing its struggling Lincoln division.

Depreciation helps

Okay, so you're well advised to choose an Asian model, but doesn't that mean you'll have to dig deep in your wallet, wiping out most of your expected savings from buying used? Not necessarily. Smart buyers can still pick up a $40,000 2008 G35 Infiniti sedan for $15,000 to $17,000. Similar savings are realized by purchasing a fully loaded Honda Accord, Nissan Maxima, or Mazda6, all of which offer similar equipment, reliability, and performance to their higher-end brethren sold by Acura, Infiniti, and Lexus, but for much, much less.

But if you want to buy a reliable and inexpensive Detroit-built luxury car, you can't do better than a 2008 Lincoln Town Car Signature for about $18,500. That's for a car that once sold for $58,599.

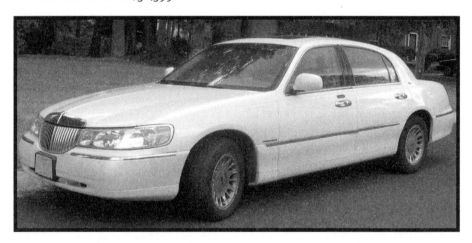

Detroit does make some good luxury cars, like the 2008 Lincoln Town Car Signature pictured above—just not that many.

Worthwhile choices

I am not a big fan of luxury cars. If I was, however, I would limit my choice to reliable vehicles that look good and are relatively easy to maintain. For me, that would be the BMW 3 Series and Hyundai's Genesis 3.8 sedan 430. The quality of these cars, the durability of their powertrains, and their overall performance cannot be faulted.

Older BMWs are almost all good buys, but the 3 Series stands out because it comes as a two-door, a four-door, a wagon, and a convertible, and has gradually evolved over the years. Unlike Mercedes and Audi, BMW models are consistently well built and keep a high residual value. A 2006 323i in good condition can be found for about $11,000. Better yet, a 2008 won't cost you more than $18,000. Drive it for four years, and then sell it for about $4,000 less—imagine, you will pay a little more than $1,000 a year to own a BMW that others paid $36,000 to buy new.

Future Luxury Cars: Asia and Europe

Let's face it: There aren't any American luxury cars that can match an equivalent Japanese model for overall reliability, durability, and value. And this isn't because Japanese products are that well made; far from it, as anyone who's purchased an engine-sludged Lexus will attest. No, it's simply because GM, Ford, and Chrysler vehicles are so poorly made that they make everyone else's look better. This fact has been reflected in the head-spinningly high depreciation rates and plummeting market share seen with most large-*cum*-luxury cars put out by the Detroit automakers. GM's rear-drive Cadillacs and Lincoln's Town Car come closest to meeting the imports in overall reliability and durability, yet they still come nowhere near the quality and performance level of many entry-level imports.

LUXURY CAR RATINGS

Recommended

Acura RL (2009-10)
Acura TL (1999–2010)

Infiniti G35 (2007–08)
Infiniti G37 (2009)

Above Average

Acura RL (1999–2008)
BMW 3 Series, 5 Series, M Series,
    Z4 (1999–2010)
Infiniti G37 (2008)

Infiniti I30 (2000–03)
Infiniti M35, M45 (2006–07)
Toyota Avalon (1999–2004)

Average

BMW Z3 (1999–2002)
General Motors DeVille (2001–05)
Infiniti I35 (2002–04)
Infiniti M35, M45 (2003–05)
Infiniti Q45 (2002–05)

Lexus ES 300/330/350, GS 300/350/430/
   450h/460, IS 250/300/350,
   LS 400/430/460/600h, SC 300, SC 400/430
   (1999–2010)
Mercedes-Benz B-Class (2006–10)
Nissan Maxima (2007–09)
Toyota Avalon (2005–09)

Below Average

General Motors CTS, CTS-V, DTS,
   STS, STS-V (1999–2010)
Infiniti G35 (2003–06)
Infiniti Q45 (1997–2001)

Mercedes-Benz 300 Series, 400 Series,
   500 Series, E-Class (1999–2010)
Nissan Maxima (1999–06)

Not Recommended

Audi A3, A4, A4 S-Line, A6, A8,
   S4, S6, TT Coupe (2000–10)

Infiniti G20 (1999–2002)
Mercedes-Benz C-Class (1999–2009)

Acura

RL ★★★★★

RATING: Recommended (2009–10); Above Average (1999–2008). Basically, this is a fully loaded, longer, wider, and heavier TL, equipped with a larger engine that produces less horsepower than its smaller brother. Watch out for the failure-prone, notchy, 6-speed manual transmission. **Ideal model year:** A $69,500 2006 can be had for around $16,500, and the much improved 2009 $63,900 3.5L V6 version will cost $33,000, or $30,900 less than its original price, and still have some original warranty coverage left. **"Real" city/highway fuel economy:** *2005 and earlier V6 models:* 13.0/9.1 L/100 km. *2006 models equipped with the 3.7L V6:* 12.9/8.4 L/100 km. *3.7 AWD:* 12.2/8.2 L/100 km. **Maintenance/repair costs:** Average; most repairs are dealer-dependent. **Parts:** Mechanical and electronic components are easily found and moderately priced. Body parts may be hard to come by and can be expensive. **Extended warranty:** Not needed, save your $2,000. **Best alternatives:** Consider BMW's 5 Series or Infiniti's I30/I35. Acura's TL sedan deserves a look, as well: it's not as expensive, and is a better performer, though passenger room is more limited. **Helpful websites:** *http://acuraforum. net; www.cbel.com/acura_cars;* and *www.acurasucks.com.*

Strengths and Weaknesses

ALERT! Poor headlight design has been a persistent problem since 2005. On the 2010 model, low-beam headlight illumination limits visibility beyond 30 metres. Before buying an RL, drive one at night.

The RL has a comfortable ride, exceptional steering and handling, top-quality body and mechanical components, good (though not impressive) acceleration that's smooth and quiet in all gear ranges, and it's loaded with goodies. The steering can be numb, however, and manual and automatic transmissions are sometimes problematic.

The 3.5 RL is loaded with the innovative high-tech safety and convenience features one would expect to find in a luxury car. These include ABS, traction control, heated front seats, "smart" side airbags, an anti-skid system, a rear-seat trunk pass-through, front and rear climate controls, and xenon headlights (get used to oncoming drivers flashing you with their headlights). The 3.5L 210–225 hp V6 mated with a 4-speed automatic transmission provides good acceleration that's a bit slower and more fuel-thirsty than the TL, partly because of the RL's extra pounds. The 2005's 300 hp V6 coupled to a 5-speed automatic (a manual shifter isn't available) resolves this problem. The car handles nicely, with a less firm ride than the TL, although steering response doesn't feel as crisp. Interior accommodations, which fit four occupants, are excellent up front and in the rear because the RL's platform is larger than the TL's. Headroom is a bit tight, though, and the 2005's smaller dimensions may irk some buyers who don't mind sacrificing performance for extra room. Be wary of the poor-performing Collision Mitigation System and run-flat tires. Also, the 2007–08 models have limited rear seating and an awkward keyless locking/starting system.

VEHICLE HISTORY: 2002—Wider tires, larger brakes, OnStar assistance, more sound deadening, and small horsepower boost (15 hp). **2005**—A major redesign reduces the car's size but it now comes with more features: standard all-wheel drive, a 300 hp V6 hooked to a 5-speed automatic, more safety and convenience features, and refreshed styling. Safety features include standard anti-skid control, front side airbags and side curtain airbags, anti-lock four-wheel disc brakes, steering-linked xenon headlights, and a navigation system. **2006**—Horsepower is cut by 10 to total 290 hp. Introduction of run-flat tires and the Collision Mitigation Braking System. **2007**—Upgraded braking. Steering-linked xenon headlights and a voice-activated navigation system are now optional features. **2008**—A couple new colours. **2009**—Returns repowered and with refreshed styling. Car carries a 300 hp 3.7L V6 hooked to a 5-speed automatic transmission.

Owner-reported problems on more recent models include frequent stalling; electrical shorts; front-wheel liner cracking; malfunctioning accessories; noisy transmission engagement and steering; a failure-prone, misshifting manual transmission; and premature brake wear, and a loud, metallic-sounding squeal when braking (see *www.cbel.com/acura_cars* and *www.acurasucks.com*).

Safety Summary

All years: Sudden unintended acceleration. • Early automatic transmission replacements. • Chronic stalling when accelerating. • Premature wearout of the front and rear brake pads. • Dash display is unreadable in daylight. **2005—** Inadequate headlight illumination:

> The vertical self adjusting headlights pose serious safety concerns on unlit roadways.... On hilly terrain, the headlights will adjust down as the vehicle starts uphill, illuminating [only] approximately 40 feet [12 m] in front of the vehicle. This also occurs when the vehicle travels over bumps and any minor changes in vehicle altitude. It is very easy to overdrive the headlights, often at speeds less than 20 mph [32 km/h]. You simply cannot see road hazards or pedestrians.

Suspension bottoms out with a full load and damages the undercarriage. **2006—** Airbags failed to deploy. • Fire ignited in the overhead door channel. • Headlights don't sufficiently illuminate the road. • Vehicle accelerates when the cruise control is engaged. **2007—**Collision Mitigation System does not perform as advertised. • Headlights flicker when car is underway. **2008—**Gas fumes infiltrate the cabin. **2009—**Sudden acceleration when pulling away from a light, accompanied by one airbag deploying and the doors refusing to open. • Gas pedal and brake pedal engage at the same time because they are mounted too close together.

Secret Warranties/Internal Bulletins/Service Tips

All years: Acura guidelines for submitting paint claims. **1999–2006—**Diagnosis and correction of drift/pull problem. **2003—**Airbag light comes on for no reason. • Troubleshooting automatic transmission malfunctions. **2004—**Sticking fuel-filler cap. **2005—**Hot weather may cause stalling, hard starts caused by vapour lock. **2005–06—**Front brake rattle, squeal. • Defective automatic door locks. **2005–07—**Low, soft brake pedal. **2005–09—**High mount stop light cover is loose, or falls off. **2005–10—**Drivetrain whistle, whine, howl. • Loose windshield side trim retainer. • Front door handle sensor won't lock or unlock the doors. **2007—**Honda USA has extended the 2007 catalytic converter warranty to 10 years/120,000 miles. Canadian Acura dealers will honour the metric equivalent of this extension. **2009—**Long crank, hard start. **2009–10—**False 'Check engine oil level' message. • Moisture in the tail lights. • Rear-view camera may be loose or aimed too low.

RL PROFILE

	2002	2003	2004	2005	2006	2007	2008	2009	2010
Cost Price ($)									
Base	54,000	55,000	55,800	69,500	69,500	63,900	63,900	63,900	63,900
Used Values ($)									
Base ▲	8,000	9,500	12,000	14,000	17,000	20,000	26,000	35,000	43,000
Base ▼	7,000	8,500	10,500	12,500	15,500	18,000	24,000	33,000	41,000

Reliability	5	5	5	5	4	4	4	5	5
Crash Safety (F)	4	4	4	5	5	5	5	5	5
Side	—	—	4	5	5	5	5	5	5
IIHS Side	—	—	—	5	5	5	5	5	5
Offset	3	3	3	5	5	5	5	5	5
Head Restraints	1	1	1	2	2	2	2	5	5
Roof Strength	—	—	—	2	2	2	2	2	2
Rollover Resistance	—	4	4	5	5	5	5	5	5

TL ★★★★★

RATING: Recommended (1999–2010). **Ideal model year:** Take a look at the redesigned and slightly enlarged 2009 models. A $40,000 TL sedan now costs $23,000 and gives you a year of factory warranty to boot. **"Real" city/highway fuel economy:** 11.7/7.7 L/100 km. **Maintenance/repair costs:** Average costs for the most part, but many repairs are dealer-dependent, which drives up servicing costs if you can't find a competent technician. **Parts:** Higher-than-average costs, but parts aren't hard to find. **Extended warranty:** Not needed. **Best alternatives:** Consider the BMW 3 Series; a redesigned Infiniti I30 or I35; Hyundai's Genesis; and the Lexus ES 300, ES 330, or ES 350. Also, take a look at Acura's CL coupe: It isn't as expensive, and it's as close as you can get to the Accord, with lots of standard bells and whistles thrown in. **Helpful websites:** *http://tl.acurazine.com.*

Strengths and Weaknesses

ALERT! Head restraints are very uncomfortable, particularly on the 2010 models. There is no fix that doesn't compromise your safety. So, take the TL for an extended test drive, and also look for side-mirror glare from the lower dash.

The TL handles well, rides comfortably, boasts impressive acceleration, and is well put together, with quality mechanical and body components. However, the suspension may be too firm for some, and the vehicle creates excessive road noise and has uncomfortable rear seating, limited cargo room, and problematic navigation system controls (see *www.vtec.net* [The Temple of VTEC], *www.acuraworld.com/forums*, *www.cbel.com/acura_cars*, and *www.autosafety.org/autodefects.html*).

Filling the void left by the discontinued Vigor, the TL combines luxury and performance in a nicely styled front-drive, five-passenger sedan that uses the same chassis as the Accord and CL coupe.

Performance enthusiasts will opt for versions equipped with the more-refined 3.2L 225/270 hp V6 mated to a 6-speed manual transmission and a firmer suspension introduced with the 2004 model. It provides impressive acceleration (0–100 km/h in just over eight seconds) in a smooth and quiet manner, without any fuel penalty. Handling is exceptional with the firm suspension but can be a bit tricky when pushed. Bumps are a bit jarring, and the ride is somewhat busier than with other cars in this class.

VEHICLE HISTORY: 2002—A new performance version based on the CL Type S, a minor facelift, new wheels and headlights, and more-comfortable seat belts. **2004**—New styling, 10 more horses, and more standard safety features like head-protecting side curtain airbags. Other improvements include a 6-speed manual tranny, a sportier suspension, high-performance tires, Brembo front brakes, and a limited-slip differential. **2007**—The return of the Type-S, last seen in 2003. Base models have a 258 hp V6 engine teamed with 5-speed automatic transmission. The Type-S has a 286 hp V6 mated to either a 6-speed manual or 5-speed automatic. Type-S also includes firmer suspension, Brembo front brakes, an upgraded interior, and better soundproofing. Other new features include an optional rearview camera, a revised instrument panel, and one-touch starting on vehicles equipped with an automatic transmission. **2009**—Complete redesign; both front-wheel drive and all-wheel drive available. Larger than the previous year's model, with more rear-seat room. Two V6 engines are offered (3.5L and 3.7L), along with electric power steering and redesigned front-seat head restraints.

Interior accommodations are better than average up front, but rear occupants of 2008 or earlier models may discover that legroom is a bit tight and the seat cushions lack sufficient thigh support. The cockpit layout is very user-friendly, due in part to the easy-to-read gauges and accessible controls (far-away climate controls are the only exception).

Common complaints involve poor body fits, electrical shorts, engine surging and stalling, premature brake and tire wear, malfunctioning airbags and accessories, the 6-speed manual transmission shifting roughly into Third gear and sometimes popping out of gear, and chronic automatic and manual transmission failures (covered by a "goodwill" warranty up to eight years). Owners point out that the window regulator may need replacing, the ignition switch buzzes, the trunk lock jams, and the rear bumper is often loose.

 Safety Summary

All years: Horn is difficult to locate in emergency situations. • Airbags fail to deploy in a collision. • Sudden, unintended acceleration. • Automatic transmission failures at high speeds; grinds when shifting from First to Second gear; and sometimes fails to downshift or upshift. • Front brake rotors warp early. • Door locks operate erratically. • Frequent tire failures. • Instrument panel is washed out in daylight. • It's easy for drivers to confuse the brake and gas pedals. **2004**—Stability control activates right front brake, causing the vehicle to swerve suddenly. • Excessive steering-wheel shake and chassis vibration often blamed on tires, but it can be caused by a defective transmission torque converter. • Cracked alloy wheel rim caused tire failure. • Headlight low beam creates a dark/blind spot. • Multiple malfunctions with the hands-free phone system. • Windshield easily broken. • Power mirrors, auto-dimming mirror, windshield wiper washer, and power-seat position memory often malfunction due to the system's fuse constantly blowing. **2004–06**—Low, soft brake pedal. **2005**—Car pulls to either side when underway. • Severe rear brake corrosion and grooving extends stopping distances. **2006**—Sudden brake and steering failures. • ABS and vehicle stabilization system fail in icy conditions. • Keys stuck in ignition and doors won't unlock after vehicle stopped. **2007**—Under-hood fire. • Sudden loss of power and lights. • Vehicle suddenly shifts from Third to Neutral. • Airbag alert constantly lit. • Premature clutch failure ($2,000). • Manual transmission frequently pops out of Third gear. • Brake and steering failure when coming to a sudden stop. • False alerts from the Fuel System light. • Driver's side window crushed driver's finger. **2008**—Premature engine timing belt failure. • Piston rod broke and destroyed the engine. • Bridgestone tire side wall blowouts. • Door stoppers don't hold the doors open when exiting the vehicle. **2009**—Lower dash reflection causes a severe side-mirror glare that creates a blind spot with each mirror. • Steering wheel lockup while driving. • Loose, rattling driver-side window. **2010**—Sticking gas pedal. • Front cloth floormats aren't securely anchored. • In cold weather, the 6-speed manual transmission is hard to shift into Third gear. • The automatic transmission slips.

Secret Warranties/Internal Bulletins/Service Tips

All years: Seat belts that fail to function properly during normal use will be replaced for free under the company's lifetime seat belt warranty. • Diagnostic procedures and correction for off-centre steering wheels. • Acura guidelines for submitting paint claims. **1999–2002**—Front, middle, or rear engine oil leaks likely caused by a too-porous cast aluminum engine block (TSB #01-041). **1999–2006**—Diagnosing and fixing a drift/pull to one side. **2004–05**—TSB #05-033 says you should install a #10A fuse if the windshield wiper washer, power-seat position memory, power mirrors, or auto-dimming mirror don't work. • A clicking or popping brake pedal may have a misaligned brake-pedal position switch plunger. Turn it around so the connector lock faces the 5 o'clock position. **2004–07**—Manual transmission pops out of gear; hard to shift into Third gear; makes a grinding noise. **2004–08**—Power steering moans, whines upon cold startup. • Front door glass reverses, shudders, or is noisy. • Cracked roof console bezel. • Interior rearview mirror loose, vibrates. • Front seatback panel loose or detaches. • Headliner sagging. • Rear shelf rattles. **2005–08**—Timing belt chirping. **2007**—Catalytic converter warranty extended to 10 years/192,000 km (120,000 miles). **2009**—Steering column makes a popping or clicking sound. • Audio speaker rattling. • AC blower changes speed. • Front door panel fabric pulls out. **2009–11**—False "Check engine oil level" message. **2009–12**—Noises from the B-pillar or moonroof area. • Tapping, clicking, or ticking noise may come from the right rear wheelwell or rear shelf.

TL PROFILE

	2002	2003	2004	2005	2006	2007	2008	2009	2010
Cost Price ($)									
Base	37,000	37,800	40,800	41,000	42,000	42,500	42,700	39,900	39,990
Used Values ($)									
Base ▲	6,000	7,000	8,500	10,000	12,500	15,500	18,000	24,000	28,000
Base ▼	5,000	6,000	7,500	9,000	11,000	14,000	16,500	22,000	26,000
Reliability	3	3	4	5	5	4	4	4	4
Crash Safety (F)	4	4	5	5	5	5	5	5	5
Side	4	4	4	4	5	5	5	5	5
IIHS Side	—	—	5	5	5	5	5	5	5
Offset	5	5	5	5	5	5	5	5	5
Head Restraints	1	1	2	2	2	2	2	5	5
Rollover Resistance	5	4	4	4	5	4	4	5	5

Audi

A3, A4, A4 S-LINE, A6, A8, S4, S6, TT COUPE ★

bad buy

RATING: Not Recommended (2000–10). Beautiful to behold; deadly to drive, and hell to repair. *Lemon-Aid* has dropped Audi's rating as low as we can because of these vehicles' failure-prone electronics, chronic electrical shorts, unreliable headlights, and terrifying DSG transmission and engine failures that can stop you dead on the highway and then shoot you forward like a slingshot. One owner filmed the entire sequence: *www.autoinsane.com/2009/08/21/news/recalls-tsbs/flash-of-death-volkswagen-audi-dsg-recall-issues-caught-on-video*.

These cars, like Mercedes and Volkswagen models, seem to quickly go downhill quality-wise after the five-year mark. **Ideal model year**: It's a risky buy, but a 2008 A3 2.0T for about $16,000 is the best of a bad lot. It hasn't been as plagued by the factory-related quality demons we've seen with other Audis. The 2008 A4 2.0T AWD is another doable buy if the car passes a rigorous pre-purchase inspection. It originally sold for $41,200, and dealers now sell the car used for $17,000. Your best strategy: Buy the A4 from a private owner for about 20 percent less than what most dealers would charge and try to get one that has some of the original warranty left. Then have your A4 serviced top to bottom by an Audi dealer. Ask for warranty coverage on all the defects that pop up. Keep all work orders that mention problems or symptoms that were never corrected, particularly powertrain glitches. Then go to a cheaper independent service centre for the rest of your servicing and get estimates for the correction of those problems that were never fixed by the dealer. File a small claims court action against the Audi dealer and Audi Canada for the cost of those repairs estimated by your independent garage.

"Real" city/highway fuel economy: *A3 2.0 6-speed manual: 10.2/7.1 L/100 km. A4 1.8 manual: 11.2/7.2 L/100 km. Quattro 3.0 manual: 13.5/8.7 L/100 km (this version burns a lot more fuel than the A4!). S4 manual: 15.8/10.2 L/100 km. A6 3.0: 11.5/8.1 L/100 km. TT Coupe 1.8 Selectronic: 11.3/7.5 L/100 km. TT Coupe 3.2: 10.9/8.1 L/100 km.* **Maintenance/repair costs:** Higher than average, and almost all repairs have to be done by an Audi dealer. Expect long delays for routine repairs. **Parts:** Very expensive, and independent suppliers have a hard time finding parts. **Extended warranty:** A good idea, considering how often the engines and transmissions need work. **Best alternatives:** Acura TL or RL; BMW 3 Series; Infiniti I30 or I35; and Lexus ES300. TT Coupe shoppers may also want to look at the BMW Z3 or Z4, Ford Mustang (2011), Honda S2000, Hyundai Genesis Coupe, and Mazda Miata. **Helpful websites:** *www.audiworld.com, www.vwvortex.com,* and *MyAudiTTsucks. com.*

 ## Strengths and Weaknesses

ALERT! NHTSA has received over 100 complaints of catastrophic fuel-pump failures on diesel models requiring major fuel-system work, including replacement of the fuel tank (total: $8,000). Owners say some Audi dealers blame the failure on the driver's use of the wrong fuel, but they usually relent when gas receipts are shown or the driver threatens to sue. **Tip:** Show the dealer *Lemon-Aid's* research of this failure and download the complaint database from *www.safercarcar.gov.* And sue if you have to.

A3

Launched as a 2006 model, the A3 is Audi's entry-level ($32,950 in 2006; $32,300 in 2011) small car. It's a conservatively styled compact hatchback with a small interior, too-light steering (be prepared to make lots of steering corrections at highway speeds), and average reliability. The base model is quite manoeuvrable and quick, thanks to the turbocharged 200 hp 2.0L 4-cylinder engine hooked to a 6-speed manumatic transmission. The AWD variant comes with a powerful 250 hp 3.2L V6 (borrowed from Volkswagen) that quiets the ride and improves handling a touch while sucking up premium fuel.

Sales of the 2006 model were quite good, prompting Audi to boost 2007 prices by almost $1,000. Fortunately, resale prices between the two model years haven't been that different. Nevertheless, 2008 models are favoured over the 2006 versions because of the fewer factory-related defects evidenced after the cars got through their first-year teething period, when product quality is at its lowest.

A4

Audi's best-selling line, these cars handle well, and are attractively styled, comfortable to drive, and provide a fairly comfortable interior. But you'd better know how to separate the wheat from the chaff, since some model years can be wallet-busters due to their rapid depreciation, poor quality, and high servicing costs.

Replacements for the Audi 90 for the 1996 model year, these alphabetically named cars are conservatively styled, often slow off the mark (in spite of the V6 addition when hooked to an automatic), and plagued by electrical glitches, mechanical breakdowns, and outrageously expensive servicing and repair costs—when you can find a competent Audi mechanic. The 4-speed automatic shifts erratically (delayed and abrupt engagement), and the 2.8L V6 engine needs full throttle for adequate performance. Handling is acceptable, on a par with the BMW 3 Series, but the ride is a bit firm and the car still exhibits considerable body roll, brake dive, and acceleration squat when pushed.

Overall quality control has improved very little over the last two decades. The automatic transmission and electrical system are the cars' weakest links and have plagued Audi's entire lineup. Normally this wouldn't be catastrophic; however, as the cars become more electronically complex, with more functions handled by computer modules, you're looking at some annoying glitches, to say the least (failure to go into gear, false obstacle warnings, etc.). Here are some other "annoyances": steering grinds, distorted windshields, brakes that fail in rainy weather, body glitches that would shame Lada, early lower control arm replacement, defective mirror memory settings, premature brake wear and then loud grinding when in Reverse, fuel-system malfunctions leading to surging and stalling, and a transmission that suddenly downshifts or jerks into Forward gear. Furthermore, servicing is still spotty because of the small number of dealers in Canada and the fact that these cars are extremely dealer-dependent (see *www. audiworld.com*, *www.vwvortex.com*, *MyAudiTTsucks.com*, and *www.thetruthaboutcars. com*).

TT Coupe

The best of the Audi lineup, but still plagued by failure-prone electrical and mechanical components, the TT Coupe is a sporty front-drive hatchback with 2+2 seating set on the same platform used by the A4, Golf, Jetta, and New Beetle. A two-seat convertible version, the Roadster, was launched in the spring of 2000. The base 180 hp 1.8L engine (lifted from the A4) is coupled with a manual 5-speed, while the optional engine uses a 6-speed manual transaxle. Shorter and more firmly sprung than the A4, the TT's engines are turbocharged.

Beautifully styled, with superb handling, the TT comes with lots of high-tech standard features that include four-wheel disc brakes, airbags everywhere, traction control (front-drive models), a power top (Quattro), a heated-glass rear window, and a power-retractable glass windbreak between the roll bars (convertible). An alarm system employs pulse radar to catch prying hands invading the cockpit area.

Problem areas reported by owners include steering-wheel clunks, excessive brake noise, early tie-rod wearout, premature wheel bearing failures, poorly performing window regulators, electrical shorts causing dash gauges and instruments to fail, premature transmission failures and grinding of the Second gear synchronizers, and loose bolts that cause the subframe to move while driving over bumps and while braking.

VEHICLE HISTORY: *A4:* **2002**—A4 is totally revamped, getting a roomier interior, a 10 hp boost to the base engine, and a 3.0L all-aluminum, 5-valve-per-cylinder, 220 hp V6 engine hooked to a new 6-speed manual transmission. Other features: brake assist, a more rigid body, and an upgraded independent rear suspension. **2003**—Addition of a convertible. **2004**—S4 returns using the A4's new design. More high-performance models and greater all-wheel-drive availability. Quattro models drop the old 5-speed for a 6-speed manual transmission. **2005**—A mid-year redesign. **2007**—S4 is restyled. **2009**—A4 lineup has been restyled and redesigned, with more power added to the S4 version, and a longer wheelbase, larger dimensions, more interior space and a new appearance shared with the other models. The sedan and Avant (wagon) variants are all-new, while the A4 and S4 cabriolet models are carried over from their 2008 configuration. **2010**—3.2L Quattro and Cabriolet are dropped and the S4 gets a supercharged 3.0L V6. *A6:* **2002**—Debut of all-wheel drive, a 2.7L engine, and adjustable air suspension. **2003**—The new RS6 debuts, equipped with a 450 hp 4.2L V8; the sporty S6 Avant adds a more-powerful V8 and sport suspension. On the downside, front-passenger seat memory is no more, and steering-wheel shift buttons are gone. **2004**—A V8 for the all-road Quattro, and a new sports model, the 2.7T S-Line sedan. **2005**—Refreshed styling and additional room and power. Wheelbase is increased and models are equipped with either a 255 hp V6 or a 335 hp V8, coupled to a 6-speed automatic transmission with manual-shift capability and all-wheel drive. Audi's MMI operating system, like BMW's iDrive, uses a centre console knob to control many of the car's accessories. All A6s now have front side airbags, side curtain airbags, and optional rear side airbags. Anti-lock four-wheel disc brakes and an anti-skid system are both standard. **2006**—A new Avant wagon and front-drive sedan spin-off. **2007**—Debut of the 435 hp V10 S6 Quattro sedan. **2009**—Restyled and equipped with a new 300 hp supercharged 3.0L V6 found on the 3.0T Quattro. Troublesome air suspension feature dropped. **2010**—The 3.2L V6 gets 10 more horses. *TT:* **2003**—All-wheel drive now found only on uplevel models; a revised grille. **2004**—A 250 hp V6, a manumatic transmission, and standard xenon headlights (thieves will love you). **2008**—Fresh styling and a new powertrain: 2.0T models get a 200 hp turbocharged 2.0L four-banger and the AWD gets a 250 hp 3.2L V6 hooked to a 6-speed manumatic transmission. **2009**—A new TTS coupe and convertible. The TTS uses a 265 hp 2.0T supercharged 4-cylinder (15 more horses than the V6 and 65 more than the basic turbo four). **2010**—The 2.0T front-drive and 3.2L Quattro model have been dropped.

Other 1996 and later Audi models are just as poorly designed and built as the A4 and its many spin-offs. For example, the A6, a reincarnation of the 100 Series, is packed with standard convenience and safety features and is a comfortable, spacious front-drive or all-wheel-drive luxury sedan. It uses the same V6 powerplant as the A4, its smaller sibling, but has 47 additional horses.

Unfortunately, the engine is no match for the car's size (0–100 km/h in 13 seconds), and steering and handling are decidedly truck-like.

The A8 competes with the BMW 7 Series and the Mercedes S-Class and loses. Equipped with a 174 hp 2.8L V6 or a 300 hp V8, the A8 is a decently performing—though equally defect-ridden—buy. Its drawbacks: a high price, subpar reliability, imprecise steering, and an aluminum body that only an Audi dealer can repair.

Launched in 1994 and powered by a turbocharged 227 hp 2.2L 5-cylinder engine, the S6 is a high-performance spin-off of the A6. Its reliability is mediocre at best, though its sporty performance leaves the A6 in the dust.

 Safety Summary

All models/years: Airbag failures. • Chronic stalling. Fuel-system contamination by debris from failed fuel pump. • Sudden acceleration. • Extremely poor wet braking on later models, caused by water contaminating the brake rotor and disc; brakes delay by almost two seconds. • Many cases of distorted windshields. **All models: 2003**—Stuck accelerator pedal. • No-starts believed to be caused by instrument cluster or steering lock/ignition cylinder failures. • CVT hesitates before engaging. • Parking brake fails to hold. • Outside mirrors don't automatically readjust. • Ice glazes the brake rotors. • Frequent failure of the windshield wiper motor and washer. • Doors fill with water when it rains. **2004**—Stuck accelerator causes sudden acceleration. • Tire jack stand collapses. • Convertible top fails. **2005**—Car constantly drifts to the right side of the roadway. • Car is a rodent magnet:

> At 2,200 miles [3,540 km], a headlight warning light came on, and I took my car to the dealership. I was told that a mouse had climbed into my engine, built a nest out of the hood insulation, and chewed through wires. Audi refused to cover any damages. This incident cost me $1,400.

Vehicle hesitates for two to three seconds when accelerating from a complete stop:

> I have almost been T-boned while trying to make a left hand turn, 3 times. The car is dangerous!! I took it in to the dealer on July the 1st. They told me then that that is the way the car is designed to operate.

A3: **2006**—Engine coolant line flange failure allows coolant to drain out:

> Engine coolant line flange failure causes engine coolant to drain from vehicle. The dealer indicates that this is common on the 2.0 engines. Part unavailable in the US (on back order). The car was parked, luckily. Could have been a major expense if on the highway. Drained within several hours while parked. If this is an issue, why isn't Audi replacing this with a metal flange instead of a plastic one?

Premature automatic transmission failure. • Wheels passed over a manhole cover, and the airbags deployed. • In warm weather, the car's fuel pump will shut off, causing the vehicle to stall in traffic. • Weak sun shade latch. • Horn may not work. **2007**—Chronic loss of power, stalling, and transmission drops into Neutral:

> On my way to work in my 2007 Audi A3—All of a sudden I lose power and my car stops accelerating and shifts into Neutral. I see that the P D N S lights are flashing so I attempt to restart my car. It starts to go again and then sputters forward without me doing anything. Luckily I wasn't far from home and was able to restart my car again and get it home while the car revved like crazy going less than 20 mph. After some research I have found that many Audi/VW's experience this in their vehicles. These are all characteristic of a faulty mechatronic unit associated with the car's DSG.

More DSG automatic transmission malfunctions:

> My DSG transmission started acting funny. When I would let off of the brake, the car would sit for a split second and then jump forward quickly as if I had blurped the throttle. Sometimes it does it twice before rolling smoothly. I[t] feels like the clutch is engaging too strongly and then letting off. Also, when coming to a stop, the transmission seems like it holds on to the gear a little too long and makes my car jump forward right before a stop. It does this in reverse also. It has caused me to go too far into the crosswalk at a stop light. It does this all of the time, not just when the engine/transmission is cold.

2008—Increase in the number of DSG manumatic transmission failures; there is no simple fix:

> My 2008 Audi A3 and its DSG transmission have exhibited irregular and dangerous shifting behavior. The transmission surges unpredictably at low speeds, particularly in 1st or Reverse with brakes off and little/no gas. Also on several occasions the transmission has completely dropped out of gear and failed to re-engage for approximately 1–2 months, however the problems have since reappeared.

2009—More DSG transmission failures:

> I am travelling on the highway in the middle lane at around 60/65 mph, the transmission (DSG) started making chunk noises and the car started to jerk, then the engine completely shut down in the middle of the highway!! Not to mention my youngest sister (10 years old) was with me. I couldn't restart the engine and I couldn't steer and/or shift without pressing on the break. I ended up in a complete stop in the middle of the highway hoped no one would hit me and thank God it didn't. I then quickly shift the gear back to "P" and fortunately the engine started again so I could get out of this hell zone. This is truly unbelievable for a new vehicle with 200 miles.

Blinking headlights and interior lights when braking. *A4:* **2006**—HID headlights flicker and often go out; fix will cost $400. • Delayed acceleration. • Power steering pump pulley separates from the vehicle. • Vehicle locks all the doors if the car is exited while the engine is running. **2007**—"Lag and lurch" when accelerating:

> I have two Audi A4's, one a 2007 sedan and one a 2008 station wagon. Both exhibit the same problem. Both have done it a number of times, mostly the sedan. When you need to scoot across opposing traffic making a left, sporadically, the car initially responds like you'd expect the gas pedal, but half a second later bogs out with basically no acceleration, so you're rolling leisurely across oncoming traffic, and then about a second later it wakes up and resumes accelerating.

Frequent stalling on the highway. • "Cam follower" inside the high pressure fuel pump may be cause of some of the stalling, loss of power incidents; it is a $1,1000+ repair:

> 2007 Audi A4 Avant. Vehicle loses power when accelerating. The failure occurred each time I would accelerate in excess of 55 mph. To correct this failure a new camshaft, cam follower, and fuel pump were installed in the vehicle for a total of $1,749.97.

> •

> This is a known issue with the cam follower and high pressure fuel pump on all 2.0T FSI motors from Audi and VW. My cam follower has a hole in it (have the part) and the HPFP is worn down because it has made contact with the cam lobe, which has been scarred. Replacement requires a new cam, HPFP and cam follower. The design however will require constant inspection of the cam follower to avoid major engine failure. All 2.0T FSI engines will experience this problem. Audi has a TSB #2013147/4 Dated June 18, 2007 that warns of this problem upon CEL light being shown. My car never showed the CEL light.

Frequent replacement of expensive coil packs and diverter valves. • Many reports that the 2.0L engine is an oil-burner. • Headlight failures caused by faulty xenon bulb or ballast. • Carpet can jam the accelerator pedal. • Driver-side seatbelt easily unlatches if an object is placed near the buckle. • Premature wearout and side bubbling of Continental tires. **2008**—Engine burns oil even after rings were replaced. • Sunroof exploded (glass pushed outward). **2009**—More fuel pump failures, causing the vehicle to shut down anywhere. • Severe steering shake. • Suspension noise caused by cracked front upper control arm bushings. • Early replacement of expensive headlight bulbs. *A6 Sedan:* **2003**—Numerous complaints of delayed braking; no brakes in rainy weather; parking brake failure; and premature replacement of the front brake rotors. • Blue-white headlights blind oncoming drivers. **2005**—Acceleration is still plagued by engine hesitation. • Right outside mirror tilts down in Reverse gear for parking but does not go back to normal until the vehicle is up to speed in Second gear. Result: No mirror while entering traffic. *TT Coupe:* **2002**—Frequent drivetrain failures. • Owners report a multitude of electrical shorts affect the radio, horn, lights, dash gauges, and controls. • Ignition coil failures. • Xenon headlights don't adequately light the roadway. **2003**—Dash panel continues to operate erratically, and gauges show false readings. **2004**—DSG transmission loses all power:

> Ultimately I had to have the mechatronic unit in the transmission replaced to fix the problem, at a cost of about $3,200.

Car jerked violently and would not change gears. • Fuel gauge failures. • Instrument cluster inoperative. **2005**—Airbag light stays on constantly. **2006**— Brake failure when making a right turn. **2008**—One vehicle burned up from a fire that ignited from the front seat wiring. • Road debris can drive the screws that secure the oil pan into the oil pan itself. • Side-view mirrors do not go out far enough to safely see the road. • DSG transmission continues to jerk and buck when shifting. **2009**—DSG manumatic transmission still locks up the gearbox. • Sudden loss of power, brakes, and steering ability.

Secret Warranties/Internal Bulletins/Service Tips

All models: 1996–2010—Silencing squealing brakes. **2000–08**—Hesitation on acceleration. **2000–10**—Low power, won't move after stopping. • Inoperative keyless entry. • Excessive oil consumption. **2005–10**—Noxious AC odours. **2006–10**—Flickering interior lighting. **2007–10**—Multiple electrical malfunctions. **2009–11**—Steering squeak when turning. *A3:* **2005–10**— Headlights go on and off. **2005–11**—Sunroof noises. • Inoperative windshield wipers. **2006–09**—No acceleration when shifted into gear. • Inoperative low beams. • Xenon headlights flicker and fail. **2006–10**—Cluster lights dim, flicker. • Door electrical malfunctions. **2006–11**—Front suspension cracking, rubbing noise. • Front, rear brake squealing. **2009**—Stiff steering. **2009–10**—Airbag light stays on. • Hard start; timing chain noise. • Automatic transmission control module update. • Inoperative headlight washer system. **2010**—TDI catastrophic fuel-pump failure; sudden engine shutdown; metal shavings found in the fuel system (an $8,000 repair awaits). Automatic transmission suddenly downshifts to M1, inviting a rear-ender. *A4, A6, S6:* **2002–05**—Vehicles equipped with the Multitronic automatic transmission buck when accelerating. **2002–08**—Noisy power steering. • Inoperative daytime running lights. **2005**—Cold engine stumble; warm engine stall. **2005–06**—Oil leak from oil filter housing. **2005–08**—Eliminating brake moan on low-speed turns. • Front window reverses direction when closing. • Inoperative sunroof switch. • Inoperative One Touch window feature. **2005–09**—Long warm-engine crank time. **2005–10**— Headlights go on and off. **2006–08**—Brake squealing. **2007–08**—Paint spots or stains on upper surfaces. **2009**—Hard start; timing chain noise. **2009–10**— Airbag light stays on. *A6, S4:* **2002–06**—TSB #05-05, October 28, 2005, notes that in models equipped with 2.7L turbocharged V6 engines, a defective auxiliary coolant pump leaks coolant from the pump body; when pump fails, coolant light comes on, warning that continued driving could cause serious engine damage. VW will install a repair kit free of charge up to seven years/160,000 km. *A6, S4, S5 Cabriolet, Q5:* **2011**—TSB #131106 says that some models with 3L or 3.2L V6 engines may experience problems with the accessory drive belt or its guide due to a guide that is out of line, causing damage to the belt. Audi will do a free inspection of vehicles it suspects of having the problem and replace the guide and the belt for free as needed. *A4:* **2002–04**—Oil leak at camshaft adjuster. **2002–04**—Hard jerking in Reverse at idle. **2002–06**—Faulty glove compartment door. • Noisy power steering. **2003–04**—Service campaign to replace the engine wire harness. **2005–06**—Remote won't lock/unlock doors. **2005–07**—Xenon headlights flicker and fail. **2005–08**—Remedy for a vehicle that pulls to one side. • Dash clicking noises. • Headlights vibrate. **2006–07**—Inoperative low beams. **2006–08**—Front, rear brake squealing. • Brakes moan when accelerating or turning. **2007**—Multiple electrical failures. **2009–11**—Sunroof noises, concerns. *A6:* **1998–2004**—Noisy power steering. **2005**—Fuel gauge reads empty with a full tank. **2005–06**—Rough-running cold engine. • Inoperative sunroof. **2005–09**—Long warm-engine crank time. **2005–11**—Sunroof noises. • Brakes moan when accelerating or turning. **2006–11**—Front, rear brake squealing. **2007**—AC doesn't cool. • Loose, broken control knobs. **2008–09**—Erratic operating radio and door locks. *TT Coupe:* **2000–10**—Excessive oil consumption. **2002–11**—Front, rear brake squealing. **2004**—Front stabilizer bar upgrade to reduce noise. **2004–05**—Xenon headlight failure. **2004–06**—Momentary delay when accelerating. • Vehicle won't go into gear. **2005–11**—Sunroof noises, concerns. **2006–09**—No acceleration when shifted into gear. **2006–10**—Cluster lights dim, flicker. **2007**—Inoperative windows, locks, and sunroof. **2007–08**—Inoperative One Touch window feature. **2007–11**—Interior buzzing vibrating noises. **2008–09**—Erratic radio and door locks. • Inoperative low beams. • Xenon headlights flicker and go out. **2007**—Loose, noisy air-intake duct. • Rear suspension rumble, rattle. **2007–10**—Headlights go on and off. • Inoperative headlight washer system. **2008–11**—Front suspension cracking, rubbing noise. **2009**—Hard start; timing chain noise. • Stiff steering.

A3, A4, A6, A8, S4, S6, TT COUPE PROFILE

	2002	2003	2004	2005	2006	2007	2008	2009	2010
Cost Price ($)									
A3	—	—	—	—	32,950	33,800	31,800	31,800	32,300
A4	37,225	37,310	34,435	34,985	35,270	35,310	41,200	41,200	38,300
A6	54,235	51,740	51,950	59,500	62,500	62,700	52,900	52,900	52,900
A8	86,500	86,500	97,750	93,90	96,250	97,190	95,000	95,000	95,000
S4	57,200	—	67,950	68,250	68,950	70,390	70,400	75,500	52,500
S6	88,500	88,500	109,000	—	—	101,900	101,900	99,500	99,500
TT	50,400	48,650	49,975	55,475	55,980	—	46,900	46,900	49,350
Used Values ($)									
A3 ▲	—	—	—	—	10,500	14,000	17,000	21,000	24,000
A3 ▼	—	—	—	—	9,500	12,500	15,500	19,500	22,000
A4 ▲	5,000	6,000	7,500	9,000	11,000	15,000	18,000	24,000	27,500
A4 ▼	4,000	5,000	6,500	8,000	10,000	13,500	16,000	22,500	25,500
A6 ▲	8,000	9,500	11,000	13,000	15,000	22,000	26,000	32,000	36,000
A6 ▼	7,000	8,500	10,000	11,500	13,500	20,000	24,500	30,000	34,000

A8 ▲	11,000	13,000	15,500	18,000	20,000	26,000	35,000	47,000	60,000
A8 ▼	10,000	12,000	14,500	16,500	18,500	25,000	33,000	45,000	57,000
S4 ▲	6,000	—	12,000	14,000	17,000	18,500	31,000	45,000	39,500
S4 ▼	5,500	—	11,000	12,500	16,500	17,500	29,500	43,000	37,500
S6 ▲	13,000	15,000	18,000	—	—	29,000	41,000	54,000	70,000
S6 ▼	12,000	14,000	16,500	—	—	27,000	39,000	52,000	67,000
TT ▲	9,000	10,000	12,000	14,000	15,500	—	25,000	29,000	36,000
TT ▼	8,000	9,500	11,500	13,000	14,500	—	23,500	27,500	34,500
Reliability (A3)	2	2	2	2	2	2	2	2	2
A4	2	2	2	2	2	2	3	3	3
A6	2	2	2	2	2	2	2	3	3
A8	2	2	2	2	3	3	3	3	3
Crash Safety (F)									
A4/S4	4	4	4	4	4	4	4	5	5
A8	5	5	—	—	—	—	—	—	—
Side (TT)	5	5	5	5	5	—	—	—	—
A4/S4	5	5	5	5	5	4	5	5	5
IIHS Side (A3)	—	—	—	5	5	5	5	5	5
A4	—	—	—	5	5	5	5	5	5
A6	—	—	—	5	5	5	5	5	5
Offset (A6)	3	3	3	5	5	5	5	5	5
A3	—	—	—	5	5	5	5	5	5
A4/S4	5	5	5	5	5	5	5	5	5
Head Restraints									
A3	—	—	—	—	3	3	5	5	5
A4/S4 (F)	5	5	1	2	3	5	5	5	5
A6	5	5	5	3	3	5	5	5	5
A8	2	2	5	—	—	—	—	—	—
TT Coupe	3	3	3	—	—	—	—	—	—
TT Roadster	5	5	5	—	—	—	—	—	—
Roof Strength (A3)	—	—	—	—	5	5	5	5	5
A4	—	—	—	—	—	—	—	5	5
A6	—	—	—	3	3	3	3	3	3
Rollover Resistance									
A4/S4	4	4	4	4	4	4	4	5	5
TT	—	5	5	5	5	—	—	—	—

Note: Reliability problems seem to be especially severe in the fifth year of ownership. The A3 has not yet been crash tested by NHTSA.

All ratings on a numbered scale where 5 is good and 1 is bad. See page 132 for a more detailed description.

BMW

RATING: *3 Series, 5 Series, M Series, Z4:* Above Average (1999–2010). *Z3:* Average (1999–2010). These cars are the best performing and most reliable vehicles Europe has to offer, but that's faint praise when one considers the overall poor quality, dangerous safety-related malfunctions, needlessly complex engineering, and exorbitant retail prices charged in Canada.

Owner feedback and internal service bulletins show these cars come with a performance and quality reputation that far exceeds what they actually deliver. As with Audi, the same safety defects are carried over year after year. Some notable examples: sudden, unintended acceleration, airbag malfunctions, hesitation upon acceleration, surging gear changes, jammed door latches that "kidnap" occupants, Turanza tires that self-destruct, and costly, poor-quality halogen headlights. Buyers of older models should be on the lookout for hidden rust damage. Door and fender seams, rocker panels, and rear-wheel openings are likely to be rust-cankered with a dash of paint used to hide the damage. **Ideal model year:** If you want the best price with good overall reliability and performance, the 2008 328i will give you all that for about $20,000, which isn't bad for a high-end car that sold new for $41,000. The 2007 5 Series is also a good bet. It builds upon the redesigned and repowered 2006 model and prices are mouth-watering. For example: a 2007 525i that sold for $58,600 can be had today for about $19,500. Or, a top-of-the-line 2007 550i that went for $78,600 now costs only (sigh) $25,500. Granted, the 2009 5 Series underwent another redesign with the 2009 models, and *Lemon-Aid* is watching to see what impact those changes will have. What would be the best Z-car? Try a 2008 Z4. Originally sold for $55,400, it will now cost you $28,000, and the car had two years to smooth out its 2006 redesign. **"Real" city/highway fuel economy:** *2.2 manual:* 11.3/7.2 L/100 km. *2.2 automatic:* 11.6/7.4 L/100 km. *2.5 manual:* 11.7/7.4 L/100 km. *2.5 automatic:* 12.3/8.0 L/100 km. *3.0 manual:* 11.7/7.2 L/100 km. *3.0 automatic:* 12.2/8.0 L/100 km. *5 Series 2.5 manual:* 11.7/7.4 L/100 km. *5 Series 2.5 automatic:* 12.5/7.6 L/100 km. *3.0 manual:* 11.7/7.2 L/100 km. *3.0 automatic:* 12.9/7.8 L/100 km. *4.4 manual:* 14.4/8.6 L/100 km. *4.4 automatic:* 13.0/8.2 L/100 km. **Maintenance/repair costs:** Higher than average, but many repairs can be done by independent garages who specialize in BMWs. Unfortunately, these experts are usually concentrated around large urban areas. **Parts:** Higher-than-average costs, and parts are often back ordered. **Extended warranty:** A good idea. **Best alternatives:** There are a number of credible alternatives to the Z Series, such as the AWD 3 Series and the Mazda6. Also look at the Acura TL or RL, and the Hyundai Genesis. **Helpful websites:** *www.roadfly.com/bmw/forums* and *www.bimmerfest.com*.

Strengths and Weaknesses

ALERT! There's no reason why Bimmers should cost so much in Canada, particularly in view of the increased value of the Canadian dollar and the high rate of depreciation with the higher-end models. Shop stateside for bargains on the higher-end models.

3 Series

The 3 Series vehicles exhibit great 6-cylinder performance with the manual gearbox, and ride and handling are commendable. Most of the small 4-cylinder engines' power is seriously compromised by an automatic transmission.

Smart shoppers who opt for the improved 2000 models will keep in mind that rear interior room is still a joke—unless you happen to be sitting there. Various upgrades make the 2001 and later models better choices, although safety- and performance-related failures are commonplace.

VEHICLE HISTORY: 2002—Entire lineup gets recalibrated steering, reshaped headrests, and an in-dash CD player. **2003**—Coupes and convertibles are restyled, along with a transmission upgrade. **2004**—Expanded availability of the sequential manual transmission. **2005**—Coupes get a sunroof (except the M3) and run-flat tires along with a tire-pressure monitor (all three items are of doubtful value). **2006**—New styling (vehicles are longer and wider than before) and more power; the much-hated, complicated iDrive is offered as an option. Debut of a premium sedan and wagon. 325i and 325xi models are powered by 215 hp engines, up from 184 hp produced by the previous model's 2.5L 6-cylinder. Wagons get a 30 hp boost. All cars come with a 6-speed manual transmission. Coupes and convertibles are carried over unchanged. **2007**—Coupes are revamped with more power (45 more horses with the turbocharged 6-cylinder), a standard 6-speed manual tranny, a larger platform, steering-linked xenon headlights that bring joy to thieves and parts suppliers, and 90 kg (200 lb.) of extra weight. Rear-drive coupes get a firmer suspension and more-comfortable seats. The new convertible has a retractable hardtop that uses a complex electronic mechanical system to open and close the roof. **2008**—Carried over with few changes except for the addition of the high-performance M3. **2009**—The 323i sedan adds heated seats, automatic climate control, and halogen headlights; 328i models receive standard glass sunroof and seats with memory settings; and the M3 performance line returns with the addition of a 335d, equipped with a diesel engine. The 2009 powertrain setup for the 3 Series is now a 2.5L inline 6-cylinder (the 323); a 3.0L inline 6-cylinder (328); a twin-turbo 3.0L inline 6-cylinder (335); twin-turbo 3.0L inline 6-cylinder diesel (335d); and 4.0L V8 (M). All except the 335d and the M models are hooked to a 6-speed manual transmission or an optional 6-speed automatic with manual shift mode. The M models offer an optional 7-speed dual-clutch automatic; the 335d uses the 6-speed automatic only. **2010**—All models return relatively unchanged.

Handling with all model years is still tricky on wet roads, despite the ASC+T traction control; rear-seat access is problematic; rear passenger space continues to disappoint; and styling is the essence of bland. The brakes, tires, engine, transmission, suspension, electrical system, and some body trim and accessories are the most failure-prone components. Paint peeling and delamination has afflicted BMW for the past several decades up through 2009. Owners who complain "energetically" are usually offered compensation:

> Paint defects on new 2009 BMW, purchased on March 2010. The paint is peeling in 4 places. Car manufacturer claims peeling is from an "external source." BMW offered a "good faith" adjustment of 50% of repair cost, but if it is a defect, it should be covered in full as part of the warranty.

BMW has always had paint problems. That defect was the principal reason for the well-known U.S. judgment, *BMW vs. Gore*, rendered on May 20, 1996, by the U. S. Supreme Court (*http://en.wikipedia.org/wiki/BMW_of_North_America,_Inc._v._Gore*). BMW was ordered to pay $2 million, but the award was reduced to $50,000 in lieu of having the case retried.

Engine overheating is also a serious and common failure on early models (see *www.straight-six.com*, *www.mwerks.com*, *www.bmwnation.com*, *www.roadfly.com*, *yoy.com/yoy/auto/m3_failure_index.html* (2002 BMW M3 Engine Failures Page), and *www.bmwlemon.com*).

5 Series

Essentially a larger, more-powerful 3 Series, the 5 Series has made its reputation by delivering more performance in a larger, more-versatile interior. The 6-cylinder and V8 engines are somewhat fuel-thirsty and occasionally a bit noisy, but they are quite remarkable, durable performers. There is no problem with rear seatroom or cargo room with the 5 Series Bimmer. Handling and ride are superb, although these weighty upscale models do strain when going over hilly terrain if they have the automatic gearbox.

Overall reliability has been very poor over the past decade. Electronic failures are the chief culprit, but brake, powertrain, and electrical problems lead the list of other persistent failings. Also, whenever a problem arises, repair costs are particularly high because of the small number of dealers, the relative scarcity of parts, and the difficulty of getting a correct, unbiased diagnosis as to the cause of a breakdown.

Owners say that premature brake wear causes excessive vibration, noise, and severe pulling to one side when the brakes are applied. The 4.0L engines are known to sometimes click, rattle, and knock due to faulty crankshaft main bearing shells or poor oil viscosity. The 3.0L 6-cylinder engines are also noted for producing an irregular clicking noise. There are some reports of water leaks through the doors and from the AC.

The 2000–07 models are plagued by airbag malfunctions; front-door and AC water leaks; automatic transmission failures; steering degradation when braking at slow speeds; cooling fan malfunctions, leading to engine overheating and fires; and a manual transmission that's hard to shift into Second gear, pops out of gear, and grinds when shifting.

VEHICLE HISTORY: 2004—Redesigned with new styling, new features, and a more-powerful V8. The 545i 6-speed is given a sport suspension teamed with run-flat tires, plus Active Steering and Active Roll Stabilization. All models still come with BMW's controversial iDrive console joystick. Critics say that the iDrive takes a University of Waterloo degree in engineering to operate, plus it's a distraction that's a safety hazard. The 545i and 545i 6-speed models use a 4.4L V8 with 325 hp, up from 290 hp. The wagon is gone. **2005**—Coupes have a new sunroof, and coupes and convertibles get a standard tire-pressure monitor. **2006**—Return of wagons, a redesigned M5, and an overall power increase. **2007**—The sedans and wagons get a power increase and new "325" monikers. **2008**—New 6-cylinder engines and a slightly restyled exterior. **2009**—535i sedan is axed.

M Series

Launched in 1996 as a four-door model, the M3 is a high-performance vehicle originally equipped with a potent 240 hp 3.0L engine (later bumped up to 3.2L), a manual shifter, a firm suspension, and 17-inch tires.

VEHICLE HISTORY: 2002—M3 gets a new 6-speed sequential manual transmission. All models are given a modified aluminum suspension, wider 18-inch tires and wheels, a new limited-slip differential, and a refreshed interior. **2007**—The M3 is dropped for one year. **2008–09**—The new M3 is now available as a coupe, sedan, and convertible, and is powered by a 414 hp 4.0L V8. **2009**—M5 offers standard electronic damper control, cross-drilled brake rotors, an M power response button, retuned sport suspension, and upgraded speed-sensitive steering. **2010**—Arrival of a Gran Turismo high-performance model. The 2010 engine lineup consists of five engines: a 3.0L inline 6-cylinder in the 528i and 528i xDrive sedan; a 3.0L twin-turbocharged inline 6-cylinder in the 535i xDrive sedan and Touring wagon; a 4.8L V8 in the 550i sedan; a 4.4L twin-turbocharged V8 in the Gran Turismo; and a 5.0L V10 in the M5. All of the above models use a 6-speed manual transmission or optional 6-speed automatic, except for the M5 and Gran Turismo. The M5 uses a 6-speed manual or optional 7-speed sequential manual gearbox, while the Gran Turismo comes with an 8-speed automatic transmission.

Owning any M3-powered BMW is a breathtaking driving experience, but at too high a cost. Servicing must be done by the book, and it's expensive, as is maintenance on all BMWs (use dealers only as a last resort). Insurance premiums are way beyond what would normally be reasonable. Another serious problem is that M-car and Z-car reliability isn't very good; owners say most of the failures that have become legendary during the past decade are related to the fuel system (frequent stalling when decelerating), electrical and climate control systems, accessories (sound system, AC, etc.), premature brake and tire wear, and poor-quality fit and finish characterized by paint delamination and poor paint application. And don't forget that the 2001s and 2002s have a serious wallet-busting, life-endangering flaw: Their engine self-destructs and has been dubbed by owners "The Engine of Damocles."

Z Series

BMW's first sports car, the two-seater Z3, debuted in early 1996 and was based on the 3 Series platform. Its 138 hp 1.9L 4-banger is outclassed by the competition (such as the Porsche non-S Boxster, the Mercedes-Benz 3.2L V6 SLK, and the Honda S2000), and you have to get the revs up past 3000 rpm to get adequate passing torque. The $17,000 2004 Z4 3.0L, with its 6-cylinder engine, is an all-around better performer and offers more features at a reasonably low price.

Dynamic Stability Control, large 17-inch wheels, and Dunlop SP Sport performance tires don't enhance handling as much as BMW pretends they do: Get used to lots of steering corrections.

The Z4 is a more feature-laden convertible, equipped with an inline 6-cylinder engine and a standard manual softtop. It still carries a base 184 hp 2.5L engine coupled with a 5-speed manual transmission; the higher-end Z4 3.0i has a 225 hp 3.0L mated to a 6-speed manual gearbox. ABS, an anti-skid system, and run-flat tires (a dubious advantage, considering cost, failures, scarcity) are standard features.

VEHICLE HISTORY: 2003—Launch of the Z4, a longer, wider variant of the Z3. The Z8's last model year. **2006**—More power, restyled, and the addition of a new hatchback coupe. The new 215 hp 3.0i boosts horses by 31 on the base convertible. Debut of the 255 hp 3.0si convertible and coupe. **2009**—The two-seater now comes as a convertible with a power-retractable roof. The fixed-roof coupe is no more. The 3.0L 6-cylinder 30i has 255 horses and a manual 6-speed, though, an optional automatic is available. A turbocharged 35i augments power up to the 300 horsepower range, and offers an optional 7-speed automatic transmission. **2010**—The Z4 returns relatively unchanged.

Safety Summary

All models/years: Sudden acceleration. • Airbag malfunctions include the bag deploying inadvertently or failing to go off in an accident. • Seat belt doesn't retract properly. • Premature failure of the magnesium alloy control arms and steering damper. • Severe suspension hop when passing over small bumps. • Transmission pops out of gear. • Multiple electrical failures. • Inoperative door latches that will make you exit through the window (if you're lucky). **All models: 2001–02**—Cooling fan failure causes engine to overheat or a fire to ignite (see *www.roadfly.com/bmw*). *320:* **2002**—Distorted windshield. *323:* **2002**—Poor steering when braking at slow speeds. • In rainy weather, brakes stiffen as they are applied, leading to extended stopping distances. • Faulty sunroof. *325i:* Transmission failure within five days of purchase. • Electrical system fire. • Sunroof glass suddenly explodes (several incidents reported). • Doors lock without prior warning. **2005–06**—When parking in an indoor garage, one vehicle suddenly accelerated as the brakes failed. **2006**—When accelerating, car delays, then surges. • Fire ignited under the hood while one vehicle was underway. • Jammed door latch forces you to open the lock with the key from the outside:

> I was at the store when the car locks jammed. The only way to get into the car was by manually using the key. The key fob would not unlock the door. The real issue was that the only door that could be opened was the drivers side all the others were jammed shut.... This is a very common problem with this make. It['s] attributed to a faulty design. See thread...*www.e90post.com/forums/showthread.php?p=3080752....*

328i: **2007**—Sudden acceleration as the car was turning into a garage. • When accelerating to merge with freeway traffic, vehicle hesitates and then surges. • Steering wheel locked when vehicle was underway. • Cracked tie rod. • Chronic electrical short circuits make most gauges and controls go haywire. • Key sticks in the ignition. • A blown fuse could deactivate the electronic door latches and force occupants to exit through a broken window; automatic locks operate erratically. • Convertible roof tries to put itself in the trunk when the trunk is closed. • Windshield cracks easily. **2008**—Chronic stalling. One fix for the stalling is to replace the fuel pump and retune the engine. However, owners say this correction creates a "turbo lag" that wasn't there before. • Electric door locks operate erratically. • Driver was locked in his car; horn could not be activated to alert passersby. • Battery loses its charge if car isn't driven frequently on trips of more than 5 km. Fog light short circuit led to a front-end fire. **2009**—More complaints of chronic stalling, run-flat tire defects, and sudden, unintended acceleration. • Owners claim Bridgestone Turanza tires are cupping so badly that the car is dangerous to drive. One owner says there is ample legal precedent to force BMW and Bridgestone to take back these defective tires:

> The BMW Bridgestone run flat tire RFT class action lawsuit reportedly concerns BMW 2006 and 2007 3 series vehicles originally equipped with Bridgestone Turanza EL42 RFT 205/55R16 or 225/45R17 run-flat tires. The lawsuit (*Chandran v. BMW of North America, LLC*, et al., Case No. 2:08-CV-02619-KSH-PS) reportedly alleges that defendants should have known that the tires were defective and prone to excessive noise and/or irregular wear, resulting in the tires needing frequent replacement and causing the vehicles to ride roughly.

330i, 330Ci: **2002**—Side airbag deploys when vehicle hits a pothole. • Vehicle overheats in low gear; tires lose air. • Vehicle slips out of Second gear when accelerating. **2003**—Chronic stalling, rough idle. • Transmission slipping. **2004**—Airbags fail to deploy. • Constant stalling • Engine bearing failures:

> The issue is the dual VANOS unit they put into the M54 engine using [D]elrin bushings and they are failing. There is a company called Dr. Vanos that fixes this issue by rebuilding the OEM VANOS with upgraded bushings. This unit cost $500.

Automatic transmission failure. • After a cold start, transmission delays going into gear for up to 30 seconds. • Distorted windshields. • Door locks operate erratically. **2005**—More delayed gear shifts. **2006**—Water enters through the door sills and causes the doors to freeze shut. *525i:* **2006–07**—Loss of engine power. • Valve lash adjuster noise. • Oil leak from the right-hand side of the engine crankcase. • Intermittent engine vibration, drone at idle. • Automatic transmission won't go into Drive or Reverse. • AC poor performance at start up or when idling. • AC stops cooling after a long drive. • Sunroof wind noises and water leaks. • Steering column noises. • Halogen low-beam headlight failure. • Electrical issues due to water intrusion. • Rear door locking issues and diagnostics. *528i:* **2008–09**—Loss of engine power.

Secret Warranties/Internal Bulletins/Service Tips

All models: Many of the service bulletins listed in this BMW section apply to other cars in the BMW lineup. If you want to check if there is an overlap that includes your car, ask a BMW dealer. If that doesn't work, go to *www.safercar.gov* and look up the service bulletins applicable to your car. As a last resort, pay $26.95 (U.S.) to Alldata (*www.alldatadiy.com/buy/index.html*) to get a digital copy of every bulletin applicable to your vehicle. *3 Series:* **2002**—Incorrect fuel gauge readings. • Rattling, tapping engine noise. • Troubleshooting navigation system malfunctions. • No 1–2 upshifts. **2003**—Harsh 3–2 and 2–1 downshifts. **2004**—Delayed Park–Drive shift. • Numerous malfunctions of telematics components. **2005–06**—Reduced engine power. **2008**—Instrument cluster displays go blank. • Intermittent engine valve lash adjuster noise. **2008–09**—Water leaks into footwell area. **2009**—Airbag warning light stays on. • No start, or reduced engine power. • Poor AC performance. • Rattling noise from the radio area. • No Reverse or Forward gear. • An oil leak at the right-hand side of the V6 engine crankcase may require that the crankcase be replaced. • Excessive engine vibration. • Silencing brake squeak and squeal. • No start, or false fuel reading. • Steering column noises. • Front suspension creaking and groaning. *5 Series:* All years: Water inside of headlight. • Erratic performance of the navigation system. *525i:* **2006–07**—Troubleshooting AC compressor noise. *528i:* **2007–09**—Automatic transmission jolt or delay when accelerating from a stop. **2009**—Reduced engine power. • Automatic transmission jumps out of Drive or Reverse into Neutral (requires a software adjustment). • Troubleshooting front seat noise. • Front brake squeak or squeal upon light brake application. • An oil leak at the right-hand side of the V6 engine crankcase may require that the crankcase be replaced. • Intermittent engine valve lash adjuster noise. • Exhaust system vibration or drone at idle. • Poor AC performance. • Steering column noises. *530i:* **2005–07**—Front brake squeak or squeal upon light brake application. • Sunroof wind noise and water leaks.

3 SERIES, M SERIES, Z SERIES PROFILE

	2002	2003	2004	2005	2006	2007	2008	2009	2010
Cost Price ($)									
320i 4d	34,900	34,950	34,950	—	—	—	—	—	—
323i 4d	—	—	—	—	35,200	35,600	35,900	34,900	34,800
325i, 328i	37,950	41,200	39,300	39,450	39,900	41,000	41,000	39,900	41,300
Convertible	52,500	52,800	53,400	54,400	55,800	56,300	56,600	56,600	56,700
330Ci Convertible	62,800	62,900	63,500	63,950	64,400	—	—	—	—
335Ci Convertible	—	—	—	—	—	66,300	66,600	65,600	69,300
550i	—	—	—	—	78,600	78,600	82,900	80,400	80,300
M/M3 2d	69,800	73,500	73,800	73,950	68,900	68,900	68,900	69,900	69,800
M Performance	—	—	—	54,300	54,200	—	—	—	—
M5 4d	104,250	105,500	105,500	—	115,500	113,300	113,300	106,900	106,800
M6 2d Coupe	—	—	—	—	130,500	130,500	128,300	121,300	121,200
M6 2d Convertible	—	—	—	—	—	140,500	138,300	131,300	131,200
Z3 1.9L/2.3L	46,900	—	—	—	—	—	—	—	—
Z3 2.8L	56,200	—	—	—	—	—	—	—	—
Z4 2.5L	—	51,500	51,800	51,900	—	—	—	—	—
Z4 3.0L	—	59,500	59,900	59,900	53,900	53,900	55,400	53,900	54,100
Z8	190,000	195,000	195,000	—	—	—	—	—	—
Used Values ($)									
320i 4d ▲	6,500	8,000	9,500	—	—	—	—	—	—
320i 4d ▼	6,000	7,000	8,500	—	—	—	—	—	—
323i 4d ▲	—	—	—	—	11,000	15,000	16,500	22,000	26,000
323i 4d ▼	—	—	—	—	9,500	14,000	15,500	20,500	24,000
325i, 328i ▲	8,000	9,000	10,500	11,500	12,500	16,500	20,500	26,000	30,000
325i, 328i ▼	6,500	8,500	10,000	11,000	11,500	15,000	19,000	24,000	28,000
Convertible ▲	12,000	13,500	15,000	17,000	19,000	23,000	29,500	35,000	42,000
Convertible ▼	10,500	12,000	13,500	16,000	17,500	21,500	28,000	33,000	40,000
330Ci Convertible ▲	13,500	15,000	17,000	18,500	20,000	—	—	—	—
330Ci Convertible ▼	12,500	14,000	15,500	17,500	18,500	—	—	—	—
335Ci Convertible ▲	—	—	—	—	—	25,500	33,500	41,500	52,000
335Ci Convertible ▼	—	—	—	—	—	24,000	32,000	39,500	49,000
550i ▲	—	—	—	—	18,000	26,000	36,000	47,000	55,000
550i ▼	—	—	—	—	16,500	23,500	34,000	44,000	52,000
M/M3 2d ▲	11,000	13,500	15,000	17,000	19,500	25,000	36,000	44,000	53,000
M/M3 2d ▼	9,500	12,000	14,000	16,000	17,500	23,500	34,500	42,000	50,000
M Performance ▲	—	—	—	17,500	18,500	—	—	—	—
M Performance ▼	—	—	—	16,500	18,000	—	—	—	—
M5 4d ▲	15,000	17,500	20,000	—	25,000	35,000	48,000	63,000	77,000
M5 4d ▼	14,000	16,500	18,000	—	24,000	32,000	45,000	60,000	72,000
Z3 1.9L/2.3L ▲	15,000	—	—	—	—	—	—	—	—
Z3 1.9L/2.3L ▼	13,500	—	—	—	—	—	—	—	—
Z3 2.8L ▲	16,000	—	—	—	—	—	—	—	—
Z3 2.8L ▼	14,500	—	—	—	—	—	—	—	—

Z4 2.5L ▲	—	14,000	16,000	—	—	—	—	—	—
Z4 2.5L ▼	—	13,000	15,000	—	—	—	—	—	—
Z4 3.0L ▲	—	16,000	17,000	18,000	19,500	24,500	29,000	34,000	41,000
Z4 3.0L ▼	—	15,000	16,000	17,000	18,500	23,000	27,000	32,500	39,000
Z8 ▲	100,000	135,000	—	—	—	—	—	—	—
Z8 ▼	90,000	130,000	—	—	—	—	—	—	—

Reliability	4	4	4	4	4	4	4	4	4
Crash Safety (F)	4	4	4	4	4	4	4	4	4
Side	3	3	3	3	5	5	5	5	5
IIHS Side	—	—	—	—	5	5	5	5	5
Offset	5	5	5	5	5	5	5	5	5
Head Restraints	1	1	1	1	—	3	3	5	5
M3	2	2	2	—	—	—	—	—	—
Convertible	—	—	—	—	—	1	1	—	—
Roof Strength	—	—	—	—	3	3	3	3	3
Rollover Resistance	4	4	4	4	4	4	4	4	5

Note: The huge price difference between entry-level models and their top-of-the-line variations narrows to almost nothing after seven years. An exception is the Z8. Although rare in Canada, it is easily found in the States and priced much less than what it would cost in Canada.

5 SERIES PROFILE

	2002	2003	2004	2005	2006	2007	2008	2009	2010
Cost Price ($)									
525i, 528i, 530i	55,200	55,500	66,500	66,500	58,600	58,600	59,900	56,200	56,100
Used Values ($)									
525i, 528i, 530i ▲	7,000	9,000	11,000	13,500	16,000	21,000	29,000	34,000	40,000
525i, 528i, 530i ▼	6,500	8,000	10,000	12,500	14,500	19,000	27,000	31,000	37,000
Reliability	5	5	4	4	4	4	4	4	4
Crash Safety									
Frontal (NHTSA)	—	—	—	—	—	—	3	3	3
Side	—	—	—	—	—	—	5	5	5
Offset	5	5	5	5	5	5	5	5	5
Side (IIHS)	—	—	—	—	—	—	2	2	2
Head Restraints (F)	—	—	1	1	1	1	5	5	5
Rollover Resistance	—	—	—	—	—	—	4	4	4

All ratings on a numbered scale where 5 is good and **1** is bad. See page 132 for a more detailed description.

General Motors

CTS, CTS-V, DEVILLE, DTS, STS, STS-V

★★✦/★★

RATING: Below Average (1999–2010). *DeVille:* Average (2001–05). These cars (except for the DeVille) put the "lack" in Cadillac. **Ideal model year:** A 2005 DeVille for about $7,500. **"Real" city/highway fuel economy:** 13.3/8.2 L/100 km. **Maintenance/repair costs:** Higher than average; repairs are very dealer-dependent. **Parts:** Higher-than-average costs, and parts are hard to find. **Extended warranty:** Your best protection is to not buy a Cadillac in the first place. For those who do, an extended powertrain warranty is the most cost-effective protection. **Best alternatives:** Acura RL or TL, Hyundai Genesis, and Infiniti G35. **Helpful websites:** *www.cadillacforums.com/forums/forum.php.*

Strengths and Weaknesses

ALERT! Another reason to take an STS for a lengthy test drive: at times 2005–08 models can turn into mobile "whoopee" cushions. For fun, get a large cup of coffee and Google "Cadillac STS farting." You will enjoy the owner tirades and Caddy mechanic comments, like this one:

> The cam that drives the recirculation door is tight and it causes a noise on the actuator arm. You have to remove the glove box to reach the actuator. The first one I did I removed the whole blower assembly to locate the noise, the next one I just lubricated. It's easy once you get the glove box out. You just have to lubricate the pin of the actuator where it goes into the cam and the noise will stop after a few cycles.

CTS

Cadillac's entry-level CTS replaced the Catera in 2003 and has quickly distinguished itself as a particularly unreliable, heavy rear-drive luxury car that purports to perform like a European sports sedan. Its extra weight destroys any pretense of fuel economy, with an estimated city/highway rating of only 13.4/7.8 L/100 km. Suggested alternatives are the Acura TL, Infiniti G35, and Lincoln Town Car.

The CTS's problematic powertrain has constantly evolved during its few years on the market because it was never made right in the first place. First-year models offered only a puny 220 hp 3.2L V6 coupled to a standard 5-speed manual gearbox or an optional 5-speed automatic transmission. The smoother and more-powerful 255 hp 3.6L V6 engine and automatic transmission powers the 2004 models. That same year, the 2004 CTS-V was launched, carrying a Corvette-derived 400 hp 5.7L V8 that is even *more* unreliable than the V6. The 2005 CTS changed over to a 2.8L V6 with 10 fewer horses and a better-performing 6-speed manual gearbox. 2006 models were given revised sport/performances packages.

Nevertheless, the above-noted powertrain changes haven't improved differential reliability, which has been a chronic problem since the CTS was launched:

> The Cadillac CTS-V rear differential is weak and may break causing this car to skid or suddenly stop, causing an accident, injury, or death. Cadillac knows of the problem and has provided some customers with warranty repair, offered 100,000 mile [160,000 km] extended warranties for others and yet denied repair for customers with similar problems. This rear differential is under rated for this car's horse power and was designed for use in the standard CTS version of this car. The rear tires have also been a problem showing early signs of wear. I had to replace my first set [of] front and rear [tires] at 8,500 miles [13,500 km]. These tires are [the] worst rated tire by consumers at *www.tirerack.com* and *www.cadillacfaq.com*.

Other problems include stability control and ABS failures; constant rear-end whine (a warning that total failure is just around the corner); early replacement of the fuel/water pump, radiator, and power windows; electrical system shorts causing lights, gauges, instruments, and power seats to malfunction; and poor fit and finish, highlighted by loud wind noise from the windshield, clunks and rattles, paint blistering and premature corrosion, and door handle, dash, and radio button plastic peeling.

Although they have better handling and are almost as comfortable as older, traditional Caddies, these front-drive luxury coupes and sedans aren't worth considering because of their dismal reliability, overly complex servicing, and dependence on parts that are impossible to find and not very durable.

The 4.3L V6, 4.1L V8, and 4.5L V8 engines and 4-speed automatic transmission suffer from a variety of terminal maladies, including oil leaks, premature wear, poor fuel economy, and excessive noise. The electrical system and related components are temperamental. Steering is noisy, the suspension goes soft quickly, and the front brakes often wear out after only 18 months/20,000 km. Problems with the digital fuel injection and engine control systems are very difficult to diagnose and repair. Premature paint peeling and rusting, excessive wind noise in the interior, and fragile trim items characterize poor body assembly.

DTS

Cadillac's front-drive DTS uses two versions of a 4.6L V8, coupled to a 4-speed automatic transmission. Its 275 horsepower can be increased to 292 with the right options or simply by purchasing the Platinum package. The DTS targets premium full-size sedans like the Buick Lucerne, Lexus LS 430, and Lincoln Town Car (Lexus and Lincoln are the better choices). Every DTS includes anti-lock braking, traction control, front torso side airbags, and head-protecting side curtain airbags. The 2006 to 2010 models have changed little.

Cadillac continued its not-so-proud history of making luxury lemons with the advent of the DTS. Owners decry hard starts and no-starts; excessive Continental

Tire noise; a key that sticks in the ignition; a gas tank cap that's difficult to open; a plastic undercarriage cover that drags on the ground; a Stability-Control Service light that remains lit; the failure of the Collision Avoidance feature's sensors; a knocking, clicking sound that comes from the steering assembly; a driver-side mirror that fails to correct for a blind spot; and distracting (to other drivers) "strobe" LED tail lights.

STS

Whopping depreciation aside, this rear-drive/AWD Seville replacement has plenty of power and versatility. The V6 engine is more powerful than the BMW 5 Series' and Mercedes E-Class's 6-cylinders, while the V8 produces slightly less horsepower than the comparable BMW but more than the Mercedes or Lexus. The 4.4L V8 STS-V was dropped for 2010.

Without question, Cadillac's switch to rear-drive or all-wheel drive considerably improves the STS's balance, handling, and overall performance. Shoppers will have to decide if the car's elegant interior and vastly superior performance make up for the loss of a little rear seatroom (it still has at least a couple centimetres more than its closest competitors, and for its unproven mechanical components, mediocre fit and finish, and untested crashworthiness.

Although complaints relative to STS reliability have been fewer than average, owners do report a number of serious safety-related failures. For example, the passenger-side airbag sensor fails to detect if the seat is occupied, and leaves the system disabled. Acceleration is erratic, the car suddenly loses power when passing another vehicle, the rear differential may suddenly lock up, and the car has poor traction in snow.

Owners report that eye-watering, throat-burning emissions emanate from the interior, principally the trunk area; the sunroof may blow out from excessive interior air pressure; the voice recognition feature executes different commands than what it is given, and prior commands can't be countermanded; the wiring harness and module under the front seat may melt; and electrical shorts play havoc with lights, gauges, and accessory systems. There have also been many complaints that the differential leaks fluid, brake pads quickly wear out and brake rotors warp prematurely, the air dam shield falls down and drags on the pavement, windshields shatter for no reason, headlights have stress cracks, and the battery dies if the car isn't started for several days.

Safety Summary

All models/years—Sudden, unintended acceleration; in one incident, vehicle suddenly accelerated, killing one person and injuring others. • Inadvertent airbag deployment, or airbags fail to deploy:

> It was December. I was 5 months pregnant. I was sitting in my 2003 Cadillac CTS warming up the car and putting eyeliner on. All of a sudden boom airbags went off first the steering wheel then driver door it made marks on my face and neck.

Excessive vibration and chronic stalling while underway:

> While traveling at moderate speed vehicle began shaking violently and losing power. The engine was missing on one or more cylinders. This seems to have been caused by a defect mentioned in TSB ID # 1609265 dated 2005. This TSB states that the crankcase vapors and engine oil will vent through the cam/valve cover seals when the crankcase ventilation system becomes blocked. The oil on this vehicle evidently vented and leaked several places including into the ignition coils causing a short.

Leaking engine oil coolant. • Wheels fall off. • Total brake failure:

> I was turning into a parking lot at a slow speed when the brakes did not engage. We took the car directly to the dealership. They recommended that we replace the tires (which we did) and then recommended that we replace the left front wheel bearing/speed sensor/hub again for the 5th time.

Many complaints of front and rear brake rotor warpage and premature pad and caliper failure. • Sudden loss of power steering, or excessive steering vibration. • Vehicle tends to wander all over the road. • Can't read speedometer in daylight. • Sun visor obstructs visibility. • Gas-tank sensor failure causes inaccurate fuel readings. • Interior lights frequently malfunction. *CTS: 2003*—Engine serpentine belt and coil failures. • Badly corroded fuel and brake line, hoses, and fittings. • When the stability control system engages, it suddenly pulls the car to the left. • Rear brake lights and plate cover fall off ($550 to replace). • Brake lights frequently burn out. • Trunk lid continually slams down. **2004**—Lower front ball joint separates from the control arm. • Transmission cooling line broke away from the radiator. **2005**—Many complaints of a rear differential axle shaft seal failure not covered by warranty. • Rear windshield suddenly shattered. **2006**—Airbag warning light is constantly lit (not part of the airbag sensor recall). • Defective middle rear brake light. • ABS light comes on and car won't brake while turning at slow speeds. • Engine timing chain breaks at 66,000 km, requiring an $8,500 3.6L V6 engine replacement. • Rear differential axle shaft seal failures continue (not covered by previous recall). **2007**—Passenger-side airbag is disabled even though an average-sized occupant is seated (not part of a previous recall). • Sudden tie rod breakage while vehicle was on the highway. • Ball joint fractured, causing the front driver's side of the vehicle to collapse. • Door latches freeze and door will swing open. **2008**—Rear window suddenly shattered. • Broken driver's seat frame: $800 to repair. • Driver's side mirror creeps upwards. • Electronic key sometimes fails to lock the vehicle. • Gas and brake pedals are mounted too close together. • Water leaks into the interior. **2009**—Key could not be removed from the ignition. • Owners feel the heater washer recall is unfair because it offers owners only $100 and disables the system. • Water leaks into the interior (a sunroof problem?). *DeVille: 2002*—Seat belts are too short for some occupants.

2003—Chronic stalling caused by electrical failure. • Instrument panel shuts down. **2004**—Vehicle caught fire while parked. • Early tie rod replacement. • Hood latch isn't secured tightly. **2005**—Headlights shut off when turning signals are enabled. • Tail lights have a "strobe effect" that blurs drivers' vision in following cars. • Door won't stay open when the car is parked on an incline. • Lengthy delay when transmission is shifted into Reverse. *DTS:* **2006**—Adaptive cruise control operates abnormally. • Cruise control fails to maintain speed when going downhill. • Steering suddenly pulls the vehicle to one side. • Total failure of the lower control arm sent the car careening out of control. • Sun reflects off the clock into driver's eyes. **2007**—Wind can blow doors shut on occupants' legs. • Many reports that the driver's right foot gets stuck between the gas pedal and the centre console. • Twilight sensors come on too early and go off too late (see *www.cadillacforums. com/forums/cadillac-forum/t-92975.html*). • Centre door post and driver-seat head restraint block the driver's view when turning or looking rearward. • Sun visor falls down on its own; fails to block the sunlight. *STS:* **2006**—Passenger-side airbag is disabled even though a 100 lb. adult is seated. • Seat bezel breaks constantly.

Secret Warranties/Internal Bulletins/Service Tips

All models/years: Reverse servo cover seal leak. • Paint delamination, peeling, or fading. **All models: 1996–2003**—Excessive oil consumption can be corrected with new piston rings if a ring-cleaning process doesn't work (TSB #02-06-01-009C). *CTS:* **2003–07**—Remedy for a front seat cushion that pops, creaks, and moves sideways on turns. **2003–12**—Drivetrain chatter or rear axle clunk: Replace the rear differential fluid. **2005–11**—Loss of engine power may be caused by water intrusion into the instrument panel (TSB #07-06-04-019D).

2008–09—Clunk noise while turning, or automatic transmission extension housing leaks. • Front brakes squeal when braking. GM suggests owners replace the brake pads with Kit #PN 25958115). Owners should ask for a partial reimbursement. • Front seat lateral movement, clunking. • Front door window drops incrementally. • Rear door windows may go down by themselves. • Front door latch freezing "Customer Satisfaction" policy: At no charge, dealers are to seal the latch housing on both front doors to prevent water intrusion:

CAMPAIGN—FRONT DOOR LATCH FREEZING

BULLETIN NO.: 09104A   DATE: JANUARY 5, 2010

2008–09 Cadillac CTS; 2009 Cadillac CTS-V. Condition: Certain 2008 and 2009 model year Cadillac CTS vehicles and 2009 model year Cadillac CTS-V vehicles registered in Canada, may have a condition where water may enter the front door latch housing and potentially freeze. If water enters the latch housing and freezes, the customer may not be able to open the front doors using the outside door handle, or the door may not latch when the door is closed. If the door does not latch, the interior lamps will illuminate, a message will display on the driver information center warning that the door is not closed, and a chime will sound for 4 seconds.

2008–10—Front door window is slow or noisy when activated. 2008–11—Noise heard when shifting between Reverse and Drive. • Inoperative low-beam headlights. *DeVille:* 2000–02—Loss of power when accelerating. • 1–2 shift concerns. 2000–04—Remedies for excessive vibration, shaking while cruising. • Troubleshooting rear suspension noise. 2000–05—Silencing a front-end clunk. • Hood blistering, premature corrosion. 2001–05—Harsh upshifts. 2003—Intermittent no-starts; no electrical power (align engine wiring junction block, says TSB #06-03-009). • Erratic transmission shifting. 2003–04—Right rear-door air leak. 2005—Difficult to move shifter out of Park. *DTS:* 2006–07—Automatic transmission slips, overheats, or won't shift. • Inoperative power seats. • Brake pulsation when travelling down steep grades (get improved brake pads). *STS:* 2005–07—Front or rear axle pinion seal leak. • Torque converter clutch surge, shudder, exhaust moan, and chuggle. • Inaccurate fuel gauge. 2005–11—Remedy for a front seat cushion that pops, creaks, and moves sideways on turns. • Drivetrain chatter or rear axle clunk can be silenced simply by replacing the rear differential fluid. 2007–08—Sunroof rattling.

CTS, CTS-V, DEVILLE, DTS, STS, STS-V PROFILE

	2002	2003	2004	2005	2006	2007	2008	2009	2010
Cost Price ($)									
CTS	—	39,900	39,200	37,800	35,555	35,780	38,900	40,485	40,650
CTS-V	—	—	70,000	70,700	68,755	70,670	—	68,995	72,045
DeVille	52,555	54,925	56,235	57,050	—	—	—	—	—
DTS	—	—	—	—	52,680	52,935	53,415	55,590	55,535
Platinum	—	—	—	—	—	—	—	—	74,675
STS V6	—	—	—	—	56,600	57,750	57,910	60,920	61,085
STS V8	—	—	—	—	69,470	71,275	68,880	70,230	70,395
STS-V	—	—	—	—	97,995	98,265	102,955	105,075	—
Used Values ($)									
CTS ▲	—	5,500	7,500	9,000	10,500	13,000	16,500	21,500	25,000
CTS ▼	—	5,000	6,500	8,000	9,000	11,500	15,000	20,000	23,500
CTS-V ▲	—	9,000	10,500	12,000	13,500	16,000	—	34,000	42,000
CTS-V ▼	—	8,000	9,500	11,000	12,500	15,000	—	32,000	40,000
DeVille ▲	4,500	5,500	7,000	8,500	—	—	—	—	—
DeVille ▼	3,500	4,500	6,000	7,500	—	—	—	—	—
DTS ▲	—	—	—	—	12,000	15,000	18,500	24,000	30,500
DTS ▼	—	—	—	—	10,500	13,500	17,000	22,000	28,500
Platinum	—	—	—	—	—	—	—	—	40,000
Platinum	—	—	—	—	—	—	—	—	37,000
STS V6 ▲	—	—	—	—	12,500	16,000	20,500	25,500	33,000
STS V6 ▼	—	—	—	—	11,000	14,500	19,000	24,000	31,000
STS V8 ▲	—	—	—	—	14,000	17,500	24,000	33,000	41,000
STS V8 ▼	—	—	—	—	12,500	16,000	23,000	31,000	39,000
STS-V ▲	—	—	—	—	16,000	19,000	31,500	49,000	—
STS-V ▼	—	—	—	—	14,500	17,500	30,000	47,000	—

Reliability	1	1	1	1	1	1	1	1	1
Crash Safety (F)									
CTS	—	4	4	4	4	4	4	4	4
DeVille	1	1	4	4	—	—	—	—	—
DTS	—	—	—	—	5	5	5	5	5
STS	—	—	—	—	—	4	4	4	4
Side									
CTS	—	4	4	4	4	4	5	5	5
DeVille	4	4	4	4	—	—	—	—	—
DTS	—	—	—	—	4	4	4	4	4
STS	—	—	—	—	—	4	5	4	4
IIHS Side									
CTS	—	—	—	—	—	—	5	5	5
DTS	—	—	—	—	3	3	3	3	3
STS	—	—	—	—	—	3	3	3	3
Offset									
CTS	—	5	5	5	5	5	5	5	5
DTS	—	—	—	—	5	5	5	5	5
STS	—	—	—	5	5	5	5	5	5
Head Restraints									
CTS	—	1	1	1	1	1	5	5	5
DTS	—	—	—	—	1	1	2	2	2
STS	—	—	—	1	1	1	1	1	1
Rollover Resistance									
CTS	4	4	4	4	4	4	4	4	4
DeVille	5	5	5	5	—	—	—	—	—
DTS	—	—	—	—	4	4	4	4	4
STS	—	—	—	—	—	5	5	5	5

Note: New Cadillacs that are far apart in their prices have almost equal worth after a few years. For example: A 2007 STS V6 sold originally for $57,750, while the V8 version went for $71,275. Today, a 2007 V6 sells for about $15,000. The V8? It will cost you about $1,500 more.

Infiniti

G20, G35, G37, I30, I35, M35, M45, Q45   ★/★★★/★★★★/★★★★

RATING: *G20*: Not Recommended (1999–2002). *G35*: Recommended (2007–08); Below Average (2003–06). *G37*: Recommended (2009–10); Above Average (2008). *I30*: Above Average (2000–03). *I35*: Average (2002–04). *M35, M45*: Above Average (2006–07); Average (2003–05). *Q45*: Average (2002–05); Below Average (1997–2001). **Ideal model year:** If you want the performance thrills for a lot less money and only 20-some fewer horses than the higher-priced G37, opt for a 2008

G35 sedan. It costs about $16,000, which is pretty good for a car that sold new for $40,000. Sure, the 2009 G37s have 7-speed automatic trannies and 6-speed manual gearboxes, but you will pay lots more for powertrains that haven't yet been time-tested, especially in the AWD versions. Plus, there are more G35s on the market. **"Real" city/highway fuel economy:** *G20:* 10.0/6.9 L/100 km. *G35 coupe:* 10.0/6.9 L/100 km. *G35 sedan:* 12.2/8.4 L/100 km. *G35 AWD:* 12.6/8.6 L/100 km. *G37 coupe:* 11.7/7.6 L/100 km. *G37 convertible:* 12.0/7.8 L/100 km. *I30 3.0:* 12.1/8.1 L/100 km. *I35:* 12.1/8.3 L/100 km. *Q45 4.1:* 13.4/9.2 L/100 km. *Q45 4.5:* 13.6/8.8 L/100 km. **Maintenance/repair costs:** Higher-than-average costs, and repairs must be done by either an Infiniti or a Nissan dealer, especially for the higher-end models that have been off the market for a few years. **Parts:** Higher-than-average costs, and hard to find:

> They found the problem...but told me that it couldn't be repaired and that the part wasn't sold separately. Instead the entire headlight assembly needed to be replaced with the light assembly costing $1,500.00 and with taxes and labour the cost would exceed $1,800.00.

Extended warranty: Not necessary. **Best alternatives:** A fully equipped Honda Accord is a better buy from a price and quality standpoint, but Accords don't have the same luxury cachet. Also consider the Acura RL or TL and the Hyundai Genesis. **Helpful websites:** *www.nicoclub.com/infiniti-technical-articles* and *http://forums.nicoclub.com*.

Strengths and Weaknesses

ALERT! Infinitis are known for excessive steering wander and tramlining (the tendency of a vehicle's wheels to follow the contours in the road surface) whenever it passes over ruts in the road. Before buying any Infiniti, take it for an extended road test.

With its emphasis on sporty handling (diluted somewhat with the '97 and later model years), the Infiniti series takes the opposite tack from the Lexus, which focuses on comfort and luxury. Infiniti models do come fully equipped and offer owners the prestige of driving a comfortable and nicely styled luxury car, but the lineup isn't as refined or as reliable as the Toyota competition.

G20

The least expensive Infiniti, 1999 and later G20s aren't as refined as their entry-level Lexus counterparts in interior space, drivetrain, or convenience features. The 140 hp engine's lack of low-speed torque means that it has to work hard above 4,000 rpm—while protesting noisily. The automatic transmission shifts roughly, particularly when passing; the power steering needs more assist during parking manoeuvres; and the dealer-installed fog lights cost an exorbitant $500 to replace. Tall drivers will find the legroom insufficient, and rear passengers will feel cramped. Trunk space is limited by the angle of the rear window.

Owner complaints target automatic transmission failures, engine coolant leaks, prematurely worn brake rotors and brake pads, excessive noise when braking, malfunctioning power seats, and clunky springs and shock absorbers.

G35

Infiniti's rear-drive, sporty luxury car was introduced in the spring of 2002. The sedan is equipped with a 260 hp engine, versus 280 hp for the coupe. Coupes are feature-laden, stretched versions of Nissan's problem-prone 2003 350Z sports car, with less power and a small fold-down back seat added. Sedans are quite long and provide sportier performance than Infiniti's front-drive I35 does. Initially, both G35s offered a 5-speed automatic transmission with manual shiftgate, but a 6-speed manual was phased in within a year. Both body styles offer four-wheel ABS disc brakes, front side airbags, and side curtain airbags (only for the front seats in the coupe). Manual transmission coupes come with more performance-oriented upgraded brakes. Alternative choices would be the Acura TL and BMW 3 Series. Owner complaints primarily concern chronic engine noise, excessive brake squealing, very poor fuel economy, a noisy manual 6-speed transmission, automatic transmission failures and erratic shifting, metal flakes in the paint (bird droppings will eat through the finish), early replacement of brake pads and rotors ($600), and excessive engine oil consumption requiring a rebuilt engine. The low-tire-pressure monitoring system must be reprogrammed by the dealer if wheels are rotated or a full-size spare tire is installed.

G37

While leaving the 2008 G35 unchanged, Infiniti launched a G37 coupe, equipped with a 330 hp 3.7L V6. In 2009 all Infiniti "G" cars became G37s equipped with the 3.7L powerplant coupled to a 6-speed manual, or a 7-speed automatic transmission. An AWD option and convertible, with a retractable hard top, were added to the lineup.

VEHICLE HISTORY: 2004—Debut of an all-wheel-drive sedan with Snow Mode that provides a 50/50 front/rear torque split. The base sedan gets 17-inch wheels; manual-shift coupes receive upgraded brakes and 18-inch wheels; the sedan variant gets a limited-slip differential. **2005**—Automatic transmission–equipped sedans share the coupe's 280 hp V6, while manual-equipped models have 18 more horses (298 hp). The all-wheel-drive G35x comes with an automatic transmission only. Models using a manual tranny use a standard limited-slip differential and sport suspension. **2007**—Sedan gets a bit more power and new styling, while the coupe stands pat. **2008**—Debut of the G37 Coupe. **2009**—All "G-cars" are now G37s. They have upgraded transmissions, a bit more horsepower, and an AWD option. **2010**—A slight restyling and upgraded seats.

I30/I35

Introduced as an early '96 model, the I30 is a sport sedan spin-off of the Nissan Maxima with additional sound-deadening material and a plusher interior. The car's interior is also roomier, but its ride is unimpressive and handling is compromised by excessive body lean when cornering. Engine and road noises are omnipresent. The redesigned 2000 model adds rear seatroom and reduces body lean considerably. I35s have a quieter and better-performing engine, a much improved ride, and more responsive handling.

VEHICLE HISTORY: 2002—Renamed the I35 and given a larger V6 engine, new styling, and more standard features.

The more-recently minted I35 models elicited more performance-related complaints than the earlier I30, which was no paragon of quality control. I30 owners report chronic suspension failures, drivetrain vibration and clunking, faulty steering, and defective transverse links, springs, and struts. I35s are known for vibration, loose steering, drivetrain noise, rattling noises, electrical shorts, excessive front-end play, incorrect fuel gauge readings, inoperative seat memory buttons, and hesitation and surging when accelerating.

Q45

Faster and glitzier than other cars in its category, this luxury sedan provides performance, while its chief rival, the Lexus LS 400, provides luxury and quiet. Up to the '96 model, the Q45 used a 32-valve 278 hp 4.5L V8 tire-burner not frequently found on a Japanese luxury compact. It accelerates faster than the Lexus, going 0–100 km/h in 7.1 seconds without a hint of noise or abrupt shifting. Unlike the base engine of the G20, though, the Q45's engine supplies plenty of upper-range torque as well. That potent powerhouse was dropped with the less-than-dazzling 1997–2001 models' 266 hp 4.1L V8. High-performance power was rediscovered, however, when the 2002–06 models returned to a more-powerful 340 hp 4.5L V8. The suspension was softened in 1994, but the car still rides much more firmly than its Lexus counterpart. The four-wheel steering is precise, but the standard limited-slip differential is no help in preventing the car's rear end from sliding out on slippery roads, mainly because of the original-equipment "sport" tires, which were designed for 190 km/h autobahn cruising. ABS is standard. There's not much footroom for passengers, and cargo room is disappointing. Fuel economy is nonexistent.

VEHICLE HISTORY: 2002—A new 4.5L V8 produces 340 hp (up from 266 hp). The transmission is a 5-speed automatic with a manual shift mode. High-end electronics are standard, including traction control, Vehicle Dynamic Control, Electronic Brake Force Distribution, tire-pressure monitors, and high-intensity xenon headlights. **2003**—A rear-axle upgrade for faster and smoother acceleration. **2004**—A rear-view camera. **2005**—A minor facelift and a recalibrated transmission for smoother shifts.

The Q45 has been exceptionally reliable throughout its model run, despite some reports of electronic computer module malfunctions and crashes, premature AC failures, power-steering problems, excessive wind noise around the A-pillars, sunroof wind leaks, and tire thumping. Paint is easily scratched and flakes off. Now that the car has been off the market for seven years, parts are harder to find and independent repairers are reluctant to fool with the electronics, hence its Average rating.

M35, M45

The 2003 M45 replaced the I30/I35 as Infiniti's mid-size, rear-drive luxury car. Powered by a 340 hp V8 engine and coupled to a 5-speed automatic transmission, the first three model years sold poorly primarily due to the car's bland design and cramped interior. The redesigned 2006 and 2007 models offer more interior room and high-tech features, like four-wheel steering, upgraded brakes, a performance-tuned suspension/transmission, and a V8 with more pep despite 15 fewer horses. M35 sedans use a 275 hp V6 that's available with rear-drive or all-wheel drive.

Owners complain of excessive oil consumption, poor tire performance with the Michelin Pilots, and a host of other problems:

> Perforated leather seats had mesh coming out, CD changer jammed, AC compressor busted, belts on the motor had to be replaced, glove box had to be readjusted, hood had to be readjusted to stop the squeaking when closing the doors, front window guides and stabilizer-inner door had to be replaced to stop all the squealing when letting the windows up/down.... [I had to] schedule another visit to see if the engine/exhaust problem could be repaired. The dealership had my car for 3 weeks...and cleaned out the combustion chamber at their cost and the day I got it back, it was still smoking out the pipes. The dealership says they know nothing else to do but to replace the motor if it's consuming oil.

 Safety Summary

G20: **2001**—Airbags fail to deploy. *G35:* **2003**—When the AC is engaged and the brakes applied, the vehicle accelerates. • Early automatic transmission replacement. • Poor upshifting from First gear. • Loss of front braking capability. • Premature wearout of brake pads and rotors. • Rear window shatters suddenly. • Seat belt cuts across the neck of small-statured drivers. • Driver's seat rocks back and forth. • Rear defroster takes forever to work. **2004**—Sudden acceleration due to pedal sticking, or when the speed control is engaged. • Transmission failures and premature brake replacement still dominate owner complaints. • Parking brake won't secure vehicle on an incline. • In one incident, ABS system locked up, flipping the car and killing the driver and two passengers. Heated air is constantly drawn in from the engine compartment. **2005**—Speed control causes the car to suddenly accelerate. Car also accelerates when brakes are applied. • Brake failure. • Car pulls to the right (service bulletins were issued for this problem, affecting 2003 and 2004 models). **2006**—Fire believed to have been caused by a defective seat heater. • Cruise control causes car to suddenly accelerate. • Stuck fuel-filler door. • Tail/brake lights are too bright; blind following drivers. **2007**—Passenger-side airbag is disabled when average-sized adult is seated. • Vehicle often hesitates when accelerating. • Dynamic Control system suddenly engages, causing the car to speed up and veer to the right. • Car seems to be constantly braking when going downhill with the cruise control engaged. • Manual transmission clutch sticks to the floor due to insufficient pressure in the line. • Sunroof explodes. • Driver-side automatic window won't go up, or operates very slowly. • Intelligent Key failures. *G37:* **2008–09**—Vehicle suddenly accelerates when brakes applied while parking:

> Experienced over six weeks five incidents of engine speed increase when braking as described by Infiniti in their bulletin ITB07-048. Reprogramming the 2008 G37 per this bulletin was unsuccessful. Dealer claims no problem because they cannot verify.

2009—Faulty electronic control module leads to engine suddenly losing power. • Severe brake judder:

> Technical Service Bulletin ITB09-037 from Infiniti states overheating of the brakes can cause judder. They recommend installing a brake backing plate, resurfacing, or replacing the rotors. I took my car to my Infiniti dealer and the plate was installed. The front rotors were resurfaced, brake pads replaced, and I still had the brake judder. I took it back and they resurfaced the rear rotors and recommended balancing and rotating tires. I did this (at my own cost) and the brake judder is still present.

Owner says rodents are snacking on his car's wiring:

> 2009 Infiniti G37 has electrical wiring insulation made of soy-based polymer. Soy based polymer is apparently biodegradable. The problem is that it is also attractive to rodents, who eat the wiring, creating electrical safety hazards. In addition to the safety hazards, it also creates an economic stressor on consumers and insurers who have to pay for repairs done to these automobiles, which Infiniti claims is not covered under any existing warranty.

2010—Sudden, unintended acceleration rears its head again. Erratic shifting of the 7-speed automatic transmission. • When cruising, vehicle shuts down. • On the convertible model front seatbelt guides don't latch as required. *I30/I35:* **2000–01**—Sudden, unintended acceleration. **2001**—Rear suspension fails. • Cruise control won't disengage when brakes are applied. **2002**—Airbags fail to deploy. • Steering wheel pulls sharply to one side when accelerating. • Poor braking. • Stalling. *M35:* **2006**—Sudden, unintended acceleration. Brake failure. • Steering is hard to control; car either pulls sharply to the right or wanders all over the road. • Frequent wheel bearing failures. • Emergency spare tire makes the car undrivable. • Driver seat frame stress crack. • Driver-side seatback may suddenly collapse due to a defective side seat hinge. • Steering wander. • Leaky sunroof. • Inaccurate fuel gauge (covered by the emissions warranty). **2010**—Unreliable braking. • 18-inch tires frequently blow out due to weak sidewalls. • Vehicle continues to wander and tramline whenever it passes over ruts in the road. • Car's steering tends to pull to the right when driving. *M45:* **2006**—Camshaft sensor failure makes the car stall out on the highway. Front-end tramlining. Steering pulls right and left. **2010**—Excessive steering wander. *Q45:* **2001**—Sudden acceleration when vehicle is shifted into Reverse gear. **2004**—Laser-controlled cruise control abruptly cuts power when passing another vehicle and doesn't work in rain or when driving into the sun at sunset.

Secret Warranties/Internal Bulletins/Service Tips

All models/years: Troubleshooting tips to correct brake pedal judder and hard starts. • Windshield cracking. • Sunroof wind noise. • Erratic operation of the power antenna. *G20:* **2001–02**—Rear brake caliper clunk, rattle, or knock. *G35:* **2003–04**—Defective seat-mounted side airbag harness may cause Airbag light to stay lit. Infiniti will relocate and secure seat-mounted side airbag connectors under Voluntary Service Campaign #P0339 (TSB #ITB10-034a, July 21, 2010). No time or mileage restrictions are indicated. **2003–06**—No-starts in cold weather. **2005**—Dash squeak and rattle repair. **2005–06**—Gap between glove compartment and dash. *I30/I35:* **2000–04**—Poor transmission performance. *G37:* **2009–11**—Troubleshooting automatic transmission malfunctions. *M35:* **2009–10**—Engine hesitation or stall at idle or very low speeds. *M45:* **2007–10**—Inoperative outside mirror actuator. *Q45:* **2002**—Engine hesitation. • Steering pull to the right; excessive vibration. • Difficult to move shift lever. • Front suspension noise. • Trunk lid hard to close. • Poor AC performance. **2002–03**—Incorrect shifting. **2002–04**—Remedy for engine knocking after a cold start. **2002–06**—Ticking, thumping noise at idle. **2004–06**—Tire-pressure monitoring system sensor seal leaks.

G20, G35, G37, I30/I35, M35, M45, Q45 PROFILE

	2002	2003	2004	2005	2006	2007	2008	2009	2010
Cost Price ($)									
G20	29,900	—	—	—	—	—	—	—	—
G35 Sedan	—	38,900	39,600	39,900	39,990	39,990	39,990	—	—
G35 Coupe	—	45,000	45,200	46,100	47,000	47,200	—	—	—
G37 Sedan	—	—	—	—	—	—	—	37,090	38,690
G37 Coupe	—	—	—	—	—	—	47,350	45,200	46,300
I30/I35	39,500	39,700	41,200	—	—	—	—	—	—
M35	—	—	—	54,800	56,100	56,400	49,400	53,700	55,500
M45	—	62,000	62,000	64,400	65,700	66,000	66,950	67,750	69,550
Q45	73,000	74,900	75,500	88,000	—	—	—	—	—
Used Values ($)									
G20 ▲	3,000	—	—	—	—	—	—	—	—
G20 ▼	2,500	—	—	—	—	—	—	—	—
G35 Sedan ▲	—	5,500	7,000	9,500	11,000	13,000	16,000	—	—
G35 Sedan ▼	—	5,000	6,000	8,500	10,000	11,500	15,000	—	—
G35 Coupe ▲	—	8,000	9,500	12,000	13,500	15,000	—	—	—
G35 Coupe ▼	—	6,500	8,500	10,500	12,500	14,000	—	—	—
G37 Sedan ▲	—	—	—	—	—	—	—	22,000	25,500
G37 Sedan ▼	—	—	—	—	—	—	—	21,500	24,000
G37 Coupe ▲	—	—	—	—	—	—	18,500	24,000	27,000
G37 Coupe ▼	—	—	—	—	—	—	17,000	23,500	26,500

I30/I35 ▲	3,500	4,000	5,500	—	—	—	—	—	—
I30/I35 ▼	3,000	3,500	4,500	—	—	—	—	—	—
M35 ▲	—	—	—	10,500	13,500	15,000	19,000	26,000	32,000
M35 ▼	—	—	—	9,000	11,000	14,000	17,500	24,500	30,000
M45 ▲	—	9,000	11,000	13,000	15,000	18,000	25,000	35,000	43,000
M45 ▼	—	8,000	9,500	11,500	13,500	16,500	23,500	33,000	41,000
Q45 ▲	10,000	12,000	14,000	15,000	—	—	—	—	—
Q45 ▼	8,500	10,500	12,500	14,000	—	—	—	—	—
Reliability	2	2	2	3	3	3	4	4	4
Crash Safety (F)									
G37 4d	—	—	—	—	—	—	—	5	5
I30/I35	4	4	4	—	—	—	—	—	—
Side									
G37 4d	—	—	—	—	—	—	—	5	5
I30/I35	4	4	4	—	—	—	—	—	—
IIHS Side									
G35	—	—	—	—	3	—	—	—	—
M35/M45	—	—	—	—	5	5	5	5	5
Offset									
I30/I35	3	3	3	—	—	—	—	—	—
G35	—	5	5	5	5	—	—	—	—
M35/M45	—	—	—	—	5	5	5	5	5
Q45—	5	5	5	—	—	—	—	—	—
Head Restraints									
G20	1	—	—	—	—	—	—	—	—
G35	—	—	—	1	1	2	2	—	—
G37	—	—	—	—	—	2	2	2	—
I35	1	1	1	—	—	—	—	—	—
M35/M45	—	—	—	—	1	1	1	1	1
Q45	—	—	—	2	2	—	—	—	—
Rollover Resistance									
G37 4d	—	—	—	—	—	—	—	5	5
I35	4	4	4	—	—	—	—	—	—

All ratings on a numbered scale where 5 is good and 1 is bad. See page 132 for a more detailed description.

Lexus

ES 300/330/350, GS 300/350/430/450H/460, IS 250/300/350, IS F, LS 400/430/460/600H, SC 300, SC 400/430 ★★★

RATING: Average (1999–2010). A bit more refined than the Infinitis, Lexus' lineup offers first-class performance but only average reliability. The powertrain is prone to dangerous stalling and surging, and the Lexus' rating has been downgraded because of serious design deficiencies relating to sudden acceleration, poor braking, and a chronic engine/transmission stumble, shudder, and surge. **Ideal model year:** Get a 2008 ES 350 for about $19,500. It comes with lots of powertrain improvements from an earlier redesign. **"Real" city/highway fuel economy:** *ES 300:* 12.3/8.2 L/100 km. *ES 330:* 11.6/7.5 L/100 km. *GS 300:* 13.1/8.6 L/100 km. *GS 400:* 13.4/9.4 L/100 km. *GS 430:* 13.3/9.3 L/100 km. *IS 300 manual:* 13.2/8.8 L/100 km. *IS 300 automatic:* 13.1/8.9 L/100 km. *LS 430:* 13.2/8.6 L/100 km. *LX 470:* 17.9/12.9 L/100 km. Real-world fuel savings may be lower by about 10–15 percent. **Maintenance/repair costs:** Higher-than-average costs, and repairs are highly dealer-dependent. **Parts:** Expensive, but parts aren't hard to find (except body panels). **Extended warranty:** Not necessary. **Best alternatives:** Look at the fully equipped Acura Legend, Honda Accord, Hyundai Genesis, Infiniti G35, and early Nissan Maxima, to provide airbags, comparable highway performance, and reliability at far less initial cost—but without the Lexus cachet. **Helpful websites:** *www.clublexus.com/forums/es350-180.*

Strengths and Weaknesses

ALERT! Be especially wary of the redesigned 2010 "active" head restraints. Owners say the restraints push the driver's head down and forward, causing considerable neck and back pain. Worst of all, there is no fix for this problem that doesn't contravene U.S. and Canadian federal safety legislation.

Head restraints aside, these are benchmark cars known for their comfort, convenience features, and good looks. Sports cars, they're not. But if you're looking for your father's Oldsmobile from a Japanese automaker, these luxury cars fit the bill. Like Acuras and Infinitis, Lexus models all suffer from some automatic transmission failures; engine sludge buildup (see *www.consumeraffairs.com/news04/2007/01/toyota_sludge_settlement.html*); early rear main engine seal and front strut replacements (front struts are often replaced under a "goodwill" warranty); and front brake, electrical, body, trim, and accessory deficiencies.

ES 300/330/350

Resembling an LS 400 dressed in sporty attire, the entry-level ES 300 was launched in 1992 to fill the gap between the discontinued ES 250 and the LS 400. In fact, the ES 300 has many of the attributes of the LS 400 sedan but sells for much less money. A five-passenger sedan based on the Camry, but 90 kg (200 lb.) heavier and with a different suspension and tires, it comes equipped with a standard 3.0L 24-valve engine that produces 181–210 horses coupled to either a 5-speed manual or a 4-speed electronically controlled automatic transmission. Like some Infiniti models, however, the ES 300 hesitates and surges when accelerating. Headroom is also surprisingly limited for a car this expensive.

ES 330s came on the scene as 2004 models and offered buyers a more-powerful 3.3L V6 that produced more horses and a bit more torque. 2005 models got very little that was new, except for power front seats with a memory feature and power door mirrors that tilt down when in Reverse.

The 2007 ES 350 arrived with new styling, more power, and additional features, but it remained an upscale Toyota Camry. It has a slightly larger wheelbase and a new 6-speed transmission, and is powered by a 272 hp 3.5L V6 instead of the ES 330's 218 hp 3.3L V6. Standard features include anti-lock braking, traction/anti-skid control, front side airbags, side curtain airbags, and front knee airbags. ES 350 competes against the Acura TL, BMW 3 Series, Cadillac CTS, and Infiniti G35.

VEHICLE HISTORY: *ES 300/330/350:* **2002**—A longer, taller body; new 5-speed automatic transmission; improved brakes, steering, and suspension; and more standard luxury features. No more standard traction control. **2004**—ES 330 (designating a 3.3L engine) debuts with 15 extra horses and larger head-protecting side airbags. **2007**—ES 350 debuts carrying a larger engine and many other improvements. **2009**—Heated seats. **2010**—Redesigned front head restraints, new interior and exterior styling; rear-seat side airbags; and an Off switch for the vehicle stability system.

Government-reported safety-related defects are surprisingly omnipresent. These reports include airbag-induced injuries; sudden acceleration; an unreliable powertrain that surges, stumbles, stalls, and shifts erratically; ABS and Goodyear tire failures; excessive vibration when underway; interior window fogging; unreadable dash gauges; poor AC performance; and a frequently disconnecting Bluetooth.

GS 300/350/430/450h

The rear-drive GS 300 is a step up from the front-drive ES 300 and just a rung below Lexus' top-of-the-line LS 400. It carries the same V6 engine as the ES 300, except that it has 20 more horses. This produces sparkling performance at higher speeds, though the car is disappointingly sluggish from a start. Fuel economy is sacrificed for performance, however, and the base suspension and tires pass noisily over small bumps and ruts. Visibility is also less than impressive, with large rear pillars and a narrow rear window restricting the view. There's not much usable trunk space, and the liftover is unreasonably high.

VEHICLE HISTORY: 2006—More power, fresh styling, a larger interior, and all-wheel drive. The rear-drive and all-wheel-drive GS 300s get a 245 hp V6 engine. The rear-drive GS 430 keeps its 300 hp V8. All models use a 6-speed automatic manumatic transmission, anti-skid/traction control, and anti-lock brakes. The GS 430 adds driver-adjustable shock absorbers and 18-inch wheels. Run-flat tires (more a boondoggle than a boon) are standard with AWD. All models have front knee airbags, front torso side airbags, and head-protecting side curtain airbags. **2007**—Entry-level models get a new 3.5L V6 that produces 303 hp, up from 245 hp with the prior 3.0L. In fact, the added horsepower beats the V8 by 13 horses, though the V8 is torquier. The lineup now: GS 350, GS 430, and GS 450h hybrid. **2008**—A slight restyling and a more powerful 342 hp 4.6L V8 engine hooked to an 8-speed automatic transmission (GS 460). **2010**—Redesigned head restraints (a painful change for some body types). GS 460 returns with a standard rear spoiler and navigation system; GS 450h hybrid has rear-seat side airbags, navigation system, and a new front grille, wheels, and rear spoiler.

Owner complaints have centred on brake failures, electrical shutdowns, prematurely worn wheel bearings, excessive front-end vibrations, fragile wheel rims, run-flat tire problems (cost, availability, performance, and durability), and electrical and fuel system malfunctions resulting in hesitation followed by sudden, unintended acceleration ("lag and lurch").

IS 250/300/350

Targeting BMW's 3 Series, this rear-drive sports-compact sedan comes with similar power and features to the BMW 325i—for a few thousand dollars less, in the case of the IS 250. Moreover, there is practically no difference in fuel economy between the manual and automatic transmission modes. The only engine is a 215 hp 3.0L inline-six (borrowed from the GS 300) mated to a 5-speed automatic transmission and incorporating Lexus' E-shift feature for manual shifting. Other important features are four-wheel ABS-equipped disc brakes, 17-inch wheels, performance tires, front seat belt pretensioners, and traction control. Just a bit narrower than the BMW 3 Series, the IS 300 is a competent performer both for routine tasks and in emergency situations. Look for models equipped with a limited-slip differential, but don't pay more for models featuring a sunroof, heated seats, or leather upholstery.

VEHICLE HISTORY: 2002—A SportCross wagon is added, which comes with an automatic transmission only. Manual-shift sedans have a firmer suspension; ABS is upgraded; side curtain/front side airbags and traction control are standard. **2006**—After dropping the slow-selling wagon, Lexus revamps its sporty small sedan along the lines of the larger GS sedans, creating two rear-drive models and an all-wheel-drive version: the IS 250 and IS 250 AWD, equipped with a 204 hp V6, and the IS 350, powered by a 306 hp V6. All IS models come loaded with the latest high-tech safety and performance features to compete primarily against the Acura TSX, BMW 3 Series, and Infiniti G35. **2008**—Debut of the IS F, featuring a

416 hp 5.0L V8. **2009**—A modest restyling and a retuned suspension. **2010**—Two new convertibles: the IS 250 C and IS 350 C.

In a nutshell, these cars stand out with a comfortable ride; a nice array of standard features; quality-looking gauges; good acceleration, handling, and braking; a low beltline for a great view; and first-class workmanship. On the other hand, rear seating is a bit cramped; the car requires premium fuel; owners report excessive road noise and tire thump; the instrument panel reflects in the windshield; seat cushions don't provide adequate thigh support; no crashworthiness data is available; trunk hinges eat up trunk space and may damage luggage; the interior doesn't feel as plush as the competition's; and the automatic transmission's manual E-shift is awkward to use and isn't as sporty as a BMW's. Other cars worth considering are the Acura TL and BMW's 3 Series.

LS 400/430/460

The Lexus flagship, the LS 400 rear-drive, arrived in 1990 with a 250 hp 4.0L V8. It outclasses all other luxury sedans in reliability, styling, and function. Its powerful engine provides smooth, impressive acceleration and a superior highway passing ability at all speeds. Its transmission is smooth and efficient. The suspension gives an easy ride without body roll or front-end plow during emergency stops, delivering a major comfort advantage over other luxury compacts. Other amenities include anti-lock brakes, a driver-side airbag, and automatic temperature control.

VEHICLE HISTORY: 2001—Totally redesigned with a sleeker body, a 4.3L V8, an upgraded suspension, and a more-spacious, reworked interior. Additional safety and comfort features are also added. **2004**—A 6-speed manumatic transmission, driver's knee-protecting airbags, steering-linked headlights, a power rear sunshade, and a tire-pressure monitor are added. Suspension, steering, and ABS systems are also upgraded. **2007**—A redesigned LS 460 gains a long-wheelbase body style, more power, and the industry's first 8-speed automatic transmission, plus a basketful of high-tech safety, performance, and convenience features. Two models are offered: the regular-sized LS 460, which is slightly longer and wider than the 2001–06 models, and the LS 460 L, which is even larger. The 278 hp 4.3L V8 is replaced by a 380 hp 4.6L V8, hence the name change from the LS 430 to the LS 460. The additional power and larger dimensions clearly target the car's main rivals: the Audi A8, BMW 7 Series, and Mercedes-Benz S-Class. **2008**—Debut of the LS 600h, a hybrid variant equipped with a 389 hp 5.0L V8 and two motor generators that boost output to 438 horses. **2009**—All-wheel drive models debut. **2010**—The LS 460 gets a restyled exterior, upgraded stereo, backup camera, and a voice-activated navigation system.

Here's an important downside: the brakes don't inspire confidence, owing to their mushy feel and average performance. Furthermore, there's limited rear footroom under the front seats, and the rear middle passenger has to sit on the transmission hump. Plus, this car is a gas-guzzler that thirsts for premium fuel.

Owner complaints over the years deal mainly with spongy brakes; main computer failures; electrical glitches; door locks that stick shut, trapping occupants; sudden, unintended acceleration; stalling caused by a faulty throttle sensor; failure of the Vehicle Stability Control to activate; and traction control that causes the vehicle to swerve unexpectedly (usually to the left).

SC 300, SC 400/430

These two coupes are practically identical, except for their engines and luxury features. The cheaper SC 300 gives you the same high-performance 6-cylinder engine used by the GS 300 and Toyota Supra, while the SC 400 uses the 4.0L V8 engine found in the LS 400. You're likely to find fewer luxury features with the SC 300 because they were sold as options. Nevertheless, look for an SC with traction control for additional safety during poor driving conditions. On the downside, V8 fuel consumption is horrendous, rear seating is cramped, and trunk space is unimpressive. Also, invest in a good anti-theft device, or your Lexus relationship will be over almost before it begins.

VEHICLE HISTORY: 2005—Upgraded shock absorbers and navigation system. **2006**—Addition of a 6-speed automatic transmission. **2007**—Convertibles get front-knee airbags. **2010**—Standard navigation system and an upgraded stereo.

 ## Safety Summary

ES 300/330/350: **All years:** Sudden, unintended acceleration. **2002**—Airbags fail to deploy. • Impossible to read speedometer and other gauges in sunlight. • Won't go into gear properly. • Warped brake rotors. **2002–03**—Chronic engine/transmission surging and stalling not fixed by computer module recalibration, switching to premium fuel, etc. **2004**—Sudden acceleration; brake failure. • Stuck accelerator. • Delayed shift and surging when accelerating still occurs frequently, despite Toyota's special campaign "fix" that involves changing the electronic module:

> This car is extremely dangerous. It's either a defective transmission or bad drive-by-wire design. The car hesitates extremely badly on acceleration. For example, when you are entering a limited access highway, if you slow down and then step on the gas, there is a long lag before the car begins to pick up speed. This lag is often a second or more. I have nearly been hit numerous times while the car makes up its mind whether it wants to move or not. The dealer has refused to fix the problem.

Transmission goes into Reverse when shifted into Drive. • Vehicle lunges forward when transmission is shifted into Reverse. • Steering pulls vehicle into oncoming traffic. • Passenger-side airbag is disabled when adult of any weight sits in the front passenger seat. • Serious blind spots caused by side rear-view mirrors. **2005**—Hesitation and then surging continues to be a major complaint category. • Sudden loss of braking capability. **2006**—Car suddenly accelerated and killed a pedestrian. • Vehicle lags and lurches. • Headlight range is too short; HID lights may ignite on impact. **2007**—Airbag on passenger side is disabled when a small adult occupies the seat. • Sudden acceleration when cruise control is engaged. • Automatic transmission flares even though foot is taken off the accelerator (car suddenly accelerates). **2008**—Car suddenly accelerated as it was being parked:

> I had almost finished parking my '08 Lexus ES 350 in a parking place at a business park when it surged forward very fast. I had not touched the accelerator. I braked hard, but the car went up over a cement divider and crashed into the car parked facing me. I had had the car one and a half years, and this was the first time it happened. I had it towed to the Lexus dealership. An inspector found nothing wrong externally, but the EDR showed I had not stepped on the accelerator before the crash, only the brake, and yet it had surged forward. I had taken the car in earlier for the recall, and had removed the mat and had something added to the software. I sold the car back to Lexus immediately as I never wanted to step foot in it again. This is a very dangerous car, and something is wrong with the electronics to cause this.

Airbags fail to deploy. • Lost steering control while underway. • Door locks open by themselves. **2009**—More sudden acceleration complaints:

> When I was going to park my car in the box in front of the hotel room, I touched the accelerator slightly to advance the two meters distant to be properly parked, then the accelerator run in high speed the brakes did not respond. To reduce the impact, I turned the wheel to the right and crashed into the hotel wall.

A fuel smell permeates the interior. • Headlights are too dim. • Windows and sunroof open by themselves. • Frequent security system false alarms. • Fuel in gas tank makes a thumping noise when the car accelerates. **2010**—Airbags failed to deploy. • Sticking accelerator. • When foot is taken off the accelerator pedal it takes several minutes for the car to slow down. • Vehicle accelerates when speed control is engaged. • Foot is easily caught between the accelerator and gas pedals. • Rear windshield distorts car headlights at night. • Driver complaints of poor rearward visibility. • Side mirrors fog up when it's raining and the outside temperature is dropping. • Navigation system malfunctions or displays inaccurate information. *GS 300:* **2002**—Fire ignites from fuel filter leak. • Sticking accelerator. • Vehicle starts without key. • Traction control engages too easily. • Inadequate headlight illumination. • Digital dash indicator washes out in sunlight. **2003**—Sudden, unintended acceleration and hesitation when accelerating. *GS 350:* **2007**—Vehicle crashed into a brick wall after suddenly accelerating; airbags didn't deploy. • Engine surged without floor mat involvement. • Fuel feed line to passenger-side fuel pump may disconnect. Xenon headlight low beam shuts off. • Side mirrors change position on their own. **2008**—Sudden, unintended acceleration. • Dim low-beam headlights and a sharp cut-off in illumination with the high beams. • Premature rear tire wear on the inside edges believed to be caused by lack of a means to make camber adjustment. **2009**—Sudden, unintended acceleration. • Cruise control may become inoperative when going uphill or downhill. • Headlights shine too low to the ground; they don't project far enough. **2010**—Road wander requires constant steering corrections. • Total brake failure. *GS 450h:* **2007**—Rear suspension collapsed as car was leaving its parking spot. • Vehicle suddenly shut down while cruising on the highway (a malfunctioning sensor is suspected). • Brake failure after passing over a bump in the road. • Vehicle may emit high levels of electromagnetic radiation emanating from the motor and/or generator (causes tingling in the hands and feet, numbness in the face, and dull headaches). **2010**—Sudden forward acceleration when the car was shifted into Drive and the brakes were applied.

Secret Warranties/Internal Bulletins/Service Tips

All models: 1997–2002—The engine warranty that was extended to eight years to cover engine oil sludge claims (see *www.autosafety.org*) has run out. Nevertheless, a case can be made in small claims court that compensation should still be given because a luxury car of this caliber should have a more durable engine. **2002**—Harsh 2–3 shift. • Troubleshooting steering pull and interior squeaks and rattles. **2002–03**—TSB #TC004-03, issued August 4, 2003, gives recalibration instructions for correcting erratic shifting. This free repair is in effect for 96 months/128,000 km (80,000 mi.). • Unreadable dash gauges. • Body creak or snap from top of front windshield. **2002–04**—Inoperative AC. **2002–05**—Countermeasures for poor shift quality. **2002–06**—Troubleshooting tips for vehicles that pull to one side when underway. • Inoperative rear power window. **2003–05**—Steering clunk, pop. **2003–06**—Windshield ticking noise. **2004**—Troubleshooting tips for a malfunctioning front-seat occupant seat belt sensor. • Vehicle pulls into oncoming traffic. *ES 350:* **2007–09**—Engine ticking noise. • Upgraded front brake pads will reduce brake pulsation. • Sunroof popping or creaking. • Vehicle won't shift out of Park. **2007–10**—Rubbing noises from rear of vehicle. *GS 300/350:* **2006–10**—Front sway bar thumping noise. *LS 460/600h:* **2007–09**—Side window wind noise at highway speeds. • Rear suspension rattle, knock. • Uncomfortable lower seat cushion. • Squawk from the brake actuator.

ES 300/330/350, GS 300/350/430/450H/460, IS 250/300/350, IS F, LS 400/430/460/600H, SC 400/430 PROFILE

	2002	2003	2004	2005	2006	2007	2008	2009	2010
Cost Price ($)									
ES 300/330/350	43,400	43,800	43,800	43,900	42,900	42,900	42,900	39,950	41,950
GS 300/350	60,700	61,700	61,700	61,700	64,300	59,750	59,900	51,900	52,500
GS 430/460	68,800	69,500	69,500	69,500	74,700	71,300	73,000	63,300	67,100
GS 450h	—	—	—	—	—	76,900	71,100	62,500	71,900
IS 250	—	—	—	—	36,300	36,400	31,900	32,350	34,400
IS 300/350	37,820	37,775	37,775	37,990	48,900	49,000	43,350	43,850	45,900
IS F	—	—	—	—	—	—	64,400	65,300	68,000
LS 400/430/460	81,900	82,800	83,200	84,900	85,700	86,440	86,500	75,900	82,900
LS 600h	—	—	—	—	—	—	132,000	118,700	119,950
SC 400/430	84,000	85,500	86,800	89,770	86,800	93,250	93,250	79,900	82,000
Used Values ($)									
ES 300/330/350 ▲	6,000	7,000	8,500	10,000	12,500	15,500	20,000	24,000	28,000
ES 300/330/350 ▼	5,500	6,000	7,500	9,000	11,000	14,000	18,500	22,500	26,000

GS 300/350 ▲	8,000	9,000	10,500	12,000	13,500	18,500	26,000	33,000	38,000
GS 300/350 ▼	7,000	8,000	9,500	11,000	12,500	17,000	24,500	31,000	36,000
GS 430/460 ▲	8,500	10,000	11,500	13,000	15,500	21,500	29,500	41,000	49,000
GS 430/460 ▼	7,500	9,000	10,500	12,000	14,000	20,000	27,500	39,000	46,600
GS 450h ▲	—	—	—	—	—	21,500	30,000	41,000	48,000
GS 450h ▼	—	—	—	—	—	20,000	28,500	39,000	45,500
IS 250 ▲	—	—	—	—	11,500	14,000	17,000	20,000	24,500
IS 250 ▼	—	—	—	—	10,000	12,500	15,500	18,500	22,500
IS 300/350 ▲	8,000	9,500	11,500	14,000	16,500	18,000	18,000	28,500	33,000
IS 300/350 ▼	7,500	8,500	10,000	13,000	15,000	16,500	16,500	27,000	31,500
IS F ▲	—	—	—	—	—	—	35,000	44,000	52,000
IS F ▼	—	—	—	—	—	—	32,500	40,000	50,000
LS 400/430/460 ▲	9,500	12,000	13,500	16,000	20,000	24,500	33,500	47,000	56,000
LS 400/430/460 ▼	9,000	11,000	12,500	14,000	18,500	22,500	31,500	44,000	53,000
LS 600h ▲	—	—	—	—	—	—	39,000	59,000	70,000
LS 600h ▼	—	—	—	—	—	—	37,000	54,000	65,000
SC 400/430 ▲	15,500	17,500	19,500	24,000	29,000	35,500	43,000	52,000	61,000
SC 400/430 ▼	14,000	16,000	18,000	22,500	27,500	33,500	40,000	48,000	56,000

Reliability	4	4	4	4	4	4	4	4	4
Crash Safety (F)									
ES 300/330/350	—	—	—	5	5	5	5	5	5
Side									
ES 300/330/350	—	5	—	5	5	5	5	5	5
IIHS Side									
ES 330/350	—	—	5	5	5	5	5	5	5
GS	—	—	—	—	5	5	5	5	5
IS 250/350	—	—	—	—	5	5	5	5	5
Offset									
ES 300/330/350	5	5	5	5	5	5	5	5	5
GS	5	5	5	5	5	5	5	5	5
IS 250/350	—	—	—	—	5	5	5	5	5
LS/LS 430	5	5	5	5	5	5	5	5	5
Head Restraints									
ES 300/350	—	3	1	1	1	2	2	2	2
GS	—	2	2	2	2	2	2	2	3
IS 250/300/350	2	2	2	2	3	3	3	3	3
LS 430/460	2	2	2	2	2	2	2	2	5
Roof Strength									
IS 250/350	—	—	—	—	3	3	3	3	3
Rollover Resistance									
ES 300/330/350	—	—	—	4	4	5	5	5	4

All ratings on a numbered scale where 5 is good and 1 is bad. See page 132 for a more detailed description.

Mercedes-Benz

RATING: *B-Class:* Average (2006–10). *C-Class:* Not Recommended (1999–2010). These luxury lemons are outclassed by most Asian luxury models, which offer more safety, reliability, and comfort for much less money. **Ideal model year:** Go for the 2008 B200 for about $15,000 and with some unexpired warranty coverage left. **"Real" city/highway fuel economy:** *B200 manual:* 9.2/6.7 L/100 km. *B200 automatic:* 9.2/7.2 L/100 km. *B200 Turbo manual:* 10.3/6.9 L/100 km. *B200 Turbo automatic:* 9.5/7.4 L/100 km. *C230 manual:* 9.5/7.2 L/100 km. *C230 automatic:* 10.2/7.1 L/100 km. *C240 manual:* 12.9/8.4 L/100 km. *C240 automatic:* 12.4/8.9 L/100 km. *C32 AMG:* 14.6/10.3 L/100 km. *C320 manual:* 12.7/8.3 L/100 km. *C320 automatic:* 11.8/8.2 L/100 km. *CL500:* 14.7/9.1 L/100 km. *CL600:* 18.4/11.6 L/100 km. *CL55 AMG:* 16.6/10.3 L/100 km. **Maintenance/repair costs:** Higher-than-average costs, and most repairs must be done by a Mercedes dealer. Look out for electronic glitches and fuel-system malfunctions. **Parts:** Highly dealer-dependent and expensive. **Extended warranty:** A smart idea. **Best alternatives:** Acura RL or TL; the BMW 3 Series; Hyundai's Genesis; and the Infiniti G35. **Helpful websites:** *www.benzworld.org* and *www.carsurvey.org/reviews/mercedes-benz/c-class.*

 ## Strengths and Weaknesses

B-Class

Mercedes' B-Class, launched as a 2006 model spun off of the smaller A-Class, looks like a mini-minivan, without any of the stylistic lines that would identify the B200 as a Mercedes product. But it does have a roomy interior and smooth-running drivetrain. A 136 hp 2.0L engine is standard, and a torquier, turbocharged 193 hp variant is optional. Although the car is quite vulnerable to crosswinds due to its extra height, overall highway performance is above average. Crashworthiness testing has not yet been done by NHTSA. The bottom line: there are half a dozen other cars that perform as well or better, with classier lines, more-extensive dealership networks, proven reliability, and good crashworthiness scores.

VEHICLE HISTORY: 2007—A telescopic steering column makes its debut. The Turbo variant gets auto-dimming mirrors, rain-sensing wipers, a removable ashtray/storage cup, heated washers, and an interior lighting package. **2008**—The B200 returns with a standard storage net on front seatbacks, cruise control, an interior light package, and more-comfortable seats. **2009**—Slightly restyled.

C-Class

Replacing the low-quality, unreliable, power-challenged, bland 190 series, the 1994 C-Class gained interior room and two new engines: a base 147 hp 2.2L and a

194 hp 2.8L 6-cylinder—a real powerhouse in this small car when coupled to the manual 5-speed transmission. The 4-speed automatic is a big disappointment—it requires a lot of throttle effort to downshift and prefers to start out in Second gear. Although this series got small, incremental power increases and additional features over the years, you don't see a major redesign until 2001. Unfortunately, the new engines and other features added at that time only add to the car's poor reliability. Engine and road noise are still bothersome, and interior space is still inadequate. Since then, these cars have coasted on the Mercedes name and been touted mainly as fuel-sippers with a high-end cachet. That's poor recompense for what little the car actually offers.

VEHICLE HISTORY: 2002—Additional rear room and storage space, more high-performance features. Variants include a wagon, and an AWD sedan and wagon. **2003**—All-wheel drive and another wagon (C240) are added, and the C230 hatchback coupe gets a new supercharged 4-cylinder engine, losing 3 horses in the process. **2005**—Restyled and joined by a high-performance 362 hp V8-equipped C55 AMG sedan. The C320 gets a 3.5L V6. **2006**—New engines and model designations, fewer body styles, and the wagons and coupes are gone. Sedans come with rear-drive and all-wheel drive. The C230 Sport gets a 201 hp V6 in place of a 189 hp supercharged 4-cylinder. The C280 Luxury has a 228 hp V6 instead of its predecessor's 168 hp engine. The C350 Sport and Luxury have a 268 hp V6 that replaces the 215 hp powerplant used by the C320. The C55 returns for its last year. **2008**—Redesigned, with a longer wheelbase and added length. **2009**—The C350 is given a Dynamic Handling Package and a rear-view mirror compass. **2010**—The entry-level C230 becomes a C250 and it carries a standard driver's knee airbag and upgraded side-view mirrors.

Owner surveys give the entry-level C-Class cars a worse-than-average rating. C-Class owners report frequent problems with sudden, unintended acceleration; slipping, or soft-then-hard shifts; drivetrain noise and vibration; and windshield squeaks. Brakes, automatic transmissions, the AC and electrical system, and computer-controlled electronic components are glitch-prone, hell to diagnose, and expensive to repair. Fit and finish is also subpar and original-equipment tires may have weak side walls.

 ## Safety Summary

All models/years: Airbags fail to deploy. • Sudden, unintended acceleration and brake failure. • Faulty gas gauge sensor. • Rear suspension bouncing makes it difficult to maintain directional control. • Car is very vulnerable to side-wind buffeting. • Window failures. • Brakes fail on incline. • When the vehicle is cold, the automatic transmission slips, sticks in gear, and shifts abruptly. • Many reports of a sudden loss of power and stalling. • Multiple electrical short circuits. • Differential failure. • Vehicle wanders over highway. **All models: 2004**—Fire ignites in the electrical wires housed in the dashboard. • Transmission fails to shift into Reverse. • Loose driver's seat. • Front windshield is easily cracked by road debris. • AC corrosion produces a noxious odour in the cabin. **2005**—Engine compartment fire. • Airbag suddenly deployed when it was not needed. • Vehicle hesitates and then slams into gear. • Instrument panel is hard to read in daylight. **2007**—Several reports that the airbag deployed for no reason. • Sudden brake failure. • No-starts due to faulty fuel pump. *C240:* Wide rear quarter panel blind spot. *C300/350:* **2008**—Airbag failed to deploy when needed. **2009**—Original equipment tires have weak, "bubbling" sidewalls. • Transmission surges when the car is accelerating. • The Electronic Stability Program (ESP) doesn't help the driver correct for over-steer. • Sudden steering lockup. • Loss of power steering. • Abrupt shifts when going into Reverse or Drive. • Hood won't latch unless it is slammed shut. • Side-view mirrors crack for no reason. **2010**—Vehicle won't shift into gear, or will suddenly shift into Reverse on its own.

Secret Warranties/Internal Bulletins/Service Tips

All models: 1997–2004—Engine oil sludge refund guidelines. **2002**—Lack of power, engine hesitation. • Inoperative cruise control. • Power-window motor locks up when closing. • Inoperative central locking system. **2002–04**—Cruise control continues to malfunction. • Harsh transmission shifts. • Transmission fluid leaks at the electrical connection. **2003–04**—Troubleshooting tips for fixing a rough-running engine. **2004**—Engine oil leaks through the cylinder head bolt threads. • Steering leaks. **2005**—Engine oil leaks from the oil-level sensor. • Harsh shifts with the automatic transmission. • Transmission fluid leaks at the electrical connector. • Inoperative central locking system and AC heater blower motor. • Steering assembly leaks fluid. • Sliding roof water leaks, rattling. • Moisture in the turn signal lights and mirrors. • Tail lights won't turn off; trunk light won't turn on. • A Service Campaign calls for the free modification of the lower door seal. **2007**—Rough shifting. • Automatic transmission shift chatter. • Steering rack leaks. • Inoperative AC blower motor. • Remedy for brake squealing. • Front-end/dash noise. • Front axle knocking when parking. • Torsion bar front-end creaking. • Inoperative turn signals. • Rear seatback rattle. • Loose head restraint. • Horn may not work due to premature corrosion of the assembly. *350:* **2009**—Oil leaks at the rear of the engine may be fixed by changing the camshaft cover plugs. • Hard 1–2 shifts. • Harsh engagement when shifting from Park to Drive. • Delayed Reverse engagement. • What to do if the automatic transmission goes into "limp home" mode. • Front axle noise when maneuvering. • Front axle dull, thumping noise when going over bumps. • Front-end suspension or steering grinding noise. • Front seat backrest noise. • Interior lights flickering. • Four-way lumbar support fails. • Internal steering gear leakage. • AC is inoperative or supplies insufficient cooling.

B-CLASS, C-CLASS PROFILE

	2002	2003	2004	2005	2006	2007	2008	2009	2010
Cost Price ($)									
B200	—	—	—	—	30,950	31,400	29,900	29,900	29,900
C230/250	33,950	34,450	35,290	36,450	36,450	38,400	35,800	35,800	35,800
C240	37,950	38,450	41,290	42,250	—	—	—	—	—

C280	—	—	—	—	42,850	42,800	—	—	—
C300	—	—	—	—	—	—	41,000	41,200	41,200
C320/C350	50,600	49,750	40,700	40,600	54,950	51,000	47,900	48,200	48,200
Used Values ($)									
B200 ▲	—	—	—	—	9,500	12,000	15,500	18,500	21,500
B200 ▼	—	—	—	—	8,500	10,500	14,000	17,000	20,000
C230/250 ▲	4,000	5,500	7,000	9,500	11,500	14,500	18,500	22,500	26,000
C230/250 ▼	3,500	5,000	6,000	8,000	10,000	13,000	17,000	21,000	24,000
C240 ▲	4,500	6,000	7,500	10,000	—	—	—	—	—
C240 ▼	4,000	5,500	6,500	8,500	—	—	—	—	—
C280 ▲	—	—	—	—	12,000	14,500	—	—	—
C280 ▼	—	—	—	—	10,500	13,000	—	—	—
C300 ▲	—	—	—	—	—	—	19,000	21,000	29,000
C300 ▼	—	—	—	—	—	—	17,500	19,500	27,500
C320/C350 ▲	6,000	7,000	8,500	11,500	13,500	15,500	22,000	26,000	34,000
C320/C350 ▼	5,500	6,500	7,500	10,000	12,500	14,000	20,500	24,500	32,000
Reliability	1	1	1	2	2	2	3	3	3
B200	—	—	—	—	2	3	3	3	3
Crash Safety (F)									
C-Class	—	4	4	4	4	4	4	4	4
Side (C-Class)	—	5	5	5	5	5	5	5	5
IIHS Side	—	—	—	3	—	—	—	5	5
Offset	5	5	5	5	5	5	5	5	5
Head Restraints (F)	—	—	2	2	3	3	5	5	5
Roof Strength	—	—	—	—	—		5	5	5
Rollover Resistance									
C-Class	4	4	4	4	4	4	4	4	4

300 SERIES, 400 SERIES, 500 SERIES, E-CLASS ★★

RATING: Below Average (1999–2010). Mercedes' quality has deteriorated because of the increased complexity of mechanical, emissions, and electronic components. **Ideal model year:** It's a toss-up as to the best E model to choose. The 2006 320E RWD comes with lots of new features and added horsepower for about $16,000 (for a car that sold originally for $75,450), while the 2007 version will cost you about $6,000 more, throws in AWD, and adds more standard safety features. **"Real" city/highway fuel economy:** E320: 13.2/8.1 L/100 km. E500: 14.4/9.1 L/100 km. E55 AMG: 16.6/10.3 L/100 km. **Maintenance/repair costs:** Higher-than-average costs, but many repairs can now be done by independent garages. **Parts:** Higher-than-average costs, and limited availability. **Extended warranty:** A good idea. **Best alternatives:** The natural inclination is to seriously consider one of the BMW variants. Don't. They are just as poorly made and unreliable. Equivalent 2001 and later 5 Series, 6 Series, 7 Series, and X5 models come with standard iDrive—a complicated cockpit electronic controller that will drive you batty. Granted, by the time the 5 Series adopted iDrive a few years later, the system was redesigned so the driver could use it without looking at the small LCD panel. The 2007 X5 incorporates iDrive's third redesign in seven years. All this effort does make for a more user-friendly operation, but the learning curve is still rather steep. Instead, consider the Acura RL or TL; Infiniti G35 series; Hyundai Genesis; and Lincoln Town Car or Mercury Grand Marquis. **Helpful websites:** *www. benzworld.org, www.troublebenz.com, www.carsurvey.org/reviews/mercedes-benz*, and *www.oil-tech.com/32million.htm*).

Strengths and Weaknesses

ALERT! One extra expense facing Mercedes C-Class owners is premature tire failure caused by Mercedes' use of larger wheels and oversized tires that have short, weak sidewalls that "bubble" and blow. Check for sidewall damage during the pre-purchase vehicle inspection.

These cars were once ideal mid-sized family sedans, until Mercedes started churning out feeble downsized models and installing failure-prone electronic and powertrain components. Nevertheless, the E-Class sedans are acceptable buys because they have been around so long, are full of nifty safety and comfort/convenience features, and provide all the interior space that the C-Class leaves out. Their major shortcoming is a weak dealer network that limits parts distribution and drives up parts and servicing costs.

VEHICLE HISTORY: *E-Class:* **2004**—Increased availability of all-wheel drive, a revamped wagon body style, and a new 7-speed automatic transmission. **2005**—A turbocharged diesel, the E320 CDI, debuts as an early 2005 model. **2006**—The E350 gets a more-powerful 268 hp 3.5L engine (47 additional horses). **2007**—New styling, more power, and additional safety features. **2009**—An improved audio system…yawn.

Quality control has traditionally been below average with the E-Class cars, although not as bad as with the C-Class models. Owners point out recurring problems with the fuel and electrical systems, causing lights, instruments, and gauges to shut off and the trunk lid to open when the engine is shut down. Other common problems include engine oil leaks; stalling and engine surging; premature rusting and paint delamination; engine problems caused by a stretched timing chain; computer module failures (in both the engine and transmission); and erratically performing, leaky, and noisy transmissions.

The 2002–07 models haven't improved much. Problem areas are similar to what's been reported with Mercedes' entire lineup, including the C-Class, CLK, M-Class, R-Class, S-Class, and SLK models. Foremost are transmission malfunctions, electrical short circuits, suspension problems, brake failures, premature wearout of key brake components, unreliable climate and audio systems, and pathetically substandard fit and finish, best exemplified by complaints that the paint peels away on the lower doors.

Safety Summary

All models/years: Frequent transmission breakdowns. • Serious, often total, electrical failures. • Chronic stalling. • Sudden, unintended acceleration. • Vehicle lags and lurches when accelerating. • Steering locks up. • No child safety locks for the rear doors. • Airbag warning light stays lit or doesn't light, and airbag deploys inadvertently:

> While driving down the highway, my passenger side curtain and rear side door airbags deployed for no reason at all.... It scared the hell out of me and nearly caused me to crash the car.

Water enters the automatic transmission control module, preventing the transmission from changing gears. • Vehicle hesitates when accelerating with gas pedal halfway depressed, then it lurches forward. • Steering locks up while turning. • Total electrical failure in traffic, leading to vehicle shutdown. • Windows don't stay up. **All models: 2003**—Faulty gateway module and software cause failure in the braking system and tire-pressure feedback. • Electrical failures can leave the vehicle with no rear brakes and limited use of the front brakes. **2004**—Sudden loss of power on the highway. • Total brake failure. • Intermittent failure of the radar-controlled cruise control. **2005**—Seat belt chime goes off when the seat is unoccupied. • Distracting reflections on the driver-side mirror; dash reflects onto the front windshield. • Faulty AC/defrost blower motor. *320:* **2005**—Failure of many brake components, some of which cannot be easily repaired. • HID headlight glare angers and blinds oncoming cars. *320 Blue:* Diesel engine surges when shifting gears, causing car to lurch forward and skid on ice. • Sudden brake failure when parking. • Electrical short circuits caused by a dried-up, cracked wiring harness. *350:* **2006**—7-speed automatic transmission failures disable steering and brake boost, ABS, and Electronic Stability Control system. • Other incidents where the tranny suddenly locks up in high gear and requires that the car be restarted to return to normal. • Automatic transmission behaves like the clutch is slipping, slowing car to a snail's pace. • Vehicle will often not start because electrical shorts have disabled the electronics. • Sunroof explodes while vehicle underway. **2007**—Vehicle will suddenly stall while on the highway. • Child opened the rear door while car was idling at a red light. • All four wheels replaced because they were bent at the rim. • Rubber ring inside the fuel tank failed, allowing fuel to leak out of the tank. **2008**—Sunroof shattered spontaneously. **2009**—Vehicle surged when the accelerator was barely pressed. **2010**—Failure-prone automatic transmission.

Secret Warranties/Internal Bulletins/Service Tips

All models: 2004—No-starts. • Harsh transmission shifts. • Steering leaks. • Sliding roof-rack cover cracks. • Wheelhouse water drain modification. • Rear axle rumbling. **2005**—Oil leaks from the oil-level sensor. • Rough automatic transmission engagement, droning, buzzing noises. • Transmission leaks fluid at the electrical connector. • Campaign to check and repair possible automatic transmission pilot bushing leakage; another campaign concerns the free cleaning of the front axle carrier sleeve and bolt replacement; a third campaign will reprogram the battery control module; and a fourth campaign will inspect or replace the alternator/regulator. • Foul interior odours. • Steering fluid leaks and steering squeal when turning. • Front-seat noise. • Sliding roof water leaks, rattling. • Moisture in the turn signal lights and mirrors. • Rear seatback rattle. • Loose passenger head restraints. • Fanfare horns may not work due to premature wiring corrosion. 350: **2006–07**—Rough transmission shifts. • Upshift/downshift chatter or shudder. • Front axle creaking, grinding, knocking noise when parking, and other front-end noises. • Brake squeal. • Steering-rack leaks. • Rivet replacement to prevent water leakage. • Inoperative AC, faulty blower motor, or compressor failure. • False oil readings. • Inoperative turn signals. • Loose front centre armrest falls off.

300 SERIES, 400 SERIES, 500 SERIES, E-CLASS PROFILE

	2002	2003	2004	2005	2006	2007	2008	2009	2010
Cost Price ($)									
280/300/350	—	—	—	—	—	45,400	65,800	65,800	—
320/Blue	68,350	69,950	72,050	73,000	75,450	67,801	68,100	68,100	—
350 AWD	—	—	—	—	57,200	53,600	74,500	74,500	62,900
420E, 430	76,150	—	—	—	—	—	—	—	—
500E/S/AWD	116,950	81,500	83,500	84,600	84,600	—	—	—	—
550 AWD	—	—	—	—	—	85,000	85,300	85,300	73,200
55/63 AMG	101,600	113,000	101,150	115,650	117,745	118,900	121,000	121,000	106,900
Used Values ($)									
280/300/350 ▲	—	—	—	—	—	21,000	27,000	31,500	—
280/300/350 ▼	—	—	—	—	—	19,500	25,000	30,000	—
320/Blue ▲	9,500	11,000	13,000	14,000	16,500	23,000	29,000	33,500	—
320/Blue ▼	8,500	10,000	11,500	13,000	15,000	21,000	27,000	32,000	—
350 AWD ▲	—	—	—	—	17,500	22,000	29,000	32,000	43,000
350 AWD ▼	—	—	—	—	16,000	20,500	27,500	30,000	40,000
420E, 430 ▲	11,000	—	—	—	—	—	—	—	—
420E, 430 ▼	10,000	—	—	—	—	—	—	—	—
500E/S/AWD ▲	8,000	9,500	12,000	14,500	16,500	—	—	—	—
500E/S/AWD ▼	7,000	8,000	10,500	13,000	15,000	—	—	—	—
550 AWD ▲	—	—	—	—	—	21,000	30,000	42,000	50,000
550 AWD ▼	—	—	—	—	—	19,500	28,000	39,000	47,000
55/63 AMG ▲	11,500	12,500	14,000	16,000	18,500	27,000	44,000	53,000	70,000
55/63 AMG ▼	11,000	11,500	13,000	15,000	17,000	25,000	41,000	50,000	66,000
Reliability	1	2	2	2	2	2	3	3	4
Crash Safety (F)	—	4	4	4	4	4	4	4	4
Side	—	5	5	5	5	5	5	5	5
IIHS Side	—	—	—	—	—	3	3	3	5
Offset	5	5	5	5	5	5	5	5	5
Head Restraints (4d)	5	5	3	3	5	5	5	5	5

Wagon	3	—	—	—	—	—	—	—	—
Roof Strength	—	—	—	—	—	—	—	—	5
Rollover Resistance	—	5	5	5	5	5	5	5	5	5

Nissan

MAXIMA ★★★

RATING: Average (2007–10); Below Average (1999–06). The 1999 models were seriously problem-prone, but the 2002 and 2004 model redesigns made matters worse and heralded a dramatic decline in quality that continued until 2007. **Ideal model year:** Upgraded powertrains, better quality control, and fresh styling make the 2008 SL the best choice at $17,500 (the car originally sold for $41,500). A 2007 is a good second-choice for $4,000 less. Be wary of the redesigned, restyled 2010 model. The addition of traction and stability control is definitely a safety plus, but nagging quality issues remain. **"Real" city/highway fuel economy:** 3.0 manual: 10.8/7.9 L/100 km. 3.0 automatic: 12.1/8.1 L/100 km. 3.5 manual: 11.5/7.3 L/100 km. 3.5 automatic: 11.6/7.9 L/100 km. **Maintenance/repair costs:** Higher than average. **Parts:** Higher-than-average costs, but parts are easy to find. Xenon high-intensity discharge (HID) headlights can cost $800 each to replace. **Extended warranty:** A must-have. **Best alternatives:** Acura Integra, RL, or TL, Hyundai Genesis, and the Infiniti G35. **Helpful websites:** *www.nicoclub.com.*

Strengths and Weaknesses

ALERT! Pull the wheels and look for corroded ABS brake sensors; another indication is a brake grinding sound heard during your test drive. Cost to fix: $1,200.

The 2002–05 models' HID xenon headlights are easily stolen and expensive to replace, a problem shared with the Acura TL, Audi S4, 2003–04 BMWs, and Nissan Altimas. Thieves pry open the hood, break the latch, and cut the battery or alarm cable. They pull the headlights from the plastic brackets to get the bulbs and the special power pack. Each bulb and ballast costs $550 to replace, and repairing additional damage can total as much as $4,000.

In 2006, Nissan settled a lawsuit with the State of New Jersey for $325,000 to cover costs of investigation and give compensation to affected owners. The state alleged Nissan knew the lights were easily stolen and failed to disclose this fact to owners.

Early models (2001 and earlier)

These front-drive sedans are very well equipped and nicely finished, but they're cramped for their size. Although the trunk is spacious, only five passengers can travel in a pinch (in the literal sense).

2002–06: More of the same

Each Maxima redesign has been followed by an increase in owner complaints of poor quality, a normal occurrence with most revamped vehicles. Usually (but not always), after a couple of years, quality rebounds and complaints diminish. But not with Nissan. Factory-related goofs, poor designs, and low-quality suppliers have kept Nissan quality in the basement for the better part of a decade, as confirmed by the post-redesign glitches emblematic of the Quest minivan.

Recent redesigns have hobbled the powertrain. Owners have difficulty controlling the engine speed with the gas pedal. There's engine popping and knocking when accelerating, surging or stalling when braking or decelerating, and transmission malfunctions galore. Premature front brake pad wear and rotor warpage; a choppy, jarring suspension; excessive front-end shaking and shimmy; faulty ignition coils; and inadequate headlight illumination continue to be major problems.

The 2004–06 revamped Maximas continue to have the following major quality problems: seat shifting; broken struts; transmission failures; harsh automatic shifting; a gear grind from First to Second; windows that are slow to roll down; paint that's easily chipped or scratched; side mirrors that won't reposition; a screeching sound that's caused by a loose heat shield; water leaks by right floorboard and through sunroof; inoperative steering-wheel stereo buttons; no-starts caused by a loose fuel-pump connector or ignition switch failure; HID lights with high beams that won't return to low and bulbs that burn out prematurely; and brake shimmy or judder (dealers lean toward all the usual suspects before they resort to the steering-rack friction adjustment that has cured the shimmy for some of the most persistent cases).

2007–10 improvements

The number of safety-related complaints posted on NHTSA's webpage (*www. safercar.gov*) has slowed to a trickle, indicating that Nissan is making more reliable and better-performing vehicles, but it has been a slow road to travel and there's still much more they need to do. Recent models still have some brake, powertrain, AC compressor, electronics, and suspension problems along with sub-par fit and finish like warped dashboards and a symphony of clicks, rattles, pops, and clunks. Hopefully, the 2010 redesign will reduce the chronic engine and transmission failures of the past. But don't bet on it.

VEHICLE HISTORY: 2002—Completely revamped, featuring a 260 hp 3.5L V6 coupled to a 6-speed manual or 4-speed automatic transmission; revised interior trim; larger front brakes; new front-end styling; and xenon headlights (a thief's Holy Grail). **2003**—GLE gets standard front side airbags. **2004**—Another redesign adds to the size and weight, along with 5 more horses. Once again, quality takes a big hit. **2005**—Improved 6-speed manual transmission. **2007**—Revised interior and exterior styling, keyless starting, and a new transmission. Sporty 3.5 SE and 3.5 SL models are offered with a 255 hp V6 coupled to a new, fuel-saving CVT automatic transmission with a manual shiftgate and six pre-selected gears.

2009—Fresh styling and additional power. All models come with a 290 hp 3.5L V6 hooked to a CVT automatic transmission, resulting in 35 more horses. **2010**—New front-end styling and standard vehicle stability control and traction control.

 ## Safety Summary

All years: Airbag failed to deploy. • Sudden loss of power, resulting in inoperative brakes and steering. • Chronic stalling. • Erratic transmission performance. • ABS failures. • Steering lock-ups and loss of brakes. **2002**—Vehicle suddenly swings to the right. • Steering wheel overheats. • Vehicle accelerates when foot is taken off accelerator. • Sudden acceleration in Reverse with gearshift lever indicating Drive. • In one incident, vehicle surged when brakes were applied while parking, and car hit a brick wall. • ABS and traction control malfunction every time car is washed. • Front wheels lock up or get no power; ABS light remains lit. • Hesitation on acceleration. • Defective mass air sensor or crank sensor causes sudden loss of power and transmission bucking and jerking. • Vehicle rolls backward when parked on an incline. • Right front wheel buckles when brakes are applied. • Faulty air control valve causes sudden acceleration. • Suspension transverse link failed, causing loss of control; owners report that cars not in the recall have the same defect. • Lower control-arm failure as in recall notice, but car isn't among those recalled. • Chronic brake failures. • Back window suddenly shatters. • Rear quarter window air leaks. • Trunk water leaks. **2003**—Passenger-side airbag deploys on its own. • O$_2$ sensor failure. • Hard-to-read instrument panel lights. **2004**—Vehicle was cruising at 100 km/h when the steering wheel suddenly locked up and the brakes failed. • In another instance, the front wheels locked up while the vehicle was in motion, causing extensive undercarriage damage. • Vehicle suddenly swerves out of control. • Vehicle suddenly accelerates in Reverse when put into Drive. • Sudden acceleration upon start-up (a faulty air control valve is suspected). • Unable to control engine speed with the accelerator pedal. • Vehicle stalls without warning in cold weather (suspect the computer module). • Many complaints that the headlights are poorly designed, placing the high beams too high for adequate visibility; drivers complain they can't see between the high and low beams. • Trunk lid and latch are hazardous when raised. • Several incidents of the SkyView roof shattering. • Sunroof opens and closes on its own. • Steering wheel overheats in direct sunlight. • The driver-side windshield washer may not work in cold weather. **2005**—Stalling and hard starts. • Engine surges when downshifting. • There is a one-second delay from when the accelerator pedal is released to when the car begins to slow down. • Engine threw a rod and had to be replaced. • Erratic transmission shifts. • Strong vibration and shimmy, probably related to faulty suspension strut assemblies that often wear out within a year. • Sudden total brake loss. • Accelerator and brake pedals are mounted too close together. • Rack-and-pinion steering assembly wears out early. • Broken axle. • Headlights don't work properly. **2006**—Airbag deployed for no reason; airbag deployed inadvertently. • Sudden, unintended acceleration. • Automatic transmission jerks and jumps. • Corroded ABS sensors produce a brake grinding sound. • Car is very difficult to steer. • Excessive steering-wheel vibration. • Crack in the rear suspension subframe. • Doors lock and unlock on their own. • Excessive windshield reflection impairs visibility. **2007**—Sudden, unintended acceleration with no brakes:

> I have a 2007 Nissan Maxima and my car shot out of a car wash and across 4 lanes of traffic and crashed into federal property. After the car was pushed from the dry option I put my foot on the brake took the car out of Neutral, put it into Drive and the car took off like a rocket. I had both feet on the brakes and had to use two hands to steer the car away from traffic.

Poor ABS brake design leads to huge repair bills due to premature corrosion of the ABS brake sensors. • Brake master cylinder failures. • Automatic transmission electronic malfunctions won't permit shifting out of First or into Second gear. • Frequent stalling on the highway. • Car jerks and transmission slips. • Incorrect fuel gauge readings (vehicle not part of the recall campaign, but has the problem). • Driver noticed the Service Engine light was lit and dealer says it was because gas cap wasn't screwed on tightly and charged him $100 to reset the computer. **2008**—Airbag alert flashes for no reason and driver must fork over $914 to get it put out. • Tire pressure warning system gives false alarms. • A four-month-old car needed its automatic transmission replaced. • CV axle broke while car was being parked. • Uncomfortable front head restraints. Michelin tires said to hydroplane at highway speeds. **2009**—Sudden, unintended acceleration. • Passenger-side airbag disabled for no reason whenever anyone occupies the seat. • Brake failures. • Wheels bend easily and cause vehicle to vibrate. • Driver's seat isn't stable when car speeds up or stops. • Tilt steering wheel locked in the extreme up position. Doors lock and unlock on their own. Original equipment tires have sidewall cracks. **2010**—Airbags failed to deploy. • Engine won't throttle down. • Engine loses power when accelerating up to 80 km/h; throttle body replaced but problem still persists. • Automatic transmission grinding; unit replaced. • Transmission won't shift into Drive. • No-starts due to a defective steering-wheel lock mechanism (#48700-JK000—often back-ordered). All Intelligent Key models are similarly affected. • Front end clunk. • Sunroof suddenly exploded. • Goodyear Eagle RS-A tire tread separation. • Front-seat passenger airbag warning light comes on for no reason; replacing the seat changed nothing. • Driver's seat moves back and forth; sometimes it won't move at all. • Large head restraint blocks driver's rearward vision. • Headlights don't provide sufficient illumination.

Secret Warranties/Internal Bulletins/Service Tips

2000–02—Doors may intermittently lock by themselves. **2000–03**—Driver's seat won't go forward or backward. • Abnormal shifting (the control valve assembly is the likely culprit, says TSB #NTB04-035). **2000–06**—Oil leaks from oil-cooler oil seal. **2002**—Erratic sunroof operation. • Driver's power seat won't move forward or backward. **2002–03**—Hesitation on acceleration. • Lack of engine power. • Sunroof operates on its own. **2002–06**—How to silence an engine ticking noise. **2003**—Troubleshooting brake noise and judder. **2003–04**—Harsh 1–2 shifts. **2004**—Cold upshift shock; abnormal shifting. • Fuel system misfires. • Hard start after a cold soak. • Engine won't crank in cold weather. •

Front brake noise. • Water leaks from roof. • Headlight fogging. • Loose headliner. **2004–05**—Exhaust rattle/buzz when accelerating. • Voluntary service campaign entails the free replacement of the rear suspension and bushing sealing for 13 years. If the subframe is too corroded, Nissan will buy back the car (see Altima "Secret Warranties/Service Tips" for the TSB confirming this important free repair). **2004–06**—No-cranks in cold weather. • Erratic gauge, AC operation. • Front power-seat malfunction. • Hard-to-move shifter. **2004–07**—Engine noise coming from the timing chain area. • ABS activates when it shouldn't. • Noisy driver's power seat. **2004–08**—Tire-pressure-monitor sensor may leak fluid. • Inoperative power-door mirrors. • Heat shield rattles. **2007–08**—Front suspension rattling. • Inoperative lumbar support. **2007–09**—If the vehicle has low power accelerating to 80 km/h, the likely cause is a defective wheel speed sensor. • Sunroof is inoperative or operates erratically. **2009**—Sunroof glass chatter, creaking, or popping. • Sunroof wind noise. • Power window "Up" and steering column adjustment may both be inoperative. • Loose headliner. • Front passenger seat shakes at highway speeds. • Voluntary Service Campaign #PC005 to replace the steering knuckle for free:

CAMPAIGN PC005—L/H REAR SUSPENSION KNUCKLE

BULLETIN NO.: NTB09-031   DATE: APRIL 23, 2009

2009 Maxima and 2009 Altima Sedan, Coupe, and Hybrid

INTRODUCTION: On some 2009 Altima and Maxima vehicles, the left hand rear suspension knuckle may not be manufactured to specification, which may result in noise or vibration under certain circumstances. Although no safety issue is presented, Nissan is conducting this service campaign to identify and replace those affected units. This service will be performed at no cost for parts or labor. **DEALER RESPONSIBILITY:** Dealers are to inspect each vehicle falling within range of this campaign that enters the service department, and if necessary, perform the indicated knuckle replacement. This includes vehicles purchased from private parties or presented by transient (tourist) owners and vehicles in a dealer's inventory.

2009–10—Transmission "booming" countermeasures. • Front power seats won't move. • Driver's seat is wobbly. • Can't turn ignition to the On position. • Fuel gauge issues. **2009–11**—Silencing a rear end squeak or clunk heard when passing over bumps.

MAXIMA PROFILE

	2002	2003	2004	2005	2006	2007	2008	2009	2010
Cost Price ($)									
Base	32,900	32,900	34,500	34,600	35,098	36,998	36,998	37,900	39,450
Used Values ($)									
Base ▲	4,500	5,000	6,000	8,000	10,500	12,500	16,500	21,500	25,500
Base ▼	4,000	4,500	5,500	7,000	9,000	11,000	15,000	20,000	23,000

Reliability	2	2	2	3	3	4	4	4	4
Crash Safety (F)	4	4	5	5	5	5	5	5	5
Side	4	4	4	4	4	4	4	5	5
IIHS Side	—	—	2	2	2	2	2	5	5
Offset	3	3	5	5	5	5	5	5	5
Head Restraints (F)	5	5	1	1	1	2	2	2	2
Roof Strength	—	—	—	—	—	—	—	3	3
Rollover Resistance	4	4	4	4	4	4	4	5	5

Toyota

AVALON ★★★

RATING: Average (2005–10); Above Average (1999–2004). A *Lemon-Aid* Recommended car for decades, the Avalon now suffers from the same "less for more" philosophy we have seen since 1997 with most of Toyota's lineup. Surprisingly, post-1996 Avalons fare better than most other Toyotas, but during the 2005–06 period, following the car's last major redesign, quality declined markedly. **Ideal model year:** If you must buy an Avalon, go for the 2008 XLS for about $19,000 (pretty good price for a car that first sold for $37,755). **"Real" city/ highway fuel economy:** 11.0/7.4 L/100 km. **Maintenance/repair costs:** Higher than average. **Parts:** Higher-than-average costs, and limited availability. **Extended warranty:** Not needed. **Best alternatives:** A fully loaded Camry, but if you want a more driver-involved experience in a Toyota, consider a Lexus ES 300 series or something in the GS 300 lineup. Other good choices are the Acura RL, or TL and the Infiniti G35 series. **Helpful websites:** *www.toyotanation.com/ forum.*

Strengths and Weaknesses

ALERT! In your pre-purchase test drive make sure the recall fix for sudden, unintended acceleration has been performed and the powertrain doesn't "lag and lurch." Also, verify that the front head restraints don't push your chin into your chest or make it impossible for seat occupants to sit all the way back.

This near-luxury four-door offers more interior space and performance than do other cars in its class that cost thousands of dollars more. Basically a front-drive, mid-sized sedan based on a stretched Camry platform, the Avalon is quick on its feet, better attuned to abrupt manoeuvres, relatively roomy.

VEHICLE HISTORY: 2005—The third-generation Avalon is restyled and is larger and more powerful. It seats five instead of six, due to new front bucket seats, and offers 2.5 cm more legroom. Toyota's 280 hp 3.5L V6 coupled to a 5-speed automatic, instead of the previous year's 4-speed, replaces the 210 hp 3.0L V6 transmission.

All models come with four-wheel ABS disc brakes, front side airbags, side curtain airbags, and a driver's knee airbag. Traction/anti-skid control is available for most models, except the Touring. Other features added to the 2005 models: reclining backrests for a split-folding rear seat, a steering wheel with telescopic as well as tilt adjustment, heated/cooled front seats, keyless starting, and xenon headlights (Touring and Limited). **2008**—A 6-speed automatic replaces the 5-speed; a restyled grille and bumper. **2009**—Standard traction control and anti-skid system. **2010**—A memory feature has been added to the exterior mirrors and driver's seat.

Quality control up through 2004 is better than average, though steering, suspension, and fuel-system components are failure-prone, and many owners have complained of engine sludge forcing them to spend thousands of dollars on engine repairs.

Owners of 2005–07 Avalons report their cars continue to have serious safety, performance, and reliability problems. And word is getting around. Says *LemonLawClaims.com* (*www.lemonlawclaims.com/toyota_avalon__problems_lemon. htm*):

> For the [2005] Avalon, [Toyota] has provided service bulletins, which alerts dealers to problems [that include] bad U-joint welds, faulty catalytic converters and a leak in the oil supply line for variable valve timing…. Transmission hesitation problems, which have plagued the automaker in the past, also have resurfaced with the five-speed automatic transmission installed in the Avalon. While the earlier transmission problems were experienced by consumers in a variety of situations, this round of trouble surfaces particularly when the driver presses the acceleration pedal for greater speed.

Other performance gripes posted by *Lemon-Aid* readers include hydroplaning, excessive body lean, highway wandering, major engine oil leaks, suspension strut failures, poor transmission performance, premature front brake repairs, faulty navigation systems, under-steering when cornering, numerous electrical system glitches, a malfunctioning laser-guided cruise control, clunky steering that vibrates and pulls to either side, and a problematic Vehicle Stability Control and Traction Control system. Body construction and assembly are no longer first class, with poor fit and finish, rattles, and water/air leaks the most common complaints. Paint spotting/flaking has afflicted all models.

 ## Safety Summary

All years: Airbags failed to deploy in an accident. • Sudden, unintended acceleration. • Excessive highway wandering. • Automatic transmission slippage. • Brake pedal goes to the floor with no braking effect. • Driver's seat rocks back and forth. • Steering wheel is off-centre. • Dash lights and gauges reflect onto windshield. • Bridgestone/Firestone, Dunlop, and Michelin tire failures. **2002**—Cruise control doesn't slow car when going downhill. • Vehicle veers to the left at high speeds. **2003**—Extended braking distances. • Front brakes appear to apply themselves. **2004**—Rear wheel seizes while vehicle is underway. • Stalling when AC is activated. • Key won't turn in the ignition. **2005**—Throttle stuck to the floor. • Hesitation and surging when accelerating. • Engine surges and then shuts off and can't be restarted. • Cruise control speed drop is hazardous:

> When my car slows down suddenly because of the car in front, there is no warning for the car behind me. Toyota was notified of this problem and told me not to use the sonar in heavy travelled roads. That is no solution. There should be a fix to make the brake lights go on when the car is slowed down by the sonar.

Brakes suddenly fail due to a faulty master cylinder. • Loose motor mounts cause noise and instability when accelerating from a stop. • Wheel bearing axle grease leaks onto front disc pad, causing poor braking. • Rear windshield distortion causes road to appear wavy and cars to appear to be swerving. • Electrical shorts. **2006**—Fire ignited in the rear middle seat from the seat heater overheating. • Engine hesitates on acceleration to merge with traffic. • WTI oil line corroded and ruptured, resulting in all of the oil leaking out of the engine. • Transmission hunts for the proper gear, lurches, and slips, and it shifts erratically at low speeds. • Navigation system doesn't function as intended. • Leaking brake master cylinder and booster may lead to loss of braking. • Sudden application of the brakes may cause the telescopic steering wheel to collapse inward. • Faulty "intermediate steering shaft" results in clunks when turning. • Laser cruise control fails intermittently. • Rough-riding Cooper Lifeliner tires. **2007**—Airbags fail to deploy. • Knee airbag deployment is alleged to have caused massive leg injuries to the driver. • When the laser cruise control is activated, rear brake lights don't come on to warn following drivers that the car is braking. • Excessive steering vibrations and pulling to the left and right. • Automatic transmission "bumps" into gear. • Inoperative push-button starter. • Ignition switch can cause keys to bend. • Smart Key ignition system can cause heart pacemakers and defibrillators to malfunction. • A $100 gas cap?

> Service Engine and many other trouble indicators at the same time. Trouble found for $80.00 loose gas cap. Days later found gas cap strap missing. Return to dealer who said the strap is what caused the poor seal so the tech removed it (as this happens all the time). Ask to purchase a replacement strap – not available. Purchased new gas cap which comes with strap (a 2 cent [item]) cost $25.00. Total cost for a known problem $100.

2008—Headlights suddenly go out:

> Driving down a dark road, the high beams would not come on. Took it to Toyota dealership and they said high beams burned out and the repair would cost $2600. The dealership stated if they were replaced, they may burn out again.

•

I just heard on the radio this morning there is a recall on the headlamps intermittently working/not working on the Prius. Please add the 2008 Toyota Avalon to this recall. On December 24, 2010, as my wife and I were leaving my daughter and son in-law's house at approx. 8:30 p.m., I used my remote start and started my car. My son-in-law looked outside and said, "You have a headlight out." It was the right front headlamp. I got in the car and turned the light switch off and turned it back on to "Auto" and both headlights came on once again. However, I had to turn them off and turn them back on to get them both working.

Headlight transformer failed; dealer estimated it would cost $2,096 to fix. **2009**—More headlight failures:

2009 Toyota Avalon; mileage at failure unknown, but less than 42,000. Both high beam bulbs exploded on the vehicle. Based on Internet research, this seems to be a known problem. Toyota issued a TSB 0044-10 on this failure 1/27/2010, yet they refuse to take ownership of the issue.

Brake failures. • Steering column telescopic lock won't stay locked. **2010**—Engaging the cruise control or applying the brakes will cause the car to suddenly accelerate. • Telescopic steering wheel suddenly collapses. • All the dash lights go out for about 10 seconds when turning or applying the brakes. • On an incline, the vehicle rolls backwards when driver's foot moves from the brake to the accelerator. • High-beam headlights shut off. • Painful front head restraints that are tilted too far forward for some drivers.

Secret Warranties/Internal Bulletins/Service Tips

1997–2002—Extended warranty will pay for engine sludge damage up to eight years, without any mileage limitation. **2000–04**—Fuel door hard to open. **2003–07**—Windshield ticking noise. **2004**—Correction for vehicle tendency to pull to the left. • Front suspension knocking. **2004–07**—Front-seat squeak. **2005–06**—Engine oil leaks. • Water leaks onto the front floor area. • Pull/drift to one side while driving. • Diagnosis and correction of steering-column noise. • Creaking and ticking noise heard from base of rear windshield. • Rear suspension thump, clunk. • Inoperative horn. **2005–07**—Rear vents blow warm air with AC on. • Front-door window won't roll up. • Windshield wiper fluid leaks. **2005–08**—Knocking noise from front of sunroof. **2005–09**—Front power seat grinding, groaning. **2005–11**—Sunroof leaks at headliner and floor areas. **2006–07**—Harsh shifting. **2007**—Rough idle, stalling. **2007–08**—Steering-wheel flutter; body vibration. **2008–10**—High-beam headlight failures will be covered by Toyota's base warranty and, thereafter, by a "goodwill" policy. Claimants should refer to TSB #004410, published January 27, 2010. If Toyota rejects the claim, go immediately to small claims court. The company's service bulletin admits Toyota goofed. **2008–11**—Underbody rattling noises. **2009–11**—Front, rear knocking noises when passing over bumps.

AVALON PROFILE

	2002	2003	2004	2005	2006	2007	2008	2009	2010
Cost Price ($)									
XL	38,365	—	—	—	—	—	—	—	—
XLS	45,135	45,560	45,830	39,900	39,900	41,135	37,755	41,840	39,285
Used Values ($)									
XL ▲	4,000	—	—	—	—	—	—	—	—
XL ▼	3,500	—	—	—	—	—	—	—	—
XLS ▲	5,000	6,000	7,500	9,000	12,000	16,000	20,000	23,000	27,000
XLS ▼	4,500	5,000	6,500	8,000	10,000	14,500	18,000	21,000	25,000
Reliability	5	5	5	3	4	4	4	4	5
Crash Safety (F)	4	4	5	5	5	5	5	5	5
Side	4	4	5	5	5	5	5	5	5
IIHS Side	—	—	—	5	5	5	5	5	5
Offset	5	5	5	5	5	5	5	5	5
Head Restraints (F)	1	1	1	1	1	1	1	5	5
Rollover Resistance	4	4	4	4	4	4	4	4	4

All ratings on a numbered scale where 5 is good and 1 is bad. See page 132 for a more detailed description.

SPORTS CARS

A Slice of "Middle-Age Crazy"

Yes, we all know that these small, low cars with high-powered, fuel-thirsty engines and seating for only two are a dangerous choice for young drivers, and scream "Mid-life crisis!" when driven by pony-tailed, open-shirted middle-aged men. They're also usually way overpriced and astronomically expensive to insure and service as they top off Helmut and Luigi's Canada Pension Plan. Most sports cars beg to be driven too fast and attract more traffic tickets than chicks.

But they're so much fun to drive, especially for those of us who missed our chance to own one in our youth because we were too poor, practical, or preoccupied with our Cavaliers, Corollas, or Beetles to give in to our primal instincts.

If real driving performance is important to you, though, remember that big isn't always better. Consider getting an agile, fun-to-drive small car, such as a used Acura Integra, Honda Civic Si, Mazda Miata, Mazda3, or Nissan Sentra SE-R. If you want to be a little more "in your face," however, it's hard to lose money with a Detroit muscle-car sportster built through 1974.

If you have a limited budget, or little experience driving a performance car, start out with one of the "sporty" makes, then move through the two-seaters, muscle cars, and then the ultimate: the luxury sports cars. Remember, though, there are some real dogs that have been run ragged or wrecked out there, so check their ratings and prior ownership carefully.

Varieties of Sports Cars

There are different kinds of sports cars to consider: traditional two-seater roadsters, styled much like the MGB of the early '70s or Mazda's Miata; sporty coupes and hatchbacks, such as the Japanese Acura Integra, Honda Civic Si,

If you want a cheap and extremely reliable sportster convertible, consider a 2008 Mazda Miata GT for $16,000–$17,000. Not bad for a car that once had a top-end price of $34,500.

Mazda MX-3, and Toyota Celica, which offer sportier styling, performance, and handling than their entry-level versions and are cheaper and more versatile to maintain than traditional sports cars; and muscle cars, which feature large engines and a few more creature comforts. The best deal in the latter category is the V8-equipped Ford Mustang with the GM Camaro or Firebird a distant second. Interestingly, that lead has increased with Ford's reworked 2011 iteration giving its V6 the power of the previous year's V8 powerplant, with better fuel economy.

There's a comprehensive forum at *www.sportscarforums.com* that goes into mind-numbing detail as to what makes a good sports car. Different cars are rated, service tips are given, and the age-old feud between domestics and imports is omnipresent and unresolved.

The biggest irony of all is that Japanese high-performance sports cars and pickups have won favour in the Deep South and throughout Canada because they deliver high-performance thrills without the service bay bills. No longer do you hear contemptuous references to Asian "rice-burners" now that Toyota and other Asian automakers are successfully racing their cars and trucks at NASCAR-sanctioned tracks.

The Downside

We all know the drawbacks. Most sports cars—or "high-performance vehicles," as they're euphemistically named—don't offer the comfort or reliability of a Honda Civic, a Toyota Celica, or even a Hyundai Tiburon. Instead, they sacrifice reliability, interior space, and a comfortable suspension for speed, superior road handling, and attractive styling. They also need a whole slew of expensive and quick-to-depreciate high-performance packages, because many entry-level sports cars aren't very sporty in their basic form. Remember, too, that used sports cars often have serious accident damage that may not have been repaired properly, resulting in serious tracking problems if the chassis is bent.

Beware of false bargains. Although a 2008 Dodge Charger SRT8 or 2009 Challenger SRT8 is a steal at $17,000 and $27,500 (they sold new for $46,395 and $46,995), the money saved will be quickly spent in high maintenance costs and frequent repairs.

Fully loaded used sports cars usually sell at a fraction of their original cost, and very few end up as collectibles. Most models that have been taken off the market—such as the Toyota Supra, Nissan 300ZX, and Chevrolet Corvette ZR1—aren't likely to become collectors' cars with soaring resale values. In fact, a 2006 Corvette 7.0L Z06 that sold originally for $90,000 in Canada can now be picked up for about $31,000! A 2012 version goes for $96,910, and it has already lost almost $10,000 of its value over the last six months.

Forget how quickly the 2006 Z06 goes from 0 to 100 km/h; check instead how fast its value drops from $90,000 to $31,000!

When buying a sports car, keep in mind that the more features you add, the less reliable the car becomes, and that there are some modifications that are more important than others. For example, good-quality high-performance tires are the first investment you should make (check the owner-polled recommendations at *www.tirerack.com/tires/reviews/MenuServlet?search=surveyComments*). Other improvements that should have a high priority are an upgraded set of brakes and suspension. And, if you have a few dollars left, consider getting a more-responsive rear end and a high-performance transmission.

SPORTS CAR RATINGS

Recommended

Mazda MX-5 (Miata) (1999–2010)

Average

Ford Mustang (2006–10)
General Motors Corvette (2005–10)

Below Average

Ford Mustang (2001–05)
General Motors Corvette (1999–2004)

Not Recommended

Ford Cobra (1999–2004)

Ford

| MUSTANG, COBRA | ★★★/★★ |

RATING: *Mustang:* The best Mustang you can buy that gives you first-class performance, great fuel economy, optimum safety features, quality craftsmanship, and a base price your gardener can afford is the...2011 Mustang V6. Anything less, and you're buying third-rate. Its $27,000 price has already fallen to $20.000. Average (2006–10); Below Average (2001–05). The 2006 version worked out many of the 2005 redesign glitches, and incremental improvements reduced factory-related defects found on earlier models. *Cobra:* Not Recommended (1999–2004). Fuel-savers beware: All 4-cylinder Mustangs should be shunned because they provide insufficient power, they aren't very durable, and the fuel savings are much less than you'd think. **Ideal model year:** Consider a 2007 LX for about $10,500. That gives the car two model years to digest its 2005 redesign anomalies and keeps you mobile for a few years until you can buy a much better-performing used 2011 version. **"Real" city/highway fuel economy:** *Mustang 3.8 manual:* 11.8/7.4 L/100 km. *Mustang 3.8 automatic:* 12.0/8.0 L/100 km. *Mustang 3.9 manual:* 11.7/7.4 L/100 km. *Mustang 3.9 automatic:* 12.3/8.2 L/100 km. *Mustang 4.6 manual:* 14.0/8.7 L/100 km. *Mustang 4.6 automatic:* 13.2/9.4 L/100 km. *Mustang Mach 1 manual:* 13.9/8.5 L/100 km. *Mustang Mach 1 automatic:* 13.8/9.5 L/100 km. *Cobra:* 14.1/9.1 L/100 km. **Maintenance/repair costs:** Average, particularly because repairs can be done anywhere. **Parts:** Average costs, and parts are often sold for much less through independent suppliers. Some parts are continually back ordered, particularly if involved in recall repairs. **Extended warranty:** A good idea for the powertrain. **Best alternatives:** GM Camaro, Honda Civic Si, Hyundai Genesis, Hyundai G35, G37, and Mazda MX-5 (Miata) or Mazda3. **Helpful websites:** *www.mustangforums.com/forum/2005-2011-mustangs-43; www. allfordmustangs.com;* and *www.flatratetech.com/community.*

Strengths and Weaknesses

ALERT! Stay away from the 2011 and 2012 Mustangs equipped with Chinese-made 6-speed transmissions. The tranny is a grenade waiting to go off.

Even if you won't be racing, get high-performance tires and "feather" the accelerator on all 2010 and earlier models. Regularly equipped Mustangs, like most rear-drive Fords, don't handle sharp curves or wet pavement very well. The rear end swings out suddenly and the car tends to spin uncontrollably. Traction is easily lost, and braking is hardly reassuring.

This is definitely not a family car. A light rear end makes the car dangerously unstable on wet roads or when cornering at high speeds, unless equipped with traction control (optional on most models). But for those who want a sturdy and stylish second car, or who don't need room in the back or standard ABS, 2001–04 and 2006–09 Mustangs are reasonably good sports car buys, thanks to their maxed-out depreciation, powertrain improvements, and fewer factory defects.

1994–2004 Mustang

Through the years, these models got four-wheel disc brakes, more-powerful engines, additional airbags, manumatic gearboxes with more gears, and a more-rigid chassis meant to reduce rattles and water leaks (which didn't work). Even more disappointing, Ford's performance- and safety-related problems were carried over year after year (see "Safety Summary"). Engines and transmissions continue to be glitch-prone: Both the V6 and V8 have a propensity for chronic surging and stalling, and they experience failed motor mounts; engine stalls when decelerating; prematurely worn clutch pressure plates; faulty differential carrier bearings; blown engine intake manifold and head gaskets; differential howling or whining (ring and pinion failures); fuel-system malfunctions, highlighted by frequent fuel-injector replacement; and poorly shifting automatic transmissions, especially from First to Second gear. Owners also frequently complain of electrical short circuits causing instrument panel shutdown and the early replacement of brake rotors, pads, and calipers.

2005–10 Mustang

Ford's reworking of the 2005 gave the Mustang a bit more muscle and slightly better performance, but the absence of ABS, an anti-skid system, independent rear suspension, and side airbags are four notable deficiencies when compared with the competition. Reliability actually went downhill during the first year of the redesign, only to improve with later models.

Nevertheless, a new subset of failures appeared with the 2005–10 cars, including tire-air leakage from faulty tire stems, rear-end howling, transmission fluid leakage, premature transmission failure, lag-and-lurch acceleration, transmission clutch slippage, sudden control-arm breakage, difficult refuelling, front end noise with low-speed turns, excessive brake noise, and electrical, fuel delivery, and fit and finish deficiencies (particularly, damage to the driver's side window from scratches caused by the hard plastic gasket on the window assembly's inner seal).

Cobra

Launched as a limited-production, high-performance 1993 sports car, the Cobra has garnered a reputation for mind-spinning depreciation, wallet-busting powertrain defects, and mediocre performance and handling. The first models came with a 240 hp V8, a firm suspension, all-disc ABS, and unique styling. In subsequent years (there were no 2000 or 2002 models), Cobras got more-powerful (yet unreliable) engines, a fully independent suspension, and hood and side scoops. The car's road performance remained seriously compromised by its loose rear end, which swings out when cornering under speed or on wet highways.

VEHICLE HISTORY: 2002—New 16-inch alloy wheels; sporty Cobra stays home again this year. **2003**—Three 4.6L V8 models: the 260 hp GT, the new 305 hp Mach 1, and the 390 hp supercharged SVT Cobra. **2005**—Restyled, with more power, more features, and a 15 cm larger wheelbase. **2007**—Debut of the high-performance Shelby GT and GT500. All models get a digital audio jack. **2008**—Debut of the Bullitt and the Shelby GT500KR, Ford's most powerful pony car ever. The Bullitt uses a 315 hp 4.6L V8 coupled to a 5-speed manual transmission, while the Shelby GT500KR carries a 540 hp 5.4L supercharged V8 engine paired with a 6-speed manual transmission.

 Safety Summary

All models/years: Serious concerns have been raised about the Mustang's fuel system failing safety integrity standards and about the tendency of the convertible's doors to jam shut in a 57 km/h frontal collision. • Sudden acceleration because of a stuck throttle. • Transmission allows vehicle to roll away when parked on an incline; emergency brake disengages. • Airbag fails to deploy; inadvertent airbag deployment. • Seat belt becomes twisted, continually tightens up when worn, or fails to retract. • Brake failure, and premature replacement of the brake master cylinder. • Side windows fall off their tracks. **2002**—Fire ignites in the wiring harness under dash area. • Wheel lug nuts fall off. • Sudden loss of steering when making a left-hand turn. • In one incident, a car left on an incline with transmission in Park and motor shut off rolled down after 10 minutes and hit a tree. • Emergency brake ratchet assembly breaks, making mechanism inoperable. • Gas spills out of fuel tank because clamps not sufficiently tightened. • Left front wheel falls off when the lower control arm and ball joint become loose. **2003**—Gas pedal can be caught by the carpet. • Sudden acceleration tied to the cruise-control mechanism. • Chronic stalling when decelerating; computer reflash doesn't fix the problem. • Automatic transmission failures. • Loss of brakes. • Spark plug blows out of the passenger-side cylinder head:

> This left me with a $4,463 repair cost to fix my car that I only owned for three months. While doing research on the Internet and asking questions in mechanic shops, it has been apparent that Ford engines have defective cylinder heads.

Water leaks through side windows. • AC condensation drips onto the exhaust pipe, rusting it out prematurely. **2004**—Throttle sticks under the carpet. • Seatback collapsed from a rear-ender; seatback bolt broke while driving. • Head restraints don't adjust enough. • Steering locks up. • Sharp tailpipe sticks out and can severely cut anyone brushing against it. • Rear window explodes for no reason. **2005**—Stuck accelerator pedal. • When slowing for a stop, engine hesitates then surges, and the automatic transmission slams into gear. • When parking, car suddenly accelerates in Drive or in Reverse. • Faulty fuel pumps blamed for frequent stalling. • The manual transmission clutch engages abruptly. • Brake fluid leaks from the master cylinder. • Brakes suddenly lock up, and in some cases, catch fire. • Parking brake cable seizes or breaks. • The powertrain "tunnel" located down the centre of the car gets extremely hot while driving. • Steering locks while turning left. • Rear strut/shock absorber support brackets rust out. • Fuel spews out the filler pipe, and gas station pumps shut off before the fuel tank is full—a problem that's carried over to the 2006 models. • When underway, flimsy hood vibrates and twists violently. • Dash panel cannot be read on a sunny day while wearing sunglasses. • Airbag warning light remains lit. • Convertible-top lifting mechanism froze halfway up; will cost $6,000 to fix. **2006**—When accelerating, vehicle hesitates then surges. • Car continues to be hard to refuel (nozzle shuts off when tank is a quarter to half full). • Side window shattered for no reason. • Windshield distortion causes wavy white lines to appear. • Broken seatback levers and side mirrors. **2007**—Mustang GT throttle stuck. • Car hesitates and then surges when accelerating. • Frequent complaints that the right control arm broke at the weld. • Fuel tank takes a long time to fill. • Clutch slippage. • Erratic shifting with the automatic transmission. • A faulty Second-gear clutch causes a whining noise and then transmission failure. • Parking brakes seize in cold weather. • Convertible top leaks and floods vehicle. • Many complaints of tires failing due to loss of tire pressure (cracked Chinese-made valve stems), having to be inflated three times weekly to maintain the proper pressure. • Saleen model rear visibility obstructed by the spoiler. • Some rear windshield defroster/defogger embedded wires don't work. **2008**—Sudden, unintended acceleration:

> Parking car into parking bay between building support and other car. With my foot on brake and at a stop I reached to place car in Park when for no reason the car accelerated over a concrete parking stop, through a ditch, out of the ditch before striking another truck head on in the parking area across the ditch. My foot was on the brake the entire time and I did not touch the shifter at all!

False tire pressure alerts. • Multiple automatic transmission replacements. • Excessive steering wheel shake. • Primary hood latch failure. • Cracked tire valve stem (a common Ford failure). **2009**—Sudden, unintended acceleration. • Frontal and side airbags failed to deploy. • Check Engine light continuously lit. • Clutch failure on the GT500:

> Ford has issued a TSB on the clutch and its flywheel indicating that heavy stop and go traffic will warp the flywheel and in turn ruin the clutch and tran[s]mission. Ford

did nothing to fix the problem (identified in the TSB, NHTSA 10032615 - TSB-09-19-11).

Brake and accelerator pedals mounted too close together. • Premature ball joint wear. **2010**—Airbag failed to deploy. • Car lurches forward when shifted into Drive. • Manual transmission grinds when shifted. • Sudden rear axle failure (the rear end carrier and axle are seizing in the housing. • AC condenser fans are vulnerable to damage from road debris. • Hood scoop may not be properly secured to the hood. • LED lights that use pulse-width modulation (PWM) produce a blinding flicker unless they are on an operating frequency above 3,000 Hertz:

It started with Cadillac's SRX around 2000, now in 2010 Ford and Volkswagen have gone overboard and just about all the vehicles they build are operating at this dangerous and deadly frequency. The operating frequency needs to be >2500 Hertz, I did test this! Police cars built by Ford are putting them in harm's way. The buses Ford and GM built are having the same issues.

Secret Warranties/Internal Bulletins/Service Tips

All models/years: Paint delamination, peeling, or fading. • Ford's seven-year "goodwill" warranty extensions usually cover powertrain and fit and finish problems. • Stalling, rough idle, long crank times, or cold hesitation when accelerating may signal the need to clean out intake valve deposits. • Excessive oil consumption likely caused by leaking gaskets, worn piston rings, poor sealing of the lower intake manifold, or defective intake and exhaust valve stem seals; install new guide-mounted valve-stem seals for a better fit as well as new piston rings with improved oil control. • A thumping or clacking heard from the front brakes signals the need to machine the front disc brake rotors. **All models: 1998–2002**—Guidelines for replacing defective ignition lock cylinders. **1998–2006**—Troubleshooting tips for correcting a rough-running engine. **1999–2004**—Manual transmission is hard to shift into Reverse or First. **2001–03**—Wind noise from the A-pillar area. **2001–04**—4.6L engine rattle. **2002**—Air leaks in the intake manifold or engine. • In 4.6L engines, oil leaks from the head gasket area. • Manual transmission clashes or grinds. **2003–04**—Hard to shift, rattling manual transmission. • Install four revised hood scoop insulators (#2L7Z-9P686-AA) to eliminate a hood rattle. **2005–06**—Erratic fuel gauge. • Parking brake cable freezes; rear brakes drag. **2005–07**—Front-end noise on bumps. • Ford finally admits it has a fuel-tank fill-up problem and offers to change the tank under warranty, according to TSB #07-21-12. • Paint blistering and early corrosion on aluminum body panels. • Abnormal, premature convertible-top wear, malfunction. **2005–08**—Water leaks onto front floor. • Exhaust system buzz, rattle. **2005–09**—Shudder on acceleration. • Loss of key gears in the automatic transmission shift sequence (see TSB on following page). • Water leak onto the front floor area. **2005–10**—4.0L V6 engine buzzing. • Rear axle vent fluid leaks and axle whine. **2006–10**—Trunk lid won't latch. **2007–09**—Airbag light stays on. **2009**—A rough-running 4.0L V6 engine may have a missing or damaged fuel injector orifice plate (an emissions warranty item).

WATER LEAK ONTO FRONT FLOOR AREA

BULLETIN NO.: 08-26-7

DATE: JANUARY 5, 2009

2005–09 Mustang

ISSUE: Some 2005–09 Mustang vehicles may exhibit a difficult to diagnose water leak in the front floor area. This may be caused by loose grommets and/or sealer skips around the cowl area, loose A-pillar window weatherstrip retainer, misaligned body harness grommet through the firewall, or a misaligned body harness grommet from the passenger door.

LOSS OF 2ND/3RD/5TH GEARS/RATIO DTC'S SET

BULLETIN NO.: TSB 09-12-12

DATE: JUNE 29, 2009

5R555/5R55N/5R55W TRANSMISSIONS—SHIFT CONCERNS, LOSS OF 2ND, 3RD AND 5TH GEAR, INCORRECT RATIO DTC'S—PROCEDURE TO INSPECT AND REPAIR SERVO PIN BORE WEAR

2002–05 Thunderbird; 2005–09 Mustang; 2002–09 Explorer; 2007–09 Explorer Sport Trac; 2002–06 Lincoln; LS 2003–05; Aviator 2002–09; Mountaineer.

ISSUE: Some 2002–09 Explorer, Mountaineer, 2007–09 Explorer Sport Trac, 2002–06 Lincoln LS, 2005–09 Mustang, 2002–05 Thunderbird and 2003–05 Aviator vehicles equipped with a 5R55S, 5R55W, and 5R55N transmission may experience shifting concerns. A loss of 2nd, 3rd and 5th gear, may have overdrive band or intermediate band failures due to servo pin case bore wear causing reduced apply pressure.

Engine squeal, chirp on cold start-up (4.0L V6). **2010**—A faulty engine balance shaft sprocket may be the cause of the 4.0L engine rattles, misfires, power loss, or no-starts. *Cobra:* **2001–05**—Rear axle shudder, chatter. **2003**—Defective engine cylinder heads or valve guides (replacement cylinder head Part #3R2Z-6049-GA). **2004**—Intermittent loss of power, no-starts. • Engine overheating.

MUSTANG, COBRA PROFILE

	2002	2003	2004	2005	2006	2007	2008	2009	2010
Cost Price ($)									
LX/Coupe	22,795	22,990	23,495	23,795	23,999	23,999	24,799	24,799	25,499
Coupe GT	31,055	31,505	31,795	32,795	32,999	33,499	33,999	33,999	36,999
Cobra	—	41,995	46,855	—	—	—	—	—	—
Cvt.	—	45,995	50,655	—	—	—	—	—	—
Shelby GT500	—	—	—	—	—	51,999	54,299	54,229	56,499
Shelby Cvt.	—	—	—	—	—	56,099	58,399	58,399	60,699
Convertible	27,465	27,760	28,095	27,995	27,999	27,999	28,899	28,899	29,699
Convertible GT	35,020	31,505	35,795	36,795	36,999	37,599	38,099	38,099	41,199
Used Values ($)									
LX/Coupe ▲	4,000	5,000	6,000	7,500	9,500	11,000	13,000	15,000	17,500
LX/Coupe ▼	3,500	4,500	5,000	6,500	8,500	9,500	11,500	13,500	16,000
Coupe GT ▲	6,000	7,000	8,000	9,000	10,500	14,000	16,500	20,500	24,000
Coupe GT ▼	5,000	6,000	7,000	8,000	9,000	12,500	15,000	19,000	22,500

Cobra ▲	—	8,000	9,000	—	—	—	—	—	—
Cobra ▼	—	6,500	7,500	—	—	—	—	—	—
Cvt. ▲	—	9,500	11,000	—	—	—	—	—	—
Cvt. ▼	—	8,500	10,000	—	—	—	—	—	—
Shelby GT500 ▲	—	—	—	—	—	20,000	25,000	31,000	38,000
Shelby GT500 ▼	—	—	—	—	—	18,500	23,000	29,000	36,000
Shelby Cvt. ▲	—	—	—	—	—	24,000	28,000	36,000	45,000
Shelby Cvt. ▼	—	—	—	—	—	22,500	27,500	34,000	43,000
Convertible ▲	6,000	6,500	7,500	9,000	11,500	13,500	15,000	18,000	21,000
Convertible ▼	5,500	6,000	7,000	8,000	10,500	12,000	13,500	16,500	19,500
Convertible GT ▲	8,500	9,000	11,000	12,000	14,500	17,500	19,500	24,500	28,000
Convertible GT ▼	7,500	8,000	9,500	11,000	14,000	16,000	18,000	23,000	26,000

Reliability	2	2	2	3	4	4	4	4	4
Crash Safety (F)	5	5	5	5	5	5	5	5	5
Convertible	—	—	—	—	—	—	5	5	5
Side	3	3	3	4	4	4	5	5	5
Convertible	2	2	2	—	—	—	5	5	5
IIHS Side	—	—	—	—	—	—	—	—	3
Side (Convertible)	—	—	—	—	—	5	5	5	5
Offset	—	—	—	—	—	—	—	—	5
Offset (Convertible)	—	—	—	3	3	3	3	3	5
Head Restraints (F)	—	—	—	—	—	—	—	—	5
Convertible	—	—	—	1	1	1	1	1	5
Rollover Resistance	5	5	5	5	5	5	5	5	5

General Motors

CORVETTE ★ ★ ★

RATING: Average (2005–10); Below Average (1999–2004). Keep in mind that premium fuel and astronomical insurance rates will drive up your operating costs. And don't discount the serious safety-related problems you're likely to experience on all models. They run the gamut of sudden steering lock-ups when underway, electrical shorts causing vehicle shutdowns, nonfunctioning parking brakes, brake failures caused by premature rotor warpage (around 16,000 km), seat belts that jam in the retractor, and, on the 2005, the top suddenly flying off (a 2002 Ford Mustang trait as well). The locked-up steering is particularly scary because it apparently has carried over to many model years, and traffic accident investigators may simply conclude that a resulting accident was because of driver inexperience or unsafe driving. **Ideal model year:** Shh! Don't tell anyone, but anything after 1962 is too big and the 1953–57 versions were handling nightmares. So that leaves my favourites: the 1958–62 models, of which I feel the 1958 Vette is the best.

Among the more recently minted models, I vote for the 2006 entry-level model for about $20,500, or less than one-third the car's original selling price. It had a year to fix the 2005 design changes and came with an upgraded 6-speed automatic transmission. **"Real" city/highway fuel economy:** *Manual: 12.3/7.7 L/100 km. Automatic: 13.2/7.9 L/100 km.* **Maintenance/repair costs:** Much higher than average, although most repairs can be done by any independent garage. Long waits for recall repairs. **Parts:** Pricey, but easy to find. Surprisingly, it is often easier to find parts for older Corvettes through collectors' clubs than it is to find many of the high-tech components used today. **Extended warranty:** Get a GM-backed supplementary warranty, or look for a recent model that has some of its original warranty left. The frequency of repairs and the high repair costs make maintenance outrageously expensive. **Best alternatives:** Ford Mustang, GM Camaro or Firebird, Hyundai Genesis Coupe, Mazda Miata, and Toyota Celica or Supra. **Helpful websites:** *www.corvetteforum.com* and *http://forums.corvetteforum.com.*

 ## Strengths and Weaknesses

ALERT! One nasty safety defect affecting many Corvettes over the past decade is sudden steering lock-up. Although it usually happens once the car has been parked, some owners report the failure while cruising on the highway. Owners say subsequent safety recalls did not fix the problem.

Corvettes made in the late '60s and early '70s are acceptable buys, mainly because of their value as collector cars and their uncomplicated repairs (though parts may be rare). Unfortunately, the Corvette's overall reliability and safety have declined over the past 40 years as its price and complexity have increased. GM has chosen to update its antiquated design with complicated high-tech add-ons rather than come up with something original. Consequently, the car has been gutted and then retuned using failure-prone electronic circuitry. Complicated emissions plumbing, braking, and suspension systems have also been added in an attempt to make the Corvette a fuel-efficient, user-friendly, high-performance vehicle—a goal that General Motors has missed by a wide margin.

Owners admit the redesigned '97 models offer improved performance, better handling, and additional safety features, but they find fault with the stiff ride, poor fuel economy, and excessive interior noise. From a reliability standpoint, these models are much more refined than earlier versions, but they are hell to diagnose and are knuckle-busters to service. And you can expect chronic engine stalling and surging, excessive engine oil consumption, an oily black buildup on the exhaust tips, and catalytic converter failures within the first five years. A real hair-raiser is the tendency of steering columns on 1977–2001 models to suddenly lock while the vehicle is underway or parked. This continues to be a widespread hazard, despite a recall to fix the defect. Says the following Corvette owner:

> This item has failed on an estimated 3,000 Corvettes throughout the U.S. Please see Internet site *www.corvetteforum.com.* As a safety professional, I see this as a hazard that Chevrolet needs to address with more severity. The loss of steering control because the steering wheel locks can lead to property loss, as well as death.

Factory-related defects on the post-2000 models are commonplace: The engine is excessively noisy; the cabins overheat; the driver's seat moves while driving; the trunk door warps; seat belts twist easily and tend to pull down uncomfortably against the shoulder; the passenger seat belt jams and won't extend or retract; smelly exhaust fumes enter the cabin, causing watery eyes and dizziness; excessive heat buildup from catalytic converters deforms the rear bumper assembly and heats up the interior even more; the glass rear window limits vision; and front and rear wheel weights sometimes fly off the wheels.

Servicing the constantly changing fuel-injection systems isn't easy, and this may be the primary reason why so many owners complain of having to take their Corvettes back to the shop repeatedly to correct poor engine and transmission performance.

The 2005–09 redesigned models have produced their own lemon grove of problems, although not as extensive a list as prior models: engine stalling and transmission jerking, electrical short circuits, lousy fit and finish, and squeaky, squealing brakes (see *www.corvetteforum.com* and *www.carreview.com*).

VEHICLE HISTORY: 2002—The Zo6 gets a 20 hp boost to 405 hp, and enhanced rear shocks, aluminum front stabilizer-bar links, high-performance brake pads, and new aluminum wheels. **2005**—Revised styling, more power, and new features. The car's wheelbase is stretched by 3 cm, and overall length shrinks by 12.7 cm. The 400 hp 6.0L V8 replaces the C5's 5.7L V8 and adds 50 more horses for good measure. Standard performance safety features still include ABS and traction/anti-skid control. Wheel diameter grows an inch to 18/19. Front side airbags remain standard on the convertible. Thief-magnet xenon headlights are newly standard, along with keyless access and ignition. **2006**—A new 6-speed automatic transmission and the return of the high-performance Zo6 model. **2007**—The two-seat V8-powered sports cars come as a coupe and a convertible. **2008**—The base engine gets a new 430 hp 6.2L V8 that can be hooked to the 6-speed manual or a 6-speed automatic transmission. Corvette Zo6 and 427 Limited models offered as coupes only, equipped with a 505 hp 7.0L V8 and mandatory 6-speed manual transmission with sporty suspension tuning, tires, and brakes. **2009**—The return of the ultra-high-performance ZR1 coupe with a 638 hp supercharged 6.2L V8. **2010**—The addition of a Grand Sport package, which replaces the previous Z51 package with wider fenders, a Zo6-style front splitter, redesigned wheels, and a tall rear spoiler. Brake cooling ducts and different gear and rear axle ratios are used this year. Manual transmission–equipped coupe models have a dry-sump oiling system and differential cooler. Other Corvettes get standard side airbags, new console trim patterns, the Zo6's tall rear spoiler on convertible models, and a revised paddle-shift control on automatic transmissions. Three engines are available: a 6.2L V8 in the coupe and convertible (including the Grand Sport), a 7.0L V8 in the Zo6, and the supercharged 6.2L V8 in the ZR1. The coupe and convertible are equipped with a 6-speed manual; a 6-speed automatic with paddle shifters is optional. The Zo6 and ZR1 use only the 6-speed manual gearbox.

Safety Summary

2002—Sudden stalling on the highway accompanied by brake failure. • Erratic transmission performance (shifts to Fourth before entering Second gear; won't shift into Second when going uphill). • Horn is hard to access. **2003**—When accelerating from a stop, vehicle fails to shift from First to Second gear and then stalls out. • Constant leaking, and failure of rear differential and suspension system. • Leaking oil pan gasket. • Annoying dash reflection onto the windshield. • Inaccurate fuel gauge. • Driver's seat belt locks up. **2004**—Defective steering, despite recall:

> The so-called "fix" GM has for the 1997–2004 Corvette column lock problem does not fix the problem. It merely puts a band-aid on the problem to protect them from lawsuits. I do not understand how this can be allowed by law. I have had to resort to an aftermarket part to fix the problem and chose to ignore the recall.

Fuel leaks found outside of the car at the fuel-tank, fuel-pump seal, and interconnecting hoses. • Fuel leakage from the crossover pipe and other fuel lines. • Steering linkage failure at the steering knuckle. • Power seat pinned driver against the steering wheel. • Clutch won't disengage. • Shifter pops out of Reverse. • Parking brake won't hold car in Neutral on a hill. **2005–06**—Corvette also "throws" its top:

> The contact stated the vehicle's roof had separated and flew off while driving 40 mph [65 km/h]. This was the second time the vehicle had problems with the roof. A NHTSA recall #06V181000 was performed in 05/06 regarding structure body: roof and pillars, however the recall did not remedy the problem.

2007—Roof panel separated while underway. • Metal pedals become very slippery in the rain. • Traction control and stability features come on when they shouldn't, causing loss of vehicle control. • Seat belt locks when driving and won't release. • Steering is unsafe:

> When driving home from the GM dealer, the vehicle skipped sideways on rough roads at a moderate speed (20–40 mph). I got online to the Corvette forum and was immediately referred to the Sep 07 Car and Driver magazine article specifically addressing this steering issue. The professional drivers in the article rate the 2007 Corvette steering as unsatisfactory.

Rear window view is distorted. **2008**—Corvettes continue to "lose their tops":

> Brand new 2008 convertible Corvette. Roof tore off driving on highway from dealership. GM currently stating not a warranty item because cables cannot break simply from the wind.

Cracked headlight lenses. • Chronic stalling. • Rear axle nut works itself loose. • Keyless start would not work and doors would not unlock. **2009**—Headliner droops and obscures rear vision. • Owner was locked in his Corvette because the power shut off once he entered the car. He had to remove the convertible top and climb out. Comments one owner who was trapped with his wife:

This vehicle is a death trap if the battery or electrical system fails or if the driver side door release cable snaps or jams in an accident. Emergency escape requires climbing through roof or into back hatch—elderly people could not do what we had to do to exit the car. There should be manual release for both doors on the doors. The batteries used by GM for these cars are notorious for quick drawdown & should be replaced at GM's expense with quality batteries such as Odyssey PC1200.

The "Service ABS System," "Service Active Handling System," and "Service Traction Control System" alerts come on and the car runs sluggishly.

My understanding is that this is a known issue for earlier years Corvettes: TSB 06.02.35.002A and TSB 06.02.35.002B. But my Corvette is a 2009 and I have the same exact problem.

2010—Owners report more "Service ABS System," "Service Active Handling System," and "Service Traction Control System" alerts.

Secret Warranties/Internal Bulletins/Service Tips

All years: A rotten-egg odour coming from the exhaust is probably caused by a defective catalytic converter, which should be covered by the emissions warranty. • Clearcoat paint degradation, whitening, and chalking, long a problem with GM's other cars, is a serious problem with the fibreglass-bodied Corvette, says TSB #331708. It too is covered by a secret warranty for up to six years. • Reverse servo cover seal leak. **1997–2002**—Tips on correcting water leaks in various areas. **1997–2004**—Remedy for a leaking rear differential. **2000–06**—Delayed automatic transmission shifts. **2003–11**—Oil leaks from engine's rear cover assembly. Should be covered by GM's eight-year emissions warranty or small claims court intervention. **2005–06**—Vibration or shudder at idle (replace power-steering inlet pressure hose). • Vehicle's top delaminates and flies off. GM will repair or replace affected roofs for free (Customer Satisfaction Program 05112D). **2005–08**—Axle nuts appear loose. **2005–09**—Tapping or scraping noise from the rear wheel area (replace wheel driveshaft nut). **2005–11**—Intermittent reduced power (repair instrument panel to body harness connector). • Crazing/cracks in transparent removable roof panel (see TSB on following page). The roof is also quite a noise-maker. Another confidential service bulletin (#08-08-67-031E) covers fixes to eliminate the snap, pop, crackle, or rattle noise coming from the roof. **2006–11**—Tips on reducing front tire chatter and rear differential "hop." **2007–08**—No-shifts, multiple electrical malfunctions. • Erratic power-window operation. **2007–09**—Premature headliner wear. Loose rear glass moulding. **2008–09**—GM agrees to pay for torn roofs and also refund money spent renting other transportation until May 31, 2011 (see TSB on following page). I'm betting any small claims court judge would find that warranty extension as cheapskate as they come. Expect the courts to extend the body warranty for this defect up to 8 years just like the existing Emissions Warranty and 8- to 10-year hybrid battery pack warranty. **2009**—Clutch spring fractures are another GM secret warranty–covered failure (pardon, I mean "Customer Satisfaction Program") that expired on July 31, 2011. After that, a small claims court judge may

CRACKS IN TRANSPARENT REMOVABLE ROOF PANEL

BULLETIN NO.: 08-08-67-001A

DATE: OCTOBER 28, 2010

CRAZING/CRACKS IN TRANSPARENT REMOVABLE ROOF PANEL (REPLACE ROOF)

2005–11 Chevrolet Corvette

CONDITION: Some customers may comment that the removable top has stress cracks developing on the right side and/or has crazing across the tint.

CAUSE: The cracking may be caused by an unsealed edge from a machining operation. The crazing may be the result of UV load. Correction: Replace the existing roof with a new one that doesn't have all the hardware attached. At time of repair, the weatherstrip retainers, weatherstrips and rear latch handles will have to be transferred from the old roof.

WARRANTY INFORMATION:

LABOR OPERATION	DESCRIPTION	LABOR TIME
B2298	Roof Lift Off Panel Replacement	Use Published Labor Operation Time

extend the expiry date. • Okay, you're not going to believe this, but it's absolutely true: GM put the wrong piston rings in its half year's production of 6.2L V8 Corvette engines. (And it took them eight months to discover this?) They have to replace the engines. Here's the proof:

CONVERTIBLE TOP COVER SEPARATION

BULLETIN NO.: 08312A

DATE: JULY 1, 2010

CUSTOMER SATISFACTION, CONVERTIBLE ROOF COVER SEPARATION—INSTALL NEW RETAINER BRACKET

2008–09 Chevrolet Corvette With Manual or Power Roof Convertible

CONDITION: Certain 2008 and 2009 model year Chevrolet Corvette manual or power roof convertible vehicles may have a condition in which the fabric roof cover may begin to separate from its retainer bracket near the top edge of the windshield. When the vehicle reaches speeds of approximately 100 mph (160 km/h) or greater, the roof cover could begin to pull away from the retainer bracket and, depending on the speed of the vehicle and duration at that speed, could tear to the rear glass. If this were to occur, the headliner would remain intact and the roof cover would not separate from the vehicle.

CORRECTION: Dealers are to install a new design retainer bracket.

CAMPAIGN—ENGINE REPLACEMENT

BULLETIN No.: 09043

DATE: MARCH 9, 2009

EXCESSIVE OIL CONSUMPTION—INCORRECT PISTON—EXPIRES SEPTEMBER 30, 2009

2009 Corvette, Equipped with a 6.2L V8 Engine

PURPOSE: This bulletin provides a service procedure to replace the engine on certain 2009 model year Corvette vehicles equipped with a 6.2L V8 engine. Some of these vehicles may have one or more incorrect oil control rings installed in the engine. This could result in high oil consumption. This service procedure should be completed on involved vehicles currently in dealership inventory as soon as possible but no later than September 30, 2009, at which time this bulletin will expire.

CORVETTE PROFILE

	2002	2003	2004	2005	2006	2007	2008	2009	2010
Cost Price ($)									
Base	62,400	68,120	69,940	67,395	67,805	68,565	69,500	66,145	67,050
Convertible	69,665	74,120	75,940	79,495	79,905	80,665	81,610	76,955	76,955
Used Values ($)									
Base ▲	10,000	12,000	15,000	18,000	21,000	24,500	28,500	34,500	42,000
Base ▼	9,000	10,500	13,000	16,500	19,500	23,000	27,000	32,000	39,000
Convertible ▲	13,500	15,500	18,000	23,500	26,000	28,000	33,000	40,000	50,000
Convertible ▼	12,000	14,000	16,000	22,000	24,000	26,000	31,000	38,000	47,000
Reliability	③	③	③	③	③	③	③	③	③

NOTE: Although U.S. testing agencies haven't crash-tested the Corvette, European agencies give the car a "Good" crashworthiness rating.

Mazda

MX-5 (MIATA) ★★★★★

RATING: Recommended (1999–2010). For over 20 years this has been an almost-perfect sports car, except for its poor braking performance on rain-slicked roadways and spotty fit and finish. The redesigned 2006–08 models are the best choices for power and performance. **Ideal model year:** The feature-laden 2009 Miata GT with some of the original warranty left is your best choice. It will cost about $23,500, which is a bargain considering its original price was $39,295. **"Real" city/highway fuel economy:** *5-speed manual: 10.1/7.6 L/100 km. 6-speed manual: 10.2/7.7 L/100 km. 6-speed automatic: 10.6/7.8 L/100 km.* **Maintenance/repair costs:** Below-average costs, and most repairs aren't dealer-dependent. **Parts:** Average costs, with good availability. **Extended warranty:** A waste of money. **Best alternatives:** Honda S2000, Hyundai Tiburon, Ford Mustang, Mazda3, Mini Cooper Clubman, Pontiac Solstice, Saturn Sky, Scion tC, and Toyota Celica. **Helpful websites:** *www.miata.net* and *www.miataforum.com*.

Strengths and Weaknesses

ALERT! Drivers who are six feet tall or taller say that the limited cabin space puts their right foot in an awkward position. It takes the weight of the entire leg, causing severe cramping. Check this out during the pre-purchase test-drive.

The base engine delivers adequate power and accelerates smoothly. Acceleration from 0–100 km/h is in the high eight-second range. The 5-speed manual transmission shifts easily and has well-spaced gears; the 6-speed adds 27 kg (60 lb.) and isn't that impressive. The vehicle's lightness, precise steering, and 50/50 weight distribution make this an easy car for novice drivers to toss around corners.

VEHICLE HISTORY: 2003—16-inch V-rated tires and strut-tower braces. **2004**—Debut of the MazdaSpeed, equipped with a 178 hp turbocharged engine, 6-speed manual transmission, sport suspension, and 17-inch wheels. **2006**—Name is changed to MX-5. Given about 6.25 cm in wheelbase, 4.25 cm more width, and 4 cm more length while gaining only about 23 kg. Base engine is a 170 hp 2.0L (166 hp with an automatic transmission), in place of the 142 hp 1.8L engine that powered the previous model. An optional 6-speed automatic transmission with steering-wheel shift paddles replaces the 4-speed automatic. Full-torso side airbags, anti-lock four-wheel disc brakes, and a manual-folding soft top with a heated glass rear window are standard features. **2007**—A retractable hardtop adds 35 kg to the car's weight. Mazda continues to offer a removable hardtop for softtop models. **2008**—GS and GT models get a driver's seat height adjuster. **2009**—All models get an improved engine and suspension; a restyled exterior; standard side airbags; and an upgraded stereo and centre armrest. GS models come with standard air conditioning, while the GT returns with a power-retractable hardtop, electronic stability control (a *Lemon-Aid* recommended feature), adjustable heated seats, auto-dimming rear-view mirror, garage opener, and satellite radio. Models equipped with the 6-speed manual transmission come with a limited-slip differential and sports suspension.

Owners' top performance gripes target the same characteristics that make other sports car enthusiasts swoon: inadequate cargo space, cramped interior for large adults, excessive interior noise, and limited low-end torque that makes for frequent shifting.

Mechanics report that it is wise to change the engine timing chain every 100,000 km. Other reported problems include crankshaft failures, leaky rear-end seals and valve cover gaskets, rear differential seal failures, leaking or squeaky clutches, hard starts and stalling, torn drive boots, transmission whining in upper gear ranges, engine and exhaust system rattles, electrical system glitches, brake pulsation, valvetrain clatter on start-up (changing oil may help), prematurely worn-out shock absorbers and catalytic converters, softtop covers that come off or break, and minor body and trim deficiencies. Redesigned 2006s have a few more fit and finish deficiencies due to their redesign. Most of the problems were fixed on the 2007s; however, there are still some reports of later models rattling and an interior leak that soaks the carpet from the driver's front area to underneath the seat.

 Safety Summary

All years: Used Miatas will likely have some collision damage; make sure you run a *Carproof.com* check online or by fax. **2002**—Interior can heat up to 54°C (130°F) because exhaust system is mounted too close to the centre console. **2003**—When accelerating from a cold start, car lurches and then stalls. • Hard starts. • Wheel rims are easily bent. • Poor headlight illumination. **2004**—Hard starts despite changing the fuel pump. • Seat belt locks up during normal driving. **2006**—Constant steering corrections are necessary due to the vehicle wandering all over the road. • In moderately cold temperatures, the power windows won't work. • It is easy to accidentally engage First gear when Reverse is required, or Reverse when First is needed. **2007**—Sudden, unintended acceleration. • "Fix-a-Flat" kit doesn't fix flats caused by a cut tire. • The point where the manual transmission clutch catches keeps moving upward. • Anchorage pins for some floor mats may be missing. **2010**—Driver's right foot cramps up due to limited cabin space.

Secret Warranties/Internal Bulletins/Service Tips

All years: TSB #006/94 gives all of the possible causes and remedies for brake vibration. • TSB #N00198 addresses complaints that the steering wheel is off-centre. • Other bulletins address the issue of musty AC odours. **1999–2003**—Clutch chatter on cold start-up. **2000–06**—Troubleshooting body vibration and steering-wheel shimmy. **2002**—Fuelling difficulty caused by gas pump shutting off early. • The 6-speed manual transmission won't shift into Fifth gear or Reverse. **2004**—Door rattling. **2004–11**—Passenger airbag deactivation light comes on for no reason. **2006**—Rough idle, hesitation. • Clutch pedal squeaking when depressed. • Abnormal heater performance. • Water leaks from top of door windows and at the front of the convertible top. • Excessive gaps between the header weather stripping and the body above the windshield; windshield adhesive oozes out onto the paint. • Console lid won't stay closed; squeaking noise. • Tire valve stem breaks when removing valve cap. **2006–07**—Manual transmission clutch hard to disengage, excessive pedal free play. • Front brakes produce a low-speed creaking noise. • Convertible-top latch rattling. • Gap in plastic door-trim panel. • Special Program MSP13 allows for the free replacement of the fuel-filler cap. • Poor AM band reception. • Water accumulation in footwells. **2006–08**—Seat belt buckle rattles, squeaks. • Audio system rattle. **2006–09**—Unstable engine idling, stalling. • Water accumulation in the footwell area. **2006–10**—Seat and seatback squeaking noises. • Upper surface dashboard may have a poor appearance. **2006–11**—Seatbelts are slow to retract. • Excessive condensation or water accumulation within the headlight assembly. • Troubleshooting tips on eliminating brake noise, judder, or dragging. • Brakes clunk, bang on initial forward takeoff. **2007**—Retractable hard top difficult to open, makes crunch noise, contacts deck panel. **2007–08**—Hard top rattles at the windshield header. **2009–11**—Inaccurate ambient temperature display.

MX-5 (MIATA) PROFILE

	2002	2003	2004	2005	2006	2007	2008	2009	2010
Cost Price ($)									
Base GX	27,695	27,695	27,895	27,995	27,995	28,095	28,195	28,495	28,995
GS	—	—	30,100	30,200	30,995	34,500	31,350	32,795	33,495
GT	—	—	33,165	34,265	33,995	34,195	34,500	39,295	39,995
Used Values ($)									
Base GX ▲	5,000	6,500	8,500	10,000	12,000	13,500	15,500	18,500	22,000
Base GX ▼	4,500	6,000	7,500	9,000	10,500	12,500	14,000	17,000	20,000
GS ▲	—	—	9,500	11,000	12,500	14,500	17,000	20,000	24,000
GS ▼	—	—	8,500	10,000	11,500	13,500	15,500	18,000	22,000

GT ▲	—	—	10,500	11,500	13,000	15,500	18,000	24,000	28,000
GT ▼	—	—	9,500	10,500	12,000	14,000	16,500	22,000	26,000
Reliability	5	5	5	5	5	5	5	5	5
Crash Safety	4	4	4	4	—	—	—	—	—
Side	3	3	3	3	—	—	—	—	—
Rollover Resistance	—	5	5	5	—	—	—	—	—

All ratings on a numbered scale where 5 is good and **1** is bad. See page 132 for a more detailed description.

MINIVANS

Minivans and Maxi-failures

The Chevrolet Uplander minivan (and its twins: the Buick Terraza, Pontiac Montana, and Saturn Relay) is as dreadful to drive as it is to inhabit. The loose steering requires constant tending at anything other than a dead stop. The suspension crashes more often than a demolition derby driver. The long wheelbase and epic turning circle make parking lot maneuvering a seemingly endless chore. (see p. 527)

After embracing Chrysler's minivans in the early '80s, disenchanted car buyers turned against Detroit's failure-prone minivans a decade later. Drivers still loved the concept, but were fed up by the low quality. So they waited in line for a Honda Odyssey or Toyota Sienna minivan: two minivans they knew were more reliable and kept a high resale value. Detroit, Mazda, and Nissan never recovered. Buyers are wary of minivans sold by these companies, regardless of their thrift shop prices. Only Chrysler, Kia, and Mazda are gaining market share.

Gone and best forgotten are Ford's godawful Windstar/Freestar, Mazda's lacklustre MPV, and GM's failure-prone Venture, Montana, Relay, Trans Sport, Terraza, Silhouette, and Outlander. You might get by with a recent-model Chrysler, if you can find a garage willing to do cheap transmission, brake, and AC repairs—year after year.

Your only real choice is Asian: Honda's Odyssey, Mazda's Mazda5 mini-minivan (for the Mazda5, refer to "Small Cars"), or a Toyota Sienna. The Mazda is a narrow six-seater that sells for much less than what Hondas and Toyotas are fetching due to the 5's low initial price and more rapid depreciation: good news for buyers, bad news for sellers.

The Recommended Mazda5 is actually a mini-minivan.

Most minivans are upsized front-drive cars that are mainly "people-movers," meaning they handle like cars and get great fuel economy. The Honda Odyssey and Toyota Sienna are the best examples of this kind of minivan. Following Honda's 2005 Odyssey improvements, its road performance, reliability, and retained value surpasse those of the front- and rear-drive minivans built by Detroit. Toyota's 2004 Sienna upgrades produced the opposite results: The Sienna became less reliable and less safe and its resale values began dropping like a stone as new Sienna prices softened.

GM's Astro and Safari minivans are rear-drive, downsized trucks that incorporate a primitive box-on-wheels design. Launched in the mid-1980s, they are dirt-cheap and offer considerable towing and hauling capabilities. On the other hand, they couldn't compete with higher-quality, more fuel-efficient, and better-performing front-drive Asian minivans, or Chrysler, for that matter. For example, the Astro/Safari's engine is located close to the front passenger compartment, thus, reducing cabin space where it is most needed and contributing to high noise levels. Getting in and out is a chore for kids, women, and seniors, thanks to the vehicle's high step-in height and single sliding rear door, which usually malfunctioned and served as a rust trap. Although these minivans are relatively rare since they were axed after the 2005 model year, they can be easily fixed by any independent garage, and parts availability and prices are better than average. Using 6-cylinder engines and heavier mechanical components, they handle cargo and passengers equally well. However, fuel economy is no match for the front-drives, highway handling is ponderous, with lots of wind buffeting and quirky braking, and the reliability of these cheap minivans is way below average. GM's rear-drive, full-sized Express and Savana vans are much more durable than its Astro/Safari, Ford Aerostar, or the front-drive Ford Windstar/Freestar. Incidentally, steer clear of any minivan equipped with an AWD powertrain. These systems are notoriously failure-prone, expensive to repair, and will keep you walking for weeks while the parts stay back ordered.

Rear-drive vans are better suited for towing trailers in the 1,600–2,950 kg (3,500–6,500 lb.) range. Most automakers say their front-drive minivans can pull up to 1,600 kg (3,500 lb.) with an optional towing package (often costing almost $1,000 extra), but don't you believe it. Owners report white-knuckle driving and premature powertrain failures caused by the extra load. It just stands to reason that Ford, Chrysler, and GM front-drives equipped with engines and transmissions that blow out at 60,000–100,000 km under normal driving conditions are going to meet their demise much earlier under a full load.

Chrysler

Chrysler has churned out millions of minivans since 1984, paying scant attention to chronic ABS, 4-cylinder engine, automatic transmission, airbag control module, electrical system, and fit and finish deficiencies, or to rust-damaged steering and suspension systems.

Indeed, Chrysler minivans caught on from their debut in 1984, when they were seen as fairly reliable and efficient people-haulers; that is, until the comprehensive warranty expired, or was cut back post-2000. Nevertheless, these minivans have continued to dominate the market despite their well-known mechanical and body problems. In fact, it's amazing how little Chrysler's defect patterns have changed during the past two decades. See *http://terpconnect.umd.edu/~gluckman/Chrysler/index* (The Chrysler Products' Problem web page), and *www.daimlerchryslervehicleproblems.com* (The Truth Behind Chrysler).

Ford

Ford's minivans went from bad to worse over two decades. Its first minivan, the 1985–97 Aerostar, had recurring brake, tranny, electrical system, and coil-spring problems. Collapsing coil springs have caused tire blowouts on all model years.

Ford's quality decline continued with the mediocre front-drive Mercury Villager, a co-venture that also produced the Nissan Quest. Both vehicles were only so-so highway performers that often resided in dealer repair bays awaiting major engine, transmission, or electrical repairs. The Villager/Quest duo lasted through the 2000 model year. The Quest continued on its own with minimal changes to its 2001–03 models. The 2004 Quest's redesign was both a conceptual and engineering disaster. First-year models were so glitch-prone and stylistically beyond the pale that Nissan sent over 200 engineers to North America to correct the defects and change the interior design. Sales have never recovered.

Ford also brought out the 1995 Windstar—one of the poorest quality, most dangerous minivans ever built; the year 2000 model logged 736 safety-related complaints at NHTSA. Renamed the Freestar in 2004, the vehicle's failure-prone fuel, braking, electrical, powertrain, and suspension (broken coil springs) systems put owners' wallets and lives at risk.

Ford compounded the Windstar's failings with its hard-nosed attitude toward customer complaints and by refusing warranty coverage for what were clearly factory-induced defects. Fortunately, there was a flood of Canadian small claims court decisions that came to the owners' aid when Ford wouldn't. These Canadian courts ruled Ford and its dealers must pay for engine and transmission repairs, even if the original warranty has expired or the minivan was bought used (see page 106).

General Motors

GM's minivans are even less reliable than Ford's. To begin with, their powertrain problems are more serious than either Ford's or Chrysler's, other mechanical components such as fuel gauges and brakes aren't dependable, and fit and finish is so bad that not even the roof can escape developing rust holes, as GM service bulletins confirm.

Asian automakers

Asian competitors don't make perfect machines either, as a perusal of NHTSA-registered safety complaints, service bulletins, and online complaint forums will quickly confirm. Asian companies, looking to keep costs down, have also been bedevilled during the past decade by chronic engine and automatic transmission failures, sliding-door malfunctions, catastrophic tire blowouts, and electrical glitches.

A word of warning about Nissan and Toyota: Yes, these importers have made fairly dependable vehicles—including minivans—for the past four decades. However, the newly redesigned Nissan Quest and Toyota Sienna minivans also have some serious factory glitches, and both automakers have learned from Detroit the art of obfuscation. Toyota's sudden, unintended acceleration, brake failures and rust-cankered trucks have tarnished the company's reputation to the point that it no longer has the public trust. Resale values are soft, and the automaker has thrown millions of dollars into dealer sales incentives and customer rebates.

Volkswagen

And, finally, we come to the automaker who pioneered the minivan concept—Volkswagen. Its vans, including the 1979 Vanagon and 1993 EuroVan/Camper, have never been taken seriously since they came to North America in 1950 with the Transporter cargo van and the nine-seater, 21-window Microbus. A reputation for poor overall quality, puny engines, and insufficient parts and servicing support continues to drive buyers away.

As part of an agreement with Chrysler, Volkswagen has sold 2009 through 2012 Routan minivans cloned from the Chrysler Town & Country. VW says it has added Euro touch steering and suspension, but most drivers will only notice a firmer ride...not always a good thing on rough roads. Another surprise that will hit families hard is that the VW version has dropped the useful Stow 'n Go and Swivel 'n Go seats. Instead, you get second-row seats on rollers.

Long-term prospects for this slow-seller are sombre. A 2009 Routan that sold for $27,975 can now be picked up for $13,500.

Larger and Smaller Alternatives

Most minivans are overpriced for what is essentially an upgraded car or downsized truck. Motorists needing a vehicle with large cargo- and passenger-carrying capacities should consider a Chrysler, Ford, or GM full-sized van, even if it means sacrificing some fuel economy. You just can't beat the excellent forward vision and easy-to-customize interiors that these large vans provide. Furthermore, parts are easily found and are competitively priced because of the great number of independent suppliers.

On the other hand, a minivan may be too large for some shoppers who want the same versatility in a smaller package capable of carrying six passengers. For them, a 2008 Mazda5 GT minivan/wagon is a good place to start. Although it originally sold for $24,815, the used value has dropped to about $11,000.

MINIVAN RATINGS

Above Average

Honda Odyssey (2006–2010)   Mazda5 (2006–10; see "Small Cars")

Average

Chrysler Caravan, Voyager, Grand   Honda Odyssey (1995–2005)
   Caravan, Grand Voyager,   Toyota Sienna (2005–10)
   Town & Country (2008–10)

Below Average

Chrysler Caravan, Voyager,   Toyota Sienna (1999–2004)
   Grand Caravan, Grand Voyager,
   Town & Country (2002–07)

Chrysler

CARAVAN, VOYAGER, GRAND CARAVAN, GRAND VOYAGER, TOWN & COUNTRY ★★★

RATING: Average (2008–10); Below Average (2002–07). **Ideal model year:** A 2009 Grand Caravan SXT for about $12,000 is your best choice. It costs $3,000 more than the 2008 version, but you will appreciate the more powerful 4.0L V6 and the extra protection provided by the unexpired portion of Chrysler's comprehensive warranty—a $3,000 value. The 2009 Grand Caravan SXT originally sold for $31,395. **"Real" city/highway fuel economy:** *Caravan 2.4 4-cylinder: 11.8/8.2 L/100 km. Caravan 3.0 V6: 12.7/8.3 L/100 km. Caravan 3.3 V6: 12.2/8.2 L/100 km. Grand Caravan 3.3 V6: 12.9/8.5 L/100 km. Grand Caravan 3.8 V6: 13.2/8.7 L/100 km. Town & Country 2.7: 15.5/10.0 L/100 km. Town & Country 4.0: 12.2/7.9 L/100 km. Town & Country AWD: 13.6/9.1 L/100 km.* **Maintenance/ repair costs:** Higher than average. **Parts:** Most parts are easy to find and reasonably priced when bought from and installed by independent suppliers. Parts needed for recall campaigns are a problem; they are often back ordered for months at a time. **Extended warranty:** Yes, mainly as protection from the powertrain, brake, and electrical system failures. **Best alternatives:** Honda's Odyssey should be your first choice, followed by the Mazda5 and Toyota's Sienna (but not the problem-plagued 2004 model). GM and Ford front- and rear-drive minivans aren't credible alternatives because of their failure-prone powertrains; brake, suspension, and steering problems; electrical short circuits; and subpar bodywork. Full-sized

GM and Chrysler rear-drive cargo vans are more affordable and practical buys if you intend to haul a full passenger load or do some regular heavy hauling, if you have physical challenges entering and exiting most vehicles, if you use lots of accessories, or if you take frequent motoring excursions. Chrysler's German-built Sprinter van is a poor alternative due to its shoddy reliability, weak parts network, and dealer-dependent servicing. **Helpful websites:** *http://dodgeforum.com/forum/ dodge-caravan-23* and *www.carcomplaints.com/Chrysler*.

 ## Strengths and Weaknesses

ALERT! Chrysler automatic transmissions fail around the 5-year/80,000–100,000 km mark. If you don't have any coverage left from Chrysler's base warranty, try to get a "goodwill" warranty extension from the dealer and Chrysler. In such cases, the usual $3,000 repair cost is split between the customer, dealer, and Chrysler. If this offer isn't made, go directly to an independent transmission specialist, who will likely fix the transmission for a third less than what the dealer would charge, or $2,000.

Here's another heads-up concerning early brake rotor warpage and pad wearout. Chrysler's inconsistent warranty policy is to replace for free front brake parts under an extended "goodwill" warranty, minus a $100 deduction, but similar failures with the rear brakes aren't covered. The owner of a 2010 Grand Caravan has this to say:

> I received a letter from Chrysler Group LLC dated Oct 24, 2011 stating "the warranty period for my front brake pads and front rotors has been extended because some of the minivans may need the pads and rotors replaced earlier than expected." It has been extended to 3 years/36,000 miles.... I believe that by writing the letter, Chrysler is admitting a defect in the manufacturing of the 2009–2011 Dodge Grand Caravan and it should be recalled.

BRAKES—FRONT END VIBRATION WHEN BRAKING

BULLETIN NO.: 05-007-11   DATE: OCTOBER 11, 2011

VIBRATION AT THE FRONT OF THE VEHICLE WHEN BRAKING AND/OR FRONT BRAKE PAD LINING LIFE (WARRANTY EXTENSION).
2009–11 Caravan/Town & Country.
OVERVIEW: This bulletin involves installing new brake linings and replacing both brake rotors as required.
SYMPTOM/CONDITION: Vibration at the front of the vehicle when braking.

Chrysler's minivans continue to dominate the new- and used-minivan markets, though they're quickly losing steam because of the popularity of crossover wagons and better-quality products from Japanese and South Korean automakers. Nevertheless, they offer pleasing styling and lots of convenience features at used prices that can be very attractive. They can carry up to seven passengers in comfort, and ride and handle better than most truck-based minivans. The shorter-wheelbase minivans also offer better rear visibility and good ride quality, and are more nimble and easy to park. Cargo hauling capability is more than adequate.

Nevertheless, these minivans can pose serious safety risks. Owners report bizarre defects such as seat belts that may strangle children, airbags that deploy when the ignition is turned on, transmissions that jump out of gear, and sudden stalling and electrical short circuits when within radar range of airports or military installations.

Other common problems include the premature wearout of engine tensioner pulleys, automatic transmission speed sensors, engine head gaskets, motor mounts, starter motors, steering columns, front brake discs and pads (the brake pad material crumbles in your hands), front rotors and rear drums, brake master cylinders, suspension components, exhaust system components, ball joints, wheel bearings, water pumps, fuel pumps and pump wiring harnesses, radiators, heater cores, and AC compressors. Fuel injectors on all engines have been troublesome, the differential pin breaks through the automatic transmission casing, sliding doors malfunction, door locks often won't lock, engine supports may be missing or not connected, tie rods may suddenly break, oil pans crack, and the power-steering pump frequently leaks. Factory-installed Goodyear and Bridgestone Turanza tires frequently fail at 40,000–65,000 km.

Fit and finish has gotten worse over the past two decades. Body hardware and interior trim are fragile and tend to break, warp, or fall off (door handles are an example). The premature rust-out of major suspension and steering components is a critical safety and performance concern. Paint delamination often turns these solid-coloured minivans into two-tones.

And as the minivan takes on its albino appearance, you can listen to a concerto of clicks, clunks, rattles, squeaks, and squeals as you drive (you'll love the reed section). Giving new meaning to the phrase "surround sound," these noises usually emanate from the brakes, poorly anchored bench seats, misaligned body panels, and suspension and steering assemblies.

VEHICLE HISTORY: 2002—Fuel-tank assembly is redesigned to prevent post-collision fuel leakage; a tire air-pressure monitor is added. **2005**—Side curtain airbags and second- and third-row seats that fold flush with the floor; AWD dropped (owners gain; repair bays lose). **2008**—Fresh styling, a more powerful engine, a larger interior, and new seating features. The shorter wheelbase Caravan model is discontinued, as is the 4-cylinder engine. All Caravans now have a V6. The 3.3L and 3.8L engines carry over from 2007, but new for 2008 is a 253 hp 4.0L engine. The 3.3L V6 teams with a clunky 4-speed automatic transmission, while the 3.8L and 4.0L engines are hooked to a 6-speed automatic. **2009**—The 3.8L six is replaced by the 4.0L V6; SXT models have an upgraded climate control system; and entry-level models add standard heated foldable mirrors and cruise control.

2010—Improved 4.0L fuel economy with the addition of Interactive Decel Fuel Shut-Off (iDFSO), which shuts off fuel during deceleration; a manual lumbar support adjuster; and stain-resistant cloth seats. Watch out for some "decontenting," especially if you plan to carry children. Some models deleted the integrated child bench seat and optional second-row swivelling bucket seats with child boosters.

Don't buy any Chrysler minivan with a 4-cylinder engine—it has no place in a vehicle this large, especially when hooked to the inadequate 3-speed automatic transmission. It lacks an Overdrive and will shift back and forth as speed varies, and it's slower and noisier than the other choices. The 3.3L V6 is acceptable for light-duty city driving; however, the 3.8L and 4.0L V6 are best for highway travel or carrying four or more passengers. The sliding side doors are a costly, failure-prone gizmo. Child safety seats integrated into the rear seatbacks are convenient and reasonably priced, but Chrysler's versions have had a history of either tightening up excessively or not tightening enough, allowing the child to slip out. Try the seat with your child before buying it. You may wish to pass on the tinted windshields as well; they seriously reduce visibility. Be wary of models featuring all-wheel drive and ABS: The powertrain isn't reliable and is horrendously expensive to repair, and Chrysler's large number of ABS failures is worrisome. Ditch the failure-prone Goodyear original-equipment tires, and remember that a night drive is a prerequisite, to check out headlight illumination, which many call inadequate.

 Safety Summary

All years/models: Sudden, unintended acceleration; owners report that cruise-control units often malfunction, accelerating or decelerating the vehicle without any warning. • Airbag malfunctions. • Carbon monoxide comes through air vents. • Defective engine head gaskets, rocker arm gaskets, and engine mounts. • Engine sag, hesitation, stumble, hard starts, or stalling. • Transmission fails, suddenly drops into low gear, won't go into Reverse, delays engagement, or jumps out of gear when running or parked. • One can move the automatic transmission shift lever without applying brakes. • Several incidents where ignition was turned and vehicle went into Reverse at full throttle, although transmission was set in Park. • No steering. • Brakes wear out prematurely or fail completely. ABS failure. • Brakes activate by themselves while vehicle is underway. • Intermittent electrical system shorts that shut down the door locks, power windows, windshield wipers, lights, mirror adjustment, and other accessories. • Many complaints of front suspension-strut towers rusting and then cracking at the weld seams; jig-positioning hole wasn't sealed at the factory. • Seatbacks fall backward. • Rear windows fall out or shatter. • Sliding door often opens while vehicle is underway, or jams, trapping occupants. • Weak headlights. • Horn often doesn't work. • Several incidents where side windows exploded for no apparent reason. • Adults cannot sit in third-row seat without their heads smashing into the roof as the vehicle passes over bumps. **2007**—Automatic transmission "bumps" into gear. • Ruptured front brake hoses. • Sudden veering to the right. **2008**—Defective (broken) tire valve stems:

I was about to add air to the front tire and was removing the cap when the valve blew apart about halfway down the stem. The tire went flat immediately. We had the dealer replace the TPM valve stem but they had to order it and it took a week to get the part. I asked them to change the other 3, but they said they will only replace one valve at a time as they fail. Sure enough, two weeks later a second valve stem failed and the tire went flat very fast.

Sliding passenger door will not stop if it catches an arm or a leg. **2009**—Vehicle may suddenly lose power. • Front wheel bearing failures. • More cracked tire valves. • Faulty gearshift assembly:

The handle fell to the floor, as did the button and the internal spring.... I now have a pointed piece of metal sticking out of my dash.

2010—Under-hood fire. Electronic throttle control comes on for no reason, producing poor or no throttle response: Restarting the vehicle fixes the problem temporarily. Brake failures. Parking brake suddenly engages while cruising; rear brakes burn up. Rear brake sensor failure causes ABS alert to activate. Headlights blink, then shut off. Loose-fitting sliding side doors produce air leaks, freeze in winter, and rattle/whistle; recall fix for the latches and seals made the problem worse for some. Leaking factory-installed sunroof allows water to collect in the console, potentially disabling the airbags or starting an electrical fire.

Secret Warranties/Internal Bulletins/Service Tips

1996–2006—Rusted, frozen rear brake drums. **2001–02**—Wind or water leaks at the rear quarter window. **2001–03**—Oil filter leaks with 3.3L and 3.8L engines (confirmed in TSB #09-001-03). **2001–04**—AC water leaks. **2001–06**—Water leaks under passenger-side carpet. **2002–07**—Power liftgate malfunctions. **2003**—Troubleshooting water leaks. • Three bulletins relating to automatic transmission malfunctions: delayed gear engagement, harsh 4–3 downshift, and excessive vibration and transfer-gear whine. **2003–05**—Crack, split and/or water leak in the upper body-seam sealer at the B- or C-pillar. **2005**—Engine squeak under light throttle. • Campaign to replace the rear AC heater tube if it is corroded; another campaign will replace the underbody heater hose at no charge. **2005–06**—AC condenser road debris damage can be prevented by installing a condenser guard supplied by Chrysler. Who pays? AC vulnerability was a foreseeable design challenge that Chrysler botched. My bet is small claims would rule the automaker negligent. **2006–07**—Silencing moonroof noises. **2007**—Troubleshooting body noises. **2008**—Harsh shifting. • Abnormal front brake pad wear. • Outside sliding-door handle is inoperative in freezing temperatures. • Roof rack howling sound. • Howl, honk from the front windshield. • Front door rattle or window won't roll down. • Exhaust system rattle, clunk. • Slow fuel tank fill; pump shuts off prematurely. **2008–09**—Roof rack crossbar adjuster corroded/seized. **2008–10**—Front wheel bearing growling, humming will be corrected by the free replacement of the front wheel bearings under a 5–year/145,000 km "goodwill" warranty extension, as outlined in TSB #02-003-11, published

September 29, 2011. • Power steering fluid leaks. • An inoperative power sliding door may only require a reflashing of the sliding-door computer module. **2009**—Remedy for front brake squeal, pulsation. **2009–10**—Correction for sliding-door binding. **2010**—Silencing transfer-gear bearing noise.

CARAVAN, GRAND CARAVAN, TOWN & COUNTRY PROFILE

	2002	2003	2004	2005	2006	2007	2008	2009	2010
Cost Price ($)									
Caravan	25,430	25,430	27,620	28,205	27,065	27,445	—	—	—
Grand Caravan	28,875	29,295	30,190	30,740	31,070	29,305	26,495	26,595	23,395
Town & Country	40,815	42,705	44,095	44,595	44,920	42,255	35,995	36,995	37,745
Used Values ($)									
Caravan ▲	2,500	3,000	3,500	4,000	5,000	6,500	—	—	—
Caravan ▼	2,000	2,500	3,000	3,500	4,000	5,000	—	—	—
Grand Caravan ▲	3,500	4,000	4,500	5,000	6,000	7,500	8,500	11,000	14,000
Grand Caravan ▼	3,000	3,500	4,000	4,500	5,500	6,000	7,500	9,500	13,000
Town & Country ▲	4,500	5,000	6,000	7,500	9,000	10,000	14,500	19,000	22,000
Town & Country ▼	4,000	4,500	5,000	6,500	8,000	8,500	13,000	17,500	20,000
Reliability	2	2	2	2	2	2	3	3	3
Crash Safety (F)									
Caravan	4	4	4	4	—	5	—	—	—
Grand Caravan	4	4	4	5	5	5	5	5	5
Town & Country	—	4	4	5	5	5	5	5	5
Town & Country LX	4	4	4	—	5	—	—	—	—
Side									
Caravan	4	4	—	—	—	4	—	—	—
Grand Caravan	5	5	—	—	5	5	5	5	5
Town & Country LX	5	5	4	4	5	—	5	5	5
IIHS Side									
Grand Caravan	—	—	—	—	1	1	5	5	5
Town & Country	—	—	—	—	1	1	5	5	5
Offset									
Grand Caravan	3	3	3	3	3	3	5	5	5
Town & Country	3	3	3	3	3	3	5	5	5
Head Restraints (F)									
Grand Caravan	—	—	1	1	1	1	2	2	2
Town & Country	3	3	1	1	1	1	2	2	2
Town & Country LX	2	2	1	1	1	1	—	—	—
Town & Country	3	3	1	1	1	1	2	2	2
Town & Country LX	2	2	1	1	1	1	—	—	—
Rollover Resistance	3	3	—	—	4	4	4	4	4

Honda

ODYSSEY ★★★★

RATING: Above Average (2006–10); Average (1999–2005). Odyssey's redesigns didn't engender as steep a decline in quality as we have seen with Kia, Mazda, Nissan, and Toyota minivan makeovers. The upgraded 2005 Odyssey generated an increase of reports concerning safety- and performance-related failures, hence *Lemon-Aid*'s downgrade of formerly Recommended recent-model Odysseys. Of particular concern are run-flat Pax tire problems, airbag malfunctions, automatic sliding-door failures, damaged AC condensers, and transmission breakdowns with erratic shifting (2000–03 models). **Ideal model year:** A 2008 EX sells for less than half ($15,000 to $16,000) what the car originally cost ($36,990) and comes slightly restyled. **"Real" city/highway fuel economy:** 2.2: 11.9/9.2 L/100 km. 2.3: 10.9/8.3 L/100 km. 3.5: 13.2/8.5 L/100 km. **Maintenance/repair costs:** Average; any garage can repair these minivans. **Parts:** Moderately priced, and availability is better than average because the Odyssey uses many generic Accord parts. **Extended warranty:** Not needed. **Best alternatives:** If you want something cheaper and quasi-reliable, consider a three-year-old Chrysler minivan or the better-built Mazda5 micro-van. If you want handling, hauling, and dependability, look to Toyota's Sienna (but not the 2004 model). Sadly, the Ford and GM front-drive minivans aren't in the running because of their self-destructing engines and malfunctioning automatic transmissions. **Helpful websites:** *www.carcomplaints.com/Honda/Odyssey, www.odysseyownersclub.com/forums,* and *www.odyclub.com/forums.*

 ## Strengths and Weaknesses

ALERT! Automatic sliding side doors can injure or kill seniors or children; be especially vigilant. Also, don't pay to replace an AC condenser damaged by road debris. Honda neglected to install a protective shield, though the company was well aware of the AC's vulnerability. Our lawyers call that negligence: Honda should pay. Finally, in your pre-purchase test drive, be wary of the newly designed 2008 and later Odyssey head restraint. It is painful to some drivers who find it tilts their head too far forward and down. One owner of a 2010 Odyssey sent the following plea to Honda:

> Touring van has extremely uncomfortable driver's seat and passenger seat due to protruding head restraints. The head rest pushes head so far forward that it causes pain in the back, neck, hips and legs due to lack of any support in the back. It does not matter where you position the seat or the head restraint. Nothing makes it comfortable. I am now having severe back pain, and stressed muscles everywhere else. I am 5'4". Please create less protruding head rests so my back can actually reach the back of the seat and my neck is not forced forward in an awkward angle.

It's easy to see what makes the Odyssey so popular: strong engine performance, car-like ride and handling, easy entry/exit, a second driver-side door, and a quiet interior. Most controls and displays are easy to reach and read, there's a lot of passenger and cargo room and an extensive list of standard equipment, and Honda is usually willing to compensate owners for production snafus after the warranty has expired.

This minivan does have its drawbacks, though. Front-seat passenger legroom may be marginal because of the restricted seat travel, and third-row seating is suitable only for children. Additionally, power-sliding doors are slow to retract, there's some tire rumbling and rattling and body drumming at highway speeds, premium fuel is required for optimum performance, and rear-seat head restraints impede side and rear visibility.

VEHICLE HISTORY: 2002—A slight restyling, 30 additional horses, disc brakes on all four wheels, standard side airbags, and additional support for front seats. **2006**—Horsepower rating cut by 11 (to 244 hp). **2007**—Two added features are a tilt/telescope steering wheel and a tire-pressure monitoring system. **2008**—Addition of a cheaper DX trim line, and restyled wheels, taillights, hood, bumper, and front grille. Also new: upgraded front seat head restraints that may literally be a pain in the neck. **2010**—LX model is gone.

Reliability is better than average, but Honda still has a few serious safety- and performance-related problems to work out. Recent examples: failure-prone sliding doors; troublesome, expensive-to-replace Pax run-flat tires; easily damaged AC condensers; and "soft," spongy brakes that extend stopping distance. The sliding doors open when they shouldn't, won't close when they should, catch fingers and arms, get stuck open or closed, are noisy, and frequently require expensive servicing. The Check Engine light may stay lit because of a defective fuel-filler neck. There's a fuel sloshing noise when accelerating or coming to a stop and an engine pinging when driving up steep hills, and the transmission clunks or bangs when backing uphill or when shifting into Reverse. There are also reports of rattling and chattering when the minivan is in Forward gear. Owners note a loud wind noise and vibration from the left side of the front windshield, along with a constant vibration felt through the steering assembly and front wheels. Passenger doors may also require excessive force to open.

Other problems include noisy steering and suspension; leather seats that split, crack, or discolour; exterior clearcoat paint that chips or discolours; the vehicle pulling to the right when underway; front-end clunking caused by welding breaks in the front subframe; accessory items that come loose, break away, or won't work; electrical glitches and defective remote audio controls; excessive wind noise at the pillars separating the front and middle seats; wheel bearings and front brakes that wear out prematurely and are excessively noisy; and transmission breakdowns, transmission seal leaks, and transmission gear whine at 90 km/h or when in Fourth gear.

Safety Summary

All years: Passenger seatbacks collapsed when vehicle was rear-ended. • Airbag malfunctions. • Sudden, unintended acceleration when slowing for a stop sign or when in Drive with AC turned on. • Automatic transmission failures. • Transmission doesn't hold when stopped or parked on an incline; gas or brakes have to be constantly applied. • Entire vehicle shakes excessively at highway speeds and pulls to the left or right. • The rear head restraints seriously hamper rear and forward visibility, and it's difficult to see vehicles coming from the right side. • Power-sliding doors are a constant danger. • Static-electricity shocks. **2002**—Axle-bearing wheel failure caused driver-side wheel to fall off. • Head restraints are set too low for tall occupants. • Rear windshield shatters from area where the wiper is mounted. • Rear seat belt unlatches during emergency braking. • Brake line freezes up in cold weather. • Abrupt downshift on deceleration. • Passenger window exploded. • Airbag light comes on for no reason. **2003**—Fire ignited in the CD player. • Fuel spits out when refuelling. • Inaccurate fuel gauge readings. **2004**—Chronic stalling even after recall; repairs to the fuel-pump relay to correct the problem. • Gas pedal will not work due to a broken throttle cable. • Sliding door crushes arms and legs. • Right-hand fingers can get caught in the gap on the steering wheel between the cruise-control buttons and the airbag area. • If vehicle is started and left in idle, the doors lock automatically. This could lock the driver out after a 10-second delay. **2005**—Child's hand was crushed in one incident by rear power-sliding door. • Run-flat tire problems:

> The tires are all worn out at 31K miles [50,000 km], and we were quoted a price of $1,300 plus tax to have them replaced. Worse yet, our nearest dealer (Flagstaff Honda) does not have the necessary equipment to service them 2 years after their release. To make things worse, we now have a flat and getting it fixed will require us to drive 50 mph [80 km/h] on a busy interstate.

2006—Engine crankshaft and motor mount failures. • Power-steering flywheel fell off. • Loss of power steering and alternator due to belt slipping when driving on rain-soaked roads. • Binding steering shaft. • AC condenser damaged by road debris. • Premature brake and sway bar replacement. • Sliding passenger-side doors still fly open and close at any time. **2007**—Engine surges while brakes feel "soft"—they can be depressed halfway down before any braking effect is felt. • Automatic transmission skips from First to Third gear; sometimes it also jerks into gear. • Brake and gas pedals still mounted too close together. • Vehicle constantly pulls to the left when underway. • Sliding door flew open on the highway; crushed a child's hand in another incident. • Rear window exploded. • AC condensers continue to be destroyed by road debris. • Tire-pressure monitor alerts driver intermittently as the outside temperature changes. **2008**—Engine surging. • No-starts:

> If the vehicle is parked facing downhill, fuel cannot flow back to the vehicle for it to start. The manufacturer stated that the vehicle could not be repaired because it was designed in that manner.

Rear-view camera has no alarm and distorts the true depth and sense of distance between objects. • A child safety seat cannot be installed safely in the middle-row centre. • Dangerous third-row seat:

> My child folded down the third row seat in my 2008 Honda Odyssey and the seat collapsed and fell on his hand, breaking three of his fingers. I contacted Honda and nothing was done.

Automatic transmission makes a loud grunting when shifting. • Excessive vibration when downshifting. • Vehicle will not drive straight after making a turn. • Rear glass window exploded as vehicle was backing out of the driveway. • Tailgate liftgate hydraulic failure allowing the liftgate to crash down. • Sliding-door craziness. • Spongy, soft, ineffective brakes. **2009**—Seat belts are too short. • Rough downshifts. • Spongy brake pedal results in the vehicle rolling past stop signs, etc. • VSA (stability control) warning light came on, and brakes suddenly were gone. • Premature replacement of the brake pads and rotors. • Liftgate hatch fell on owner's head. • Power windows open on their own. • Rear window shattered for no reason. • Sticking fuel-filler door and power-sliding door. **2010**— Fire ignited. • Sunroof suddenly exploded. • When decelerating or accelerating, transmission slams into gear, usually between 80 and 100 km/h. • Transmission slips and shakes. • Fuel odour invaded the cabin because rodents had eaten through the fuel line at the top of the fuel tank. • A loud grinding sound when brakes are applied. • Power steering failures. • Passenger door lock won't open the door. • Sliding-door failures in cold weather or when ice forms; latch does not disengage.

Secret Warranties/Internal Bulletins/Service Tips

All years: Honda TSBs allow for special warranty consideration on a "goodwill" basis by the company's District Service Manager or Zone Office. • There's an incredibly large number of sliding-door problems covered by a recall, and a plethora of service bulletins too numerous to print here. Ask Honda politely for the bulletins or "goodwill" assistance. If refused, subpoena the documents through small claims court, using NHTSA's complaint and service bulletin summaries as your shopping list. **1999–2003**—Deformed windshield moulding. **1999– 2006**—Troubleshooting vehicle pull or drift to one side. **2003**—Engine cranks but won't start. • ABS problems. • Fuel-tank leak. **2003–07**—Honda has a secret warranty extension that covers paint defects up to 7 years (no mileage or prior ownership limitation), says TSB #08-031, issued January 8, 2010. Although this service bulletin is specifically for blue metallic paint defects, the coverage can be easily extrapolated to cover any other Honda or colour, as indicated in TSB #10- 002 "Paint Defect Claim Information," issued January 20, 2010. **2005**—Windshield noise remedy. • Correction for middle-row seat that won't unlatch. **2005–06**—Noise remedy for the power steering, front brakes, front wheel bearings, windshield, sliding door, and exhaust system. **2005–07**— Drivetrain ping, squeal, or rattle. • Power steering pump whine or buzz. • Power seat won't move forward or backward. **2005–09**—Engine timing belt chirp. •

Sliding door doesn't open all the way. • Power door locks continually lock while driving. **2005–10**—If the steering wheel is hard to turn at low speeds, Honda will replace the steering pump for free up to 7 years/100,000 miles (TSB 11-039, available in the U.S.). **2007**—Delayed First gear engagement. • Insufficient AC cooling at idle. **2007–08**—If the brake pedal feels low and spongy, the dealer should replace the ABS/TCS or VSA modulator control unit under warranty, says Honda TSB #07-045 issued March 5, 2009. **2008**—Engine knocking or ticking at idle. **2008–09**—Water accumulates in the inner tail lights in the tailgate. **2008–10**—Gap between the front passenger's airbag lid and the dashboard. • Front door glass opens/closes slowly or sticks.

ODYSSEY PROFILE

	2002	2003	2004	2005	2006	2007	2008	2009	2010
Cost Price ($)									
LX/DX	31,900	32,200	32,400	32,700	33,200	33,300	33,590	33,590	31,690
EX/DX	34,900	35,200	35,400	35,900	36,400	36,900	36,990	36,990	—
Used Values ($)									
LX/DX ▲	4,500	5,500	7,000	8,000	11,000	13,000	14,500	19,000	21,000
LX/DX ▼	4,000	5,000	6,000	7,000	10,000	12,000	13,500	17,500	19,500
EX ▲	6,000	7,000	8,500	9,500	12,000	14,000	16,500	21,500	—
EX ▼	5,000	6,000	7,500	8,500	10,500	13,000	15,000	20,000	—
Reliability	4	4	4	4	4	4	4	4	4
Crash Safety (F)	5	5	5	5	5	5	5	5	5
Side	5	5	5	5	5	5	5	5	5
IIHS Side	—	—	—	5	5	5	5	5	5
Offset	5	5	5	5	5	5	5	5	5
Head Restraints (F)	—	—	—	**2**	**2**	**2**	5	5	5
Rollover Resistance	4	4	4	—	4	4	4	4	4

Toyota

SIENNA ★★★

RATING: Average (2005–10); Below Average (1999–2004). A resurgence of safety-related defects carried over to the 2005 model following the 2004 Sienna's redesign. Although the Sienna was excluded from Toyota's initial sudden-acceleration recall, it is apparent the 2004 and later models have had the same problem (see "Safety Summary"). **Ideal model year:** A 7-passenger 2008 Sienna LE for about $16,000; it's well-appointed, has traction and stability control, and costs much less than half what it sold for originally ($37,225). **"Real" city/highway fuel economy:** 3.0: 12.4/8.8 L/100 km. 3.3: 12.2/8.1 L/100 km. 3.5: 11.7/8.1 L/100 km. AWD: 13.1/9.0 L/100 km. 3.5L AWD: 13.3/9.5 L/100 km.

Maintenance/repair costs: Average; very dealer-dependent. **Parts:** Cheap Sienna parts van be found in the Camry parts bin. **Extended warranty:** Only for the problematic 2004 and 2005 powertrains. **Best alternatives:** Honda CR-V, Mazda5, and a heavily discounted, well-checked-over (AC, brakes, and powertrain especially) Chrysler minivan. **Helpful websites:** *www.carcomplaints.com/Toyota/ Sienna* and *www.toyotanation.com.*

 ## Strengths and Weaknesses

ALERT! If you have children, stay away from any minivan with the automatic sliding-door feature. It can put your child at serious risk, says this parent:

> My 17-month-old's head got jammed between the right rear wheel and the right rear door panel while the electric door slid open. Even though my wife pulled on the door handle the door kept sliding open. My baby's head was crushed between the tire and door panel. This is a very unsafe design as my wife tried to stop the door from sliding back and the door kept moving. My car is a 2011 model.

The Sienna is Toyota's Camry-based front-drive minivan. Some of the Sienna's strong points are standard ABS, stability and traction control; side airbags (LE, XLE); a smooth-running V6 engine, and a more-refined transmission; a stable ride and quiet interior; a fourth door and easy entry/exit; and better-than-average reliability. Its weak areas: V6 performance is compromised by the AC and the automatic transmission powertrain; it lacks the trailer-towing brawn of rear-drive minivans; and sliding doors won't close, won't open, and are hazardous to children and seniors.

The redesigned 2004 Sienna has more interior room than previous models (accommodating up to eight passengers), is better-handling, rides more comfortably, and uses a more-powerful, fuel-efficient 230 hp 3.3L V6 engine. However, the 2007 Sienna's 3.5L V6 is a better powerplant that's more suited to highway use.

Reliability can be problematic, with a large cluster of redesign-related deficiencies appearing around the 2004–05 model years and continuing into the 2010 model year. The most serious concerns are self-destructing, sludge-prone engines (1998–2002 models) and defective automatic transmissions that "lag and lurch" (1998–2010). Many other failure-prone mechanical and body components continue to compromise the Sienna's safety and performance, including electrical shorts; stalling when the AC engages; collapsing rear hatch struts and faulty power-sliding doors; premature brake wear; 3.5L engine "piston-slap" a clunk or banging in the driveline; and expensive, hard-to-find, run-flat tires:

> The dealer could not mount the tire on the rim and had to send it to a special tire place, because th[ese] are special rims, I have been told. The price for this one tire was $269.56 including mounting, balancing and sales tax. Since this type of a van with Run-Flat tires does not come with a spare tire. They told me it is not necessary

to have one. What will happen when you are in the middle of the wilderness in the country. Yes you can drive over 100 miles on the flat tire, but when you get to the next town and they have to order this tire and it can take days before they get one.

The vehicle jolts or creeps forward when at a stop, forcing you to keep your foot firmly on the brake. Also, owners report distracting windshield reflections and distorted windshields; sliding-door defects; the window or sunroof suddenly shattering; easily chipped paint; and various other body glitches, like a hard-to-pull-out rear seat, water leaks, and excessive creaks and rattles.

VEHICLE HISTORY: 2004—New styling, larger dimensions, more power, more safety options, and about 90 extra kilograms. The not recommended optional AWD adds even more weight and includes problematic run-flat tires. A 230 hp 3.3L V6 and 5-speed automatic transmission add 20 more horses. Power windows for the sliding rear side doors are newly standard, and the CE and LE can carry eight with a removable second-row bench seat. A hideaway third-row bench seat folds into the floorwell, *à la* Honda's Odyssey, but the Sienna's 60/40 split adds to its functionality. **2005**—Dual front power seats. **2006**—Standard front-side and curtain-side airbags. **2007**—A 266 hp 3.5L V6 replaces the 215 hp 3.3L V6 as Sienna's sole engine. **2008**—Standard traction and stability control offered on all models. **2009**—CE 7-passenger Sienna gets rear privacy glass and power flip-out rear side windows. **2010**—Toyota added a front-wheel drive, seven-passenger Limited model; it had been an all-wheel drive only.

 ## Safety Summary

All years: Airbag malfunctions. • Sudden unintended acceleration:

> These vehicles no longer use the traditional mechanical cable between the pedal and throttle, it is all controlled electronically. I honestly believe that Toyota has a serious problem in this drive-by-wire electrical circuit that enables a faulty signal to be sent to the throttle valve that will enable it to go wide open. There have been so many cases that there is even a book by Clarence Ditlow called *Sudden Acceleration: The Myth of Driver Error* written to refute NHTSA findings that most incidents of sudden acceleration are caused by driver error. It accuses auto manufacturers of withholding evidence that would prove that there is a serious problem in this technology. Toyota acknowledged that they have a problem but they are blaming it on car mats. In the case of my van, there is no way that car mats caused the sudden acceleration, it was clear that it was electronically-driven. Car mats causing all the documented Toyota vehicle sudden acceleration cases is highly unlikely.

When accelerating from a stop, vehicle lags then lurches forward. • Chronic transmission failures. • Vehicle rolls down the driveway while in Park. • When proceeding from a rolling stop, acceleration is delayed for about two seconds. • Child can knock gearshift lever into Drive from Park without key in the ignition. • Sluggish transmission downshift; vehicle sometimes seems to slip out of gear when decelerating. • Skid-control system lock-up. • Rapid brake degradation (glazed and warped rotors). • A multiplicity of sliding-door defects covered by internal bulletins. • Windshield distortion; shatters spontaneously. • Reflection of the dashboard onto the windshield impairs visibility. • Slope of the windshield makes it hard to gauge where the front end stops. **2004**—Fuel-tank leakage after recall repairs; leaking fuel line. • Complete loss of brakes. • Sliding door catches passenger's arm or leg; manual door doesn't latch properly (particularly when windows are open); door opens when turning, jams or closes when vehicle is parked on an incline:

> Our two-year-old son pulled on the sliding door handle, and the door began to open (we thought the child locks were on, but this was not the case). He was surprised and was afraid of falling out of the van, so he just held onto the handle. As the door was opening, his head then was dragged between the sliding door and the side of the van. But the van door did not stop opening. It just continued opening, exerting even more force on our son's head. Fortunately we were able to grab the door and forcefully pull it back closed before our son was horribly injured.

Small brake lights inadequate. • Daytime running lights blind oncoming drivers. **2005**—Airbag deployed for no reason while vehicle was underway. • Airbag is disabled when passenger seat is occupied. • Hesitation when accelerating, then sudden acceleration. • Laser-controlled cruise control jerks back to former speed when the way seems clear. • Gearshift lever can be accidently knocked from Fourth to Reverse. • Vehicle Stability Control engages when it shouldn't. • Brake pedal stiffens intermittently. • Run-flat tires don't signal driver when they are damaged; may catch fire:

> 2005 Toyota Sienna has Bridgestone run flat tires and the back right passenger tire went flat, then smoked and caught fire.

When the rear windows are down, the door will not stay open. • Rear hatch may fall:

> The liftgate on a power liftgate 2005 Toyota Sienna will not stay open. It has come down and whacked my wife and I on the head many times. I found out the replacement is $450.

Automatic interior light shut-off fails intermittently, draining the battery. • Rear heater core leaks coolant. • Front heater airflow is inadequate. **2006**—Seat belt unbuckled during a collision. • Head restraints cannot accommodate tall people. • Power steering cuts out intermittently. • Increased engine speed when stopped. • Vehicle pulls to the right. • Rear disc clip rust causes the caliper piston to stay extended and keep the disc brake pad in contact with the disc. • Windshield optical distortion causes eye strain, headaches, dizziness. • Second-row passengers have no armrests for support and are thrown into the side windows when the vehicle turns. **2006–07**—Tire-pressure monitoring system gives false alerts. **2007**—Hesitation and then sudden acceleration ("lag and lurch") continues. • Tires often have side wall bulges. **2008**—Airbags did not deploy in a side collision. • Seatbelt tightened around child's stomach; he had to be cut free. • If battery power is cut from a collision or power drain, front seat passengers may be locked in. One young mother had this to say:

> There should be an override where if the battery power is lost everything automatically unlocks—and there should be a way to open the trunk from the inside! I am freaked out to think of getting in an accident and no one being able to get in to help out my kid(s). This is a huge safety concern!

When making a left-hand turn it is easy to hit the cruise control "Resume" button and suddenly accelerate. • Hood suddenly flew up and broke the windshield when vehicle was underway. • Tire inflation warning light stays on constantly. • Faulty HomeLink garage opener transmitter. **2009**—Sticking cruise control. • Power sliding doors are still dangerous:

> I have a 2009 Toyota Sienna mini-van with automatic sliding doors. These doors are an accident waiting to happen. Unlike an elevator door that will immediately reverse if someone or something is in its path. The Sienna's doors continue to close unless forcibly pushed back to retract with a serious amount of strength. My arm has been bruised and I could only imagine a child's hand being caught. It's inconceivable to me how these doors do not operate on the same premise as an elevator. Very dangerous!

> •

> Our automatic sliding door was opened but would not close. No amount of tugging, finessing, or cursing would make it shut. Children were stranded in Phoenix heat in August because the vehicle was unsafe to drive with a door that could not be closed. There are many mentions of this exact problem on various blogs and all report difficulty in getting Toyota to offer a solution that didn't cost $1–2K. Almost all owners reported the "fixed" doors to have failed in some way again with dealers refusing to cover the cost of the second (or third) fix.

Rear sliding doors won't stay open if vehicle is parked on the slightest incline. • Total brake failure. • Power rear hatch struts fail, allowing the hatch to come crashing down. **2010**—Severe accident injuries occurred when the airbags didn't deploy during a collision and the seatbelt retractor failed. • The slightest touch of the gear shift lever shifts the car into Neutral. • Sienna didn't come with a spare tire even though the owner's manual said that a spare tire was included. • Rear hatchback door doesn't close manually or with the remote. • Sliding side door doesn't latch; door hinge and latch were changed, but problem remains. • Sunroof suddenly shattered. • Brakes require a great deal of effort to stop the vehicle.

Secret Warranties/Internal Bulletins/Service Tips

All years: Sliding-door hazards, malfunctions, and noise are a veritable plague affecting all model years and generating a ton of service bulletins. • Owner feedback confirms that front brake pads and discs will be replaced under Toyota's "goodwill" policy if they wear out before 2 years/40,000 km (in spite of Toyota's pretensions that brakes aren't a warrantable item). • Rusting at the base of the two front doors will be repaired at no cost, usually with a courtesy car included. **2003–05**—No-start in extreme cold. **2003–09**—Upper, lower windshield ticking noise. **2004**—VSC activates intermittently when it is not needed. • New ECM calibration for a poorly shifting transmission (TSB #TC007-03). • Rear disc brake groan (TSB #BR002-04). • Intermediate steering shaft noise on turns. • Front-door area wind noise (TSB #NV009-03). • Power-sliding door inoperative, rattles (the saga continues). • Backdoor shudder and water leaks. • Seat heaters operate only on high. **2004–05**—Remedy for hard starts in cold weather. • Transmission lag, gear hunting. • Premature brake pad wear. • Fuel-injector ticking. • Inoperative AC light flashing. • AC blower or compressor noise; seized compressor. **2004–06**—Silencing engine ping, knock. • Power-hatch door shudder and leakage. • Power-sliding door rattles. • Excessive steering effort in high road-salt areas. **2004–07**—Back power-sliding doors are hard to close. • Back power-door shudder. **2004–08**—Front power-seat grinding, groaning. • Remedy for front brake pads that wear out prematurely. **2004–10**—Front seat squeaking. • Sliding doors don't operate smoothly (change the lock assembly). • Sliding-door rattle. • Brake rattle, buzz from driver's side of the dash. **2007**—Inoperative front, sliding-door windows. • Front-seat squeak. **2006–09**—No shift from Park. **2007–08**—Engine compartment squeaking.

SIENNA PROFILE

	2002	2003	2004	2005	2006	2007	2008	2009	2010
Cost Price ($)									
Sienna CE 4d	29,335	29,060	30,000	30,000	30,800	31,200	31,750	28,990	29,500
Sienna LE 4d	32,985	31,925	35,000	35,420	36,255	36,860	37,225	37,225	33,900
Used Values ($)									
Sienna CE 4d ▲	4,500	5,500	6,500	8,000	10,500	12,000	14,000	17,500	20,000
Sienna CE 4d ▼	3,500	5,000	5,500	7,000	9,000	11,000	12,500	16,000	18,500
Sienna LE 4d ▲	5,500	6,500	8,000	9,500	11,500	13,500	16,500	20,000	23,000
Sienna LE 4d ▼	5,000	6,000	7,000	9,000	10,000	12,000	15,000	18,500	21,000
Reliability	4	4	4	3	3	3	3	3	3
Crash Safety (F)	5	5	5	4	4	4	4	4	4
Side	4	4	4	5	5	5	5	5	5
Offset	5	5	5	5	5	5	5	5	5
Side (IIHS)	—	—	—	3	5	5	5	5	5
Head Restraints (F)	—	—	—	1	1	1	1	1	1
Rollover Resistance	4	4	4	4	4	4	4	4	4

All ratings on a numbered scale where 5 is good and **1** is bad. See page 132 for a more detailed description.

VANS

What's the attraction of full-sized vans? Simple: they're cheap used and easier to handle and maintain than a "recreational vehicle" (RV). Sure, they may not be sleek, fuel-efficient, or sexy, their styling is likely decades old, and their popularity has certainly waned, but large vans are versatile carriers that have more grunt than front-drives and are much more reliable as well. Okay, they *are* fuel-thirsty. But I'll bet that'll be the last thought on your mind when you pass more fuel-efficient front-drive minivans stuck on the side of the road with cooked engines or burned-out transmissions.

There are also some safety reasons for choosing a large van, including excellent outward visibility, plenty of room to sit away from a deploying airbag and housing, and the inclusion of electronic stability control as a standard feature. SUVs and other vehicles are also less likely to run up over the frame and crash into the van's passenger compartment.

Handling, though, is definitely not carlike (regardless of hype to the contrary); expensive suspension modifications may be needed to produce a reasonable ride and manoeuvrability. Rear visibility is also problematic, so be sure to invest in the biggest and best rear-view and side-view mirrors available. Vans will require some additional driving skills due to their large size and truck platforms that make for ponderous handling. They are very susceptible to crosswinds, they wander at highway speeds, and they demand greater driver attention simply to corner safely and to park in the city.

15-Passenger "Killer" Vans

15-passenger vans are particularly hazardous. Often used to shuttle sports teams, church groups, and airport passengers, they are three times more likely than regular vans to roll over when carrying 10 or more passengers, according to NHTSA. This is because the van's centre of gravity unexpectedly shifts up and to the back, and excess baggage adds to this instability.

In the past five years, two horrific 15-passenger van accidents have occurred in Canada. The first, in Bathurst, New Brunswick, resulted in 13 dead and led to Nova Scotia, New Brunswick, and Quebec outlawing the vans for school use.

Said the mother of one of the high school students killed in the crash:

> Passengers in 15 seat vans have no protection because these vans were not designed to carry human beings. Passengers in a 15-seat van collision are ejected from the vans and killed when they suffer massive injuries.

The latest accident occurred in February, 2012 near Kitchener, Ontario and resulted in the death of 11 passengers.

The courts have ruled that these vans are inherently dangerous. Ford paid $37.5 million in a 2004 Kentucky van crash case after a Scott County jury found the automaker's 15-passenger van responsible for two deaths.

Chrysler Vans

Chrysler's full-sized, American-built rear-drive vans (the Tradesman and Ram Van or Ram Wagon series) are Above Average buys that have always been more reliable than Chrysler's front-drive minivans, like the Grand Caravan. But rear-drives in good condition are hard to find, as 2003 was their last model year. Don't forget that these full-sized vans may also need expensive repairs generated by blown transmissions, collapsed ball joints, and premature wearout of brake components. On the other hand, the problems are well known and easily fixed by independent garages. Ram Van prices are also quite reasonable, with fully equipped 2000 to 2003 models selling for less than $2,000. Crashworthiness is fairly good as well: 2001 through 2003 models scored four stars out of five in frontal collision occupant protection and three stars for rollover resistance.

When Chrysler dumped its full-sized vans, the company chose the overpriced and under-performing Mercedes/Freightliner Sprinter to fill the gap in its van lineup. Not Recommended by *Lemon-Aid*, the Sprinter was a sales flop from the start. North American sales were repatriated from Chrysler and are now overseen by Mercedes and Freightliner.

A 2009 Sprinter Cargo Van originally sold in Canada for $45,600 and is now worth about $24,000. Ouch!

The Sprinter is an expensive van, retailing for almost $20,000 more than the discontinued Van Wagon. Crashworthiness is also problematic. NHTSA-tested rollover resistance for the 2008 through 2010 models was rated one star out of five. Other disadvantages: Service is provided by only a few select dealers, parts are hard to find, and depreciation is brutally fast. A 2009 version passenger van now sells for $26,000; its original price was $51,215.

Ford and GM Vans

Both automakers are struggling with their vans due to a stalled economy and high fuel prices. GM has hedged its bets by shoehorning the Duramax 6600 diesel engine into its large vans, making them less fuel-thirsty and more attractive to frugal buyers. However, this is too little, too late. Many remember the Duramax's poor past performance and are angry that the old GM warranty is worthless now that the automaker has come out of bankruptcy.

Ford's Econoline joins GM in the middle of the pack in terms of value for dollar. Servicing this Ford van is a breeze due to the large number of generic parts in Ford's truck parts bin and the few changes made to the E-150 series over the years. As with all full-sized vans, depreciation is your friend, allowing you to pick up a 2008 Econoline XL for about $11,500. Its original selling price was $32,599.

GM has substantially redesigned its full-sized vans within the past few years to improve both their handling and the ride, and to add important safety features like stability control, ABS, and additional airbags. Following this redesign, GM has led the Detroit pack with better-handling and smoother-riding models than those available from Ford or Chrysler.

Some of the more-common problems shared by all three automakers: engine and drivetrain breakdowns, brake failures, premature brake and suspension/steering wearout, AC failures, electrical and computer module glitches, and defects in both manual and sliding doors.

The reason why there's such similarity in the defect trending among Asian and Detroit van builders is that they all get their key components from a small band of suppliers. And, as they cut supplier profits, quality goes down the drain. Hence, as Toyota and Honda become more skinflint in their supplier payouts, they, too, see a corresponding quality decline, evidenced by engine and transmission defects and sliding-door failures.

Note: Individual full-sized van ratings are found in the Appendix (page 523)

SPORT-UTILITY VEHICLES

Large SUVs—Low Prices

Unrest and talk of war in the Middle East and China's insatiable quest for fuel—at any price—have sent gas prices soaring and savaged full- and mid-sized SUV sales, forcing Detroit's automakers to drop negotiated prices by thousands of dollars and creating a market shift to downsized and "crossover" models.

Used SUVs, like the Ford Expedition and Excursion, the Jeep Grand Cherokee, and the GM Suburban, Yukon, and Tahoe are selling for a song. Imagine: Three-year-old large SUVs are worth less than half their original suggested retail price. Of course, poor fuel economy and high insurance costs need to be figured into your overall cost estimate. Still, a $25,000 savings can buy a whole lot of gas, not counting the reduced GST or HST, insurance premiums, and dropped $1,500 "freight charge."

Dealers are offering $10,000 discounts on leftover full-sized SUVs—even more if they're option-loaded models, while prices for compact and family-sized cars are higher than ever. In fact, no SUV larger than Honda's CR-V or Toyota's RAV4 has a secure future.

Small SUVs, like the Ford Escape, Honda CR-V, Hyundai Tucson, and Mazda Tribute, are selling as fast as they are being traded in. Buyers are attracted by the more-reasonable used prices, better fuel economy, and easier handling than larger SUVs. Plus, there are plenty of used downsized SUVs available, as many five-year leases expire.

Safety

One of the main reasons buyers choose sport-utility vehicles is the safety advantages they offer their drivers, at the expense of others on the road. The large windshield and high seating give the driver a commanding view of the road ahead, though rear vision may be obstructed by side pillars, rear head restraints, or the spare tire hanging off the back end. As we react more slowly with age, increased visibility comes in handy (a few extra seconds of warning can make a big difference). Improvements have also been made with three-point seat belts in the front and rear, seat belt pretensioners, optional adjustable brake and accelerator pedals, four-wheel anti-lock brakes, electronic stability control, a high centre brake light, adjustable head restraints on all seatbacks, side head-protecting airbags, side-door beams, and reinforced roofs to protect occupants in rollovers.

Reliability and Quality

In the last decade, many domestic and imported SUVs were rushed to market with serious quality and performance deficiencies. How much you spent was irrelevant: SUVs have their own luxury lemons. Mercedes' 1997–2006 M-Class luxury sport-utilities, for example, are nowhere near as reliable as today's entry-level Hyundais.

During the past couple decades, the Detroit Three haven't closed the quality gap with Asian automakers. Yes, much has been written about how Chrysler, GM, and Ford were raising their quality standards, but the benchmark was already in the sub-basement. Dodge's Durango has a barely acceptable reliability score. Jeep's Cherokee and Grand Cherokee have been afflicted by serious brake, body, AC, and powertrain defects, and the Jeep Commander is mediocre at best. The Jeep Wrangler's been around forever, yet its quality is barely acceptable. And don't forget another oldie, the Ford Explorer: The most popular SUV ever produced was probably the least reliable, most dangerous vehicle Ford ever built (yes, even worse than the automaker's "You light up my life" Pinto).

GM's post-2000 SUVs are the best of Detroit's worst. Their relatively recent redesigns (the Acadia, Enclave, Traverse, and Terrain) have better safety and performance scores, but reliability is still the pits, with serious engine, transmission, and fit-and-finish defects. After five years of use (about when the warranty ends), buyers would be wise to get an extended warranty or dump these vehicles.

"Crossovers"

Advertising hype for a tall wagon, the term describes most family-sized vehicles that incorporate unibody construction, a relatively high seating position, four-wheel drive (usually), a good amount of cargo space, and seating for at least four. Crossover models embrace a wide range of sizes. Some models are styled like traditional SUVs, others may look like downsized SUVs or upsized wagons (Pontiac Vibe and Toyota Matrix), and an emerging type resembles a mini-minivan (Mazda5).

SPORT-UTILITY RATINGS

Recommended

Honda CR-V (2002–10)   Hyundai Tucson (2005–10)

Above Average

Ford Escape/Mazda Tribute (2008–2010)

Average

Ford Escape/Mazda Tribute (2002–2007)
Ford Escape Hybrid (2005–10)
GM Escalade, ESV, EXT, Denali, Suburban,
    Tahoe, Yukon, XL (1999–2010)

Lexus RX 300, RX 330, RX 350 (2000–06)
Lexus RX 400h andd 450h (2006; 2010)
Toyota RAV4 (2010)

Below Average

Chrysler TJ Wrangler (1999–2010)
Lexus RX 300, RX 330, RX 350 (2007–09)

Toyota RAV4 (1999–2009)

Not Recommended

Lexus RX 400h (2006–09)

Chrysler

TJ WRANGLER	★ ★

RATING: Below Average (1999–2010). **Ideal model year:** A 2008 Wrangler Sahara. It has lots of safety, performance, and convenience features carried over from the 2007 redesign, and costs only $11,000, far less than its $26,995 original price. Try to get a Wrangler with some unexpired factory warranty left. **"Real" city/highway fuel economy:** The 5-speed manual and 6-cylinder engine give you the best fuel economy. *2.4 4-cylinder automatic:* 15.7/12.1 L/100 km. *3.8 6-cylinder manual:* 14.1/10.8 L/100 km. *3.8 6-cylinder automatic:* 14.1/10.3 L/100 km. *4.0 6-cylinder automatic:* 16.8/11.7 L/100 km. **Maintenance/repair costs:** Average. **Parts:** Inexpensive and not hard to find. **Extended warranty:** Only for the transmission. **Best alternatives:** Honda CR-V or Element, Hyundai Tucson, and Subaru Forester. But remember, none of these other models can follow the Wrangler off-road. **Helpful websites:** *www.carcomplaints.com/Jeep/Wrangler* and *www.wranglerforum.com/f33.*

 ## Strengths and Weaknesses

ALERT! Insurance industry figures show a much-higher-than-average number of accident injury claims, aggravated by a high incidence of sudden rollovers when drivers exceed the Jeep's very low tolerance for sporty driving.

A direct descendent of the original Jeep, the 1941 Willys MB, the Wrangler should be every off-roader's first car. It's primitive, capable, and fun to drive. Plus, the Wrangler's not a bad looker for Saturday night cruising along Yonge or Burrard, and short commutes with the 6-speed manual transmission or the 4-speed automatic are a breeze (for 2003 and later models).

Best choice: an improved, second-series 2007–10 model for both on- and off-roading capability. The 2007 model's complete redesign gave it more power, more interior room, better off-road capability, and more on-road refinement. It has more standard features and handles much better than earlier versions.

You will have to take some bad with the good, however: a wobbly, noisy, rough-and-tumble ride; vague, imprecise steering; mediocre braking; cramped rear seating; little storage space; a canvas top that is a chore to open and leaks like a sieve; plastic windows that don't stay clean for long; a high step-in; some powertrain and body shortcomings; and mediocre fuel economy.

VEHICLE HISTORY: 2003—An optional 4-speed automatic is introduced. SE models use the Liberty's 147 hp 2.4L 4-cylinder engine, and the X, Sport, Sahara, and Rubicon versions carry a 190 hp 4.0L inline-six powerplant. **2004**—Unlimited gets larger and longer. **2005**—A 6-speed manual transmission replaces the 5-speed. **2007**—A new 205 hp 3.8L V6 with 15 more horses than the 4.0L V6; Electronic Stability Program; electronic roll mitigation; dual-stage airbags; seat-mounted side airbags and Occupant Classification System; increased ground clearance; larger wheels and tires; enhanced Dana front and rear solid axles; Command-Trac and Rock-Trac transfer cases; new electric axle lockers; and a revamped front sway bar. Also, a stiffer frame, a 5 cm (2 in.) longer wheelbase, 9 cm (3.5 in.) wider track, lower spring rates, better brakes, and a retuned suspension. The three-piece hardtop is also new. **2009**—Trailer Sway Control added. **2010**—*Wrangler*: The base Wrangler X has been renamed the Sport. New features include upgraded seats, new gauges, a full-length floor console, a new bumper, and Interactive Decel Fuel Shut-Off, which cuts the fuel supply on deceleration for better gas mileage. *Sahara and Rubicon*: new wheel finishes and a more "user-friendly" soft top.

Factory-related defects have always plagued these vehicles, although the cars have gotten marginally better after their 2007 redesign. Premature front brake wear is a frequent complaint. Owners say that the 5-speed and 6-speed manual transmissions don't shift smoothly. The 6-speed grinds when going into Reverse, or pops out of Reverse. The 5-speed constantly grinds when shifting or when in Neutral with the clutch depressed; the shifter won't come out of or go into gear, may suddenly pop out of gear, and sticks in Second when hot or when accelerating in First or Second; and the Fifth gear suddenly disengages. One dissatisfied owner says:

> There have now been four transmissions in my Jeep, and all have had problems with noise, shifting into and out of gear, and getting stuck in gear.

Another owner had to replace the transmission at 600 km (370 mi.). Clutches aren't very durable (and squeal a lot). Watch out for transfer-case malfunctions, engine overheating, engine and transfer-case oil leaks, worn-out steering components and suspensions (ball joints, especially), and ignition-component malfunctions.

Windshield cracks going up the middle are a common failure. Body welds and seams are susceptible to premature rusting, and there have been frequent complaints about peeling paint and water leaks. The worst leaks occur at the bottom of the windshield frame. An easy way to check for this is to examine the underside of the frame to see if there's excessive rust. This has consistently been a problem area for Jeeps; hence, all the ads for aftermarket windshield frames. The good news is that you can replace the windshield frame and all of the seals relatively cheaply.

Safety Summary

All years: Failures that crop up repeatedly are malfunctioning airbags; fuel-tank leaks; fuel-pump failures; malfunctioning fuel gauges; sudden, unintended acceleration; chronic engine stalling when accelerating or decelerating; clutch master and slave cylinder leaks; premature brake wear; and brake failure—there have been several incidents of sudden brake loss where the pedal goes all the way to the floor with no braking effect (corrected by replacing the master cylinder). Other brake complaints include a seal leak in the power-brake booster that might cause a brake failure; the brake drum not keeping its shape; the vehicle pulling to the left when braking; the rear brakes suddenly locking up while driving in the rain and approaching a stop sign; and the vehicle going into open throttle position when brakes are applied. **1995–2003**—Manual and automatic transmission failures. **2003**—Driveshaft fell out while vehicle was underway. • Vehicle slips into Neutral from Drive. • Sudden axle and steering failure. • Seat belts unlatch too easily. **2004**—Left-front axle seal leak. • Gas-line leaks. • Seized front brakes. • Defective steering stabilizer responsible for steering shudder. **2004–05**—Partial loss of control when passing over bumps or railroad tracks. **2005**—Carpet causes accelerator pedal to stick. **2006**—Excessive front shimmy. • Windshield cracks. • Faulty 6-speed manual transmission:

> The clutch rod comes out of the floor board and attaches to the clutch pedal with a clip/attachment that bolts into the clutch pedal. The problem here is, as part of their new design, the clip or attachment piece can break very easily and disable your Jeep.

2007—ABS may suddenly lock up while underway. **2008**—Fire ignites in the engine compartment. • Chronic stalling and no-starts linked to a faulty C-Bus module. • No-start due to the WCM computer module failure (a $400 repair). • Overheated transmission spilled fluid onto the exhaust, which caused a fire. • Transmission failure: 6-speed transmission violently jumps out of gear when accelerating in First gear. • Early clutch failures. • Prematurely worn-out front end torsion bar. • Severe front end "wobble" and "wheel hop" when passing over small changes in the road surface like an expansion joint, rippling of the road, or a small pothole):

> My brand new 2008 Jeep Wrangler X 4×4 began the dreaded "death wobble" (loss of steering control) around 550 miles [890 km]. Thought I was about to "die". Happened 4 more times until I got it to the dealer. After searching Jeep forums and such, I

found that 1000s of Jeep owners have experienced this problem, with many Jeep models. And, I learned that Chrysler does not consider the death wobble an issue.

Fuel overflows whenever refuelling. • Hood rises up several inches with headwinds, or when a large truck passes. • Defective turn signal switch. • Gas tank replaced due to a faulty emissions valve. • Driver's head poorly protected:

There is a poorly designed bracket right behind the driver's and [front] passenger's head. The bracket has a sharp metal corner right behind the front drivers and passengers heads. If there [was] even a small accident, there would be significant trauma to the head if they were to hit the bracket.

2009—Manual transmission popped out of gear. • Clock spring module fails, causing loss of stability control. • When refuelling, the tank often overflows. • Driver's side brake lines worn through. Vehicle not part of the recall in place to fix this problem. • Hood shakes violently when trucks pass from the other direction. Jeep is aware of the hood latch problem and has a Customer Satisfaction Program in place to assist owners, or so they say. • Front suspension suddenly collapsed:

While driving 65 mph, the entire front suspension broke, almost causing a crash. The contact pulled over and look[ed] under the vehicle and noticed that the axles were split in two places.

2010—Underhood fires are quite common. • During fill-ups, fuel spews out of the tank. • 6-speed manual transmission pops out of First gear. • Violent vehicle shake after passing over small bumps in the road. • Severe front tire "cupping." • Headlights suddenly shut off. • Premature failure of the heater core.

Secret Warranties/Internal Bulletins/Service Tips

1997–2005—Tips on repairing a leak in the engine rear main oil seal. 1997–2006—Tips on plugging door leaks. 1999–2004—A rough idle may require the installation of a fuel-injector insulator sleeve. 2001–05—If the vehicle tends to drift, install upgraded ball joints. 2003—Manual transmission may have defective Third gear weld. 2005—Manual 6-speed won't stay in gear. 2007–08—Oil seepage at front of engine. • No-crank, no-start due to a defective wireless control module. • Water leaks onto dash and console areas. • Steering rubbing sound when cornering. • Body tapping or knocking sound. 2007–09—Excessive steering vibration when passing over rough surfaces. • Difficult fuel fill. • Wind noise and water leaks from the windshield/soft top header. 2007–10—Manual transmission pops out of First gear when upshifting. • Hard starts, no-start, or dead battery. • Special Campaign #J34 for free replacement of the steering damper hardware. 2008–10—Warranty is extended to 7 years/70,000 miles to cover the replacement of the automatic transmission cooler line on vehicles equipped with a 3.8L engine. 2009–10—Transmission fluid may overheat; a chime will be installed to alert the driver when this happens. This is a Customer Satisfaction Program, not a safety recall. 2010–11—Chrysler will repair, free of charge, a noisy right rear door latch.

TJ WRANGLER PROFILE

	2002	2003	2004	2005	2006	2007	2008	2009	2010
Cost Price ($)									
TJ, SE	21,000	21,340	21,995	22,910	23,230	19,995	19,995	19,995	20,595
Sahara	28,120	28,715	29,950	—	—	26,450	26,995	27,195	27,495
TJ Rubicon	—	29,425	30,420	31,790	32,210	28,150	28,595	30,195	30,495
Unl. Rubicon	—	—	—	33,250	33,160	29,895	30,595	32,195	32,495
Used Values ($)									
TJ, SE ▲	2,500	3,500	4,000	5,000	6,000	7,000	10,000	11,500	14,000
TJ, SE ▼	2,000	3,000	3,500	4,000	5,500	6,500	8,500	10,000	12,500
Sahara ▲	4,000	5,000	5,500	—	—	9,000	11,500	16,000	19,000
Sahara ▼	3,500	4,500	5,000	—	—	7,500	10,000	14,500	18,000
TJ Rubicon ▲	—	4,500	5,000	6,000	7,500	9,500	12,500	19,000	20,500
TJ Rubicon ▼	—	4,000	4,500	5,500	6,500	8,500	11,000	17,500	19,500
Unl. Rubicon ▲	—	—	—	6,500	8,500	10,000	13,000	20,000	22,000
Unl. Rubicon ▼	—	—	—	6,000	7,000	8,500	11,500	18,500	20,500
Reliability	2	2	2	2	2	3	3	3	3
Crash Safety (F)	4	4	4	4	4	5	5	5	5
IIHS Side	2	2	2	2	2	1	1	1	1
Offset	3	3	3	3	3	5	5	5	5
Head Restraints	1	1	1	1	1	2	2	2	2
Rollover Resistance	3	3	—	4	4	4	4	3	3

Ford/Mazda

ESCAPE, TRIBUTE, ESCAPE HYBRID ★★★

RATING: *Escape, Tribute:* Above Average (2008–10); Average (2002–07). The Escape and Tribute's safety-related problems involve the brakes, steering, and electrical system. *Escape Hybrid:* Average (2005–10). **Ideal model year:** Worth $13,000, a 2009 Escape XLT V6-equipped front-drive will cost just a little over half the car's original price of $26,699. Plus you get lots of extra power, possibly some unexpired factory warranty, and more standard features. **"Real" city/highway fuel economy:** *2.3 4-cylinder:* 9.7/7.3 L/100 km. *2.3 Hybrid:* 6.6/7.0 L/100 km (hybrids are more economical in the city). *3.0 V6:* 13.3/9.9 L/100 km. **Maintenance/repair costs:** Average. **Parts:** Reasonably priced and usually not hard to find, although, the coolant pump's high failure rate keeps it on back order. **Extended warranty:** Only for the transmission. **Best alternatives:** The Honda CR-V, Hyundai Tucson, Jeep Wrangler, Mitsubishi Outlander, and Nissan Xterra. **Helpful websites:** *www.carcomplaints.com/Ford/Escape* and *www.carcomplaints. com/Mazda/Tribute.*

Strengths and Weaknesses

ALERT! 2012 will be the Hybrid's last model year. This move is likely to drive down the car's resale value and make parts and servicing more problematic. The C-Max hybrid and C-Max Energi plug-in hybrid, two small minivan models, will replace the Escape Hybrid for the 2013 model year. The C-Max hybrid will be more than 25 percent more fuel-efficient than the Escape Hybrid.

Launched as 2001 models, both the Escape and Tribute combine a carlike ride and handling—thanks to an independent rear suspension and front MacPherson struts—with the ability to drive in the snow and carry up to five passengers and their luggage. Neither vehicle is an upsized car or a downsized truck—they're four-doors that sip fuel, look like sport-utilities, and drive like sedans.

VEHICLE HISTORY: *Escape, Tribute:* **2005**—A quieter engine and 26 more horses with the 2.3L Duratec 4-banger. The V6 engine uses upgraded engine mounts and computers to smooth out the idle and improve throttle response. Safety is also enhanced with dual-stage airbags, side curtain airbags, head restraints and three-point safety belts for all seats, "smart" seat sensors, and larger-diameter four-wheel disc and anti-lock brakes. Other enhancements include a fully automatic 4×4 system; front shocks that are larger in diameter; a new stabilizer system; a floor-mounted shifter; new headlights, fog lights, grille, and front and rear ends; different gauges; upgraded seat cushions; more storage space; additional sound-absorbing materials (though it still lets in excessive wind noise); and alloy wheels. **2008**—New interior and exterior styling; speed-sensitive electric power steering; standard electronic stability control, and side curtain airbags. The manual transmission has been dropped. **2009**—Gasoline models receive new 4- and 6-cylinder engines that promise improved performance and better fuel economy. The new 6-speed automatic transmission replaces the previous 4-speed automatic. *Escape Hybrid:* **2005**—This gasoline-electric hybrid is equipped with a 2.3L 4-cylinder engine, a 65 kW electric motor, and a 28 kW generator. It has off-road and towing capability, plus acceleration comparable to the Escape's 200 hp V6 engine. **2008**—Restyled inside and out and given additional features. No change in size or power. **2009**—A 171 hp 2.5L 4-cylinder engine replaces the 153 hp 2.3L four; the optional 3.0L V6 gained 40 hp for a total of 240.

Most owner complaints target powertrain reliability, like chronic stalling and hard starts; engine oil leaks (engine crankshaft out of spec); automatic transmission gear-hunting; loss of Reverse gear; transmission fluid leaks; frequent short circuits; a cruise control that turns itself off; faulty side windows; front wheels that let ice form, causing excessive vibrations; lots of squeaks, rattles, and wind noise; poor fit and finish; and engine hesitation when the AC is engaged.

Safety Summary

Escape, Tribute: **2001–04**—Stalling; sudden, unintended acceleration; airbag and brake malfunctions; and frequent transmission replacements are major problems. **2002**—Gas-tank filler pipe allows fuel to spill out when refuelling. **2002–04**—

Cruise control won't deactivate. • Rear window explodes. **2003**—Fire ignites due to faulty fuel injectors. • Throttle cable jams. • Poor starting. • Rainwater leaks at the driver window pillar area, shorting out the electrical system. **2005**— Accelerator sticks. • Faulty transmission pump shaft causes vehicle to jump out of gear and not shift. • Excessive steering play. • Constant pulling to the left when underway. • Passenger-door latch failure causes door to fly open. • Airbag disables when an average-sized passenger occupies the front seat. • Sunroof explodes. • Fog lights afflicted with stress cracks. **2006**—Driver's window suddenly shatters. • Brakes fail. **2006–07**—Liftgate fails:

> I was knocked out and pinned by the rear hatch door of our 2006 Ford Escape. I opened the rear hatch and leaned in to remove some items from rear of the Ford Escape and the hatch came slamming down, hitting me in the back of the head and rendering me unconscious (I am not sure as to how long). I came to face-first inside the Ford Escape with the door pinning me down and my feet hanging out the rear.

2007—Fire ignites in the trunk area. • In one incident, driver-side airbag and seat belt failed in a head-on collision. • Passenger-side airbag is disabled even though a small adult occupies the seat. • All four wheels suddenly lock up while the vehicle is underway. **2008–09**—Airbags failed to deploy. **2008**—Throttle binds. • Automatic transmission cooler leaks fluid and then the transmission self-destructs; fluid is flammable:

> I went to this website: *www.carcomplaints.com/Ford/Escape/2008/transmission/ transmission_cooler_failure-TSB_exists.shtml* and found many people are having transmission issues.

Car hesitates when accelerating; gas pedal has to be pumped, which causes vehicle to accelerate faster than desired. • Many complaints of no power steering, or steering lockup; repair cost can range from $1,000 to $1,700. • Brake pedal went to the floor without braking (broken throttle cable suspected). • Rear hatch window shatters for no reason. **2009**—Engine timing chain cover frequently cracks. • Window exploded as hatch door was closed:

> It was like the window exploded sending glass all over the driveway behind the vehicle. The window cost almost $60 to replace and the Ford body shop estimated almost $1,300 damage to the hatch finish for the nicks and scratches from the broken glass. We contacted Ford but they refused to cover any of the damage. Our insurance covered the cost of the repairs except for our $250 deductible. We found a web site where there [are] 31 incidents of Escape rear windows shattering [reported]. We believe there must be a defect in the glass or window design and want to go on record that this is a problem with the Ford Escape.

Jerky acceleration. • Automatic transmission often slips into Neutral. • Broken left front axle. • Transmission fluid leakage. • Seat belt retractor locks and won't release the passenger. • Passenger side airbag disables itself for no reason. White flakes blow from the AC (see TSB #09-21-6). • Tire pressure monitoring system sends out false alerts. *Escape Hybrid:* **2005**—Sudden shutdown while underway, allegedly due to a defective water pump. • Shifter gets stuck in Park. **2005–06**—Loss of power:

> As fleet manager, I have experienced engine failure on all three 2006 Ford Escape Hybrid vehicles. During each failure, the main engine shuts down and the vehicle goes to straight electrical power, which could cause a wreck in situations where a rapid drop in speed could cause an accident. The failure has happened on all three hybrids at about 15,000 miles [24,000 km] and now again at 36,000 miles [58,000 km]. The dealership replaces the water pump that supplies coolant to the electric motor after each failure. I feel that this situation should be reported due to the fact that I researched *Edmunds.com* and this problem is well documented in their CarSpace automotive [forums]. Ford needs to re-engineer this system.

2005–07—Loss of brakes and steering. **2006**—Fuel tank slow to fill; frequent pump shut-offs. **2007**—Occupants are trapped by their seat belts that must be cut away due to over-ratcheting. • Vehicle will suddenly lose power at any time:

> One of the times it stopped, I was stopped at a red light, the light turns green, I am accelerating to get on the highway and it cuts off again at about 30–40 mph. Cars are behind me and honk and I have nowhere to go but to the side of the road slightly, wait a few seconds and turn it back on. Very scary.

Erratic braking; ABS failures; Stop Safely Now and Service Brake System alerts are often lit; plus, the master brake cylinder travel sensor and ABS control assembly and tone ring don't last very long. **2008**—Sudden, unintended acceleration. • Dashboard electrical system goes out while driving, setting off a concerto of alarms and an instrument and gauge light show. • Steering may lock up until brakes are applied. • Escape continues to suddenly shut down; dealers keep ordering new motor coolant pumps to mitigate, but not resolve, the problem. • Cracked tire valve stems cause the original equipment to lose air. **2009**—Vehicle destroyed following an under-hood fire that originated in an electrical wire cable located on the passenger side of the engine wire harness near the ABS unit. • Owners report the steering continues to lock up and braking capability may be cut by 90 percent as all kinds of chimes and lights come on. **2010**—Back glass shattered as the tailgate was being closed. • Many reports of the glass shattering for no reason at all. • Rear liftgate window suddenly exploded (see TSB-11-2-9 VISIBILITY: GLASS, SIDE/REAR). • When filling up, fuel leaks from under the car. • Vehicle lurches and lags when accelerating.

Secret Warranties/Internal Bulletins/Service Tips

All models/years: Engine hydromount insulator and rear driveshaft replacement. • No forward transmission engagement (yes, the forward clutch piston, the cause of so many Windstar and Taurus/Sable failures, once again rears its ugly head). • Rear axle pinion seal leak. • Driveline grinding and clicking. • Possible leak in the transmission converter housing near the cooler line. •

Intermittent loss of First and Second gears. • Possible causes for a lit malfunction indicator light. • EGR valve failures. • ABS light may stay lit. **All models:** **2001–02**—Harsh, delayed upshifts • Defective door latches. • Power-steering leaks. **2001–03**—3.0L engine stalling remedy. **2001–04**—Engine misfire troubleshooting tips. • Correction for a sagging rear headliner. **2001–05**— Diagnostic and repair tips for an unstable idle, transmission shuddering, and steering pull and drifting. • Poor shifting in cold weather; install a Cooler Bypass Kit. • Slow-to-retract seat belts. **2001–06**—3.0L engine ticking noise. • Driveline whine. **2001–07**—Heater core leakage. **2001–09**—Suspension noise when turning. **2002**—Coolant, oil leakage from engine cylinder head area. • Defective Duratec engines. • Brake squealing. • Wheels make a clicking sound. **2001–10**— Underbody creak, squeak noise. **2003**—Automatic transmission shudder and whine. • Powertrain throttle body service replacement. • Front wheel bearing noise. • Rear shock leak and noise. **2003–04**—False activation of Parking Assist. ("Stop, there's something behind you! Just kidding.") You know what's most worrisome? Ford says this device may be operating as it should. **2003–06**— Inoperative AC; compressor leakage. **2003–08**—Remedy for excessive wheel/tire vibration. **2005**—Engine overheating. • Troubleshooting engine hesitation, miss. • An engine oil leak from the oil dipstick or front/rear crankshaft seals can be fixed by installing a Heated PCV Kit. • Rear brake noise. **2005–06**—Hard starts may require a recalibrated PCM; the half-hour labour charge is covered by the emissions warranty, says TSB #05-26-1. **2005–08**—Engine stalling when accelerating or stopping. • Slow fuel fill. **2005–09**—Drivetrain fluid leak from the PTU vent. **2005–10**—A front end click or pop noise may come from the front stabilizer bar. **2006–08**—Engine camshaft ticking noise. **2007–08**—Free tire valve stem inspection, replacement. **2008**—Engine drive belt idler pulley bearing noise. • Engine grinding, rattle noise. • 3.0L engine oil leak from the dipstick or crankshaft seal. • Transmission cooler fluid leak. • Wind noise, whistle at cruising speed. **2008–09**—Steering column pop, clunk when turning. • All instrument cluster warning lights come on intermittently. • Uncommanded liftgate opening or closing. • Exterior heated mirror glass cracking. • Front grille chrome peeling. **2008–10**—Steering wheel vibration can be remedied by installing a special damper Ford has devised. • Special Ford fix for steering column pop or clunk. • Windows squeak, grind when operated. • Ignition key binds in ignition cylinder. • Washer nozzles leak fluid onto the hood. • Poor radio reception. **2009**—Ford Customer Satisfaction Program #10B15100419-001 (secret warranty) was set up April 19, 2010, to cover the cost of reprogramming the Power Control Module to reposition the solenoid regulator valve and eliminate bore wear. Mechanics are also empowered to replace the valve body, overdrive, and forward clutch. Ford says these measures are needed to increase the transmission's durability. • Automatic transmission fluid leaks from the dipstick tube. • Exterior door handles may be hard to open and may not be flush. **2009–10**—Automatic transmission sticks in Fifth gear (reprogram the power control module). A harsh-shifting automatic transmission requires the same remedy. • Harsh engagements, shifts, or starts in Fifth gear from a start signal there's an open signal in the output shaft speed sensor or the main control lead frame connector. • Automatic transmission axle shaft seal fluid leak. • AWD models may produce a vibration, rumble, and/or excessive exhaust noise in cold temperatures. **2009–11**— The rear axle may produce a "hoot" noise on light acceleration just before the 1–2 shift.

ESCAPE, TRIBUTE, ESCAPE HYBRID PROFILE

	2002	2003	2004	2005	2006	2007	2008	2009	2010
Cost Price ($)									
XLS/XLT 4×2	21,510	21,595	21,895	22,795	23,000	23,000	23,999	23,999	24,499
XLS/XLT 4×4	24,190	30,300	27,825	28,125	28,399	28,399	27,800	27,499	27,999
Tribute 4×2	22,415	22,790	22,790	24,495	24,595	—	22,295	22,560	23,450
Tribute 4×4	25,065	25,575	25,445	27,295	27,395	—	26,990	26,245	27,145
Hybrid 4×2	—	—	—	33,195	33,599	33,600	31,499	32,399	34,899
Hybrid 4×4	—	—	—	35,925	36,399	36,399	33,899	34,799	37,299
Used Values ($)									
XLS/XLT 4×2 ▲	3,000	3,500	4,000	4,500	5,000	5,500	8,000	10,500	14,000
XLS/XLT 4×2 ▼	2,500	3,000	3,500	4,000	4,500	5,000	6,500	9,000	12,500
XLS/XLT 4×4 ▲	4,000	4,500	5,000	5,500	6,000	7,000	9,500	11,500	15,000
XLS/XLT 4×4 ▼	3,500	4,000	4,500	5,000	5,500	6,500	8,500	10,000	13,500
Tribute 4×2 ▲	3,000	3,500	4,000	4,500	5,000	—	8,000	11,000	13,500
Tribute 4×2 ▼	2,500	3,000	3,500	4,000	4,500	—	7,000	9,500	12,000
Tribute 4×4 ▲	5,000	5,500	6,000	6,500	7,000	—	10,000	12,000	14,500
Tribute 4×4 ▼	4,000	5,000	5,000	6,000	6,500	—	8,500	10,500	13,000
Hybrid 4×2 ▲	—	—	—	4,000	5,500	6,500	7,500	11,500	20,500
Hybrid 4×2 ▼	—	—	—	3,000	4,500	6,000	7,000	10,500	19,000
Hybrid 4×4 ▲	—	—	—	5,000	7,000	7,500	8,500	12,000	22,000
Hybrid 4×4 ▼	—	—	—	4,000	6,000	7,000	8,000	10,500	20,500
Reliability	2	2	2	2	3	4	4	4	4
Crash Safety (F)	5	5	5	4	4	4	3	5	5
Side	5	5	5	5	5	5	5	5	5
Side IIHS	1	1	1	5	5	5	5	5	5
Offset	2	2	2	3	3	3	3	5	5
Head Restraints	—	—	—	3	3	3	3	5	5
Roof Strength	—	—	—	—	—	—	2	2	2
Rollover Resistance	3	3	—	3	3	3	3	3	3

General Motors

ESCALADE, ESV, EXT, DENALI, SUBURBAN, TAHOE, YUKON, XL ★★★

RATING: Average (1999–2010). Ratings have remained high because safety and reliability problems have abated. **Ideal model year:** A 2008 V8-equipped Chevrolet Tahoe LTZ 4×4 (original list price $64,595) will give you a more powerful engine, lots of safety and performance features, and a cut-to-the-bone price ($23,500). **"Real" city/highway fuel economy:** *Tahoe and Yukon 4.8, with or without 4×4: 16.9/12.7 L/100 km. Tahoe, Suburban, Yukon, Yukon Denali, and Yukon XL 5.3 4×4: 17.1/12.6 L/100 km; 6.0: 17.3/12.5 L/100 km.* **Maintenance/repair costs:** Higher than average. The early Suburban's many mechanical and body deficiencies boost its upkeep costs. One saving grace, however, is that it can be serviced practically anywhere. **Parts:** Good supply of inexpensive parts. **Extended warranty:** An extended warranty is a good idea, but it isn't critical. **Best alternatives:** Choose a 2007 GMC Acadia or an identical 2008 Buick Enclave. Don't become mesmerized by a luxury nameplate on a practically identical model. Alternatively, a full-sized van or extended minivan may be a better choice if off-road capability isn't a priority. If size isn't your primary concern, look to more-reliable Asian SUVs that are less costly to operate. **Helpful websites:** Go to *www.carcomplaints.com/Chevrolet/Tahoe* and then key in "Escalade," "Suburban," "Yukon," or the hybrid variants.

 ## Strengths and Weaknesses

ALERT! As fuel prices have risen, these large SUVs have become cheaper and cheaper on the used car market. Again, don't worry about the extra gas these vehicles burn—the cost is nowhere near what you will have saved on the purchase price. Inasmuch as oil prices are expected to rise as we go into the winter of 2012–13, buying one of these SUVs at that time will save you a bundle.

The GMC Yukon and Denali and the Cadillac Escalade share the basic Tahoe/Suburban design but differ in styling, options, and price. Although these models are some of GM's best-performing large SUVs, they can't match the Japanese competition in overall reliability and quality control. Plus, spending over $47,650 (2009 Tahoe 4×2) for the cheapest model in this series is way too much. Used models at about half that price, perhaps. New? You've gotta be kidding.

Don't sell these models short, however. They have a lot to offer, like standard stability control, a fuel-saving cylinder-deactivation feature, a lavishly appointed interior, a good selection of instruments and controls, a good variety of competent engines that are great for trailering, a large and comfortable cabin that adds passenger and cargo space (with the redesigned 2007s), high ground clearance, a rattle-resistant body, and slow depreciation. The Suburban and Yukon XL are the largest heavy-hitters of this group, and they actually acquit themselves quite well, with reasonably predictable handling and more than enough power for most driving needs.

But there are important disadvantages: These vehicles lose value quickly, and the 4-speed automatic transmission wastes fuel and hinders powertrain performance. A high step-up takes some acrobatics, the wide turning circle complicates parking, and braking is barely acceptable. Furthermore, get ready for bizarre electrical short circuits that require an exorcist's intervention and transmission clunks that GM says is a "normal characteristic of these SUVs."

Other complaints include faulty fuel pumps, premature brake wear, excessive suspension and steering vibrations, vague steering, a suspension that provides a too-compliant, wandering ride, and excessive road and engine noise.

VEHICLE HISTORY: 2002—More standard features, such as AC, power windows, power front seats, heated power mirrors, and rear climate controls. **2003**—An anti-skid system, four-wheel steering, and adjustable pedals. **2005**—The StabiliTrak anti-skid system becomes standard for all Tahoe and 1500 models, and swing-out rear cargo doors are gone. **2006**—No more Quadrasteer; Yukons get a 5.3L V8 that uses gasoline and ethanol. Standard stability control. An Active Fuel Management cylinder shutoff system saves gas while cruising. **2007**—More power (the 5.3L V8 comes with 320 hp versus 295 hp), new styling, a larger interior, and additional features like improved second-row seats, a revised navigation system, a power liftgate, and a rear obstacle-detection feature. These models provide more-agile handling, much better steering and braking responses, and a more-comfortable and controlled ride. **2008**—A gas/electric hybrid and a 380 hp 6.2L V8 for the Tahoe LTZ and Yukon Denali rear-drives. For heavy-haulers, the best choice, though, is the 5.7L gas engine mated to an electronic 4-speed automatic. This matchup provides gobs of torque at low rpm, making these part-time 4×4s great for towing, stump pulling, or mountain climbing. **2009**—Tahoe *et al*: A new 6.2L V8 on the LTZ; a 6-speed automatic transmission on all non-hybrid models; standard Bluetooth connectivity; all three rows of seats are three-passenger; the LTZ has standard heated and cooled power seats; and OnStar has a Stolen Vehicle Slowdown feature. Tahoe Hybrid now has standard power-adjustable pedals; while the Yukon Hybrid returns with a more aerodynamic exterior and low-rolling-resistance tires. **2010**—Tahoe comes back with a few new revisions shared with its brothers, especially relating to fuel economy: the 6.2LV8 is discontinued, while the 5.3L V8 gains E85 ethanol capability and cam phasing and will be used in a new Tahoe XFE model, available as a mid-interim introduction, providing an estimated return of 14.3 L/100 km in the city and 9.3 L/100 km on the highway. Other changes include a single-speed transfer case as the default choice on four-wheel-drive models, with the two-speed transfer case optional; a USB connector for playing and charging music devices; an enhanced battery saver mode when running accessories; and a universal garage door opener on the LTZ model.

GM's diesel engines provide a good compromise between power and economy, although they have been plagued by malfunctions for decades and have never been the equal of the Cummins used by Chrysler.

As far as highway performance is concerned, these are the best SUVs sold by the Detroit automakers…ho-hum. Overall reliability improved with the 2007 redesign—then it nosedived, with the drivetrain, brakes, electrical system, and fit and finish cited as the worst offenders. There have been lots of complaints relative to poor driveability and factory-related defects that include excessive wander and vibration, hesitation when accelerating, transmission failures, wheel bearings wearing out after only a year's use, and incredibly loud squeaking brakes. Other complaints pertain to the premature replacement of brake rotors, AC squealing, and electrical, fuel, and exhaust system malfunctions. Body assembly and paint application is below standard.

Suburban, Yukon XL

Although it's classed as a full-sized SUV, the Suburban is really a combination of a station wagon, a van, and a pickup. It can carry nine passengers, tow just about anything, and go anywhere with optional 4×4.

These vehicles didn't change much until the launch of the 2000 models. Chevrolet restyled the Suburban by setting it on the Silverado/Tahoe/Yukon platform and using generic parts from the same parts bin. With the changeover, GMC's Suburban name was swapped for the Yukon XL, while the Chevrolet division soldiered on, keeping the Suburban name alive.

The Suburban and Yukon XL are GM's largest sport-utilities: Handling has improved considerably, but fuel economy remains atrocious. Improvements include a wider and taller body; new 5.3L and 6.0L V8 engines that replace the 5.7L and 7.4L engines, and a turbocharged diesel V8; an automatic transmission with tow/haul mode for smoother shifting; standard front side airbags; and four-wheel disc brakes. Rear leaf springs have been replaced by rear coil springs.

Cadillac Escalade

This is GM's pop culture party wagon, favoured by rappers and politicos. Cadillac's first truck, the 1999 Escalade 4×4, was nothing more than a warmed-over GMC Yukon Denali covered with ugly, poorly designed side cladding in an effort to disguise its parentage. The redesigned 2002 Escalade got many improvements, including an EXT version (a Suburban/Avalanche clone with additional luxury features), a 6.0L V8, and a more-refined AWD system.

VEHICLE HISTORY: 2003—A longer ESV and Escalade EXT, an all-dressed version of the Chevrolet Avalanche SUV/pickup truck. Other changes include standard power-adjustable gas and brake pedals and second-row bucket seats for the wagons. **2004**—A tire-pressure monitor, trailering package, and satellite radio are added. **2005**—An improved cooling system and upgraded interior trim and gauges. **2006**—Standard electronic stability control. **2007**—More power and fresh styling. The only engine is a 403 hp 6.2L V8; it replaces the 345 hp 6.0L V8. A 6-speed manumatic is the sole transmission available. New standard features include curtain side airbags, power-adjustable pedals, and leather upholstery. Wagons get a standard power liftgate with opening glass and heated first- and second-row seats. **2008**—A new Tahoe Hybrid debuts, equipped with a 332 hp 6.0L V8. The ESV is available for the first time with rear-wheel drive; EXTs are AWD only. **2009**—6-speed transmission and heated seats. **2010**—This year sees a number of changes: The 6.2L V8 now incorporates Active Fuel Management, a feature that shuts off half the cylinders when full power is not required, while the 6.0L V8 used in the 2-Mode Hybrid can run on E85 ethanol fuel. Other changes include standard front side airbags, a revised inner door design, and a USB connection for music players.

Safety Summary

All models/years: Sudden, unintended acceleration. • Airbags frequently fail to deploy, or deploy when they shouldn't, causing severe trauma. • Braking is terrible—one of the worst in the sport-utility class (100–0 km/h: 50 m). • Tire, steering, door lock, transmission, ABS and brake rotor and pad, and engine head gasket and exhaust manifold failures. • These SUVs wander all over the road and will require constant steering corrections, particularly when buffeted by crosswinds. • Vehicle vibrates excessively and jerks to one side when braking. • Seat belt tightens progressively; in one incident, a child had to be cut free from a locked-up seat belt. • Gas tank leaks fuel. • Fuel pumps often need replacing. • Gas fumes permeate the interior. • Rear liftgate window explodes. • Chronic electrical failures. **All models: 2003–10**—Airbags fail to deploy in rollovers or in high-speed frontal collisions, and OnStar fails to activate. *Tahoe, Yukon:* **2002**—Loose steering feels unstable, causes vehicle to wander. • Faulty transmission; delayed shifts. **2003**—Vehicle can be shifted out of Park without pressing the brake pedal. • Rear passenger doors don't lock properly. **2005**—Overheated fuel-pump wiring. • Wheels intermittently lock up while driving. • Transmission slips from Drive to Neutral. **2006**—Driver's seatback suddenly collapses. **2007**—Automatic transmission failure. • Transmission slips when accelerating after morning start-up. • Brake rotors quickly become deeply grooved. • Instrument panel cannot be read during the day. • Faulty wheel bearings. • Heated seats don't work. • Wipers start on their own (defective wiper module). • Car locks itself, and liftgate opens on its own:

> The electric rear liftgate opens while driving 50 mph [80 km/h]. The failure also occurs while the vehicle is parked. The liftgate opens just enough so that all of the doors continuously lock and unlock and the interior lights illuminate.

2008—Fire ignited in the cigarette lighter area. • Airbag warning light is constantly lit. • When accelerating, there is a transmission delay and then the engine surges. • Persistent vibration problems. • Back brake grinding indicative of prematurely worn out brake rotors. Owners say this happens on all four wheels, but rear wheels tend to go first. • Excessive side-to-side movements in lateral winds, or when following high-profile vehicles. • Electrical short circuits cause instrument panel lights, gauges, and controls to go haywire. Then doors lock and unlock on their own as the windshield wipers suddenly come on. Car acts as if were possessed by Detroit demons. **2009**—Frequent stalling. • Loss of braking capability as Service Brakes and Service StabiliTrak alerts come on. • Door locks continue to lock and unlock at will; intermittent failure of instrument panel gauges. • Frequent steering rack and pinion gear failures. • Rear window and top hinges suddenly break off. **2010**—Accelerator stuck as the car was passing another. Cause? A faulty accelerator pedal position sensor. • Support bracket weld to transmission dipstick tube broke loose. Tube could pop out of transmission and leaking oil could ignite on the exhaust. • In snow conditions wipers freeze and don't clean the windshield. • Chrome-plated interior door handle peels and cuts fingers. *Tahoe Hybrid: 2008*—In a sudden stop, the Stow 'n Go seat slams against the driver and passenger seats. • Door locks quit locking; dealer says the fix will cost $350 per door. GM insiders blame the wiring harness. • Early transmission replacement. • Power brake failure after the hybrid battery pack loses power:

> The warning indicators illuminated on the instrument panel. Suddenly, there was no response when the brake pedal was depressed. The driver experienced extreme difficulty stopping the vehicle and had to slam on the brakes. The vehicle was able to slow down upon reaching its destination. The OnStar device was engaged and recommended that the engine be turned off and restarted. Immediately, the computer system reset itself; however, the failure recurred the following day.

2009—Multiple incidents of uncontrolled acceleration when driving on cruise control. *Yukon: 2005*—Instrument panel gives bizarre readings or simply goes out when vehicle is started. • Chronic stalling. • Headlight fuse burns out constantly. • Spare-tire security device doesn't work as described in manual. *Suburban, Yukon XL: 2002*—Dash lights reflect into mirror and are too bright. • Gas tank hard to refuel, causes premature shutoff. **2003**—Vehicle lunges forward when stopped. • Sudden brake loss. • Premature tie-rod wearout. • Steering shaft failure and differential leaking. • Cab reverberation causes ear pain (not a problem with later models). **2004**—Vehicle fails to accelerate when merging into traffic. • Sharp pull to the right when accelerating, and then vehicle snaps to the left when foot is taken off the accelerator. • Excessive on-road vibration at 110 km/h; vehicle becomes very unstable. • Defroster doesn't clear entire windshield and stops working intermittently. • When using the turn signal, the flashers are activated. • When accelerating from a stop, transmission jumps into gear after a long delay. • Complete transmission replacement followed by chronic electrical system failures. • While driving, tailgate window falls inward. • Inoperative emergency brake. *Suburban: 2005*—Vehicle rolls backward when parked on a hill. • Sudden brake loss. *Yukon XL: 2005*—Frequent no-starts. • Transmission shifts harshly when put in Reverse, or is slow to engage Drive. • StabiliTrak fails to activate. • Driver's seat moves on its own; inoperative seat memory. • Rear heater inoperative. *Escalade: 2006–07*—LED tail lights are distracting. **2007**—Inadvertent side airbag deployment. • Hesitation when accelerating. • Retractable steps don't work. **2004–10**—V8 engines may leak oil at the rear of the cylinder block (see following page). **2007–09**—Side airbag deploys if door is slammed. • Engine oil leak from oil cooler hose connection. • Power liftgate opens partly, then reverses. • Door wind noise and water leaks. • Second-row seat rattles; hard to latch or unlatch. • Troubleshooting various electrical problems. **2008–09**—Tire low pressure alert stays on. *Tahoe, Yukon: 1999–2004*—Paint delamination, peeling, or fading. **1999–2005**—No Reverse, Second, or Fourth gear may be caused by a defective reaction sun gear. **2007–09**—Steering squawk and binding. • Outside door handle pulls out of base. • Clunk noise at stop or when accelerating. • Remedy for noise coming from the front windshield. • Inoperative keyless entry. • Wavy, warped wheelhouse fender liners. **2007–11**—Troubleshooting tips for silencing

OIL LEAKS AT REAR OF CYLINDER BLOCK

BULLETIN NO.: 05-06-01-034I   DATE: SEPTEMBER 23, 2009

5.3L, 5.7L, 6.0L, 6.2L, 7.0L—ENGINE OIL LEAK AT REAR COVER ASSEMBLY AREA (ENGINE BLOCK POROSITY RTV REPAIR PROCEDURE)

2004–07 Buick Rainier; 2008–09 Buick LaCrosse Super, Allure Super (Canada Only); 2005–10 Cadillac CTS-V; 2007–10 Cadillac Escalade, Escalade ESV, Escalade EXT; 2003–09 Chevrolet TrailBlazer; 2003–10 Chevrolet Corvette; 2004–06 Chevrolet SSR; 2005–10 Chevrolet Silverado, Silverado SS; 2006–07 Chevrolet Monte Carlo SS; 2006–09 Chevrolet TrailBlazer SS; 2006–09 Chevrolet Impala SS; 2007–10 Chevrolet Avalanche, Suburban, Tahoe; 2009–10 Chevrolet Colorado Pickup; 2010 Chevrolet Camaro; 2003–09 GMC Envoy; 2003–10 GMC Sierra; 2004–05 GMC Envoy XUV; 2007–10 GMC Yukon XL, Yukon Denali, Yukon XL Denali; 2009–10 GMC Canyon; 2004–06 Pontiac GTO; 2005–08 Pontiac Grand Prix GXP; 2008–09 Pontiac G8 GT; 2009 Pontiac G8 GXP; 2005–09 Saab 9-7X 5.3i; 2008–09 Saab 9-7X Aero; 2003–10 HUMMER H2; 2006–10 HUMMER H3 with 5.3L, 5.7L, 6.0L, 6.2L, 7.0L VORTEC(TM) GEN III or GEN IV V8 Engine (All Aluminum Block Gen III and Gen IV V8 Engines).

CAUSE: Upon initial diagnosis, it may be determined that the leak is coming from the rear cover gasket. This condition may be caused by engine block porosity on the sealing surface. This issue pertains to aluminum block applications only.

front suspension noises. *Suburban, Tahoe, Yukon, Yukon XL:* **2007–12**—Engine oil leak at oil cooler hose/pipe assembly. • It may be necessary to lower the headliner assembly and add foam to stop roof panel fluttering or rattling. • TSB shows how to reset the detent spring if the sun visor fails to stay up. • Tips on repairing warped fender liners. **2008–09**—Side window problems. *Suburban, Yukon XL:* **2000–05**—Tips on silencing a differential whine are found in TSB #03-04-17-001E. **2002–09**—Front axle whine or click. **2003–05**—Faulty AC and audio (replace RSA module). **2007–09**—Clunk noise when stopping or accelerating. • Power liftgate opens partly, then reverses. **2007–10**—Sunvisor falls down. **2008–09**—Multiple side window problems. *Escalade:* **2006–07**—A Low Oil level indicator light or a visible oil leak may signal the need to reseal the oil-pressure sensor. **2007**—Liftgate malfunctions. • Wind noise from the rear liftgate area. • Inoperative power-assisted running boards. • Steering gear fluid leaks. • Water leak guide. • Silencing buzz, rattles from the instrument panel. • High-pitched whistle heard while driving. • Driver-seat squeak or creak. • Squeak, scratching noise heard from the upper door area (replace the roof-drip weather stripping). • Rear suspension rubbing, clunking noise. • Inoperative keyless entry feature. • Front-bumper paint peeling. **2007–08**—A noisy AC compressor or serpentine belt can be silenced by reprogramming the PCM computer module. An AC that defaults to full Hot or full Cold requires the same reprogramming. • Third-row seat won't fold flat or requires great effort to release seatback. • Great effort to close hood. • Outside door handle may loosen or crack. **2007–09**—Power liftgate opens partly, then reverses. • Side door wind noise and water leaks. • Fixing various electrical malfunctions. **2008–09**—No-crank, no-start, dead battery, and no audio output from the radio (replace the amplifier). • AC not cold enough. • Power steering fluid leakage. • Multiple side window problems.

ESCALADE, SUBURBAN, TAHOE, YUKON PROFILE

	2002	2003	2004	2005	2006	2007	2008	2009	2010
Cost Price ($)									
Escalade	72,700	74,970	70,675	71,405	71,805	71,730	72,175	78,535	84,575
Suburban	45,875	46,670	46,680	49,820	47,000	46,935	48,455	50,795	51,880
Tahoe	42,680	42,530	44,105	45,615	42,795	45,455	45,895	47,650	49,290
4×4	50,385	42,530	48,870	47,785	47,175	49,255	47,155	51,635	53,750
Tahoe Hybrid	—	—	—	—	—	—	66,125	67,415	68,625
Tahoe Hybrid 4×4	—	—	—	—	—	—	69,125	70,415	71,610
Yukon 4×4 Denali	—	—	66,180	66,940	63,645	64,550	66,295	70,910	72,535
Yukon XL/SLE	46,895	47,290	44,720	50,415	47,665	47,595	48,855	51,205	51,880
Yukon Hybrid	—	—	—	—	—	—	66,885	68,255	68,625
Yukon Hybrid 4×4	—	—	—	—	—	—	69,885	71,235	80,300
Used Values ($)									
Escalade ▲	6,500	8,000	10,500	13,500	17,000	24,000	29,000	36,000	52,000
Escalade ▼	5,500	7,000	9,000	12,000	15,500	22,500	27,000	33,500	49,000
Suburban ▲	5,500	7,000	8,500	10,500	13,500	15,500	19,500	25,000	31,000
Suburban ▼	5,000	6,000	7,500	9,000	12,000	14,000	18,000	23,500	29,000
Tahoe ▲	5,000	6,000	7,000	8,500	10,000	14,000	16,500	21,500	27,000
Tahoe ▼	4,500	5,500	6,500	7,500	8,500	12,500	15,000	20,000	25,000
4×4 ▲	5,000	6,000	7,000	8,500	10,500	14,500	17,500	22,000	31,000
4×4 ▼	4,500	5,000	6,000	7,500	9,000	13,000	16,000	20,500	29,000
Tahoe Hybrid ▲	—	—	—	—	—	—	22,500	29,500	37,000
Tahoe Hybrid ▼	—	—	—	—	—	—	20,500	27,500	35,000
Tahoe Hybrid 4×4 ▲	—	—	—	—	—	—	23,500	31,000	39,000
Tahoe Hybrid 4×4 ▼	—	—	—	—	—	—	22,500	28,000	37,000
Yukon 4×4 Denali ▲	—	—	10,500	12,000	14,000	17,500	23,000	32,000	41,000
Yukon 4×4 Denali ▼	—	—	9,500	11,000	12,500	16,000	21,000	30,000	38,000
Yukon XL/SLE ▲	6,500	7,500	9,000	10,500	13,500	16,000	19,500	25,000	31,000
Yukon XL/SLE ▼	5,500	6,500	8,000	9,500	12,000	14,500	18,000	23,500	29,000
Yukon Hybrid ▲	—	—	—	—	—	—	22,000	29,500	37,000
Yukon Hybrid ▼	—	—	—	—	—	—	25,000	28,000	35,000
Yukon Hybrid 4×4 ▲	—	—	—	—	—	—	25,000	31,000	39,000
Yukon Hybrid 4×4 ▼	—	—	—	—	—	—	22,500	29,000	37,000
Reliability									
Tahoe, Yukon	3	3	3	3	3	3	3	3	3
Suburban, Yukon XL	2	2	2	2	2	2	2	2	2
Crash Safety (F)									
Suburban, Yukon XL	4	4	4	4	4	5	5	5	—
Tahoe/Yukon	3	4	4	4	4	5	5	5	5
Escalade	3	4	4	4	4	5	5	5	5
Side (Tahoe)	—	—	—	—	—	5	5	5	—
Escalade	3	4	4	4	4	5	5	5	—
Suburban	4	4	4	4	4	5	5	5	—

All ratings on a numbered scale where 5 is good and **1** is bad. See page 132 for a more detailed description.

Rollover Resistance								
Escalade	—	—	—	3	3	3	3	3	3
Tahoe/Yukon	2	2	3	3	3	3	3	3	3
Suburban	3	3	—	3	3	3	3	—	—

Note: IIHS has not tested these vehicles.

Honda

CR-V ★★★★★

RATING: Recommended (2002–10). Take solace in knowing that, even if you pay too much, you can drive this bantam 4×4 a decade or longer without paying huge repair bills. **Ideal model year:** Real penny-pinchers need to get a 2009 LX 4WD for about $15,500 versus its original selling price of $29,790. If you also have some of the base warranty left, that's a bonus. A good second choice is the 2007 version for $11,500. **"Real" city/highway fuel economy:** 10.9/8.9 L/100 km. **Maintenance/Repair costs:** Average, except for AC compressors and electronic components; easily repaired at independent garages. **Parts:** Easily found and reasonably priced (they come mostly from the Civic parts bin). **Extended warranty:** Extended warranty is unnecessary. **Best alternatives:** The Hyundai Tucson or Santa Fe, Mazda5, and Subaru Forester. **Helpful websites:** *www. carcomplaints.com/Honda/CR-V* and *www.crvownersclub.com*.

Strengths and Weaknesses

ALERT! During your pre-purchase road test be especially watchful for two common performance deficiencies: On 2005–08 models there is a hard pulling when accelerating or coming to a stop. As one owner of a 2008 CR-V reported to NHTSA:

> Many other owners in [the] U.S. have the same problem. [See *www.topix.com/forum/ autos/honda-cr-v/TCU5MEVBRLJO6CTIK*.] The car always pulls to the right even with 4 brand new tires, both front and back alignment done with correct reading. I visited 3 times to Honda dealer regarding this problem and they could not fix it.

A second problem to be wary of is painful front head restraints. CR-Vs from 2008 and later may be fitted with poorly-designed head restraints that force your chin into your chest. Owners say this awkward position causes excruciating pain to the neck, back, and hip on even short drives.

Combining sport-utility styling with minivan versatility, this SUV is essentially a restyled Civic with 4×4 capability added. After its '97 launch, the car changed little until the revamped 2002 came out. The small power boost and improved chassis added in 2002 give additional interior space and provide improved functionality. The CR-V's Civic-based platform incorporates a four-wheel independent suspension that shortens the nose and frees up more rear cargo room. The base 160 hp 2.4L i-VTEC 4-cylinder engine is offered with either a 5-speed manual or a 4-speed automatic transmission (through the 2004 models). The 2002–05 versions don't look that different from their predecessors, though they are a bit longer, wider, and higher. The interior, however, underwent a major change, with more space for both passengers and cargo, and more user-friendly features and controls.

Owners laud the CR-V's many standard features; impressive steering and handling, particularly around town; easy front entry and exit; top-quality fit and finish; comfortable seating with lots of passenger room; innovative use of storage space; easily storable flip-folding seats; plastic cargo floor panel *cum* picnic table; fair fuel economy; and superior reliability.

There are some performance deficiencies: for example, there's no low-range gearing for off-roading; a long history of severe steering pull to the right when accelerating ("torque steer"); jittery ride on less-than-perfect roadways; excessive engine and road noise; the 2005 redesign reduces front legroom slightly; and the rear cargo door opens to the street, rather than the curb. Fuel economy is okay, but nowhere near Honda's or Transport Canada's overly optimistic figures.

VEHICLE HISTORY: 2002—Restyled and given more power, interior room, and features, like a side-hinged tailgate and new interior panels. **2005**—Standard side curtain airbags, skid control, and ABS; an upgraded 5-speed automatic transmission; and minor styling changes. **2007**—A new platform borrowed from the Civic, and a restyled interior and exterior that includes a new swing-up tailgate and a hiding spot underneath the cargo floor for the spare tire. These changes make the car wider and shorter than the previous year's model and enhance ride and handling, especially in turns. Cargo is also easier to load and unload. **2010**—Refreshed styling with increased horsepower and fuel economy.

 ## Safety Summary

All years: Sudden acceleration. • Airbags fail to deploy, or deploy for no reason. • Chronic stalling. • ABS lock-up. • Premature tire and brake wear. • AC condenser is vulnerable to damage caused by road rocks and other debris. Other vehicles have a protective screen in place. **2002–03**—Hood suddenly flies open while cruising. **2003**—Driver-side and rear centre seat belts unbuckled when car was rear-ended. **2004**—Steering wheel freezes while making a turn. • Wheel lug bolt breaks off. • Removable picnic table caused serious head injuries in a rollover accident. • Gas spews out of filler tube when refuelling. • Water can enter the fuel tank from gas-cap vent. • No seat belt extender available. **2004–05**—Many reports of engine fires after oil has been changed. **2006**—Vehicle won't hold its alignment settings. • Seat belt fails to retract. **2007**—Poor acceleration, followed by surging. • Sudden stalling while underway. • Vehicle is unstable when passing over a grooved highway. • Automatic transmission failures. • Defective engine oil seal. • Visibility impaired by windshield lamination. • Frequent AC failures blamed on road debris, but a missing AC condenser shield is the likely cause. • False alerts displayed by the tire-pressure warning system. **2008**—Broken motor mount bolts. • Windshield wipers fail to clean the windshield of snow; instead, they trap the ice and become frozen. • Low-beam headlights give inadequate illumination. • Premature failure of the AC compressor ($1,200 for a rebuilt unit). • Vehicle sporadically locks out occupants. • CR-V cannot be driven at 40 km or more with the rear window open. The noise inside the cabin is painfully loud. • Bent or broken wheel studs. • Rear tires can't be aligned due to cambers lacking adjustment mechanism; this leads to tire "cupping" and tire replacement every 20,000 km. • Vehicle steering shimmies and vibrates; plus, it won't track straight on the highway at any speed, despite the replacement of the steering rack. **2009**—Sudden, unintended acceleration, especially when the vehicle is in cruise control mode. • Loss of braking ability. • Owner was sitting in car with the engine off, and the doors locked on their own. • Sharp pull to the left or right when accelerating. • Rodents love snacking on Honda's soy-coated wiring:

> The contact owns a 2009 Honda CR-V. The contact stated that mice were able to gain entry into the interior of the vehicle through the heating system and began nesting within the heating system and the glove box. The mice were chewing on different components of the vehicle which is a potential safety hazard. He called the dealer who advised him to put moth balls in the vehicle.

2010—Fire ignited in the rear of the vehicle. • Once stopped, vehicle will lunge forward. • Transmission constantly hesitates to downshift, especially from Fifth gear, due to throttle lag. Also, there is considerable driveline vibration. • Tire pressure warning sensor doesn't always warn of low tire pressure. • Sunroof suddenly exploded while vehicle was cruising down the highway at 100 km/h.

Secret Warranties/Internal Bulletins/Service Tips

All years: Keep in mind that Honda service bulletins almost always mention that "goodwill" extended warranties may be applied to any malfunction. **1999–2007**—Vehicle pulls/drifts to one side. **2002**—Rattling from the passenger grab handle area and above the doors. **2002–03**—Front brake clicking noise caused by faulty lower retaining clips on the front brake pad that may be replaced for free under a "goodwill" program. • Engine stumbles or stalls after a stop. **2002–04**—Troubleshooting a rear brake grinding noise. • Correcting harsh or noisy automatic transmission downshifts when slowing down. **2002–05**—Remedy for a rattle, grind, or growl coming from the A-pillar of the front-right side of the vehicle when turning left. **2002–06**—Water leaks into the interior from behind the dash. • Rear seat won't fold up. **2002–07**—Moan or groan from the rear differential. **2003**—Coolant in the oil pan. **2005–06**—Front suspension clicks while driving over bumps or turning. **2007**—Power steering pump seizure. Honda will cover the cost of this repair under Campaign #08-070. • Inoperative power windows. • Low Tire Pressure light stays on. • Distorted image in driver's outside mirror. • Wiper won't park or turn off. **2007–08**—Poor AC performance on acceleration; AC hoots or whistles. • Headliner rattles or buzzes when driving. • Tailgate rusting near licence plate trim. • Exhaust system squeaks. • False low tire pressure alert. **2007–09**—Inoperative windshield washer pump. • Roof rack whistling at high speeds. **2007–11**—Rear brakes grind or thump. A new brake pad will fix the problem says Honda TSB #10-020, published May 20, 2011. **2008**—Cold engine whine may be corrected by replacing the engine oil pump. **2008–09**—Headliner sagging near the liftgate. **2010–11**—Fluid leaks from rear of vehicle. • Low power on acceleration requires only a software update, says Honda.

CR-V PROFILE

	2002	2003	2004	2005	2006	2007	2008	2009	2010
Cost Price ($)									
SE/LX	26,900	27,300	27,200	28,200	29,300	27,700	27,790	27,790	26,290
4×4	—	—	—	—	—	29,700	29,790	29,790	28,290
Used Values ($)									
SE/LX ▲	5,000	5,500	6,500	8,000	9,000	11,000	13,000	15,000	17,500
SE/LX ▼	4,500	5,000	6,000	7,000	8,500	10,000	11,500	13,500	16,000
4×4 ▲	—	—	—	—	—	12,000	13,500	16,000	19,000
4×4 ▼	—	—	—	—	—	11,000	12,500	14,500	17,500
Reliability	5	5	5	5	5	5	5	5	5
Crash Safety (F)	5	5	5	5	5	5	5	5	5
Side	5	5	5	—	—	5	5	5	5
IIHS Side	2	2	2	5	5	5	5	5	5
Offset	5	5	5	5	5	5	5	5	5
Roof Strength	—	—	—	—	—	2	2	2	2
Head Restraints	—	—	—	1	1	5	5	5	5
Rollover Resistance	3	3	—	4	4	4	4	4	4

Hyundai

TUCSON ★★★★★

RATING: Recommended (2005–10). With this better-made Kia Sportage twin, you get a lot of features for your money, but a peppy 4-cylinder engine isn't one of them. **Ideal model year:** A 2007 Tucson GL V6 front-drive is your best choice. Originally retailed for $26,395, it now sells for about $10,500. **"Real" city/highway fuel economy:** *2.0 4-cylinder:* 10.6/7.9 L/100 km. *V6:* 11.9/8.4 L/100 km. **Maintenance/repair costs:** Much lower than average. **Parts:** Easily found and reasonably priced. **Extended warranty:** Not necessary. **Best alternatives:** Honda CR-V and Nissan Xterra. **Helpful websites:** *www.hyundaiforum.com* and *www.hyundaikiaforums.com*.

Strengths and Weaknesses

ALERT! As part of your pre-purchase road test, pay particular attention to the performance of the automatic transmission. It has been problematic through the 2010 model year.

Hyundai's smallest sport-utility is built on a strengthened and stretched Elantra platform powered by the Elantra's engine, and offers the addition of four-wheel drive. This said, true handling enthusiasts will want to throw their lot in with the RAV4 or Ford/Mazda Escape/Tribute to get their performance thrills. Still, the Tucson is fairly cheap, comes well equipped with standard side airbags and stability control, and has earned NHTSA five-star front and side crashworthiness ratings. It also brakes well, gives a comfortable ride, has a roomy interior, and comes with fewer factory defects than either the RAV4 or Escape/Tribute. Another advantage is that the Tucson has changed very little over the years, so one model year is about as good as another.

VEHICLE HISTORY: 2007—No more GL 4-cylinder with all-wheel drive. **2008**—Standard cruise control added to all automatic transmission-equipped models. **2009**—A slight restyling. **2010**—A new 2.4L 4-cylinder provides more horsepower than the V6 it replaces. The standard 6-speed manual transmission in the base GL is joined by an optional 6-speed automatic, while the GLS and Limited trim lines use the automatic exclusively. The GL and GLS come in front-wheel and all-wheel drive, while the Limited is all-wheel only. All 2010s come with hill descent control and hill start assist.

Some minuses: It's underpowered, has a bland interior, mediocre handling, sluggish steering, limited rear visibility, numerous first-year factory-related deficiencies, a noisy suspension, and only average fuel economy. Owners have reported failures related to the cruise control, automatic transmission, manual transmission shift-lever cable assembly, and stability-control module. Fit and finish is not the best; a conclusion driven home every time water pours in from behind the glove box:

> Upon removing the glove box and pulling out the cabin filter, I noticed the water coming down through the AC system...similar complaint filed on service bulletins. Car was parked on a 10 degree angle nose end down. Water leak through and near electrical components and near passenger side airbag.

Safety Summary

All years: Airbags fail to deploy. **2005**—A faulty Electronic Stability Program module can cause the vehicle to stall and the ABS to suddenly engage, and can result in the vehicle going out of control. This has happened to vehicles that have been recalled and "fixed" for the problem and to cars that aren't included in the recall. • Manual and automatic transmissions suddenly fail to go into gear. • Power steering fails while passing through small pools of water on the road. **2005–06**— The passenger-side airbag is disabled even though an adult occupies the seat. **2007**—Head restraints cause neck stiffness and headaches. • Rear window explodes for no reason. **2008**—Firewall insulation ignited. • Sudden, unintended acceleration. • Rear of the vehicle slides as if it were on ice. • Excessive shaking when underway. • Electronic stability control activates when it is not needed. • Wiper inoperative in snow storm. • Horn doesn't always work. **2009**—Sudden, unintended acceleration. • Airbag failed to deploy. • Horn failure even after the clock spring was replaced. • Windshield wiper fluid leaks out of reservoir filler neck. **2010**—Intermittent engine surging: The ESC and DBC lights will come on; the brakes will lock; and when you press on the gas pedal the RPMs shoot up, but the car doesn't move. • Transmission slips. • Transmission lockup occurs around 90 km/h. • Sudden downshifting. • Snow accumulates under the front windshield wipers. • Vehicle sways from left to right when it's driven on the highway.

Secret Warranties/Internal Bulletins/Service Tips

2005—Harsh automatic transmission shifting. **2005–08**—A humming noise may come from the 4×4 coupler. **2005–09**—No movement in Drive or Reverse. • Fluid may leak from the area around the automatic transmission torque converter or between the transaxle and the transfer case. • Correcting harsh gear engagement. • Tips on silencing a rattling sunroof. **2006–07**—Troubleshooting complaints relative to a cloudy paint condition. **2006–08**—Harsh, delayed shifting. **2008**—Free TCM software update. • Self-activating antitheft alarm. • Sunroof creaking, ticking. **2010**—Troubleshooting harsh, delayed shifts by the automatic transmission. • Incorrect operation of the transmission solenoids will cause the transmission to perform erratically and the Check Engine warning to light up.

TUCSON PROFILE

	2005	2006	2007	2008	2009	2010
Cost Price ($)						
GL	19,995	20,596	21,195	22,995	22,995	22,999
V6	24,865	25,695	26,395	26,495	26,495	26,699
GLS	28,725	29,995	30,795	26,795	26,795	26,799
Used Values ($)						
GL ▲	5,000	6,000	9,000	11,500	14,500	16,500
GL ▼	4,000	5,000	7,500	10,500	13,000	15,000
V6 ▲	7,000	8,000	11,000	13,500	15,000	18,000
V6 ▼	5,500	7,000	9,500	12,000	13,500	16,500
GLS ▲	7,500	9,000	11,500	14,000	16,000	17,500
GLS ▼	6,500	7,500	10,000	13,000	15,000	16,500

Reliability	4	4	5	5	5	5
Crash Safety (F)	5	5	5	5	5	5
Side	5	5	5	5	5	5
IIHS Side	3	3	3	3	3	5
Offset	3	3	3	3	3	5
Head Restraints (F)	—	1	1	1	5	5
Roof Strength	1	1	1	1	1	5
Rollover Resistance	—	4	4	4	4	4

Lexus

RX 300, RX 330, RX 350/RX 400H, 450H ★★★/★★

RATING: *RX 300, RX 330, RX 350:* Average (2000–10) Lexus has followed Toyota's example of cutting content to keep prices low, except that Lexus started the process a decade later. Unfortunately, when there's less content, then quality, safety, and reliability suffer, owner dissatisfaction increases, and resale values plummet. Lexus is now scrambling to recapture market share by cutting new car prices, which results in used models costing less.

Lemon-Aid alerted readers to Lexus safety hazards almost a decade ago. Our ratings have been lowered progressively since we noted that many models had engine sludge problems, dangerous automatic transmission delayed shifts, sudden acceleration, unreliable brakes, inadequate and theft-prone headlights, and weak rear hatches that kept falling on people's heads.

RX 400h and 450h: Average (2006; 2010); *RX 400h:* Below Average (2007–09). Essentially a more fuel-frugal RX model with plenty of horsepower and full-time AWD, but these Japan-built SUVs are ridiculously expensive and dangerous to drive. They are brake-challenged whenever passing over bumpy terrain, and their frequently delayed shifts and engine surges can be deadly either from a rear-ender when you stall, or from a T-bone collision that cuts your car in half as it suddenly accelerates into traffic. If you must go "green," get a cheaper used Ford Escape Hybrid. **Ideal model year:** The 2000 to 2006 models are good buys, except for the 2004s. Of that group, your best bet is the 2006 AWD RX 330 for $16,000, a far cry from the car's original $50,500 selling price. True, the 2007s got a horsepower boost and a 6-speed automatic transmission, but their redesign glitches have caused trouble through 2009, judging from owner complaints and internal service bulletins. The 2010 model looks promising, but it is too soon to be sure of its long-term reliability. **"Real" city/highway fuel economy:** *RX 300:* 9.7/13.0 L/100 km. *RX 330:* 9.0/12.8 L/100 km. *RX 350:* 9.0/12.4 L/100 km. *RX 400h:* 8.1/7.5 L/100 km. *RX 450h:* 6.7/7.2 L/100 km. **Maintenance/repair costs:** Higher than average; most repairs are dealer-dependent and expected to cost more for hybrid repairs. **Parts:** Dealers have a quasi-monopoly on parts and can blame high charges on supply lines disrupted by Japan's recent earthquake and tsunami. **Extended warranty:** Not needed. **Best alternatives:** *RX 330 and 350:* The Ford Edge, GM Acadian or Traverse, Honda Pilot, Hyundai Santa Fe Limited or Veracruz SE, Nissan Murano SL or Xterra 5, and Toyota Highlander Limited. **Helpful websites:** *http://us.lexusownersclub.com; www.lemonlaw.com/ wordpress/toyota-sudden-acceleration;* and *www.germancarforum.com/pit-general-discussion/3318-lexus-makes-reliable-cars-well-not-anymore.html.*

Strengths and Weaknesses

ALERT! Can you live with a car that rolls backwards when stopped for a light or traffic on an incline? Find out during your pre-purchase test drive.

Here are some of the RX series pluses. *RX 300:* Strong powertrain performance; handles well; fully equipped; top-quality mechanical components and fit and finish; pleasant riding (better than the Acura MDX and the Mercedes M series); plenty of passenger room; very comfortable seating; lots of small storage areas; and easy entry and exit. *RX 330:* Quieter, longer, wider, slightly taller, a bit more powerful, and with a longer wheelbase than its predecessor. Comfortable rear seats are adjustable and are easily folded out of the way. Better interior ergonomics, and ride comfort doesn't deteriorate with a full load. Much better emergency handling than with the RX 300. Improved fuel economy; can take regular unleaded fuel. *RX 400h:* Mind-spinning depreciation, which is good news for hybrid buyers.

Now, for some of the RX series faults, and there are many. *RX 300:* Pricey, and it's too big and heavy for sporty handling. No low-range gearing for off-roading, and traction control is optional. Thick roof pillars obstruct outward visibility. Instrument displays wash out in direct sunlight. Tilt steering wheel may not tilt sufficiently for some drivers. Expect lots of wind noise, squeaks, and rattles in addition to wind roar from the moonroof. Limited rear storage area, with a high liftover and excessive wind noise. Takes premium fuel. *RX 330:* Additional power is undermined by the added kilos. Dangerous shift delay when downshifting with the automatic transmission. There's considerable body lean when cornering, the suspension bottoms out easily, steering could be more sensitive, and there's excessive bouncing and body roll with original-equipment shocks. Front and rear seat cushions lack thigh support. Thick rear roof panels continue to obstruct visibility. No third-row seating, and the sloping rear end cuts into cargo space. The power rear door is slow to open, and the moonroof takes up too much headroom. Reduced ground clearance. The optional navigation system screen washes out in sunlight. *RX 400h:* Makes you a captive customer of Toyota/Lexus and limits where you can go for servicing. The $3,000 (U.S.) battery replacement may require a bank loan to pay off. The vehicle takes an unusually long time to start; slow and vague steering; and the instrument panel power gauge is too small. The 18-inch wheels and beefy P235/55R18 tires don't enhance fuel efficiency.

VEHICLE HISTORY: First launched in Canada as a 1999 model, the RX 300 is a compact luxury sport-utility based partly on Toyota's passenger-car platform. It's a bit longer and wider than a Jeep Grand Cherokee, and it's sold as either a front-drive or permanent all-wheel drive. Available only with a 4-speed automatic transmission and a Camry/Lexus ES 300–derived, upgraded 220 hp V6, the RX 300 handles competently on the highway but isn't suitable for off-roading because of its lack of low-range gearing and its tall, four-door wagon body.

RX 330 and 350

The RX 330 eclipses the old model with its many luxury features and extra-cost gadgets, extra interior room, and an upgraded powertrain. On the other hand, competing minivans have more utility, more room inside, more seats, and even, as in the Toyota Sienna, four-wheel drive.

The RX 330 and 350 offer all-wheel drive, a good ride, a plush and innovative interior, great all-around visibility, plenty of power, better-than-average quality, and acceptable reliability. Not bad for a bestselling SUV cobbled together from ES 350, Camry, and Sienna parts. On the downside, these cars have a history of sudden, unintended acceleration and "lag and lurch" drivetrains, cold engine piston "slap," and premature, costly brake pad and rotor replacements.

RX 400h and 450h

The RX 400h Lexus hybrid debuted as a 2006 model, joining other hybrid models like Honda's Insight and Civic, Ford's Escape, and Toyota's Prius and Highlander. Toyota hopes that by putting the hybrid system in a luxury Lexus, it will get back the high costs of hybrid technology—clearly, an impossible dream.

The 230 hp 3.3L engine has been detuned to just 208 horses; however, when coupled with the 68 hp electric motor, there's a net gain in horsepower. Like the Prius, the RX 400h operates by allowing the gasoline and electric motors to kick in when the engine load varies. For example, the electric motor is used when accelerating from a stop or in city traffic, while the gasoline engine is useful for highway cruising. If you floor the accelerator, both motors work in unison to give you the extra horsepower needed (posting 0–100 km/h acceleration scores of about 7 seconds). Nevertheless, Lexus hybrid technology isn't as refined as that of the Honda Accord hybrid, which shuts down half the engine's cylinders when carrying a light load to save even more gas.

Fortunately, there's no need to recharge the battery pack. That's done by the gasoline-engine generator. Toyota guarantees the battery for eight years. A new pack will cost about $3,000 (U.S.)—about what the vehicle will be worth eight years from now.

VEHICLE HISTORY: *RX Series:* **2004**—Completely redesigned. **2005**—Rain-sensing wipers and an eight-way front passenger power seat are standard features. **2007**—The RX 330 gets a 3.5L V6 and is renamed the RX 350. Also new: a tire pressure monitoring system and a larger rear-seat entertainment display screen. **2008**—All models get a new grille, vehicle stability control cut-off switch, and chrome-plated door handles. **2010**—The RX 350 has been redesigned, while the hybrid version, temporarily discontinued for 2009, returns as the RX 450h. RX 350 models have been restyled and come with a more responsive V6 engine, and an all-new 6-speed automatic transmission. *RX 400, and RX 450h:* **2007**—This year's hybrid adds on-demand electronic four-wheel drive, 18-inch alloy wheels, power sunroof, LED taillights, and self-levelling high-intensity discharge headlamps (HID). **2009**—No changes. In fact, the car was temporarily discontinued until mid-2009 when it was replaced by the 2010 RX 450h.

Other reasons to be wary of a hybrid-equipped vehicle: Fuel economy is hyped by 15–40 percent; cold weather performance isn't as fuel-efficient; repairs and servicing are dealer-dependent; highway rescuers are wary of cutting through the high-voltage electrical system to save occupants; there's no long-term reliability data; the vehicles have a faster-than-average rate of depreciation; and you have to drive several hundred thousand kilometres to amortize the hybrid's start-up costs.

RX Series models and hybrids have declined in quality and safety for most of this decade. In particular, 2004 was a watershed year for brake, transmission, and headlight failures. The automatic transmission lurches between gears and lags in shifting at low speeds, making the car vulnerable to rear-enders. The fuel gauge gives inaccurate readings, and there have been some minor electrical shorts, prematurely worn brake calipers and warped rotors, excessive brake noise, and a variety of interior squeaks and rattles. Also, there are some body trim defects, and the instrument panel display may be too dim. The continuously variable transmission on the RX 400h has had a checkered past, with early failures reported by other automakers (like Saturn) who used a similar CVT design; independent repairers are unable to service it. Sudden, unintended acceleration and engine surging make for risky winter driving. If your Lexus has some of its warranty left, don't let Toyota/Lexus give you the run-around by claiming a problem is "normal." Any car that suddenly accelerates, or hesitates, then surges is *not* operating normally

 Safety Summary

All models/years: Many reports of sudden, unintended acceleration while in Drive, when shifted into Reverse, or when applying the brakes to cancel cruise control:

> Accelerator sticks. I had a 2002 Lexus RX300 and the accelerator kept sticking. I took it to the Austin TX Lexus dealer in Spring 2008 and reported it. They said there was nothing wrong. I sold the car and bought a new 2008 RX350 and it does the same thing.

Drivetrain lags and lurches when accelerating or decelerating. • Airbags fail to deploy. • Cruise control won't release. • Rear hatch closes on driver's neck. • Side windows shatter for no reason. Vehicle rolls backwards when idling on an incline. **2002**—Vehicle rolls backward when stopped on a hill. **2003**—Major rear blind spot. **2004**—Many complaints that brakes fail because of a faulty brake booster. • Suspension may cause car to pull into oncoming traffic. • Poor headlight illumination. • Dash reflects onto the windshield. • **2004–09**—A Lexus owner who is also a physician says the vehicle emits a dangerously powerful electromagnetic field in the cabin:

> Our two 2007 Lexus RX-350 (and all models 2004–2009) have electromagnetic field near the dashboard of approximately 100 milliguass. This is causing our knees and hand cells to degenerate as Lexus has not done an adequate job of providing Faraday cage or shielding from EMF. This reading of 100 Milliguass is what you find under high voltage transmission lines and studies have linked 2 to 3 milliguass to childhood Leukemia, cancer, headaches or cell de[ge]neration. I contacted Lexus customer service but they brushed off our safety concern, saying most household appliances produce EMF. For reference, 2010 Lexus RX-350 or current model ES-350S have 15 to 20 milliguass. Therefore Lexus has technology to shield but has done an inadequate job of shielding 2004–2009 Lexus RX-350 by [not] issuing a recall.

2005—Xenon headlights are often stolen. • Headlight low beam falls short. • Exhaust fumes are sucked into the cabin if the rear hatch is left ajar. **2006**—Engine destroyed by sludge. • Extended stopping distance caused by brake fluid leaking from the brake booster, making the master cylinder inoperative. • Blue-tinted headlights blind oncoming drivers. **2007**—No brakes. • Oil line burst. • Inhalation of white dust emitted from the AC heat vent may cause severe respiratory distress:

> We searched the Internet and found out this is not an isolated event. Lots of people have the same problem with the white dust. Some of them (even a three-year-old child) also developed health problems. Lexus admitted the white dust was from corrosion of the coating material inside the AC/heat vent system. This is a health safety issue. As a physician, myself, I believe Lexus has the responsibility to inform the public. Lexus knew of this problem as early as June of 2007. Lexus has already replaced evaporators in many cars in 2007–2008.

Backup lights are too dim. • Airbag warning light comes on for no reason. **2008**—Airbag is disabled when the front passenger seat is occupied. • Again, rear backup lights don't seem bright enough. • Driver needs to floor brake pedal before brakes catch. • Engine surges when vehicle goes downhill. **2009**—Cruise control doesn't disengage when brakes are applied. • Loss of brakes and steering. • Brakes work erratically on bumpy roads. • Brake and gas pedal mounted too close together. • Accumulated snow may cause the rear hatch struts to fail, sending the hatch crashing down. **2010**—Airbag failed to deploy. • Rear liftgate opens by itself while the car is moving. • Bubble in tire sidewall. • With strong winds or when travelling at high speed, wipers don't clean the windshield. • Navigation system cannot distinguish height of highways and can lead you to driving off an overpass. • Tire pressure sensors appear to be over-sensitive. • Flimsy front bumper. *RX 400h:*

2006—Sudden acceleration. • Surging when brakes are applied makes for risky winter driving. • Sudden brake loss; brake slippage after passing over bumpy terrain. • Erratic cruise-control operation. • Vehicle constantly pulls to the left. • Complete loss of power steering. • While driving on the highway, car will stall out. 2007—Intermittent loss of braking capability. • Airbag light stays on. • More reports that the white "dust" that blows into the cabin through the AC air vents could be hazardous. 2008—Sudden acceleration when the brakes are applied. 2008–09— Brakes disengage for a few seconds when passing over a rough surface:

> It appears to be precisely the same problem now being reported with the Prius braking system. Toyota/Lexus basically ignored us when we complained and the problem is not fixed.

2009—When turning at an intersection, there was no acceleration and then a sudden engine surge ("lag and lurch"). 2010—Sudden brake failure on the freeway. *RX 450h:* 2010—Sudden, unintended acceleration. • The vehicle has difficulty maintaining speed when going up a steep incline. • Be wary of the traction control system when passing over lightly snow-covered roads. The wheels lock up when the brakes are applied and all steering control is lost. • Vehicle surges when braking. • Tires wear out prematurely at the inner edge. • If you hit a bump in the road, vehicle may stall out and lose all braking capability.

Secret Warranties/Internal Bulletins/Service Tips

All models/years: Free engine sludge repairs. • There are dozens of bulletins that address the correction of various squeaks and rattles found throughout the vehicle. **All models: 2002**—Drivetrain vibration. **2002–03**—Troubleshooting front brake vibration. **2002–06**—Diagnosis and repair of vehicles that pull excessively to one side. **2003–10**—Windshield ticking. **2004**—Front brake vibration remedy. • Drone, vibration upon acceleration. • Front suspension creaking and knocking. • Hatch area creak or tick. • Glove box and instrument panel rattles. **2004–05**—No-start in cold weather. • Front-door window noise. • Free headlight theft-prevention kit. **2004–06**—Rear door–stay improvement. • Unacceptable power backdoor operation. • Fuel tank shield rattle. **2004–07**—Troubleshooting dash rattles. • Front seat squeak. **2004–08**—Front power seat grinding, groaning. **2004–09**—Transmission fluid or gear oil leaks from the transfer case vent. • Plugging water leaks at the liftgate area. **2004–10**—Remedy for brake rattle, buzz heard near the driver's side dash. • Power back door noise. **2006–09**—Countermeasures to reduce white dust emitted through the AC air vents. • Multiple warning lights; can't shift out of Park. • Moonroof auto-close function inoperative. **2007**—Engine timing cover oil leaks. • Engine squealing. • Loose shift lever. • Moonroof rattle. **2007–08**—Oil leak from the engine camshaft housing. • Replace engine VVTI oil hose free of charge. **2007–09**—Driver's door rattle. **2007–10**—Engine ticking noises. **2007–11**—Oil control valve will be replaced under warranty. **2008–09**—Transfer case fluid leak. **2010**—Dust powder blows in from dash vents. • Steering groan when turning the steering wheel. • Front seat track noise. **2010–11**—Steering column rattle. *450h:* **2010**—Steering groan when turning the steering wheel. **2011**—Dust powder blows in from dash vents.

RX 300 SERIES, 400H, 450H PROFILE

	2002	2003	2004	2005	2006	2007	2008	2009	2010
Cost Price ($)									
RX	51,250	51,600	49,900	50,200	50,500	51,550	51,550	42,950	46,900
400h	—	—	—	—	62,200	62,250	62,250	53,650	—
450h	—	—	—	—	—	—	—	—	58,900
Used Values ($)									
RX ▲	8,500	10,000	12,000	13,500	16,500	20,000	22,000	29,000	35,000
RX ▼	7,500	9,000	10,500	12,500	15,000	18,500	20,500	27,000	32,000
400h ▲	—	—	—	—	19,000	23,000	29,000	35,000	—
400h ▼	—	—	—	—	18,000	21,000	27,500	33,000	—
450h ▲	—	—	—	—	—	—	—	—	42,000
450h ▼	—	—	—	—	—	—	—	—	39,000
Reliability	4	4	3	3	3	2	2	3	3
Crash Safety (F)	4	4	5	—	—	4	5	5	5
RX 400h	—	—	—	—	—	—	5	—	—
RX 450h	—	—	—	—	—	—	—	—	5
Side	5	5	5	—	—	—	5	5	5
RX 400h	—	—	—	—	—	—	5	—	—
RX 450h	—	—	—	—	—	—	—	—	5
Side IIHS	—	—	—	—	—	—	—	—	5
Offset	—	—	5	5	5	5	5	5	5
Head Restraints	—	—	1	1	1	1	1	1	5
Rollover	3	3	—	—	—	—	4	4	4
RX 450h	—	—	—	—	—	—	—	—	4

Toyota

RAV4 ★★

RATING: Average (2010); Below Average (1999–2009). This small SUV is an impressive performer that carries a remarkable array of standard features suitable for limited off-road tasks. But there is a serious downside: The car's faulty powertrain, bad brakes, and erratically functioning cruise control can put your life in danger. **Ideal model year:** A 2008 V6-equipped, front-drive RAV4 is your best choice. It got upgraded airbags, had two years to work out 2006 redesign errors, has fewer safety-related complaints recorded by NHTSA, and now costs only about $10,500, much less than its original price of $31,200. **"Real" city/highway**

fuel economy: *Pre-2006 models: 10.7/8.1 L/100 km. 2006–07 models: 10.1/7.8 L/100 km. V6: 11.1/7.7 L/100 km. 2008 and later models: 9.5/6.9 L/100 km. V6: 10.8/7.4 L/100 km. 4×4-equipped 2008 and later models: 9.7/7.2 L/100 km. V6: 11.1/7.7 L/100 km.* **Maintenance/repair costs:** Below average. **Parts:** Moderately priced and fairly easy to find from independent suppliers. **Extended warranty:** A good idea as the RAV4 quality decline continues. **Best alternatives:** Honda CR-V and Hyundai Tucson or Santa Fe. Other choices worth looking at are the Nissan Xterra or X-Trail and Subaru's Forester. **Helpful websites:** *www.toyotaownersclub.com*; *www.toyotanation.com*; *www.arfc.org/complaints/2009/toyota/rav4*; and *www.carcomplaints.com/Toyota/RAV4.*

Strengths and Weaknesses

ALERT! Three things to check in your pre-purchase roadtest: 1. The RAV4's wheel studs. They are easily broken. 2. Make sure the front head restraints aren't painful to use. 3. Verify if you can drive this car as if it were a manual. Owners say the RAV4's engine doesn't produce enough torque at idle to hold the vehicle in place on an incline. This requires modulating the brake and accelerator to keep the car from rolling backwards as if it had a manual transmission.

A cross between a small car and an off-road wagon with a tall roof, the RAV4 is Toyota's entry into the mini-sport-utility market. It has attractive lines, a high profile, and two drivetrains: permanent 4×4 or front-drive (which doesn't include low-range gearing but has a locking centre differential). The car is based on the Camry platform and features a four-wheel independent suspension and unibody construction. The 2005 and earlier models ride and handle like stiffly sprung, small-wheelbase cars; later models are a bit smoother. Like Honda's CR-V, the RAV4 is an upsized car that has been made more rugged with the addition of AWD, larger wheels, more ground clearance, and a boxy body.

Following the car's 2006 redesign, two engines were offered: a 166 hp 4-cylinder and a 269 hp V6—coupled to an automatic transmission. ABS and traction/anti-skid control are standard. Front-drive RAV4s have a limited-slip differential. Hill ascent/descent control is standard on V6 models and on seven-passenger 4-cylinder models. RAV4s have a side-hinged rear gate that makes for difficult curbside loading. The second-row seat is a split-folding bench that moves fore and aft and has a reclining seatback. The optional third-row seat folds into the floorwell.

VEHICLE HISTORY: 2004—Given the Camry's 2.4L engine, rear disc brakes, vehicle skid control, a revised suspension and steering, a tire-pressure monitor, and optional side curtain airbags. **2006**—A major redesign gives the 2006 a V6 and a small horsepower boost for the 4-cylinder engine as well as new styling, a longer wheelbase, additional length, more width, more cargo room, and third-row seating to carry a total of seven passengers. **2007**—Standard front seat-mounted side airbags and roll-sensing front and rear head/side curtain airbags. **2009**—The 2008's 166 hp 2.4L 4-cylinder engine is replaced by a 179 hp 2.5L four.

The peppy 6-cylinder engine provides excellent acceleration while sipping fuel. The car has adequate 4-cylinder acceleration, good handling, and a smooth ride (the four-door model has a handling advantage over the two-door version); more than enough headroom and legroom for all passengers; more cargo space than most passenger cars with the four-door (but the two-door version reduces that cargo capacity by half); a split rear bench seat that folds for extra cargo space; easy access and a low liftover; and a nicely equipped four-door version (the two-door is spartan, though adequate).

But owners aren't all happy, and they report the following problem areas: serious throttle delay followed by engine surging; the automatic gearbox reduces engine performance; excessive road and engine noise; and seriously compromised rearward visibility caused by the RAV4's convertible top, high headrests, and spare-tire placement.

The V6 throttle is super-sensitive and tough to modulate, leading to jerky acceleration and rough low-speed shifts; speed control constantly shifts in and out of gear; tall drivers will find the cockpit cramped; wide rear roof pillars obstruct rearward view; second-row seats give insufficient legroom; third-row seats are hard to access; and the glove box lid and headliner are cheap-looking.

Quality control has declined over the past five years, with countless reports of "lag and lurch" when accelerating. A faulty speed control causes the transmission to shift constantly in a jerky manner, making the engine race:

> The response has been the same—that's just what Toyotas do. The problem: when accelerating from a stop when my 2008 RAV4 has been idling, the car hesitates. There is a second or 2 during which there is no power. Then, the power kicks in and the car jumps forward, not because the pedal is sticking but because the car suddenly "catches up" with the gas pedal.

"Torque steer" makes the car unstable when merging or accelerating to pass. Rodents munch on the soy-based electrical wiring. The suspension clunks when making slow-speed turns. The brakes screech, squeal, or grind even after the pads have been replaced. Other noises: dash and windshield cowl rattling (worse in low temperatures) and rear suspension creaking when accelerating from a stop. To a lesser degree, owners tell of rear-view mirror and windshield cowling vibrations as well as minor electrical shorts. The AC and heating display is nearly impossible to read in daylight.

 ## Safety Summary

It's important to note that the RAV4's 2006 redesign coincided with a dramatic uptick in safety-related failures reported to NHTSA. From 2005 to 2009 the complaint tally is as follows: **2005**—42; **2006**—351; **2007**—275; **2008**—138; and **2009**—130 complaints posted at *www.safercar.gov*.

All years: Airbag malfunctions. • Sudden, unintended acceleration • Intermittent hesitation when accelerating or making a slow turn ("lag and lurch"). • Loss of brakes and frequent brake pad replacement. • Windshield is easily chipped. • Vehicle pulls to one side when accelerating; alignment and tires are not the cause. • Rear window suddenly shatters. **2002**—Brake pedal is too small. **2002–04**—Fire ignites in the engine compartment. **2004–05**—Fuel-hose leakage. **2006**—Passenger-side airbag shuts off even though an adult occupies the seat. • More complaints of engine hesitation and surging when accelerating or when coming to a stop:

> My 2006 Toyota RAV4 has a non-responsive throttle. On many occasions, when you give it gas it does nothing, then it takes off like a rocket. I have nearly been in accidents because I pull out from a stop and the throttle is unresponsive while traffic is bearing down on me.

2007—Sudden loss of steering. • Faulty cruise control and engine hesitation when accelerating (a common Toyota problem over the past decade). **2008**—Stuck accelerator:

> It happened only once and hasn't repeated. It was while approaching an intersection red light fortunately with no cars in front of me. I was able to overcome the acceleration by standing on the brake and shifting into neutral. When Toyota came out with the recall for floor mats my car was not one of the models with those type of floor mats and the mats in the car are fastened down. Toyota's current recall does not include this model and a check of the accelerator pedal confirms that this is not one of the current pedal replacements. My vehicle was produced in Japan not the USA. I suspect that this was more of an electronic problem than a pedal problem. I'm concerned that it could happen again. Since my year and model is not on the recall.

> •

> Driving into a parking space, doing a little under 5 mph. The car suddenly surged forward. I applied the brake even harder and the ABS engaged. Fortunately I missed the BMW parked in front.

> •

> I own a 2008 Toyota RAV4, with a VIN that begins with a 'J', but I have experienced a problem with acceleration when I depress the brake pedal. It has happened about 3 times in the last 4 months.

Many reports of sudden brake loss. • Weak defroster:

> Under certain weather conditions (wet snow, ice & freezing temps) the defrost system will not keep ice from forming over about 3/4 of the windwhield. After 10 to 12 minutes of driving it is necessary to stop and scrape ice from the windshield and wipers. It's not a good idea to stop on narrow mountain roads in a blizzard.

Driving with the rear windows open creates intolerable air pressure. • Rear tire cover blows off the car. • Car is a rodent "bed and breakfast":

> The contact owns a 2008 Toyota RAV4. The contact noticed mice entering the vehicle when it was parked. The vehicle was taken to an authorized dealer for diagnostic testing. The mechanic stated that the failure was due to the air filter not having a screen to prevent the mice from entering the vehicle. The technician recommended that traps be set to catch the mice.

2009—Sudden, unintended acceleration accounts for almost all of the 130 complaints. • Airbag failed to deploy. • Engine camshaft secret warranty applied on a case-by-case basis. • Brake pedal too close to the accelerator. • Brake pads and rotors wear out prematurely. • Loose driver's seat. • All four tires had to be replaced because they were bald. • Under-hood fire. • Windshield wiper inverted like an umbrella strikes the left wiper blade, causing both blades to fail, after damaging the windshield. • Flimsy hood. • Fuel gauge gives incorrect readings. **2010**—Nearly 150 complaints sent to NHTSA; 75 would be normal. The majority of the incidents reported concern sudden, unintended acceleration. • Passenger-side airbag turns itself off even though a normal-sized occupant is seated. • Sometimes the cruise control doesn't disengage when the brakes are applied or the lever pulled. • Wheel studs break frequently. No, it is not due to over-torquing the lug nuts. Owners suspect a low grade of steel is the culprit. • Backdoor closed on driver's hand as vehicle was unloaded. • Head restraints are painful:

> There are numerous forums and message boards on the Internet on which drivers of newer vehicles such as this one are complaining about extreme pain being caused by these headrests. In my case in particular, the malpositioning of the headrest is causing vertebrae in my neck, along with my upper two ribs, to be pushed out of place. This condition causes extreme pain, headaches, and fatigue. Additionally, the middle of the head being pushed so far forward, and no support for the neck, would seem to me a very dangerous combination if a high-speed crash were to occur.

Gas tank leaks. • Vehicle rolls back when stopped on an incline. • Brake and gas pedals are mounted too close together. • False low tire pressure alerts. Rodents chewed up the wiring harness. • Rear windshield wiper traps snow where the spare tire is mounted and freezes.

Secret Warranties/Internal Bulletins/Service Tips

2002–06—Correction for vehicles that pull to the right when accelerating. **2003–11**—Windshield ticking noise considered a factory-related problem (T-SB-0142-08, published July 29, 2008). **2004–10**—Front-seat squeaking. **2006**—Engine timing cover oil leaks. **2006–07**—Automatic transmission shift lever doesn't move smoothly. • Water leaks onto the passenger floorboard. • Front-door locks may be inoperative in cold weather. **2006–08**—Engine compartment squeaks. • Steering clunk, pop, knock. **2006–09**—Engine ticking noise. • Multiple warning lamps lit; no shift from Park. • Brake rattle, buzz heard from the driver's-side dash area. • Inoperative moonroof. **2006–10**—No-crank, no-start requires the installation of a revised neutral switch assembly. • Rough idle. • Loose sun visor mount. • Automatic transmission whining noise. **2007**—Paint stains on horizontal surfaces. **2008**—Water drips from the headliner near the A-pillar.

RAV4 PROFILE

	2002	2003	2004	2005	2006	2007	2008	2009	2010
Cost Price ($)									
4×4	24,420	24,485	24,485	24,585	28,700	29,300	29,400	26,500	27,230
V6	—	—	—	—	31,200	31,800	31,900	29,100	29,845
Used Values ($)									
4×4 ▲	4,500	5,500	7,000	8,500	10,000	12,000	13,500	15,500	19,000
4×4 ▼	4,000	5,000	6,500	7,500	9,000	10,500	12,000	14,000	17,500
V6 ▲	—	—	—	—	11,000	12,500	15,000	18,000	20,500
V6 ▼	—	—	—	—	10,000	11,000	13,500	16,500	19,000
Reliability	4	4	3	3	3	3	3	3	3
Crash Safety (F)	4	4	4	4	5	5	5	5	5
Side	5	5	5	5	5	5	5	5	5
IIHS Side	1	1	1	1	5	5	5	5	5
Offset	3	3	5	5	5	5	5	5	5
Head Restraints (F)	—	2	2	2	2	2	2	5	5
Roof Strength	—	—	—	—	3	3	3	3	3
Rollover Resistance	3	3	3	—	4	4	4	4	4

TRUCKS

Pickup Picks

When choosing a pickup, consider cost, safety, reliability, performance, and style—in that order. Start small with reliable entry-level Honda, Mazda, or Nissan offerings. If you need more brawn and performance and must buy something Detroit-made, go for a 150-series Ford pickup. Ford's 250-series and higher aren't in the running due to their larger number of failures involving more components. GM's Sierra and Silverado trucks are good second choices, but Chrysler Rams aren't. The Rams have serious powertrain, brake, and electrical system failures; fit and finish is also the worst of the Detroit Three.

Be prepared for subpar reliability, high maintenance costs, rapid depreciation, and abysmally poor fit and finish on all Detroit-bred models. This includes Chrysler's much-vaunted Cummins diesel engine. Recent iterations of the Cummins have proven to be almost as quality-challenged as the Ford Power Stroke and GM Duramax (*www.mycarlady.com/2009/01/28/2009-cummins-diesel-problems-continue*).

Cummins diesel problems are primarily related to the 2006–10 models and mostly concern the turbocharger and emissions component failures that stop the truck dead in its track. Says one owner:

> I have had constant problems with this emission system where the particulate filter plugs up constantly causing more fuel to be injected into the particulate and causing very poor fuel mileage, along with carbon soot residue on the bed of the truck from the exhaust. The last 3 visits to the dealership would get the warning light turned off just to have it come back on a few days later. I have a 2002 Dodge with the 5.9 liter, and have never had a problem like this.

What about Toyota's Tacoma and Tundra? Steer clear of both models. Too many owner complaints of sudden acceleration, poor braking, suspension deficiencies, steering failures, and rust-damaged undercarriages.

TRUCK RATINGS

Recommended

Honda Ridgeline (2007–10)	Nissan Frontier (2005–10)

Above Average

Ford/Mazda Ranger, B-Series (2008–10)	Nissan Frontier (1999–2004)
Honda Ridgeline (2006)	

Average

Ford F-Series (2007–10)

Ford/Mazda Ranger, B-Series
  (1999–2007)

General Motors C/K, Sierra, Silverado
  (2006–10)

Below Average

Chrysler Ram (2002–10)

Ford F-Series (1999–2006)

General Motors C/K, Sierra,
  Silverado (1999–2005)

Not Recommended

GM Hybrid (2005–10)

Toyota Tacoma (2002–10)

Toyota Tundra (2000–10)

Chrysler

RAM

RATING: Below Average (2002–10). Rams are mediocre buys; however, when equipped with a manual tranny and an older diesel powertrain, they are adequate for most chores, even with their "death wobble" suspension/steering assemblies. **Ideal model year:** Get a 2009 redesigned front-drive Ram for about $14,000; quite a savings over the pickup's $23,795 original price. **"Real" city/highway fuel economy:** *3.9 4×2: 15.9/11.0 L/100 km. 5.2 4×4: 18.9/13.1 L/100 km. Hemi V8 with Multi-Displacement System: 13.9/8.8 L/100 km. V6: 12.2/8.1 L/100 km.* Pre-2006 models' average real-world fuel consumption has been reported at 21.0 L/100 km. **Maintenance/repair costs:** Higher than average. **Parts:** Parts distribution has hit the skids since Chrysler's bankruptcy. Prices are unreasonably high and often back ordered. **Extended warranty:** Yes. Invest in extra powertrain protection if no more of the factory warranty is left. By limiting it to the powertrain you will save almost $1,000. **Best alternatives:** Ford Ranger, Honda Ridgeline, Mazda B Series, and Nissan Frontier V6 and Rogue. **Helpful websites:** *www.carcomplaints.com/ Dodge/Ram_1500; www.ramforumz.com;* and *www.mycarlady.com/2009/01/28/2009-cummins-diesel-problems-continue.*

 ### Strengths and Weaknesses

ALERT! "Death wobble" describes the intense bounce and shimmy that follows whenever Ram trucks pass over a bump or pothole in the road. The shimmy can be so bad, drivers can lose steering control. Chrysler has just announced a recall that affects 242,780 Ram pickups manufactured between 2003 and 2011. This includes all 2008 Ram 1500, and 2003–2011 Ram 2500 and 3500 Heavy Duty trucks.

NHTSA says these trucks may have a defective left tie rod ball stud that can fracture during a low-speed parking manoeuvre:

This condition could result in the potential loss of directional stability in the left hand front wheel, increasing the risk of a crash.

To remedy this potential problem, dealers will inspect the tie rod ends and replace them free of charge, if needed; an alignment may also be done.

Another potential problem to check out before purchase is the driver's shoulder belt. Many owners say its high position causes the webbing to rub the driver's neck raw.

Not a spectacular performer with its weak standard powertrain hookup (corrected in its 2009 redesign), the Dodge Ram is a full-sized pickup that mirrors Ford's and GM's truck lineups. The 2004 and later 1500 series models come with a 3.7L V6 base engine and optional 4.7L and 5.7L V8s. The latter engine is called the Hemi, and it's sold only with a 5-speed automatic transmission. The V6 and 4.7L V8 offer a manual transmission or a 4- or 5-speed automatic, respectively. Automatics include a tow/haul mode for heavy loads. Chrysler plays the nostalgia card with its 345 hp 5.7L Hemi high-performance engine, last seen as an allegedly 425 hp powerhouse offered from 1965 to 1971. It is sold with the 1500 series heavy-duty Ram pickups and the Dodge 300C/Magnum wagon. Drivers can expect to shave about three seconds off the 1500's time of 0–100km/h in 10.5 seconds, all the while praying that the engine doesn't kill the tranny.

The Ram's strong points: bargain resale prices, cylinder deactivation for better fuel economy and more power, and plenty of interior room and convenience features. The 4.7L V8 is a good alternative to the larger, more fuel-thirsty Hemi version.

Some of the sore points with the 2006–10 models: You won't get the fuel economy, safety features, or manoeuvrability of other full-sized pickups. The ride is jiggly, at best; scary, at worst, when passing over bumps and potholes; the interior is Kmart kitsch; and the climb up to the lofty cab may need a Sherpa's boost.

Pre-2006 models are even cheaper to buy, and they offer average quality combined with assertive styling, a high-tech engine, full-time 4×4, adequately sized cabs with good stowage utility, one of the longest and roomiest cargo boxes available, and a comfortable and well-designed interior with easily accessed and understood instruments and controls. The 1500 series models have better handling, improved steering, and fewer rattles. Other pluses: powerful Hemi, V8, and V10 engines; a bit more reliable Cummins diesel; good trailering capability; a smooth-shifting automatic transmission (when it's working right); and four-door versatility.

But there are minuses with pre-2006 models, as well: The 1500 series engines may be outclassed by Ford and GM powerplants. The resurrected Hemi V8 is quite fuel-thirsty and has had a number of quality problems over the past few years. Considering Chrysler's inability to make reliable and safe ball joints, ABS brakes, and automatic transmissions, the 2005's engine cylinder deactivation feature may become a problem as these trucks reach their critical fifth year of use. The 2500 and 3500 models were left in the Jurassic Age until the 2006 redesigned models came on board. Outdated mechanical components, like an inconvenient transfer case and a solid front axle, make for an unstable ride (on 2500s and 3500s only); 4×4 must be disengaged on dry pavement; V6 acceleration is poor; steering response is slow; controls aren't easy to calibrate; the 1.8 m (6 ft.) bed looks stubby; and the high hood hides obstacles from view. Chrysler ties with Ford for very poor fuel economy at a real-world average of about 21.0 L/100 km (11 mpg). And as with Ford and GM trucks, Rams have also had a disturbingly large number of safety- and performance-related defects reported to NHTSA.

VEHICLE HISTORY: 2002—Revamped handling and ride comfort. The 1500 models get more-aggressive styling, two new engines, roomier cabs, and optional side airbags. The two-door extended Club Cab is axed, Quad Cabs are given four front-hinged doors, and short-box models gain 7.6 cm (3 in.) of cabin length at the expense of bed length. The 4×4-equipped Rams get an independent front suspension. **2003**—2500 and 3500 series are revised and given the Hemi 345 hp 5.7L V8 and rack-and-pinion steering. **2004**—An expanded model lineup that includes a Hemi-powered Power Wagon off-roader and the SRT-10 Quad Cab, equipped with the Dodge Viper's 500 hp 8.3L V10 engine. **2005**—More models available with manual transmissions (hmm…word must be spreading that the automatics are grenades with a pulled pin). **2006**—The 1500 gets weather seals, a stiffer frame, a softer front suspension, reduced-drag brake calipers, high-intensity headlights, an electrically operated front-axle disconnect system, a revised interior and body style (Mega Cab), and constrained layer (quiet steel) technology in the dash panel area—improvements that should reduce clunks, rattles, and wind noise. There's also a cylinder cut-off system to boost fuel economy—if it functions properly (feeling lucky?). The Mega Cab option can seat six passengers in comfort, which wasn't possible with earlier models. Comfort is enhanced through reclining rear seats that split, fold down, and move forward. Hauling capacity is more than adequate with the Mega's "mega" engine, a 345 hp 5.7L Hemi V8 mated to a heavy-duty 5-speed automatic transmission. **2007**—A new 350 hp 6.7L inline-six Cummins Turbo Diesel (25 more horses than the 2006 version), and the debut of the Class 3 Chassis Cab, equipped with either a 330 hp 5.7L Hemi V8 or a torquier Cummins Turbo Diesel V8. **2008**—The 310 hp V8 replaces the 235 hp 4.7L. **2009**—Redesigned and restyled with added power, comfort, and convenience features. Ram 1500s are available with three engines: A 215 hp 3.7L V6; a 310 hp 4.7L V8; and a 390 hp 5.7L Hemi V8. The 390 hp engine replaces 2008's 345 hp 5.7L Hemi. The V6 comes only with a 4-speed automatic transmission, V8s get a 5-speed automatic. The V6 is only available on rear-wheel-drive models. A new Crew Cab replaces the previous Mega Cab. The 2500 and 3500 models also use the 5.7L V8 with 5-speed automatic, along with an available 6.7L inline 6-cylinder Cummins turbodiesel with 6-speed automatic or 6-speed manual transmission. **2010**—All-new heavy-duty models; all models get a 700-amp battery; SLT and Sport models add a tire pressure monitoring system; and the Sport adds an automatic transfer case.

Fit and finish and powertrain, suspension, steering, brake, electrical, and fuel-system components are still not top quality. Owners mention that rust spots appear within a year and seem to have an affinity for the truck bed and front bumper. Vehicles that are painted white look the worst. • Dashboard cracks are another sign of Ford's poor-quality materials. • Hemi engines have had problems with broken valve springs and rear main seal leaks. The Cummins diesel engine has performed acceptably well, except for frequent engine emissions hardware problems shutting the truck down, or making it "limp" home.

Other owner-reported problems: Electrical fire at the power disbursement box under the hood; sudden transmission and differential failures; and the accelerator pedal jams while backing up. Be wary of front differential damage caused by road debris striking the unprotected housing. Poorly performing brakes must be adjusted at almost every oil change; the rear brake hubs and front brake pads wearout prematurely (5,000 km); and the ABS fails completely. The weak stabilizer bar is easily bent when passing over potholes; the lack of an anti-sway bar on the rear axle in the trailer towing package means excessive swaying, causing steering instability; and some trailer hitches are cracked. Very loose steering allows the vehicle to wander all over the roadway, and a defective steering pump causes loss of steering control. Owners complain of constant pulling to the right on the highway; excessive vibration when approaching 100 km/h; excessive shimmy after hitting a bump or pothole; clunk or rattle felt in the steering wheel after running over a rough surface; and a faulty steering gearbox. Expect inadequate cooling because of AC freeze-up and a strange odour coming from the AC ducts. There's a clunking or rattling noise from the front suspension, a ringing noise from the rear of the vehicle, and a shudder when the truck pulls away from a stop while near maximum gross vehicle weight rating (GVWR), and on the 3500 series, front disc brake noise. The absence of a fuel tank baffle allows gas to slam forward and back in the tank, subjecting connections to stress and causing early failure. The ignition fuse link blows intermittently, shutting down the vehicle. The Ram suffers from fragile front ball joints; transmission seal leakage; and oil-filter adaptor plate and speed-sensor oil seepage. The obstructive rear door latching mechanism prevents easy access to the rear seat and the lap belt rides too high on the abdomen, while the shoulder belt lies too close to the neck and jaw.

 ## Safety Summary

All models/years: Sudden acceleration. • Chronic stalling. • Airbag malfunctions. • Brake pedal goes to floor without any braking effect. • Severe pull to the side when braking. • Warped rotors and worn-out brake pads. • When parked, vehicle rolls down an incline. • Frequent transmission failures and fluid leaks. • Overdrive engages poorly in cold weather. • Vehicle wanders excessively at highway speeds. **All models: 2002**—Front end jumps from side to side when vehicle passes over uneven pavement, or it easily hydroplanes when passing over wet roads. • Premature brake master cylinder failure. • Differential and rear axle bearing fail prematurely. **2003**—Accelerator pedal falls off. • Front suspension collapse. **2004**—Fire ignites in the driver-side rear wheelwell. • Stalling Hemi engine (a faulty EGR valve is the suspected culprit). • Wheel bearing failure. • Rear axle breaks. **2005**—Electrical fire ignites in the engine compartment. • Vehicle speeds up when going downhill. • Early ball joint failure. **2006**—Tie-rod failures. • Gas and brake pedals are mounted too close together. **2006–07**—Automatic transmission slips out of Reverse and grinds. **2007**—Front control arm (suspension/steering) breaks:

> This caused the tire to dislocate from the vehicle. The tire, ball joint, brake system and hoses stayed attached to the rim of the tire. This caused the vehicle to drop and surge to the right, then collide with another vehicle.

Engine oil sensor failures. • Dashboard cracks may impair airbag deployment. • Michelin tire failures. **2008**—Sudden acceleration. • Airbag malfunctioned, but could not be repaired due to a lack of the required part. • Gas spills out of the filler tube. • Windshield wipers fall off. • Floor mat may jam the accelerator. • Electronic transfer case computer module failures lock up the transmission. • Steering wheel lockup when turning left. • Wheel lug nuts may fail:

> Upon hitting a slight dip in the road, my left front wheel sheared from the lug nuts and rolled away, while my truck wheel hub and rotor slammed into the asphalt and grinded 15 feet to a stop.

Sudden failure of the outer tie-rod ends. • "Death wobble" when passing over bumps. • At 70 km/h excessive shake and severe pull to the right (after recall repairs were performed to prevent this problem):

> The vehicle is not able to properly maintain a lane in traffic when there are changes in road texture, pot holes, or if there are road deterioration issues. These changes cause the vehicle to bounce out of control and it makes it difficult to safely maneuver the vehicle in traffic.

Premature front shock and tire tread wear. • There is no way to lower the headlights:

> A truck is made to carry weight in the back end or pull a trailer, both of which makes the front of the truck raise in height. While pulling my trailer I receive about 100 cars per hour that flash their high beams just as they approach me causing me to be blind for a second or two...While driving through Sacramento in a rain storm at night I could not see the reflectors that mark the lanes and came close to having an accident because my headlights were so high.

2009—Sudden, unintended acceleration:

> The contact owns a 2009 Dodge Ram 1500. The contact stated that while driving 60 mph, the vehicle abnormally accelerated to 115 mph. The contact noticed that the accelerator had become stuck in the open throttle position and he then attempted to dislodge the accelerator pedal in order to stop the unintended acceleration. The

vehicle was taken to the dealer for diagnosis and repairs. The dealer replaced the accelerator pedal and removed the floor mat, however, the failure recurred after repairs.

Airbag failed to deploy. • No defrosting. • Excessive accelerator pedal vibration. • Spare tire jack won't support the Ram 1500's weight. • No brakes. • Warped rear brake rotors. • Drivers find the rearview mirror too small. • Horn intermittently doesn't work. • Chrome trim around the shifter reflects the sun into the driver's eyes. **2010**—Sudden, unintended acceleration. • Airbags failed to deploy. • Rear axles fracture frequently. • Many complaints that the rear wheel seized and the driveshaft detached from the vehicle, punctured the fuel tank, and flattened the spare tire. • Snow packed in around transmission and transfer causing shifter linkage to seize. • Fuel tank doesn't fit properly on the bracket designed to hold it in place. • Fuel filler neck pops out when refuelling. • Complete brake failure. • Corroded tire pressure sensors can lead to tire failure. • All four doors can be easily blown shut or close inadvertently because they are not held back securely. • Headlights and taillights suddenly go out. • Painfully loud noise and vibration when driving with rear windows down.

Secret Warranties/Internal Bulletins/Service Tips

All models: 1999–2008—Paint delamination, peeling, or fading. • An erratically shifting automatic transmission may require only a recalibrated PCM or TCM. Check out this solution before spending big bucks. **2001–04**—Water leaks on passenger-side floor (Dakota also affected). **2002–04**—Water leaks at grab handle. **2002–05**—PCV system freezes up in cold temperatures. **2003**—Low start-up oil pressure with the Hemi engine requires the replacement of the oil-pump pick-up tube. • Poor idle and coasting. • Lack of air from floor vents. **2004**—Brake kit should be installed to eliminate brake shudder, vibration. • Power-window binding or slow operation. **2004–05**—Water leaks at the roof marker lamps. **2004–08**—Sunroof makes a ratcheting sound. **2004–09**—Remedy for fuel overflow or fuel nozzle shutting off. **2005–06**—Delayed shifting. **2005–10**—Lower door hinge popping, groaning noise. **2006**—Electrical malfunctions; no-crank. • Sunroof glass not flush with roof; won't close. • Lack of airflow from rear seat heater duct. **2006–07**—Steering pull or shudder when brakes are applied. • Water leaks onto the rear floor area. **2006–08**—Horizontal paint etching. **2007**—Automatic transmission torque converter shuddering. • Transmission defaults to neutral. **2009**—Steering wander may require installation of a steering shaft kit. • Under a special warranty extension campaign, Dodge will replace free of charge torn seat cushion covers or seat cushions. • Hood squeaking, creaking sound on turns or when passing over bumps. • AC hissing noise. **2009–10**—Quad rear doors won't lock or unlock. • Water leaks diagnostic tips. • Under Customer Satisfaction Notification K23, Dodge will replace a corroded front bumper for free. No mileage or time limitations have been imposed. • Another Campaign will tackle poor AC performance by replacing defective air door actuators free of charge. **2009–11**—Excessive steering wheel vibration on the 1500 model may require a new steering wheel assembly under warranty, says

Chrysler. • Fuel filler housing pops out of opening. • A wind noise from the front door area can be silenced by adding more soundproofing material under warranty.

RAM PROFILE

	2002	2003	2004	2005	2006	2007	2008	2009	2010
Cost Price ($)									
D-150, 1500	23,255	23,865	24,910	26,975	26,020	26,395	26,995	23,795	26,495
Quad Cab	27,280	26,900	—	—	—	—	—	—	—
SRT-10	—	—	61,000	58,465	61,555	—	—	—	—
Used Values ($)									
D-150, 1500 ▲	3,000	3,500	4,500	5,500	7,000	9,500	12,000	14,500	16,500
D-150, 1500 ▼	2,500	3,000	4,000	5,000	5,500	8,500	10,500	13,000	15,000
Quad Cab ▲	4,000	5,000	—	—	—	—	—	—	—
Quad Cab ▼	3,000	4,000	—	—	—	—	—	—	—
SRT-10 ▲	—	—	10,000	13,000	17,000	—	—	—	—
SRT-10 ▼	—	—	8,500	11,500	15,500	—	—	—	—
Reliability	3	3	3	3	2	2	2	2	2
Crash Safety (F)	4	4	5	5	5	5	5	5	—
Ext. cab	—	—	—	5	5	—	—	—	—
Quad cab	—	—	—	5	5	—	—	—	—
Side	—	—	3	—	—	—	—	—	—
Quad Cab	4	5	3	—	—	—	—	—	—
Side (IIHS)	—	—	—	—	—	—	—	2	2
Offset	5	5	5	5	5	5	5	5	5
Head Restraints (F)	—	3	3	3	1	1	1	5	5
Roof Strength	—	—	—	—	—	—	—	2	2
Rollover Resistance	3	3	—	4	4	4	4	4	—

Ford

F-SERIES ★★★

RATING: Average (2007–10); Below Average (1999–2006). Entry-level F-Series trucks are versatile and brawny haulers, with much-improved handling, a quieter ride, and a more-comfortable interior incorporated into the 2005 model's redesign. Quality control, however, only got slightly better. Until 2009, it remained mediocre at best and life-threatening at its worst. This isn't news to owners. Over the past two decades, they have suffered with poor-quality powertrain components and serious safety-related defects like sudden tie-rod separation, torsion bar failures, unintended acceleration, and complete loss of braking. **Ideal model year:** Get a 2009 front-drive Regular Cab XL for about

$14,000; it will have had a couple of years to digest its last redesign and some remaining factory warranty can provide much-needed powertrain protection. **"Real" city/highway fuel economy:** Very poor; average real-world fuel economy hovers around 21.0 L/100 km—equal to the Dodge Ram's. 4.2 4×2: 15.1/11.1 L/100 km. 4.6 4×2: 16.2/11.3 L/100 km. 5.4 4×2: 17.4/12.3 L/100 km. 4.2 4×4: 15.9/12.2 L/100 km. 4.6 4×4: 17.4/12.9 L/100 km. 5.4 4×4: 18.6/13.6 L/100 km. **Maintenance/repair costs:** Higher than average, but easily repaired by independent garages. **Parts:** With the exception of Power Stroke diesels, parts are generally widely available from independent suppliers and are of average cost. **Extended warranty:** An extended powertrain warranty is a must to counter Ford's well-known powertrain glitches. **Best alternatives:** Honda, Mazda, and Nissan pickups are a lot safer and more reliable. Even a Ranger/Mazda B Series are worth considering. Be wary of Toyota's Tacoma and Tundra rust-prone and "runaway" pickups and GM's quality-challenged trucks. **Helpful websites:** *www. carcomplaints.com/Ford/F-150* and *www.fordf150.net/forums.*

Strengths and Weaknesses

ALERT! During your test drive, pay careful attention as to how the tranny shifts and if the acceleration is steady and straight. Gear "hunting" is a common complaint from owners. Also look for early brake caliper and rotor wear.

In Ford's glory days, it and GM were the only pickup games in town and relations with parts suppliers were cordial. Now, Chrysler, Honda, Nissan, and Toyota are gobbling up Ford's market share and supplier relations are testy at best. Buyers are clamouring for more versatile and reliable trucks that mix high-tech features with dependability and are covered by stronger warranties. Unfortunately, Ford's F-Series revamp in 2005 was too little, too late, and wasn't corrected until the latest redesign of the 2009 models, which gave these pickups more power, passenger room, and features.

The Ford 4.2L V6 is rated better in fuel economy than the 4.6L V8, but the V8 gets better mileage in the real world. The V6 also was known for oil pump problems, so it has been dropped from the reworked F-150. An engine Ford should have dropped, but didn't—the 300 hp 5.4L V8—is known for chronic production glitches. It features three valves per cylinder, variable-cam timing, and an electronic throttle control that dealer mechanics are still trying to master.

Safety features on the 2005 and later F-150s were augmented to include multi-stage front airbags; a sensor to determine if the front passenger seat is empty; five three-point seat belts, with the front shoulder belts integrated into the seats; and a LATCH (lower anchors and tethers for children) system to facilitate the installation of child safety seats.

The 2006 and earlier F-150s' underpowered base V6 engine and 4.6L V8 don't have sufficient passing power. Other pre-2007 problems: questionable engine, transmission, suspension/steering, and brake performance and reliability; poor braking performance with four-wheel ABS; and an uncomfortable rear seat. The climate-control system is a bit slow in warming up the cabin. There's no left footrest on some models, and the cramped and upright rear seats can't match GM's for comfort. Cargo flexibility is compromised by the second-row layout. An inordinate number of serious safety-related complaints have been collected by NHTSA, with cruise-control switch fires, tie-rod end and front torsion bar failures, and steering vibration and drivetrain shudder heading the list. Watch out for violent body shaking when passing over a bumpy highway and for severe dash glare onto the front windshield. Warranty payouts have been unacceptably Scrooge-like in the past, and fuel economy is astoundingly poor.

The 2007 and later F-150s have easy and predictable handling; a pleasant ride on bad roads; well-thought-out ergonomics, instruments, and controls; and fourth-door access. With a few exceptions (like tacky cloth seats), base models are nicely appointed, with lots of handy convenience features and a classy interior.

One serious defect, afflicting 2007 and later models, is collapsing tie rods/torsion bars in the steering/suspension system that throw the truck out of control when they fail. Ford has sent a letter to owners asking them to *please* have their vehicles inspected and repaired—at their own cost, of course. Engine and automatic transmission breakdowns top the list of owners' complaints, which extends to failure-prone engine gaskets, timing belt tensioners, oil pumps, fuel injectors, fuel and ignition systems, and drivelines (principally clutches). If that weren't enough, owners have also been burdened with poor-quality front and rear brake components that include premature pad and caliper replacement and chronic rotor warping; faulty powertrain control modules that cause sudden stalling at full throttle; excessive vibration felt throughout the vehicle; front suspension and steering problems; inadequate AC cooling; and early replacement of the AC compressor. There are also body defects up the wazoo, including a vibrating sun roof, cracked door hinges, and blistering paint on more recent versions.

VEHICLE HISTORY: 2003—Lightning models receive a stiffer rear suspension to support a 635 kg (1,400 lb.) payload. **2005**—All models redesigned. **2007**—F-250 and F-350 pickups offer a new 350 hp 6.4L V8 diesel engine to replace the quality-plagued 6.0L diesel. **2008**—A new flexible-fuel 5.4L V8 equips most models. Ford readies the big changes for its 2009 redesign. **2009**—More power and passenger room. A 248 hp 4.6L V8 hooked to a 4-speed automatic transmission replaces the 202 hp V6 as the base engine. A 292 hp version of the 4.6L and a 310–320 hp 5.4L V8, both matched to a 6-speed automatic, also come on board. **2010**—No more flareside box and only two box lengths are offered with the SuperCab.

 Safety Summary

All models/years: Tie-rod and front torsion-bar failures send the truck out of control. • Dangerous front-end bounce. • Sudden acceleration and chronic stalling, mostly blamed on the poor design and positioning of the accelerator and brake pedals. • Sticking accelerator pedal. • Frequent automatic transmission failures; transmission slippage. • Airbag malfunctions. • Brake failure as pedal goes to the floor. • Wheel lug nut failures. • Firestone and Goodrich tire-tread separation. • Gas and brake pedals are mounted too close together. **All models: 2000–02**—Windows suddenly shatter while vehicle is underway. **2002**—Fire ignites under the power-adjusted seat mechanism. • Headlights and dash lights fail intermittently. • Small wheel hubs cause vehicle to vibrate excessively. **2003**—Faulty EGR valve causes throttle to stick wide open and brakes to fail. • Rear axle failure; wheel comes off. • One truck's left front wheel separated, and the truck ran into a wall. • Harley Truck Owners Club (*www.nhtoc.com*) reports that rubber strips on stainless steel gas pedals peel off, making the pedal too slippery. • Fuel-tank leakage. **2004**—Driving with rear window open makes the cabin vibrate violently. • Painful, high-pitched noise comes from the dash area. • Tire chains cannot be used. • Wiper leaves a 15 cm blind spot near the driver's side pillar. **2004–05**—Tailgate falls off. • Excessive vibration and rear-end shudder at highway speeds. **2005**—Many complaints of sudden, unintended acceleration with complete loss of braking capability. • When parked on an incline, vehicle slips out of gear and rolls downhill. • Tire jack won't raise truck high enough to allow the mounting of a fully inflated spare. • Faulty ignition keys. **2006**—Many complaints of 5.4L V8 engine hesitating or stalling when accelerating. • Reports of faulty fuel pumps leaking fuel onto the exhaust system. • Poorly designed suspension causes the vehicle to jump and shake wildly when passing over a small bump in the road. • Rack-and-pinion steering falls apart. • Sudden brake loss. • Ice accumulates in the wheels. • Many complaints relative to prematurely worn Hankook DynaPro original-equipment tires. **2006–07**— Unintended acceleration when braking, or when the cruise control is enabled. **2007**—Steering failure in rainy conditions. • Fuel gauge shows empty when the tank is full. • Vision hampered by dash reflection (glare) onto front windshield. • Tire valve stem cracking. **2008**—Two separate fires: one ignited under the hood; the other was sourced to the passenger-side dash area. • Fuel poured out of the gas tank from a faulty plastic connection to the fuel pump. • Many reports of sudden, unintended acceleration. • The accelerator pedal is too large and can be applied when one is braking. • Starter gear shaft self-destructed. • The Special 60th Edition Ford F-150's driveline vibrates excessively. • AC blows hot air only. • Cracked front upper door hinges. • Hankook P235 75R17 tires aren't very durable and Dill tire valve stems on all tires are prone to cracking. • Vehicle side steps aren't sturdy. • Ford's stated towing capability for the F-150 may be dangerously inaccurate:

> I think it a crime that Ford's put towing weights on their web sites and in booklets and it is false. We bought [a] Ford 150 in March so that we could tow our 32' travel trailer that weighs 7,000 lbs. All documentation states it can pull 9,000 lbs. We have pulled our unit 3 times and every time we pray that we make it to our destination and home safely

2009—Sudden, unintended acceleration. • 6-speed automatic transmission allows the truck to roll backwards when stopped on a grade. • Automatic transmission slips, chatters, surges, and slams into gear. • Water accumulation in the right side kickplate. • Deep grooves in brake rotors. • Smart junction box failure caused the headlights to go out. • Loss of brakes. • Seat belt tightened up and would not release a child. **2009–10**—Tips on silencing engine compartment clicking noises. • Drivetrain slip/bump on acceleration, or braking. • Drivetrain shudder on hard acceleration. • Transmission fluid leakage around the transmission bulkhead connector sleeve. **2009–11**—Excessive automatic transmission shifter effort in cold conditions. **2010**—Accelerated inboard rear brake pad wear. A special brake kit will be installed under warranty. *F-250:* **2005**—Faulty diesel engine fuel injectors and exhaust system cause sickening exhaust fumes to enter the cabin. • When the diesel engine is turned off for fuelling, it cannot be restarted. • Engine blows because of a faulty camshaft fuse. • Frequent fuel-pump failures. • Truck will not shift down automatically when carrying a load. • On the highway, the truck vibrates excessively and sways uncontrollably. **2006**—Automatic transmission gear slippage and stalling. • Transmission suddenly downshifts, abruptly slowing down the truck. • Recessed gauges and windshield glare impair visibility. • Vehicle stalls just as the accelerator pedal is released. **2007**—Truck is easily stolen:

> All it took for a thief to break into my Ford F-250 was, what the police officer determined, a flat-head screwdriver. It is extremely disturbing to think that all a person has to do is jam a screwdriver under the plate, for the door handle/lock plate, pry down, and the door pops open.

Engine goes to idle with no response to the accelerator. • Violent shaking when passing over a bumpy highway. • Severe dash glare onto the front windshield. *F-350:* **2008**—Diesel exhaust fumes enter into the cabin. • Long delay when accelerating. • Converter/transmission snap ring and solenoid failures. • Multiple brake failures. • When towing a trailer, the brakes don't work at low speeds (10–15 km/h). • Defective brake booster and engine oil pump. • Weak coil springs won't support a plow. **2009**—Sudden loss of power. **2010**—Double the number of complaints that are normally posted on NHTSA's website (*www.safercar.gov*). The complaints mostly involve transmission, brake, and electrical failures. • Sudden, unintended acceleration. • Chronic stalling. • Truck stalls when turning, as power steering and power brakes are lost. • Automatic transmissions known for harsh, violent downshifting, shuddering, and seizing. • Transmission slams into gear when upshifting, as well. • Sudden steering seizure. Frequent brake failures. • Water pools into the headliner corners.

Secret Warranties/Internal Bulletins/Service Tips

All models: 1999–2002—High idle speeds; throttle sticks in cold weather. **1999–2005**—Ford will install a special axle kit to stop rear axle noise. Ford's bulletin admission of this defect is actionable in small claims court if the company won't pay for the six-hour repair. • Water leaking from the roof flange area accumulates in the headliner. The leak may also occur at the cab floor pan area. • Drivetrain drive-away shudder or vibration. **1999–2006**—A driveline clunk may signal that the slip yoke needs lubrication. Check this out before spending money on more-involved tests or repairs. • Tips for correcting a rough idle. • Paint delamination, peeling, or fading. • Troubleshooting broken intake manifold studs. **2000–05**—Seat belts slow to retract. Engine power loss in hot weather. • Vacuum or air leaks in the intake manifold and engine. • Faulty ignition switch lock cylinder. **2003–06**—Inoperative AC; compressor leakage. **2004**—Faulty handle cables could make it impossible to open the doors from the inside. **2004–05**—Remedy for warm engine knocking or ticking. • Correction of axle chatter, shudder, or vibration during low-speed turning. • Remedies for steering-wheel and body vibrations. • Upgraded brake rotors will be installed to stop brake shudder and vibration. • Cooling fan noise on trucks equipped with 4.6L and 5.4L engines. • Butyl bed pad removal to prevent corrosion. **2004–07**—Aluminum body panel corrosion. **2004–08**—Power-steering-line fluid seepage in cold weather. • Excessive steering-wheel vibration (80–105 km/h). • High-speed driveline vibration. • Intermittent brake vibration, shudder. • Side cowl panel may pop up. • Power steering fluid leakage in cold weather. • Tailgate rattle. • Erratic fuel gauge readings:

ERRATIC FUEL GAUGE/MIL ON/DTC P0460/P0463

BULLETIN NO.: 08-2-9   **DATE: FEBRUARY 4, 2008**

2004–08 F-150; 2006–08 Mark LT

ISSUE: Some 2004–08 F-150 and 2006–08 Mark LT vehicles, built before 12/3/2007, may exhibit erratic fuel gauge operation or illuminated malfunction indicator lamp (MIL) with diagnostic trouble codes (DTCs) P0460 or P0463, and/or Instrument Cluster Module DTC B1201. This may be caused by sulfur contamination in the fuel causing an open or high resistance in the fuel level sender.

ACTION: Install a new fuel level sender following the service procedure instruction sheet provided in the fuel sender kit.

WARRANTY STATUS: Eligible Under Provisions Of New Vehicle Limited Warranty Coverage and Emissions Warranty Coverage.

Is that clear? This is a warrantable item. Don't pay a cent for this fuel gauge repair (estimated non-warranty cost: $300).

2005—Engine stalls when shifting into Drive or Reverse, or when coming to a stop. • Hard starts; rough running; engine won't crank. • Like with the Dodge Ram, there's excessive steering-wheel shimmy after passing over bumps. **2005–07**—Power rear sliding window may need a new motor. • Power windows are slow to roll up. **2005–08**—Sunroof water leaks. • Troubleshooting steering wheel nibble, vibration. • Cannot control AC output temperature. • Grinding noise heard when the AC changes modes. • Banging, clunking front suspension noise when driving in cold temperatures. **2005–10**—Inadvertent transmission lock-up during 1–2 shifts. **2006–08**—Shudder on acceleration and deceleration; binding in turns. **2007–08**—Engine RPM flare during 3–4 upshift; runs rough, hesitates after a cold start; misfires while cruising; idler pulley noise after a cold start. • Free tire valve stem inspection or replacement. **2009**—Engine, shift hesitation. • Erratic operation of the automatic transmission. • Steering assist varies. **2009–10**—Low frequency hot idle engine knocking noise. • Right driveshaft slip, bump condition. • Shudder, vibration upon acceleration. • Water leak near right-hand assist handle.

Diesels: **2003–04**—Remedies for 6.0L diesel engines that lose power, have fuel in oil, or run roughly are covered in TSB #03-14-6. **2003–05**—Troubleshooting tips for misfire, lack of power, excessive smoke, and excessive cranking to start. Keep in mind that Ford *must* pay for this troubleshooting and repair under the little-publicized, though much-longer, emissions warranty. **2003–06**—TSB #06-9-7, issued May 15, 2006, gives more diagnostic and repair tips for poorly performing diesel engines. **2003–07**—Erratic automatic transmission shifting over 90 km/h. **2008–09**—Customer Satisfaction Campaign #09B08 will replace the 6.4L diesel engine injectors for free, plus give you a free oil filter and oil change, no matter the mileage or number of previous owners. **2008–09**—Cold weather automatic transmission failures on vans and trucks equipped with a 6.4L diesel engine and a 5R11OW transmission. • One-way clutch failure is common. Ford will cover the failure under its warranty.

F-SERIES PROFILE

	2002	2003	2004	2005	2006	2007	2008	2009	2010
Cost Price ($)									
XL	23,310	23,380	22,850	23,840	22,499	22,499	22,199	24,199	24,599
Fireside STX	—	—	—	—	—	27,099	26,699	—	—
Used Values ($)									
XL ▲	3,000	4,000	4,500	5,000	6,000	8,500	10,500	14,500	17,000
XL ▼	2,500	3,500	4,000	4,500	5,500	7,000	9,000	13,000	15,500
Fireside STX ▲	—	—	—	—	—	10,000	11,500	—	—
Fireside STX ▼	—	—	—	—	—	8,500	10,500	—	—
Reliability	2	2	2	3	3	4	4	4	4
Crash Safety (F)	5	—	5	5	5	5	5	5	—
Side	5	5	—	—	—	—	—	5	—
Ext. cab	4	4	—	—	—	—	—	5	—
Side (IIHS)	5	—	—	—	—	—	—	5	5
SuperCrew	5	5	—	—	—	—	—	5	—
Offset	1	1	5	5	5	5	5	5	5
Head Restraints (F)	—	—	1	1	1	1	1	5	5
Rollover Resistance	—	3	4	4	4	4	4	4	—
4×4	—	2	4	4	4	4	4	4	3

Ford/Mazda

RANGER/B-SERIES ★★★★

RATING: Above Average (2008–10); Average (1999–2007). Mazda pickups are generally the least expensive of the "gang of three" small Japanese pickups (Mazda, Nissan, and Toyota). From the 1994 model onward, your Mazda is really a Ford

Ranger. Overall, both the Ford and Mazda are acceptable buys, but their highway performance is mediocre. Powertrain defects are worrisome for their frequency and their high repair cost. **Ideal model year:** Get a 2009 XL front-drive Ranger that sells for $7,500. It originally cost $15,899. Earlier, cheaper Rangers have too many powertrain, suspension, and brake failures. **"Real" city/highway fuel economy:** 4×2 and 2.5: 11.7/8.8 L/100 km. 4×2 and 3.0: 14.0/9.4 L/100 km. 4×2 and 4.0: 13.9/9.7 L/100 km. 4×4 and 3.0: 14.8/10.6 L/100 km. 4×4 and 4.0: 14.7/10.9 L/100 km. **Maintenance/repair costs:** Below average; the wide availability of cheaper, independent garages keeps costs down. **Parts:** Parts are easy to find and relatively inexpensive when bought from independent suppliers. **Extended warranty:** A toss-up. Most components are fairly durable, except for some powertrain, brake, and electrical glitches. **Best alternatives:** A Dodge Ram, equipped with manual transmission and a Cummins diesel, a Honda Ridgeline, or a Nissan Frontier V6. **Helpful websites:** *www.carcomplaints.com/Ford/Ranger*; *www.therangerstation.com/forums/forumdisplay.php?f=86*; and *http://forums. mazdaworld.org/109-b-series-truck*.

Strengths and Weaknesses

ALERT! Get behind the wheel to ensure you have a good view of the road and cabin instruments and gauges. The low seat has been troublesome for short-statured drivers. These small pickups are also noted for out-of-round brake rotor wear. Pull the car's wheels and check the rotors and discs before purchase.

Good engine performance (4.0L V6), well-designed interior, comfortable seating, user-friendly control layout, four-door extended cab, good off-road handling, and good resale value. On the minus side: a fuel-thirsty 3.0L V6, a harsh ride, excessive braking distance, the 4×4's extra height hinders easy entry and exit, rear doors are hinged at the back and won't open independent of the front doors, the spare tire can be difficult to remove, and many safety-related complaints reported to NHTSA. Assembly and component quality are average. Reliability isn't impressive. Owners note some engine problems (poor idle, surge, and stalling), erratic transmission performance and failure, and brake and fuel system problems. Other negatives: wind noise from the windshield cowl, top-of-door glass seal, or the weather stripping moulding area; water leaks through the rear window; mediocre AC performance; and premature paint peeling and delamination.

VEHICLE HISTORY: 2002—Models joined by an XLT FX4 off-road 4×4 model, which comes equipped with heavy-duty suspension, 31-inch tires, a heftier skid plate, and tow hooks. **2003**—3.0L V6 engine gets eight more horses. All models add thicker glass and more insulation. **2006**—A slightly restyled exterior. **2009**—No more 3.0L V6. Model lineup is reduced to a 143 hp 2.3L 4-cylinder or a 207 hp 4.0L V6. **2010**—Side airbags and electronic stability control. *Mazda Tribute:* **2010**—V6 engines run on E85 fuel; improved fuel economy; automatic locking doors; and auto-dimming rearview mirror/backup camera on the GTs.

Safety Summary

All models/years: Ford Ranger and Mazda B-series passengers slam their heads into the back glass during sudden stops or in rear-end collisions. • Steering-wheel lock-up. • Excessive shaking when cruising. • Malfunctioning airbags; burns caused by airbag deployment. • Defective tie-rod. • When parked on an incline with shifter lever in Park and the vehicle idling, the truck jumped into Neutral and rolled away. • Transmission failures:

> Ford tech consultants revealed that this is happening to many Ford Rangers, but no recall has been issued. Apparently, the torque on the transmission was increased without redesigning the transmission or seals to be able to withstand the higher load.

Driveshaft sheared off while driving at high speed. • Fuel leaks (tank and fuel lines). • Sudden acceleration, often when braking. • A faulty idle air control valve may be responsible for the vehicle not decelerating properly. • Stalling. • Complete loss of ABS. • Gas and brake pedals are too close together. • Brakes don't work properly, with stuck brake calipers, overheating, and excessive pad and rotor wear. • Windshield wiper comes on by itself, or won't come on at all. • Tire-tread separation. *Ranger:* **2002**—A large number of serious safety-related incidents have been reported. • Sudden acceleration after vehicle jumps from Park into gear. • Premature replacement of clutch slave cylinder. • Complete brake failure because of a defective idle control, among other causes. • Rear shock absorbers quickly wear out. • Front tire falls off because of defective carter pin. • Interior and exterior lights go out intermittently. **2003**—Throttle sticks as pedal sinks to the floor. • Misaligned driver-side door allows wind and water entry. **2004**— Chronic stalling, loss of power. • Stuck accelerator. • Airbags failed to deploy. • Vehicle left in Park with the engine idling shifted into Reverse. • Transmission slippage; slams into gear. • Frequent brake lock-up when brakes are applied. • When the front seat was pushed rearward, a window popped out. • High rear head restraints block side and rear visibility. • Odometer can't be seen in daylight. **2006**—Many reports that a faulty inertia switch causes the truck to stall randomly. • Leaking drivetrain seals cause the pinion bearing to fail ($1,000 U.S. to repair). • Front wheel bearing failures. • Wipers come on when they shouldn't and won't engage when they should. **2007**—Fire ignites in the passenger-side dash airbag housing. • Airbag failed to deploy. • Sudden failure of the front control arm. • Side doors shake and rattle at highway speeds. • Excessive shimmy and shake at 70 km/h. • Exterior mirrors are too small. • Ice and snow build up in the grooves of the wheels. • Many complaints of cracked tire valve stems that cause tires to rapidly lose air on the road. **2008**—Fire ignited from fuel leaking from the gas tank. • The non-tilting steering wheel hampers tall drivers from lifting their foot from the gas pedal to apply the brakes. • The brake and gas pedals are too close together and placed at the same height. **2009**—Truck won't slow down after the gas pedal is released. • Rotors need to be turned after a year's use. • Excessive steering shake. • In cold weather, doors freeze shut. • Continental Conti-Trac tire sidewall blows out. **2010**—Sudden, unintended acceleration after cancelling cruise control. • Fuel line split. • Short-statured drivers do not have enough seat elevation to see the roadway. • High-frequency vibration from the engine that numbs driver's hands after an hour or so of driving. Interestingly, similar comments have been posted on the Internet by owners of other Ranger model years. • The tailgate fell off the truck.

Secret Warranties/Internal Bulletins/Service Tips

All models: Keep in mind that Ford service bulletins will likely also apply to Mazda, and Mazda's to Ford. *Ranger:* **1993–2008**—Paint delamination, peeling, or fading. *B-series:* **All years:** TSB #006/94 outlines all the possible causes and remedies for brake vibration or pulsation. **1998–2005**—Driveline clunk remedy. **2001–10**—4.0L engine buzzing. **2002–03**—Noisy manual transfer-case shifter. **2002–09**—Rear brake "grabbing." **2007–10**—Delayed automatic transmission gear engagement. **2008–11**—Window chatter/shudder when operated. **2008**—Coolant leak from the block heater. **2010**—Engine rattle, tick on cold start-up. *Mazda 2300:* **2002–09**—Rear drum brakes grabbing. **2007–09**—Engine drone, moan at idle. **2007–10**—Cold starts produce a high idle speed. • Delayed gear engagement.

RANGER/B-SERIES PROFILE

	2002	2003	2004	2005	2006	2007	2008	2009	2010
Cost Price ($)									
Ranger/XL	18,595	17,395	16,775	17,810	18,299	18,299	15,399	15,899	17,799
B2300/3000	16,680	16,995	17,395	17,595	17,995	17,995	14,995	15,250	15,795
B4000 4×4	27,495	28,840	28,495	28,695	27,295	27,496	22,375	18,995	18,895
Used Values ($)									
Ranger/XL ▲	2,000	2,500	3,000	3,500	4,500	5,000	6,000	8,000	9,500
Ranger/XL ▼	1,500	2,000	2,500	3,000	4,000	4,500	5,000	7,000	8,500
B2300/3000 ▲	1,500	2,000	2,500	3,000	3,500	5,500	7,000	7,500	8,500
B2300/3000 ▼	1,500	1,500	2,000	2,500	3,000	4,000	6,000	6,500	7,500
B4000 4×4 ▲	3,500	4,000	4,500	5,000	6,000	7,500	8,500	10,000	12,500
B4000 4×4 ▼	3,000	3,500	4,000	4,500	5,500	6,500	7,500	9,000	11,000
Reliability	3	3	3	3	3	3	4	4	4
Crash Safety (F)	4	4	4	4	4	5	5	5	—
Side	5	5	5	5	5	5	5	5	—
Offset	3	3	3	3	3	3	3	3	3
Head Restraints (F)	—	—	5	5	**1**	**1**	**1**	**1**	5
Rollover Resistance	3	3	—	3	3	3	3	3	—

Note: Although a new Mazda B4000 4×4 once cost almost $10,000 more than the Ford Ranger, this difference is now just a few thousand dollars.

All ratings on a numbered scale where 5 is good and **1** is bad. See page 132 for a more detailed description.

General Motors

RATING: Average (2006–10); Below Average (1999–2005). *Hybrid:* Not Recommended (2005–2010). **Ideal model year:** Buy a 2008 front-drive Silverado for $12,500; hopefully, the 2007 redesign glitches will have been corrected by then. This way, you keep your buy-in low, there may be some factory warranty left, and can sell the truck after a few years for $8,000. The pricier 2010s are also a good choice principally for their side/curtain airbags, fuel-sipping variable-valve engine timing and six-speed automatic transmission. All for $17,000 (price new: $26,260). A same year Hybrid (not Recommended) would cost almost $30,000 (price new: $47,505). **"Real" city/highway fuel economy:** *4.3 V6 manual: 14.1/9.5 L/100 km. 4.3 V6 automatic: 14.6/10.6 L/100 km. 4.8 V8 automatic: 14.6/10.5 L/100 km. 5.3 V8 automatic: 16.2/12.0 L/100 km. 5.3 V8 automatic hybrid: 10.4/13.2 L/100 km. 6.0 V8 automatic: 16.6/11.7 L/100 km.* **Maintenance/repair costs:** Upkeep costs for these trucks are high; use independent garages to keep costs down. **Parts:** Mechanical parts are widely available and reasonably priced due to the proliferation of independent suppliers. **Extended warranty:** A good idea for the powertrain, judging by consumer complaints and the high incidence of diesel engine deficiencies. **Best alternatives:** A Dodge Ram with a manual transmission and a Cummins diesel, Ford's Ranger or Mazda's 2300/4000, Honda's Ridgeline, or Nissan's Frontier V6 or Rogue. **Helpful websites:** *www.gmtruckclub.com/forum/forum.php; www.carcomplaints.com/Chevrolet/Silverado;* and *www.carcomplaints.com/Chevrolet/1500_Pickup.*

Strengths and Weaknesses

ALERT! Get used to a clunk sound when the automatic transmission changes gear. GM says it's "normal." Yes, it is—for General Motors. And, don't forget the head restraints (especially on the 2009 and later models). Can you really endure driving with your chin tucked into your chest? A deal-breaker? You bet.

Similar to Detroit's other pickups, these models are classed as 1500 half-ton, 2500 three-quarter-ton, and 3500 one-ton models. They come with a wide range of engine options, body styles, and bed sizes. The "C" designation refers to 4×2, and the "K" designation to 4×4. The 3500 series offers a four-door cab with a full rear seat. The variety of cab and cargo bed combinations, along with a choice of suspensions, makes these pickups adaptable to just about any use. Standard features include one of the biggest cabs among pickups, a fourth door, a three-piece modular truck frame, rack-and-pinion steering, and four-wheel disc brakes with larger pads and rotors.

An AutoTrac AWD drivetrain allows the driver to select an automatic mode that delivers full-time 4×4 (particularly useful if you live in a snowbelt area), while a

4-speed automatic features an innovative tow/haul mode that stretches out the upshifts to tap the engine's power at its maximum. GM also offers a potent family of four Vortec V8s in addition to a 6.6L turbodiesel (360 hp), 16-inch tires and wheels, and the highest minimum ground clearance among the Detroit pickups.

Chevy and GMC full-sized pickups are good domestic workhorses—when they're running. Of course, that's the problem: They're not dependable. On the one hand, they have a large, quiet cabin and give relatively easy access to the interior. On the other hand, their size and heft make for lousy fuel economy, a mediocre ride, and subpar handling and braking. Resale value? Don't ask.

For over a decade, Sierras and Silverados have been plagued with severe vibrations that GM has routinely ignored. Owners have nicknamed their trucks "Shakerados," and they say that the new frame braces added to the 2001s to stop the shakes haven't worked (see *agmlemon.freeservers.com/index.html*).

Never-ending powertrain and brake repairs and complaints of excessive vibration often sideline the vehicle for days at a time, and dealer repair suggestions often don't make any sense. GM plant workers claim that the porous frame used on both Sierras and Silverados cracks behind the cabin and near the tow hook.

The 1999–2006 models got many new features that make them more powerful, versatile, and accommodating, and they're safer than previous models. However, these changes also make them less reliable than the pickups they replaced. Major powertrain, brake, suspension, electrical system, and body deficiencies have turned these "dream machines" into motoring nightmares.

The 6.0L Duramax diesel has always had serious reliability and performance problems. The base 4.3L V6 needs more grunt, the transmission hunts for the right gear and produces an incessant whine, the base suspension provides a too-compliant ride, and there's insufficient room for the driver to reach between the door panel and seat to access the seat-adjusting mechanism. An incredibly high number of performance- and safety-related complaints regarding 2006 and earlier models have been reported to NHTSA and confirmed through confidential bulletins, whistle-blowers, and disappointed owners.

2007–10 Sierra and Silverado

The 2007 redesign produced mediocre trucks with only marginally improved performance and reliability. Improvements include a larger cabin, higher ground clearance, good noise insulation, and a rattle-resistant body. You will also find a more-stylish interior; user-friendly instruments and controls; large, supportive seats; lots of leg clearance; and wide-opening doors with useful pull-lever handles.

On the other hand, there are many minuses with the newer models: Hybrid systems and cylinder deactivation haven't produced promised fuel savings. You still get a mediocre ride, problems with brakes and steering are omnipresent, and handling continues to be compromised by lots of body roll and under-steer when cornering, and by serious chassis shake when going over potholed roads. Quality control is only slightly better than with previous models.

VEHICLE HISTORY: 2003—Quadrasteer expands to other models; an improved electrical system and passenger-side airbag sensor; a new centre console; and dual-zone temperature and steering-wheel controls. **2004**—Standard cruise control, power door locks, and a CD player. **2006**—A new 360 hp 6.6L V8 turbodiesel engine late in the model year; Quadrasteer option dropped. **2007**—Active Fuel Management cylinder deactivation with the 5.3L V8; more-powerful engines (the 4.8L V8 gets 10 more horses, the 5.3L gets five more, and the 6.0L gets 22 more); a 980 kg (2,160 lb.) payload rating; and towing capability boosted to 4,763 kg (10,500 lb.). Also, a reinforced chassis, upgraded suspension and steering systems, a larger cabin and bed, and new exterior and interior styling. Standard stability control on Crew Cabs. **2008**—A minor instrument panel revision. **2009**—A hybrid model for the 1500; a new 403 hp 6.2L V8; and a 6-speed automatic transmission. **2010**—Side/curtain airbags on all 1500 models; most engines add E85 flexible fuel capability; the 6.0L option on non-hybrid 1500 models is dropped; variable valve timing is standard with the 4.8L and 5.3L engines; and a 6speed automatic transmission is added to all models equipped with the 5.3L engine.

Safety Summary

All models/years: Sudden, unintended acceleration. • Airbag fails to deploy. • Intermittent loss of power steering. • Brake failures (pedal goes to the metal with no braking effect) with ABS light constantly lit. • Brake pad failure and warped rotor. • Parking brake doesn't hold. • ABS doesn't engage; results in extended stopping distances and wheel lock-up. • Chronic stalling. **All models: 2002**—Fire ignites in the dash. • Throttle sticks. • Chronic engine surging when braking. • Automatic transmission suddenly downshifts when accelerating, as engine surges then clunks into gear. • Passenger-side front end suddenly collapses (replace outer tie-rod end). • Steel wheel collects water that freezes and throws wheel out of balance. • Steering-column bolt comes apart. • Interior rear-view mirror distortion. • Dimmer switch overheats. • Driver's seatback will suddenly fall backwards. • Head restraint blocks vision to right side of vehicle. **2002–04**—Steering wheel locks up while driving. **2003**—Fire ignites in the engine compartment. • Cracked transmission transfer case. • Automatic transmission slips when shifting from First to Second gear. • 4×4 shifts erratically, causing serious highway instability. • Seat belts lock up. • Tailgate pops open. **2004**—Front axle assembly collapses. • Sway bar mounting bracket breaks, causing the frame and mounting bar to come off. • Brakes are too soft and set too close to the accelerator pedal. • Cruise control surges when going downhill. • Transmission suddenly jumps from Second gear to Reverse. • Tailgate falls apart. • Doors won't unlock in cold weather. • Driver's door window shatters for no reason. • Hood coil spring fails. • Jack slips off the vehicle. • Side mirrors constantly vibrate and are easily scratched when wiped clean. **2005**—Airbag warning light comes on, even when seat is occupied by an adult. • Sudden acceleration and chronic stalling:

> Diesel system has a problem transferring fuel into the truck for use. It runs out while the front fuel tank is still full of fuel. The fuel tank never reads over half full.

Transmission slips when accelerating, making the truck an easy target when turning into an intersection. • Sudden driveshaft failure:

> GMC Sierra 1500 Crew Cab; while driving at interstate speed, the drive shaft fell off the vehicle and shattered. There was substantial damage to the underside of the vehicle, including muffler, yoke, heat shield, and drive shaft.

The 4.3L engine and 4-speed automatic transmission work poorly together, constantly downshifting and gear hunting when going up an incline. • On diesels, fuel gauge and transfer pump fail repeatedly. • Rear diesel tank sprays fuel on the highway. • Vehicle is hard to move from a stopped position; feels like the rear brakes are locked up (change master cylinder). • Front brakes seem to stick, then overheat and catch fire. • Front doors won't close properly. • Jack bends under weight of vehicle and collapses. **2006**—Erratic cruise-control performance:

> When you are driving using the cruise control and start up a hill the truck slows down at least 10 miles an hour [16 km/h] then suddenly without warning the cruise control system jolts the truck forward trying to compensate for the loss of speed....It has happened to us going up hills and around hilly curves. If I did not keep both hands on the wheel I very well could have lost control and crashed.

Rear drum brakes perform poorly. • Loose steering. • Front tires rub against the suspension when the steering wheel is turned to the extreme. • Automatic door lock cannot be overridden. • Headliner falls down. **2006–07**—Hard-shifting manual transmission. **2007**—Passenger-side airbag is disabled even though an adult is seated. • The 5.3L V8 with Active Fuel Management will not idle properly or slow down in a timely manner. • Steering, brake lock-up. • Dash gauges are hard to read in daylight (especially the speedometer). • Truck bounces all over the road. • Failed welds under the front seat. • Windshield distortion. • Inoperative tire-pressure monitor system. • Cracked tow hitch receiver. **2008–09**—Failure of door lock actuators. **2008**—Vehicle will suddenly stall while underway. • Erratic AC performance. • Fire ignites near the transmission. • Premature wearout of the brake pads and rotors. • Windshield cracking under the driver-side moulding. • Rear driver-side tire/wheel fell off. **2009**—Vehicle caught fire due to a defective under-hood wiring harness. • In another fire, the origin was determined to be the electronic control module in the front dash area. • A third fire reportedly started in the passenger-side dashboard area, also while parked. • Sudden, unintended acceleration. • Airbag fails to deploy. • Both curtain side airbags deployed when truck went over a pothole • Poorly designed head restraints. Short drivers will have their head pushed too far forward. • Engine suddenly shuts down. Driver must wait five minutes, then re-start. • Cruise control doesn't slow down the vehicle on grades or small slopes. • Overheated door wiring can burn a hole in the interior door panel. • Child can open the doors while truck is in motion. • Doors shake and rattle when driving, despite recall to change the striker plate (hinges, latches, and seals were all replaced. • Weak brake pedal back pressure causes the brakes to feel spongy as they go all the way to the floor. Driver has to continually pump the brake to stop:

> Really bad in an emergency stop or when you have a light trailer on that doesn't require separate brakes on trailer. I had it both on 1500 4×4 2008 GMC and on the same 2009 Chevy I have now.

Premature brake rotor (warped) replacement. • Headlights flicker constantly. They flash on and off whenever the brakes are applied. • Sun visors don't block the sun's rays sufficiently. • Passenger's rear window shattered while the pickup was parked. • General AmeriTrac tires have premature wear on the sides and flat spots on the tread. • Spare tire fell from underneath the 2500 Silverado. It was determined the tire was too heavy for the supporting brackets. **2010**—Defrost doesn't work well, especially when it is raining:

> When the air temp starts to drop to about 35 degrees the truck automatically turns off the air conditioner compressor and if there is any moisture on the coil it is then blown into the cab of the truck and severely fogs up the inside windows making it impossible to see out. Had to pull over and keep windows down until the moisture evaporated. (Shower effect on mirror.)

Side seat bracket rusting. • Weak car jack; would not raise the truck to change a tire. • General AmeriTrac tires are prone to early tread separation. • Premature front brake pad wear; spongy brakes.

Secret Warranties/Internal Bulletins/Service Tips

All models: 1999–2004—Prematurely worn and noisy brake rotors and pads may be replaced with higher-quality aftermarket parts for about half the price. • GM says in TSB #00-05-23-005B that owners should invest in a GM mud flap kit (Part #15765007) to make their rear brakes last longer. Again, save money by shopping at independent retailers. • Inoperative power windows. • Remedy for steering-wheel clunk. • Suspension clunk, slap. **1999–2005**—Install an exhaust system flex pipe kit to stop an exhaust moan, vibration. **1999–2007**—Engine misfire may be due to an ECM ground terminal that has corroded with rust. Inspect the main engine wiring harness ground terminal (G103) for this condition. **1999–2009**—Silencing rear leaf spring noise. **2000–04**—Troubleshooting delayed gear engagement. **2001–02**—Troubleshooting tips to correct no-starts, a blank PRNDL, or slow or no automatic transmission engagement. **2001–03**—The torque converter relief spring and lube regulator spring may need to be changed to correct automatic transmission delayed shifts or loss of power. • TSB #01-07-30-043 and 03-07-30-031 explain why the automatic transmission may slip or leak. **2001–05**—Fuel gauge reads empty on trucks with a spare tank. **2002**—1–2 shift shudder. •

Clunk noise from under the hood. • Shudder or vibration when accelerating from a stop. • Water leak at the roof centre clearance light. • Inability to control temperature setting. • Intermittent failing of the tail lights, backup lights, or trailer harness. **2002–09**—Front axle whine or click. **2003**—Harsh automatic transmission 1–2 shifting; slipping likely caused by a faulty pressure control solenoid. **2003–04**—Inoperative front power window. **2004–10**—Underbody pop, clunk when turning. **2005**—Troubleshooting tips for poor automatic transmission performance. **2005–11**—Reduced engine power (repair instrument panel to body harness connector. **2006–07**—V8 engine oil leaks. • AC doesn't cool; noisy compressor. **2007**—No-starts; loss of power. • Power-steering leaks. • Water leaks into the rear footwell area. **2007–08**—Sunroof water leak onto headliner. • Front fender buzz, rattle. • Compressor, serpentine belt noise. • AC defaults to full Hot or full Cold. **2007–09**—Flare and/or harsh 2–3 shifts. • Oil leak at oil cooler hose/pipe assembly. • Clunk noise when stopping or starting out. • Buzzing, snapping, or popping exhaust system. • Door wind noise and water leaks. **2007–10**—Rear suspension clunking noise. • Excessive interior wind noise. • Engine valve lifter tick noise at startup. • Inoperative heated seats. • Warped fender liners. • Troubleshooting sunroof leaks. • Sun visor fails to stay in place **2007–11**—Engine valve lifter tick noise at start-up (V8 engines with Active Fuel Management). • Inoperative low-beam headlights. • Front end suspension noises. • Exhaust heat shield buzz. • Squeak noise from rear of vehicle. Excessive interior wind noise. **2007–12**—Engine oil leak at engine oil cooler hose/pipe adapter to engine. Warped/wavy fender liners. **2008**—Campaign for tire bead inspection and free tire replacement if needed. **2008–09**—Side door window problems. • Water leaks onto driver's side floor. **2008–11**—Steering fluid leaks. **2009–10**—Causes of reduced engine power. **2009–11**—Front brake pulsation, vibration (install upgraded brake pads). • Exhaust system leak, rattle, or rumble. **2010–11**—Excessive cabin moisture/reduced window cleaning signals the need to reprogram the AC ventilation system. *Diesel engines:* **1999–2002**—Special policy covers fuel injection pump failure up to 11 years/193,000 km:

SPECIAL POLICY ADJUSTMENT (REPLACE INJECTOR)

BULLETIN NO.: 04039   DATE: JUNE 2004

2001–02 Silverado/Sierra (6.6l Duramax Diesel)

CONDITION: Some customers of 2001–02 model year Chevrolet Silverado and GMC Sierra vehicles, equipped with a 6.6L Duramax Diesel (RPO LB7—VIN Code 1) engine, may experience vehicle service engine soon (SES) light illumination, low engine power, hard start, and/or fuel in crankcase, requiring injector replacement, as a result of high fuel return rates due to fuel injector body cracks or ball seat erosion.

SPECIAL POLICY ADJUSTMENT: This special policy covers the condition described above for a period of 7 years or 200,000 miles (320,000 km), whichever occurs first, from the date the vehicle was originally placed in service, regardless of ownership. The repairs will be made at no charge to the customer.

2001–04—Free O-ring replacement. **2001–06**—Troubleshooting a turbocharger failure. **2004–10**—Oil leak at charge air cooler/air inlet adapter. • Drive belt chirp, squeal at cold idle. **2007–09**—GM says 6.6L Duramax diesel ticking is acceptable. **2008**—Free replacement of the turbocharger vane position sensor on the 6.6L diesel.

C/K, SIERRA, SILVERADO PROFILE

	2002	2003	2004	2005	2006	2007	2008	2009	2010
Cost Price ($)									
Sierra, Silverado	22,410	23,330	24,070	24,925	22,650	28,245	28,395	23,990	26,260
Hybrid	—	—	—	35,140	42,040	33,025	—	46,725	47,505
Used Values ($)									
Sierra, Silverado ▲	4,000	4,500	5,000	6,000	7,500	10,500	13,000	15,000	17,500
Sierra, Silverado ▼	3,500	4,000	4,500	5,500	6,500	9,000	11,000	13,500	16,000
Hybrid ▲	—	—	—	8,000	9,000	11,500	—	24,000	30,000
Hybrid ▼	—	—	—	7,000	8,000	10,000	—	22,500	28,500
Reliability	2	2	3	3	3	3	3	3	3
Hybrid	—	—	—	2	3	3	3	3	3
Crash Safety (F)	—	—	4	4	4	5	5	5	5
Ext. cab	3	4	4	4	—	5	5	5	5
Hybrid	—	—	—	—	—	—	—	5	5
Side	—	—	—	—	—	1	5	5	4
Side (NHTSA)	—	—	—	—	—	5	5	—	3
Offset	2	2	2	2	2	5	5	5	5
Head Restraints	1	1	1	1	1	3	3	3	3
Rollover Resistance	—	—	4	4	4	4	4	4	4
Ext. cab	3	4	4	4	4	4	4	—	4
Ext. cab 4×4	3	3	4	4	4	4	4	—	4
Hybrid	—	—	—	—	—	—	—	4	4

Note: Hybrid prices are all over the board. Drive a hard bargain.

Honda

RIDGELINE ★★★★★

RATING: Recommended (2007–10); Above Average (2006). An almost perfect pickup, except for its high initial buy-in price, which can be easily avoided by buying used. A big plus is that Honda's first-year vehicles and redesigns haven't been as glitch-prone as Detroit's reworked products, Toyota's redesigned Sienna, or Nissan's revamped Quest. **Ideal model year:** A 2007 EX-L front-drive for $15,000 is the best buy; the truck will have depreciated about $25,000 and Honda will have had ample time to correct most of the first-year production mistakes. The 2009 model is another good buy if you want a bit more engine power and torque. It will cost you $8,000 more than the 2007 version (price new: $40,790). **"Real" city/highway fuel economy:** 14.4/10.1 L/100 km. **Maintenance/ repair costs:** Very low due to good quality control and the availability of servicing at any Honda dealership or independent garage. **Parts:** Mechanical parts are widely available and reasonably priced due to the proliferation of independent suppliers. Body parts may be costly and in short supply due to Honda's quasi-monopoly of body panels. **Extended warranty:** A waste of money. These pickups are too well made to need any extra warranty help. Also, if a vehicle failure falls outside of the warranty period, Honda has been generous in granting "goodwill" coverage to pay for the repairs. **Best alternatives:** The Dodge Ram with a manual transmission and a Cummins diesel, Ford's Ranger or F-Series, a Mazda B-Series, or a Nissan Frontier V6 or Rogue. **Helpful websites:** *www. carcomplaints.com/Honda/Ridgeline* and *www.ridgelineownersclub.com/forums.*

Strengths and Weaknesses

ALERT! Some drivers' power seats "rock" back and forth; clearly a warrantable item. Here's the catch: some dealers are saying the problem is "normal" and delaying repairs until the warranty has expired. Don't let this happen. The seat and mechanism could cost $1,000 to replace.

The Ridgeline, built in Alliston, Ontario, is Honda's first truck—a crew cab cloned from the company's Pilot sport-utility. It's about as long as the Explorer Sport Trac and comes with lots of standard features like all-wheel drive, a 5-speed automatic, Vehicle Stability Assist (electronic stability control) with traction control, ABS, front side airbags and full-length side curtain airbags with rollover sensor, and power locks, windows, and mirrors. The 2006–10 models haven't changed much, except for a minor exterior and interior restyling of the 2009s.

This pickup has quite a lot going for it, beginning with deflated prices due to slumping truck sales throughout the industry. Very smooth engine performance with exceptionally quick, carlike throttle response; agile handling and enhanced ride comfort, thanks to front and rear independent suspension; and good braking. The truck uses a smooth and reliable 5-speed automatic transmission borrowed from the Pilot and extra traction can be obtained by using a dash-mounted button to lock in power to the rear wheels. The vehicle is well appointed, with plenty of innovative and easily accessed cabin storage compartments; large, user-friendly cabin instruments and controls; plenty of rear legroom; and rear seats that can be stowed vertically, creating extra storage space. The versatile box has a trunk built into the floor, accessed through a tailgate that swings out as well as down; the bed surface has a strong plastic protective layer with tie-down hooks and tire indents to carry motorcycles or an ATV; and there's no rear wheelwell intrusion into the bed area. Excellent fit and finish; and the unibody construction reduces body flexing and creaking, keeping road noise to a minimum. Good quality control.

Some of the Ridgeline's minuses: It's overpriced for a compact truck; acceleration is a bit slower than with competitive V6-equipped pickups; there are no powertrain options; it lacks low-range gearing; low-speed steering is a bit slow; it is not built for heavy-duty hauling, towing, or serious off-roading; and there's excessive body lean when cornering. Rear visibility is hampered by the sloping sides and small rear window, rear-seat padding is thin, the seatback is too upright, leather trim isn't very durable, door openings are a bit narrow, and tailgate latches often jam shut.

Owner complaints include hesitation when accelerating and fuel pump, tie-rod, and suspension strut failures. There are some complaints of water leaking into the cabin, windshield stress cracks, and wipers overwhelmed by heavy snow. The truck bed is easily scratched, and early Ridgelines don't support trailers with surge brakes. When pulling a trailer, make sure you are within the recommended towing range: some owners report that their rear axle collapsed. Cracked wheel rims are common.

Safety Summary

2006—Fire originating in the AC. • Airbags fail to deploy, and seat belts malfunction in a collision. • Some child safety seats cannot be installed. • Accelerator surging. • Engine shuts down suddenly; must be replaced. • Fuel tank is easily punctured by road debris. • Parking lights will not stay lit. • Tire jack will not raise vehicle high enough to change a tire. **2007**—Child safety seat tether strap fails to lock. • Gas and brake pedals mounted too close together. **2008**—Engine surging. • Rear side window implodes. • Many reports that the AC wiring harness melts. • Wipers work well until they pack the snow on the bottom part of the windshield and then they quit. • Tailgate cables loosen. • The car jack can barely lift the car and bends at its maximum height (see *www.ridgelineownersclub.com/forums/showthread.php*). **2009**—Overheated automatic transmission. • Vehicle constantly pulls to the right. **2010**—Rear passenger window exploded for no reason. • Weak door latches often fail, forcing passengers to hold the door closed. • Ice collects inside the wheel rim causing the vehicle to shake excessively when driven. • Windshield wipers are mounted too low; they get stuck whenever snow collects on the windshield and cowl.

Secret Warranties/Internal Bulletins/Service Tips

2006–07—Automatic transmission is hard to shift into Fourth gear. • Vehicle pulls, drifts to one side. • Drivetrain ping, squeal, or rattle upon light acceleration. • Rear differential noise, judder on turns. • Steering wheel, interior squeaking noise. **2006–08**—Timing belt chirping. **2006–09**—Parking brake won't release in cold weather because of water infiltration. • Noise and judder when turning. **2006–10**—Steering column clicking when turning. **2006–11**—Rear seat leg doesn't fold flat. **2009–10**—Headliner vibrates or rattles. • Whistling from the front door windows. • Gap between the front bumper and the fender/headlamp. **2009–11**—Tailgate won't open in swing mode; handle is stiff. • Front seats squeak and creak.

RIDGELINE PROFILE

	2006	2007	2008	2009	2010
Cost Price ($)					
LX/DX	35,200	35,600	35,820	34,490	34,990
EX-L	39,700	40,300	40,520	40,790	41,490
Used Values ($)					
LX/DX ▲	12,000	15,000	18,000	22,000	25,500
LX/DX ▼	10,500	13,500	16,500	20,000	24,000
EX-L ▲	13,000	15,500	20,000	23,500	30,000
EX-L ▼	11,500	14,500	18,500	25,000	28,500
Reliability	4	5	5	5	5
Crash Safety (F)	5	5	5	5	5
Side	5	5	5	5	5
Side (IIHS)	5	5	5	5	5
Offset	5	5	5	5	5
Head Restraints	2	2	2	5	5
Rollover Resistance	4	4	4	4	4

Nissan

FRONTIER ★★★★★

best buy

RATING: Recommended (2005–10); Above Average (1999–2004). Nissan has hit a home run with its Frontier. Year after year, this "Baby Titan" pickup performs well without any major complications, bypassing the serious design glitches found with Nissan's earlier Titans. It's as good as the Mazda and Honda competition, and is more frugal and better performing than GM's puny, Isuzu-bred Canyon/Colorado munchkins. Sure, the pre-2005s are mediocre performers; nevertheless, they are reliable, relatively inexpensive, competent for light chores, easy to maintain, and fun to drive. Plus, they won't "run away" from you like Toyota's Tacoma and Tundra pickups. **Ideal model year:** A 2007 V6-equipped King Cab SE front-drive for $9,000 is the best choice as far as cost is concerned. But from a cost, safety, and performance standpoint, you can't beat the better-equipped 2010 version of the same model for $15,000 (price new: $26,248). **"Real" city/highway fuel economy:** *2.5 4-cylinder: 10.7/8.7 L/100 km. 2.5 4-cylinder automatic: 12.6/9.2 L/100 km. 4.0 V6: 13.5/10.1 L/100 km. 4.0 V6 automatic: 14.4/10.2 L/100 km. 4.0 V6 4×4: 14.8/10.6 L/100 km.* **Maintenance/repair costs:** Upkeep costs for these pickups are relatively low. **Parts:** Mechanical parts are widely available and reasonably priced due to the generic nature of most Frontier parts and the proliferation of independent suppliers. **Extended warranty:** Not needed. **Best alternatives:** A Honda Ridgeline, Mazda B-Series, or a Nissan Rogue are all good buys. Chrysler's Ram is also an acceptable choice as long as you choose the Cummins diesel and manual transmission. **Helpful websites:** *www. carcomplaints.com/Honda/CR-V* and *www.crvownersclub.com/forums.*

Strengths and Weaknesses

ALERT! Sprayed-on bedliner may have holes and cracks that extend to the width of the box. Inspect the box before purchase. Also, verify if the truck can fill up with fuel automatically without gasoline spewing out the filler tube.

Introduced in 1985, these pickups perform better, are more comfortable, and aren't as rust-prone as their Datsun predecessors. The different 4-cylinder engines offered through the years have all provided adequate power and reasonable reliability. Although the powerful 6-cylinder is more fuel-thirsty, it's the engine of choice for maximum hauling and off-roading versatility.

You won't have to look far to find a reasonably priced Nissan pickup. These small pickups, like Mazda's trucks, didn't cost much when they were new, and their used prices have drifted downward accordingly. On newer models, though, you'll find prices have firmed up on popular two- and three-year-old crew-cab pickups and downsized sport-utilities. Depending on the year, you'll find a standard 4- or 5-speed manual or an optional 3-, 4-, or 5-speed automatic. Later 4-speed automatics have a fuel-saving lock-up torque converter, but a manual transmission will get the most power and economy out of these motors. The 4×4 option is available with either manual or automatic hubs. The manual version is a pain because you have to stop and turn the hubs. Furthermore, manual transmissions have poorly designed clutches that result in slave cylinder, disc, and pressure plate failures:

> Inherent design flaw. Brake master cylinder and clutch system share same fluid reservoir. Poss brake failure may result. I am a retired GM master mechanic, I possess more skills on car[s] and trucks than most. This system really requires redesign possible conversion to linkage clutch throw-out bearing system and a more heavy-duty flywheel (not dual mass) and more like a stage 2 or stage 3 competition clutch configuration.

The automatic isn't much better because it can't be engaged above 50 km/h, and to disengage it you have to stop and back up a metre or two. These pickups handle impressively well, though, and they provide a firm but reasonably comfortable ride, although some owners say the bucket seats fit only bucket bottoms and rear-seat comfort is an oxymoron. The King Cab is a must for tall drivers.

2004 and earlier models

Okay choices, but not the best vintage for performance and value. Standard four-wheel ABS on some models; a user-friendly interior layout; fairly reliable; an acceptable ride over smooth roads; and reasonably good handling.

The negative side? The 4.0L will run on regular fuel (wink, wink; nudge, nudge), but 91-octane is recommended. Test-drive your choice for engine performance—

Nissan has been notorious for overrating their engines. You will also find poor steering feedback, a cheap-looking interior, and limited rear seating on base models. There's a history of engine exhaust intake manifold failures; drive shaft and ball joint defects that cause excessive vibration; premature front brake wear; electrical short circuits; and minor trim and accessory defects.

Poor 4-cylinder acceleration is a given; there's lots of body lean when cornering; braking is mediocre; the Crew Cab has a small cargo bed; and there are few standard features. Some owners report drive shaft carrier bearing failures on earlier models and lots of engine, wind, and tire noise. The automatic transmission shifter obstructs the view of the climate controls and blocks access to the wiper switch. A choppy ride over uneven terrain ("rear-end hop") is accentuated if you are carrying an empty load and the slow, vague steering offers little feedback.

Other disadvantages: difficult rear entry and exit (King Cab); limited rear legroom on the hard rear bench seat; low seats make the height-adjustment feature essential for many drivers; and the King Cab's rear jump seat is laughably small. The cabin looks like plastic central, and many gauges are too recessed to be easily read. Expect mediocre fuel economy on 2001–05 models. There have been some safety complaints relative to sudden acceleration and brake failures.

2005–09 models

These newer Frontiers are significantly improved pickups that are larger, more powerful, easier to handle, and safer than previous models. The entry-level King Cab carries a 152 hp 2.5L 4-cylinder engine, while most other Frontiers use a 265 hp 4.0L V6. A 5- and 6-speed automatic replaced the 4-speed. A new dual-range 4×4 set-up with shift-on-the-fly electronic control, rack-and-pinion steering, and a slew of handling improvements was also carried over this year. Overall, these models carry better-performing, more powerful engines (especially with the V6 and vehicles equipped with a manual transmission); the new 5-speed automatic transmission shifts more smoothly than the previous 4-speed, and it conserves fuel. They boast nice handling; a very comfortable ride up front; are fairly reliable; and have a high resale value.

VEHICLE HISTORY: 2002—The regular-cab model is dropped, Crew Cabs are offered with a long bed, and all pickups get a restyled interior. **2003**—6-cylinder engines for the 4×4s and Crew Cabs get 10 more horses. **2006**—Additional trim items. **2007**—Debut of Crew Cab SE and LE Long Bed models that are 330 mm, or 13 inches longer than the previous bed. **2009**—Front end is slightly restyled. **2010**—New safety features and side/curtain airbags on all models and electronic stability control on all V6-equipped models. The SE and LE 4×4 get standard hill start and descent control assist. Box lengths are now 1.8 m (6 ft.).

Frontier pickups have always been reliable and versatile haulers. Most models initially used a lethargic 143 hp 2.4L 4-cylinder, supplemented by a better-performing 180 hp 3.3L V6 and a barely-worth-the-trouble, premium-fuelled, temperamental supercharged 210 hp V6 variant. The King Cab V6 addition gave these pickups the power boost they lacked in the past. ABS is standard on the rear wheels and optional on all four wheels. It's standard, however, on all recent 4×4s and Crew Cabs and on the Desert Runner.

Safety Summary

2001–02—Airbags fail to deploy. **2002**—Automatic transmission jumps out of Park into Reverse. • Leaking fuel tank. • Brake failure. • Sudden loss of power caused by defective oxygen sensor or Nissan speed limiter kicking in. • Controller fuse blows repeatedly, shutting down vehicle. • Gas and brake pedal set too close together. • Tail light fills with water. **2003**—Sudden, unintended acceleration when brakes are applied. • Engine has to be shut down to turn off AC if defroster is engaged. **2004**—Truck slips out of Park and rolls downhill. • Excessive vibration caused by corroded upper and lower ball joints. **2005**—Truck won't start because of a corroded fuel-sending unit. • Power-assisted driver-side mirror can't be adjusted to eliminate a blind spot. • Tailgate falls off due to its poor design. • Tailgate gap allows sand or other fine material to spew out. • Water leaking into the tail light can cause the truck to shut down. **2006**—Rollover airbags deploy for no reason. • Powertrain transfer case sticks in 4×4. • Gas and brake pedals are mounted too close together. • Right front wheel falls off due to the shearing of the wheel lug nuts. • Rear brake assembly bolts fall out, and the disc caliper flies off. • Transmission doesn't hold a vehicle stopped on an incline. • Many complaints of loss of steering due to a defective steering-column bearing. **2007**—Engine surges when brakes are applied. • Poor braking. • Steering pulls suddenly to the right, or doesn't return to centre. • Electronic computer module failure causes the vehicle to suddenly shut down. **2008**—Inadvertent airbag deployment. • Airbag is disabled when the passenger seat is occupied. • Brake master cylinder failure. • Cruise control may not stay on. • Loose rear brake caliper nut. • Excessive wind buffeting. **2009**—Brake and gas pedal are mounted too close together. • Brake pedal falls to floor when fully pressed. • Notoriously weak manual transmission clutch. • Incorrect fuel readings. • Driver-side sun visor doesn't stay in place. • Tire jack won't raise the vehicle high enough to change the tire. • Tailgate falls off when opened; may affect Frontiers back to 2005 models. **2010**—Front passenger-side airbag is disabled when a normal-sized adult occupies the seat. • Sudden loss of brakes. • Automatic transmission slippage. • Plan on 15-minute fuel fill-ups in order to keep fuel from spewing out the filler pipe. • "Hands-free" cell phones sold by Nissan dealers are of poor quality, say some owners. • Early clutch failure on the 6-speed manual transmission. • Prematurely rusted rear bumper. • Sprayed-on bedliner may have holes and cracks that extend to the width of the box.

Secret Warranties/Internal Bulletins/Service Tips

1999–2002—Troubleshooting tips for noisy, hard transfer-case shifting. • Loss of supercharged engine power. • Surging, no automatic transmission upshifts. • Steering pull during braking. • Silencing bearing noise from the transfer-case area. • Knocking noise above idle. **2000–03**—ABS warning light stays lit. **2001**—Warm air from fresh air vents. • Speedometer may not work. **2003**—Remedy for

AC that won't turn off. **2003–04**—Cold engine start-up rattle. **2004–05**—Troubleshooting spray-in bedliner defects. **2005**—More engine rattles. • Free body control module sub-harness to improve electrical connection for trailering. **2005–06**—Right front seatback rattles and moves sideways. **2005–07**—Buzzing, whining engine timing chain. • Engine chirping, squealing. • Jump seats won't stay up while driving. **2005–08**—Drivebelt noise on startup. • Low airflow from front AC air vents. • Sunroof doesn't seal correctly. • Erratic fuel gauge readings. **2005–09**—Rear driveshaft support bearing noise. **2005–10**—Rear differential axle seal leaks. • Inoperative AC blower motor. • Engine buzz, whine from timing chain area. • Front suspension popping, squeaking, and clunking. • Driveshaft U-joint noise, vibration. • Heat shield rattling. **2005–10**—Buzz, whine from engine timing chain area. • AC water leaks onto the passenger side of the carpet. **2005–11**—Excessive engine vibration or noise may be caused by a defective engine mount. • Tips for troubleshooting low-speed front brake noise. **2007–08**—Sunroof malfunctions. • Inoperative "auto up" power window. • Right front seat back vibration at highway speeds. **2007–09**—Sunroof inoperative or operates erratically. **2008**—Engine bump, thump felt on light acceleration. • AC refrigerant leaks from connections. • Troubleshooting brake judder, "feel," and noise. • Front door window rattles, creaks when windows are partially open. • Left turn signal won't cancel after turning. **2009**—Nissan will re-weld the torsion tube (it was welded out of specification and can become heavily corroded) free of charge under Voluntary Service Campaign #PC007.

FRONTIER PROFILE

	2002	2003	2004	2005	2006	2007	2008	2009	2010
Cost Price ($)									
4×2	22,890	23,498	23,450	22,998	24,298	24,448	24,448	22,598	24,098
4×4	27,553	27,398	27,400	28,998	29,598	29,748	29,748	28,148	30,048
Used Values ($)									
4×2 ▲	3,500	4,500	5,000	6,000	7,500	10,000	11,000	13,000	16,000
4×2 ▼	3,000	3,500	4,500	5,500	6,000	8,500	9,500	11,500	14,500
4×4 ▲	4,500	6,000	7,000	7,500	8,500	11,500	14,500	16,500	20,000
4×4 ▼	4,000	5,000	6,000	7,000	7,500	10,000	13,000	15,000	18,500
Reliability	5	5	5	5	5	5	5	5	5
Crash Safety (F)	4	4	4	4	4	4	4	4	4
Ext.	—	—	—	—	3	3	4	4	4
Side	5	5	4	5	5	5	5	5	5
Side (IIHS)	—	—	—	5	5	5	5	5	5
Offset	2	2	2	5	5	5	5	5	5
Head Restraints	—	—	—	1	1	1	1	1	3
Roof Strength	—	—	—	5	5	5	5	5	5
Rollover	3	3	—	—	3	3	3	3	3

All ratings on a numbered scale where 5 is good and 1 is bad. See page 132 for a more detailed description.

Toyota

RATING: Not Recommended (2002–10). Originally a low-tech, unadorned pickup, it was more reliable during its early years. Recent models are more refined and more failure-prone. They have been downgraded due to their propensity for serious sudden, unintended acceleration and for the presence of other life-threatening safety-related design defects. **Ideal model year:** A 2006 front-drive that's not rust-afflicted for $6,500. **"Real" city/highway fuel economy:** 4×2, 2.4, and *automatic:* 11.1/8.8 L/100 km. 4×4 and 2.7: 13.1/10.4 L/100 km. 4×4 and 3.4: 13.6/10.9 L/100 km. 4×2 and 4.0: 13.5/10.1 L/100 km. 4×4 and 4.0: 15.0/10.9 L/100 km. **Maintenance/repair costs:** Upkeep costs for these trucks are high; use independent garages to keep costs down. **Parts:** Mechanical parts are widely available and reasonably priced due to the proliferation of independent suppliers. **Extended warranty:** A good idea for the powertrain, judging by consumer complaints and the high incidence of engine deficiencies. **Best alternatives:** A Dodge Ram, equipped with a Cummins diesel hooked to a manual transmission, Honda's Ridgeline, the Mazda B-Series, or a Nissan Frontier V6. **Helpful websites:** *www.carcomplaints.com/Toyota/Tacoma* and *www.toyotanation.com/forum/forumdisplay.php?f=164.*

Strengths and Weaknesses

ALERT! Check out the spare tire car jack; owners have found it to be weak and unsteady. Pull the wheels and pay particular attention to the brake rotors and discs. Owners says two years' use is the maximum one can expect with the discs; three years for the rotors. When changing the brakes, go to an independent repairer who offers an extended warranty for better-quality brake parts. Finally, when considering a 2010 model, drive it at night to verify how well the low-beam headlights illuminate the roadway. Many owners say they can see no more than two car lengths ahead.

Toyota has been building good cars for quite a while, but its pickups have always missed the quality and performance mark because they were undersized, underpowered, and glitch-prone. Their mechanical reliability is no longer any better than that of American pickups, which is shameful. Tacomas don't offer a lot of razzle-dazzle or carlike handling, and their powertrain hesitation and surging can be dangerous to life, limb, and your pocketbook.

2004 and earlier models

Competent V6 engine performance; rugged, impressive off-road capability; good braking, when the brakes work as they should; a roomy interior; and relatively good build quality. The Tacoma's traditionally high resale value and reasonable fuel economy has kept operating costs down in the past.

Earlier versions are known for their mediocre ride, poor wet-weather handling, and lots of engine and road noise. They have less towing capability than domestic competitors, and may not meet the stated towing capacity (be very wary). Bereft of many standard features offered by competitors; the front seat is set too low and far back; cushions are too small in the rear seat, where legroom is limited; climate controls are obstructed by the cupholders; and difficult entry and exit require a higher step-up than with other 4×4 pickups. They come with a smaller bed than what's offered by other automakers and the StepSide bed is quite narrow.

There have been many reports of powertrain, brake (especially with 2000–03 models), and AC failures; electrical shorts; premature front brake wear; and subpar fit and finish (excessive paint chipping, wind noise, and water leaks). Some report that the truck is hard to start, the engine seizes after ingesting water when the vehicle passes through a puddle, and the inadequate lumbar support with the driver's seat is painful on long drives.

2005–08 models

More powerful 4- and 6-cylinder engines give smoother performance without guzzling much fuel; ride and handling are improved with firmer, shorter springs, gas shocks, a limited slip differential, and larger tires; towing capability increased by 680 kg (1,500 lb.); additional interior room makes back seats acceptable for adult passengers. Upgraded interior and a new composite cargo bed with extra storage compartments and adjustable tie-down anchors. Additional safety features like side curtain airbags.

While adding features to make these trucks safer, Toyota neglected other areas that present serious safety risks. For example, handling can be extremely dangerous, due to hazardous cruise control malfunctions and engine surging when braking. Overall performance is still somewhat truck-like; the 6-speed manual transmission is a bit clunky at times; rear drum brakes are not as efficient as disc; and the bed is still quite small.

Redesigned for the first time in 10 years, the 2005 Tacoma targeted the Dodge Dakota crowd with a powerful V6 and a 6-speed manual/5-speed automatic transmission to counter Dodge's at-the-time less sophisticated powertrain set-up. Set on the same platform as the 4Runner and Lexus GX 470, recent Tacomas are about 15 cm (6 in.) longer, 10 cm (4 in.) wider, and 5 cm (2 in.) taller than 2004 and earlier versions.

This compact pickup is available as a Regular Cab, Xtracab, or Double Cab (a four-door crew cab) in 4×2 or 4×4. There's no denying the added convenience of four doors, but the Double Cab also provides a 60/40 folding rear bench seat for more versatility. The 236 hp V6 beats Dodge's 215 hp 3.7L V6, Ford's 202 hp 4.2L V6, and GM's 200 hp 4.3L V6. Available engines on 2004 and earlier models are a 2.4L and 2.7L 4-cylinder and a 3.4L V6. A dealer-installed supercharger package gives the

V6 59 additional horses. The shift-on-the-fly 4×4 system is optional on 4×4 trucks and standard on the 4×4 SR5 V6.

VEHICLE HISTORY: 2003—Standard ABS and upgraded child restraint anchors. **2005**—Larger, more powerful, and equipped for the first time with side curtain airbags. **2005**—Redesign makes it bigger and more powerful. Towing capacity goes from 3,500 lbs in 2004 to 5,000 lbs for 2005. **2007**—No more Prerunner; Access Cab returns as a two- or four-wheel drive; the Double Cab is 4×4 only. **2009**—New 4-cylinder 4×4 Access Cab model; standard side and curtain airbags; head restraints, vehicle stability control and traction control, and LED combination taillights. **2010**—4×2 X-Runner dropped.

The 2005's changes brought their own set of problems to subsequent model years, including chronic cruise control and transmission breakdowns; oil leaks between the transmission and crankshaft; assorted short circuits; water leaks onto the floorboard from the A-pillar; easily chipped paint (rocker panels, lower doors, and front of the bed sides); tailgates that fail while vehicles are underway; and acid sprayed around the engine compartment by the Delphi battery. Cabin mount bolts and bushings contract and loosen in cold weather, resulting in a loud banging noise in the cabin area.

Reliability has been compromised during the past several decades by lapses in quality control, leading to expensive V6 engine head gasket failures through 2004. Automatic transmission and brake problems have carried over to the latest models.

 ## Safety Summary

All years: The Tacoma is Toyota's poster child for incidents of sudden, unintended acceleration:

> Over a period of several months after purchasing a new 2007 Toyota Tacoma, I experienced five incidents of brake/acceleration problems finally resulting in a crash. First incident: Stopped at a traffic light with my foot on the brake, the truck lunged forward a few feet. The dealership told me they could not find any problem. A month later, stopped in a gas station drive with my foot on the brake waiting to exit, the rear wheels began spinning out of control. I pressed on the brake as hard as I possibly could to keep from entering traffic. Three weeks later, approaching the bottom of a hilly sharp turn, I tapped the brakes to slow down. Again the rear wheels accelerated to a high rate of speed. I could not stop the truck to keep from striking a van in front of me so I crossed over a double yellow line to avoid a collision. It took about a thousand yards to gain control.

Airbag malfunctions. • Brake failures, overheating, extended stopping distance, and prematurely worn calipers and rotors. • Vehicle wanders all over the road after hitting a bump. • Firestone, Goodyear, and Dunlop tire-tread separation. • Loose or poorly fitted trip panels. **2002**—Brake and gas pedal mounted too close together. • Automatic transmission shudders, clunks, surges, shifts erratically, and jumps from gear to gear. • Transmission line blows out. • Water enters the cabin through the driver-side support handle. • Poorly designed jack handle makes for risky tire-changing. **2003**—Sudden rollover. • Engine surging caused by a defective throttle actuator control. • Loss of power caused by a faulty throttle body sensor (maybe the second defect could "cure" the first?):

> You can only open the throttle body butterfly the first 25% with the pedal, then the computer opens it the rest of the way. These throttle by wire [or highly-responsive accelerators] are crapping out left and right. [Toyota claims they are covered under the less-generous 3 year/60,000 km bumper-to-bumper warranty and not the 5 year/100,000 km powertrain warranty].

Truck sways and pitches excessively. • Shifter can be accidentally bumped and will shift into Neutral. • Front seats rock back and forth. • Water leaks through the passenger door onto the driver-side floor. • Doors don't close fully or lock. • Broken wheel lug nuts:

> While the inspector was placing the tires back onto the truck, two of the wheel studs broke on the front hub. He stated that this happens on almost every 2000–2003 Toyota pickup they work on. He even showed me that the stud wasn't cross-threaded and removed the stud from the lug nut using a pair of pliers. The stud came right out with little pressure.

2004—Several incidents of fires igniting while vehicles are being driven. • Front airbags don't deploy as required. • Transmission jerks when going into gear. • Parking brake hits driver's knee. • Seat lumbar supports cause lower back pain. **2005**—6-speed manual transmission has serious judder and shifts only with considerable difficulty. • Skid plate catches air and causes the vehicle to shake violently at highway speeds. • Exhaust crossover pipe hangs below the transfer-case mount and can be easily crushed when off-roading. This would allow carbon monoxide to enter into the cabin. • Left-turn signal quits intermittently. • Right side mirror vibrates excessively (especially on windy days) and also creates a large blind spot in the right front quarter of the vehicle. • Tailgate is dangerously weak, unable to support normal weight without bending out of shape. **2006**—Surging when braking, particularly on vehicles equipped with cruise control. • Throttle sticks. • Erratic cruise control/transmission operation causing violent gear shifts into the wrong gear. • Transmission pressure plate failure. • Sun visor drops down when pushed forward. • Water leaks through the firewall. **2007**—More than the average number of safety-related complaints for Toyota vehicles, including many hair-raising incidents where the vehicle suddenly accelerates during braking. • Many complaints that the cruise control suddenly goes into Overdrive. • Extremely fast idle and engine surge after a cold start. **2008**—Airbags failed to deploy. • Sudden rear differential lockup. • More reports of sudden, unexpected acceleration. Toyota's answer: "The vehicle is performing as designed." • Loss of brakes after passing over a pothole or a speed bump. • Excessive steering, suspension vibration. • Suspension bottoms out with a light load. • A child's booster seat will not fit in the rear seat. • Rainwater/drops accumulate on door window and mirror. • Contrary to claims, plastic bed cannot tie down motorcycles. **2009**—Sudden, unintended acceleration caused by a "demented" Tacoma:

> My 2009 Toyota Tacoma has a demented mind of its own when it comes to unexpected acceleration. I will describe what it has done at least 10 times in the year and a half since I (unfortunately) purchased it. As I take my foot off the accelerator and apply it to the brake, the engine speeds up to more than 7,000 rpm. I continue pressing on the brake which starts to slip. To avoid a crash I must quickly shift the transmission into neutral. As the engine reaches maximum rpm's, it then dies back to an idle. It is not the floor mat or the acceleration pedal causing this.

Owners complain that the driver has to "put the pedal to the metal" for acceptable braking; others report complete loss of braking capability. **2010**—Airbags failed to deploy. • Sudden, unintended acceleration still occurs after the recall "fix." • Vehicle constantly shudders when driven. • Clutch slippage. • When slowing down and then speeding up, transmission takes time to "hunt" for the proper gear. • Brake and accelerator pedals are mounted too close together. • Complete brake failure without any prior warning. • Fuel pump sometimes runs on after the ignition switch has been turned off. • Rodents are using the car as a "snack bar":

> While driving at speeds of 25 mph, the vehicle stalled. The Vehicle Stability Control (VSC) warning light illuminated on the instrument panel immediately after stalling. The vehicle was towed to the dealer and they advised him that rodents crawled into the vehicle and were chewing on the wires underneath the vehicle. The dealer also stated that he found a rodent "nest" in the engine compartment.

Secret Warranties/Internal Bulletins/Service Tips

All years: If there is a delay when shifting from Park or Neutral to Reverse, Toyota will install an upgraded B3 return spring, B3 Brake piston O-rings, and a low-cost modulator spring to correct the problem. Toyota doesn't say if the repair will be covered by its base warranty or "goodwill"; however, a good rule of thumb is that any transmission malfunction, like a delay in this case, would be the automaker's responsibility for at least the first 7 years/160,000 km. • Musty odours emanating from the AC may be caused by a blocked evaporator-housing drain pipe. • Consult TSB #BR94-002 and #BR95-001, where the company outlines all the possible ways brake pulsation/vibration can be further reduced. Incidentally, this problem has affected almost all of Toyota's cars and trucks over the past decade. **1997–2004**—Tips on plugging body water leaks. **1999–2002**—Tube step knocking, squeaking, and rattling fix. • Loose fender flare pad. • Tearing of the seat material on Double Cabs. **2001–03**—Special Service Campaign relative to the fuel inlet protector. **2001–04**—Front door window pane improvement. • Dash pad rattle repair tips. **2002**—Off-centre steering wheel. • MIL stays lit. **2002–06**—Correction for vehicles that pull to the side. **2003–04**—Intermittent hard cranking. **2004–10**—Front seat squeaks. **2003–11**—Tips for silencing an upper or lower windshield ticking noise. **2005**—Front cowl water leaks. **2005–07**—Intermittent no-starts. • Front brake noise when brakes applied while backing up. • Harsh rear spring ride. •

Windshield wind noise. **2005–08**—Oil leaks from the engine timing cover. • Rear differential howl, whine. • Driveline vibration. • Bent rear tailgate. **2005–09**—Suspension squeaks. **2005–10**—Manual transmission clutch slippage. • Harsh rear suspension ride with heavy loads. • Rattling on rough roads. • Water leaks onto rear carpet. **2005–11**—Manual transmission rattles in Neutral. • AC blower ticking, clicking, and squealing, or only operates on High. • Turn signal lens bubbles or is distorted. • A harsh-riding rear suspension. • Rear suspension squeaking when passing over bumps. **2007–10**—AC defrosts poorly; insufficient output. • Blower motor squealing when cold.

TACOMA PROFILE

	2002	2003	2004	2005	2006	2007	2008	2009	2010
Cost Price ($)									
Base	21,920	22,370	22,570	22,125	22,535	22,635	22,760	20,215	21,355
4×4	28,065	29,400	29,240	29,560	29,660	29,660	29,785	24,845	25,995
Used Values ($)									
Base ▲	3,500	4,000	5,000	6,000	7,000	8,500	10,500	13,000	14,500
Base ▼	3,000	3,500	4,000	5,500	6,000	7,000	9,000	11,500	13,500
4×4 ▲	5,000	6,000	7,000	8,000	9,000	12,000	13,000	14,500	16,500
4×4 ▼	4,000	5,000	6,000	7,000	7,500	10,500	12,000	13,000	15,000
Reliability	3	3	2	2	2	2	2	2	3
Crash Safety (F)									
4×2	4	—	—	5	5	5	5	5	5
Ext. Cab	3	3	3	5	5	5	5	5	—
Double	—	4	4	—	—	—	—	—	—
Side									
4×2	5	—	—	5	5	5	5	5	5
Ext. Cab	3	3	3	5	5	5	5	5	5
Double	—	5	5	—	—	—	—	—	—
Side (IIHS)	—	—	—	5	5	5	5	5	5
Offset	3	3	3	5	5	5	5	5	5
Head Restraints	—	—	—	—	—	5	5	5	5
Roof Strength	—	—	—	2	2	2	2	2	2
Rollover	2	4	4	—	4	4	4	4	4
Ext. Cab	—	2	—	—	4	4	4	4	4

TUNDRA ★

bad buy

RATING: Not Recommended (2000–2010). The rating has been downgraded because the competition has safer, better-performing models, better quality control, and cheaper prices. The many instances of sudden, unintended acceleration, brake and transmission failure complaints, and severe "bed bounce" are other negative factors. **Ideal model year:** The 2010 Tundra Regular Cab DLX 4.6 front-drive (without the bouncing and rear-end hop) for $15,000. **"Real" city/highway fuel economy:** 4×2, 3.4, and *manual:* 14.3/11.1 L/100 km. 4×2, 3.4, and *automatic:* 14.1/10.9 L/100 km. 4×4, 3.4, and *manual:* 15.4/12.1 L/100 km. 4×4, 3.4, and *automatic:* 14.4/12.3 L/100 km. 4×2, 4.0, and *automatic:* 12.7/9.7 L/100 km. 4×2, 4.7, and *automatic:* 15.6/11.9 L/100 km. 4×4, 4.7, and *automatic:* 15.4/12.6 L/100 km. 5.7 V8, and *automatic:* 15.6/11.9 L/100 km. 4×4, 5.7 V8, and *automatic:* 15.4/12.6 L/100 km. **Maintenance/repair costs:** Upkeep costs for the Tundra are outrageously high (imagine, a complete paint job every couple of years). Use independent garages to keep repair costs down. **Parts:** Mechanical parts aren't widely available, and prices are what the market will bear. Tundras aren't widely supported by independent parts suppliers. **Extended warranty:** A good idea for the powertrain, judging by consumer complaints and the high incidence of diesel engine deficiencies. **Best alternatives:** A Dodge Ram equipped with a Cummins diesel hooked to a manual transmission, Honda's Ridgeline, the Mazda B-Series, or a Nissan Frontier V6. **Helpful websites:** *www.carcomplaints.com/ Toyota/Tundra* and *www.tundratalk.net/forums.*

Strengths and Weaknesses

ALERT! How resistant are you to "shaken driver syndrome"? Don't buy a 2007–10 Tundra without a road test. Hundreds of owners report that the bouncing about is severe, and Toyota has sent out a bulletin describing the problem and fix (see "Secret Warranties").

Larger, stronger, safer, and roomier than its T100 predecessor, the 2001 Tundra was Toyota's first serious foray into the lucrative, though crowded, full-sized pickup market. Unfortunately, Toyota's new truck wasn't quite full-sized and sales suffered.

Toyota corrected that shortcoming with its 2004 models by stretching the Dana-built frame to make the Tundra more competitive with Detroit's Big Three pickups. Unfortunately, this increase in size was accompanied by a continuing decline in overall quality, which was never seriously addressed in subsequent years. Two engines, a 190 hp 3.4L V6 and a 240 hp 4.7L V8, are offered up to the 2005 model year, when the 4.0L came on board.

More power, performance, convenience, and value were added by twin-cam V8 acceleration; low-range gearing for off-roading; a smoother, quieter ride; a roomier Double Cab (2004); easier front access; better fit and finish; standard transmission and upgraded engine oil coolers; and the passenger-side airbag that can be switched off with a key.

Yet the Tundra couldn't shake its early image as a poorly designed, low-quality, glitch-prone pickup. Owners point out that the steering and suspension design is so bad that the truck can easily go out of control when passing over slightly irregular roadways. Electronics and brakes continue to be seriously weak areas, and fit and finish is deplorable.

2006 and earlier models

Less engine torque than the competition; difficult rear exit and entry; 4×4 can't be used on dry pavement (unlike the GM Silverado and Sierra); excessive body sway, and tends to be quite bouncy; poorly performing rear brake drums; rear-hinged back doors on the Access Cab don't open independently of the front doors; no four-door Crew Cab model available; and the V8 requires premium fuel. The 2003 and earlier models aren't as roomy in the rear half of the extended cab as other extended full-sized trucks—you feel like you're entering a Dodge Dakota or Ford Ranger. Paint is not up to Toyota standards. Dash LCDs are unreadable with sunglasses. Weak door indents; bland styling; and an incredibly high rate of safety-related defects involving sudden, unintended acceleration, and brake, airbag, and seat belt failures.

VEHICLE HISTORY: 2002—The Limited gets a standard in-dash CD changer, anti-lock braking, and keyless remote entry. **2003**—A new V8-equipped Access Cab StepSide model. New features include ABS, a redesigned grille and bumper, power-sliding rear window (Limited), 17-inch wheels (optional on the SR5), and a revamped centre console. **2004**—A more powerful, brawnier Double Cab that gains 30 cm (12 in.) in wheelbase and length and 7 cm (3 in.) in width. **2005**—More power, new transmissions, and optional side curtain airbags; a 245 hp 4.0L V6 replaces the 190 hp 3.4L; a 6-speed manual transmission replaces the 5-speed, and a 5-speed automatic replaces the 4-speed; the 4.7L V8 gets 42 more horses. **2007**—A redesigned Tundra. It's larger, more powerful (now equipped with an optional 381 hp 5.7L V8), and better appointed. **2008**—More variations with the Double Cab and CrewMax models, standard power front bucket seats, heated mirrors and mudguards. Limited version gets standard front and rear parking assistance. **2009**—Standard windshield de-icer and the 4×4 Double Cab and Crew Max get additional standard equipment. The 4×4 Double Cab Limited has been axed. **2010**—A 4.6L V8 replaces the 4.7L V8; standard 6-speed automatic transmission; and a standard driver's knee airbag.

The Tundra's safety-related defects, low quality, and poor reliability got worse with this last redesign. Owners report chronic stalling and surging, frequent brake failures, excessive brake caliper and rotor wear, premature transmission replacements, engine manifold rust-outs, paint peeling, and poor-quality original-equipment tires. The 2007 and 2008 models have mostly been plagued by the above-mentioned problems, plus faulty camshafts and torque converters, cracking tailgates, and even more cases of paint scratches and peeling:

> Paint is very thin (one coat). Paint cannot even be washed without scratching. Truck has scratches on it from leaning over the bed, also around all the door handles from just opening the doors, not to mention all the marks around the door and tailgate from just our hands.

Other deficiencies include excessive front-brake vibration or pulsation that makes the truck almost uncontrollable and causes it to shake violently when brakes are applied. Brake drums and rotors warp within 7,000 km; steel wheels rust prematurely; the automatic transmission binds; and overall transmission performance is poor. The ABS make a loud banging sound upon engagement; the 4×4 system grinds and pops out of gear; there's chronic rear axle noise and suspension knocking; V8 engine knocking when started in cold weather; and excessive drivetrain vibration at 100 km/h.

With many of the above deficiencies, owners say that Toyota often dismisses the problems as "normal," or blames customers for its own manufacturing errors while stonewalling legitimate claims.

 ## Safety Summary

All years: Sudden, unintended acceleration. • "Lag and lurch" acceleration. • Airbags fail to deploy. • Seat belt/retractor failures. • Vehicle rolls away after it is put in Park and the emergency brake is applied. • An incredibly high number of brake complaints relative to brake failures, rotor and drum warping, and excessive vibration/shudder. • Brakes overheat and fade after successive application; extended braking distance. • Ball joint failure causes wheel to separate. **2002—** Cab separates from chassis. • Automatic transmission goes into the wrong gear or slams into gear. • Sudden brake lock-up. • Lug nuts are easily broken when tightened. • Bent wheel rims. **2003—**Vehicle stalls out. • Engine oil leaks. • Sudden tie-rod failure can cause Tundra to flip. • Transfer-case malfunction leads to reduced power and excessive vibration. • Faulty transmission Overdrive causes engine surge. **2004—**Many reports of the ball joint or lower control arm suddenly failing on vehicles not included in the recall to fix the problem. • Broken wheel lug nuts. • Defroster draws carbon monoxide into the cab. • Rear window pops out, sunroof explodes. **2005—**Automatic transmission failure (won't go into gear, or jumps out of Drive into Neutral). • Cruise control downshifts two gears on slight upgrades. • Extreme pulling to the left and right. • Driver's captain chair rocks back and forth. • Faulty tire-pressure monitoring system. **2006—**Vehicle suddenly shuts down. • Malfunctioning cruise control. • Sudden brake loss. • When fuelling, the filler nozzle will eject from the vehicle. **2007—**Instruments and gauges are not readable in daylight. • Headlights are difficult to aim properly. • Heat duct falls and blocks access to the brake pedal. • Truck is bouncy on the highway; described by one owner as producing excessive cab shake, wobble, and jerkiness. **2008—**Driver severely injured after a sudden acceleration crash:

> I approached a turn, and removed my foot from the accelerator and applied the brake, but the accelerator remained stuck down, the vehicle's speed exponentially increased and as a direct result I lost control of the truck and it slammed into a tree going 65 miles + per hour. The result is that the truck is "totaled". I will live with permanent injuries, including broken neck, ribs, hip and partial paralysis.

Many complaints of "lag and lurch" acceleration. • "Piston slap" caused by the 5.7L V8 engine piston hitting against the cylinder wall. • Vehicle was in Park with the engine running and the parking brake engaged when the truck rolled backwards down a hill and crashed into a building. • Transmission and transfer case failures. • Tundra bounces all over the highway and shakes violently when approaching 100 km/h:

> Anyone familiar with "shaken baby" syndrome will recognize this defect. On certain sections of pavement and at certain speeds, this vehicle sets up a harmonic vibration and shakes so violently that infants are at risk. The events are easily repeated and are known to the manufacturer.

•

> A Google search of Tundra rumble strip vibration will yield information on the issue. Los Angeles Toyota motor sales officials have nicknamed the problem "the rumble strip" because the slippage causes vibration similar to the sensation of driving over the wake-up strips at the side of highways. The rumbling usually lasts several seconds. But the problem sometimes worsens to the point that some owners can't shift into certain gears. The problem has been reported only in six-speed transmissions, which are linked to the popular 5.7-liter V-8 engine. Since the 2007 Tundra's February launch, the 5.7-liter engine has been installed in 70 percent of about 135,000 Tundras sold. That means the problem could affect nearly 100,000 vehicles.

Premature wheel bearing failure. • Ventilation system allows rodents to enter the ductwork from the engine compartment. Consequently, the cabin air is laced with rodent feces, which may sicken occupants who breathe the air. **2009**—Sudden, unintended acceleration. • Toyota asked owner to pay for recall repair:

> Contacted Toyota dealership as part of pedal/floor mat recall. Told that I would have to purchase separate retainer to secure floor mat. Does not make sense to have a recall and then insist that customers pay for Toyota's failures and defects. The safety retainer should have come with the vehicle. It does in other vehicles.

Automatic transmission "hunts" for the right gear and slips when in gear. • Early driveshaft replacement. • On 2007–2010 models, Tundra headlights can blind approaching drivers. **2010**—More complaints of unintended acceleration after the recall fix. • Ultra-sensitive gas pedal makes it difficult to accelerate without lurching. • Owners experience random power losses. • Vehicle stalls out due to a defective camshaft sensor. • Warped brake rotors cause excessive shaking when the brakes are applied. • Severe road bounce when cruising:

> I was driving on the freeway when I heard a loud bang. I pulled over and engine oil was dumping out of the engine onto the ground. I had the truck towed to Stevinson West Toyota—they took the engine apart and found multiple holes in the engine block. They are still not telling me the source of this engine failure. Toyota is telling me this is a one time occurrence, but I have been finding multiple problems with other Tundras (2007–2010), including a *USA Today* article from 2007, "Toyota fixing engine failures in new Tundra trucks." And, while our truck has been in the shop, we spoke with another Tundra owner (2009; in the same shop) who had a similar issue.

Exact issues from some other Tundras online (*www.tundrasolutions.com/forums/tundra/186091-engine-blew-4k-miles/*)!!!

Severe road bounce when cruising. • Rear shock absorber broke through the truck bed.

Secret Warranties/Internal Bulletins/Service Tips

2000–04—If the AC doesn't sufficiently cool the cabin, TSB #AC004-04 says the water control valve is the likely culprit. **2000–05**—Troubleshooting front and rear brake vibrations. • Front-door window rattles. **2001–03**—Oil pressure gauge reads abnormally low. • Front brake repair tips. **2002–06**—Remedy for vehicle pulling hard to the left or right. **2003–11**—Tips for silencing an upper or lower windshield ticking noise. **2004–10**—Front seat ticking. **2005–09**—Front power seat grinding and groaning. **2007**—Automatic transmission shifter slide binding. • Rear brake squeak. • Tailgate latch won't open. **2007–08**—Troubleshooting a no-start condition. • Transfer case not shifting in cold temperatures. • Drivetrain clunk or thunk. • Front differential howl or growl. • Instrument panel rattles. • Condensation drips from dome lamp headliner. • Loose driver-side air vents. **2007–09**—Gap between A-pillar and instrument panel. • Rust on steel step boards. **2007–10**—Tube step pad cracking, lifting. • Front driveshaft ticking. • Snow ingestion into air cleaner box. • Front end grinding noise when in four-wheel drive. • Rear differential growl, whine. • A choppy ride that can be severe at times with the extended cab version. Don't pay for this modification; Toyota made the mistake:

CHOPPY RIDE

BULLETIN NO.: T-SB-0270-10   DATE: SEPTEMBER 13, 2010

INTRODUCTION: Some 2007–10 Tundra vehicles may exhibit a body vibration when driving under certain road conditions. A newly designed cab mount has been developed to improve this condition. **NOTE:** The Tundra performs similarly to other long wheelbase trucks on choppy, broken concrete surfaces. The enhanced cab mounts of this TSB reduce the amplitude of body vibrations caused by uneven road surfaces, but they do NOT eliminate the sensation entirely. Also, reducing speed by as little as 5 mph has a considerable positive effect in reducing body vibration.

2007–11—Rear driveshaft clunk, thunk noise. • Inoperative front power seat.

TUNDRA PROFILE

	2002	2003	2004	2005	2006	2007	2008	2009	2010
Cost Price ($)									
Base	23,520	23,520	24,565	25,580	26,100	25,255	23,475	23,855	25,310
4×4 V6/V8	29,270	29,270	30,320	30,650	31,080	29,320	27,540	27,400	28,795

Used Values ($)

Base ▲	3,500	4,000	5,000	5,500	7,000	8,500	10,000	12,000	15,500
Base ▼	3,000	3,500	4,500	5,000	5,500	7,500	8,500	10,500	14,000
4×4 V6/V8 ▲	5,000	5,500	6,500	7,000	8,000	9,500	11,500	13,500	16,500
4×4 V6/V8 ▼	4,500	5,000	5,500	6,500	7,000	8,000	10,000	12,000	15,000
Reliability	2	1	1	1	1	1	1	2	2
Crash Safety (F)	4	4	4	4	4	4	4	4	4
Side	—	—	—	5	5	—	—	—	—
Extended	5	5	5	5	5	—	—	—	—
Side (IIHS)	—	—	—	—	—	5	5	5	5
Offset	5	5	5	5	5	5	5	5	5
Head Restraints	—	—	—	3	3	5	5	5	5
Roof Strength	—	—	—	—	—	5	5	5	5
Rollover	—	—	—	—	3	3	3	3	3
Extended	3	3	—	—	3	3	3	3	—

All ratings on a numbered scale where 5 is good and **1** is bad. See page 132 for a more detailed description.

Appendix
BEATERS, NEWBIES, AND ORPHANS

Here we include thumbnail sketches of some of the vehicles we passed over in Part Three.

First, a word about residual values. Prices that are listed in this Appendix will drop as we go through 2012–13. To get the most current resale value for almost any vehicle in Canada and see what its predicted value will be three and five years down the road, use the VMR website at *www.vmrcanada.com/canada_makes.htm*. This is an excellent site that continually updates used values for everyday vehicles, whether they are "beaters" or exotic or collector cars. VMR also links searchers to NHTSA's recalls and service bulletin databases.

"Beaters," or "minounes," as they are called in Quebec, are my favourite kind of car, and I suspect that feeling is shared by most *Lemon-Aid* readers. The more I see the newer auto offerings, the more thankful I am for "beaters"—cheap, older cars that may not be all that pretty or refined, but they are mostly reliable and easy to find.

In my 42 years of writing *Lemon-Aid*, I have seen an interesting vein of regret from Baby Boomers who say their first "beater" was the best car they ever owned, and they wish they had never given it up.

"Newbies" are vehicles that are relatively new to the market. These vehicles are included here because there is insufficient data from service bulletins and real world driving data from owners to make a full assessment of the vehicle's worth. They are usually risky buys because they don't have a large parts inventory and mechanics are relatively inexperienced at finding likely failures and choosing the least expensive "fix."

Then we have "orphan" cars—vehicles that are no longer built, or whose parent company has been sold many times to different automakers or has gone bankrupt. Saab is a prime example. Fiat, Jaguar, and Volvo may be the next to fall.

As the automobile industry shakes off the Great Recession and its bankruptcies, I am concerned that cars are getting so complicated that the average driver has little choice for servicing and must go to the dealership where that vehicle is sold. This is a scary thought because it gives dealers a servicing monopoly and cuts out independent repairers who build their customer base through honest and competent service. Beaters break automaker/dealer monopolies and allow motorists to go where service is the best and cheapest.

Sport-Utilities

Anyone buying a sport-utility that's a decade old or older is asking for trouble, because many SUVs are worked hard off-road. The danger of rollovers for vehicles not equipped with electronic stability control is also quite high. Safety features are rudimentary, dangerous, and unreliable (especially ABS); overall quality control is very poor; and performance and handling cannot match today's models.

Pickups

For over three decades, most all of the small Japanese pickups have been good performers, with the exception of Toyota, which has been handicapped by serious chassis rust, brake failures, and sudden, unintended acceleration. Toyota will repair or buy back 1995–2000 **Tacoma** pickups affected by rust-damaged structural frames. An estimated 813,000 Tacomas from this era are still on North American roads and may be affected, especially if driven in areas with snow where road salt is used. The excessive rusting is caused by inadequate anti-corrosion undercoating applied at the factory.

In spite of its own suspension-caused instability, the Toyota **Tundra** beats out Nissan's **Titan** for quality control. Although Toyota has had a number of powertrain, brake, suspension, and fuel delivery problems, the scope of these deficiencies doesn't come close to the Nissan Titan's problems, which comprise all of the above, plus accessories and body fit and finish. Mazda's **B-Series** trucks are particularly vulnerable to powertrain, suspension, brake, and fuel system failures. But interestingly, fit and finish is better with Mazda than with other Asian automakers. **Nissan's** small trucks, like the **Frontier** and **Rogue** are the most reliable, although body fit and finish and accessories (AC, sound system, brakes, and electrical systems) are problem-prone.

The paucity of owner complaints and relatively benign nature of Honda's service bulletins confirm that the **Honda Ridgeline** has had far fewer performance and reliability/durability complaints than have comparable makes from Mazda, Nissan, or Toyota.

Depreciation Quirks

Depreciation varies considerably among different vehicle types and models. For example, Asian minivans depreciate a bit more slowly than cars, and diesel cars and trucks hold their value better than gas-powered vehicles do.

Gas-electric hybrids, which have been on the market since 1999, apparently lose their values at about the same rate as conventional cars. Undoubtedly, this is because used-car buyers are afraid they may have to replace costly high-tech components, like the $3,000 battery pack. As Canadians keep their vehicles longer, this major expense is inevitable. One exception: fuel price hikes early in 2012 pushed up the Toyota Prius resale value about 5 percent.

10 Beater Rules

1. Try to buy a vehicle that's presently being used by one of your family members. Although you may risk a family squabble somewhere down the road, you'll likely get a good buy for next to nothing, you'll have a good idea of how it was driven and maintained, and you'll be able to use the same repair facilities that have been repairing your family's vehicles for years. Don't worry if a vehicle is almost 10 years old—11 years is becoming the norm for Canadian ownership, particularly the farther west you go.

2. Buy from a private seller. Prices are usually much cheaper, and sales scams are less frequent.

3. Cut insurance and fuel costs. Use the Internet (*www.insurancehotline.com*) to compile a list of models that are the cheapest to insure. Be wary of diesel-equipped or hybrid cars that may require more-expensive dealer servicing and thus wipe out any fuel-consumption savings. Also, pay attention to the quality and performance of your fuel-efficient choice: A fuel-sipping 2001–03 Ford Focus will likely have higher repair bills than gas bills, and a 4-cylinder minivan, though cheap to run, can make highway merging a nightmare.

4. Find out the vehicle's history through a franchised dealer, CarProof, or provincial licensing authorities. Then, have an independent garage (preferably CAA-affiliated) check out the body and mechanical components.

5. Look for high-mileage vehicles sold by rental agencies like Budget Rent A Car—a company that offers money-back guarantees and reasonably priced extended warranties.

6. Refuse all preparation or "administration" fees, as well as 50/50 warranties where the repair charges are submitted by the seller.

7. Stay away from vehicles or components known for having high failure rates. American front-drives, for example, have more-frequent failures and costlier repairs than rear-drives. "Orphaned" American models like the Ford Taurus/Sable and Windstar or GM front-drive minivans are also poor choices because of low-quality components and inadequate servicing support from dealers who wish these cars were never made. Other sinkholes: any vehicle equipped with a turbocharger or supercharger or with multiple computers (BMW's 7 Series, for example); Cadillacs with 4.1L engines and/or front-drive; and Chryslers with sludge-prone 2.7L engines or 4-speed automatic transmissions. If the engine has a timing chain instead of a belt, you will save a fortune. Timing chains frequently survive the lifespan of the engine, whereas timing belts must be replaced every 70,000–100,000 km.

8. Steer clear of European models. They are often money pits. Parts and competent, reasonably priced servicing will likely be hard to find, and quality control has declined considerably over the past decade.

9. Buy five-year-old Hyundais, if you want Asian car quality at a fraction of the cost for a Japanese make. Also try to avoid early Kias or Daewoos. Instead, look for five- to 10-year-old single-owner Japanese models.

10. Run away from any dealer offering you a used car lease. You will pay far more for the vehicle than you should and the seller can stick you with high finance costs and hundreds of dollars in sundry fees.

Cars

Acura

The mid-sized 2003 Acura **CL** is an Above Average buy; the 1997–2002s are Average, due to serious first-year factory glitches and powertrain problems. 1998 saw the debut of the 2.3L engine; 2003 CLs have plenty of power from the quiet, smooth-running 3.2L V6. And handling is better than average, thanks to an upgraded suspension, variable assisted steering, and 16-inch wheels.

A 2003 CL is now worth between $5,000 and $7,500 (new models sold for $37,800); 1997–2002 prices vary from $3,000 to $4,500. Add $500 for the Type S (260 hp).

Owners have reported that the 2003 models have troublesome gearboxes. Sudden, unintended acceleration and hesitation problems are thought to be transmission-related also. Premature brake pad and caliper wear and warped brake rotors continue to be serious problems.

Based on the Honda Civic, the Acura **Integra** evolved into more of a sports car than an econocar. Dramatically redesigned for 1994, the 1994 through 2001 models provide a smoother ride than previous versions, and crash protection was augmented by the use of front airbags (1996 frontal collision protection was rated four stars by NHTSA). The powerful VTEC engine, however, requires lots of shifting, and interior room is problematic. Nevertheless, these are the benchmark cars for optimum savings, performance, and quality. Expect to pay $4,500 to $5,500 for a 2001 SE.

What Integras give you in mechanical reliability and performance, they take away in poor quality control on body components and accessories (what do you expect after 10 years?). Water leaks, excessive wind noise, low-quality trim items, and plastic panels that deform easily are all commonplace.

The 2002–06 Acura **RSX** is built on the Civic platform and is powered by a base 160 hp 2.0L twin-cam iVTEC 4-banger or a torquier 210 hp variant used by the high-performance Type S. Three transmissions are available: the first two, a 5-speed manual and a 4-speed automatic, are offered with base models, while a 6-speed manual is found on the Type S. Both engines are torquier than the powerplants they replaced; however, the base engine has more useful commuting low-end torque than the so-called sportier Type S engine. Your best buy would be a much-improved 2005 model that sells for $7,500–$9,000. Add $1,000 for the Type S.

The RSX appeals to drivers who want to shift fast and often, and who don't mind a firm ride. The car is well appointed; has good acceleration and handling above 3000 rpm; provides user-friendly gauges and controls; brakes well, especially with the Type S; gives good fuel economy; depreciates slowly; has garnered a five-star frontal crash rating for both the driver and front-seat passenger, and a four-star front side-impact rating; and has head restraints that IIHS rates Good up front and Average in the rear. The car has high-quality construction, except for brakes, electronics, and transmission components.

On the downside, the car exhibits so-so acceleration in lower gears and compromised acceleration with the automatic; vague heavy steering; limited front and rear passenger space; excessive road and engine noise; and rear visibility obstructed by small side windows, thick roof pillars, and a tall rear deck. Peruse transmission complaints at *forums.clubrsx.com*.

BMW

The BMW 2008–10 **1-Series** is an Average buy, even though it's a joy to drive—most of the time. BMW's entry-level car comes as the 128i and 135i, and as either a two-door coupe or convertible with a power-folding soft top. These vehicles are equipped with a 230 hp 3.0L inline 6-cylinder that's shared with the 3-Series. The turbocharged 135i produces 300 hp. All models carry a 6-speed manual transmission, though the 128i offers an optional 6-speed automatic. For the 2011–2012 model year, the top-end 135i offers an optional 7-speed automated manual transmission; in the past, this has been a problematic transmission. The best model/year choice is the 2009 128i Coupe, which originally sold for $33,900 and can now be picked up for $21,500; the Convertible version costs $26,500. Going upscale to the 135i Coupe and Convertible will cost $27,000 and $31,000, respectively. These small luxury cars are known for sporty acceleration, a generally smooth drivetrain, responsive steering, precise handling, good outward visibility, average depreciation, and acceptable fuel economy. Overall reliability and depreciation have been average, but the car's styling has created a stir. *L.A. Times* car columnist Dan Neil has this to say:

> The new 1 Series BMW is ugly. Seriously ugly. Ugly with X-wings locked in attack formation…The 1 Series looks like it needs a jowl lift to repair its prolapsed cheeks. Or perhaps a truss. With the downward bowed accent lines running along its flanks, this car looks like it has suffered a high-speed hernia.

Expect harsh riding—you feel every bump in the road; poor outward visibility with the convertible top up; and a big let down with fuel consumption. Owners also report chronic fuel pump failures covered by a 10-year secret warranty:

> As I pulled out into the road, the Engine light came on and the car had reduced power. The car (with only 5500 miles [8,850 km] or so) was shaking violently when going under 10 miles [16 km] an hour. The RPMs fluctuated at idle to where the car almost stalled several times. I drove the 15 or so miles [24 km] home with my flashers on as the car was having trouble. The above is a description of a HPFP failure on the N54 engine. I would say many, many people get a bad fuel pump. BMW has covered the part for 10 years/120K miles [193,100 km], but it will fail again. There is no fix at this point. Just a new pump that eventually gives way. I know people who are on their

4th pump. Just do a Google search on "BMW HPFP" and see what comes up. The 135I, 335I, 535I [and] Z4 35I all have the N54 engine, and they all suffer from this defect. Loss of power really concerns me, what if I was going 65 mph [105 km/h] on a highway when the pump decided to fail? I brought the car into the dealership, and explained the long cranks and loss of power etc...and they explained BMW has to approve all fuel pump swaps. Got a call 2 days later to say they will replace the pump. In addition to the new pump, I will be getting a software update as well.

Other drawbacks: ABS malfunctions; early ignition coil, clutch plate, and DTC traction failures; run-flat tire alerts come on for no reason; cramped interior is awkward to get in and out of; and few storage spaces. No crashworthiness data is available.

Chrysler

The 2004–07 **Crossfire** is an expensive, low-volume luxury sports coupe that also gets a Not Recommended rating. Its cramped interior, high windowsills, and low roofline combine to create a claustrophobic cabin that's hard to get used to. Crashworthiness scores for the 2004–05s are quite good, with five stars given for frontal occupant protection, side protection, and rollover resistance; 2007s got similar marks.

Crossfire owners reported numerous safety defects to NHTSA, though. Some, like the one below, are particularly frightening:

Lack of power when at a stop, even though you might be mashing in the gas pedal (pedal to the metal). So if you fear for your life when you're in the middle of an intersection and your car won't move, don't worry because it's normal.

Other problems include sudden acceleration when the brakes are applied; high-performance tires and a low-slung body that impair safe handling in inclement weather; airbags that fail to deploy; chronic stalling; transmission breakdowns; a manual transmission that abruptly slips out of First gear into Neutral; defective wheel bolts that lead to the wheel separating from the car; a short circuit in the dash wiring harness that poses a fire risk; $400 wheel rims that are easily bent in normal driving; front and rear strut failures; headlights that don't adequately illuminate the road; lights that dim at stoplights and at idle; and erratic voltage (possibly due to a faulty voltage regulator) that fries powertrain computer modules and other electronic components. Yikes!

Depreciation has also been brutal: A 2007 base coupe Ltd., which cost $48,050 new, is now worth $9,000–$10,500—a good price for a bad car. There is no "good" Crossfire model to choose from; all models will cause you no end of grief.

The **Neon** is a Not Recommended buy throughout its 2000–05 model run. These are low-quality, fuel-thirsty small cars that devour engine head gaskets and brake calipers, so what savings you realized from an unbelievably low price will be lost through high maintenance costs that will creep even higher as the parts supply dries up. Remember, Chrysler is notoriously slow in distributing parts for cars it no longer makes; waits of several months are commonplace for some components.

The Neon does offer a spacious interior and responsive steering and handling. Nevertheless, it's seriously handicapped by an antiquated, feeble, and fuel-thirsty 3-speed automatic gearbox, a DOHC 4-cylinder 150 hp powerplant that has to be pushed hard to do as well as the SOHC 132 hp engine, and a mushy base suspension.

The 2003 Neon was renamed the SX 2.0 in Canada. Later refinements gave it a softer, quieter ride while enhancing the car's handling and powertrain performance. Quality didn't improve much and the car was discontinued in 2005.

Chrysler tried to make its low-end Neons more appealing and more profitable by adding expensive high-performance features that made the car less reliable, complicated servicing, and drove down the car's resale value. For example, the 2004 SRT4 equipped with a turbocharged 215 hp 2.4L 4-cylinder engine hooked to a manual 4-speed transmission sold originally for $26,950; it's now worth $3,500.

Reliability has always been the Neon's worst problem. Owners report costly automatic transmission failures, engine motor mounts that last only a few years, an AC system noted for condenser and compressor failures, a plethora of electrical short circuits, interior noise and water leaks, and uneven fit and finish, along with poor-quality trim items, like paint delamination and cracked dashboards.

The 2004–05 models are not better made. Owners of these newer models say early failure of the front control arms and suspension bushings is commonplace, starter rust-out causes no-starts; the AC is inadequate; the automatic transmission shudders when shifting; when the car is passing through puddles, the engine can self-destruct after ingesting water though the air-intake port; and the engine noticeably loses power when windows are lowered, the sunroof is open, or the AC is engaged.

The 2001–10 **PT Cruiser** is Not Recommended. It has been off the market for three model years and Chrysler's "benign neglect" of the model has set owners adrift with limited servicing and almost no warranty support. Quality is seriously lacking in mechanical and electronic components. And the abysmally bad fit and finish could have been a Larry, Curly, and Moe summer project. There is no ideal model year, however, the $10,500 2009 LX wagon is reasonably priced and likely to have some warranty left. A last-year 2010 version costs about $4,000 more and all it offers is ABS brakes on all four wheels.

The PT Cruiser is essentially a fuel- and space-efficient small hatchback minivan. It's noted for good fuel economy (regular fuel), nimble handling around town, good braking, lots of interior space, and easy access.

Forget about hot-rod power with the base engine, though. The 150 hp 2.4L 4-cylinder powerplant is not very smooth-running and, when matched with the automatic transmission, it struggles when going uphill or merging with highway traffic. This requires frequent downshifting and lots of patience. Costlier turbocharged models will give you plenty of power, but you risk some steep repair bills. The automatic transmission has little low-end torque, forcing early kickdown shifting and deft manipulation of the accelerator pedal. High-speed handling isn't impressive; hard cornering produces an unsteady, wobbly ride because of the car's height. The ride is firm, with lots of interior engine, wind, and road noise.

Some of the safety-related problems reported to NHTSA include sudden, unintended acceleration; side airbags not deploying; prematurely worn control arm bushings (the car wobbles at all speeds and pulls to the right); tire aluminum valve stem failures; a plastic part of the seat adjustment mechanism fails and the seat suddenly readjusts whenever the vehicle goes over a bump (cost to fix: $300); repeated loss of brakes; side rear window may suddenly shatter; and the driver must punch the centre of the steering wheel several times to shut off the horn.

The 2005–10 models score four stars with the NHTSA; 2007 and 2008 convertibles weren't tested. Side impact crashworthiness wasn't tested on the 2005–06 Cruiser, either.

IIHS gave the 2006–10 Cruisers a "Good" rating for frontal impacts; side protection for the 2008–10 models was "Poor"; and 2006–10 model head restraints were judged to be also "Poor."

Reliability is problematic for all model years, with frequent drivetrain complaints that include chronic stalling, faulty valve cover gaskets causing oil burning, and faulty automatic transmission control modules forcing the drivetrain to gear down to "limp home" mode; or the front axle may break while the car is accelerating. Power-steering pump units and steering units are also frequently replaced and there are many reports of steering clockspring failures. Side-wind instability also seems to be a generic problem. Instrument panels are difficult to read in the daylight. Tall drivers beware: The windshield is uncomfortably close, and overhead traffic lights will disappear. Wide pillars obstruct the view; headrests are too high, block vision, and are unstable; short circuits kill the lights and gauges, or else cause the lights to flicker and dim; doors lock and unlock on their own; water may leak through the passenger-side window; an annoying wind noise is produced when driving with the rear window or sunroof open; and paint delamination gives the original paint job a chalky colour. See *www-odi.nhtsa.dot.gov/complaints*, *www. ptcruiserlinks.com*, *http://terpconnect.umd.edu/~gluckman/Chrysler/index.html* (The Chrysler Products' Problem Web Page), *www.daimlerchryslervehicleproblems.com* (The Truth Behind Chrysler), and *www.autosafety.org/autodefects.html*.

Ford

1981–2000 Ford **Escort/Lynx/Tracer** front-drive small cars are cheap to buy and economical to operate, if you get the right vintage. Expect a comfortable, though jittery, ride and adequate front seating for two adults. *Lemon-Aid* gives these cars a Not Recommended and a Below Average rating, because this is a Dr. Jekyl and Mr. Hyde car. The 1981–90 models were lemons with their chronic brake, powertrain, and electrical system failures in addition to Ford's lack of parts and servicing support in Canada. In 1991, though, the car was upgraded with quality Mazda 323 and Protegé components, available from Ford or Mazda dealers. Almost instantly, the frog turned into a prince and Escorts were hopping off dealer lots. So spend the additional loonies and get the more reliable, better-performing year 2000 ZX2 for about $1,000. Other models can be bought for about $500. Incidentally, the slightly cheaper base Escort has three-star (average) front, side, and rollover crash protection; the ZX2 has only a one-star side crashworthiness score.

Ford's 1999–2006 **Taurus** and **Sable** are the worst cars *Lemon-Aid* has rated in 42 years. A 2006 Taurus for $6,000—a car that originally sold for $25,099. Is that a bargain, or what? No! Both the Taurus and the Sable, Taurus's unindicted co-conspirator, are bargain-basement traps that will quickly deplete your savings, make you take forced marches, and give you a crash course in making emergency electrical and powertrain repairs. These quintessential lemons make the Ford "You Light Up My Life" Pinto and Vauxhall Firenza look good. They are easy to find and dirt cheap because their owners can't wait to get rid of them before they pay another $4,000 in powertrain repairs (if they're lucky). And the extra engine and transmission warranty protection you'll have to buy will wipe out any savings realized from the low selling price.

Although they lack pickup with the standard 4-cylinder engine, these mid-sized sedans and wagons are competent family cars, offering lots of interior room, nice handling, a good crash rating, and many convenience features. From a performance standpoint, the best powertrain combination for all driving conditions is the 3.0L V6 hooked to a 4-speed on the family sedan.

The first generation Taurus LX was *Motor Trend* magazine's Car of the Year for 1986 and placed on *Car and Driver*'s annual Ten Best list from 1986 to 1991. Two examples of why most automobile journalists can't be trusted.

The 4-cylinder engine is a dog that no amount of servicing can change. It's slow, noisy, prone to stalling and surging, and actually consumes more gas than the V6. The 3.0L 6-cylinder is noted for engine head bolt failures and piston scuffing and is characterized by hard starting, stalling, excessive engine noise, and poor fuel economy. Transmission cooler lines leak and often lead to the unnecessary repair or replacement of the transmission. Plus, there are many reports of sudden coil spring breakage puncturing tires, and throwing vehicles out of control.

Bland but solid-looking, the spacious 2005–07 Ford **Five Hundred** and **Freestyle** (an SUV wagon clone) front-drive and AWD family sedans failed to capture buyers' hearts at first, due to a combination of high gas prices, mediocre highway performance, and early reports of poor-quality powertrain and other components affecting the 2005 through 2007 models.

The 2008–2010 **Taurus** and **Taurus X** are the Five Hundred and Freestyle's renamed, restyled carryover models that have a more-powerful 260 hp 3.5L V6 hooked to a 6-speed automatic transmission and are equipped with a retuned suspension. Both cars are rated Average buys.

The Ford Five Hundred.

A plus for buyers is that prices are depressed, but quality has improved markedly with these renamed models. Consequently, 2008–10 models represent Average buys, while the 2005–07 years are rated Below Average. Used 2005 versions are selling for only $5,000; 2006 models are worth barely $6,500; and 2007s go for $7,000–$8,500. Tack on another $1,000 for an AWD variant. A 2008 Taurus goes for $8,500 to $10,000, while a 2010 SE version costs $12,500–$14,000. This time, AWD will cost another $1,500 more.

Crash test scores are impressive: Front and side crash protection are rated at five stars, and rollover resistance scored four stars. 2007s come with side airbags.

Look out for problems related to the engine, automatic transmission, fuel supply, and ignition (unintended acceleration, hard starts, stalling, and dieseling).

Owners report that the transmission jumps out of Park into Reverse, has no intermediate or Second gear for descending mountains, and often hesitates as it hunts for the right gear. Also, the engine surges and lurches when accelerating; and brake and suspension components require early replacement.

Old Mercury **Cougar** and Ford **Thunderbird** models are Not Recommended from both a reliability and performance perspective. The early rear-drives (1985–97), now worth $500 to $2,000, were plagued by powertrain, electrical, suspension, and brake defects; the 1999–2002, now worth $1,000 to $3,500, are front-drive iterations that carry over these same deficiencies and add more problems common to Ford's front-drives, namely, gear "hunting" and drivetrain failures. As for the resurrected 2003–05 Thunderbird's low rating, its lackluster highway performance and quality shortcomings clearly showed that Ford was "pimping nostalgia" with a warmed-over, less reliable version of what was once a classic car. It's surprising that a 2005 version still commands $14,500 to $16,000; collectors predict that price will drop to $10,000 within the next three years.

1999–2002 Mercury **Cougars** are Not Recommended despite their attractive styling, easy handling, and low $2,000–$3,500 price for a base 2002. For these low prices, owners have to put up with mediocre acceleration in the base models; problematic transmission performance; a narrow, claustrophobic interior for a four-seater; limited rear seat room; obstructed rear visibility; an ugly and superfluous trunk-lid spoiler; and excessive interior noise.

1999–2008 Mercury **Grand Marquis** models are Average buys, offering good overall reliability, reasonably low prices, and acceptable highway performance. On the other hand, powertrain, electrical system, and brake failures are endemic with the Grand Marquis and its **Crown Victoria** and Lincoln **Town Car** twins.

Other shared minuses include excessive engine noise, poor fuel economy, no electronic stability control, no curtain airbags, and low IIHS side-impact marks without side airbags. Yet these large sedans can be bargain buys as their owners bail out and sell them for next to nothing as fuel prices increase.

Get the 2006 high-end and fully-loaded LS Ultimate. It's a $42,799 car that's now worth $8,000 to $9,000. 2008 models are good second choices. They are little-changed, are likely to have some of the original warranty left, and cost between $11,500 to $13,000.

These rear-drive cars are especially well suited to seniors, who will appreciate the roomy interiors and convenience features (although entry and exit may require some acrobatics). The high crash protection scores and ease of servicing are also major advantages. Handling, though, is mediocre and can be downright scary on wet roads, where the car can quickly lose traction and fishtail out of control.

As is the case with most full-sized sedans, high insurance premiums and fuel costs have walloped the resale value of both models, making these cars incredibly good used buys. The only caveat is to make sure the undercarriage, powertrain, electronics, and brakes are in good shape before you ink a deal.

General Motors

The 1999–2005 GM **Alero** and **Grand Am** are rated Below Average buys due to their mediocre road performance and chronic engine, transmission, brake, and electrical system failures. If there is a bright side, it is that these cars can be repaired anywhere since they use inexpensive, easily found generic parts. Also, these cars are cheap: A 1999 Alero GX goes for $1,000 to $1,500, while a 2005 Grand Am SE is worth $4,000 to $5,500. Nevertheless, keep aside a few thousand dollars for powertrain and brake repairs.

Grand Ams and Aleros from 1999 to 2005 are well-appointed with many more standard features, like traction control, than offered with previous versions. They have a competent V6, good steering and handling, and are easily serviced. Some of their disadvantages include a mediocre ride over rough terrain, excessive

4-cylinder noise, and a noisy interior. Also expect difficult rear-seat access (coupe), awkward radio controls, rear visibility that's obstructed by the spoiler, problematic trunk access, and annoying body creaks.

Overall quality control is poor and crashworthiness is inconsistent. Owners report expensive engine and automatic transmission failures and premature brake pad and rotor wear. Also mentioned are electrical problems; suspension squeaks; and substandard body assembly that produces more squeaks and rattles, water leaks, and poor paint adhesion. NHTSA says the Grand Am merits an Above Average score for frontal collision occupant protection and rollover resistance, but frontal offset, side protection, and head restraint effectiveness vary between Poor and Average.

The 1999–2003 GM **Aurora** and **Riviera** are orphaned cars that haven't been built for almost a decade. They are rated Not Recommended buys because they are unreliable, expensive-to-service gas guzzlers. Resale values have nosedived, making these cars attractive buys to gullible shoppers who can't resist a bargain 2003 Buick Riviera or Olds Aurora for $3,000 to $4,000. Be prepared to pay higher than average repair costs; if you can find a mechanic willing to tackle a repair job, this will solve only half your problem. The remaining worry will be finding parts. Most of the complicated electronic and emissions hardware is hard to find and junkyards have almost been picked clean. NHTSA and IIHS give both cars Above Average crashworthiness scores.

There are still many generic deficiencies affecting the automatic transmission (torque converter constantly engages and disengages); engine, fuel, and electrical systems; computer modules; AC compressor; brakes (rotor warpage and premature pad replacement); steering; suspension; and fit and finish (surface rust and poor paint quality are the most common body complaints for all model years). Because of their problematic brakes, these cars usually have a pronounced low-speed shudder/vibration and severe pull that intensifies when passing over uneven terrain or when braking.

The Aurora is a front-drive Olds luxury sedan that uses the same basic design as the Riviera but doesn't share the same major mechanical features or popular styling. A 2003 model will cost about $5,000. The Aurora's main advantages are its sporty handling and unusual aero styling. In contrast to the Riviera, the Aurora seats only five and offers a 4.0L V8 derived from the failure-prone, hard-to-repair Cadillac 4.6L V8 Northstar engine. Acceleration is underwhelming (this is a heavy car) but adequate for highway touring. Road and wind noise are omnipresent, and the trunk's small opening compromises its ability to handle odd-sized objects.

The 1999–2002 GM **Camaro** and **Firebird** are Above Average buys that were dropped for the 2003 model year. Fun to drive and easily repaired, these early cars are more reliable than the Mustang, despite having elicited similar safety-related complaints such as airbag deployment injuries, sudden acceleration, brake failures, and steering loss. Be especially wary of brake rotor warpage, which requires rotor replacement every two years (about $300 each time). Bargain-hunter alert: Although these cars originally sold for $40,000, today you can pick up a used 2010 V8-equipped Camaro for about $26,500. But you can also do quite well with the cheaper base coupe equipped with a high-performance handling package. Other money-saving advantages: repairs can be done by any independent garage, parts are plentiful, and the cars always draw buyers.

The Camaro and Firebird (*above*) are relatively reliable and fun to drive.

Above Average crash protection scores (except for head restraints, which were rated Poor by IIHS). Like all rear-drive Detroit iron, handling is compromised by poor traction on wet roads and a suspension that's too soft for high-speed cornering and too bone-jarring for smooth cruising. The Z28, IROC-Z, and Trans Am provide smart acceleration and handling but at the expense of fuel economy—a small drawback, however, when you save thousands buying used. How many thousands? For example, a potent, head-turning 2002 Firebird Trans Am convertible can be had for $8,000 to $9,500. A same-year Camaro convertible will cost three thousand less. Convertibles carry a $1,000 premium over the coupe.

Stick with the 1996–2002 models for the best performance and price. Overall, they are much better performers than previous models, and additional standard safety features are a plus.

Owners report premature automatic transmission failures, a noisy base engine, and excessive oil consumption with the larger engine. Fuel economy is unimpressive, the AC malfunctions, the front brakes (rotors and pads, mostly) and MacPherson struts wear out quickly, servicing the fuel-injection system is an exercise in frustration, electrical problems are common, and gauges operate erratically. Body problems are frequent. These include door rattles, misaligned doors and hatches, roof water and air leaks, a sticking hatch power release, and poor fit and finish. Owners also complain that the steering wheel is positioned too close to the driver's chest and the low seats create a feeling of claustrophobia. Visibility is limited by wide side pillars, and trunk space is sparse with a high liftover. (See *www.autosafety.org/autodefects.html* and *www.sportscarforums.com.*)

GM's 2005–07 **G6** is rated Below Average. The G6 is a mid-sized replacement for the Grand Am and is built on GM's 2004 Chevy Malibu platform. It comes with a weak, fuel-thirsty 2.4L 4-cylinder engine and a barely competent 219 hp 3.5L V6— much less power than what's offered with most of the family-sedan competition. A $27,995 2006 GT is now worth $5,000–$6,500. Crash test scores vary considerably; 2005–06 frontal and side crash protection are scored five and three stars, respectively, and rollover resistance scored between four and five stars. The 2007 and 2008 models, however, garnered five stars in all three categories.

These cars have major reliability problems that may put both your life and your wallet in danger. The most frightening of these is the problem with the steering system, which can suddenly lock up, throwing your car out of control. Owners of 2005–08 models who lose power steering can get the unit fixed for free under Special Coverage Adjustment #10183, dated July 20, 2010. GM will replace the failed components free of charge up to 10 years/100,000 mi. (160,000 km). 2006–07 G6 models also can get their catalytic converter replaced free of charge up to 10 years/120,000 mi. (193,000 km) under Special Coverage Adjustment #10134, dated November 17, 2010.

The 1999–2005 **Park Avenue** is given a Below Average rating. Originally sold for $47,545, a 2005 model is now worth $6,000–$7,500. A 1999 version can be picked up for $2,500. Crash ratings are very good, with four-star scores for front, side, and rollover crash protection.

These front-drive cars provide lots of room (but not for six), as well as luxury, style, and—I'm going to regret saying this—performance. Granted, plenty of power is available with the 205 hp 3.8L V6 engine and the 240 hp supercharged version of the same powerplant. On the other hand, owners decry the car's ponderous handling; over-assisted steering; obstructed rear visibility; hard braking accompanied by a severe nosedive; interior gauges and controls that aren't easily deciphered or accessed; and surprisingly high fuel consumption.

Park Avenue models have compiled one of the worst repair histories among large cars. The main problems are the starter, engine, brakes, steering, alternator, automatic transmission, fuel system, and electrical system (including defective PROM and MEMCAL modules), plus the badly assembled, poor-quality body hardware. The 3.0L V6 engine is inadequate for a car this heavy, and the 3.8L has been a big quality disappointment. Maintenance costs are higher than average, but thankfully, repairs aren't dealer-dependent.

Pontiac's 1976–94 **Sunbird** (renamed the **Sunfire** in 1995) was GM's smallest American-built car, along with its twin, the Chevrolet **Cavalier**. Discontinued in 2005, these models are rated Below Average due to parts shortages and powertrain failures. The 2004 models received above-average crashworthiness scores, except for side protection, which IIHS rated Poor. The 2003–05 models carried the better-performing 2.2L Ecotec 140 hp 4-cylinder engine. Expect to pay $2,500 to $4,000 for a 2005 Cavalier VL four-door, and half as much for a 2002 or earlier version. These prices are predicted to drop by half over the next three years.

General Motors/Daewoo

The **Optra, Optra5,** and **Forenza** are three Non-Recommended compact cars that were sold from 2004 through 2008. Unfortunately, they weren't as versatile or reliable as the Japanese and South Korean competition. The puny 119 hp 2.0L 4-cylinder engine has only 16 more horses than the equally underpowered entry-level Aveo.

Depreciation has hit these models hard, making them cheap to acquire. Their poor quality and unreliable parts supply will wipe out those savings, though. Known in the U.S. as the Suzuki Forenza, the 2004 Optra was a uniquely Canadian car that sold for $16,190, or almost $3,000 more than the same model-year Aveo. Presently, a 2004 Optra or Optra5 hatchback is worth between $2,000 and $2,500; a 2008 model goes for $6,000 tops.

Crashworthiness is better than average for all model years, except for the 2004's "Average" IIHS rating for side crash protection. IIHS also says head restraint protection is "Poor."

General Motors/Saturn

General Motors' entire Saturn lineup: the **S-Series, L-Series,** and **ION,** sold from 1999 through 2007 are Not Recommended. Not only did GM close the money-burning division in 2007, but the company never did bring Saturn's quality control up to a competitive level. Quality control was the pits, especially as it related to powertrain dependability. Even GM's less-pretentious models, like the Cavalier and Aveo or the minuscule Metro and Firefly, offered better quality and value for your money.

Saturn's later entries, like the Aura, Sky, and Outlook SUV, were marginally better buys from a performance and styling perspective, but in the end they became just as problem-plagued. Now that Saturn has been closed, parts like the CVT transmission and powertrain components will be almost impossible to find at a fair price. Alternative models to consider are the Honda Civic LX (up to the 2011 model year), Hyundai Elantra, Mazda3, Ford Focus (2005 and later), Nissan Sentra or Versa, and Toyota's Corolla.

Saturn's entry-level S-Series models are as low-tech as you can get and have remained virtually unchanged until replaced by the 2003 ION. The base model provides a comfortable driving position, adequate instrumentation and controls, unobstructed visibility, good braking, dent-resistant body panels, and better-than-average crashworthiness scores. But, balancing these advantages, buyers have to contend with excessive engine noise, limited rear seatroom, glitch-prone anti-lock brakes and serious factory-related defects.

In an attempt to save money by adapting a European car to the American market, Saturn brought out the **L-Series' LS**, **L-Sedan**, and **LW Wagon**, derivatives of GM's own quality-challenged Opel Vectra. Some major differences, however, include a lengthened body, a softer-riding chassis for a more comfortable ride, and the use of a homegrown 137 hp 2.2L 4-banger constructed with failure-prone aluminum components. The higher-priced models have a roomy interior with a full range of convenience features, plus a good V6 powertrain matchup that provides a firm ride and impressive high-speed stability and braking.

The Saturn **ION** is a larger, more comfortable, and more powerful vehicle than its S-Series predecessor. Early IONs were powered by a 140 hp 2.2L 4-cylinder engine and Saturn followed up with the ION 2 and 3, which came with a 145 hp 4-cylinder and an optional 175 hp 4-cylinder. The Red Line coupe used a supercharged 205 hp 4-cylinder engine hooked to a manual transmission.

The ION's many deficiencies mirror those of the S-Series coupe and its L-Series big brother. The only added wrinkle is the CVT transmission, which, despite an extended warranty following widespread quality complaints, is only good for the trash heap. In the meantime, ION and VUE SUV owners are likely to face long servicing waits and mind-boggling depreciation.

All of the above cars have lost most of their resale value since being dropped by GM. Prices vary from $1,500 for a 2002 base model, up to $4,000 for a 2007 Red Line version.

TSBs and owner complaints indicate that a variety of major quality problems are likely to crop up throughout all model years. These include self-destructing engines; poorly welded exhaust systems; alternator and AC compressor failures; chronically malfunctioning automatic transmissions; a host of body defects, led by paint delamination, rattles, and wind and water leaks; and failure-prone brake, ignition, fuel, and electrical systems. (Are flickering, dimming lights your cup of tea?)

Saturn crashworthiness is Above Average as tested by NHTSA; however, IIHS gives low marks for side collisions and head restraint protection.

The Saturn **Astra** (2007–08) and **Aura** (2008) are two Not Recommended cars. Both models are recent arrivals that are relatively fuel frugal and not as failure prone as the VUE, but now that Saturn has left the marketplace, servicing for the low-volume Astra and Aura is more problematic, and resale values are dropping. The compact Astra is a warmed-over Belgian-built Opel that carries a 138 hp 1.8L 4-cylinder engine coupled to a 5-speed manual or 4-speed automatic transmission. The 2008 Aura is a mid-sized car that may be powered by a 219 hp 3.5L V6 (down from 224 horses in the 2007 model) or a 252 hp 3.6L V6 hooked to a 6-speed automatic transmission. The 2008 hybrid variant uses a 164 hp 2.4L 4-cylinder engine that has six fewer horses than the previous year's Green Line (hybrid) model. Auras have been afflicted by some brake, suspension, and body glitches. Owners of 2008 models who lose power steering can get the unit fixed for free under Special Coverage Adjustment #10183, dated July 20, 2010. GM will replace the failed components free of charge up to 10 years/100,000 mi. (160,000 km).

Astras appear to be slightly better built. Although the base price for the Astra was given as $17,910, many dealers discounted them to less than $12,000. Today, a 2008 Astra sells for $5,500–$6,500. Auras suffer from a similarly high rate of depreciation: A 2008 that originally sold for $24,240 can now be found for $7,500–$9,000. The Astra hasn't been tested by NHTSA; the Aura got the agency's top five-star rating for frontal and side protection and four stars for rollover protection.

The Saturn **Sky** and Pontiac **Solstice** convertibles (2007–08) went through only three model years before the Saturn and Pontiac divisions began closing down. Both vehicles are rated Below Average following owner reports of powertrain, fuel, electrical, and brake system problems, plus very poor fit and finish. The Sky and Solstice received four stars for front and side crashworthiness and five stars for rollover protection. A 2008 Sky convertible that originally sold for $33,125 is now worth $11,00 to $12,000; the high-performance Red Line version sells for about $2,000 more.

On 2004–07 Saturns, a defective power steering assist control module will be replaced free of charge up to 10 years/160,000 km, says GM Service Bulletin #10187, issued July 20, 2010. If GM balks, ask for a small claims refund since GM's bulletin commitment was made after its bankruptcy:

CAMPAIGN—POWER STEERING LOSS OF POWER ASSIST

BULLETIN NO.: 10187   DATE: JULY 20, 2010

SPECIAL COVERAGE ADJUSTMENT—POWER STEERING ASSIST
2004–07 Saturn ION
CONDITION: Some customers of 2004–07 model year Saturn ION vehicles, equipped with electric power steering, may experience a sudden loss of power steering assist, which could occur at any time while driving the vehicle.
SPECIAL COVERAGE ADJUSTMENT: This special coverage covers the condition described above for a period of 10 years or 100,000 miles (160,000 km), whichever occurs first, from the date the vehicle was originally placed in service, regardless of ownership.
Retailers are to replace the power steering motor. The repairs will be made at no charge to the customer.

A similar free replacement program exists for the 2006–07 fuel pump module. Again if GM balks, or says the policy only covers certain regions, get your money from small claims court using the service bulletin below:

CAMPAIGN—FUEL PUMP WARRANTY EXTENSION

BULLETIN NO.: 09275A   DATE: MARCH 3, 2010

SPECIAL COVERAGE ADJUSTMENT—FUEL ODOR OR SPOTTING ON GROUND—REPLACE FUEL PUMP MODULE.
2006–07 Chevrolet Cobalt; 2006 Pontiac G4; 2006–07 Saturn ION; and 2007 Pontiac G5
The plastic supply or return port on the modular reservoir assembly (MRA) may crack. If either of these ports develop a crack, fuel will leak from the area. The customer may notice a fuel odor while the vehicle is being driven or after it is parked. If the crack becomes large enough, fuel may be observed dripping onto the ground and vehicle performance may be affected.
SPECIAL COVERAGE ADJUSTMENT: This special coverage covers the condition described above for a period of 10 years or 120,000 miles (193,000 km), whichever occurs first, from the date the vehicle was originally placed in service, regardless of ownership. Dealers are to replace the fuel pump module. The repairs will be made at no charge to the customer.

The Not Recommended Saturn **VUE** (2002–08), the company's oldest model since the L-Series was dropped in 2005, is no longer sold since the Saturn division shut down in October 2010. Stay away from the problem-plagued GM-bred 4- and 6-cylinder powerplants and opt instead for the more durable Honda V6 first used in 2004. The CVT is another failure-prone component to avoid.

Hyundai

The **Genesis Sedan** and **Coupe** are two Hyundais worth buying. The 2009–10 Sedan is rated a Best Buy and the Coupe is ranked an Above Average car. The 2010 3.8L GT Coupe can be found for around $22,500 and a 2010 V8 Tech Sedan will cost about $10,000 more.

Hyundai's Sedan targets BMW and Mercedes-Benz big spenders with rear-drive cars that are loaded with high-tech safety, performance, and convenience features. You get quick and smooth acceleration with the refined V6 (a V8 is optional); excellent, no-surprise handling; and good fuel economy. The interior is tastefully done with most features and instruments well within reach. Not only is the cabin roomy, but it accommodates 6-foot-plus passengers quite well, especially in the rear seating area. The Genesis Coupe and Sedan have also earned impressive five-star crashworthiness rankings (2009–10 models). NHTSA-posted safety-related owner complaints for the 2009 Sedan: sudden loss of power on the highway due to a faulty throttle sensor; a stuck throttle; a jerky acceleration as the transmission "hunts" for the proper gear; premature wearout of Dunlop original-equipment tires; intermittent short circuits that cut out the interior lights; and the steering may have a severe left or right pull, says one owner:

> Research this problem on the Internet through Google under the heading "Hyundai Genesis steering issue and left or right pull" and you will get more than [one] hundred similar complaints from new owners since the 2008/2009 model release. I have been to the dealer 3 times to fix this issue within 3000 miles—but Hyundai dealers are just performing alignments...that don't fix the problem.

Both the V6 and V8 engines produce less torque at higher rpm than do some competitors, the ride can be twitchy at times, and there's excessive body roll during hard cornering. Hyundai mechanics say the suspension is tuned for a full load, so anything less makes the vehicle wander.

The smaller 2010 Genesis Coupe was launched a year after the sedan and targets the Chevrolet Camaro and Ford Mustang. The coupe is a different animal that maximizes the vehicle's highway performance through a high level of driver input. Original-equipment Dunlop tires may be too sensitive to the crown of the road. Navigation and audio system controls are cumbersome. Hyundai recommends premium fuel for extra horsepower from the V8, but it's not worth the higher fuel cost for just eight more horses.

NHTSA-logged safety-related complaints for the 2010 model include sudden, unintended acceleration; an acceleration "flat spot" that causes the Coupe to almost "die out" when accelerating; premature transmission failure; lurching when put into gear; traction control that doesn't work on occasion; and the severe steering pull and the car's inability to track in a straight line. Owners add that the hood bolts come off; the hood is often misaligned, causing lots of hood buffeting; a raw fuel smell pervades the cabin; and the brakes lock up for no reason.

Hyundai's 1997–2008 Above Average **Tiburon** is a steal for buyers who want some high-performance features without spending much money. Essentially a sportier variant of the Elantra, this is a fun-to-drive budget sport coupe with a good overall reliability record. Since dealer maintenance and repair costs can be a bit higher than average, owners usually go to independent garages to get cheaper inspections and repairs. Used prices vary from $2,500–$8,000 for 1997–2008 models. On early models, the base 16-valve 1.8L 4-cylinder engine is smooth, efficient, and adequate when mated to the 5-speed manual transmission. The 1998 versions use a stronger 145 hp 2.0L engine, and the $2,500 to $4,000 2003 GT is powered by a sizzling 2.7L V6.

Crashworthiness and rollover resistance as tested on the 2004 model have been outstanding: five stars for frontal and side occupant protection and four stars for rollover resistance. 2007 models did almost as well, with five-star frontal protection and four-star side and rollover protection ratings. The 2008s got four stars for side and rollover protection. Head restraints were judged Poor up to the 2003 models, but Good thereafter.

Although no serious defects have been reported, be on the lookout for oil leaks, body deficiencies (fit, finish, and assembly), harsh shifting, clutch failures, slipping between gears (with the automatic), and brake glitches (premature front brake wear and excessive brake noise).

Jaguar/Land Rover

Ford's entry-level 2000–08 **Jaguar S-Type** and the **XF series** are two of the many Jaguar models that are Not Recommended. As Europe continues to go through its present economic crises, Jaguar sales have worsened while Rover is just getting by. Owners claim recent build quality is early Jurassic; reliability is reliably unreliable, and servicing is inconsistent and costly. Parts availability suffers from an inefficient U.K./Ford/Tata alliance (Tata is an Indian conglomerate) and parts costs reflect the added commission of each member of that alliance. The S-Type is an attractively styled small rear-drive luxury sedan that shares its platform with the Lincoln LS. The S-Type's V8 engine provides plenty of power, and the car handles well. Nevertheless, it's a terrible buy due to its clunky, failure-prone automatic transmission; limited cargo room; unreliable engine, electronics, and fuel delivery system; and frequently needed brake repairs.

Resale prices reflect a stunningly high depreciation rate. A 2006 S-Type that sold for $64,295 is now worth $11,500. It is expected to lose half that value within the next three years. The 2010 XF Luxury, which sold originally for $61,800 is now worth $37,000. In three years, it is projected to sell for $21,350. Other examples: A $62,000 2008 S-Type 3.0 sedan is now worth $19,500—less than a third of its original cost. Surprisingly, an entry-level 2008 Land Rover LR2 SE 3.2-6 is worth about the same as the Jaguar above. Although this is good news for used car buyers, the high cost of Jaguar and Land Rover maintenance and repairs will cut deep into the savings realized from the cars' low purchase price.

Kia

Kia's 2004–09 **Amanti** models get a Below Average rating; the **Magentis** earns an Above Average score for its 2007–10 models; an Average rating for the 2005–06 versions; and a Below Average rating for the 2001–04s. Of these two vehicles, the 2009 Magentis LX V6 is the better buy. It originally sold for $24,295 and can now be picked up for $12,500. The low price, added features, better performance, dependable servicing and parts supply, and likelihood of some non-expired warranty coverage are all pluses.

Carrying the Hyundai XG350's 3.5L V6 and 5-speed manumatic transmission, the 2004 Amanti is Kia's first large sedan. Amanti's styling is different from the XG350's, though, and it sits on a 5 cm longer wheelbase and a 10 cm longer body, giving it about 180 additional kilograms that erode overall handling, on-road performance, and fuel economy. The car originally came with a modicum of safety and convenience features, like anti-lock four-wheel disc brakes, front and rear side airbags, and side curtain airbags. Unfortunately, the much-recommended traction/anti-skid control is offered only as an option. A 2008 V6 will cost $13,500.

Amanti reliability has been worse than average, characterized by rapid brake and tire wear, electrical short circuits, chronic front-end noise, and fuel problems that cause the engine to start poorly, suddenly shut down, jerk when accelerating, or hesitate and then surge. Fit and finish is also problematic, with owners complaining of multiple water and air leaks.

Amanti highway performance is very disappointing. Engine power is unreliable, steering is imprecise, handling is clumsy, and body roll is excessive. Crash tests carried out by both NHTSA and IIHS have given both cars better than average crash ratings since 2001, except for a "poor" rating for the 2001–05 Amanti's head restraints and the 2001–05 Magentis's side crash protection.

Sold in the States as the Optima, the front-drive, five-passenger Magentis sedan is basically a Hyundai Sonata without traction control. It comes with a twin-cam 138 hp 2.4L 4-cylinder or an optional 170 hp 2.7L V6 hooked to a 4-speed automatic transmission (V6s have the Sonata's separate gate for manual shifting and four-wheel ABS). The 2009 model was restyled and given a power boost. Entry-level models were powered by a 175 hp 2.4L 4-cylinder engine. A 194 hp 2.7L V6 is found on the EX and SX.

The Magentis is nicely appointed, provides good V6 performance with the 5-speed automatic, handles competently, and rides comfortably. There's also plenty of front headroom and better-than-average fuel economy with regular fuel. The car is a bit better built than Kia's other models, but fit and finish is still inferior to other Asian makes.

Unfortunately, this car has some major weaknesses that include mediocre braking; limited rear headroom; a small trunk opening; faulty door locks that trap occupants; considerable body lean when turning; excessive tire, wind, and suspension noise; a poorly performing 4-speed automatic transmission; a wimpy 2.4L 162 hp 4-cylinder engine; and a weak dealer network. Owner complaints deal primarily with harsh shifts, stalling, brake failures, faulty door locks, poor servicing, electrical shorts, AC overheating, subpar fit and finish, premature brake pad and rotor wear, and sudden acceleration (maybe wimpy is good). Rattling fuel caps will be replaced free of charge under Campaign SA006.

Lincoln

Lincoln model ratings go from bad to good depending upon whether the car is front- or rear-drive and how long it has been on the market. For example, the Not Recommended 1999–2002 **Continental** is a luxury lemon cobbled together from leftovers fallen out of the Taurus and Sable parts bin. Other model ratings include the **LS:** Average (2000–06); **Town Car:** Recommended (1999–2010); **Zephyr:** Average (2006); and **MKZ:** Above Average (2007–10). In a nutshell: Rear-drives are generally more reliable buys than front-drive versions. For example, the discontinued 1988–2002 front-drive Continentals are dirt-cheap, mediocre performers. Servicing has become more problematic as parts dry up and knowledgeable mechanics die off, leaving you with a garaged car that's more of a sculpture than a conveyance. The rear-drive Town Car and LS ($8,000 for a 2006 LS) are the best choices for quality and performance. A 2008 MKZ ($13,500) and its 2006 Zephyr predecessor ($7,000) are also quite competent performers that are good second choices. Town Cars haven't changed much over the years. Look for a $19,000 2008 Signature L model, with 60,000 to 80,000 km on the clock.

These large luxury cruisers are proof that quality isn't always proportional to the money you spend. Several designer series offer all the luxury options anyone could wish for, but the two ingredients most owners would expect to find—high quality and consistent reliability—are sadly lacking, especially with the front-drive versions. The front drives are noted for poor-quality brakes, automatic transmissions, electrical systems, body hardware, and subpar fit and finish. NHTSA-recorded safety complaints also target more front-drive than rear-drive Lincolns, with engine, transmission, airbag, and brake failures cropping up repeatedly over the years. Crashworthiness ratings from NHTSA and IIHS are mostly four- and five-star, except for the 2001–02 Town Car's one-star award and the Continental's two-star score for head restraint protection, and the 2006 Zephyr/MKZ, which received three-star scores for side, offset, and roof protection.

What about the trade-off in better fuel economy with the front drives? Don't count on it. What little fuel savings you'll enjoy will be eaten up in brake, transmission, and suspension repairs.

The rear-drive Town Car shares most of its parts with the fairly reliable Crown Victoria and Grand Marquis, and is easily found with little mileage and at bargain prices. Cheaper high-mileage units are frequently sold by airport limousine companies and taxi services that run the airport shuttle service.

The car's rear-drive configuration is relatively inexpensive to repair, and parts aren't hard to find. Nevertheless, the Town Car is still afflicted with many generic problems that appear year after year. Some of the more common problems: transmission, AC, and electrical system failures and body hardware fit and finish deficiencies.

The LS rear-drive sedan comes with a high-performance 200 hp variant of the Taurus 3.0L V6, mated with an optional manual or standard automatic gearbox. A better engine is the 250 hp 3.9L V8 (based on the Jaguar XK8 coupe's engine) coupled with a semi-automatic transmission. The 2001 version adopted standard traction control and the 2002–06 models changed very little over the years. And the car was dropped in mid 2006.

AC, body, powertrain, and electrical system glitches are commonplace. Owners also report jerky transmission shifting, excessive drivetrain and body noise and vibrations, and inconsistent braking response.

Ford's smallest Lincoln ever, the mid-size, entry-level 2006 Zephyr was sized and priced below the rear-drive Lincoln LS that it replaced. It's essentially a luxury-equipped spin-off of the front-drive Ford Fusion and Mercury Milan mid-size sedans, vehicles that are quite similar to the Mazda6. Zephyr carries a 221 hp V6 engine hooked to a 6-speed automatic transmission, plus all of the most important safety features. Zephyr's name was changed to MKZ in 2007.

Mercedes Benz

Below Average–rated **Smart** minicars are an embarrassment to Mercedes-Benz, a company that is proud of its over-the-top, high-performance, and high-end vehicles. So why does Mercedes sell the Smart econocar? Because no one else wants it. In fact, the Smart franchise has gone from Mercedes to independent dealers and back again, all in the past decade. Now, the car is back under Mercedes' wing until it's dropped altogether. The 2009–10 models are rated Below Average; earlier versions are Not Recommended. Although the post-2008s are a bit improved in performance and quality control, there are many cheaper, more reliable Asian-, European-, and Detroit-hailed small cars—like the Ford Focus,

Honda Fit, and Civic (through 2011); the Mazda2 and Mazda3; Nissan's Sentra; and the VW TDI. These are all frugal runners that are more refined and easier to service and repair.

This European toy car is not suited for North American roads and will lose more than half its original value after three years of use. If you are cruising at 120 km/h, you're killing its little engine. Plus, there's the Smart's lethargic acceleration, tiny wheels that transform small potholes into moon craters, and a stiff-riding short wheel base that compromises emergency handling.

The Smart's poor highway performance hasn't gone unnoticed by a number of independent auto publications, including these two:

> Beyond the [Smart] Fortwo's safety concerns, it also has sluggish acceleration, even for a subcompact car. It is low on utility since it offers seating for just two and only 12 cubic feet of cargo space (and that's only if you're willing to obscure the rear window). Test drivers also complain loudly about the car's sluggish transmission and the fact that the engine requires premium gasoline.
>
> U.S. NEWS AND WORLD REPORT
> JULY 21, 2010

> Herky-jerky automatic gearbox, seats only two, gets buffeted on the highway by stiff crosswinds and big trucks.
>
> EDMUNDS.COM

Smarts depreciate much too quickly for a small car that one would imagine to be in high demand by fuel-frugal drivers. For example, sold new for $16,700, a used 2006 entry-level Smart Fortwo Coupe now goes for $3,000 to $4,500; a new $19,700 2006 entry-level convertible now sells for between $6,000 and $7,000. 2010 prices are a bit more than double those of the 2006 models.

Service costs aren't cheap; after all, why should dealers give you the lowest prices and best service if you have nowhere else to go? Dealers much prefer to focus on high-end Mercedes products. Smart sales have declined smartly during the past few years as more refined American and European competitors hit the streets. As a result, few independent suppliers stock Smart parts, and dealers get annoyed when asked to look for some obscure Smart part in the back of the warehouse while the little car takes up valuable bay space and their mechanics' time.

An extended warranty is a good idea, but the estimated $2,000 cost is a budget-buster for such a cheap used car. Plus, It'll only keep you longer in a dealer network that doesn't want you.

Finally, the Smart is not as green or as frugal as environmentalists claim, since its estimated 41 miles per U.S. gallon (premium) (5.7L/100 km) is no climate saver, though the diesel fuel economy at an estimated 74 mpg (3.2L/100 km) is impressive. Yet the diesel advantage has been mitigated by soaring diesel prices up to $1.23 a litre in Canada versus $1.29 a litre for regular fuel. In the States diesel fuel sells for $4.42 per gallon versus $3.81 a gallon for regular fuel.

As for reliability and safety concerns, the Smart receives mixed reviews. Reliability figures on the 2008 model compiled by *Consumer Reports* magazine show serious deficiencies affecting the transmission, body hardware, fuel and electrical systems, and overall fit and finish.

As for crashworthiness the little tyke does quite well. NHTSA has given the 2008 through 2010 Smart Fortwo (2-door) a four-star rating for frontal protection and a five-star score for side occupant crash protection. Rollover resistance was given three stars for those same model years. IIHS has given the 2008 through 2010 Smart a Good rating for frontal and side-impact occupant protection, as well as roof strength. Head-restraint effectiveness was judged Acceptable.

Second-generation models come with standard electronic stability control and side curtain airbags. For reliability and overall highway performance, all first-generation Fortwos (built through 2007) come up far short.

Common complaints include chronic stalling; the transmission "hanging up" in gear during hard acceleration or sticking in Park so the car must be towed; myriad short circuits (most common: door locks that won't lock and interior lights that behave erratically); premature ball joint wear; blower motor failures; the ABS warning light coming on due to a faulty brake light switch; defective tire valve stems; inaccurate fuel gauge readings; polycarbonate roof panels that often need replacing (spider cracks); and an assortment of other body glitches.

Mitsubishi

Mitsubishi sold the following 2005–08 models in Canada: the compact **Lancer ES** ($15,998); the mid-sized **Galant DE** ($23,998); and the **Eclipse GS** ($25,498), **GT** ($32,998), and **Spyder** ($35,148 for the 2005). A convertible **Spyder GS** version returned as a $31,998 2007 model, and is now worth about $11,500. Earlier 2005 Spyder GS versions can be found for $7,000–$8,500, while a 2008, which originally cost $32,298, is now only $15,000. As for the Lancer and Galant versions, the 2007 Galant ES (there wasn't a Lancer for that model year) sells for about $7,500. 2005 and 2006 Galants are worth $5,500 and $6,500, while the cheaper 2005 and 2006 Lancers go for $3,500 and $4,500. Only three models were sold in 2010: the **Galant, Lancer,** and **Lancer Sportback**. They are now worth $15,000, $9,500, and $13,500.

These entry-level front-drive econocars run the gamut from the cheap and mundane ES to the high-performance street racer called the OZ Rally. Yes, Mitsus depreciate faster than most Japanese vehicles, but if you're shopping for used models, that's an important advantage. And don't forget: Mitsubishis are just as reliable as other Asian makes, and can be serviced practically anywhere. There's not much to dislike with the **Lancer**, and that's why we've given it an Above Average rating. You get spirited acceleration with the OZ Rally's turbocharged engine, excellent frontal and offset crashworthiness scores, and good overall quality. The only drawbacks: The base engine is a bit horsepower-challenged (especially with the automatic transmission), you can expect some parts shortages, and side crashworthiness is below average.

The **Galant** is another Above Average Mitsubishi. It's reasonably priced, carries competent 4- and 6-cylinder powerplants, handles very well, enjoys good crashworthiness scores, and is fairly reliable, as was its Colt predecessor over a decade ago. On the downside, some model years don't have a manual transmission to make full use of the car's spirited engine, and rear-seat entry and exit can take some acrobatics.

The **Eclipse** is an Above Average, beautifully styled, reasonably priced sporty coupe; however, its on-road performance lags behind its looks. As with other Mitsubishis, early models quickly lose their value, making the car a bargain if bought used. A $23,857 2003 model sells for $3,500; a $23,998 2004 is now worth $5,000; and a $35,148 2005 Spyder (if you get the cheapest model available) is now worth almost $9,000.

There are two engine choices available: a 162 hp 2.4L 4-banger and a 263 hp V6. A manual 5-speed is standard, but the optional automatic 5-speed and the 6-speed manual are better performers. Both engines have plenty of grunt throughout their power range when mated to a manual gearbox. Handling is exceptionally good on all models, but the sportier GT and Spyder are better than the rest (a 2009 Spyder GT-P convertible runs about $21,000). Some of the Eclipse's deficiencies include an automatic transmission that isn't quick enough for confident highway merging; frequent shifting with the manual transmission; and, with the automatic tranny, real-world fuel economy that's much less than promised.

Porsche

The **Boxster**, **Cayenne**, and **Cayman** have parlayed Porsche's legendary racing cachet into a half-dozen bestselling high-performance sports car models. Nevertheless, these are high-maintenance cars that are dealer-dependent and failure-prone, earning them a Not Recommended rating.

They are also outrageously overpriced in Canada. Shop in the States and you will see savings of up to $40,000 (CDN). Porsche was forced to cut its Canadian prices by almost 10 percent when the Canadian dollar increased value in September 2007. Now that the dollar is stronger once again, adroit haggling could get you a new Porsche in the States for less money than a used one would cost in Canada.

A Porsche is a source of worry about service, repairs, theft, depreciation, high insurance costs, and premature wear and tear from cold and snow. Recent consumer complaints show that even the entry-level Boxster hasn't escaped the typical Porsche factory-induced defects affecting the engine, transmission, electrical system, brakes, and fit and finish. Making the reliability failings hurt more is the company's attitude that its cars are "perfect," and what problems that do occur are caused mainly by "driver abuse." Much to most owners' surprise and contrary to what Porsche dealers will tell you, Porsches do depreciate quickly. For example, a 2009 Boxster that originally sold for $58,400 is now worth about $36,000. Other Porsche models also lose much of their value during the first few years they are on the road. Although originally priced at $100,400, a 2004 911 Carrera is now worth one-third of that amount, or about $30,000; in three years that figure is predicted to drop to $16,000. So much for a Porsche being a solid investment.

But these are exceptional cars that are famous for high-performance acceleration and handling and impressive braking. As with most sports cars, you can expect lots of engine and road noise, acrobatic entry and exit, cramped rear seating, and limited storage space. *Consumer Reports* and internal service bulletins confirm that all model years have a higher-than-average number of factory-related problems, highlighted by engine, transmission, fuel system, and fit and finish deficiencies.

Saab

All Saab model years are rated Not Recommended, principally because the automaker declared bankruptcy in December 2011. The most popular models are the 9-3 and 9-5. Both models suffer from an abundance of defective components that imperil the cars' reliability and your own financial solvency. Be especially wary of powertrain, electrical, and fuel system breakdowns; brake failures; and poor fit and finish.

One bit of good news is that General Motors says it will cover any warranty remaining on vehicles sold under its ownership of Saab, which ended in February 2010. GM estimates its warranty will cover a majority of the about 48,000 Saabs still under warranty in the U.S. and 9,000 in Canada. Saab owners can also hold their selling dealer responsible for damages arising from the bankruptcy or manufacturing defects without any time limitation (see *Lemon-Aid*'s Jurisprudence section in Part Two).

NHTSA has given the 9-3 four stars for frontal crashworthiness and rollover resistance; side crash protection was awarded five stars. The 9-5 D remains untested by NHTSA. IIHS rated the 9-3's frontal offset, side, and rear crash protection as "Good." The 9-5's frontal offset crash protection was given a "Good" rating and side impact protection scored "Average." Head restraints were rated "Average." The 9-7X models got the worst scores among the Saabs tested by the IIHS; frontal offset protection was given an "Average," side crashworthiness was judged to be "Marginal," and restraints were rated "Poor." A 2007 9-3 model that sold new for $35,135 is now worth $8,000. A $43,450 9-5 is worth $10,500. The same two models of 2009 vintage now sell for $12,500 and $15,500.

Volkswagen

Volkswagen's **Phaeton** full-sized luxury sedan was greeted by underwhelming sales and restrained dealer enthusiasm when it was launched in Canada as a 2004 model. After all, who in their right mind would buy a $96,500 V8 VW sedan that is now worth barely $14,000? 2006 was the car's last year in Canada, and those models vary in value between $18,000 for the entry-level model and $25,000 for the top-of-the-line W12 four-passenger version that originally sold for $144,000. The Phaeton's platform is shared with the Bentley Continental GT, and some powertrain components are also used in the Audi A8. No crashworthiness scores are available and owner feedback has been insufficient to offer a reading on the long-term reliability of these vehicles.

Minivans and Vans

Ford

The 1995–2003 Ford **Windstar** and 2004–07 **Freestar** are Not Recommended front-drive minivans. The Freestar is a Windstar in disguise, with the same poor-quality components and lousy fit and finish that made driving hell for Windstar owners. The Windstar is infamous for atrocious quality control (particularly, with such vital powertrain components as the engine and automatic transmission), stonewalled owner complaints, and life-threatening defects. The Honda Odyssey and Toyota Sienna (but not the 2004) are good alternative choices. Some full-sized Ford (Econoline), and GM (Chevy Van, Vandura, Express, or Savana) rear-drive cargo/passenger vans are more reliable and practical buys, even if they cost a bit more to fuel. 2002–03 Windstars sell for $1,000–$2,000; 2004–07 Freestars cost between $3,000 and $7,000.

Ford can call it the Windstar or the Freestar; the fact remains that owners call it a "death trap." Sure, the Windstar combines an impressive five-star crash safety rating, plenty of raw power, an exceptional ride, and impressive cargo capacity. But these minivans have failure-prone engines, self-destructing automatic transmissions, collapsing rear axles, "Do I feel lucky?" brakes, and unreliable electrical systems.

The Windstar's rust-prone coil springs frequently break, blow out the front tire, and make the minivan uncontrollable. As solace, Ford says it will pay for coil breakage up to 10 years on vehicles registered in rust-prone regions. Another rust-induced safety hazard is self-destructing rear axles. More than half a million 1998–2003 Windstars were recalled to replace rust-damaged rear axles that could separate and cause the vehicle to careen out of control. It is estimated that a third of those vehicles were never fixed because owners got tired of waiting for the parts.

While on the subject of crashes, 2001–03 Windstars earned only three stars out of five by the IIHS for occupant protection in frontal offset collisions, while the 2006–07 Freestar did worse in the IIHS side crash, scoring only one star.

Another counterpoint to Ford's Windstar crashworthiness boasting is the frightening archive of Windstar/Freestar safety-related failures compiled by NHTSA. Owners report sudden stalling, acceleration, steering loss, exploding windows, horn failures, wheels falling off, sliding doors that open and close on their own, and vehicles rolling away while parked.

Other safety-related deficiencies include the lack of head restraints for all seats on early Windstars and a digital dash that's often confusing, failure-prone, and expensive to replace. Drivers must also contend with mediocre handling, restricted side and rear visibility, and an abundance of clunks, rattles, and wind and road noise.

Freestar: Too little, too late

Built on a modified Taurus platform, the Freestar gives you the same uninspired, though predictable, carlike handling characteristics of Ford's mid-size family sedans. You'll also find many of the horrific engine, automatic transmission, electrical, suspension, and brake system problems experienced by Taurus and Sable owners.

Ford's denial of owner claims has been blasted in small-claims court judgments across Canada. Judges have ruled that engines and transmissions (and power-sliding doors) must be reasonably durable long after the warranty expires, whether the vehicle was bought new or used, notwithstanding that it was repaired by an independent or that it had the same problem repaired earlier for free. The three best engine judgments supporting Ford owners are *Dufour v. Ford Canada Ltd.*, *Schaffler v. Ford Motor Company Limited and Embrun Ford Sales Ltd.*, and *John R. Reid and Laurie M. McCall v. Ford Motor Company of Canada* (see Part Two of this guide).

Dangerous doors

We noted previously that the courts have slammed Ford for allowing dangerously defective sliding doors to go uncorrected year after year. Typical scenarios reported by owners include the following: a sliding door slammed shut on a child's head while the vehicle was parked on an incline; passengers are often pinned by the door; the door reopens as it is closing; the door often pops open while the vehicle is underway; a driver's finger was broken when closing a manual sliding door; and the handle is too close to the door jam, which is a hazard that has been reported on the Internet since 1999. Owners also report that the 2003 Windstar's automatic sliding door opens by itself or the door will not power open, and the door lock assembly freezes.

In *Sharman v. Formula Ford Sales Limited, Ford Credit Limited, and Ford Motor Company of Canada Limited* (Ontario Superior Court of Justice (Oakville), No. 17419/02SR, 2003/10/07), Justice Shepard awarded the owner of a 2000 Windstar $7,500 for mental distress resulting from the breach of the implied warranty of fitness plus $7,207 for breach of contract and breach of warranty. The problem: The Windstar's sliding door wasn't secure and leaked air and water after many attempts to repair it. Interestingly, the judge cited the *Wharton* decision, among other decisions, as support for his award for mental distress (see page 115).

2004–10 **Econolines** are Average buys, but earlier 1999–2003 versions are rated Below Average. The 2010 **Transit Connect** merits an Average rating. Easily found at reasonable prices, these E-series vans don't possess any glaring virtues or vices; they perform in a manner similar to that of the Chrysler and GM large, rear-drive vans. Overall reliability is on par with similar Chrysler and GM full-sized vans.

One of the better buys among the Econolines is the 2008 Wagon XL. Selling for $11,500 (new: $32,599) it has a restyled front-end that increases engine airflow; more responsive steering and front and rear suspensions; additional load-carrying capability; and improved seats. Chassis improvements include a better-tuned suspension, larger sway bars, revised rear shock absorbers. There is better road feedback and reduced steering effort plus an upgraded braking system with larger rotors and calipers.

The Ford Club Wagon, which is an Econoline dressed up for passenger duty, offers lots of room with capacity to spare for luggage. Nevertheless, full-sized vans have a very high floor, long panelled windows, and seats that are bolted to the floor—unlike most minivans, which feature powered middle windows and seats that stow into the floor or fold to the side.

There are a number of sound reasons for buying a used Ford Econoline: It's more reliable than any Detroit front-drive; all models are reasonably well equipped; it carries a more-refined powertrain and brakes that were phased in with the 2004s; and it has a good control and instrument layout, adequate interior room, and an acceptable ride. Negatives: It's huge and heavy with sloppy handling, similar to the Ram lineup. With earlier vehicles, excessive braking distances and harsh transmission shifting and hunting are the norm. Get used to limited second-row legroom and lots of engine, wind, and road noise. Quality control isn't the best, especially in regards to the failure-prone 6.0L diesel engine, alternators, and AC compressor.

2001–03 Econolines scored poorly for rollover protection in NHTSA-run crash tests (two stars), though the same model years scored four stars for frontal crash protection.

Ford engine defects are legion, with turbocharger, high-pressure pump, oil pump, and injector malfunctions, and with EGR valve coking, when unburned deposits coat the valve and cause power loss, surging, and stalling. Electrical, fuel, and ignition systems are constantly on the fritz. The 3- and 4-speed automatic transmissions, steering and suspension components (lower steering shaft/tie rods), and brakes (calipers, pads, rotors, and torn rear caliper boots) have also come under considerable criticism.

Body fit and finish are typically below average, and have been that way for the past several decades. Premature rusting hasn't been a serious problem since the mid-1980s (except for rusted-out oil pans), but water does leak into the cabin, principally through the windshield, doors, and third-brake light. Paint delamination and peeling are also quite common.

The newer **Transit Connect** is more reliable than the Econoline models, but its overall performance is worse.

Sold worldwide for the past decade, the Transit Connect is essentially an easily accessed, capacious rolling box with traction control; an anti-skid system; a vehicle tracking device; and an Internet connection. Handling is fairly good, though fuel economy is only acceptable. It can seat two, four, or five passengers and uses minivan-like sliding rear side doors and two rear "barn doors" similar to a commercial van. Powered by a puny 136 hp 2.0L 4-cylinder engine and a rather primitive, fuel-thirsty 4-speed automatic transmission, the Transit is longer, wider, and heavier than a Focus. It is aimed at the small-business commercial market and fits between the discontinued compact Chevrolet HHR and the recently ditched humongous and problematic Dodge Sprinter. NHTSA gives the van a five-star rating for protection from frontal- and side-impact injury; the wagon got a similar rating but added four-star rollover protection. IIHS hasn't tested the Connect, yet.

Owners report that the Transit Connect has lethargic acceleration caused by a sluggish, uncertain transmission and it's very vulnerable to side winds. Interior materials look cheap; tall head restraints and closed rear quarter panels limit visibility; drivetrain pedals are too close to each other for such a wide interior and the pads are unusually small; the navigation feature is glitch-ridden; and there's a symphony of engine and road noise that transform the interior into a Jamaican steel drum. Owners can expect problems with premature brake wear and powertrain malfunctions due to the Transit's heft. Internal service bulletins target various water leaks; excessive steering play, noise; and rear brake thumping or knocking. NHTSA-posted owner complaints are incredibly few, listing the following incidents: Traction control causes the van to stall in traffic; no-starts due to a faulty PCM module; and early wearout of the starter, brake rotors, pads, and calipers, wheel bearings, and hubs.

General Motors

GM's 1999–2005 **Astro** and **Safari** run-of-the-mill, squarish "bread box" minivans are Average buys. They are easy to repair, and cost only about $4,500 for a 2005 version. Stay away from the unreliable all-wheel-drive models, though:

they're expensive to repair, parts are always on back order, and repairs don't last long.

More a utility truck than a comfortable minivan, the Astro and Safari are built on a reworked S-10 pickup chassis. As such, they offer uninspiring handling, average-quality mechanical and body components, and relatively high fuel consumption. Best alternatives depend upon how much interior room and power you need. For example, a full-sized, rear-drive GM van like the Savana or Express can give you both the pulling power and interior space for camping or running a small business.

The GM Safari.

2000–05 models are a bit more reliable and better performing than previous models, inasmuch as they underwent considerable upgrading by GM. Nevertheless, buyers should pay extra attention to the following areas: automatic transmission clunk; electrical system shorts; excessive vibration transmitted through the AWD; sliding-door misalignment and broken hinges; heating and AC performance hampered by poor air distribution; electronic computer module and fuel-system glitches that cause the Check Engine light to remain lit; hard starts, no-starts, or chronic stalling, especially when going downhill; and poor braking performance (brake pedal hardens, and brakes don't work after going over bumps or rough roads) and expensive brake maintenance. NHTSA rates frontal crashworthiness and rollover protection as Average and side occupant protection as Above Average. On the other hand, IIHS rates the head restraints and offset collision protection as Poor.

Lemon-Aid doesn't recommend any front-drive minivan built by General Motors or Ford, including GM's 1999–2009 **Montana**, **Montana SV6**, **Relay**, **Silhouette**, **Terraza**, **Uplander**, and **Venture**. Minivan orphans, these aove vehicles should have never left the factory. They are unreliable and dangerous, as evidenced by their automatic transmission and engine head gasket/intake manifold gasket failures and sliding doors that may crush children.

These minivans are enticingly cheap and similarly priced. For example, the 2009s go for $9,000 to $10,000; the 2006s sell for $3,500 to $4,500; and the 2002s are practically given away for $2,000 to $3,000. Seating is limited to five adults in the standard models (two up front, and three on a removable bench seat), but this is increased to seven on other models. Seats can be folded down flat, creating additional storage space.

Passengers who require mobility assistance may use an optional Sit-N-Lift power seat system that provides convenient access to the right-hand second-row seating area and is capable of lifting 300 pounds. Operated via remote control, the power bucket seat rotates and then extends out of the vehicle before lowering for easy entry and exit. This enables a person with limited mobility to enter and exit the vehicle without needing someone to lift them. For added safety, the seat only operates when the vehicle is in Park and the door is open.

Thousands of these minivans were fitted with this unique invention from GM since they were first offered with the 2003 minivan models. If you can't find a minivan with this feature already installed, selected GM dealerships can install it as a $5,000 U.S. aftermarket option (see *www.gm.com/vehicles/services/gm_mobility*).

Crashworthiness doesn't vary much among these identical minivans. The 2005–09 models got the best scores in all categories, except for head restraint protection and IIHS frontal offset tests. As with most minivans, be wary of vehicles equipped with a power-assisted passenger-side sliding door—it's both convenient and dangerous. Despite an override circuit that should prevent the door from closing when it's blocked, a number of injuries have been reported. Furthermore, the doors frequently open when they shouldn't and can be difficult to close securely.

All models and years have had serious reliability problems—notably, faulty rear-seat latches; abysmal fit and finish; side-door glass that pops open; chronic sliding-door malfunctions; a badly mounted sliding door; automatic transmission breakdowns; AC evaporator core failures; wind buffeting noise around the front doors; engine head gasket and intake manifold defects; premature wearout of the inner and outer tie rods; electronic module (PROM) and starter failures; a poorly performing automatic transmission; premature front brake component wear, brake fluid leakage, and noisy braking; squeaks, rattles, and clunks in the instrument panel cluster area and suspension; and short circuits that burn out alternators, batteries, power door lock activators, and the blower motor.

The 2003–10 **Express** and **Savana** are Above Average buys; earlier 1999–2002 versions are rated Average. These rear-drive full-sized vans are better buys than the Ford Econoline and cheaper and more easily serviced than Chrysler's 2004 and later German-bred Sprinter.

These vans are low-priced bargains because the recent increase in fuel costs drove so many buyers away. Surprisingly, even though gasoline is cheap again, used van prices have stayed in the basement. Passenger versions are usually heavily customized and can mean great savings to second owners who get once-expensive options for practically nothing. Expect to pay $2,000 to $4,000 for the 2001–05 models and $6,000 to $14,000 for 2006–10 models.

GM's full-sized vans come with a large array of powerful engines; multiple wheelbase configurations; a comfortable, soft ride; reasonably good transmission and brakes; plenty of interior room; and dual side-access doors. They are also quite easy to convert to the needs of drivers or passengers who use wheelchairs. On the other hand, base models are poorly equipped, and their interior is cheap-looking and rather spartan. The automatic transmission has always been a bit clunky, brakes wear out early, and body fit and finish is bottom-drawer. As with all large vans, handling is ponderous and fuel-economy is nonexistent. NHTSA gave the 2008–10 models five stars for frontal impact occupant protection and three stars for rollover resistance.

Owner complaints target diesel injectors and oil cooler lines, turbochargers, and other diesel maladies. Other problem areas: doors, tires, AC, ABS sensors, brake pads and rotors, paint (delamination, peeling), suspension, catalytic converter, steering gearbox, the power-steering pump, starter, EMC fuses, electrical system, fuel sending unit, and fuel.

Hyundai/Kia

Yes, Hyundai and its Kia division have made some bad vehicles, and we don't have to go as far back as the trouble-prone trio: the 1984 Pony, 1985 Stellar, or 1986 Excel. Instead, we can point to more contemporary junkers like the discontinued 2007 Hyundai **Entourage** minivan and its Kia twin, the aging 2001–2012 **Sedona**. Both cars are Not Recommended buys from their launch dates to the present because they are so unreliable and poorly made. Nevertheless, these minivans attract bargain hunters due to their low resale price and user-friendly, roomy, versatile, and comfortable interior. Think of Hyundai's seven-seat Entourage as a Sedona twin with styling borrowed from the Hyundai Santa Fe SUV. A 2008 Kia Sedona EX for about $9,500 is the best of the bad. It's two model years removed from the 2006 redesign and is full of important safety, performance, and convenience features. The 2008 Entourage GL costs $3,000 more. It's not worth the extra dough.

NHTSA has given these models a five-star crashworthiness rating since 2001; IIHS has been equally favourable, except for its "Average" score given for frontal offset crash protection with the 2002–05s.

Until their 2006 revamping, poor fuel economy and mediocre handling were the nemesis of these two minivans. However, the upgraded V6 engine provides much more power while posting fuel economy numbers that are similar to those of the competition. Performance is still compromised by less-than-agile handling and a stiff ride. Owners' ears are assailed by excessive engine and wind noise, braking is mediocre, and overall quality control, especially fit and finish, is embarrassingly bad.

Poor reliability has traditionally been the Sedona/Entourage's weakest link. The greatest concerns: brake pads and rotors; AC compressor; fuel and electrical systems; engine (misfiring, head gasket leaks, and timing chain wearout), transmission (failures and lock-ups); hard starts or no-starts; faulty throttle position sensors that cause chronic stalling or bucking when accelerating; and overall body construction, especially sliding door glitches (sometimes the result of a faulty door motor, but more often attributable to an electrical malfunction in the control mechanism) and subpar side window mouldings. See *www.kia-forums.com* and *www.autosafety.org/autodefects.html*.

Mazda

A $3,500–$5,500 Not Recommended buy, the 2002–06 Mazda **MPV** is a particularly risky purchase because it's an orphaned low-volume model served by a dealership network that is reluctant to service a vehicle that requires hard-to-find parts and constantly breaks down. Mazda threw in the towel and dropped the MPV after the 2006 model year.

Early MPVs embodied many of the mistakes made by Honda's first Odyssey: Its 170 horses weren't adequate for people-hauling, and it was expensive for what was essentially a smaller van than buyers expected. Crashworthiness scores are mixed: NHTSA gives the MPV an Above Average rating for frontal and side crash protection and an Average score for rollover resistance. IIHS rates head restraints and side protection as Poor. Offset crash protection received an Average score.

Mercedes Benz

Next, we come to Mercedes-Benz and its problem-wracked foray into luxury sport-utilities, first launched in 1997. Known collectively as the **M-Class**, these SUVs are Not Recommended from 1998 to 2010. Even though they cost a bundle new, these luxury SUVs are "all hat and no cattle." Smart shoppers know the ML320, 350, 500, and 550 models depreciate about 50 percent after five years (a $60,000 2008 ML350 has already dropped to $27,500). The ML350 was launched as a 2003 model and sold for $50,600; it's now worth about $9,500. A 2005 ML500 that originally sold for $68,690 is now worth approximately $14,500. The main drawbacks of these luxury lemons are poor quality control; unreliable, limited servicing; and so-so parts availability. Owners report engine, automatic transmission, brake, master cylinder, fuel pump, oxygen sensor, and mass airflow sensor failures; electrical system shorts; prematurely worn brake pads and rotors; and lousy fit and finish that produces water leaks, rattles, and paint defects.

Nissan/Ford

The 1993–2002 Ford **Villager** and 1993–2009 Nissan **Quest** are two more poor-quality and badly designed minivans that are rated Not Recommended. Even though it was larger, more powerful, and better appointed than the old 2002 Quest and its Villager variant, the 2004 Quest's redesign was so poor that sales never recovered and the 2010 model was dropped altogether. Major engineering goofs and poor-quality body and electrical components still plague the Quest through the 2012 model. Although any Quest purchase is a "leap into the abyss," the $11,500 2008 SL version is the best buy in what is a terrible lot. It is fairly well-equipped and sells for about a third of its original price. A 2002 final-year Mercury Villager is now worth between $2,000 and $3,000. NHTSA gives the minivans its top, five-star crash protection ranking, except for the four stars given for rollover resistance. IIHS gave a "poor" rating for the 2004–10 head restraints and to the 2001 Quest for offset crash protection.

1993–2003 Quest/Villager

Smaller and more carlike than most minivans, the pre-2004 Villager and Quest are sized comfortably between the regular and extended Chrysler minivans. The early minivans' strongest assets are a 170 hp 3.3L V6 engine plus carlike ride, handling, and cornering achieved from borrowed Nissan Maxima parts.

These fuel-thirsty minivans are quite heavy and the 3.0L and 3.3L engines burn lots of fuel to carry the extra weight; GM's 2.8L engines produce more torque, without as much of a fuel penalty. Other minuses: the interior looks cheap, suspension is too soft, rear-seat access can be difficult, and the control layout can be a bit confusing.

Most owner-reported problems involve excessive brake noise and premature brake wear, door lock malfunctions, interior noise, and driveline vibrations. There have also been many reports of engine exhaust manifold and crankshaft failures that cost up to $7,000 to repair. Other problems include electrical shorts; brake failures because of vibration, binding, or overheating; premature front disc, rotor, and pad wear; chronic stalling, possibly because of faulty fuel pumps or a shorted electrical system; and loose steering with veering at highway speeds.

Fit and finish is subpar. Owners complain of doors opening and closing on their own and poorly fitted panels that produce a cacophony of wind noise, squeaks, and rattles, as well as water leaks, paint defects, and premature rusting.

2004–10 Quest

A totally different minivan than its predecessor, the 2004–10 Quest is an Altima/Murano spin-off that is larger, more powerful, and better equipped than before. It's also less reliable. Skyroof leaks and dangerous sliding doors are quite common. Owners also complain of malfunctioning engines, prematurely worn-out engine timing chains on 2007 models (replacement cost: $3,300 U.S.), and early replacement of transmissions, brake pads and rotors, and Pax run-flat tires:

> I own a 2007 Nissan Quest with the Michelin Pax Run-Flat tire system. The Pax Run-Flat Tire System is a defective product. I purchased the car in November 2007. By 13 months, at 18,000 miles, 2 of the tires had worn to the point where the dealer said they needed to be replaced. At 20,600 miles we had all 4 tires replaced.

> •

> The shop has had the vehicle for more than 35 days and he does not know when it can be retrieved. The shop does not have the tires and the liner that are needed to repair the tire.

Goodyear tires are also notorious for premature wear and poor performance on these minivans (see *www.tirerack.com*).

Volkswagen

The 2009–10 **Routan** is Not Recommended. A Chrysler minivan cousin with a German accent, the Routan is a seven-seat spin-off of the RT platform used by the Chrysler Town & Country and Dodge Grand Caravan. 2010 was its last model year in Canada. It was manufactured in Windsor, Ontario, alongside Chrysler's minivans and featured revised styling and firmer suspension tuning. Price: $28,075–$50,575 (very soft). Strong points: A tauter suspension and an interior that's plusher than what Chrysler offers. The 251 hp 4.0L V6 is a good performer and the van provides a comfortable ride. The cabin is also relatively quiet. Weak points: On the Canadian market for only two model years (2009 and 2010). Depreciation? A 2009 top-of-the-line $50,000 Execline is now worth about $30,000. If you are offered a Routan at a ridiculously low price, run—don't walk—away; it has all of the Caravan's problems without the warranty or servicing backup. Some of the more common safety complaints concern transmission failures, which means the transmission locks up in traffic; a poorly designed backup camera; unsafe child safety seat positioning; a power sliding door that can crush a child's hand; and unsafe power-assisted rear seats. Crashworthiness: NHTSA gives the Routan five stars for front and side crashworthiness and four stars for rollover resistance.

Sport-Utilities

Acura

Rated Above Average, the Acura **RDX** is marketed as the SUV version of Acura's sporty TSX. This luxury crossover combines an innovative powertrain (turbocharger, etc.), lots of safety gear, high-tech standard features, a sporty platform, and a versatile, plush interior. It was launched as a 2007 model, and has remained relatively unchanged, except for an engine upgrade on the 2008. 2007–10 crashworthiness scores are impressive: five stars given for front and side crash protection and four stars earned for rollover protection. A 2007 version can be bought for $16,000, or about $25,000 less than its original selling price.

Some complaints: Road noise is omnipresent, and the ride is stiff. You get the impression that the RDX is trying too hard to target the BMW "sporty" SUV market, especially since the 42 buttons and knobs mounted in the centre console area copy BMW's earlier confusing iDrive cockpit controls.

The Acura **MDX** gets an Above Average rating for the 2007–10 models, but just an Average score for the 2001–06 versions. The 2007 improvements made a world of difference to the car's road performance and comfort. Still, why spend $20,500 (2007) for a warmed-over Odyssey when you can do better with the cheaper 2007

Honda Pilot ($14,500)? The 2010 MDX returned with a revised V6 and a restyled interior and exterior. Not much improvement for its $37,000 used price tag (new: $51,990).

On the plus side, the MDX accelerates well, with plenty of low-end power. It's nicely appointed, has a roomy interior with a standard third-row seat, and employs a gas-saving engine cylinder deactivation system. 2007 and later models have successfully tackled most of the negatives found with 2006 and earlier models, and the 2007's extra horsepower is a critical improvement. The MDX's real-world fuel economy is mediocre, and premium fuel is required. The steering wheel can't be adjusted for reach, forcing small drivers to sit perilously close to the airbag housing. Reliability shouldn't be a problem, unless you actually believe this vehicle can go off-road. If so, make sure you get an extended warranty and find a friendly garage. Buying the second-series model in March 2007 or later will save you from some of the first-year glitches commonly found with most reworked makes. 2007 and later models have registered only a few complaints, concerning premature brake wear, minor electrical shorts, AC compressor failures, and some fit and finish concerns.

NHTSA's 2004–10 MDX crashworthiness scores are hard to beat: five stars for front- and side-impact occupant protection; four stars for rollover resistance, except for the 2004, which wasn't tested. 2003 models earned four stars for front-impact and rollover protection, while side-impact crashworthiness was given five stars. 2002 models were the earliest versions crash-tested and they scored five stars for front and side occupant safety and four stars for rollover resistance. IIHS qualifies 2001–12 models' frontal offset, side protection, and head restraints as "Good." One discordant note: 2003–06 model head restraints were judged to be "Poor."

Audi

The 2009–10 **Q5** is a Below Average buy, mostly due to Audi's history of factory-related glitches and its "lag and lurch" powertrain. The Q7's smaller brother, it's a stylish five-passenger luxury crossover compact full of high-tech gadgetry, with everything ready to go awry. Most notable is the car's adaptive suspension that allows for firm, sporty handling, if so desired. The Q5 power comes by way of a 270 hp 3.2L V6 and the latest rear-biased version of AWD. The car is stylish; full of luxury appointments; has good acceleration and excellent handling; and is full of nifty safety, performance, and convenience goodies. On the other hand, the Q5 is way overpriced when compared with prices stateside; there's limited rear seatroom and cargo space; and, in the best German tradition, controls are needlessly complicated. Servicing is highly dependent upon a weak dealer network; parts are problematic; and servicing quality is spotty. Owners report excessive wind noise; hard and delayed upshifts and downshifts between First and Second gear; and sometimes, when coming to a stop, the transmission downshifts just as the engine suddenly surges. NHTSA awarded five stars for front and side crashworthiness and four stars for rollover protection. IIHS gave its top, "Good," rating for frontal offset and side protection. Head restraint effectiveness is also rated "Good."

The 2007–10 **Q7** is Not Recommended for similar reasons as the more recent Q5—it's outrageously overpriced in Canada and quality is lacking even more so than with its smaller brother. Granted, it does handle well, although the ride is a bit stiff, and is full of the latest techno safety, performance, and convenience features.

The Q7 is a VW Touareg/Porsche Cayenne combo with an Audi badge and new powertrains that have yet to be tested. Off-road prowess is not as great as the Touareg's or Cayenne's; fuel economy is not impressive; ride quality is ho-hum; rear visibility is limited; and the third-row entry/exit is problematic. Furthermore, early owner feedback indicates that this large crossover AWD wagon has a host of factory-related defects affecting its fuel and electrical systems, powertrain components, and fit and finish—exactly the problems owners find with Porsche and VW models. Poor servicing and recurring factory glitches are to be expected. NHTSA gives the Q7 five stars for front and side crash protection and four stars for rollover resistance. IIHS gives its top, "Good," score for frontal offset, side, and head-restraint protection. A 2009 entry-level 3.6 version sold new for $54,200; it is now worth about $37,500.

Chrysler

The Chrysler **Aspen 4×4** is a Not Recommended model that's essentially a $49,995 Dodge Durango with a different front grille. It lasted only three model years (2007–09). A 2007 Aspen is worth $14,500, or $4,000 less than a 2008; a 2009 version will set you back $25,000. The Aspen was rated five stars for frontal collision occupant protection and three stars for rollover protection.

Ford/Lincoln

The 2007 Ford **Edge** and Lincoln **MKX** are Not Recommended models that sold new for $32,999 and $42,399, respectively. A 2007 Edge is now worth $15,500; an MKX goes for $20,500. These practically identical small car–based SUVs use the Mazda6 platform, share Volvo CX-7 parts, and take their styling cues from the Ford Fusion. In the past, an infusion of Mazda parts has always helped bring up the quality of Ford's cars and trucks, including the Escort/Tracer, Probe/MX6, and Escape/Tribute. However, mixing in Volvo components when China-owned Volvo cannot guarantee timely parts delivery creates added risks. The 3.5L V6 (265 hp) mated to a 6-speed automatic transmission makes both vehicles better-than-average performers. Big minuses are mediocre fit and finish and the absence of third-row seating. Crash test scores are excellent, though.

General Motors

The 2007–10 GM **Acadia**, **Enclave**, and **Outlook** are practically identical mid-sized models that are rated Below Average buys mainly due to their high cost, poor fuel economy, subpar reliability, and lousy fit and finish. The trio sold new for $36,495 (2007), $40,895 (2008), and $33,990 (2007), respectively. Today, they're worth $12,000 (2007), $17,000 (2008), and $8,500 (2007). They all offer front-drive/all-wheel-drive powertrains and use a car-based platform that incorporates a third-row seat that's suitable for adults, allowing for a maximum of eight passengers. Power is provided by a 288 hp 3.6L V6 mated to 6-speed automatic transmission. Standard safety features abound. A wide stance and low centre of gravity reduce the threat of a rollover. NHTSA crashworthiness scores are quite good: five stars for front- and side-impact occupant protection and four stars for rollover resistance.

Some of the minuses inherent in GM's new crossover trio: the new 6-speed tranny has yet to prove itself, and the V6 powerplant is a mixed-breed design from Australia, Germany, Sweden, and North America that was first introduced on Cadillac's CTS sedan and SRX SUV crossover. CTS and SRX complaints logged by NHTSA and others frequently mention engine and transmission/differential failures, and early 2010 *Consumer Reports* member survey results show some automatic transmission problems with the 2007–09 models.

The Cadillac **SRX** is a Not Recommended, failure-prone mid-sized rear-drive or all-wheel-drive luxury crossover. It has been on the Canadian market since 2004, then selling for $52,250 as a front-drive SUV, and $63,965 for a V8 AWD. Today, the same vehicles are worth $6,000–$8,000 and $9,000–$11,000, respectively. 2008 models offer the best trade-off in features and price: $17,500 for the rear-drive 3.6L V6 (new: $46,695); $1,000 more for the AWD version (new: $49,320); $19,000 for the rear-drive 4.6L V8 (new: $60,300); and $19,500 for the AWD variant hooked to the 4.6L V8 powerplant (new: $62,925).

SRX owners report frequent transmission and differential breakdowns in addition to brake and electrical failures and fit and finish deficiencies. The 2004–07 models earned four stars for front crashworthiness and five stars for side-impact protection. The 2008–09s got similar ratings, but they also scored three stars for front-drive rollover resistance and four stars for AWD rollover protection. 2010 models earned five stars for front and side crash protection and four stars for rollover resistance.

General Motors/Hummer

The 2003–08 GM Hummer **H2** SUV and SUT (the SUT being a pickup version launched in 2005) are Not Recommended due to their overall poor reliability, mediocre highway performance, and head-spinning depreciation. Furthermore, since GM shut down its Hummer division, warranties and servicing aren't worth much. A 2004 H2 SUV that originally sold for $73,500 is now barely worth $13,000–$14,500; a 2008 SUV or SUT that sold for $67,700 new has already lost half its original value. Outward visibility is severely compromised by the small windshield and wide roof pillars, and NHTSA hasn't crash tested the H2 yet. Still, the H2 is a good off-road performer (it uses the Tahoe's previous generation platform), and it appeals to those who like ultra-macho styling.

The more moderately priced 2006–10 Hummer **H3** is also Not Recommended, mainly because its mechanicals are derived from the poor-quality GM Canyon/Colorado. Depreciation is unusually rapid: a $40,995 2008 H3 now fetches $9,500. Like its big brother, the H3 is a good off-roader, but for this attribute you must sacrifice reliability, access, visibility, a quiet interior, and a comfortable ride. The base engine is noisy, has little grunt, and is a gas-guzzler. It was replaced by a 3.7L engine in late 2007. A 300 hp 5.3L V8 powers the 2008 H3 Alpha variant. NHTSA has given the H3 its top, five-star rating for frontal and side crashworthiness, beginning with the 2006 model, although passenger protection is rated only four stars for frontal impacts.

Hyundai

Hyundai hit a bulls-eye when it brought out the Recommended **Santa Fe** mid-size crossover SUV for the 2001 model year. Based on the Hyundai Sonata platform, this sport-utility does almost everything right, providing acceptable acceleration with the 185 hp 2.7L V6 and the 174 hp 2.4L four-banger. More power and good fuel economy can be achieved with the optional 242 hp 3.3L or 276 hp 3.5L V6. Automatic transmission shifts are generally smooth and predictable, though powertrain computer module malfunctions sometimes screw up the shift sequence; and steering is effortless and precise; making this SUV fairly agile in most driving situations. Passengers are treated to a comfortable, controlled ride and standard stability/traction control and full-body side curtain airbags ensure that the Santa Fe is sure-footed and crashworthy. There's lots of interior room; and the spacious interior allows for an optional pair of flat-folding third-row seats. Tall drivers will, nevertheless, need more headroom. Owner complaints are rare. NHTSA and IIHS gave the Santa Fe their top ratings for offset and front- and side-impact protection. Rollover resistance got four stars, and head-restraint effectiveness was rated "Good."

Redesigned for the first time in 2007, the revamped Santa Fe is larger, with more interior amenities, and offers stronger engines. It's still competitively priced, has improved build quality, and provides standard safety and performance features that cost a lot more when bought with competing models. It comes with front-drive or with all-wheel drive.

The best Santa Fe models to buy are the 2008 GL 3.3L V6 AWD (a year after the 2007's redesign) for $13,500 and the face-lifted 6-speed automatic 2010 3.5L GL front-drive for $19,500. 2.0L and 2.2L 4-cylinder turbodiesels, producing 184 hp and 200 hp, were also launched in 2010.

Owner-reported problems: sudden acceleration accompanied by loss of braking; the vehicle frequently shuts down when underway; the passenger-side airbag is disabled when an average-sized passenger is seated; sudden brake failure, with the brake pedal going to the floor with no effect; horn needs to be pounded in the right spot to activate; rear window explode for no reason; excessive engine and steering vibration when underway; door lock failures; low-beam headlights don't give far enough illumination; steel belts may unravel on Bridgestone Dueler tires; and the tire-pressure monitor system light comes on for no reason.

There are few service bulletins covering factory-related defects, except for creaking, ticking sunroofs; automatic transmission malfunctions; transmission defaults to the "failsafe" mode; harsh transmission engagement; and no-starts in Park or Neutral.

Jeep

All Jeeps are Not Recommended (Wrangler excepted). To be fair, the Jeep's tendency to roll over isn't as high as that of other small sport-utilities; parts aren't yet hard to find; and servicing, if not given with a smile, at least isn't accompanied by a snarl or head-scratching. Early Cherokees, CJs, and Wagoneers have been known for rattle-prone and rust-cankered bodies, air and water leaks, electrical glitches, and high-cost brake maintenance. Expect to spend $1,500–$2,500 (tops) for a decade-old entry-level CJ or Wrangler. A 2008 Grand Cherokee Laredo sells for about $15,500, much less than its $41,095 original sales price.

Kia

The Above Average 2009–10 Kia **Borrego** truck-based SUV lacks the refined ride comfort and handling found in other luxury three-row SUVs, due to its truck-like body-on-frame construction. Nevertheless, the V6 performs quite well in all driving situations and can handle heavy loads with ease. The V8 cranks up the towing capability to 7,500 lb., with plenty of power in reserve for serious stump pulling. There's also a smooth-shifting automatic transmission, a quiet interior, user-friendly controls, ample third-row seating, a standard trailer hitch and electric harness, and standard stability control. NHTSA gives the Borrego five stars for frontal and side occupant crash protection. Rollover protection was given four stars. There have been few owner complaints over reliability, so far. Owners report that the Borrego gives a hard, jolting ride; has poor emergency handling; provides head restraints that are too close to the back of the head; lacks a power tailgate; and burns much more fuel than represented. Owners also say that the vehicle sticks in Drive once underway, or suddenly accelerates. Borregos tend to wander along the road and pull to the right when accelerating, requiring constant steering corrections. The best Borrego buy is the 2010 V6 LX, which sells for $22,000 (not bad for a 4×4 that sold new for $37,395).

Land Rover

See Jaguar/Land Rover.

Mazda

Mazda's 2007–10 **CX-7** and **CX-9** models, rated Above Average, premiered in Canada in 2007 for $31,995 and $39,595, respectively, with an AWD version costing about $2,000 more; they are now worth $11,000 and $14,500. 2008 models now sell for $13,000 and $17,000.

The sporty five-passenger CX-7 is a well-appointed, four-door crossover SUV based on the Mazda5 and Mazda6. It isn't suitable for off-roading, even though it looks like it could go anywhere. The turbocharged 4-cylinder engine is taken from the MazdaSpeed6 and has performed well. Nevertheless, CX-7 owners report some problems with the brakes, fit and finish, and engine, transmission, fuel, and climate control systems. The CX-9 has had fewer complaints, though the brakes, suspension, climate control system, and fit and finish (mostly paint) remain the most troublesome. Both models have earned high crashworthiness rankings: five stars for occupant protection in front and side impacts, and four stars for rollover resistance.

Porsche

2007–10 Porsche's **Cayenne** is a Not Reccomended buy, mainly due to its limited servicing network, mediocre performance, and outrageously high retail price—reserved for Canadians who are too naive to know they're being scammed. In fact, we're paying a retail price that is still way too high, even after having been cut by more than $10,000 following *Lemon-Aid*'s criticism of Porsche's greed in late 2007. For example, Canadian dealers sold the 2006 V6, V8, and AWD V8 Turbo Cayennes for $60,100, $80,100, and $126,900, respectively. Meanwhile, these luxury SUVs sell for $43,400, $57,900, and $93,700 in the States. Incidentally, used 2006 Canadian versions of the above models cost $18,500, $22,500, and $33,000.

First launched as a 2003 model, the Cayenne skipped the 2007 model year and returned as a 2008 model. Cayenne does have some limited off-road capability, thanks to its low gearing, sophisticated electronics, and Touareg-sourced V6 engine, as well as Porsche V8 and twin-turbo variants. Transmissions consist of a 6-speed manual and a 6-speed automatic. On-road capability is a big disappointment, however, since the vehicle lacks Porsche's usual handling prowess. Furthermore, many of the cabin controls are needlessly complex and confusing. Crashworthiness has not yet been rated.

Subaru

The 2003–06 Subaru **Baja** is a Below Average all-wheel-drive crossover. It provides the handling and passenger-carrying characteristics of a car, with the open-bed versatility and, to a lesser degree, the load capacity of a pickup truck (think of a small 1959–60 Chevrolet El Camino, or a mini GM Avalanche). Baja's unibody platform borrows heavily from Subaru's Legacy and Outback.

The car is too small to offer much that is useful or fun. Still, poor sales mean deeply discounted used prices. For example, a 2006 version that sold new for almost $30,000 is now available for $8,000 to $9,500. Some of the Baja's minuses: uncomfortably upright rear seating; the bed is too short to carry a bike without extending the tailgate as part of the bed; there's no 5-speed automatic transmission; and the absence of a folding midgate means the flip-and-fold versatility isn't as practical as Subaru pretends.

Toyota

The 2007–10 Toyota **FJ Cruiser** takes its inspiration from the Toyota FJ40 Land Cruiser, built between 1956 and 1983. First model year 2007s sold for $30,000 and are now worth $12,500; 2008 used prices are only a couple of thousand dollars more. The Cruiser is an Above Average buy that competes especially well off-road against the Ford Escape, Honda Element, and Nissan Xterra. It is powered by a competent 239 hp 4.0L V6 that can be used for either two- or four-wheel drive. A 5-speed automatic transmission comes with both versions, and a 6-speed manual gearbox is available with the all-wheel drive. Although the FJ's turning circle is about 1.5 m larger than those of similar-sized SUVs, off-roading should be a breeze, if done carefully. Interestingly, NHTSA crashworthiness scores for front and side impacts are five stars; however, rollover protection merits only three stars. This is disappointing and is almost never seen with vehicles that are equipped with electronic stability control.

Of course, if you don't mind driving a really old Toyota, there's nothing wrong with a 1987–89 Toyota **Land Cruiser**, which sells for about $2,000. Just be sure to pull the wheels off to examine the brakes, check for undercarriage corrosion, and make sure the engine head gasket is okay.

Volkswagen

The Volkswagen 2005–10 **Touareg** is a Not Recommended model that is living on borrowed time due to poor sales and quality-control deficiencies. Restyled in 2007, it's now cleaner-burning and more fuel-efficient. Crashworthiness ratings have also been quite good: 2004–06 models earned four stars for frontal crash protection and five stars for side impacts. 2007 models did even better with five stars granted for frontal and side protection and four stars given for rollover resistance. Nevertheless, the Touareg has been earning a bad reputation for poor reliability and expensive servicing ever since it was first launched as a 2005 luxury SUV listed at $55,010 (now worth $11,000–$13,000); a new 2010 entry-level Comfortline V6 sold for $45,300; it now sells used for $30,000 and is predicted to be worth only $23,000 in the next three years.